D0742037

Orders, Production, and Investment —
a Cyclical and Structural Analysis

NATIONAL BUREAU OF ECONOMIC RESEARCH
Studies in Business Cycles

Orders, Production, and Investment— a Cyclical and Structural Analysis

VICTOR ZARNOWITZ

University of Chicago and National
Bureau of Economic Research

National Bureau of Economic Research

NEW YORK

1973

Distributed by Columbia University Press

NEW YORK AND LONDON

Copyright © 1973 by the National Bureau of Economic Research
All Rights Reserved
Library of Congress card number: 70-171576
ISBN: 0-87014-215-1
Printed in the United States of America

NATIONAL BUREAU OF ECONOMIC RESEARCH

OFFICERS

Arthur F. Burns, *Honorary Chairman*
Walter W. Heller, *Chairman*
J. Wilson Newman, *Vice Chairman*
John R. Meyer, *President*
Thomas D. Flynn, *Treasurer*
Douglas H. Eldridge, *Vice President-Executive Secretary*

Victor R. Fuchs, *Vice President-Research*
Edwin Kuh, *Director, Computer Research Center*
Hal B. Lary, *Vice President-Research*
Robert E. Lipsey, *Vice President-Research*
Edward K. Smith, *Vice President*

DIRECTORS AT LARGE

Atherton Bean, *International Multifoods Corporation*
Joseph A. Beirne, *Communications Workers of America*
Arthur F. Burns, *Board of Governors of the Federal Reserve System*
Wallace J. Campbell, *Foundation for Cooperative Housing*
Erwin D. Canham, *Christian Science Monitor*
Solomon Fabricant, *New York University*
Frank W. Fetter, *Hanover, New Hampshire*
Eugene P. Foley, *James A. Reed & Co., Ltd.*
Eli Goldston, *Eastern Gas and Fuel Associates*
David L. Grove, *International Business Machines Corporation*
Walter W. Heller, *University of Minnesota*

Vivian W. Henderson, *Clark College*
John R. Meyer, *Yale University*
J. Irwin Miller, *Cummins Engine Company, Inc.*
Geoffrey H. Moore, *Bureau of Labor Statistics*
J. Wilson Newman, *Dun & Bradstreet, Inc.*
James J. O'Leary, *United States Trust Company of New York*
Alice M. Rivlin, *Brookings Institution*
Robert V. Roosa, *Brown Brothers Harriman & Co.*
Boris Shishkin, *Washington, D.C.*
Arnold M. Soloway, *Jamaicaway Tower, Boston, Massachusetts*
Lazare Teper, *International Ladies' Garment Workers' Union*
Donald B. Woodward, *Riverside, Connecticut*

Theodore O. Yntema, *Oakland University*

DIRECTORS BY UNIVERSITY APPOINTMENT

Moses Abramovitz, *Stanford*
Gardner Ackley, *Michigan*
Charles H. Berry, *Princeton*
Francis M. Boddy, *Minnesota*
Otto Eckstein, *Harvard*
Walter D. Fisher, *Northwestern*
R. A. Gordon, *California*
Robert J. Lampman, *Wisconsin*

Kelvin J. Lancaster, *Columbia*
Maurice W. Lee, *North Carolina*
Almarin Phillips, *Pennsylvania*
Lloyd G. Reynolds, *Yale*
Robert M. Solow, *Massachusetts Institute of Technology*
Henri Theil, *Chicago*
Thomas A. Wilson, *Toronto*

DIRECTORS BY APPOINTMENT OF OTHER ORGANIZATIONS

Eugene A. Birnbaum, *American Management Association*
Emilio G. Collado, *Committee for Economic Development*
Thomas D. Flynn, *American Institute of Certified Public Accountants*
Nathaniel Goldfinger, *American Federation of Labor and Congress of Industrial Organizations*
Harold G. Halcrow, *American Agricultural Economics Association*

Walter E. Hoadley, *American Finance Association*
Douglass C. North, *Economic History Association*
Charles B. Reeder, *National Association of Business Economists*
Willard L. Thorp, *American Economic Association*
W. Allen Wallis, *American Statistical Association*
Robert M. Will, *Canadian Economics Association*

DIRECTORS EMERITI

Percival F. Brundage
Gottfried Haberler

Albert J. Hettinger, Jr.
George B. Roberts

Murray Shields
Joseph H. Willits

SENIOR RESEARCH STAFF

Gary S. Becker
Charlotte Boschan
Phillip Cagan
Solomon Fabricant
Milton Friedman
Victor R. Fuchs
Raymond W. Goldsmith

Michael Gort
Daniel M. Holland
F. Thomas Juster
John F. Kain
John W. Kendrick
Irving B. Kravis
Edwin Kuh

Hal B. Lary
Robert E. Lipsey
Benoit B. Mandelbrot
John R. Meyer
Jacob Mincer
Ilse Mintz
Geoffrey H. Moore *

M. Ishaq Nadiri
Nancy Ruggles
Richard Ruggles
Anna J. Schwartz
Robert P. Shay
Carl S. Shoup †
George J. Stigler
Victor Zarnowitz

* On leave.
† Special consultant.

Relation of the Directors to the Work and Publications
of the National Bureau of Economic Research

1. The object of the National Bureau of Economic Research is to ascertain and to present to the public important economic facts and their interpretation in a scientific and impartial manner. The Board of Directors is charged with the responsibility of ensuring that the work of the National Bureau is carried on in strict conformity with this object.

2. The President of the National Bureau shall submit to the Board of Directors, or to its Executive Committee, for their formal adoption all specific proposals for research to be instituted.

3. No research report shall be published until the President shall have submitted to each member of the Board the manuscript proposed for publication, and such information as will, in his opinion and in the opinion of the author, serve to determine the suitability of the report for publication in accordance with the principles of the National Bureau. Each manuscript shall contain a summary drawing attention to the nature and treatment of the problem studied, the character of the data and their utilization in the report, and the main conclusions reached.

4. For each manuscript so submitted, a special committee of the Board shall be appointed by majority agreement of the President and Vice Presidents (or by the Executive Committee in case of inability to decide on the part of the President and Vice Presidents), consisting of three directors selected as nearly as may be one from each general division of the Board. The names of the special manuscript committee shall be stated to each Director when the manuscript is submitted to him. It shall be the duty of each member of the special manuscript committee to read the manuscript. If each member of the manuscript committee signifies his approval within thirty days of the transmittal of the manuscript, the report may be published. If at the end of that period any member of the manuscript committee withholds his approval, the President shall then notify each member of the Board, requesting approval or disapproval of publication, and thirty days additional shall be granted for this purpose. The manuscript shall then not be published unless at least a majority of the entire Board who shall have voted on the proposal within the time fixed for the receipt of votes shall have approved.

5. No manuscript may be published, though approved by each member of the special manuscript committee, until forty-five days have elapsed from the transmittal of the report in manuscript form. The interval is allowed for the receipt of any memorandum of dissent or reservation, together with a brief statement of his reasons, that any member may wish to express; and such memorandum of dissent or reservation shall be published with the manuscript if he so desires. Publication does not, however, imply that each member of the Board has read the manuscript, or that either members of the Board in general or the special committee have passed on its validity in every detail.

6. Publications of the National Bureau issued for informational purposes concerning the work of the Bureau and its staff, or issued to inform the public of activities of Bureau staff, and volumes issued as a result of various conferences involving the National Bureau shall contain a specific disclaimer noting that such publication has not passed through the normal review procedures required in this resolution. The Executive Committee of the Board is charged with review of all such publications from time to time to ensure that they do not take on the character of formal research reports of the National Bureau, requiring formal Board approval.

7. Unless otherwise determined by the Board or exempted by the terms of paragraph 6, a copy of this resolution shall be printed in each National Bureau publication.

(Resolution adopted October 25, 1926, and revised February 6, 1933,
February 24, 1941, and April 20, 1968)

To Lena, Steven, and Arthur

Contents

Tables

Charts

Preface

THIS book was developed from a study mainly concerned with the characteristics of manufacturers' new orders as a type of leading indicator of general business changes.[1] Although limited in scope, this work gave early recognition to the "dynamic and critical role of the demands represented by the new order series." Attempts to gain a better understanding of this role led to a much more extensive and intensive inquiry than was initially contemplated. Completion of the book seemed near some time ago, but it was delayed by other work and then by the consequent need to update the empirical contents of the manuscript.

This study deals primarily with the cyclical aspects of selected variables and their relationships. However, it also includes some analysis that might be termed "structural," for example, regression estimates based on time series for different industries and types of processes. It covers a rather wide ground: short-term order-production sequences, relationships between delivery period and price changes, investment commitments and expenditures, orders and inventories, etc. This diversity reflects the diversity of orders, their structure, and their functions. The unifying element is also provided by orders, an expression of effective demand that in one form or another appears in each of the areas covered.

At the National Bureau, many individuals cooperate to produce a book, in ways that make it proper to acknowledge their contributions collectively; consequently, this report is truly "A Study by the National Bureau of Economic Research." Another institution to which I owe thanks for the generous provision of time and assistance for research is the Graduate School of Business of the University of Chicago. I also wish to acknowledge the aid of a Ford Foundation faculty research fellowship in 1963–64.

I am most indebted to Geoffrey H. Moore for his encouragement, suggestions, and comments, which helped me in every stage of this

[1] A report on this phase of my work was published as "The Timing of Manufacturers' Orders During Business Cycles," in Geoffrey M. Moore, ed., *Business Cycle Indicators*, Vol. I, Princeton University Press for the National Bureau of Economic Research, 1961, Chap. 14.

study. Rosanne Cole gave me helpful advice and supervised some computations. An early version of parts of the manuscript benefited from the criticisms of Millard Hastay, Ruth P. Mack, and Thomas M. Stanback, Jr.; a later version, from a review by Ilse Mintz and Robert Eisner. Valuable comments on Chapter 5 were made by Zvi Griliches. Chapter 7 incorporates, with modifications, parts of an earlier paper of mine,[2] which received useful comments from George Stigler and Jacob Mincer, among others. Thanks are also due to Geoffrey H. Moore, Charles B. Reeder, and Emilio G. Collado for their service and valuable advice as members of the Board of Directors reading committee.

I am grateful to the following persons for aid in collecting and interpreting data on new and unfilled orders, shipments, and inventories: Lawrence Bridge and Genevieve B. Wimsatt of the U.S. Department of Commerce, Bureau of Economic Analysis; Julius Shiskin, Office of Management and Budget; and Maxwell R. Conklin and Shirley Kallek of the Bureau of the Census. They and others helped me to avoid some errors but bear no responsibility for any remaining deficiencies.

Assistants to whom I am indebted for their able help with the statistical work in its successive phases are: Nadeschda Bohsack, Moon-Young Cha, Joan Chen, Gerald Childs, Paul Halpern, Leopold Koziebrodzki, Lee Severance, Dorothy Suchman, and Josephine Su. I wish also to give credit to Maude Pech, Johanna Stern, and the late Sophie Sakowitz for assistance in the detailed interpretation of the data; to Joan Tron, Virginia Meltzer, and Ester Moskowitz for skillful and efficient editing; and to H. Irving Forman for a clear and careful presentation of the charts.

[2] *Unfilled Orders, Price Changes, and Business Fluctuations,* Occasional Paper 84, New York, NBER, 1962 (reprinted from *Review of Economics and Statistics,* November 1962).

Orders, Production, and Investment —
a Cyclical and Structural Analysis

1

INTRODUCTION

ON AN AVERAGE trading day in 1969, new orders worth roughly $2.6 billion were received by United States manufacturers. They originated in firms engaged in trade, construction, transportation, utilities, mining, and in manufacturing itself; they also originated in the government sector. They ranged in size from a small hosiery order placed by a local retailer to a huge order for sheet steel placed by a national automobile manufacturer. These orders signified intentions to buy a variety of consumer and producer goods.

Many orders are filled when they are received, from finished staple stocks; others are filled on short notice, from current production; still others are filled from future output a number of weeks or even months hence, because of time-consuming production processes (such as those for heavy or specialized equipment) or crowded production schedules, or both. Finally, some orders never reach the final stage of output or delivery, but are canceled by one of the transactors.

Problems of the Study

The findings that are available from earlier studies mostly concern the cyclical timing of certain order series. For example, it is known that the cyclically more sensitive new orders tend to lead at business cycle turns: the group is represented in each of the successive lists of leading indicators selected by the National Bureau of Economic Research.[1]

[1] See Geoffrey H. Moore and Julius Shiskin, *Indicators of Business Expansions and Contractions*, Occasional Paper 103, New York, NBER, 1967. Besides including new orders for durable manufactured products and machinery and equipment industries, the lists of indicators also include the series on building contracts, which are in a sense also "new orders" for investment goods.

But a survey of a larger number of order series for various industries and products shows that there is considerable difference in the characteristics of the series, including timing; for example, several of the series examined in Moore's studies were not acceptable as indicators. What is the nature and meaning of such differential features? What classification of new orders will reveal systematic differences in their behavior, and will further explain this behavior?

Customer orders received in advance of production represent quantities or values currently demanded that may, and typically do, differ from the quantities or values currently produced or shipped.[2] Differences between new orders and shipments represent changes in the stock of unfilled orders — in the backlog of revealed but not yet satisfied demand. Orders data may thus be helpful in studies of determinants and effects of changes in demand, being, as will be demonstrated later, preferable in this role to the commonly used data on production, deliveries, or outlays. This is the major reason for analytical interest in the statistics of new and unfilled orders.

Advance orders and contracts are particularly important in the demand for capital goods. Investment projects give rise to commitments to acquire productive plant and equipment: commercial and industrial construction contracts, orders for machinery, tools, etc. As a rule, completion of these projects requires a substantial period of time. And such projects are highly individual, even though some of their elements may be fairly standardized. Because of the long gestation periods and the individualized nature of these projects, the difference between time series on commitments and realizations is of special analytic and empirical interest.

There are some rather conspicuous openings for exploration. Firms that have sustained increases in the flow of new orders received would be expected to plan for correspondingly larger outputs of the products for which demand is apparently expanding; a similar statement should,

---

[2] Of course, any order that is placed and accepted at an agreed upon price refers to a stated quantity demanded that is equal to the quantity to be supplied. The discrepancies between the rates of new orders and shipments at a given point of time arise because the process of filling orders takes time. Clearly, there is no practical way here of distinguishing between the schedules of demand and supply for specific new orders, only between points on different schedules. Nevertheless, the distinction can be interesting, and the above clarification does not impair the validity of this and the following statements in the text.

mutatis mutandis, apply to the impact of a decrease in ordering. But how close is this relation, and how is it influenced by other relevant factors such as price reactions, inventory position, and backlogs of unfilled orders? How well, in effect, are changes in output or shipments anticipated by movements in new orders of the corresponding industries? In particular, what are the timing aspects and other characteristics of these relationships at turns in the business cycle?

This last question is again particularly important for fixed investment, where shipments and expenditures actually lag at business cycle turns. Does the tendency for business capital outlays to lag contradict those hypotheses that ascribe to investment the prime causal role in business cycles? Not necessarily, since it can be shown that investment *commitments* do lead at turns in the business cycle. Such early timing is an enabling—if by no means a sufficient—characteristic of an important cyclical "mover." But can we account for the main factors that determine the changes in investment commitments? In particular, which of these influences may be responsible for the lead of commitments?

These are broad and difficult questions, and I can claim only to have made some progress with them. The present study has moved to these problems from its initial goal of describing the behavior of manufacturers' new orders with particular reference to their apparent tendency to lead at peaks and troughs of business cycles. To understand the role of new and unfilled orders, it is necessary to examine both the basic relations between the two as well as the relation of both to output and shipments. The analysis must recognize certain essential distinctions between modes of organizing production, and between different market groupings of industrial output. For example, new orders tend to be coincident with shipments for consumer staples and other "shelf goods," but to lead by substantial lengths for most items of producers' durable equipment. The timing of expenditures is similar to that of shipments. Hence, the widely adopted view that expenditures represent "effective demand" seems to have more justification for consumer goods than for capital goods: it may be argued that for capital goods, it is new orders and contracts that reflect effective demand. An analogous argument applies to large components of government demand, particularly defense products, where long delivery lags are the rule.

Data and Procedures

My first task is to review systematically the available raw materials. These consist of time series (some quarterly, but mostly monthly) on new orders received by various groups of manufacturing companies, and of corresponding series for the related activities of production, shipments, and unfilled orders. There are about a hundred new-order series, covering various periods between 1870 and the present, but mostly the interwar and recent years. For most of these series, matching data on the related processes could also be procured. Most of the figures are industry aggregates in current dollars: adjustments for price-level changes have been made in some cases, and data representing changes in physical quantities have also been employed. For most purposes, seasonally adjusted series are used.

The collected materials are rather substantial, considering the relative scarcity of orders data. But it should be noted that many of the series are short, and that the collection contains some duplication (major industry aggregates are included along with their components; and, in some cases, we use more than one source of series for the same industry and process). Also, the data give very unequal representation to different categories of industrial product. Although this is because the incidence of advance ordering is itself unevenly distributed, the inevitable result is that the samples for some categories are quite small.

Data for orders and related variables are from regular government sources and trade association statistics, except for a few special compilations. In addition, data on price changes, investment expenditures, inventories, and a number of related economic variables have been used in several parts of this book.

The procedures applied to these statistical materials include tools developed in the business cycle studies of the National Bureau, some of which have been modified for our purposes. There are measures of timing relations, comparisons of amplitudes of fluctuations, summary results of time series decomposition, indexes of conformity to business expansions and contractions, patterns of cyclical movements, diffusion indexes, etc. — all products of a method designed to describe cyclical behavior and estimate cyclical relations. Extensive use was also made of several standard methods of statistical inference and econometrics: correlation and regression analysis with discrete and distributed, as well as fixed and variable, lags; ranking techniques; significance tests; some elements of probability calculations; etc. In short, the diversity of the phenomena and problems dictated the use of an assortment of tools; no commitment to a unified set of well-defined methods seemed possible or indeed desirable for our purposes.

Usually, when the theory fails to insure the correctness of any single, fully developed hypothesis, experimenting with alternative model specifications cannot be avoided without sacrificing possible gains of information. Such exploratory approaches had to be used in this study, and the results, as always, must be viewed with caution.[3] However, care has been taken to reveal all that has been done, so as *not* to mislead the reader, "as if the final hypothesis presented is the first one, whereas in fact it is the result of much experimentation."[4] Where possible, replication, with the aid of new or different sets of data, was used as a partial remedy. These principles of procedure often result in lengthy, and sometimes tedious, exposition. However, in the conflict between a treatment that is tiresome but informative, and a treatment that is more elegant but less revealing or potentially misleading, I strongly favor the former.

Plan of the Book

This report has four substantive parts. Part I, consisting of four chapters, relates new orders to later stages of production—outputs and shipments. It considers first the role of orders in the process of industrial production (Chapter 2); compares next the amplitude and frequency of fluctuations in new orders with those of the related production and shipments data (Chapter 3); proceeds to compare the timing of turning points in these series (Chapter 4); and closes with a regression analysis of the lagged relations between shipments and new orders (Chapter 5).

Part II is concerned with causes and consequences of changes in un-

[3] The familiar reason for this is that the experimentation involves an unknown loss of "degrees of freedom"; as a consequence, the usual standard error statistics tend to overrate the accuracy of the resulting estimates.

[4] See H. Theil, *Economic Forecasts and Policy*, Amsterdam, 1958, p. 207.

filled orders and inventories. Chapter 6 is a survey of the evidence bearing on the behavior and role of order backlogs. Chapter 7 contains an analysis of the relation between the changes in unfilled orders, in delivery periods, and in prices. Chapter 8 is a discussion of the cyclical aspects and major determinants of purchasing for inventory, especially the links between orders, production, and inventory investment.

The focus of Part III is on the cyclical behavior and relation of investment commitments and expenditures. In Chapter 9, new orders for producers' durable equipment and construction contracts for industrial and commercial plants are related to the corresponding capital outlays; other indicators (anticipations) of investment in plant and equipment and other corresponding commitments data such as those on new capital appropriations are also considered. In Chapter 10, evidence on various factors influencing fixed-investment commitments and realizations is assembled and reviewed.

Part IV offers an analysis of the behavior of manufacturers' new and unfilled orders during business cycles and attempts to relate it to other important cyclical processes. Chapter 11 presents and interprets measures of cyclical conformity and timing for new and unfilled orders. Chapter 12 examines the patterns of cyclical change in orders, production, investment, and related variables.

To a large extent, this book is, of necessity, technical. Each chapter includes at the end a fairly comprehensive summary of the major findings and interpretations. The reader who is both interested in the main results and impatient with the complications and details involved might wish to start by consulting the chapter summaries and also the conclusions assembled in Chapter 13. He thus could first survey the entire field and then select for further study those parts that are of most interest.

Finally, there are several appendixes, containing supplementary material.

PART I

THE RELATIONSHIPS BETWEEN
NEW ORDERS, PRODUCTION, AND
SHIPMENTS

2

THE ROLE OF ORDERS IN
INDUSTRIAL PRODUCTION

Manufacture to Stock and to Order

Two Contrasting Models and Their Significance

It will be helpful to introduce two simple models: one, pure production to stock, and the other, pure production to order. In the first, new orders are shipped immediately upon receipt and hence are virtually synchronous with and equal to shipments. Orders that cannot be so filled are either not placed or not accepted; thus, in the absence of advance orders in the real sense, there are no backlogs. The firm has to maintain, at all times, a sufficiently large unsold inventory of finished products to meet current sales. In contrast, the second case, by assuming production to order only, implies that there are no *unsold* stocks of the finished product.[1] Lacking such stocks, the firm cannot, of course, handle orders for immediate delivery and is limited to advance orders.[2]

A manufacturing concern is typically a multiproduct firm, often with a highly diversified output. Some of its products may be made to stock and others to order. Some may also shift from one category to the

---

[1] This ignores cancellations of orders, which may give rise to some unsold finished stocks, but the qualification is probably not a major one. The relevant data are scanty, but they indicate that cancellations are relatively unimportant (see the second part of this chapter, beginning with the section "Comparing Long-Term Average Levels of Orders Received and Filled"); and cancellations that occur after the items ordered have been produced must be least frequent because of the large risk of loss, which the seller will try to avoid.

[2] To formulate these two models algebraically, let n_t and s_t be the flows of orders received and shipped, respectively, during the tth unit period, say month, and let z_t be the corresponding flow of output or production. Then $n_t - s_t = u_t - u_{t-1} \equiv \Delta u_t$, and $z_t - s_t \equiv q_t - q_{t-1} \equiv \Delta q_t$, where u_t is the backlog, i.e., stock of unfilled orders, and q_t is the finished-product inventory on hand, both measured at the end of period t. In pure production to stock, $n_t = s_t$ and $\Delta u_t = 0$ in each period, so that u_t is always zero. In pure production to order, $z_t = s_t$ and $\Delta q = 0$ in each period, so that q_t is always zero.

other at certain times. In particular, a product normally sold from stock may temporarily be made to order when orders for it run at peak levels and customers allow lags on their deliveries. But there are good reasons to believe that some goods are produced to order and others to stock because of certain "structural" considerations.

Production will not be to stock if the costs of stocking the product in finished form exceed the costs of having to meet demand exclusively from future outputs. Under this condition, production will be to order if it promises to be sufficiently profitable to be undertaken at all. The costs that must be considered include intangibles that are not easily assessed in dollars (or any other comparable units). Usually, the comparison will take the form of probability considerations involving expected values of the respective net costs. The principal factor is the cost of not selling the stocked product or, more accurately, selling it only at a loss — what might be called a "liquidation loss." If there is a long delay before the sale can be accomplished, substantial carrying charges may arise, but these are often not nearly as important as the liquidation loss. On the other hand, the main cost of not having an item in stock is the loss of potential sales or customer goodwill when there is excess demand. This, however, implies that the customer is not willing to wait for delivery. Clearly, if buyers generally expect immediate deliveries, the product will have to be held in stock.

It may be well to note that manufacture to order need not be characterized by small *total* inventories, only by small stocks in finished-product form. Manufacturers of products made to order will normally hold inventories of purchased materials, which may include, along with "raw" commodities, various fabricated items such as standardized parts, components, and supplies. These stocks help to keep the delivery periods as short as competition requires (given the existing technological constraints). The higher the average degree of fabrication of these stocks, the better they can perform this function. But, presumably, with increased fabrication the inventories will also be increasingly sensitive to the liquidation losses, which, by assumption, are prohibitively large at the finished-product stage, as viewed by the manufacturer.[3]

[3] Cf. J. A. Bryan, G. P. Wadsworth, and T. M. Whitin, "A Multi-stage Inventory Model," *Naval Research Logistic Quarterly*, March–June 1955 (reprinted in T. M. Whitin, *The Theory of Inventory Management*, 2nd ed., Princeton, N.J., 1957, pp. 281–98).

Furthermore, the finished product itself will often be held in stock by the distributor who ordered it from the manufacturer. The distributor, by assumption of the stock-holding function, will then have enabled the manufacturer to produce to order.[4]

Types of Goods Made to Order

The goods for which manufacturers demand, and their customers must allow, "lead times" in filling orders are those that can be held in producer inventory only at very great cost and risk for one or more of the following reasons: (1) The product must precisely meet individual consumer specifications that are virtually unpredictable; (2) the product is, in its finished form, physically or economically perishable, even though it is made from materials that are durable; (3) the product has an extremely unstable or sporadic demand, which is very difficult to forecast.

In the first category belong many diverse goods purchased by expert buyers for special industrial purposes. The extreme subgroup consists of items so differentiated by the buyers' requirements that each customer's order must be handled separately in production; there is no possible combination of orders into batches that can be executed jointly by the producer. Thus, many types of machine tools are highly specialized, with models built to perform a single operation with maximum speed and efficiency.[5]

Such uniqueness of orders clearly imposes limitations, which may be severe, upon the scale of operations and size of a firm. A job machine shop is an example. But manufacture to order is not by any means restricted to these individually differentiated orders. A much larger share of it is accounted for by orders that, while retaining certain individual features, can nevertheless be aggregated into batches to be processed and filled together. Thus, many steel and other metal products are made to customers' specifications regarding dimension and chemical composition. Fabricated plates and sheets are cut to size to

---

[4] It has often been asserted that it is irrelevant *who* is holding the inventories, and for *certain* problems this is undoubtedly true. However, for other important problems the economic identity of the inventory holder is very relevant. This will be made clear at several points in this study.

[5] Moreover, competition within this industry largely involves changes in design and quality, the success of which depends to a great extent upon close cooperation between builder and prospective user. This industry characteristic should also favor production to order—and it may apply even to those equipment varieties that have more general uses and are therefore capable of considerable standardization.

fill specific orders; structural steel is produced in several hundred different shapes and sizes.[6]

The second category consists of products that cannot be stored over longer periods or in larger quantities without losing much of their value or causing excessive cost or risk. The timing of the production of such items is not influenced by changes in the raw material supply, because the material they are made of can be stored (or used for producing other goods). Products of this kind will be made only to the extent that they can be promptly shipped to outside users or used by their producers. Some producer nondurables belong in this category; for example, certain chemicals (such as explosives) deteriorate with age and/or are dangerous to store.[7] But, other than such special producer goods, most of this class consists of style-sensitive consumer goods. Thus, women's dresses are rapidly made and shipped to order to the distributors, to be sold to consumers before the garments go out of fashion. Only in lines that sell particularly well will a dress manufacturer risk producing a certain stock against the expected seasonal requirements. In most lines, he will only prepare samples and perhaps some small stock to meet the first orders for the coming season. This applies to many other apparel items, especially in the higher-priced lines.

Goods that are less affected by the vagaries of fashion are also primarily manufactured to order if there are specific requirements of the buyers that reflect the varying preferences of the individual consumer in style, color, size, and material. Shoe production, for example, is mostly on an order basis.[8] This then is an overlap of categories 1 and 2.

The third category includes producer durables that are made to order because they are sold to a small number of large companies at infrequent intervals and in quantities varying widely according to the changing business situation in the consuming industry. Railroad equipment, such as rolling stock and rails, offers a classic example. Goods

---

[6] Cf. Jack Hirshleifer, "The Firm's Cost Function: A Successful Reconstruction," *Journal of Business*, July 1962, pp. 235-55. Hirshleifer uses examples from nonmanufacturing industries (transportation and electric power) to illustrate production to aggregated rather than individual orders.

[7] The damage in case of accident is, of course, directly related to the size of stock. According to an early report, business in this industry is predominantly to order and average stocks seldom exceed seven to ten days' production (dynamite) or a month's supply (black powder). See Edwin G. Nourse and Associates, *America's Capacity to Produce*, Washington, D.C., Brookings Institution, 1934, p. 290. Commerce data for 1923-31 (discontinued later because of small coverage) indicate an average of about two weeks' output for stocks of all high explosives.

[8] Ruth P. Mack, *Consumption and Business Fluctuations: A Case Study of the Shoe, Leather, Hide Sequence*, New York, NBER, 1956, p. 142.

will be produced only upon order if they are characterized both by sporadic or unpredictable demand and by the high cost of filling even the smallest possible order. For example, locomotives or ships cannot be ordered in less than one unit, and even one such unit is very expensive.

Furthermore, even goods that have none of the characteristics which would make their production to stock obviously inadvisable – goods that are staple, low priced, in popular demand, and not perishable – may be produced to order under conditions of great instability and uncertainty. After the painful experiences of the 1930's, the textile industry's concern with the frequent recurrence of both heavy stock accumulations and drastic production curtailments led to an intensive reevaluation of the merits of manufacturing to stock. This was done even for cotton print cloth, a highly standardized product with a diversified demand.[9] In fact, a number of cotton textile products that are only slightly differentiated are woven mostly to order. Textile mills operate in conditions of high short-run instability. Demand for their products is volatile, with strong seasonal patterns as well as cyclical influences. More importantly, there are short but sharp speculative ordering movements that chiefly reflect the anticipation by professional textile buyers of changing prices and shifts in popularity. These fluctuations in buying are extremely difficult to forecast. The cost of output curtailments is high, but so also is the risk of carrying large unsold stocks.[10]

A Criterion for Determining the Prevalent Type of Manufacture

For a good made only to stock, unfilled orders (U) are nil.[11] For a good made only to order, total inventory in finished-product form (Q) is small: Unsold finished stocks tend to be nil (see note 1, above), and

[9] See Hiram S. Davis, "Controlling Stocks of Cotton Print Cloth," *Inventory Policies in the Textile Industries*, No. 5, Washington, D.C., Textile Foundation, 1941.

[10] To what extent these conditions are peculiar to the textile industry, I am not prepared to say. However, it is reported that certain staple materials used in construction (an industry which also faces very unstable demand) are frequently produced to order. The function of wholesaling them and maintaining adequate inventories for that purpose is customarily assumed by distributors; so the manufacturer is largely relieved of the finished-stock burden. Because of this, he sometimes offers the distributors protection against price rises between the receipt of an order and the time of shipment, and the benefits of price declines during the same period. For some historical examples, see Temporary National Economic Committee, *Geographical Differentials in Prices of Building Materials*, Monograph No. 33, 76th Cong., 2nd sess., Washington, D.C., 1940, pp. 66 and 288.

[11] Capital letters denote aggregative variables for individual or major industries, while small letters refer to microvariables (e.g., u is unfilled orders of a given product held by an individual firm; U is unfilled orders of an industry or group of firms). The available data pertain as a rule to aggregative variables. The equations in note 2, above, are valid, *mutatis mutandis* (when expressed in common units such as current-dollar or constant-dollar values) for the aggregative variables as well as the micro ones.

sold stocks would accumulate in large volume only if deliveries lagged behind output by long intervals, which is unlikely. Certainly, Q would in this case be very small *relative to* U. Industries for which there are data on both Q and U cannot be working to stock only; as a rule, they include both production to order and production to stock in various proportions. By comparing the average levels of the Q and U series for these industries, one may determine the relative importance of the two types of production. The larger the proportion of its output that is made to order, the closer an industry will come to resemble the model of pure manufacture to order—and the lower will be its typical Q/U ratio. Conversely, the larger the proportion of its output made to stock, the closer an industry will approach the opposite extreme—and the higher its typical Q/U.

Specifically, one must average the monthly values of Q for each complete calendar year covered by the data, then do the same with U; compute the ratio of these averages $(\bar{Q}/\bar{U})$ for each year; and judge from these ratios, expressed as percentages, whether for the given industry $\bar{Q}/\bar{U}$ is typically larger than 100 or smaller than 100 (or whether it is merely varying around 100 with no systematic preponderance of either $\bar{Q}$ or $\bar{U}$). If $\bar{Q}$ typically exceeds $\bar{U}$, production to stock is said to prevail; if $\bar{U}$ typically exceeds $\bar{Q}$, production to order prevails.

The method must allow for the presence of pronounced cyclical fluctuations in the stock-backlog ratios. During a vigorous expansion of demand for its output, an industry is likely to experience both a fall in its finished-goods inventory and a rise in its unfilled orders. Conversely, contracting demand will be associated with increases in unsold stocks and decreases in order backlogs. Hence Q/U should move inversely to cycles in the given industry's business. Indeed, the ratios studied show a strong inverted conformity to the business cycle at large. They tend strongly to increase between a peak and a trough year, and to decrease between the trough and the subsequent peak year (the dates being those of the National Bureau annual reference chronology).

Table 2-1 takes account of the cyclical factor in the movement of the stock-backlog ratios by presenting the averages of these ratios separately for the expansion (including peak) years and the contraction (including trough) years. In the late 1950's and early 1960's, unfilled orders had a strong downward trend in most manufacturing industries, while finished inventories continued to show a strong upward trend.

Consequently, the Q/U ratios have increased sharply. As a result, the ratios are high for many years in the "expansion" class, since there were few contraction years in the postwar period. Nevertheless, the averages — medians are used to avoid distortion by the unrepresentative extreme items — are in all but a few cases higher for the contraction and trough years than for the expansion and peak years (compare columns 7 and 8). For the individual industry and product series, which cover the interwar and early postwar years, the differences between the two categories are typically large.

If the $\bar{Q}/\bar{U}$ percentage ratios were higher than 100 in each of the contraction and trough years and lower than 100 in each of the expansion and peak years, I would interpret this to mean that the industry in question showed no consistency in working either primarily to order or primarily to stock, but was merely subject to cyclical shifts in which either one or the other type of production prevailed. But there is no example of such behavior of the ratios in the available data. Instead, the annual series of the average $\bar{Q}/\bar{U}$ ratios, although they all fluctuate cyclically, group themselves easily into two major categories: those which in most years — expansion and contraction alike — move substantially above the level of 100, and those which move in a parallel fashion below that level.[12] The former, then, may be regarded as representing goods typically made to stock and the latter as representing goods typically made to order. In the individual-product sample of Table 2-1, the two groups are about equal in number. The inclusion of peak years in the measures for expansion and of trough years in the measures for contraction could bias the results, since the averages of the ratios in expansion years other than the peak year and of the ratios in contraction years other than the trough year need not necessarily show the inverse cyclical conformity that is generally indicated in Table 2-1. (This has been pointed out to me by Geoffrey Moore.) Separate averages were therefore computed for four subsets of data: expansion, peak, contraction, and trough years. With very few exceptions, the median $\bar{Q}/\bar{U}$ ratios turned out to be larger for the contraction than for the expansion years as well as larger for the trough than for the peak years. The exceptions are slight: They relate either to cases in which only one or two observations are available for the subsets to be compared (mainly the

[12] Only about 10 per cent of the more than 600 observations fall in the zone about the critical level of the ratios, between 80 and 120.

Table 2-1

Average Ratios of Finished Stocks to Unfilled Orders, Forty Industries and Products, Various Periods, 1913–64

| Industry or Product [a] | Period Covered [b] (1) | No. of Years Covered [c] | | No. of Years in Which [d] | | Median of $\bar{Q}/\bar{U}$ Ratios [d] | | |
		Exp. and Peak Years (2)	Cont. and Trough Years (3)	Q/U < 100 (4)	Q/U > 100 (5)	All Years Covered (6)	Exp. and Peak Years [e] (7)	Cont. and Trough Years [e] (8)
Primary metals								
Merchant pig iron (OR)	1919–26	5	3	7	1	66.2	56.9	75.4
Steel sheets (OR)	1919–36	11	7	17	1	34.4	44.7	30.6
Fabricated metal products								
Steel barrels and drums, heavy type (OR)	1933–54	17	5	22	0	2.2	2.4	0.7
Oil burners (ST)	1929–52	17	7	6	18	228.4	190.7	588.6
Bathtubs (ST)	1919–31	7	6	5	8	150.9	102.8	261.8
Lavatories, sinks, and misc. enameled sanitary ware (ST)	1919–31	7	6	4	9	261.4	261.4	333.8
Wire cloth (OR)	1924–39	10	6	3	13	271.4	164.8	463.1
Clay and glass products								
Illuminating glassware (ST)	1923–37	10	5	0	15	304.3	223.6	408.6
Face brick (ST)	1923–35	8	5	1	12	325.2	284.5	359.0
Lumber and wood products								
Total hardwoods (ST)	1925–31	4	3	0	7	494.9	479.9	591.2
Southern pine lumber (ST)	1929–55	19	8	0	27	515.3	477.2	647.0
Do.	1947–64	14	4	0	18	586.2	556.3	644.8
Western pine lumber (ST)	1947–64	14	4	0	18	435.7	463.0	388.6
Douglas fir lumber (ST)	1947–64	14	4	2	16	161.4	159.4	165.2

Oak flooring (ST)	1913–55	31	12	17	26	138.7	138.1	157.1
Do.	1947–64	14	4	4	14	147.5	147.5	176.5
Maple flooring (OR)	1929–54	18	8	11	15	140.3	140.3	173.8
Do.	1947–64	14	4	15	3	76.2	65.6	89.2
Paper and paper products								
Boxboards (OR)	1924–32	4	5	6	3	56.7	56.0	112.5
Paper, excl. building paper, newsprint, and paperboard (ST)	1934–55	17	5	15	7	62.6	62.0	72.1
Textile products								
Hosiery, total (ST)	1924–30	4	3	1	6	130.6	146.5	130.6
Women's full fash. hosiery (ST)	1928–39	8	4	0	12	299.9	282.2	375.8
Knit underwear, cotton, wool and mixtures[e]	1934–38	4	1	3	2	98.1	93.6	150.8
Rayon cut from own fabrics (ST)	1934–38	4	1	0	5	363.1	340.9	471.0
Sheets (ST)	1928–38	7	4	3	8	179.6	135.0	210.8
Denims (OR)	1928–38	7	4	10	1	77.8	77.8	84.1
Wool, menswear (OR)	1935–39	4	1	5	0	42.7	38.8	71.1
Women's wear[e]	1935–39	4	1	3	2	83.0	77.8	107.2
Carded cottons, wide plain print cloth (OR)	1928–38	7	4	8	3	80.5	80.5	89.9
Combed cottons, lawns (ST)	1930–31; 1933–38	4	3	1	7	202.3	131.1	376.4
Colored yarn shirtings (OR)	1934–38	4	1	5	0	12.4	12.8	10.9
Staple rayons, taffeta[f]	1934–39	5	1	5	1	59.0	58.9	106.4
Cotton yarn								
Carded weaving (OR)	1928–38	7	4	11	0	36.9	29.1	43.6
Carded knitting (OR)	1928–38	7	4	11	0	26.5	20.8	26.0

(continued)

17

Table 2-1 (concluded)

Industry or Product [a]	Period Covered [b] (1)	No. of Years Covered [c]		No. of Years in Which [d]		Median of $\bar{Q}/\bar{U}$ Ratios [d]		
		Exp. and Peak Years (2)	Cont. and Trough Years (3)	$Q/U < 100$ (4)	$Q/U > 100$ (5)	All Years Covered (6)	Exp. and Peak Years [e] (7)	Cont. and Trough Years [e] (8)
Textile products (cont.)								
Worsted yarn								
Bradford knitting (OR)	1935–39	4	1	5	0	34.4	34.8	28.6
Broadwoven goods (OR)	1946–64	15	4	19	0	41.0	42.0	41.0
Major-industry aggregates [g]								
Primary metals (OR)	1948–55	6	2	8	0	13.9	13.6	24.0
Do.	1953–64	9	3	12	0	24.4	17.4	27.5
Machinery, total (OR)	1946–55	7	3	10	0	17.9	15.8	23.1
Do.	1953–64	9	3	12	0	21.4	20.7	22.1
Transportation equipment (OR)	1946–55	7	3	10	0	6.0	5.4	6.6
Do.	1953–64	9	3	12	0	3.5	3.6	3.4
Paper (OR)	1946–55	7	3	10	0	44.6	35.7	58.9
Durable goods industries, total (OR)	1939–55	13	4	17	0	11.3	11.3	13.0
Do.	1953–64	9	3	10	0	16.6	16.0	17.2
Nondurable goods industries, total (ST)	1939–55	13	4	4	13	162.1	162.1	189.5
Do.	1953–64	9	3	0	12	284.7	282.7	286.7
All manufacturing industries (OR)	1939–55	13	4	17	0	22.6	22.6	26.6
Do.	1949–62	10	4	14	0	29.3	23.6	36.1

Notes to Table 2-1

Source: Steel barrels and oak flooring (1947–64): U.S. Department of Commerce, Bureau of the Census; wire cloth: Wire Cloth Manufacturers' Association; illuminating glassware: Illuminating Glassware Guild; face brick: American Face Brick Association; total hardwoods: Hardwoods Manufacturers' Institute; western pine lumber: Maple Flooring Manufacturers' Association; textiles, except series on staple rayon, cotton yarn, worsted yarn, and broadwoven goods: Hiram S. Davis, "Inventory Trends in Textile Production and Distribution," Number Seven of *Inventory Policies in the Textile Industries,* The Textile Foundation, Washington, D.C., 1941, p. 27; textile products not in preceding source and primary metals: U.S. Department of Commerce, Office of Business Economics. For sources underlying the remaining items see Appendix A.

a (ST) signifies goods made primarily to stock; (OR), goods made primarily to order.

b Identifies the complete calendar years for which the average ratios of finished stocks to unfilled orders were computed.

c Identified according to the annual reference chronology of the National Bureau. For the calendar-year dates of business cycle peaks and troughs in the United States see A. F. Burns and W. C. Mitchell, *Measuring Business Cycles,* New York, NBER, 1947, Table 16, p. 78.

d $\bar{Q}/\bar{U}$ denotes ratio of finished-goods inventory ($\bar{Q}$) to unfilled orders ($\bar{U}$), in percentage terms. The ratios are based on monthly averages of Q and U for each calendar year covered.

e The evidence of the ratios is inadequate for classifying this item as either "to order" or "to stock," due to the shortness of the record and the apparently dominant influence of the cyclical factor in the movement of the ratios above and below 100.

f The product is described in monographs on management policies in the textile industries as being sold from current as well as future output. See text and note 14.

g For each of the industries except paper products, two sets of measures are shown, one based on the OBE data for the years before 1956 and the other based on the current Census data (1963 revision) that cover the later years as well.

contraction years) or to small and uncertain differences (which are in several instances reversed when means instead of medians are used). For the aggregate series which start in 1946 or 1948, the category "contraction years" (excluding trough years) is empty, because none of the recent business declines lasted more than thirteen months. In no case did the re-examination of the ratios lead to a revision of the classification in Table 2-1, column 9, which distinguishes the products made primarily to order from those made primarily to stock.

Interindustry Comparisons of Stock-Backlog Ratios

Some of the products covered in Table 2-1 would be expected to be manufactured primarily to order and some primarily to stock. On the whole, the results obtained by using the $\bar{Q}/\bar{U}$ ratios conform to such expectations. For example, the ratios are low in both good and bad business years for steel sheets, which we know are made largely to specification. The ratios are extremely low throughout for steel barrels and drums, a heavy item of industrial equipment. They run with perfect or high consistency below the level of 100 for those textile products which are style-sensitive or must meet individual buyer requirements: woolen menswear fabrics, colored yarn shirtings, and cotton and worsted yarns. On the other hand, the ratios are typically high (greater than 100) for a variety of staple products: textiles such as hosiery and sheets; construction materials such as southern pine lumber and face brick; and residential building equipment such as oil burners and bathroom fixtures.[13]

However, it must be noted that the dichotomy employed, while emphasizing one important distinction between types of business operation in manufacturing, glosses over another, no less important distinction between modes of adjustment to varying demand. A firm should be able to avoid building a large finished inventory even though it produces goods without having sold them previously on contract. The adjustment of output and price, if sufficiently prompt and large, should minimize the volume of both finished stocks and unfilled orders. (Indeed, the extreme model of perfect competition without uncertainty can be conceived, in which instantaneous market price reactions would prevent the appearance of stocks and backlogs alike.) Although these output and price variations perform a major role in adjustment to business fluctuations, in practice (for reasons to be explored later) they still leave room, in many diverse industries, for product inventories and order backlogs whose average volumes and changes are large.

Where the average levels of both product inventories and order backlogs ($\bar{Q}$ and $\bar{U}$) are small relative to average output ($\bar{Z}$) or shipments ($\bar{S}$), one would assume that the firms rely largely on price-output adjustments and succeed in selling their outputs currently. The comparison of the $\bar{Q}/\bar{U}$ ratios alone does not permit isolation of the elements of the "sell-as-you-make" policy from those of the "sell-before-" and "sell-after-you-make" policies.[14] However, from the available data it

<hr/>

[13] A unique case is presented by maple flooring, where the stock-backlog ratios show a strong decline between the prewar and the recent postwar period. Here the averages for 1929–54 all exceed 100, while those for 1947–64 are less than 100; so a reclassification from ST to OR is required under our criterion.

[14] Note that if output is sold shortly before it comes off the machine, some backlog of orders will

appears that where $\bar{U}$ is large relative to $\bar{Q}$, it is also typically large relative to $\bar{S}$, which tends to validate the notion of manufacture to order described here and the selection of the industries that are representative of this category.

The one significant exception to this among the major industries that report unfilled orders is paper. In this industry finished inventory tends to be smaller than the unfilled orders backlog (see the industry aggregate and compare also "boxboards" and "paper, excl. building paper . . ." in the product section of Table 2-1) but the backlog itself is very small — on the average not more than about two-thirds of monthly shipments. (Of all major manufacturing industries for which unfilled orders are reported, paper alone has a $\bar{U}/\bar{S}$ ratio of less than 1, as shown in Table 6-5, below.) Hence current price and output adjustments would be expected to be very important in the paper industry, and they are, particularly output adaptability.[15]

When the figures for finished stocks and unfilled orders are not physical-volume data for individual commodities but value data for multiproduct industries, the ratios must be viewed in the light of the probability that Q and U represent aggregates of different goods. A predominance of Q over U could then mean that most of the items produced by the given industry are made typically to stock, but it could also mean that the items made to stock, even though less numerous than the others, have a larger value weight.[16] Nevertheless, there is little ambiguity about the evidence in Table 2-1, which clearly confirms that production to order prevails heavily in such industry groups as

exist at any time, though it cannot be larger than the amount of work started in production (assuming that no real "advance" orders, i.e., commitments of output of future production periods, are accepted). Finished stocks do not come into existence, and yet the product is made in anticipation of immediate needs of the market, not in fulfillment of contracts for delivery in the more distant future. It follows that unfilled orders may exceed finished stocks for an industry whose principal policy is "make and sell" rather than "make to order."

[15] The relationship between new orders, production, and shipments of paper is close, and the lags involved are mostly short (see Chapter 4). Information from the American Paper and Pulp Association confirms that, while paper products are produced in large measure to order in accordance with the evidence of our $\bar{Q}/\bar{U}$ ratios, the lags of output and shipments relative to new orders are usually very short. The reasons given are the continuous nature and fairly short duration of fabrication processes and the great adaptability of equipment to production of various items. But prices, too, seem to be more flexible here than in many other manufacturing industries (see Chapter 6).

The pattern of rayon taffetas is similar. Judging from the slender information on the Q/U ratios that is here available, this product would be classified as manufactured to order, but the prewar Textile Foundation study (see source note to Table 2-1) refers to this case as exemplifying a policy of selling from current output.

[16] The ratios for textile products show how heterogeneous the output of a major industry can be when it is classified according to whether the goods are made to order or to stock (Table 2-1, listings for individual products of the industry).

primary metals, machinery, and transportation equipment, as would be expected.[17]

Furthermore, the ratios for the comprehensive major-industry aggregates show that industries which produce mainly to order are dominant in the composite of all durable manufactures. In contrast, production to stock apparently prevails within the aggregate of nondurable goods industries. In appraising this last finding, however, one must remember that all of the major nondurable goods industries report inventory figures, while only four of them—textiles, leather, paper, and printing and publishing—report unfilled orders. For the large part of the nondurables sector that includes food, beverages, apparel, tobacco, chemicals, petroleum, and rubber, new orders are considered to be equal to "sales" (or value of shipments) in the current compilation of the Department of Commerce. For most of the products of these industries the assumption that orders backlogs are negligible should be realistic. (Note that these are, in part, products of industries in which continuity of operation is particularly important for cost reasons; in part, goods whose rates of supply in the short period are subject to only a very limited control by the manufacturer; and, in part, commodities whose producers face fairly stable and predictable demand conditions.) However, some of the component industries of these major groups undoubtedly do receive advance orders which may at times accumulate to substantial volumes.[18]

Finally, for total manufacturing (last two lines of Table 2-1), the ratios again suggest that sectors working to order outweigh those working to stock, despite the inclusion here of the seven major nondurable goods industries "without unfilled orders." No doubt, the ratios can

[17] The points made in this and the following paragraphs are demonstrated in Table 2-1 with the aid of both the most recent series on manufacturers' orders and inventories (as revised in 1963; see Table 2-1, note g) and the data before 1953.

[18] Backlogs of purchasing orders from distributors and retailers are certainly *not* negligible in at least a large part of the apparel industry, which is characterized by small companies that are probably particularly anxious to keep finished inventory low because of the risks inherent in the seasonality and sensitivity to style changes of their operations. In fact, the National Credit Office, Inc., has collected quarterly information on unit production, shipments, stocks of piece goods, *and unfilled orders* from a panel of more than one hundred clothing manufacturers for a few recent years. In the seven quarters between the fall 1950 season and the spring 1952 season, unfilled orders of menswear manufacturers amounted most often to about one-half and sometimes to more than three-fourths of the manufacturers' cuttings (see W. A. Bennett and R. S. White, "Menswear, Past, Present, and Future," *Dun's Review,* August 1952, pp. 29 and 60–66). It may be, however, that the unfilled orders for lines of apparel still more "perishable" from the point of view of the seller (such as women's dresses) would be much smaller because rates of output and deliveries are adjusted with particular rapidity to swings in new business for such articles.

give only a crude indication of how total manufacturing is divided between industries operating to order and industries operating to stock. But as far as this evidence goes, it is unequivocal in pointing to (1) a sharp contrast between the order-oriented durables and the stock-oriented nondurables, and (2) the strikingly high importance of sectors producing to order within the manufacturing division as a whole.[19]

It must be admitted that the period covered by the aggregate data (1939–64) mostly includes years of good or excellent business conditions: the rapid wartime expansion and the generally prosperous postwar times. But even in 1939, which was quite a poor year, finished stocks amounted to no more than 88 per cent of unfilled orders for all manufactures (48 per cent for total durables and 229 per cent for total nondurables).

None of these results should be understood to imply that any neat divisions can be made within industry aggregates between production to stock and production to order. Diversified outputs of large companies would often include both categories in variable proportions. Dependable quantitative information on this subject is scanty or nonexistent, and presumably hard to acquire; the indirect and rough measures presented here must not be viewed as compensating for the deficiencies in the data. Nevertheless, the evidence from the $\bar{Q}/\bar{U}$ ratios has claims to both reasonableness and usefulness. It is consistent not only with what is known in general about the industries under study but also with differences in relative timing and amplitudes that are observed for series classified according to type of manufacture (see Chapters 3 and 4, passim). Further evidence bearing on the importance of unfilled orders (and therefore of production to order) in industries covered by the new Census data on manufacturers' shipments and orders (1963 revision) is given in Appendix A (Table A-2 and text).

[19] On the logic of our test, i.e., assuming that the stock-backlog ratios tend to be considerably higher (lower) than 100 for all goods made typically to stock (to order), the range of the ratios for total manufacturing (from 23 to 36) in Table 2-1 would indicate that the greater part of industrial production is organized on an order, and not on a stock, basis. If the contrary situation were true and production to stock were prevalent, then the average level of Q/U would have to exceed 50. For even if the average for all sectors working to stock were as low as 100 and that for all sectors working to order as low as zero, the over-all ratio could not be lower than 50 as long as production to stock accounted for not less than half of total manufacturing output (it would equal 50 if it accounted for precisely half of the total). But we expect the average for the stock-oriented industries to be substantially above 100 and the average for the order-oriented industries to be higher than zero (but significantly lower than 100). This makes it even more certain that an over-all average ratio considerably lower than 50 still indicates the prevalence of production to order.

Interpreting Orders Data:
The Importance of Cancellations

Loose Intentions or Firm Commitments?

Much of the preceding analysis implicitly assumes that orders received by manufacturers represent declarations of serious decisions, rather than indications of loose intentions, to buy. A company would hardly be able or willing to engage in production to order, unless it viewed the bulk of its orders as "firm" in this sense. The test is, of course, actual experience: When the proportion of cancellations is steadily high, orders cannot long be regarded as firm commitments. The legal contractual arrangements and industrial customs regarding orders generally reflect the economic considerations that are decisive for the issue; but the economic factors are likely to vary, perhaps not just between industries but also over time, while laws and customs are relatively rigid.

Where production is largely to stock but some advance orders are being received, the usefulness to the company of such orders as predictors of demand should depend on their firmness (as well as their size relative to the total company output). Interesting questions arise here of how advance orders are used in this role and what predictive value they possess, but the available aggregative data, in which advance orders are mixed with orders filled from stock, are clearly not designed to help in examining such questions.

Information of two kinds can be used to appraise the role of order cancellations: reports on trade practices and the evidence of time series. Unfortunately, both sources are meager. The quantitative evidence of time series is by far the more important of the two, and it will permit us to draw some guarded inferences.

First, however, let us refer to some reports on the terms of sale contracts in individual industries. These suggest that establishing and varying the rules on cancellation privileges is one of the instruments by which sellers can influence the course of ordering. But such privileges are often negotiated between the firm placing and the firm receiving the order, and are thus determined by the buyer as well as the seller.

Sales agreements differ substantially in regard to the interrelated clauses on cancellations, acceptances, and deliveries. Consider the following illustrations of the diverse rules accepted by companies in different industries. In the early post-World War II period (a time when "seller's markets" predominated), cancellations were (1) precluded altogether on ordered goods in process of manufacture or on special sizes, shapes, etc. (rayon, steel, and structural clay and pottery products); (2) allowed, provided the buyer answered for the possible losses to the seller (paper); (3) permitted, along with changes of orders, in cases of mutual consent only (foundry equipment); and (4) acknowledged as a privilege of the producer in the event of his inability to secure the necessary materials and parts (electrical supplies and appliances). Purchase contracts featuring an "escalator clause," providing for an increase in sale price in the case of a rise in the costs of the seller, were frequent in many industries, but in some (e.g., chemicals) they also reserved to the buyer the right not to accept the shipment if he deemed the price increase excessive or otherwise unwarranted.[20]

This differentiation occurs partly because customary trade practices vary among industries, and partly because of other factors, such as changing business and market conditions, new legal decisions, mutual confidence of buyer and vendor, etc. Systematic and substantial *interindustry* differences in cancellation privileges reduce the usefulness of the order series for individual industries as general business indicators.[21]

Comparing Long-Term Average Levels of
Orders Received and Filled

In most of the series based on directly reported new-order figures, orders canceled during the reporting period have not been deducted. Take a series on gross new orders for a given industry or product and a corresponding series on output or shipments. Assuming the two are strictly comparable in coverage, the average level of the new orders over a long period of time should exceed the average level of the shipments only by the average amount of cancellations (orders include both the advance orders and orders filled or shipped directly from stock). This is the rationale of the simple procedure followed in Table 2-2.

[20] See G. Clark Thompson, "Industry's Terms and Conditions of Sale," National Industrial Conference Board, *Studies in Business Policy,* Conference Board Report 26, New York, 1948, passim; and F. R. Lusardi, "Purchasing for Industry," in *ibid.*, Report 33, New York, 1948, p. 22.

[21] Cf. "An Appraisal of Data and Research on Businessmen's Expectations About Outlook and Operating Variables," *Report of Consultant Committee on General Business Expectations Organized by the Board of Governors of the Federal Reserve System,* September 1955, p. 133.

Table 2-2
Comparison of Average Annual Levels of Gross New Orders, Shipments, and Production, Selected Industries or Products, Various Periods, 1916–55

	Gross New Orders Minus Shipments or Production	
	Amount[a] (1)	Per Cent of New Orders[b] (2)
MERCHANT PIG IRON (THOUS. LONG TONS), 1919–26[c] (8) Orders[d] = 4,156		
Shipments	−583	(14.0)
Production	−553	(13.3)
STEEL SHEETS (THOUS. NET TONS), 1919–36[c] (18) Orders[d] = 2,416		
Shipments	+21	0.9
Production	−48	(2.0)
MACHINE TOOLS, DOMESTIC (MILL. DOL.), 1946–63[c] (18) Orders[d] = 467		
Shipments	+44	9.4
MACHINE TOOLS, FOREIGN (MILL. DOL.), 1946–63[c] (18) Orders[d] = 80		
Shipments	+6	7.4
WOODWORKING MACHINERY (THOUS. DOL.), 1921–39[c] (19) Orders[d] = 10,697		
Shipments	+91	0.9
FOUNDRY EQUIPMENT (MONTHLY AV. SHIPMENTS, 1922–24 = 100), 1925–39[c] (15) Orders[d] = 123		
Shipments	+6	4.6
RAILROAD FREIGHT CARS (NO. OF CARS), 1913–55[c] (43) Orders[d] = 69,561		
Shipments	+2,877	4.1
RAILROAD PASSENGER CARS (NO. OF CARS), 1911–55[c] (45) Orders[d] = 1,048		
Shipments	−16	(1.5)
RAILROAD LOCOMOTIVES (NO. OF LOCOMOTIVES), 1920–40[c] (21) Orders[d] = 698		
Shipments	+2	0.3

(continued)

Table 2-2 (concluded)

	Gross New Orders Minus Shipments or Production	
	Amount [a] (1)	Per Cent of New Orders [b] (2)

FURNITURE (NO. OF DAYS PROD.), 1924–46 [c] (23)
  Orders [d] = 259

Shipments	+34	13.1

BOXBOARD (THOUS. SHORT TONS), 1924–32 [c] (9)
  Orders [d] = 2,512

Production	−13	(0.5)

PAPERBOARD (THOUS. SHORT TONS), 1938–55 [c] (18)
  Orders [d] = 9,254

Production	+111	1.2

PAPER, EXCL. BUILDING PAPER, ETC. (THOUS. SHORT TONS), 1934–55 [c] (22)
  Orders [d] = 7,579

Shipments	+32	4.2
Production	+2	0.2

OAK FLOORING (MILL. BOARD FT.), 1912–55 [c] (44)
  Orders [d] = 411

Shipments	−5	(1.2)
Production	−8	(1.9)

SOUTHERN PINE LUMBER (MILL. BOARD FT.), 1916–55 [c] (40)
  Orders [d] = 7,084

Shipments	−23	(0.3)
Production	+35	0.5

BATHTUBS (THOUS. PIECES), 1918–26 [c] (9)
  Orders [d] = 901

Shipments	+77	8.5

LAVATORIES (THOUS. PIECES), 1918–31 [c] (14)
  Orders [d] = 1,047

Shipments	+59	5.6

KITCHEN SINKS (THOUS. PIECES), 1918–31 [c] (14)
  Orders [d] = 1,102

Shipments	+62	5.6

Notes to Table 2-2

Source: See Appendix A.

ᵃ The units are those indicated for the individual industry. The averages are based on annual totals of the series for new orders, shipments, and production for each calendar year over the period covered by that industry.

ᵇ Ratio of the amount shown in column 1 to the amount of orders of the industry, multiplied by 100. The percentages that correspond to the negative values in column 1 are shown in parentheses. Because of rounding, the figures may differ from those computed by calculating the ratios from the levels and differences shown in the table.

ᶜ Identifies the complete calendar years covered by the corresponding series for gross new orders and shipments or production. The number of years is given in parentheses.

ᵈ Gross new orders, average annual level.

In this table, average annual amounts of gross new orders are presented for eighteen industries or product groups in column 4; in each case, the figure is the mean of annual totals for all the complete calendar years covered by the given series (the periods and units used are identified in columns 2 and 3). Similarly, mean annual levels relating to the same periods were calculated in the same units for shipments and, where data permitted, also for outputs of the same industries. Algebraic differences computed by subtracting the mean levels of shipments or production from the mean levels of gross new orders are listed in column 5 and are shown as a percentage of the levels of orders in column 6. There are sixteen comparisons with shipments (including two for machine tools, where separate figures are available for domestic and foreign transactions) and seven with production.

The expected sign of the differences in column 5 is a plus (indicating positive cancellations), but in eight of the twenty-three cases the differences are negative. This presumably means that the coverage of the order series is less than that of shipments or production; so the comparisons in these cases are inconclusive. However, in percentage terms these differences are quite small for each case but merchant pig iron. Where the differences are positive, most of them are again small; several amount to less than 1 per cent of the average level of gross new orders (column 6). The figures that suggest very low typical cancellation amounts are found for heavy equipment such as railroad locomotives, but also for diverse investment goods and materials (woodworking machinery, steel sheets), and even some standardized items (paper and paperboard, southern pine lumber). On the other hand, in a few instances the excess of gross orders over shipments is relatively large, notably so for furniture (13 per cent), machine tools (7–9 per cent), and the three items of sanitary ware (6–9 per cent).

Separate data on cancellations are available for machine tools, woodworking machinery, and furniture. Expressing cancellations as a percentage of gross new orders in terms of the average annual levels, the following figures are obtained: for domestic machine tools, 8.8; foreign machine tools, 6.4; woodworking machinery, 2.6; and furniture, 8.1. These percentages are lower than the corresponding entries in Table 2-2, column 6, except for woodworking machinery, but the discrepancies are not disturbingly large.[22] The figures computed directly from the cancellation data are presumably the more accurate estimates.

As will be shown presently, cancellations fluctuate greatly over time; in some periods, they are much larger and more important than the averages of Table 2-2 indicate. Undoubtedly, duplications of orders in times of rapid increases of demand and cancellations of orders in times of large decreases of demand combine to exert a disturbing influence in some of the individual industries to which the data refer.[23] On the average, however, cancellations appear to be relatively small for a large variety of products, including most items produced to order, such as locomotives and (according to industry reports) fabricated structural steel.

In general, one would expect sales contracts to be less easily revocable for the larger order-unit and high-cost goods than for smaller and less expensive items; also, less for specialized than for standardized, general-purpose products. The one case that would seem to contradict this expectation is machine tools, which are highly specialized but show a relatively high incidence of cancellations. However, this is mostly due to the large rise in cancellations during 1950–53 (see the next section), when military and defense-related contracts became very important for many durable goods industries, including machine tools.

---

[22] The largest discrepancy is for the furniture series, which is perhaps associated with the particular measurement units used for this item. According to the source of these data (the public accounting firm of Seidman and Seidman, Grand Rapids, Michigan), because of the variation in the number of firms reporting each month, the figures are "shown in number of days' production or sales, based on current ratios. . . . The original data are based on value" (see *Survey of Current Business, Annual Supplement*, 1932, p. 297).

[23] Thus, according to the Enameled Sanitary Ware Manufacturers' Association, "orders shipped are the best current index of the industry. Orders received are likely to pyramid during periods of great activity to be followed by cancellations if the demand drops off" (*Survey of Current Business*, May 1922, p. 81). See last three lines of Table 2-2 for figures on the average level and proportion of cancellations for these products.

Such contracts have special characteristics because they originate in the largest single source of buying power, the defense system of the federal government, and reflect certain centralized decisions based largely on noneconomic considerations. The latter may cause heavy bunching of military and related orders at certain times (during a war crisis) and sharp curtailments or withdrawals at others (when hostilities decrease and peace prospects improve).[24]

In an early (c. 1936) unpublished study of building construction, Arthur F. Burns expressed the presumption that cancellations of construction contracts are much less important than cancellations of orders for most commodities. Data to test this hypothesis are not available, but the preceding argument supports it strongly. A decision to build and equip a new industrial plant, for example, represents a commitment over a long span of the future that typically involves far greater costs and risks than a decision to alter the rate of production of a plant already in existence.

Gross and Net Orders

Unlike all other series of new orders in our collection, which are compiled directly from company data for this variable, the aggregative value series of the Department of Commerce are derived indirectly. The reporting unit is here, as in nearly all other compilations of orders data, the firm that has received the orders. The method consists in adding to the estimates of manufacturers' sales (recorded at the time of shipment) the corresponding figures on changes in the backlog of unfilled orders. This procedure results in estimates of new orders net of cancellations.[25]

[24] Apart from such major episodic factors, defense orders, in their short-term movements, are likely to be quite sensitive to a host of minor random influences. The average unit size of these orders will presumably be large and the average number of orders per unit of time will be small if the unit is short (a month or a quarter), e.g., military contracts for aircraft and ships. Orders with these characteristics would be expected to show large irregular short-period fluctuations — to be heavily bunched in one period and very sparse in another. (See Chapter 4 on aircraft orders and aggregate defense obligations.)

[25] That the sum of sales and the change in unfilled orders gives *net* new orders follows from two definitional propositions: (1) the value of all orders accepted but not filled or canceled equals the change in backlogs over the period; and (2) sales measure the value of orders filled. Let N_t^* denote the value of gross new orders accepted; D_t, orders filled (delivered); and C_t, cancellations in period t; N_t, S_t, and U_t have been defined before. Then we have

$$U_t - U_{t-1} \equiv \Delta U_t \equiv N_t^* - D_t - C_t$$
$$S_t \equiv D_t.$$

Adding the foregoing gives $\Delta U_t + S_t \equiv N_t^* - C_t$. But we already know that $N_t = \Delta U_t + S_t$; thus N_t equals $N_t^* - C_t$ (i.e., it is net of cancellations).

The Commerce estimation method also implies that the cancellations that occur in the current month (t) are reflected in the current estimate of net new orders (N_t). But it is the orders received in past months that probably account for a considerable part of current cancellations; the orders just received seem least likely to be canceled. A systematic variation over time in the age or vintage of canceled orders, if it exists, would be an interesting phenomenon that should be taken into account in appraising the impact of new orders on production, shipments, etc. To illustrate, suppose that cancellations are high at about the time of the downturn and shortly thereafter, and that they refer to "old" orders placed in mid-expansion or the early boom. Then new orders recorded in that phase of the business upswing will have been overstated, in the sense that lower estimates would have led to better (less optimistically biased) predictions of future shipments (i.e., of the values of S at the assumed downturn phase). Unfortunately, information about the composition by vintage of the canceled orders is not available. Data on unfilled orders are not decomposed that way either; if they were, many interesting problems in the analysis of short-run behavior of orders and production, including this one, could be treated much more effectively.

Independent evidence on the behavior of manufacturers' orders since 1949 is provided by series compiled by Standard and Poor's Corporation. These are monthly indexes (1949 = 100) based on dollar values. They have a much smaller sample base than the Commerce series; hence they are considerably more erratic. The indexes for new orders are compiled directly, gross of cancellations.[26]

Chart 2-1 compares the Commerce value aggregate for all industries reporting new orders as distinct from shipments, with Standard and Poor's composite index. (Excluded in both cases is a large part of the nondurable goods sector for which the value of new orders is assumed to equal the value of shipments.) The two series are plotted to uniform logarithmic scales, a standard procedure in most of the charts in this book. [On these scales, vertical distances denote equal relative changes, permitting direct comparisons between all kinds of (nonnegative) data.]

[26] Because of their narrow coverage, the component-industry indexes from the Standard and Poor's compilation are used in this book largely as supplementary evidence. However, in Appendix B, the charted behavior and cyclical timing measures of the indexes for shipments, unfilled orders, and new orders are discussed at some length. The indexes are presented there for 1949–58, for which they have been seasonally adjusted by the National Bureau.

Chart 2-1

Department of Commerce and Standard and Poor's Estimates of Total Advance Orders for Durable and Nondurable Goods, 1949–58

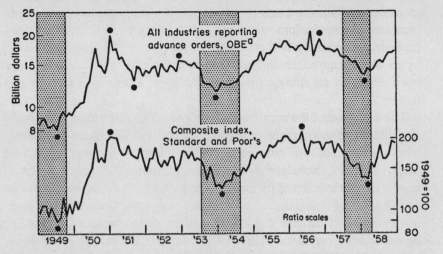

Note: Shaded areas represent business cycle contractions; unshaded areas, expansions. Dots identify peaks and troughs of specific cycles.

[a] Includes all durable goods industries and four major nondurable goods industries reporting unfilled orders.

The periods of general business contraction are shaded, another arrangement followed in most of these charts. It is clear that the two series have very similar systematic movements—trends and cyclical fluctuations. Both their timing and their relative amplitudes are much alike.

The one significant difference is in 1952. There the Commerce series shows an upward movement which, while mild, is yet sufficiently long and clear to qualify as a specific-cycle expansion. In Standard and Poor's index, on the other hand, the corresponding movements are considerably shorter and weaker: a retardation superimposed upon the contraction that began early in 1951, rather than a cyclical expansion.

The reason for this is not easily determined, since the two samples differ greatly in size and to some extent also in composition, but an important part of the explanation is probably the contrast between a net and a gross orders series. In some durable goods industries, especially those with heavy military contracts, cancellations increased very substantially when the threat of a further intensification or an extension of the Korean conflict subsided and the chances of a truce increased. Thus net orders (Commerce) dropped much more rapidly than gross orders (Standard and Poor's) from their Korean peak levels. The increase in cancellations was temporary. When cancellations returned to their substantially lower normal levels, net orders moved upward, again closely approaching the value of gross orders, which may have been declining all along, or perhaps were just leveling off temporarily (Chart 2-1).

The coverage of the component industries in the Standard and Poor's compilation is too narrow to allow detailed comparisons with the Commerce series for the corresponding industries.[27] However, for one major industry, nonelectrical machinery, an independent survey of new orders is conducted by the economics department of the McGraw-Hill Publishing Company, and these data have some interesting features not available elsewhere. Like the Standard and Poor's series, they are indexes based on dollar values of new orders, gross of cancellations, beginning in 1949. But they are designed to concentrate on that part of nonelectrical machinery output which represents industrial equipment serving the needs of private nonagricultural producers. An effort is thus made to exclude from these indexes orders for defense products, consumer durables (household appliances), and farm machinery. The resulting totals cover seven types of machinery and, since 1957, are also divided into domestic and foreign orders.[28]

Despite the differences in the coverage and estimation methods, there is a substantial similarity between the McGraw-Hill index and the Commerce series on the aggregate value of new orders for total nonelectrical machinery (Chart 2-2). Again, this applies to the longer systematic movements, i.e., to the trends and cycles. The short irregular movements are usually more frequent, if not longer, in the index than in the aggregate, but at times (e.g., in 1951) the opposite is true. There are probably opposite factors at work here: the smaller sample

[27] Some further observations on this point are made in Appendix B.
[28] The seven components are pumps and compressors, engines and turbines, construction machinery, mining machinery, metalworking machinery, office equipment, and other industrial machinery. Indexes are available for all these categories (since 1957, for foreign as well as total new orders). The data are published without seasonal adjustment, except for total new orders, for which the adjusted figures are also given. The base period was 1950 until March 1963, when it was replaced by the average 1957–59 = 100. New seasonal adjustment factors were also introduced at that time (see release of the McGraw-Hill Department of Economics, March 4, 1963, Part III).

Chart 2-2
Department of Commerce and McGraw-Hill Estimates of
New Orders for Nonelectrical Machinery, 1949–62

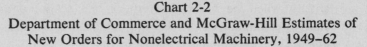

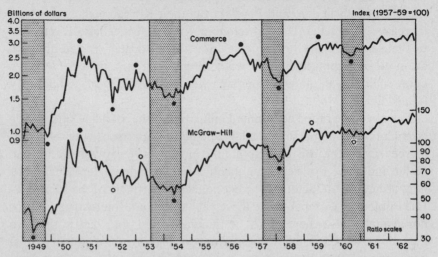

Note: Shaded areas represent business cycle contractions; unshaded areas, expansions. Dots identify peaks and troughs of specific cycles; circles, short cycles or retardations.

tends to make the index more erratic, while the deduction of cancellations tends to add to the variability of the Commerce series.

The kind of difference between the course of the net and gross orders in 1952 that was observed for the comprehensive series in Chart 2-1 is not produced here, except perhaps faintly (see Chart 2-2). This may be related to the exclusion of military orders from the McGraw-Hill series. The other differences between the two nonelectrical machinery estimates which appear significant (in 1956 and 1959–60) may also reflect the discrepancies in coverage more than the effects of cancellations.

The role of cancellations can be isolated from other factors in the machine tool industry, for which data relating to orders are particularly rich. Chart 2-3 compares domestic net new orders for machine tools with the corresponding gross orders. The two monthly series stay close together most of the time but move apart in certain periods, particularly in 1952–53. Their behavior during that phase of the Korean con-

Chart 2-3

Gross and Net Domestic Orders, Metal-cutting Machine Tools, 1946–63

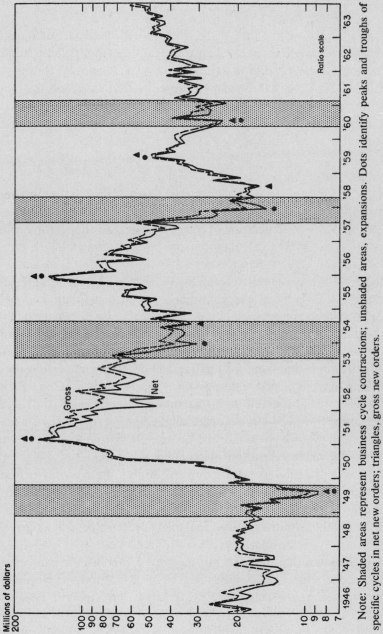

Note: Shaded areas represent business cycle contractions; unshaded areas, expansions. Dots identify peaks and troughs of specific cycles in net new orders; triangles, gross new orders.
Source: National Machine Tool Builders' Association.

flict illustrates strikingly the developments discussed before in connection with Chart 2-1.

The timing of the two series at peaks is nearly identical, but at troughs there are some differences. These suggest that net orders would at times turn upward earlier than gross orders (see Chart 2-3 for the years 1956 and 1958). It will be shown presently that cancellations tend to lag behind orders received; they were declining sharply during most of 1954 and again in 1958, which explains the net-gross discrepancies observed at these troughs.

Cancellations

Orders for industrial products can be canceled for a number of reasons: (1) a change of mind by the would-be purchaser (he no longer wants his order filled because of actual or expected changes in business conditions or revised calculations: the costs of completing the transaction appear greater than the costs of withdrawing); (2) an analogous change by the prospective supplier or vendor; (3) nonfulfillment of contract, or unsatisfactory performance, or disagreement on how the order was to be or was executed (this may be by either party to the transaction or third parties such as subcontractors); (4) liquidation of "surplus" orders by the firm that had placed them (these are tentative, informal orders implying no binding commitment; multiple orders of this kind may be placed at certain times, particularly when a tight supply situation is suspected, to insure timely delivery; after the required items are received, the remaining "duplicating" orders are rescinded).

If cancellations have a "normal" range and rise well above it, would not such an increase be a sign of economic distress, like a similar movement in business failures, for example? An affirmative answer implies that the rise in cancellations can be accounted for primarily by the first two causes, i.e., a deterioration in business conditions or expectations that forced the withdrawal of a great many orders placed at a time when business was better or was expected to improve.

To the extent that they are thus motivated, increases in cancellations should occur mainly during business recessions, perhaps with a short lead where the worsening of conditions was anticipated. This would imply a tendency toward inverted cyclical behavior. In the data on cancellations, however, positive cyclical patterns prevail, modified somewhat by lags and secondary movements. Thus the postwar series for machine tools shows three troughs which follow the business cycle revivals in 1949, 1954, and 1958 by short intervals (see the upper curve in Chart 2-4). It also shows three peaks, a high one early in 1952 (the advanced stage of the "Korean" expansion), and lower ones in 1956–57 and late 1960, again at the close of an upswing or shortly afterward.

A comparison of Charts 2-4 and 2-3 indicates a substantial positive correlation between cancellations and new orders, with cancellations lagging behind new orders. At peaks, cancellations lagged gross new orders by long intervals, at troughs by intermediate or short intervals, as shown in the accompanying table.

Date of Peak in Gross Orders	Lead (−) or Lag (+) of Cancellations (mos.)	Date of Trough in Gross Orders	Lead (−) or Lag (+) of Cancellations (mos.)
		Aug. 1949	+6
Feb. 1951	+12	July 1954	+3
Dec. 1955	+18 [a]	Aug. 1958	+1
July 1959	+14		
Average	+14.7	Average	+3.3

[a] Cancellations had a double-peak configuration in 1956–57 (see Chart 2-4). This comparison is based on the second, higher peak; had the first one been used, a lag of five months and an average of 10.3 months would have resulted.

The positive association between new orders and cancellations can be explained very simply by the assumption that a certain proportion of orders received will usually be canceled. Given that probability, it is clear that a rise in new orders, which usually results also in a rise in order backlogs, would lead to an increase in cancellations. When there is a larger number of orders on the manufacturers' books, the number of cancellations that fall into the third category above is likely to be greater, too. A large influx of orders during a buying boom may also involve a certain amount of multiple orders (as in category 4) that are subsequently liquidated. In short, cancellations of all types are likely to increase (decrease) in response to expansions (contractions) in the volume of industrial orders.

Chart 2-4

Cancellations of Domestic Orders for Metal-cutting Machine Tools, Dollar Values and Ratios to Gross New Orders, 1946–63

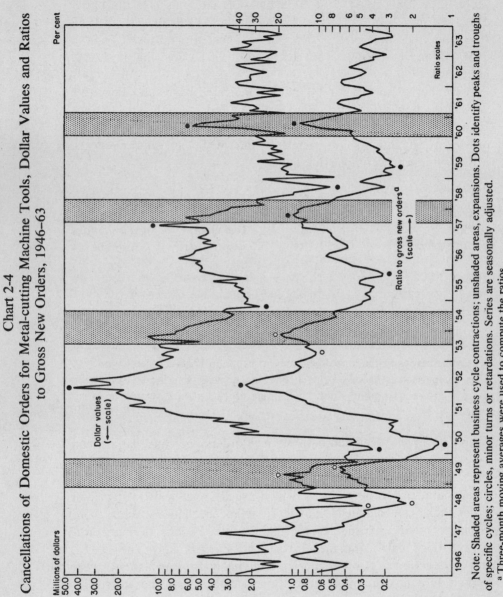

Note: Shaded areas represent business cycle contractions; unshaded areas, expansions. Dots identify peaks and troughs of specific cycles; circles, minor turns or retardations. Series are seasonally adjusted.

[a] Three-month moving averages were used to compute the ratios.

The argument seems to apply primarily to the number of orders rather than their aggregative value. One would not necessarily expect cancellations to rise if a rise in total value of orders reflected an increase in the average order size, rather than the number of orders outstanding. There is, after all, no presumption that the probability of cancellation is greater for large orders than for small ones. The available data measure the value or physical volume, not the number, of orders; consequently, these propositions cannot be tested directly. But the distinction between numbers and values is probably not very important in practice, since there is presumably a strong correlation between the two, especially for the large systematic movements in orders, which are here of main interest.

However, to explain that cancellations vary in a positive correlation with the volume of orders because they form a stable proportion of that volume is a gross oversimplification of what actually happens. The second curve in Chart 2-4 shows that the ratio of cancellations to gross new orders undergoes fluctuations similar to those of the cancellations themselves.[29] In other words, when incoming business and backlogs expand, cancellations increase not only absolutely but also relative to orders received. Furthermore, the timing discrepancies between cancellations and orders must be considered as a factor modifying the basic positive association of these two variables. Cancellations lag considerably; so, their peaks occur when new business is already sharply falling and their troughs when it is already sharply rising (compare Charts 2-4 and 2-3). Here, then, is an element of inverse relationship between cancellations and a particular indicator of business conditions, namely, the rate of change (not the level) of new orders.[30]

Data for woodworking machinery extending over the interwar period confirm that new orders and cancellations are positively correlated (Chart 2-5). Cancellations are here again small and highly erratic; their major movements are distinct in the original data but somewhat blurred by the short irregular variations; therefore, it might be useful

[29] Relative movements in cancellations are larger than those in new orders and dominate the changes in the ratio. The ratio lags somewhat behind cancellations partly because it is based on smoothed series (unsmoothed, it is extremely erratic). Gross new orders were used in the denominator but similar results would have been obtained with unfilled orders (judging from the behavior of total backlogs of machine tool orders, since separate backlog figures for domestic orders are not available).

[30] The change in new orders, which often turns ahead of the level, is of course a very early indicator. But the inverse relation in question is clearly meaningful and not just a reflection of timing divergencies (which can produce spurious associations of this kind between leading and lagging series).

Chart 2-5

New Orders and Cancellations, Woodworking Machinery, 1921–39

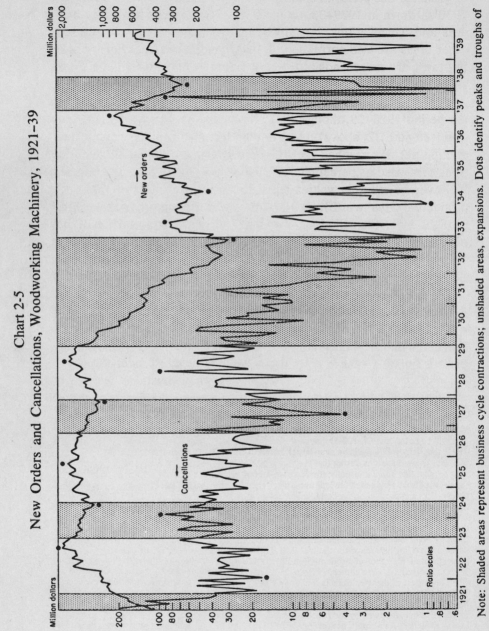

Note: Shaded areas represent business cycle contractions; unshaded areas, expansions. Dots identify peaks and troughs of specific cycles.

to visualize this series in smoothed form. The large swings during the 1930's—down in 1929-33, up in 1933-37—stand out in both new orders and cancellations, but smaller movements in the two series at other times are also correlated. Lags of cancellations prevail at peaks, but there are more leads at troughs, and the timing dispersion is considerable.[31]

Finally, there is also some supporting evidence for furniture orders in the period 1923-29, though these data must be interpreted with caution (see note 22, above). Here new orders measured in value of production per day reached their highest levels in 1926, as did cancellations measured as percentage of new orders. In 1928-29, new orders had average monthly values equal to those of production (about 28 production days' worth); by 1934, they had declined to the equivalent of eight days. Cancellations dropped in the same period from 12 to 7 per cent of new orders. However, cancellations remained very low, with some tendency to decline, in 1934-36 when new orders were definitely improving, and seemed to lag behind new orders at peaks.

The furniture data are difficult to evaluate not only because of the way they are measured but also because they are subject to strong yet rather variable seasonal influences. These reflect a particular institution of the industry, the great furniture markets held four times (in some periods twice) a year in certain key centers of the trade.[32]

---

[31] The months of lead (−) or lag (+) of cancellations at peaks in gross orders, based on unsmoothed, seasonally adjusted data, are: January 1923, +13; October 1925, +3; January 1929, −3; June 1933, +5; March 1937, +7. The average is −5.0 months. At trough dates, the figures are: June 1924, +6; October 1927, −5; March 1933, −5; September 1934, −4. The average is −2.0 months.

It will be noted (see Chart 2-5) that cancellations declined from a very high level in the first half of 1921; they may well have been even larger earlier in the 1920-21 recession. Direct evidence on the behavior of cancellations during that sharp downswing is very scant, but data for a few textile products suggest that some unusually strong spurts in the amounts of orders canceled occurred in 1920 (as shown directly by series for knit underwear and indirectly by the steep declines in new and unfilled orders and production for cotton goods, all in the second half of 1920; see Department of Commerce, Bureau of the Census, *Record Book of Business Statistics*, Part I, *Textiles*, Washington, D.C., 1927, pp. 31-33, 37-38). These indications are consistent with the statement by Simon Kuznets that ". . . the wholesaler even if he waits for the filling of his order, may cancel it if conditions change. Such cancellations were epidemic during 1920, and although resorted to with great reluctance, they are still providing an escape for the wholesaler. The manufacturer is committed to a far greater degree since all his costs of production are already expended" (*Cyclical Fluctuations, Retail and Wholesale Trade, United States, 1919-1925*, New York, 1926, p. 181).

[32] The largest of these exhibits is the American Furniture Mart in Chicago, but New York, High Point (N.C.), Grand Rapids, and San Francisco are also important (see Kenneth R. Davis, *Furniture Marketing*, Chapel Hill, N.C., 1957, particularly pp. 88-89, 154-60). The January market is the most active one, followed by the June–July market, while the others (in the spring and fall) are much less in evidence. As a result, new orders often show sharp seasonal peaks in January and secondary peaks in the mid-year (especially in the 1920's). Two seasonal troughs preceding the main market months are also conspicuous in the furniture orders data: a longer slack in the spring, centered on

The Variability of Orders and the Behavior of Production

How Firms React to Fluctuations in Orders

Time series on new orders give evidence of great variability in the demand flows for many manufactured products.[33] Few of the many series examined fail to show sizable cyclical fluctuations, and the great majority are also subject to pronounced "irregular" movements from month to month. Seasonal variations, too, are marked in many of these series; but they are presumably less troublesome as a source of instability because they are essentially periodic and therefore more predictable.

To a large extent, fluctuations in manufacturers' new orders are translated into fluctuations in production. In many industries, conditions of substantially elastic supply seem to prevail over broad ranges of variation in the output rates. Such conditions favor the use of production adjustments in response to changes in demand. But even within the range of elastic supply it would not be advisable for the firm that faces highly unstable flows of customer orders to permit its output flows to be equally unstable. To have each small, short, up-and-down movement in new orders followed by a similar movement in production would be costly and, to the extent that it is avoidable, imprudent. In fact, a large proportion of this variation is smoothed out in the output flows through appropriate production scheduling. The resulting divergencies between sales and output are reflected either in product inventory changes or in order backlog changes, depending on whether sales are executed from stock (so that they coincide with shipments) or from future production (so that they coincide with advance orders).

This role of stocks and backlogs as "buffers" or "shock absorbers"

April, and a sharp short low in December. Cancellations, on the other hand, show steep peaks in December and secondary peaks in April or May, and troughs in January–February and in the third quarter of the year. In short, seasonally, the pattern of cancellations is almost an inverted image of the pattern of new orders. This contrasts with the positive relation prevailing in the longer movements of these series.

[33] The statements made in this paragraph are verified in Chapter 3. As argued before, new orders come closer to measuring actual market demand than do figures on current manufacturing activity (production or shipments). The term "demand" is used here rather loosely to mean the volume or value demanded at a given price instead of the function linking the quantities demanded to different hypothetical prices (and other relevant variables). It is believed that where the term is so used no serious risk of misunderstanding is involved.

implies also that prices do not change greatly in response to these short variations in new orders. There is indeed no good reason why even prices in highly competitive markets should be so "flexible" as to react to each small quirk in buying which does not force any major decisions concerning the production levels. Where sellers set prices, consideration of the costs and risks, which will often appear large, would inhibit frequent price alterations and revisions.

The larger *cyclical* movements in buying or ordering are normally associated with similar major movements in production, as would be expected. But an expansion of output is limited by existing capacities, while that of new orders is not. When advance orders reach rates exceeding those of capacity production and this condition of "excess demand" prevails for some time, a cumulative expansion of the order backlog is, of course, bound to occur. Where the process is observed, it must be inferred that prices did not rise sufficiently and in time to prevent it. To be sure, prices do increase when unfilled orders expand, but they do so typically in a lagging fashion. The massive backlog accumulations of recent history reflected growing delivery delays in several major manufacturing industries, and it can be argued that prices would have risen more in the absence of these delays (Chapter 7).

If their degree of "firmness" is sufficiently high, the accumulated orders represent a precontracted volume of work to be done by the supplying firm and the resources it employs. When the demand falls off again, a firm that emerges from the boom with a large backlog of such orders can maintain satisfactory levels of production for some time by drawing upon the backlog. Although the flow of new orders into the backlog would now proceed at rates smaller than the outflow orders filled (and the process would involve a return to shorter average delivery periods), it might take considerable time before a large backlog would be reduced enough to lose its usefulness as a means of stabilizing production.

The role of backlog and delivery-period adjustments in production to order has an analogy in the role of changes in finished-goods inventories in production to stock. A manufacturer may decide to produce in excess of current demand when business is slack but expected to improve in the not too distant future. This would keep equipment and labor working for stock at times when they would otherwise be partly idle or laid off; the unsold stock thus accumulated would await liquidation during the recovery. Of course, unsold stock will often accumulate because of failure to forecast sales correctly rather than as a result of this planning for output stabilization. If production continues to increase for some time after sales have begun to decline, and is cut only with a lag (which is a frequent result of insufficient foresight), this adds to the amplitude of output fluctuation and thus to output instability. Certainly, whatever their cause, changes in finished inventories need not always result in steadier operations. But an inverted pattern of movements in those stocks — increases during contractions and decreases during expansions in activity — is in itself an indication that some stabilization of production relative to fluctuating demand has been achieved, whether deliberate or not.[34]

Examples of Production Stabilization

Chart 2-6 suggests that there are great differences among the various lines of manufacturing in the urgency, method, and effectiveness of producers' efforts to mitigate the consequences of demand instability. Each of the four selected products has distinct characteristics that can be presumed representative of a larger class of goods.[35]

1. Freight cars illustrate the class of large-sized equipment made only to order, in time-consuming production processes. Makers of these capital goods face an extremely unstable flow of demand which they manage to convert into a flow of current operations that is no more than moderately variable.

2. Steel sheets represent goods made mostly to order, with much shorter production and delivery periods. The fluctuations of demand for this item, while quite pronounced and erratic, are markedly smaller in percentage units than the movements in freight car orders, and much more faithfully reproduced in the corresponding activity series. However, production of steel sheets is noticeably smoother than new orders, and shipments are somewhat smoother than production.

3. The boxboard-paperboard series exemplify goods that are either shipped from stock or are manufactured promptly upon receipt of order. Here unfilled orders are persistently low (as a rule less than one month's output), and new orders and production move largely together.

[34] Moses Abramovitz, *Inventories and Business Cycles*, New York, NBER, 1950, pp. 260–62.
[35] The selection, originally guided only by a comparative reading of the graphs, was later rationalized in the light of the classification of goods by type of manufacture and the underlying measures of the unfilled orders–finished stock ratio.

Chart 2-6
Selected Series on New Orders, Production, and Shipments, Four Commodities, Various Periods, 1919–38

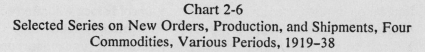

1. Freight Cars, 1919-1931

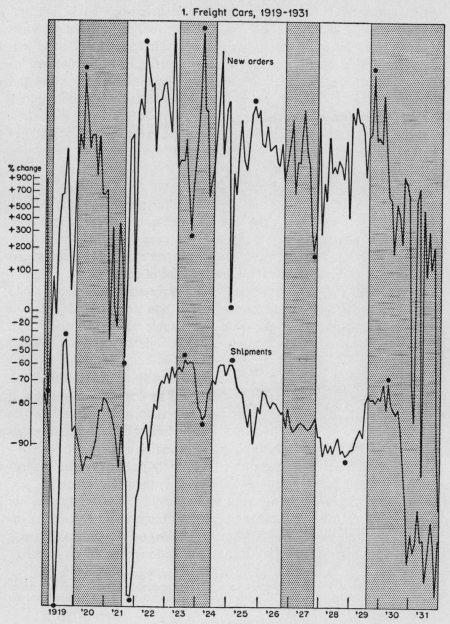

Chart 2-6 (continued)

2. Steel Sheets, 1919–1936

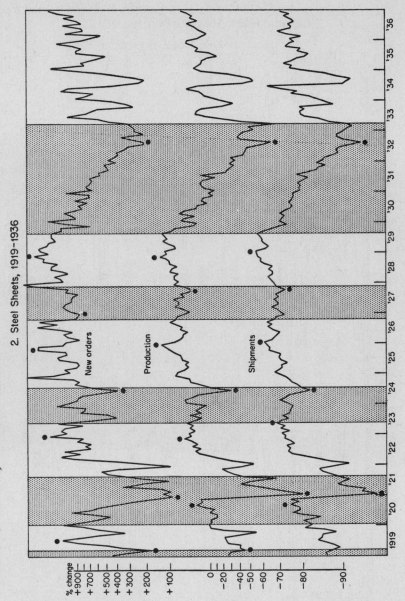

46

Chart 2-6 (concluded)

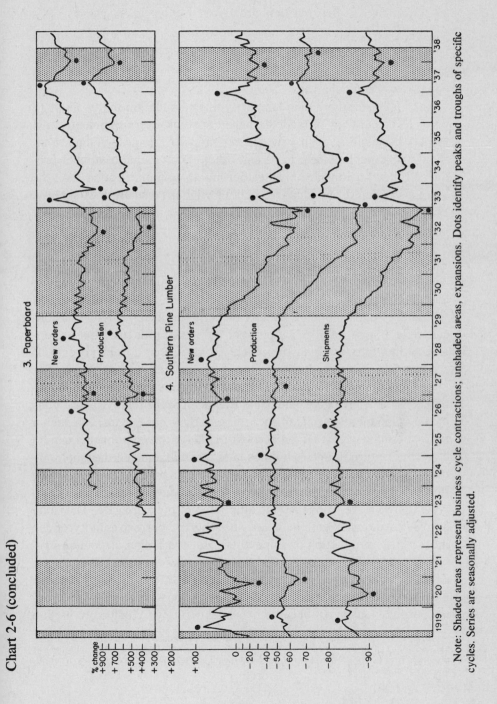

3. Paperboard

New orders

Production

4. Southern Pine Lumber

New orders

Production

Shipments

% change
+900
+700
+500
+400
+300

+200
+100
0
-20
-40
-50
-60
-70
-80
-90

1919 '20 '21 '22 '23 '24 '25 '26 '27 '28 '29 '30 '31 '32 '33 '34 '35 '36 '37 '38

Note: Shaded areas represent business cycle contractions; unshaded areas, expansions. Dots identify peaks and troughs of specific cycles. Series are seasonally adjusted.

47

The variability of demand is rather mild, so there is much less need and scope for output stabilization. Indeed, it takes a close inspection of the paperboard curves to detect where some degree of stabilization has apparently been achieved.

4. Finally, southern pine lumber typifies a situation that is likely to prevail for many goods made primarily to stock. Here shipments must in part be identical with new orders; the two are closely similar, although shipments appear to be smoother. The volume of lumber produced follows a considerably steadier month-to-month course than the volumes ordered and shipped, behind which it usually lags slightly. Hence, it would seem that much of the smoothing has been achieved by means of stock rather than backlog adjustments.

Implications of Dealing with Aggregates

Since single-product manufacture is seldom encountered in practice and even less often in statistics, comparing the course of new orders with that of corresponding production activities usually involves a considerable amount of aggregation over different products.[36] Let us consider a multiproduct industry which works against advance orders. If rises or falls in orders for its various products all reached their peaks or troughs at precisely the same time, the relative amplitude of movements in the aggregate would equal the mean of the relative amplitudes of the components weighted according to their base levels. But such a perfect confluence in timing is most unlikely; the components can be expected to turn at different times, and this will dampen the amplitude of the aggregate as compared with the weighted mean amplitude. Other things being equal, the greater the dispersion in the timing of the components the more dampened the amplitude of the aggregate. The same applies to the aggregate or index showing the current activity of the industry (its production or shipments). But the timing dispersion may well be very different for the component order series than for the component activity figures. If it is greater for the latter—perhaps because of differences of production or delivery periods for the various products of the industry, or because firms deliberately schedule production

[36] Of course, even in single-product manufacture, order and production figures are aggregative in the sense of being the sum for all firms engaged in making the given commodity. The implications of this are in certain respects analogous to those of product aggregation, although probably of considerably less practical importance.

of the diverse items so as to mitigate short-term variations in their total outputs—then this is in effect another mechanism whereby much of
the oscillation in new orders received is averaged out in the time-path
of the industry's current activity.

Major Factors in Timing of Orders and Production

Model Sequences and Expected Lags

Pure production to order implies a logical sequence—which is also
the time sequence—of three stages of operation: (acceptance of) new
orders, output, and shipments. The lag of output behind new orders
may well be long, due either to a long production period, or a long delay
before new orders are started in production, or both. The lag of shipments behind output would usually be short, perhaps less than one
month and indiscernible in monthly data. This we assume because there
is no general reason why such goods, once produced, should not be
shipped promptly to their purchasers. (All finished inventories are *sold*,
and it is in the manufacturers' interest to schedule operations so as to
avoid accumulating goods in stock awaiting shipment.)

In pure production to stock, the timing of new orders and shipments
is coincident when the unit period is not too short, say, one month. The
association of orders with *output* is less simply described. Conceivably,
output could move with, or precede, orders and shipments. Statistical
evidence, however, shows that output of finished nonperishable staples
made from storable materials—a class of goods best suited to be produced primarily "for the market," i.e., not against specific orders—
tends to *lag* behind shipments, though mostly by short intervals. There
are various possible reasons for this. It is usually very difficult to fore-
see turning points in demand, not only for products sold on advance
contracts but also for products sold from stock. Changes in the rate
of current manufacturing operations will presumably require some time
for completion (increases are likely to be particularly time consuming
at higher levels of capacity utilization); consequently, anticipations of
shifts in demand, even if correct, will not lead to timely adjustments of
the production schedules, unless they are formed far enough in advance. Moreover, the sales forecast will not be regarded as justifying

action which is costly and not easily revocable (especially when changes in the labor force are involved), unless the judgment about the future is sufficiently long range and is held with sufficient confidence.[37]

Arguing by inference from the model sequences, one can form certain definite expectations regarding the lags of output and shipments vis-à-vis new orders for products that are identifiable by type of manufacture:

1. Output of staples made for the market may *tend* to lag behind demand as measured by sales or orders shipped from stock. But output of precontracted goods lags behind demand as measured by sales (orders received in advance of production) *constantly,* in what is a necessary relation, not just a tendency. This is logically an important qualitative difference.

2. The lags of shipments relative to new orders should usually be negligible for goods ordinarily sold from stock. In the case of an item shipped from inventory directly upon receipt of an order, this lag obviously approximates zero. In times of booming business, however, the delivery periods [38] will lengthen as rising demand exhausts the available product inventory and exceeds the capacity of the firms to fill orders on receipt, causing unfilled orders to accumulate. For goods made to order, of course, the shipment lags are always positive and never zero, because production always intervenes between the date of the advance sales contract and the date of shipment, and production always requires some time.

"Production period," defined as the average amount of time needed to produce a unit of a given item, is a loose term and indeed an elusive concept. In modern continuous mass production of standardized goods, this period will often be very short; one may neglect it in writing the production function without any input-output lags. A popular car, for example, may be produced at the rate of 2,000 automobiles per day, or three per minute. But the production of a new model of a car requires

---

[37] The argument presented in the above paragraph follows the lines of explanation given in Abramovitz, *Inventories,* pp. 256–62; see *ibid.* for a more detailed analysis of the forces involved.

[38] For stylistic variety and convenience, the lags of shipments behind new orders are sometimes called the "delivery periods" or "delivery lags." It is, of course, recognized that the dates of shipment and delivery are separated by the time needed for transportation, but this interval should usually be short — less than the unit period in our data, which is one month or one quarter. Disregarding the difference between shipments and deliveries in terminology will cause no error in the context of this study.

months of research, planning, designing, and testing. In job-order production of capital equipment to customer specifications, the situation is often similar. The production periods for the more standardized goods manufactured to order may fall anywhere between these extremes. Clearly, the production periods depend on and change with the available technology, but the conditions determining what we have labeled the "type of manufacture" are here again relevant.

The measures of the average lag of output relative to new orders disclose some marked interindustry differences which accord with the above considerations. The longest lags by far are concentrated in the area of "heavy" capital goods produced to order (Chapter 4).

On the other hand, short-term fluctuations in the duration of output lags for a given industry cannot, as a rule, be ascribed to changes in the average production period over time. Technological developments may produce trends in the production periods, but one would not expect them to cause cyclical movements in the latter. Instead, the short-term changes in the output lags are apparently related to changes in the backlog position and capacity utilization of the firms that fill the orders.

Where customer orders anticipate and commit future output, whether because of a consistent policy of the firm (as in regular manufacture to order) or temporarily under pressure of booming demand (as may be the case even for items that are at other times well stocked by manufacturers and promptly available), the time interval between the acceptance of an order and its material execution cannot be shorter than the minimum production period involved. But when demand continues high for some time and advance orders pile up, the average interval between booking a new order and the beginning date for the work on it must lengthen relative to the essentially stable production period. Thus, of the two components of the total order-output intervals—the time the order has to wait before it is started in production, and the time needed for the actual production process—the former may then indeed become much the longer one. Certainly the former will have increased, often substantially, while the latter may have shortened or lengthened somewhat (efforts to rush orders through may succeed to a certain extent, or they may be "overdone" and self-defeating), but probably it will not have changed much.

Since in such times finished output is presumably promptly accepted by the buyer, the argument can be stated directly in terms of the order-shipment lags. These delivery lags, then, will lengthen in the advanced stages of expansion as a result of an increase in the "waiting periods" on the accumulated orders.

Problems of Measurement and Aggregation

Tracing the history of any particular order to ascertain how much time elapsed between the date it was accepted and the date it was produced or shipped is often impossible and rarely practical. Our measures of timing of new orders relative to shipments and production (Chapter 4) are based on aggregative time series data in which individual orders cannot be identified. In a large part, these measures refer to the length and regularity of intervals between the similar specific-cycle turns in new orders and output or shipments—peaks or troughs which apparently bound corresponding upward and downward movements. Here the lags of activity relative to orders are observed only at certain critical turning points, not in the continual succession which can be presumed to be their characteristic. However, much if not all the evidence from the series being compared is shifted and weighed in identifying the turning points in the series. Also, additional measurements of such lags can be derived by matching and comparing the timing of the turns in shorter movements that these series exhibit.

Lagged regressions provide a different method in which all the observations in the related time series are utilized. The criterion of maximum correlation can be applied to establish the optimal lags. In ordinary regression analysis, however, the lags are assumed to be constant for each given relationship, whereas the lags here considered are likely to show certain systematic changes over time, as already noted.

These considerations suggest the use of both timing comparisons and regression analysis as complementary tools. Further steps will lead to regressions incorporating distributed and variable lags.

Random variation is one major source of measurement difficulties; aggregation is another. The former affects strongly the method of timing comparisons. Large, short, and erratic movements often obscure the cyclical behavior of the series compared and make the dates of their turning points uncertain. Thus, even in the most straightforward case of a single product manufactured to order, occasional lapses from the expected timing sequence may be encountered for technical reasons. While this problem can be lessened by using averages of the individual measures, there are few series that are sufficiently long to provide representative timing averages.

Industry aggregates represent typically diversified multiproduct firms. Hence they often cover goods made to order as well as goods made to stock. The problems of interpretation caused thereby could be very serious, but for the most part do not turn out so in practice. As suggested by the evidence presented earlier in this chapter, many of the industrial aggregates are marked by a prevalence of one or the other type of manufacture. Where this is so, average lag measures tend to reflect, albeit in muted form, the timing patterns expected of the dominant category.

Table 2-3 provides a hypothetical illustration of the differential timing sequences that would be generated by a given flow of new orders under two assumptions regarding the proportion of business handled from stock. We abstract in this scheme from several features that add to the complexity of the empirical relations between new orders and current production activities: incoming business is taken to move in smooth (but not symmetrical) cycles; no representation is given to the process of subduing the fluctuation in output relative to that in orders which was briefly discussed before; and simple, constant timing associations between the corresponding series are assumed throughout. Two models are distinguished, one in which three-fourths of orders received are filled from future production (A) and one-fourth from stock (B), the other in which the proportions are reversed (that is, component A accounts for one-fourth and B for three-fourths of total new business). For A it is assumed that output, equal to shipments, lags new orders by two periods; for B, that output lags new orders and shipments, which are equal, by one period. In Model One, where A outweighs B three to one, timing characteristics of A prevail in the relation between the *totals* for new orders, output, and shipments. In Model Two, where the weights are reversed in favor of B, timing characteristics of B dominate the aggregate relations. But timing observations depend also on the way in which new orders vary about their turning points. Thus at the last trough in new orders in Model One (period 10), the timing of shipments turns out to be different for the totals than for the dominant component A (see columns 2 and 6). This can be due only to the particular pattern of the rates of change in orders during the contraction preceding this trough (periods 6–10). Unlike the expansion

Table 2-3
Timing of Output and Shipments Relative to Orders Under Two Assumptions About the Proportion of New Business Handled from Stock

Period	Total New Orders (N_A+N_B) (1)	Component A Output $(Z_A = S_A)$ (2)	Component B Shipments $(S_B = N_B)$ (3)	Component B Output (Z_B) (4)	Total Output (col. 2 + col. 4) (5)	Total Shipments (col. 2 + col. 3) (6)	Unfilled Orders (A only) — Monthly Change (col. 1 minus col. 6) (7)	Unfilled Orders (A only) — Total U (col. 7 cumulated) (8)	Finished Stock (B only) — Monthly Change (col. 5 minus col. 6) (9)	Finished Stock (B only) — Total Q (col. 9 cumulated) (10)
					MODEL ONE [a]					
1	100		25							
2	92(T)		23(T)	25				150		50
3	104	75	26	23(T)	98	101	+3	153	−3	47
4	120	69(T)	30	26	95(T)	99(T)	+21(P)	174	−4(T)	43
5	128	78	32	30	108	110	+18	192	−2	41
6	132(P)	90	33(P)	32	122	123	+9	201(P)	−1	40(T)
7	124	96	31	33(P)	129	127	−3	198	+2	42
8	112	99(P)	28	31	130(P)	127(P)	−15(T)	183	+3(P)	45
9	108	93	27	28	121	120	−12	171	+1	46
10	100(T)	84	25(T)	27	111	109(T)	−9	162(T)	+2	48(P)
11	116	81	29	25(T)	106	110	+6	168	−4	44
12	140	75(T)	35	29	104(T)	110	+30	198	−6	38
13		87		35	122					

1	100		75	75	94	103		50		150
2	92(T)		69(T)	69(T)	101	113	+1	51		141
3	104	25	78	78	116	122	+7(P)	58	−12(T)	129
4	120	23(T)	90	90	126	129(P)	+6	64	−6	123
5	128	26	96	96	131(P)	125	+3	67(P)	−3	120(T)
6	132(P)	30	99(P)	99(P)	126	117	−1	66	+6	126
7	124	32	93	93	115	112	−5(T)	61	+9(P)	135
8	112	33(P)	84	84	109	103(T)	−4	57	+3	138
9	108	31	81	81	102(T)	114	−3	54(T)	+6	144(P)
10	100(T)	28	75(T)	75(T)	112	130	+2	56	−12	132
11	116	27	87	87	134		+10	66	−8	124
12	140	25(T)	105	105						
13		29								

Note: Q is finished stock; N, new orders; S, shipments; U, unfilled orders; and Z, production. The subscripts A and B refer to the two components. T denotes a trough and P, a peak, in the series.

[a] It is assumed that component A accounts for three-fourths, B for one-fourth, of total new orders. For A: $Z_A(t) = S_A(t) = N_A(t - 2)$. For B: $S_B(t) = N_B(t)$, and $Z_B(t) = S_B(t - 1)$. Initial levels: $N_A = 75$ and $N_B = 25$ (to period 1); $U_A = 150$ and $Q_B = 50$ (in period 2); U_B and Q_A are zero throughout.

[b] It is assumed that component A accounts for one-fourth, B for three-fourths, of total new orders. Initial level and time paths of new orders (N_A and N_B) are the same as in Model One. Initial level of $U_A = 50$ and $Q_B = 150$ (in period 2); U_B and Q_A are zero throughout. Equations for Z_A, S_A, Z_B, and S_B are the same as in Model One.

(periods 2–6), which shows a retardation before this peak, this contraction ends on a reaccelerated decline.

The lead of new orders relative to shipments results in a cyclical movement of unfilled orders that conforms positively to the cycle in demand (new orders), while the lead of shipments relative to output results in a movement of finished stock that conforms negatively (columns 8 and 10). The *leads* alone are sufficient to produce these patterns; no particular assumptions about the relative *amplitudes* of new orders, shipments, and output are necessary for that. But in fact new orders are subject to larger fluctuations than shipments. This results in larger amplitudes of the corresponding movements in the unfilled orders backlog, both absolutely and relative to shipments. Similarly, if output fluctuates less than orders shipped on receipt, the inverted cycles in finished inventory are correspondingly increased.

The Structure and Variability of Lags in Filling Orders

Let s_t be a firm's shipments of a certain product and n_t be new orders for that item which the firm has received, with t relating to some short unit period, say, one month. In general, s_t can be viewed as a weighted sum of new orders previously received. Thus,

$$s_t = \alpha_0 n_t + \alpha_1 n_{t-1} + \alpha_2 n_{t-2} + \cdots = \Sigma \alpha_i n_{t-i}, \; i = 0, 1, \ldots, m, \quad (1)$$

where the summation extends from i to m, and m reaches as far back as necessary to cover the entire relevant past.

In practice, some of the α's will, of course, be zero. In particular, for production to stock, $\alpha_0 = 1$ and $\alpha_j = 0, j = 1, 2, \ldots, m$, when it is assumed that shipments can always be executed from stock without any significant delay. Similarly, in the simplest case of production to order with a constant delivery period k, all the α coefficients would be zero, except that of n_{t-k}; for example, if $k = 2$ (months), then $\alpha_i = 1$ for $i = 2$ and 0 for $i \neq 2$.

However, where manufacture to order is involved, there will ordinarily be more than one nonzero (positive) α coefficient in an equation such as (1); that is, the lags will be distributed rather than simple. For some products, it may be meaningful to think of a technologically defined minimum delivery period, but even there longer periods are feasible and may under certain circumstances be economically preferable. Technology alone does not determine production schedules, which rather are influenced by economic factors such as demand expectations, supply conditions including availability and prices, and the like. In particular, a firm will, *ceteris paribus,* prefer a more stable flow of output to one that varies greatly, since large short-term variations in the production rates add to the costs. The attempt to stabilize operations is likely to involve some smoothing of the impact of new orders by scheduling production to make it less variable than the incoming business. This means a policy of substituting distributed for simple delivery lags; for, in the case of a single constant delivery period k, the flow of output and shipments would be just a replica of the flow of new orders, lagged by k, and this is precisely what the firm would *not* want, assuming that it desires to reduce the variability of s_t.

Another reason is that the rate per unit period at which new orders are received may at times exceed the rate at which the orders can be filled. This happens when the incoming business strains the capacity to produce, and it implies a lengthening of the average delivery periods agreed upon by the contracting parties or imposed upon the buyer. In terms of the distributed lags, this means a shift in the weights, which are now lighter for the more recent and heavier for the more distant past. Hence, not only are the lags distributed, but they are also variable: in times of high capacity utilization the longer lags become more and the shorter lags become less important.

When applied to aggregates comprising groups of firms (industries) and groups of products, we shall have, analogously to (1),

$$S_t = a_0 N_t + a_1 N_{t-1} + a_2 N_{t-2} + \cdots = \Sigma a_i N_{t-i}, i = 0, 1, \ldots, m, \quad (1a)$$

with the summation taken over the same range as in (1). Aggregation supplies additional reasons for the delivery lags being distributed rather than simple. Even in a single-product industry, summation over different firms would work in this direction, since the delivery periods are unlikely to be always identical for all the firms. In a multiproduct industry, aggregation over the different products also is likely to result in a differentiation of the lags.

Typically, the available data are industry totals, so that (1a) rather than (1) can be estimated. In all applications of (1a) as a regression model based on time series data, the estimates of the a's have, of course, the meaning of temporal averages. They represent the average effects upon S_t of N_t, N_{t-1}, etc. Even if at any given time the delivery lag for any item were of the simple rather than distributed type, variations over time in these orders-to-shipments intervals could produce sufficiently large deviations from the mean to make the distributed-lag model superior to the simple-lag model. Thus the results of such regressions incorporate the combined effect of all the involved types of aggregation — over firms, products, and time.

As usual, aggregation is necessary to simplify and generalize but it also creates problems. Changes in the product mix, for example, will affect the results of applications of (1a) to industry totals. But to the extent that such changes in the aggregates involved are random rather than systematic, they would cause no bias and could be disregarded. And in some cases where they do matter, some disaggregation may be possible and helpful.

Those changes in the delivery lags, however, which come about because of cyclical changes in resource utilization present a different and more substantive problem. They are systematic and may occur at any level of industry aggregation. They can, therefore, be neither ignored nor handled by disaggregation. The answer lies in studying the lags in the context of business cycles; separately at peaks and at troughs, for example, or as a function of the demand pressure (which may be measured by the ratio of unfilled orders to shipments or indexes of capacity utilization).[39]

Manufacturers' Orders as Target and Tool of Forecasts

On the Quality and Functions of Orders Forecasts

Uncertainty about future demand, when sufficiently high, contributes a motive for production to order. If the sales of a specific product can be fairly accurately predicted, then this item, whatever its other characteristics, is likely to be produced to stock rather than to order (assuming, of course, that production is expected to be profitable). It is where sales appear to be particularly difficult to predict and where the costs of acting upon wrong forecasts are punitive that production will follow advance orders.

[39] Evidence bearing on these relationships is presented in several parts of this book: in the comparisons of the amplitudes of new orders, output, and shipments during cyclical and shorter movements (Chapter 3); in the estimates of lags of shipments and output behind new orders (Chapters 4 and 5); and in the discussion of the behavior and function of unfilled orders (Chapter 6).

Nevertheless, forecasts of future sales exist even in manufacturing to order, presumably because they are needed for planning purchases of materials in the short run and also for planning production, fixed investment, and the work force in the long run. For nonelectrical machinery, an industry in which production to order prevails, forecasts of new orders are collected by the McGraw-Hill Publishing Company. The forecasts are reported quarterly for the industry as a whole and for six subgroups [40] by 50 to 60 large companies; they begin in 1956 and cover spans of one to four quarters ahead. Seasonally adjusted indexes, 1950 = 100, are compiled by McGraw-Hill from these forecast figures, to match series on the actual flow of orders reported in the same form.

Recently, an accuracy analysis of the aggregate forecasting index for all companies reporting in 1956–65 has been carried out by George Terborgh.[41] The performance of this forecasting series was found to be very poor, as illustrated in Table 2-4. In fact, the deviations of predicted from actual changes have on the average been larger than the actual changes themselves (compare columns 4 and 5). This implies that predicting that there would be no change from the last known level of new orders would have yielded smaller errors than predicting with the index based on the companies' reported forecasts; in other words, the forecasts in the aggregate have been worse than the extrapolations of the last level.

This finding shows the forecasting index for nonelectrical machinery orders to be definitely inferior to most forecasts by business economists of such series as GNP and its major components and industrial production. These forecasts have typically been better than the simple last-level projections; and most of the GNP and industrial production forecasts in the postwar period show better over-all scores than even the more sophisticated extrapolations of past trends or of the relations between several recent values of the series concerned. This is true for predictions of the next two or three quarters and of the average annual values.[42]

The errors increase systematically with the span of the forecast, as can be seen by reading down columns 1–4 in Table 2-4. This would be

[40] See note 28 above. Construction machinery is combined with mining machinery.

[41] Machinery and Allied Products Institute, *Capital Goods Review*, No. 64, Washington, D.C., December 1965.

[42] See Victor Zarnowitz, *An Appraisal of Short-Term Economic Forecasts*, Occasional Paper 104, New York, NBER, 1967.

Table 2-4

Average Errors of Forecasts and Average Actual Changes, New
Orders for Nonelectrical Machinery, Quarterly, 1956–65
(per cent)

Span of Forecast[a] (no. of quarters)	Mean Absolute Error of Forecast[b]				Mean Absolute Change in Actuals,[c] 1956–65 (5)
	1956–58 (1)	1959–62 (2)	1963–65 (3)	Total Period, 1956–65 (4)	
One	7.2	3.7	6.0	5.4	4.7
Two	8.9	6.4	9.9	8.1	7.4
Three	11.1	7.8	16.0	11.1	10.6
Four	10.3	8.3	19.0	12.1	12.5

Source: Machinery and Allied Products Institute, *Capital Goods Review*, December 1965.

[a] Interval between the last quarter for which actual orders are known at the time of forecast and the quarter to which the forecast refers. For example, for a forecast made in mid-January the last known quarter is the fourth quarter of the preceding year; the forecast with the one-quarter span refers to the first quarter of the current year (in which the respondent stands); the two-quarter span reaches into the second quarter of the current year; etc. The forecasts are made in January, April, July, and October.

[b] Averages taken without regard to sign over the deviations between actual and predicted percentage changes from the base quarter to the target quarter. The first forecast covers II-1956; the last, III-1965.

[c] Averages taken without regard to sign over the actual percentages changes from the base quarter to the target quarter. Comparable to the corresponding entries in column 4.

expected, and it has been shown elsewhere for a variety of aggregative forecasts.[43] But the average change in the observed values also increases with the span (column 5). In fact, the rise in the actual change is faster than that in the average forecast error; so the errors, when taken relative to the changes, *decrease* with the predictive span. This means that the forecasts improve somewhat relative to the extrapolations based on the no-change assumption when the distance between the base and the target period is lengthened, until, for the four-quarter span, the forecasts appear to be slightly more accurate than such "naive-model" extrapolations.[44]

[43] *Ibid.*, Chap. 5.
[44] Among the GNP and industrial production forecasts reviewed in *ibid.*, one can find some sim-

The forecasts for the subperiod 1959–62 were definitely more accurate than those for either the earlier (1956–58) or the later years (1963–65). The worst forecasts were made in the most recent years (except for the shortest forecasts, which were worst in 1956–58; compare columns 1–3 in Table 2–4). This, as noted in the evaluation by the Machinery and Allied Products Institute, probably occurred because in 1959–62 the reported nonelectrical machinery orders showed a fairly steady and moderate advance of the kind that is often expected and comparatively easy to predict. In contrast, the same series experienced in the earlier period a substantial decline and recovery in connection with the 1957–58 business recession. The decline was missed, which gave rise to large overestimates of the level of orders during the recession, while the subsequent improvement was significantly underrated. The forecasts have generally failed to signal the cyclical turns in this period (they seem to have done somewhat better in this respect during the declines of orders in 1960–61 and 1962). As for the 1963–65 period, it was characterized by a steeper rise of orders than that observed in the recent past. Even though this new, faster advance was quite steady, forecasters continued to underestimate it by large margins; they "simply refused to believe that the trend could be maintained." [45]

The McGraw-Hill series shows the average predictive performance of all companies reporting, not the performance of any single one of them. No doubt, some of the respondents have done better than the average, and others have done worse. I have no knowledge of any company scores, but, if the experience with other groups of forecasts is a guide, the better-than-average scores should be decidedly a minority. In terms of the summary measures of error over time, the average forecast for a group is typically more accurate than most of the forecasts for individual members of the group because the former is helped in the long run by the cancellation of individual errors of opposite sign. [46]

Few sources of potential strength seem to exist for microforecasts of advance orders, and none are clearly reliable. Current inquiries from

ilar examples of longer forecasts being better than the short ones in comparison to the naive model here employed, although counterexamples also exist and the observed relations are not very strong or regular. When compared to the more effective extrapolations of trends or autoregressive relations, forecasts typically come out worse rather than better for the longer spans (see *ibid.*, Table 18 and the text).

[45] *Capital Goods Review*, No. 64, December 1965.

[46] See Zarnowitz, *Appraisal*, Chart 6 and text.

old and prospective customers may provide some guidance; but they are probably at best short-run indications and may well be too sporadic or informal to be really helpful. One can presume that sales experience or knowledge of the past behavior of orders received should work to improve the company forecasts; but the past record will be of little assistance where the inflow of new orders is irregular. It would not be surprising, therefore, if the ability to predict new orders on the level of the individual firm were generally quite limited, as the above evidence for nonelectrical machinery suggests it is.

However, another possible, partial reason for the weakness of these forecasts is that the effort invested in them is rather small because the needs they are to serve are modest. As argued earlier, advance orders themselves represent an important guide to production, thereby preempting, at least in part, the function which in manufacture to stock must be performed by sales forecasts.

Sales Forecasts and the Predictive Properties of Orders

New orders are difficult to predict as such but, once known, should be decidedly helpful in predicting shipments (often referred to as "sales"). They certainly make a better tool than a target of forecasts.

If new orders help businessmen to predict their sales more accurately, then the sales forecasts should be better in those industries which receive advance orders for large proportions of their outputs. Recent evidence suggests that sales anticipations are indeed substantially better predictors in the durable goods sector of manufacturing, where production to order is generally important, than in the nondurable goods sector, where this is not the case.

These results come from Michael Lovell's study of new data from the Quarterly Manufacturers' Inventory and Sales Anticipation Survey conducted by the Office of Business Economics, Department of Commerce.[47] This survey, initiated in the fall of 1957, was at first (through 1958) semiannual; continuous and comparable observations on anticipated and actual values are available only for a short period ending in 1963, since later figures are on a revised basis. While the older sales anticipations data, of more limited coverage and perhaps of lower qual-

---

[47] Michael C. Lovell, "Sales Anticipations, Planned Inventory Investment, and Realizations," in *Determinants of Investment Behavior*, Universities–National Bureau Conference 18, New York, NBER, 1967.

ity, give poor or indifferent results, the predictive performance of the present series appears to be more satisfactory.[48]

The OBE survey collects figures on sales expected in the current and the immediately following quarter, as well as reports on actual sales in the preceding quarter. The "second anticipations," which refer to the current quarter, are only in part forecasts and very short-term at that. They reflect in about equal measure the knowledge of actual current sales, since the survey is taken close to the middle of the quarter to which they refer. Their deviations from the corresponding figures on actual sales would be expected to be small and essentially random.[49] It is therefore not surprising that the correlations between these anticipations and actual sales are high for most industries. But it is worth noting that they are definitely higher for durable goods than for nondurables. The adjusted determination coefficients ($\bar{r}^2$) are .962 for the durables aggregate and .620 for the nondurables one.[50]

The first anticipations relating to the next quarter are of more interest. As would be expected, they show lower correlations with actual sales than do the second anticipations, which have a much shorter span. On the whole, however, these correlations are still fairly high for the durable goods industries: the coefficients $\bar{r}^2$ exceed .8 for two, and exceed .5 for five of the seven components of this sector. For the aggregates of durable goods, $\bar{r}^2 = .738$. The results for the nondurable goods industries are, again, considerably worse, e.g., four of the seven $\bar{r}^2$ coefficients for the components of this sector are less than .5. The coefficient for the aggregates of nondurable goods is .483.

An industry that does receive advance orders for many of its products may of course still have relatively poor sales forecasts because

[48] The older data include the Railroad Shippers', *Fortune*, and Dun and Bradstreet surveys, and the sales anticipations data reported as a by-product of the Commerce-SEC annual survey of intended business expenditures on plant and equipment. They have been evaluated in numerous studies, notably Robert Ferber, *The Railroad Shippers' Forecasts*, Urbana, 1953; F. Modigliani and O. H. Sauerlander, "Economic Expectations and Plans in Relation to Short-Term Economic Forecasting," *Short-Term Economic Forecasting*, Studies in Income and Wealth, Vol. 17, Princeton for NBER, 1955, pp. 261–351; Peter B. Pashigian, "The Accuracy of the Commerce-SEC Sales Anticipations," *Review of Economics and Statistics*, November 1964, pp. 398–405; and several papers in *The Quality and Economic Significance of Anticipations Data*, Universities–National Bureau Conference 10, Princeton for NBER, 1960.

[49] Compare Robert Eisner's "Comment" on Lovell's paper, in *Determinants of Investment Behavior*, p. 595.

[50] Furthermore, four of the seven major component industries listed for the durable goods sector show $\bar{r}^2 > .9$, and the remaining three have $\bar{r}^2$ of the order of .7. The seven component nondurable goods industries covered have substantially lower $\bar{r}^2$ coefficients, ranging from .8 down to less than .2. See Lovell, "Sales Anticipations," Table 3, p. 546.

of the greater variability of its sales (or for other, individually probably less important reasons which may make some series harder to predict or some forecasters less able or less lucky than others). By the same token, an industry selling mainly from stock may have a relatively good forecasting record. There are apparent illustrations of this in some of the differences in the performance of sales anticipations among the component durable goods industries.[51]

Lovell also presents measures for the predictive accuracy of the new OBE anticipations data relative to a naive model of the "same as last level" variety.[52] Once more, according to these ratios of average absolute errors, the durable goods industries have produced much better sales forecasts than the nondurable goods ones. All the ratios for the durables are less than 1, that is, the errors of the anticipations average less than those of the naive model (the former being used in the numerator and the latter in the denominator of each ratio). The ratio for the aggregate durable goods sector is 0.42. The ratios for the nondurables are generally higher and exceed unity for two industries. The ratio for aggregate nondurables is 0.64.

Further tests by Lovell consisted of regressions of actual sales change on anticipated sales change, seasonal dummy variables, and a trend term. Presenting partial correlations of actual with anticipated change, Lovell notes that "while these partial coefficients are quite high in a number of durable industries, it is apparent . . . that the anticipated change makes a negligible contribution toward predicting the seasonally adjusted actual change in most nondurable industries." [53]

Using the same detailed anticipations data, furnished by courtesy of the Office of Business Economics, I was able to reexamine the relations between actual and anticipated sales, including new orders re-

[51] Nonautomotive transportation equipment, an industry producing largely to order with highly variable sales, shows a low $\bar{r}^2$ of .325. The group of other durables, where production to stock is more important and sales are much less variable, has a higher $\bar{r}^2$, .537. (But this group comes out worst of all durables in comparisons with a naive model, which are described in the next paragraph.)

[52] The model produces extrapolations $E_t^{**} = A_{t-4}(A_{t-1}/A_{t-5})$, where A_{t-i} denotes actual sales i quarters earlier. This amounts to adjusting the same quarter of the preceding year by the recently observed trend (or, alternatively, to adjusting the preceding quarter for the change observed last year, since $E_t^{**} = A_{t-1}(A_{t-4}/A_{t-5})$; thus the formula involves a crude seasonal correction). The test was introduced by Ferber in his 1953 study (see reference in note 48).

[53] Lovell, "Sales Anticipations," pp. 548–49. The partial correlation coefficient, squared and adjusted for degrees of freedom, is .444 for aggregate durables. Corresponding measures are reported for only three nondurable goods industries, where they are less than .1. Even for the second anticipations, the partials are insignificant for the nondurables (here the sectoral value of the partial is reported and equals .022; the corresponding coefficient for the durables is .552).

ceived ahead of the target period. It was possible to match data for six-teen quarterly intervals in the period III-1959–II-1963 and to cover four major durable goods industries. Tests confirmed that the sales an-ticipations are best treated as seasonally unadjusted. Regressions with seasonal dummy variables were selected as the most acceptable method of handling the problem.

Second anticipations, issued in the first half of the target quarter, are more closely associated with actual sales than are new orders received in the preceding quarter. This accords with expectation and, because of the partial overlap and the short predictive span involved, is viewed more as a sign of consistency and reasonable promptness of current information about sales than as a mark of superior ability to forecast. In Table 2-5, therefore, only the first anticipations, which refer to the next quarter, are included. The table presents regressions of the form

$$S_t = a + bS^a + cN_{t-1} + w_1D_1 + w_2D_2 + w_3D_3 - u_t, \qquad (2)$$

with S_t = actual sales in quarter t; S^a = first anticipations of sales (is-sued in the first half of quarter $t - 1$); N_{t-1} = new orders received in quarter $t - 1$; D_i $(i = 1, 2, 3)$ = seasonal dummy variables which equal unity in the ith quarter and zero in all other quarters; and u_t = residuals. Only new orders received in quarter $t - 1$ are incorporated in these regressions; the term N_{t-2}, representing the earlier orders, proved to be of little or no significance when used instead of N_{t-1}, and there is no need here to use both.

In three of the four industries covered in Table 2-6, new orders (N_{t-1}) are shown to be more closely associated with actual shipments or sales (S_t), than are the first sales anticipations (S^a). For primary iron and steel the latter variable has a negative (but in all likelihood not significant) coefficient. For both machinery industries, the partial correlations of S_t with N_{t-1} (column 6) are higher than those of S_t with S^a (column 5). In transportation equipment, however, the situation is reversed: here S^a is highly significant and N_{t-1} is not.

If the partial r of S_t with S^a, net of the effects of N_{t-1} and D_i, is sig-nificantly positive, then S^a must have some predictive value that is not contained in new orders (N_{t-1}); indeed, this coefficient (or better, its squared and adjusted form) is a measure of the net contribution of S^a to the prediction of S_t. At the same time, if the partial r of S_t with N_{t-1}, net of the effects of S^a and D_i, is significantly positive, then N_{t-1} must

Table 2-5
Regressions of Sales (Value of Shipments) on Sales Anticipations, New Orders,[a] and Seasonal Terms, Four Major Manufacturing Industries, Quarterly, 1959–63

Industry	Constant Term[b] (1)	Regression Coefficients[b]		Adjusted Determination Coefficient (4)	Partial Correlation Coefficients[c]	
		b (2)	c (3)		(5)	(6)
Primary iron and steel[d]	2.359 (0.914)	−0.216 (0.250)	.616 (.177)	.618	−.310	.797
Machinery, except electrical	−0.834 (0.699)	0.457 (0.137)	.641 (.117)	.961	.726	.866
Electrical machinery	−0.028 (0.968)	0.423 (0.241)	.609 (.202)	.818	.486	.690
Transportation equipment[e]	−4.540 (3.435)	1.177 (0.402)	.224 (.240)	.800	.698	.297

[a] Equation (2) is used for the estimate. For the notation, see the text. The coefficients of the dummy variable, $D_i - w_1$, w_2, and w_3 — in that order, are: primary iron and steel: 0.052, 0.311*, 0.031; machinery, except electrical: 0.102, 0.274*, −0.525*; electrical machinery: −0.217*, −0.062, −0.404; transportation equipment: −0.636*, 0.570, 0.318. Most of these coefficients are smaller than their standard errors; those that are larger, and possibly statistically significant, are marked with an asterisk.

[b] Column 2 gives the coefficient of S^a. Column 3 gives it for N_{t-1}. The standard errors are in parentheses beneath the coefficients.

[c] Column 5 shows the partial correlation coefficient of S_t with S^a, net of the effects of N_{t-1} and the seasonal factors D_i; column 6, the partial of S_t with N_{t-1}, net of the effects of S^a and D_i.

[d] Excludes three quarters strongly affected by a major steel strike: III-1959, IV-1959, and I-1960.

[e] Total of automotive and nonautomotive.

have some predictive power that was not used in the sales forecast S^a. Where that coefficient is large, as it is for the primary iron and the two machinery industries, the forecast could presumably be much improved by better utilization of the available information on recently received orders.[54]

[54] This paragraph and the following one apply certain concepts developed in Jacob Mincer and Victor Zarnowitz, "The Evaluation of Economic Forecasts," in J. Mincer, ed., *Economic Forecasts and Expectations: Analyses of Forecasting Behavior and Performance*, New York, NBER, 1969.

Measures of direct association between S^a and N_{t-1} give us an idea of how important recent orders are as a codetermining factor or "ingredient" of first sales anticipations. These correlation statistics are shown in Table 2-6. They suggest that the anticipations of primary iron and steel and machinery sales have much in common with new orders, even net of the seasonal influences (first three lines, columns 1–3). The lowest correlations are obtained for transportation equipment, where, it will be recalled, S^a has been relatively efficient as an estimator of S_t, while N_{t-1} has been poor in this role (Table 2-6, last line). It is, of course, sensible for the anticipations to have a weaker association with orders whenever the latter are less helpful in predicting sales.

The addition of orders received in quarter $t - 2$ contributes little to the correlations in Table 2-6, except for nonelectrical machinery, where the combined effect of N_{t-1} and N_{t-2} on S^a is strong (third line).

Finally, a *caveat* must be issued: it should be clear that the correlations in Table 2-6 are generally not high enough to yield results con-

Table 2-6

Correlations of Sales Anticipations with New Orders and Seasonal Terms,[a] Four Major Manufacturing Industries, Quarterly, 1959–63

| | Correlations[b] of S^a with N_{t-1} and D_i | | | | Correlation[c] of S^a with N_{t-1}, N_{t-2}, and D_i | |
| | Simple (1) | Partial (2) | Multiple (3) | Adjusted and Squared (4) | Multiple (5) | Adjusted and Squared (6) |
Industry						
Primary iron and steel[d]	.644	.508	.761	.369	.872	.591
Electrical machinery	.598	.554	.632	.199	.686	.231
Machinery, exc. electrical	.442	.562	.601	.149	.879	.668
Transportation equipment	.142	.260	.566	.073	.590	.023

[a] For the notation, see the text accompanying equation (2), above.

[b] The simple correlation is of S^a with N_{t-1}. The partial is of S^a with N_{t-1}, net of the effects of D_i. The multiple is of S^a with N_{t-1} and D_i. Column 4 shows $\bar{R}^2$, the adjusted coefficient of determination.

[c] The multiple correlation coefficient is in column 5. Column 6 shows the adjusted coefficient of determination.

[d] Excludes three quarters affected by the steel strike: III-1959, IV-1959, and I-1960.

ventionally regarded as significant after adjustments have been made for the degrees of freedom. The numbers of observations are small (13 to 16); consequently, the adjustments reduce the coefficients substantially. The values of $\bar{R}^2$ in Table 2-6 are accordingly low, except for the above-mentioned case of nonelectrical machinery (columns 4 and 6).

Summary

The demand for some goods is so differentiated or unstable or sporadic, and consequently the cost of storing them unsold in finished form is so high, that these goods are produced primarily to order rather than to stock. For products that are typically made to order, the average ratios of finished inventories to unfilled orders (Q/U) are relatively low, while for products that are typically made to stock the Q/U ratios are high. Although they tend to fall in prosperous times and rise in sluggish ones, the ratios generally exceed 1 ($Q > U$) in most nondurable goods industries and are generally less than 1 ($Q < U$) in most durable goods industries. Manufacture to order is particularly important in metals, machinery, and nonautomotive transportation equipment — industries producing mainly capital goods.

Cancellations of orders received by manufacturers appear to be on the average relatively small for a variety of products, but they have been large at certain times on military and defense-related contracts. The amount and rate of cancellations increase with, but lag behind, new orders.

New orders (N) and shipments (S) tend to coincide in production to stock. In contrast, N leads S in production to order, with output (Z) intervening. Here changes in unfilled orders that reflect adjustments of delivery periods can absorb much of the variation of incoming business, thus making the course of Z and S considerably smoother than the course of N.

New orders for many manufactured goods are highly variable in the short run and difficult to predict. Sales forecasts are likely to have frequent serious errors and, if the costs of acting on wrong sales forecasts are critically high, production tends to follow advance orders. Forecasts of future sales (new orders) exist even in manufacture to order but they presumably have a less important function than in production to stock and may command less care and attention. Certainly the available evidence indicates that company forecasts of incoming orders tend to have little predictive value.

Advance orders, while themselves poorly predicted, can help businessmen predict their sales more accurately. Thus, sales anticipations appear to be substantially better predictors in the durable goods industries, where production to order is generally important, than in the nondurable goods sector, where this is not the case.

To conclude, in a large segment of the economy orders perform an important role in guiding production. Quantitative evidence on the relationships involved is unfolded in the chapters that follow.

3

SIZE AND FREQUENCY OF FLUCTUATIONS

THIS CHAPTER DEALS principally with the amplitude aspects of the relations between new orders, production, and shipments. It describes the comprehensive series for the postwar period, in current and constant dollars, with the aid of charts and comparisons of relative cyclical amplitudes. The analysis is then extended to data for individual industries, for selected economic indicators, and for the interwar period. Measures based on statistical decomposition of the time series by type of movement are used in this part of the chapter.

Postwar Cycles in Comprehensive Series

Current Data on New Orders and Shipments of Major Industries

The main body of data on the value of manufacturers' new orders and shipments is the monthly compilation by the U.S. Department of Commerce, which goes back to the Industry Survey established in 1939 by the Office of Business Economics (OBE). The OBE data cover the years after World War II and are given in changing prices of the period; the over-all totals for the durable and nondurable goods sectors begin in 1939.

In 1957, the processing of the Industry Survey was transferred within the Commerce Department to the Bureau of the Census, which published, in October 1963, a major revision of the survey series on manufacturers' shipments, orders, and inventories.[1] The new Census

[1] Bureau of the Census, *Manufacturers' Shipments, Inventories, and Orders: 1947–1963 (Revised)*, Washington, D.C., 1963.

data carry the totals for durable goods industries, nondurable goods industries, and all manufacturing, back to 1947; the series for component industries and the newly introduced market-grouped categories, back to 1953.

The revised data set differs from the old one in several respects: (1) The coverage of the survey has been broadened significantly, particularly with regard to large companies; (2) the sample design has been revised as a probability sample to give better representation of the entire manufacturing universe; (3) improved industry reporting and new benchmark levels have permitted a reorientation from a company base to a divisional or establishment base; (4) as a result, the new survey is able to provide more detailed and homogeneous industry figures as well as aggregates for market categories which cut across the industry groups, separating materials from final products and, among the latter, consumer goods from industrial equipment, defense items, etc.[2]

Because of these differences in concept or estimation procedure, the old and new component series differ rather substantially, though primarily in level and much less in change characteristics such as amplitudes and timing. Before the 1963 revision was published, I had completed an analysis of the earlier data, and the charts and tables that follow are based in part on that analysis. However, much of this work was replicated with the aid of the new series, to keep the study as up to date as possible and to incorporate the presumably improved statistical information now available. A warning is due here that these latest data are not strictly comparable with the earlier series used for the years before 1953, though care has been exercised to avoid any inferences that could be invalidated by such noncomparabilities. Only for the most comprehensive aggregates are the currently published series continuous over the entire postwar period.

In the Commerce data of all vintages, the comparability of the orders and shipments figures is assured by the method of their estimation: the value of new orders in any month t is derived by adding to the value of shipments in the same month the *change,* centered on t, in the estimated end-of-month totals of unfilled orders. This procedure is ap-

[2] For a further discussion of these and some other features of the Commerce data and some comparisons of the old and new series, see *ibid.*

plied to data before seasonal adjustment. The resulting figures are net of cancellations.[3]

Chart 3-1 shows the most comprehensive of the Commerce series. The pair of series plotted in the middle relates to all durable goods industries and that at the bottom to the group of four nondurable goods industries reporting unfilled orders (textiles, leather, paper, and printing and publishing). The pair of series plotted at the top of the chart relates to the total manufacturing sector and thus covers, in addition to the above two groups, those nondurable goods industries for which new orders and shipments are assumed to have equal values. In this and the following charts, new orders and shipments are drawn to the same semilogarithmic vertical scales and superimposed upon each other for each industry or group of industries. All series are shown in seasonally adjusted form.

Chart 3-2 covers those major-industry components of the Commerce set for which matching figures on new orders and shipments were published in the 1963 revision. Where the latest revised figures are not available for the period before 1953, data of the previous vintage are used to cover the earlier postwar years. The results should not be treated as continuous series, as indicated in the charts which keep the two segments separate. But comparisons of levels and longer movements show good over-all agreement between the new and the old data, as illustrated by the overlaps provided in Chart 3-2 for the years 1953–54.

Main Differences Between Industries and Changes over Time

The charts serve several basic purposes both in this chapter and in the following one, which is concerned with the timing relations between new orders and shipments. They are designed to bring out the relative levels and amplitudes of the paired series. Their inspection corroborates some of our earlier results. New orders tend to exceed shipments on the rise and to fall short of them on the decline. Not only the cyclical fluctuations but also the short "irregular" movements are seen to be typically larger in new orders than in shipments. The markings for the turning points emphasize the evident tendency of new orders to move ahead of shipments.

[3] See Chapter 2, note 25, for the definitions underlying the estimation of N_t as the sum of ΔU_t and S_t.

Chart 3-1

Value of Manufacturers' New Orders and Shipments, All Manufacturing, Durable Goods Industries and Nondurable Goods Industries Reporting Unfilled Orders, 1947–65

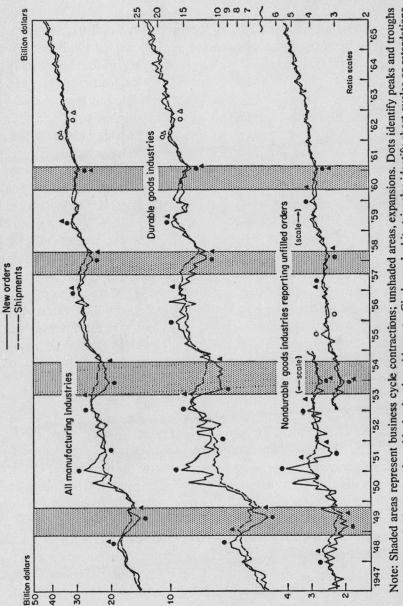

Note: Shaded areas represent business cycle contractions; unshaded areas, expansions. Dots identify peaks and troughs of specific cycles in new orders; black triangles, shipments. Circles and white triangles identify short cycles or retardations in new orders and shipments, respectively. Series are seasonally adjusted.

Source: Bureau of the Census.

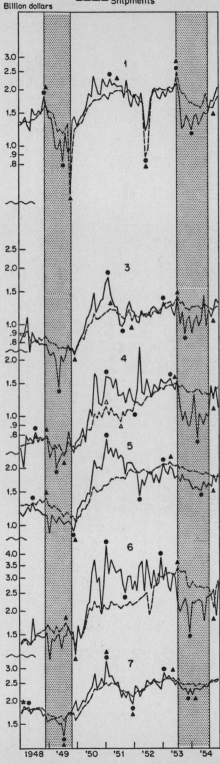

Note: Shaded areas represent business cycle contractions; unshaded
areas, expansions. Dots identify peaks
and troughs of specific cycles in new
orders; black triangles, shipments.
Circles and white triangles identify
short cycles or retardations in new orders and shipments, respectively.
Series are seasonally adjusted.

Source: 1948–54: U.S. Department
of Commerce, Office of Business Economics; 1953–65: Bureau of the
Census.

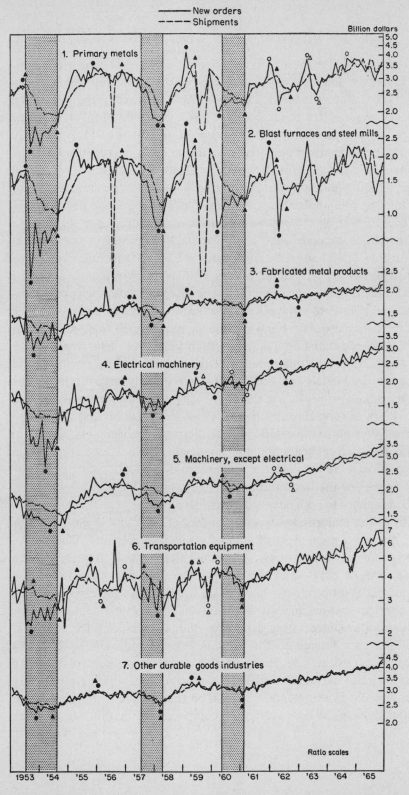

New orders

Shipments

Billion dollars

1. Primary metals

2. Blast furnaces and steel mills

3. Fabricated metal products

4. Electrical machinery

5. Machinery, except electrical

6. Transportation equipment

7. Other durable goods industries

Ratio scales

1953 '54 '55 '56 '57 '58 '59 '60 '61 '62 '63 '64 '65

75

However, while these characteristics are general and often con-spicuous, the intensity and regularity with which they appear vary greatly for different industries and periods. First, there is the smoothing effect of aggregation: the series that cover broad divisions of industry are in general less erratic than those relating to the more narrowly defined components (compare, e.g., the over-all aggregates in Chart 3-1 with the major-industry series in Chart 3-2, for new orders and shipments, separately). This, of course, is merely one manifestation of the familiar rule applicable to various types of economic process.

Second, new orders and shipments move much closer together in the nondurable goods sector of manufacturing than in the durable goods one. The nondurable aggregates in Chart 3-1 include only those industries that report unfilled orders (textiles, leather, paper, and print-ing and publishing). The other components of the sector, with consider-ably larger values of production and sales, work predominantly to stock and for them new orders and shipments are assumed to be identical in the Commerce statistics. Thus, had I plotted the all-inclusive series for the nondurables, the differences between orders and shipments would have appeared much smaller still. As it is, relatively large discrepancies between the two series for the four-industry group reporting unfilled orders are observable only in the 1948–49 recession and during the Korean War period in 1950–51; for the new set of data beginning in 1953, the discrepancies are small indeed. Another fact apparent in Chart 3-1 is more familiar: the amplitudes of fluctuations are consider-ably larger for the durable than for the nondurable goods industries, and this applies to both new orders and shipments.

Third, the major-industry components of the durable goods sector also display a great deal of diversity in these respects (Chart 3-2). The difference between new orders and shipments is greater, and the fluctuations of both series are much larger, in primary metals than in fabricated metal products. Orders are more erratic for electrical than for nonelectrical machinery and show less systematic cyclical devia-tions from shipments (persistent and large deviations for electrical machinery are limited to the Korean War period and the 1953–54 recession). Orders for transportation equipment have particularly large irregular movements of very short duration, which are radically smoothed out in shipments. This will be shown to reflect primarily the relationships in the nonautomotive component of that industry, which is dominated by large and expensive items (aircraft, ships, railroad equipment) that are produced to order, often with long delivery periods. The automotive component (motor vehicles and parts) shows, in contrast, only small divergencies between new orders and shipments, and behaves typically like an industry which produces primarily to stock.[4] In the remaining group of "other durable goods industries" new orders and shipments also run close to each other, with shipments being smoother and lagging but slightly. This group is composed mainly of stone, clay, and glass products, furniture, and lumber, which are largely items made to stock or (like furniture in part) made to order but with rather short delivery periods.

Finally, the relations concerned have undergone certain changes over time which are reflected in our charts. In the period since 1958–60, new orders and shipments differed much less than in the previous twelve or fourteen years covered. This implies that the changes in unfilled orders have become smaller in the first half of the 1960's. Direct evidence that this has indeed happened is given in Chapter 6, and shows that backlogs of manufacturers' orders generally have markedly diminishing fluctuations around downward or horizontal trends during these latter years.

On the whole, there is a one-to-one correspondence between the major movements in new orders and shipments, but a significant divergence from it occurred in 1950–52. The outbreak of the Korean War caused a rush of forward buying motivated by fear of shortages and price rises; this receded at the end of 1950 when hope spread that the conflict might end soon, but another wave of buying started when the war was intensified by Chinese intervention. These rises brought new orders to levels far above those of shipments, thus leading to a very large accumulation of unfilled orders. When new orders declined in 1951–52, shipments of durable goods continued to increase, though at a slower pace, reflecting work on the previously accumulated orders (Chart 3-1). The continued rise of shipments is particularly evident in industries with longer average delivery periods, such as nonelectrical machinery and (nonautomotive) transportation equipment; in contrast, shipments declined in 1951 in response to the fall in new orders in

---

[4] In fact, unfilled orders of motor vehicle manufacturers are relatively small, consisting as they do largely of military orders; the bulk of production here is represented by automobiles which are shipped to dealers who hold the inventory of finished cars.

industries working largely to stock or with short delivery lags, such as the nondurables and the group of "other durables" (Chart 3-2).

Relative Cyclical Amplitudes of the Major-Industry Series

Table 3-1 presents percentage amplitudes of cyclical rises and falls for the series that were presented in Charts 3-1 and 3-2. With very few exceptions, the current value of new orders (N) rose more in percentage units than the value of shipments (S) in each successive expansion of these series. Similarly, N as a rule fell more than S in each of the successive specific contractions.[5]

Since the amplitudes of the rises are based on the initial low levels and those of the falls on the initial high levels, the former are in a sense overstated and the latter are understated. Using average cyclical levels as bases would correct for this "bias," which should be recognized in reading the table. However, for our comparisons, which aim mainly at differences between variables and industries, the simpler measures applied are deemed adequate. As the effects of the base differences on rises and falls tend to cancel each other, the over-all averages taken without regard to sign (column 11) would be but weakly influenced by this technical factor.

The series have upward trends and their rises are substantially larger than their falls, as illustrated in the charts and demonstrated in the measures of Table 3-1. This difference is real enough and quite general, even though it should be somewhat discounted because of the base effects just noted. More interestingly, the relative amplitudes of rises show a tendency to decline in three successive episodes: They were on the whole smaller in 1958–59 than in 1954–57 and smaller in the latter period than in 1949–53. However, the most recent rises of the 1960's (which were still in progress at the time of this analysis), have already exceeded the earlier expansions of the mid- and late 1950's, though not, in general, those of 1949–53 (compare columns 2, 4, 6, and 8). A tendency for the recent declines to become progressively smaller is also observable in Table 3-1 (compare columns 1, 3, 5, and 7). Of course, these differences themselves are in part a reflection of the

[5] The apparent exceptions are due to special causes or are not really significant. Thus the primary metals figures for 1948–53 (Table 3-1, columns 1 and 2) are affected by the steel strike in 1949, which caused a lower trough level in shipments than in new orders (compare Chart 3-2). Elsewhere the differences between the amplitudes are negligible in those cases in which the movement of S seems to exceed the movement of N (see the totals for nondurable goods in Table 3-1).

growth trends; for example, it would take a much larger absolute rise in 1961–65 than in 1949–53 to produce the same relative rise, because the series had reached a much higher level in 1961 than in 1949. Nevertheless, it is worth noting that the relative fluctuations in these series have in general become markedly smaller in the recent years than they were earlier in the postwar period (see Charts 3-1 and 3-2 and Table 3-1).

Along with the reduction in the percentage amplitudes of cyclical movements, in shipments as well as new orders, the excess of the amplitudes of new orders over those of shipments has also tended to decrease. Thus the ratios of the relative amplitudes of shipments to new orders have increased in each of the successive contractions and in each of the successive expansions of the period 1953–61 for the total durable goods sector.[6]

It is well known that production and employment tend to undergo much larger fluctuations in durable goods industries than in nondurable goods industries. The same is true of both new orders and shipments: The cyclical amplitudes of orders are more than 3 to 5 times larger in durables than in nondurables, and those of shipments are more than 2 to 3 times larger (the differences are smaller for rises than for falls; compare columns 9–11 for total durable and total nondurable orders and shipments). Among the nondurables, however, the industries that report unfilled orders (textiles, leather, paper, and printing and publishing) show considerably larger fluctuations than the rest, as can be inferred from the averages in the last four lines of the table.

Of the major industries in the durable goods sector, primary metals and, particularly, its blast furnaces component, persistently had the largest cyclical amplitudes in percentage terms, both for rises and falls. Transportation equipment had smaller movements, while electrical and nonelectrical machinery series fluctuated less and the fluctuation of the fabricated metals series, on the whole, was still less. The "other durable goods" category shows the smallest amplitudes of all, in most instances and on the average. These rankings have been quite persistent in both expansions and contractions, particularly since 1953. Also, the ranks of the industries according to the amplitudes for

[6] The ratios for the four postwar contractions (1948–49, 1953–54, 1957–58, and 1959–61) are 0.47, 0.63, 0.79, and 0.86, respectively. The ratios for the four expansions (1949–53, 1954–57, 1958–59, and 1961–65) are 0.76, 0.67, 0.73, and 0.84.

Table 3-1

Percentage Amplitudes of Cyclical Expansions and Contractions, Value of New Orders (N) and Shipments (S), by Major Industries, 1948–65

	Percentage Rise (+) or Fall (−) in Series [a]								Av. of Periods with Rise [d]	Av. of Periods with Fall [d]	Av. Amplitude of Rises and Falls [d]
N or S	1948–49 Fall (1)	1949–53 Rise [b] (2)	1953–54 Fall (3)	1954–57 Rise (4)	1957–58 Fall (5)	1958–59 Rise (6)	1959–61 Fall (7)	1961–65 Rise [c] (8)	(9)	(10)	(11)
ALL MANUFACTURING INDUSTRIES											
N	−20	+72	−17	+36	−12	+26	−8	+50	+46.0	−14.3	30.2
S	−14	+64	−10	+29	−11	+20	−6	+44	+39.4	−10.0	26.7
DURABLE GOODS INDUSTRIES, TOTAL											
N	−32	+135	−27	+57	−24	+41	−14	+63	+73.7	−24.6	49.1
S	−15	+102	−17	+38	−19	+30	−12	+53	+55.7	−15.7	35.8
PRIMARY METALS, TOTAL											
N	−38	+97	−47	+128	−48	+110	−42	+76	+102.7	−43.9	73.3
S	−40	+132	−30	+68	−36	+54	−28	+50	+76.2	−33.6	54.9
BLAST FURNACES, STEEL MILLS											
N	n.a.	n.a.	−53	+175	−58	+166	−58	+118	+153.1	−53.7	104.7
S	n.a.	n.a.	−38	+94	−43	+71	−37	+68	+77.7	−39.6	58.7
FABRICATED METAL PRODUCTS											
N	−33	+102	−27	+54	−14	+24	−10	+40	+55.0	−21.0	38.0
S	−16	+80	−14	+37	−12	+18	−8	+31	+41.4	−12.5	27.0

ELECTRICAL MACHINERY

N	−22	+155	−42	+81	−18	+34	−4	+69	+84.6	−21.4	53.0
S	−12	+120	−21	+29	−13	+32	−1	+59	+60.1	−11.8	35.9

MACHINERY, EXCEPT ELECTRICAL

N	−21	+100	−26	+68	−24	+33	−11	+76	+69.3	−20.4	44.9
S	−18	+93	−19	+42	−12	+18	−6	+57	+52.5	−13.9	33.2

TRANSPORTATION EQUIPMENT

N	−12	+140	−30	+91[e]	−33	+40	−18	+87	+89.6	−23.1	56.3
S	−13	+122	−18	+50[e]	−24	+32	−12	+63	+66.8	−17.0	41.9

OTHER DURABLE GOODS INDUSTRIES[f]

N	−16	+84	−21	+23	−12	+27	−9	+46	+44.8	−14.7	29.8
S	−10	+62	−14	+19	−10	+22	−7	+40	+35.9	−10.4	23.1

TOTAL NONDURABLE GOODS INDUSTRIES

N	−11	+34	−5	+22	−2	+12	−0.1	+36	+27.6	−4.5	15.2
S	−12	+33	−4	+23	−3	+12	+0.3	+35	+25.4	−4.8	15.1

TOTAL NONDURABLES WITH UNFILLED ORDERS[g]

N	−16	+52	−11	+26	−6	+21	−5	+50	+37.1	−9.6	23.3
S	−16	+40	−8	+23	−5	+16	−3	+46	+31.5	−8.0	19.8

Notes to Table 3-1

Note: The amplitude measures in columns 3–8 for all industries and those in columns 1 and 2 for all manufacturing, total durable goods, and total nondurable goods industries are based on the new Census data (1963 revision). For the other industries, the measures in columns 1 and 2 are based on the earlier OBE data (the revised series for the component industries begin in 1953).

[a] The annual dates given refer to the expansions and contractions in total manufacturers' shipments. The corresponding movements in the component series may have different dates. As a rule, the amplitude of each successive rise and fall in the given series is measured between the average standings of the seasonally adjusted series in the three-month periods centered on the initial and terminal turns, and all amplitudes are expressed in percentages of the initial-turn levels. However, the high levels attained by the series late in 1965 were used as terminal values for the measured amplitudes of 1961–65 (column 8), even though the expansions apparently still continued at the time this analysis was being performed; hence these figures refer to truncated movements and in this sense understate the (currently unknown) "true" amplitudes of the rises that began in 1960–61.

[b] In this period, new orders for durable goods rose to steep peaks in 1950–51, then declined sharply in 1951, finally increased erratically and moved slowly in 1952 (see Charts 3-1 and 3-2). For some industries, these movements can be matched with those of shipments. To make the results for the different industries more comparable, amplitude measures for these additional movements are not included in the table, but they are shown below:

	Total Durable		Primary Metals		Fabricated Metal Products		Other Durable Goods	
	N	S	N	S	N	S	N	S
1949–51 rise	+87	+52	+111	+110	+172	+61	+87	+52
1951–52 fall	−22	−12	−36	−41	−38	−6	−22	−12

[c] Significant retardations interrupted these rises in 1962 in several major industries (see Charts 3-1 and 3-2). The following tabulation illustrates the magnitudes of the movements involved.

	All Manu- facturing		Total Durable		Primary Metals		Blast Furnaces		Fabri- cated Metal Products	
	N	S	N	S	N	S	N	S	N	S
1961–62 rise	+14	+14	+22	+20	+64	+33	+82	+28	+16	+7
1962 fall	−2	−1	−4	−2	−27	−13	−38	−18	−4	−3

[d] The averages in column 11 are taken without regard to sign, but not those in columns 9 and 10. Because of rounding, the figures shown may differ from ones computed directly from the listings in columns 1–8.

(continued)

Notes to Table 3-1 (concluded)

e Short but substantial declines interrupted these rises in 1955–56 (see Chart 3-2). The amplitudes of the increases that started in 1953–54 and ended in 1955 were +82 and +42 for new orders and shipments, respectively; those of the declines in 1955–56 were −18 and −14.

f Includes stone, clay, and glass products; lumber and wood products; furniture; instruments and related products; and miscellaneous, including ordnance.

g Includes textile mill products; leather and leather products; paper and allied products; and printing and publishing.

new orders and shipments have tended to be remarkably similar: the Spearman rank correlation coefficients (r_s) exceed .85 for each of the six periods with rise or fall in 1953–65. The correlations between the ranks based on average amplitudes are perfect $(r_s = 1)$ for rises and for rises and falls combined, while the correlation for falls is .86.

The high degree of cyclicality and volatility of new orders received by such industries as iron and steel, transportation equipment (particularly nonautomotive), and machinery, confirms the long-held idea that investment demand is often very unstable. While shipments (and output) fluctuate much less than new orders, they nevertheless vary considerably more in these industries than elsewhere in the manufacturing sector. And it is in these industries that production is to a large extent order oriented, resulting in order leads of substantial analytical and predictive interest.

Market Categories

For the new Census series, industry data have been regrouped into major market sectors covering consumer goods, equipment, and materials. The composition of these "market categories" follows below.[7]

Home goods and apparel: Knitting and floor covering mills; apparel; household furniture and fixtures; leather products (other than industrial and cut stock); kitchen articles and pottery; cutlery, handtools, and hardware; household appliances; ophthalmic goods, watches, and clocks; and miscellaneous personal goods.

Consumer staples: Food and beverages; tobacco manufactures; die-

[7] This is a short description; for a detailed listing of the SIC industries included, see Census, *Manufacturers' Shipments (Revised)*, App. B.

cut paper and board; newspapers, periodicals, and books; and drugs, soaps, and toiletries.

Equipment and defense items, except automotive: Furniture and fixtures, other than household; machinery, electrical and other (excluding household appliances and some others); aircraft, shipbuilding, railroad and streetcar equipment; scientific and engineering instruments; and ordnance.

Automotive equipment: [8] Motor vehicles and parts; motorcycles, bicycles, boat building, trailer coaches; and tires and tubes.

Construction materials, supplies, and intermediate products: Wood products (except containers); building paper; paints; paving and roofing materials; stone, clay, and glass products (other than kitchen articles, pottery, and glass containers); and building materials (fabricated metals) and wire products.

Other materials and supplies and intermediate products: Fats and oils; broad-woven fabrics and other textiles (except those in home goods and apparel); wooden and glass containers; pulp, paperboard, and other paper products; printing and publishing (except the items in consumer staples); chemicals and allied products: industrial, fertilizers, and miscellaneous; petroleum and coal products (except paving and roofing materials); rubber and plastics (except tires and tubes); leather, industrial products, and cut stock; primary metals; fabricated metal products: cans, barrels, and drums, and others n.e.c.; internal combustion engines; machine tools and machine shops; electrical industrial apparatus, electronic components, and other electrical machinery n.e.c.; aircraft parts; photographic goods, watch cases; and other durable goods, except personal and ordnance.

In short, these groupings provide both a division between final products and materials and a further division of final products between consumer goods and equipment for business and government use.

In addition, data for the following three "supplementary market categories" are available (for consumer durables only since 1960):

Consumer durables: Same as home goods and apparel (above), except that knitting and floor covering, apparel, and the leather products are excluded.

---

[8] This is treated as a separate market grouping, instead of being divided between consumer goods, equipment (buses and trucks), and materials (motor vehicle parts), because the Industry Survey reports do not separate the value of cars and trucks.

Defense products: Communication equipment; complete aircraft; aircraft parts; and ordnance (part of group 3 above).

Machinery and equipment industries: Machinery, except electrical (excluding farm machinery and machine shops); electrical machinery (excluding household appliances, communication equipment and electronic components); shipbuilding; and railroad and streetcar equipment.

Chart 3-3 presents the seasonally adjusted series on new orders and shipments for each of the nine market categories just described as well as for total materials (which includes the "Construction materials" and "Other materials . . ." groups identified above). It is clear that the goods purchased by the consumer are overwhelmingly made to, and sold from, stock. New orders and shipments of these classes of goods move closely together and show very small, and for the most part apparently random, differences. In particular, N and S are virtually identical for consumer staples. The two variables are somewhat more differentiated for home goods and apparel, but here too the deviations are generally small, except during the decline and initial rise associated with the 1953–54 recession. The series for consumer durables are very short, since they begin in 1960. They closely resemble their counterparts for the home goods group, which covers the same products along with some nondurables.

In contrast, the equipment series cover in large part goods manufactured to order, and the picture they present is very different. In 1953–58, particularly, new orders for nonautomotive equipment and defense products moved in much wider swings than shipments, which also lagged behind the orders by long intervals. In 1959–62, a period marked mostly by sluggish increases and retardations in these series, the deviations between N and S became considerably smaller and predominantly erratic; but in 1963–65, when business moved up more briskly, new orders again repeatedly rose faster than shipments, only to fall back occasionally to the level of the latter. Throughout, shipments of equipment have followed a much smoother course than the highly volatile orders. New orders for defense products have been especially erratic, moving up and down in large seesaw patterns every few months. However, longer movements superimposed upon those irregular oscillations are also evident in the defense series during the 1950's. The timing of these movements was unfavorable as far as the business cycle is concerned: defense orders declined sharply just be-

Chart 3-3

Value of Manufacturers' New Orders and Shipments, Consumer Goods, Equipment, and Materials, Ten Market Categories, 1953–65

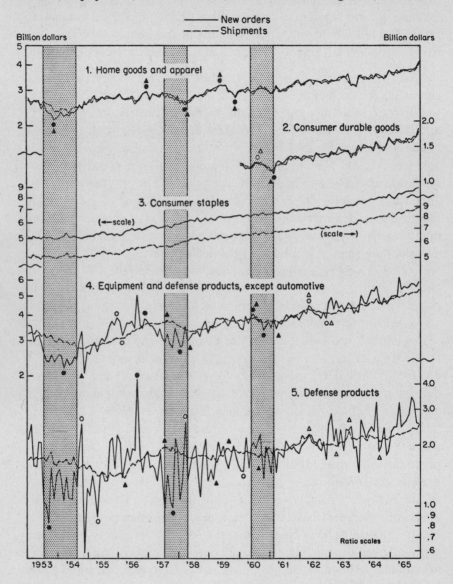

Chart 3-3 (concluded)

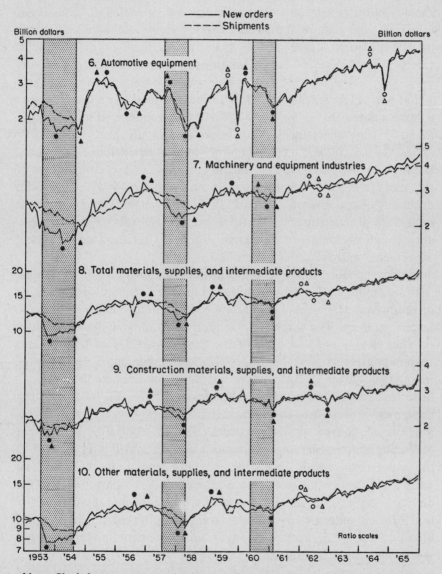

— New orders
--- Shipments

Billion dollars

6. Automotive equipment

7. Machinery and equipment industries

8. Total materials, supplies, and intermediate products

9. Construction materials, supplies, and intermediate products

10. Other materials, supplies, and intermediate products

Ratio scales

1953 '54 '55 '56 '57 '58 '59 '60 '61 '62 '63 '64 '65

Note: Shaded areas represent business cycle contractions; unshaded areas, expansions. Dots identify peaks and troughs of specific cycles in new orders; black triangles, shipments. Circles and white triangles identify short cycles or retardations in new orders and shipments, respectively. Series are seasonally adjusted.

Source: Bureau of the Census.

fore and during the 1953–54 recession and again in 1956–57, prior to the downturn of aggregate economic activity in mid-1957. The recent (1963–65) increase in the short-period volatility of total equipment orders is also to a considerable extent (though by no means exclusively) due to renewed large variations in defense orders (see Chart 3-3).

The series for machinery and equipment industries represent transactions related to the business outlays on "producer durable equipment."[9] They share much of their coverage with the corresponding series for nonautomotive equipment (other than defense products), but include also some types of machinery classified as components of the market group "Other materials and supplies and intermediate products." On the whole, new orders of the machinery and equipment industries are apparently smoother than new orders for total nonautomotive equipment and defense products, but the longer cyclical movements in these series are similar.

Unlike nonautomotive transportation equipment (aircraft, ships, railroad equipment), which is produced to order, usually with long lags of output and shipments behind new orders, motor vehicles are made largely to stock. The graph for automotive equipment shows N and S moving closely together most of the time (Chart 3-3), while the corresponding series for total transportation equipment differ by large amounts (Chart 3-2). Automotive orders follow a course that is only a little less smooth than that of shipments, while total transportation equipment orders are, in contrast to shipments, very erratic. This implies, of course, that new orders for transportation equipment excluding automobiles are even more erratic, and this is evident in the older data, which do distinguish between "motor vehicles and parts" and "other transportation equipment" (see Chart 3-4). But the charts suggest, too, that the divergence between the time paths of N and S for nonautomotive (and total) transportation equipment is in part also cyclical, i.e., reflected in longer and systematic movements, not just in very short irregularities.

Other evidence, on timing and on size of unfilled orders (Chapters 4 and 6), will confirm these statements. Meanwhile, let us merely note that motor vehicle manufacturers hold relatively small amounts of

[9] New orders for these industries will be used extensively in Part IV, below.

Chart 3-4
Value of New Orders and Shipments for Two Components of the
Transportation Equipment Industry, 1949–61

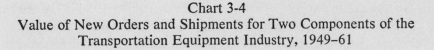

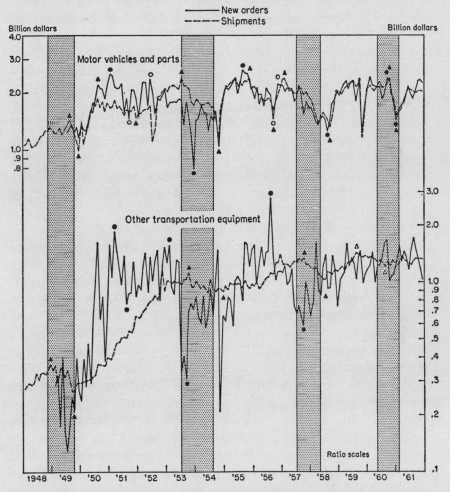

Note: Shaded areas represent business cycle contractions; unshaded areas, expansions.
Dots identify peaks and troughs of specific cycles in new orders; black triangles, shipments. Circles and white triangles identify short cycles or retardations in new orders and
shipments, respectively. Series are seasonally adjusted.

Source: U.S. Department of Commerce, Office of Business Economics.

unfilled orders (for most of them the reported backlog figures are confined to military orders). The bulk of their production is represented by automobiles shipped to dealers, who then hold the finished car inventory for sale. Although cars come in a great variety of models, colors, and combinations of accessories, among which the buyer may choose as he wishes, individual customer specifications, as communicated to the dealer, are as a rule readily met by producers, without any significant delays in delivery.

It should be added that, according to the old series (Chart 3-4), new orders for motor vehicles did have much larger amplitudes than shipments in the years 1951–54, which include the Korean conflict and its aftermath. If this was so, it is possibly due in large part to military orders; but it seems idle to speculate about the matter, especially since the quality of these data is quite uncertain. In any event, after 1955 the two series, even according to the old data, show little difference in amplitudes and nearly coincident timing.[10]

Of the two parts of "materials, supplies, and intermediate products" (Chart 3-2), the group relating to construction had somewhat larger irregular, but smaller cyclical, fluctuations than the other, much larger group. The latter includes the highly cyclical metalworking industries, which is clearly reflected on several occasions, such as the long lead of new orders relative to shipments for this group at the 1953–54 upturns (compare the corresponding graphs in Charts 3-2 and 3-3).

Relative Cyclical Amplitudes of the Market-Category Series

Table 3-2 presents for the market groups the same information on the size of successive cyclical movements in new orders and shipments as Table 3-1 gave for the major industries.[11] The format is in both cases the same, and so is the general observation that N rises and falls more than S for each of the groups, with great regularity.

Comparisons of the amplitudes recorded in the different subperiods also merely yield a confirmation of what has been noted before: The

[10] The series for motor vehicles and parts in Chart 3-4 show much more erratic behavior in 1953–61 than do the corresponding series for total automotive equipment in Chart 3-3. While the latter data represent a somewhat larger aggregate, this difference may be due more to the smaller size of the samples underlying the older data in Chart 3-4. The cyclical movements, however, are broadly similar in the two charts, which is reassuring about the internal consistency of this evidence.

[11] Two categories, consumer staples (1953–65) and consumer durables (1960–65), are not included in this table. As seen in Chart 3-3, these series are dominated by upward trends and show no identifiable cyclical fluctuations.

declines tend to become smaller, while the latest rises already rival those of 1954–57 (the rises of 1958–59 were definitely the smallest but also the shortest in the recent years). Again, increases in the amplitude ratios S/N are frequently observed, as illustrated by the following results for home goods and apparel (HG), nonautomotive equipment and defense (NAE), machinery and equipment industries (ME), and total materials, supplies, and intermediate products (MSI).

Fall	HG	NAE	ME	MSI		Rise	HG	NAE	ME	MSI
1953–54	0.63	.48	.62	.50		1954–57	0.70	.65	.59	.68
1957–58	0.89	.45	.63	.83		1958–59	0.91	.40	.59	.87
1959–61	1.25	.33	.71	.91		1961–65	1.03	.69	.78	.88

The group of home goods and apparel has the smallest cyclical rises and falls in both new orders and shipments. Moving on to progressively larger average percentage amplitudes, construction materials and other materials rank second and third for new orders, followed by automotive equipment, defense products, and nonautomotive equipment. The rankings for shipments are similar,[12] but they differ in two respects from those for new orders: the ranks of defense products are consistently lower for S and the ranks of automotive equipment are consistently higher. This reflects two facts: (1) The production smoothing process is highly effective for the defense items, which have large backlogs and long delivery periods (the amplitudes of N are here, on the average, about two and a half times larger than those of S); and (2) in contrast, there is very little smoothing, if any, in the automotive group.

In short, the fluctuations of both new orders and shipments tend to be smallest for consumer goods, larger for materials (particularly the "Other materials" group, which includes the sensitive metalworking industries), and by far the largest for equipment. The groups with greater relative amplitudes are also, on the whole, the groups with greater weights of products manufactured to order. However, as an important special case, the automotive category represents a segment of the economy where the demand is highly variable but production is not "to order" in the sense used here. For this category, current pro-

---

[12] The r_s coefficients are .77 for periods of rise, .60 for periods of fall, and .71 for all six episodes in 1953–65.

Table 3-2

Percentage Amplitudes of Cyclical Expansions and Contractions, Value of New Orders (N) and Shipments (S), Nine Market Categories,[a] 1953–65

	Percentage Rise (+) or Fall (−) in Series[b]						Av. of Periods with Rise[d] (7)	Av. of Periods with Fall[d] (8)	Av. Amplitude of Rises and Falls[d] (9)
N or S	1953–54 Fall[c] (1)	1954–57 Rise (2)	1957–58 Fall (3)	1958–59 Rise (4)	1959–61 Fall (5)	1961–65 Rise (6)			
HOME GOODS AND APPAREL									
N	−19	+30	−9	+22	−8	+34	+28.5	−12.3	20.4
S	−12	+21	−8	+20	−9	+35	+25.3	−9.4	17.3
NONAUTOMOTIVE EQUIPMENT AND DEFENSE									
N	−33	+54	−20	+35	−9	+58	+48.9	−20.8	34.9
S	−16	+35	−9	+14	−3	+40	+29.2	−9.7	19.2
DEFENSE PRODUCTS									
N	−49	+88	−48	+27	−3	+84	+66.3	−33.7	50.0
S	−19	+36	−11	+10	−6	+34	+26.9	−12.2	19.5
NONAUTOMOTIVE EQUIPMENT, EXCLUDING DEFENSE									
N	−49[e]	+199	−31	+46	−13	+68	+104.5	−31.3	67.9
S	−24	+59	−14	+26	−11	+52	+45.7	−16.0	30.9
MACHINERY AND EQUIPMENT INDUSTRIES									
N	−34	+81	−27	+32	−7	+69	+60.7	−23.1	41.9
S	−21	+48	−17	+19	−5	+54	+40.2	−14.5	27.4

AUTOMOTIVE EQUIPMENT									
N	−16	+51'	−34	+69	−22	+88	+69.5	−23.9	46.7
S	−22	+50'	−32	+65	−23	+83	+65.6	−25.6	45.6
MATERIALS, SUPPLIES, AND INTERMEDIATE PRODUCTS									
N	−24	+47	−18	+31	−11	+42	+40.1	−17.3	28.7
S	−12	+32	−15	+27	−10	+37	+32.4	−12.4	22.4
CONSTRUCTION MATERIALS, ETC.									
N	−17	+41	−15	+29	−12	+33	+34.3	−14.6	24.5
S	−7	+31	−10	+23	−12	+31	+28.1	−9.5	18.8
OTHER MATERIALS, ETC.									
N	−21	+45	−19	+33	−11	+47	+41.7	−17.1	29.4
S	−12	+33	−16	+29	−10	+40	+33.9	−13.1	23.5

[a] For composition of these categories, see text.

[b] See Table 3-1, note a.

[c] The high levels from which these series start in 1953 were used as the base for the measures in this column, even where such levels cannot be positively identified as specific-cycle peaks.

[d] The averages in column 9 are taken without regard to sign, but not those in columns 7 and 8. Because of rounding, the figures shown may differ from ones computed directly from the listings in columns 1–6.

[e] Refers to the decline in the second half of 1953, which interrupted the very large irregular movements in the first half of the year (see Chart 3-3).

[f] There are additional movements in these series. To maintain comparability with the other groups, these movements are not included in the table. The amplitudes of the short but steep rises in 1954–55 were +73 in new orders and +64 in shipments; those of the ensuing declines in 1955–56 were −26 and −24; and those of the rises in 1956–57 were +18 and +19 (compare Chart 3-3). Had these measures been included, the averages in columns 7–9 for machinery and equipment industries would have been somewhat smaller (+61.7, −24.3, and 43.0 for new orders; and +57.6, −25.0, and 41.3 for shipments).

93

duction operations, as measured by shipments, follow quite faithfully the large short-term variations in demand, as measured by new orders.

Series in Constant Prices

In undertaking to compare new orders with production, one is confronted with a major gap in the data: the unavailability of aggregate volume estimates for new orders. In an attempt to bridge this gap, we have corrected the Department of Commerce estimates of the current value of manufacturers' new orders for changes in prices. This adjustment was applied to the major industry series in the OBE compilation for the years 1948–58; at the time, the revised Census data were not yet available. The deflating indexes used for these corrections are essentially combinations of the appropriate components of the Bureau of Labor Statistics wholesale price index.

Deflation procedures, even when carefully executed, seldom produce more than crude approximations, for the difficulties and pitfalls are many. Without fully describing at this point the procedures and data employed,[13] two special problems are discussed. The first concerns the timing of orders and price data; the second, the pricing of goods made to specific orders.

To the extent that manufactured products are priced at the time the orders for them are received and accepted, it is precisely to the new-order series that the current price indexes would be applicable as deflators. Clearly, too, where the products so priced are not shipped immediately but require some time for production and delivery, the same indexes would often fail to be properly applicable as deflators of the data on the value of output or shipments. For the latter would then be recorded at the price of the period in which the order was accepted rather than at the price of the period in which the order was delivered, and the two may well differ. Of course, for new orders shipped from stock, whose value equals that of shipments of the same period, no complications of this sort can arise; as a rule, the current price is the right one to use for both the new order and the sales series.

What if the price was not contractually fixed at the time the order had been accepted? Where time-consuming production processes are involved, the long-term contract may provide that the price of the output shall be adjusted according to the changes in the input prices during

[13] See Appendix C.

the period set for the completion of the order. Such escalation provisions, based as a rule on the BLS wholesale price index, are common in certain industries.[14] In such cases, the precise contract sum (price of the preordered output at the time the order is accepted) is unknown. But if no other price has been specified at that time, then the price of the current (i.e., the order-acceptance) period can be presumed to apply; any subsequent price changes cannot, and need not, be taken into account in a deflation procedure whose aim can only be correction for current, not future, price changes.

Conceptually, then, the only real difficulty seems to be with those new orders that are contracted for at price levels different from those prevailing in the current period. This need not cause serious difficulty in practice.

The difficulty of pricing custom-made equipment gives rise to an important deficiency of the price data. The wholesale price indexes measure essentially the price movements in primary markets, where the goods are first sold commercially, ordinarily in large lots. But there is no "market price" in this sense for unique products, that is, for goods made to order and designed to meet individual customer specifications, such as planetarium equipment or an airliner. Although many of the technical or quality characteristics of such products may have a common valuation which they implicitly contribute to the product's transaction price, this price may vary with each buyer, since each purchase is likely to involve a different bundle of product attributes. The BLS has not found it possible to price directly such items as "ships and railroad stock, fabricated plastic products, and some machinery which is largely custom-made."[15]

The series of manufacturers' new orders in constant (average 1947–49) prices are presented in Chart 3-5 for the comprehensive industry groups and in Chart 3-6 for the major component industries. These series show much weaker upward trends than their undeflated counter-

[14] Cf. M. E. Riley, "The Price Indexes of the Bureau of Labor Statistics," in *The Relationship of Prices to Economic Stability and Growth,* Compendium of Papers Submitted by Panelists Appearing before the Joint Economic Committee, 85 Cong., 2nd sess., Washington, D.C., 1958, p. 114. The author notes that "virtually all of the heavy power-generating equipment produced is made under an arrangement by which the contract sum is adjusted for changes in the prices of selected materials and components between the initiation and completion of the job. Federal shipbuilding contracts contain similar provisions."

[15] "Wholesale Price Index," in U.S. Bureau of Labor Statistics, *Techniques of Preparing Major BLS Statistical Series,* BLS Bulletin 1168, Washington, D.C., 1954, p. 84.

On the construction of price deflators for the industries not covered in the BLS data (such as nonautomotive transporation equipment and printing and publishing), see Appendix C.

Chart 3-5
New Orders and Shipments in Constant Dollars and Production Indexes, All Manufacturing, Durable and Nondurable Goods Industries, 1948–58

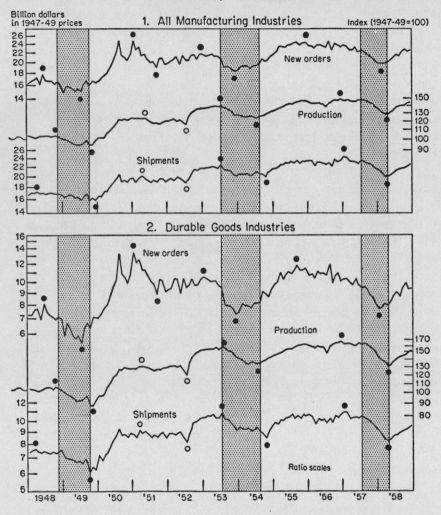

Chart 3-5 (concluded)

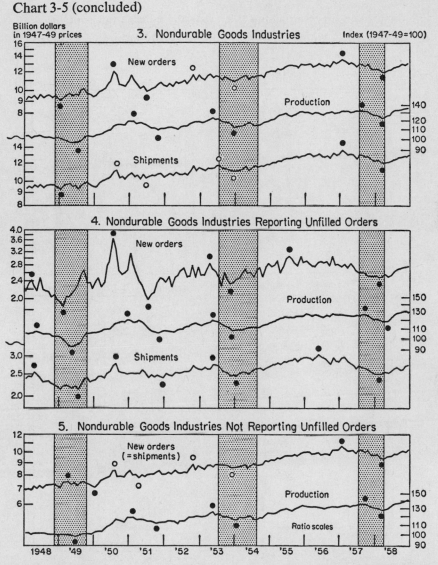

Note: Shaded areas represent business cycle contractions; unshaded areas, expansions. Dots identify peaks and troughs of specific cycles; circles, retardations. Series are seasonally adjusted.

Chart 3-6
New Orders and Shipments in Constant Dollars and Production Indexes, Ten Major Manufacturing Industries, 1948–58

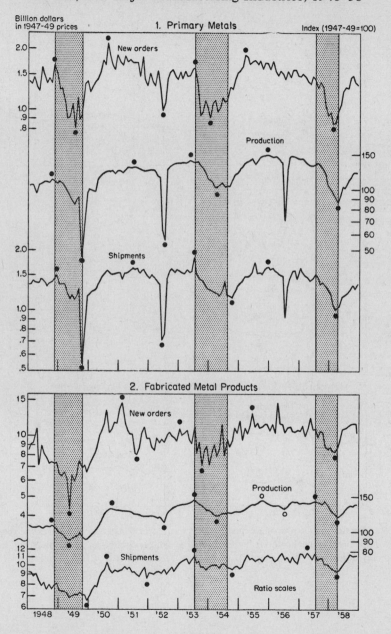

Chart 3-6 (continued)

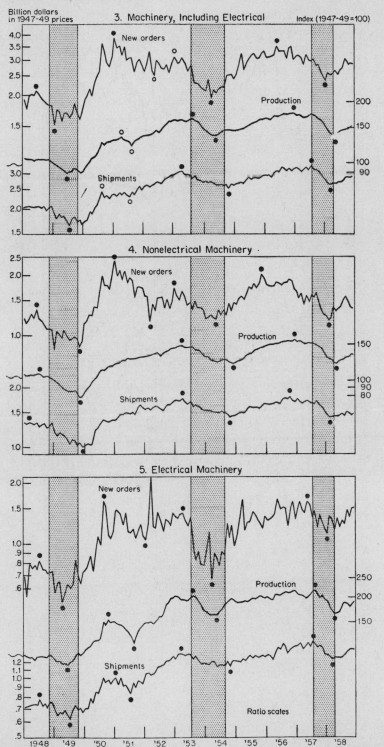

Billion dollars in 1947-49 prices

3. Machinery, Including Electrical

Index (1947-49=100)

4. Nonelectrical Machinery

5. Electrical Machinery

Chart 3-6 (continued)

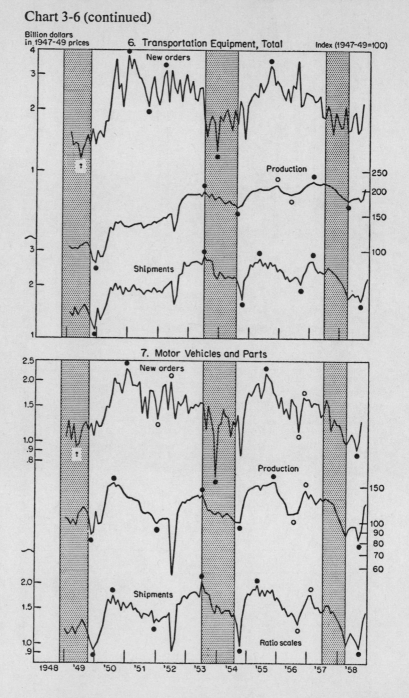

Billion dollars
in 1947-49 prices

6. Transportation Equipment, Total

Index (1947-49=100)

7. Motor Vehicles and Parts

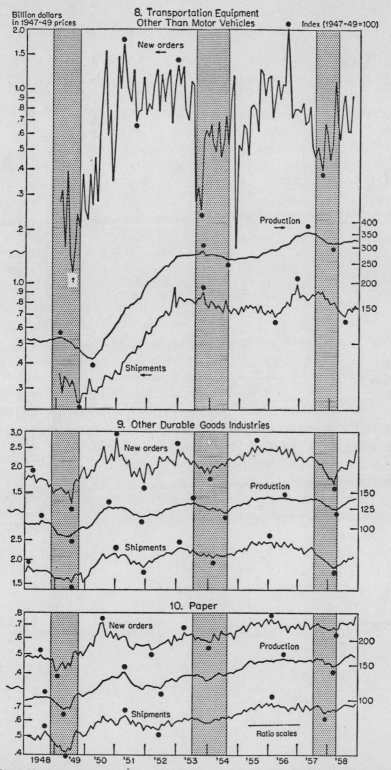

**8. Transportation Equipment
Other Than Motor Vehicles**

Billion dollars
in 1947-49 prices

● Index (1947-49=100)

New orders

Production

Shipments

9. Other Durable Goods Industries

New orders

Production

Shipments

10. Paper

New orders

Production

Shipments

Ratio scales

Note: Shaded areas represent business cycle contractions; unshaded areas, expansions. Dots identify peaks and troughs of specific cycles; circles, retardations. Series are seasonally adjusted.

parts, which would, of course, be expected in view of the tendency for industrial prices to rise during most of the period covered. The short-term movements, on the other hand, were largely unaffected by the adjustment. The reason for this is that the price deflators are very smooth and stable, while the new-order series to which they were applied are much more volatile.

The observed differences in cyclical behavior between the corresponding constant-price series and current-price series are largely of the kind to be expected as a result of trend elimination. Thus, the amplitudes of the specific-cycle expansions tend to be somewhat smaller than those in the constant-price series. On the other hand, cyclical declines are often larger in the deflated than in the undeflated figures, but these differences are neither considerable nor systematic.

In addition to new orders in real terms, Charts 3-5 and 3-6 show, for each of the major industries or groups cover 1, the corresponding series on output and real shipments. Output is represented by the appropriate components of the monthly Federal Reserve Index of Industrial Production (1953 revision, 1947–49 = 100).[16] The series for shipments were constructed by deflating the OBE current-value figures by means of the same price indexes that were used to deflate new orders. To the extent that prices actually changed during the delivery periods, this clearly results in errors for goods which were made to order and priced as of the period in which they were ordered. On the other hand, in some cases current price deflators might apply better to shipments than to new orders; and in production to stock they should apply equally to both. In any event, there is no good practical alternative to the simple current-price deflation procedure we have adopted; any more elaborate method would merely be pretentious, for it would have to be based on necessarily arbitrary assumptions about the time aspects of pricing the made-to-order goods.

[16] For production, as for new orders and shipments, revised data became available after this analysis was completed. Examination of the new series indicates that our findings would not be materially affected by the use of the revised data.

Indexes for three industry groups (other durable goods and nondurable goods industries with and without unfilled orders) were computed by combining the Federal Reserve indexes for the component industries with weights derived from the 1947 value added weights used in the FRB compilation. Separate indexes for automotive and other transportation equipment were obtained through the courtesy of the Federal Reserve Board for the period before 1956, the year in which the published series for these industries begin.

Relative Movements of Real New Orders,
Output, and Real Shipments

Major fluctuations in quantities ordered are typically reproduced, with lags, in the course of output, so that the phase-to-phase correspondence between these series is strong. But the cyclical movements are systematically larger in real new orders than in the corresponding output, and these differences are particularly pronounced for the durable goods industries.

The sequence of corresponding cycles in new orders and production may be interrupted by a wave of advance buying characterized throughout by an excess of the ordering rates over the capacity output rates. The statistical expression of a concentrated buying movement of this sort would be an "extra" cycle in new orders, absorbed largely by a gradual expansion of output and to a certain extent also by cancellations. Our materials include a single but very significant episode illustrating such developments: the 1950–51 phase of the Korean War as experienced by a large segment of durables manufactures. The chart for the durable goods sector as a whole shows production moving along a virtually horizontal plateau in the last quarter of 1950 and the first half of 1951, in contrast to new orders (measured net of cancellations), which first climbed to unprecedented peak levels in August 1950 and again in January 1951, then declined steeply through the first quarter of 1951. The principal point here is that throughout this period new orders were received at high rates exceeding those of current shipments, and the behavior of shipments mirrored that of production. New orders never fell below the level of shipments; so their contraction merely reduced the rates at which the backlog of unfilled orders, already very large, continued to increase. Total output of durables dipped only slightly in the summer of 1951, when the decline in new orders was nearly completed, but it remained close to its top levels and soon started moving gradually upward again, reflecting the upturn in buying in the last quarter of the year. After the mid-1952 steel strike, finally, the expansion of output resumed a more vigorous pace, feeding on the backlog which was then at its peak level, even though the recovery of new orders was only moderate and quite hesitant throughout. Thus both the huge 1950–51 humps and the irregular 1951–52 rise in new orders were translated into an almost continuous and gradual expansion of output.

Chart 3-6 suggests that these developments, which show up well on the graph for the total durable goods sector, are attributable mainly to nonelectrical machinery and transportation equipment (other than motor vehicles). In the other major component industries of the sector, the "Korean" cycles in quantities ordered did reappear in the time path of production, although in a strongly subdued form.

The cyclical paths of real shipments are closely similar to those of output of the corresponding durable goods industries, in both amplitude and timing. For a technical reason, output indexes overstate the degree to which the short irregular movements of new orders are smoothed out in scheduling production; the series on shipments involve less rounding and therefore retain more of the erratic components than do the output indexes.[17] This, however, is about the only major and persistent difference between the charted production indexes and deflated shipments series that the eye can detect.

A difficulty arises at this point because many of the individual industry components of the Federal Reserve production indexes are based in part on data for shipments. One saving feature is that shipments are often combined with inventory changes to get deflated value-of-output data. Also, the use of Census value data (after deflation) is mostly limited to the estimation of the annual indexes, whereas the monthly intrayear movements are based largely on the BLS man-hour data. Nevertheless, the close similarity of output indexes and deflated shipments in our charts is doubtless in some part a statistical artifact due to the incorporation of the shipments data in the production indexes. This is more true for the longer trends than for the shorter movements, with which I am primarily concerned, and it is also more true for some industries than for others.[18]

The contrast between real new orders on the one hand and output and real shipments on the other is well expressed in the two metalworking and the two machinery-producing industries, but it is particularly strong in transportation equipment. This is due primarily to the

[17] The Federal Reserve production indexes that are used are rounded off in a relatively drastic manner, to exclude fractions of an index point. The OBE series, on the other hand, are expressed in millions of dollars, while a monthly value of new orders or shipments will run into billions of dollars; as a result, the minimum changes in these series are many times smaller than those that can be expressed by the production indexes.

[18] Production indexes for steel mill products, a subgroup of primary metals, rely directly on data on mill shipments. This is the only one of the larger industrial subdivisions so affected, according to the descriptions in the Federal Reserve publications.

nonautomotive component of the latter group (Chart 3-6). It is clear that these observations support our earlier findings concerning the major importance of production to order in this large area of durable goods manufacturing. Also consistent with our earlier analysis is that for the "other durable goods industries," where production to stock has a greater weight, the differences among the three series are relatively small and real shipments at times (e.g., in 1955–58) resemble real new orders more than production.

For the group of nondurable goods industries reporting unfilled orders, real shipments follow the general cyclical course of output but at times show more similarity to deflated new orders (see 1950 and 1956–57 in Chart 3-5). It is, of course, necessary to assume that deflated new orders and shipments are equal for the large group of nondurable goods industries that do not report backlogs, since this is implied in the compilation of the underlying current-value data. The series for the total nondurable goods sector represent weighted composites of the figures for the above two groups and behave accordingly: most of the time, shipments and new orders move closely together, with production following along a fairly parallel course. There is a significant difference, however, in the early phase of the Korean War (1950–51), when two sharp but short bursts of advance buying were, to a large extent, smoothed out in both output and shipments of nondurable goods.

Relative Cyclical Amplitudes of Output and the Deflated Series

Table 3-3 summarizes measures of the amplitude of each successive expansion and contraction for all series covered in Charts 3-5 and 3-6. The amplitudes are expressed, as before, in percentages of the initial-turn levels.

The average amplitudes are larger for deflated new orders than for either output or deflated shipments of the corresponding industries. This holds true for expansions as well as contractions, and hence for total cycles (Table 3-3, columns 1–6). In virtually every set of average amplitudes for individual matched movements in each series, S and Z each exceeds N.[19]

---

[19] Some individual comparisons do not conform to the rule but these are concentrated in one period and the deviations are easily explained. The 1952–53 expansions in output and real shipments were larger than the 1951–52 expansions in real new orders for most durable goods industries. This is

Table 3-3

Average Percentage Amplitudes of Cyclical Expansions and Contractions of Output, New Orders, and Shipments in Constant Prices, by Major Manufacturing Industries, 1948–58

| Industry | Average Percentage Amplitudes of Real New Orders (N), Output (Z) and Real Shipments (S) | | | | | | Ratios of Average Percentage Amplitudes, All Cyclical Movements[c] | | |
| | Expansions[a] | | | Contractions[b] | | | | | |
	$\bar{N}$ (1)	$\bar{Z}$ (2)	$\bar{S}$ (3)	$\bar{N}$ (4)	$\bar{Z}$ (5)	$\bar{S}$ (6)	$\bar{S}/\bar{N}$ (7)	$\bar{Z}/\bar{S}$ (8)	$\bar{Z}/\bar{N}$ (9)
All manufacturing	+29	+21	+18	−13	−8	−7	.60	1.08	.65
Durable goods, total	+54	+30	+27	−25	−12	−14	.53	1.00	.53
Primary metals	+67	+66	+61	−39	−35	−36	.92	1.02	.94
Fabricated metal products	+66	+27	+24	−27	−11	−10	.35	1.12	.40
Electrical machinery[d]	+76	+50	+40	−24	−19	−11	.52	1.31	.68
Machinery, except electrical[d]	+63	+51	+43	−28	−20	−19	.67	1.14	.76
Motor vehicles and parts[e]	+73	+47	+48	−40	−32	−33	.72	0.95	.68
Transportation equipment excl. motor vehicles[e]	+329	+132	+123	−64	−8	−19	.36	0.99	.36
Other durable goods industries[f]	+37	+23	+23	−20	−11	−13	.63	0.94	.59
Nondurable goods, total	+19	+16	+15	−8	−6	−6	.79	1.00	.79
With unfilled orders[g]	+43	+19	+17	−21	−9	−11	.42	1.08	.45
Textile-mill products[e]	+86	+25	+25	−34	−18	−17	.36	1.05	.37
Leather and leather products[e]	+31	+17	+19	−23	−16	−17	.67	0.89	.59
Paper and allied products[e]	+47	+43	+39	−14	−11	−12	.85	1.04	.88

ᵃ Movements corresponding to the 1949–51, 1952–53, and 1954–57 expansions in total manufacturing production (the rises in individual series may have different dates). The figures are averages of the percentage changes during the three expansions.

ᵇ Movements corresponding to the 1948–49, 1951–52, 1953–54, and 1957–58 movements in total manufacturing production (contractions all, except for some retardations in 1951–52; the declines in individual series may have different dates). The figures are averages of the percentage changes during the four contractions.

ᶜ Based on averages of rises and falls during the six expansion and contraction periods (see notes a and b). The averages are taken without regard to sign.

ᵈ Based in part on unpublished data received from the U.S. Department of Commerce, Office of Business Economics (OBE).

ᵉ Based on unpublished data received from OBE and seasonally adjusted by the electronic computer method for NBER.

ᶠ Includes professional and scientific instruments; lumber; furniture; stone, clay, and glass; and miscellaneous industries.

ᵍ Includes textiles, leather, paper, and printing and publishing.

The differences between the amplitudes of deflated shipments and output, on the other hand, are in most cases small, and almost always much less than the corresponding differences between the amplitudes of deflated shipments and new orders. Moreover, the differences between S and Z, unlike those between N and either S or Z, have no marked tendency to agree in sign. Of the 59 comparisons for the ten major industries covered, 35, or nearly 60 per cent, show output to have larger amplitude than shipments ($Z > S$) and the rest show the opposite.[20]

Columns 7–9 in Table 3-3 present the ratios of average relative amplitudes of real shipments to real new orders ($\bar{S}/\bar{N}$), output to real shipment ($\bar{Z}/\bar{S}$), and output to real new orders ($\bar{Z}/\bar{N}$). The corresponding ratios must satisfy the simple multiplicative rule $(\bar{S}/\bar{N}) \times (\bar{Z}/\bar{S}) = \bar{Z}/\bar{N}$.[21] This is a rough attempt to discriminate between the average effects that changes in unfilled orders and in finished-product stocks

clearly the consequence of developments in the early phase of the Korean War (1950–51). At that time, output and shipments of durables moved along a high ceiling; new orders climbed to unprecedented levels and then declined swiftly, but always exceeded shipments. The huge backlog of long-term orders thus accumulated, plus the effects of the mid-1952 steel strike, explain the large relative size of the output expansion of late 1952–53.

[20] For expansions, about 70 per cent of the comparisons show $Z > S$; for contractions; there is nearly an even division among instances in which $Z > S$ and $Z < S$.

[21] For some purposes, it would be more convenient to use differences instead of ratios, and actually I have examined both, but there is no point in duplicating this analysis. The multiplicative rule for the ratios (see text above) is replaced for the differences by the additive rule: $(\bar{S} - \bar{N}) + (\bar{Z} - \bar{S}) = \bar{Z} - \bar{N}$.

have upon the size of cyclical movements in output relative to the size of cyclical movements in real new orders. The relation of the amplitudes $\bar{Z}/\bar{N}$ is attributed entirely to the interaction of backlog changes and stock changes, the contribution of the former being measured by $\bar{S}/\bar{N}$ and the contribution of the latter by $\bar{Z}/\bar{S}$. In other words, we are dealing here with the relative role in manufacturing of "backlog adjustments" and "stock adjustments" (as introduced in Chapter 2); the role of the current price adjustments is suppressed by the use of deflated values.

A $\bar{Z}/\bar{N}$ ratio of less than 1 indicates a reduction in the cyclical amplitude (stabilization) of production. All these entries in Table 3-3 are less than 1 (column 9). The amplitude ratios suggest that the proximate reason why outputs are much more stable than new orders is that shipments fluctuate much less than new orders; it is not that outputs fluctuate less than shipments, for actually the amplitudes of Z and S differ little; when they do differ, the effect is often to cause increased rather than decreased cycles in production. Most of the $\bar{Z}/\bar{S}$ ratios for the combined rise-and-fall amplitudes exceed 1 (column 8), and the same applies to expansions; for contractions the record is more mixed, with relatively low ratios prevailing in the durable goods sector. In total manufacturing both the expansions and the contractions are on the average larger in output than in shipments. Industries with high (low) $\bar{Z}/\bar{N}$ values also have high (low) $\bar{S}/\bar{N}$ values, whereas the ratios $\bar{Z}/\bar{N}$ and $\bar{Z}/\bar{S}$ show no significant correlations except for contractions.[22]

These measures suggest that the net effects of accumulations and decumulations of finished inventories are relatively weak and more often destabilizing than stabilizing. In contrast, the net effects of changes in backlogs of unfilled orders appear to be as a rule stabilizing and strong.

Unpublished OBE data for subdivisions of the major manufacturing industries were used to construct some preliminary estimates for three groups of industries representing primarily the production of consumer durable goods, equipment, and materials. This was done in an early

---

[22] The correlation coefficient (r) for $\bar{Z}/\bar{N}$ with $\bar{S}/\bar{N}$ for expansions is .926; for contractions, .760; and for all cyclical movements, .949. The corresponding figures for the correlation of $\bar{Z}/\bar{N}$ with $\bar{Z}/\bar{S}$ are .288, .569, and .040.

attempt to approximate for new orders and shipments some of the market-category data as provided in the FRB compilation for industrial production.[23] The resulting group aggregates were adjusted for price changes by means of the BLS wholesale price indexes.[24]

Despite their relative crudeness, these estimates are not devoid of interest; however, only a broad summary of what they show seems warranted. The average percentage amplitudes of cyclical movements are larger for equipment and the consumer durables group (which includes the volatile motor vehicle industry) than for materials. This applies to all three variables, i.e., to $\bar{N}$, $\bar{Z}$, and $\bar{S}$ (see tabulation below).

Average Percentage Amplitudes
(rise and fall)

	Real New Orders ($\bar{N}$)	Output ($\bar{Z}$)	Real Shipments ($\bar{S}$)
Consumer durable goods	45	33	32
Equipment	49	31	27
Materials	31	25	22

The cyclical movements of real shipments for the equipment group are on the average only a little more than half the size of the corresponding movements of real new orders; for consumer durables and materials, the fluctuations of shipments are reduced relative to those of new orders by approximately 30 per cent. That the smoothing or stabilizing effect of backlog variation is particularly strong for equipment would be expected; that it is still considerable for the other groups deserves some emphasis.

For equipment and materials, the relative amplitudes of rise and rise-and-fall are on the average larger in output than in shipments, suggesting again some (not very strong) destabilizing effects of finished-inventory changes. For contractions, however, $\bar{Z}/\bar{S}$ is 1 or less.

[23] The new Census data of the 1963 vintage include market-category series that are undoubtedly superior to these estimates. However, the new series (introduced earlier in this chapter; see Chart 3-3 and text) do not extend back before 1953 and have not been analyzed in deflated form.

[24] The deflators for the three groups were, respectively, the index of consumer durable goods prices, the index of producer finished goods prices, and a weighted combination of price indexes for materials and components used in manufacturing and construction (1957–59 = 100).

The above interpretation of the average amplitude relations makes no allowance for the differences in timing of the cyclical movements that are being compared. This, however, can hardly be a source of significant error in our broad conclusions. Cyclical phases in the corresponding series of new orders, output, and shipments show a high degree of positive conformity and are well matched in our measurements. Even the longest of the time intervals between the paired turning points in these series are short relative to the duration of the cyclical phases. The results based on the averages seem representative and strong enough; consequently, it is unlikely that they would be materially altered by minor adjustments of the method applied. Moreover, they are supported by independent evidence on the cyclical behavior of manufacturers' finished-goods inventories and unfilled orders (Chapter 10).

Evidence for Other Series and Periods

Average Amplitudes of Component Movements:
37 Industries, 1953–63

Amplitude measures of a different type are obtained from computer programs for seasonal adjustment based on the ratio-to-moving-average method.[25] Here each series is divided into three components, Cy (the cycle-trend), Se (the seasonal), and I (the irregular). Each monthly value of the original series (Or) is assumed to be a product of the three, i.e., $Or = Cy \times Se \times I$, and the seasonal adjustment reduces the series to $Cy \times I$. Monthly percentage changes are computed for the original and seasonally adjusted series and also separately for each of the component series. When these figures are averaged without regard to sign, the result is five measures of average month-to-month percentage change (AMPC) relating to the original series $(\overline{Or})$, the seasonal factor series $(\overline{Se})$, the seasonally adjusted series $(\overline{CyI})$, the trend-cycle series $(\overline{Cy})$, and the irregular series $(\overline{I})$.[26]

---

[25] For a detailed description of this method, see Julius Shiskin, *Electronic Computers and Business Indicators,* Occasional Paper 57, New York, NBER, 1957; and Julius Shiskin and Harry Eisenpress, *Seasonal Adjustments by Electronic Computer Methods,* Technical Paper 12, New York, NBER, 1958. The seasonal adjustment and time series analysis program was developed at the Bureau of the Census and the National Bureau of Economic Research by Julius Shiskin and associates.

[26] The AMPC for the seasonally adjusted series, $\overline{CyI}$, is computed by dividing the moving seasonal factors into the corresponding figures of the original series, month by month. $\overline{Cy}$ is the AMPC

The relations among these measures are also of interest. In particular, attention must be given to $\bar{I}/\overline{Cy}$, the ratio that shows the size of the irregular relative to that of the cyclical component, on a single month basis. When the ratios $\bar{I}/\overline{Cy}$ are computed for periods of two, three, or more months, their value declines rapidly because the cyclical amplitude ($\overline{Cy}$) cumulates steadily, while the irregular amplitude ($\bar{I}$) remains about the same. On a month-to-month basis, the irregular factor is usually larger, often much larger, than the cyclical factor. As the span over which the percentage changes are computed is increased, however, the value of $\bar{I}$ sooner or later falls below the value of $\overline{Cy}$. A measure labeled MCD (index of months required for cyclical dominance) records the number of months in that span for which the ratio $\bar{I}/\overline{Cy}$ first declines below 1.

Finally, there is another simple measure that has a time dimension, but which takes into account only the direction and not the amplitude of changes in the series. The "average duration of run" (ADR) is the average number of consecutive months during which a series has been moving in the same direction.[27] Table 3-4 presents the monthly percentage amplitudes of the cyclical and irregular components, as well as the related measures $\bar{I}/\overline{Cy}$, MCD, and ADR, for a large number of paired current-dollar series on new orders and shipments compiled by the Bureau of the Census.[28]

The amplitude figures for the major industries and the still more comprehensive sectoral aggregates tend to be substantially smaller than the averages of movements in the component series. This is presumably because divergencies in timing result in partial smoothing out of the component fluctuations in aggregation. But in all cases, for comprehensive groups and their individual components alike, the average monthly percentage changes are greater in new orders than in

in a fifteen-month weighted moving average (Spencer graduation) of the seasonally adjusted data. (We shall often refer to $\overline{Cy}$ as the "cyclical" component, although it contains also trend elements. The series in our samples are often not long enough to show pronounced secular trends, whereas their cyclical sensitivity is typically high.) $\bar{I}$ is the AMPC in the monthly ratios of the seasonally adjusted series to its Spencer graduation.

[27] For a full description of this measure, see W. Allen Wallis and Geoffrey H. Moore, *A Significance Test for Time Series*, Technical Paper 1, New York, NBER, 1941; and Geoffrey H. Moore, *Statistical Indicators of Cyclical Revivals and Recessions*, New York, NBER, 1950, App. A.

[28] The series themselves are published for a much smaller number of major industries, but the descriptive statistics shown here were published in full industrial detail in 1963 as a part of the major revision of the official data formerly known as the Industry Survey (see text and note 1 at the beginning of this chapter).

Table 3-4
Average Monthly Percentage Amplitudes of Irregular (*I*) and Cyclical (*Cy*) Components and Related Measures in New Orders (*N*) and Shipments (*S*), Thirty-seven Industries, 1953–63

Industry	N or S	Seas. Adj. Series $\overline{Cyl}$	$\bar{I}$	$\overline{Cy}$	Ratio: $\bar{I}/\overline{Cy}$	MCD[a]	ADR[b]
All manufacturing	N	1.92	1.52	0.98	1.55	2	1.98
	S	1.35	0.98	0.75	1.31	2	2.55
Durable goods	N	3.79	3.25	1.61	2.02	3	1.67
	S	2.04	1.42	1.19	1.19	2	2.91
Primary metals	N	7.28	5.96	3.68	1.62	2	2.36
	S	5.21	3.98	3.24	1.23	2	2.91
Blast furnaces, steel mills	N	13.20	11.76	4.63	2.54	3	2.22
	S	3.55	2.45	2.54	0.96	1	2.76
Nonferrous metals	N	5.65	5.34	1.98	2.70	3	1.81
	S	3.45	2.73	1.87	1.46	2	1.99
Iron and steel foundries	N	5.82	5.05	2.46	2.05	3	1.74
	S	3.31	2.42	1.82	1.33	2	2.28
Fabricated metal products	N	5.55	5.32	1.42	3.75	4	1.52
	S	2.03	1.75	0.81	2.16	3	2.16
Cutlery, hand tools, hardware	N	8.33	8.25	1.66	4.97	5	1.56
	S	4.41	4.20	1.12	3.75	4	2.05
Building materials and wire products	N	6.49	6.18	1.46	4.23	4	1.56
	S	2.94	2.81	0.83	3.39	4	1.79
Machinery, except electrical	N	4.20	3.97	1.34	2.96	3	1.71
	S	1.46	1.19	0.90	1.32	2	1.95
Engines and turbines	N	10.82	10.32	2.14	4.82	6	1.76
	S	6.46	6.18	1.84	3.36	4	1.51
Farm machinery and equipment	N	9.44	8.86	2.16	4.10	4	1.74
	S	5.31	4.78	1.81	2.64	4	2.08
Construction, mining and material handling	N	6.65	6.33	2.34	2.71	3	1.69
	S	3.78	3.08	1.82	1.69	2	2.64
Metalworking machinery	N	9.02	8.67	2.46	3.52	4	1.81
	S	6.15	5.41	2.67	2.03	3	2.01
Machine tools, accessories, etc.	N	5.34	5.04	1.93	2.61	3	1.58
	S	3.47	2.96	1.67	1.77	2	2.03
Special industry machinery	N	8.29	7.92	2.35	3.37	4	1.54
	S	5.23	4.96	1.45	3.42	4	1.76
General industrial machinery	N	5.34	5.14	1.34	3.84	4	1.47
	S	3.66	3.41	1.27	2.69	3	1.67
Office and store machines	N	5.42	5.11	1.37	3.73	4	1.64
	S	3.08	2.80	1.08	2.59	3	1.85

(continued)

Table 3-4 (continued)

Industry	N or S	Seas. Adj. Series $\overline{Cyl}$	$\overline{I}$	$\overline{Cy}$	Ratio: $\overline{I}/\overline{Cy}$	MCD[a]	ADR[b]
Durable goods (cont.)							
Electrical machinery	N	7.48	7.26	1.99	3.65	4	1.60
	S	2.50	2.17	1.05	2.07	3	1.87
Transmission and distribution equipment	N	10.11	9.68	2.03	4.77	6	1.55
	S	3.59	3.32	1.33	2.50	3	1.81
Electrical industrial apparatus	N	10.95	10.40	2.72	3.82	4	1.52
	S	3.70	3.33	1.44	2.31	3	1.80
Household appliances	N	8.49	8.08	2.13	3.79	4	1.69
	S	6.23	5.80	2.31	2.51	3	1.67
Radio and TV	N	11.19	10.77	2.96	3.64	4	1.71
	S	7.98	7.02	3.20	2.19	3	1.83
Communication equipment	N	12.31	11.78	2.65	4.45	5	1.60
	S	4.22	3.68	1.91	1.93	3	2.15
Electronic components	N	10.66	10.07	2.60	3.87	4	1.63
	S	4.38	3.81	2.04	1.87	3	1.97
Transportation equipment	N	11.28	10.96	2.38	4.61	5	1.52
	S	3.62	3.02	1.68	1.80	3	2.19
Motor vehicle parts	N	12.77	12.00	3.52	3.41	4	1.71
	S	4.27	3.57	2.11	1.69	2	2.03
Aircraft and parts	N	266.43	261.40	5.47	47.79	6	1.52
	S	3.91	3.69	1.11	3.32	4	1.62
Shipbuilding and railroad equipment	N	26.44	25.84	4.26	6.07	6	1.52
	S	6.71	6.17	2.41	2.56	3	1.67
Scientific and engineering instruments	N	12.24	11.75	2.24	5.25	6	1.49
	S	3.21	2.89	1.14	2.54	3	1.85
Ordnance	N	14.12	13.79	3.11	4.43	6	1.62
	S	4.66	4.08	2.02	2.02	3	1.81
Household furniture	N	4.25	3.87	1.36	2.85	4	1.98
	S	3.38	3.03	1.29	2.35	3	2.03
Selected nondurable goods industries							
Broadwoven fabrics	N	6.23	5.88	1.52	3.87	5	1.69
	S	3.35	2.94	1.41	2.09	3	1.91
Knitting mills	N	8.10	7.66	1.87	4.10	5	1.74
	S	3.49	3.06	1.30	2.35	3	1.92
Leather, industrial products, and cut stock	N	12.23	11.81	1.79	6.60	6	1.84
	S	3.58	3.29	1.03	3.19	4	1.87

(continued)

113

Table 3-4 (concluded)

Industry	N or S	Average Monthly Amplitude of				MCD[a]	ADR[b]
		Seas. Adj. Series $\overline{Cyl}$	$\bar{I}$	$\overline{Cy}$	Ratio: $\bar{I}/\overline{Cy}$		
Selected nondurables (cont.)							
Pulp and paperboard mills (except building paper)	N	2.38	2.24	.69	3.25	4	1.64
	S	1.51	1.12	.88	1.27	2	2.40
Newspapers, books, and periodicals	N	3.86	3.80	.64	5.94	6	1.49
	S	1.46	1.37	.45	3.04	3	1.81

Source: Bureau of the Census, *Manufacturers' Shipments, Inventories, and Orders, 1947–1963 (Revised)*, Washington, D.C., 1963, Appendix F, Parts VI and VII. For description of the measures, see text and note 25.

[a] MCD signifies months required for cyclical dominance.

[b] ADR signifies average duration of run of seasonally adjusted series.

shipments (in terms of the seasonally adjusted series, $\overline{Cyl}_n > \overline{Cyl}_s$, where n denotes new orders and s, shipments; see Table 3-4, column 1). Also without exception, the irregular component is larger in new orders than in shipments, that is, $\bar{I}_n > \bar{I}_s$ (column 2). The cyclical component in new orders exceeds its counterpart in shipments, $\overline{Cy}_n > \overline{Cy}_s$, for all but four of the thirty-seven industries listed (column 3). These measures, then, are in full agreement with the observations made earlier for the amplitudes of cyclical rises and falls in the major-industry series.[29] Indeed, along with similar results for other sets of data,[30] they emphasize the virtual ubiquity of the rule that N is both

[29] The $\overline{Cy}$ estimates enable us to compare the size of cyclical movements in different series, the task for which the relative cyclical amplitudes were previously used. The latter depend upon identification of the specific-cycle turns in the series: They measure the size of the *total* movement between such turns. The $\overline{Cy}$ figures, while also computed from seasonally adjusted data, measure changes in *smoothed* series on a *per month* basis; they do not require any explicit dating of the specific-cycle turns.

[30] Measures of average amplitudes of component movements have been computed for a large number of other series, notably the paired indexes of new orders and shipments for fourteen manufacturing industries in Standard and Poor's *Industry Surveys*. These independently collected data confirm strongly the findings reported in the text and provide some related evidence; in particular, they show that seasonal variations, too, are in most cases substantially larger in new orders than in shipments. However, to keep this discussion from becoming excessively long and detailed, these additional measures are relegated to Appendix D.

more cyclical and more irregular than S wherever the two variables differ.

The irregular-cyclical ratios $\bar{I}/\overline{Cy}$, taken over one-month spans, are larger for new orders than for shipments in all industries except one (column 4). The MCD index—the number of months required for the ratio $\bar{I}/\overline{Cy}$ to fall below unity—tends likewise to be larger for new orders. However, the MCD indexes are much less sensitive than the $\bar{I}/\overline{Cy}$ measures, and are sometimes equal for new orders and shipments; that is, $(MCD)_n \geq (MCD)_s$ (see the figures in brackets, column 4). Finally, the average duration of run, ADR, is inversely related to both $\bar{I}/\overline{Cy}$ and MCD, since it is larger for smooth than for erratic series; and, with but two exceptions, $(ADR)_n < (ADR)_s$ (column 5).

To facilitate an appraisal of these relations, ratios were computed of the corresponding measures for S and N.[31] These figures indicate how much smaller the movements of shipments are when compared with the movements of new orders; lower fractions are associated with greater reductions of the amplitudes. Many comparisons point in the expected direction. Thus, the ratios based on the comprehensive aggregates are throughout lower for the durable goods industries than for all manufacturing, which includes those nondurables that are produced to stock only (e.g., the $\overline{CyI}_s/\overline{CyI}_n$ figures are here .538 and .703, respectively). Consumer durables, such as household appliances, radio and television, and furniture, which tend to come in rather standardized models and are mass produced, have relatively high ratios: 0.7–0.8 for the seasonally adjusted series and irregular components and 0.9–1.1 for the cyclical components. In contrast, producer goods—most of the machinery and equipment items and materials supplied by the metalworking industries—have, as a rule, substantially lower ratios, varying from 0.2 to 0.6 for the averages $\overline{CyI}$ and $\bar{I}$, and from 0.5 to 0.9 for $\overline{Cy}$. The ratios for aircraft and parts are fractional and far lower than those for any other industry, especially for the seasonally adjusted series and irregular components. Other transportation equipment, instruments, and ordnance also have relatively low ratios.

The sample of nondurable items covered by these measures is small and biased in the sense that it includes only those nondurable goods in-

---

[31] The discussion that follows is based on a tabulation of five ratios—$\overline{CyI}_s/\overline{CyI}_n$, $\bar{I}_s/\bar{I}_n$, $\overline{Cy}_s/\overline{Cy}_n$, $(\bar{I}/\overline{Cy})_s/(\bar{I}/\overline{Cy})_n$, and $(ADR)_n/(ADR)_s$—which is not shown here; however, the ratios can, of course, be readily computed from the paired entries in Table 3-4.

dustries in which production to order is particularly important (see Table 3-4). Nevertheless, it is interesting to observe that the ratios for publishing and some textile and leather products are as low as the ratios for many equipment items or metal products. On the other hand, pulp and paperboard mills show a cyclical ratio of 1.275, one of four ratios exceeding unity and the highest in the collection.

The reduction of amplitudes is found to be decidedly greater for the irregular than for the cyclical movements. The ratios $\bar{I}_s/\bar{I}_n$ are, in almost all cases, smaller than the ratios $\overline{Cy}_s/\overline{Cy}_n$; the average of the former is 0.444 and that of the latter is 0.747 for the thirty-seven industries included. The ratios $\overline{CyI}_s/\overline{CyI}_n$, which can be viewed as weighted averages of the two component ratios, are larger than $\bar{I}_s/\bar{I}_n$ and smaller than $\overline{Cy}_s/\overline{Cy}_n$, but are as a rule considerably closer to the former than to the latter (their average is 0.482).

The ratios $(\bar{I}/\overline{Cy})_s/(\bar{I}/\overline{Cy})_n$ are, with a single exception, less than 1, averaging 0.581. This shows that the weight of the irregular relative to the cyclical movements is greater for new orders than for shipments. These ratios also show the extent to which the short erratic variations in N are more effectively smoothed out in S than are the longer cyclical changes, for they equal $\bar{I}_s/\bar{I}_n$ divided by $\overline{Cy}_s/\overline{Cy}_n$.

Since the ADR index is a measure of *duration* only, and ignores the *size* of the fluctuations, it need not always suggest the same degree of irregularity as the $\bar{I}/\overline{Cy}$ ratio. For example, a series may move up and down frequently in short erratic oscillations, but the latter may be small relative to the cyclical swings; or, conversely, the irregular movements may be less frequent but larger. The ratios $(ADR)_n/(ADR)_s$ average 0.844 and are on the whole larger than the ratios $\bar{I}_s/\bar{I}_n$ and $(\bar{I}/\overline{Cy})_s/(\bar{I}/\overline{Cy})_n$, which means that the frequency of the erratic movements is reduced relatively less than their size in the transition from new orders to shipments.

Cyclical and Irregular Components of New Orders and Other Comprehensive Indicators

This section summarizes the evidence on the relative amplitudes of selected comprehensive series, so as to compare new orders with several important economic indicators, in particular those relating to investment. Table 3-5 shows that the averages $\overline{CyI}$, $\bar{I}$, and $\overline{Cy}$ are all larger for the aggregates of new orders than for the corresponding production indexes. The measures of $\bar{I}/\overline{Cy}$ and MCD are also larger for new orders, while those of ADR are smaller. This is true for the interwar as well as for the post-World War II period (see lines 1–5 and 10–15), although it should be noted that the comparability of the interwar measures suffers from the limited industrial coverage of the available new-order series. As would be expected, production, like shipments, is typically much smoother than new orders and subject to smaller cyclical movements.

It is well known that sales and production tend to be more stable for nondurable than for durable goods. In Table 3-5, this is clearly reflected in both the interwar and the postwar comparisons between total and durables production (lines 4–5 and 14–15). For new orders, similarly, the amplitude measures $\overline{Cyl}$, $\overline{I}$, and $\overline{Cy}$ are smaller for all manufactures than for durable manufactures (lines 1 and 2).

Among the durables, it is the orders for capital goods, such as machinery and equipment, that have particularly large cyclical and irregular amplitudes. One tends to associate investment with high volatility and large fluctuations, and the figures in Table 3-5 are consistent with this notion. However, the average size and frequency of fluctuations of different types and phases of investment vary greatly. Thus, commercial and industrial construction contracts (floor space) show much larger cyclical and irregular amplitudes than new orders (compare lines 2–3 and 10–12 with lines 6 and 16, respectively).[32] By adding up for each month the value of new orders for machinery and equipment and the value of industrial and commercial building contracts, a comprehensive series of investment commitments (line 17) is obtained, with amplitudes similar to, but somewhat larger than, the equipment-orders component (lines 12 and 17). It is particularly interesting to compare the amplitude figures for new orders and contracts for plant and equipment with the corresponding measures for expenditures on plant and equipment; the former appear to be 2 to 4 times larger than the latter (lines 8 and 12). This contrast parallels that existing between new orders and production, and must be due to a similar smoothing process.[33]

[32] While the contracts series differ from the new-order series in breadth of coverage, this is unlikely to be the source of the observed amplitude differences. The prewar data and the Standard and Poor's indexes of new orders have a much narrower coverage than the postwar Commerce figures, but all of these series show substantially smaller amplitudes than the commercial and industrial building contracts.

[33] The timing of cyclical turns in the spending by business for fixed-capital formation tends to be roughly coincident with the average cyclical timing of production or shipments of investment goods. Both production and expenditures lag behind orders—contracts by intervals of several months. For the discussion of the investment orders data and what they show, see Chapters 9 and 10.

Table 3-5
Summary of Measures of Irregular (*I*) and Cyclical (*Cy*) Components for Comprehensive Series on New Orders and Selected Indicators, Interwar and Post-World-War-II Periods

Line		$\overline{CyI}$ (1)	$\overline{I}$ (2)	$\overline{Cy}$ (3)	$\overline{I}/\overline{Cy}$ (4)	ADR[a] (5)	MCD[b] (6)
			Average Monthly Amplitude of				
	INTERWAR PERIOD						
1	New orders, composite index, 1920–33	7.7	6.4	3.4	1.9	2.13	3
2	Durables, 1920–33	8.5	7.1	3.9	1.8	2.43	3
3	Durables, 1929–39	7.8	6.5	3.8	1.7	2.18	3
4	Indus. prod., total, 1919–39	2.3	1.4	1.7	0.8	5.71	1
5	Durables, 1919–39	4.0	2.3	2.8	0.8	4.61	1
6	Comm. & indus. bldg. contracts, 1925–39	12.5	12.0	3.7	3.3	1.81	4
7	Resid. bldg. contracts, 1925–39	8.9	7.8	3.9	2.0	1.95	3
8	New incorporations (no.), 1923–39	4.2	4.1	1.0	4.2	1.65	4
9	Average, 12 aggregative series, 1919–39	5.1	4.5	1.9	2.2	2.67	2.7
	POST-WORLD WAR II PERIOD						
10	New orders, composite index, 1949–56	6.4	5.8	2.0	2.8	1.77	3
11	Durables, 1948–60	5.6	5.0	2.0	2.5	1.94	3
12	Machinery and equipment, 1948–60	6.1	5.6	2.2	2.5	1.68	3
13	Shipments, composite index, 1949–56	3.0	2.7	1.1	2.4	2.14	3
14	Indus. prod., total, 1947–56	1.1	0.7	0.7	0.9	3.52	1
15	Durables, 1947–56	1.7	1.1	1.0	1.1	4.07	2
16	Comm. & indus. bldg. contracts, 1948–60	12.4	11.9	2.8	4.3	1.62	5
17	New investment orders and contracts, 1948–60	6.4	5.9	2.2	2.7	1.59	3
18	New private nonfarm dwelling units, 1948–60	4.1	3.4	2.0	1.7	2.29	3
19	New business incorporations, 1948–60	3.0	2.6	1.3	2.0	2.19	3
20	Change in business inventories, 1947–58	n.a.	7.1	3.4	2.1	5.9	n.a.
21	Plant & equipment expenditures, total, 1947–58	n.a.	1.3	1.1	1.2	12.8	n.a.
22	Average, 12 aggregative series, 1947–56	4.9	4.4	1.4	2.7	2.3	3.0
23	25 indicators, 1947–58	n.a.	3.4	1.7	1.6	3.8[c]	2.3[c]
24	11 leading	n.a.	6.5	2.8	2.2	2.3[d]	3.1[d]
25	9 coincident	n.a.	1.2	0.8	1.5	3.4[e]	1.9[e]
26	5 lagging	n.a.	0.6	1.0	0.8	9.2[f]	1.3[f]

Notes to Table 3-5

Source: Lines 1 and 2: Department of Commerce indexes in physical terms, 1923–25 = 100. Durables include iron and steel (6 items); railroad transportation equipment (3 items); stone, clay, and glass (2 items); furniture, lumber (5 items), and flooring (2 items). The composite index also includes textiles (3 items), and paper and printing (3 items).

Line 3: National Industrial Conference Board index of the value of new orders for durable goods, 1935–39 = 100.

Lines 4, 5, 14, and 15: Federal Reserve Board index, 1947–49 = 100.

Lines 6, 7, and 16: F. W. Dodge Corporation series in units of floor space (millions of square feet).

Lines 8 and 19: Compiled by R. G. Dun & Co. (after 1933, Dun and Bradstreet, Inc.).

Line 9: Includes: (1) Wholesale price index, excluding farm products and foods, 1926 = 100, BLS; (2) index of factory employment, 1947–49 = 100, BLS; (3) industrial common stock price index, dollars per share, Dow-Jones; (4) index of business activity, AT&T; (5) see Source, line 6; (6) see Source, line 7; (7) see Source, line 8; (8) freight carloadings, thousands of cars per week, Association of American Railroads; (9) bank debits outside New York City, billions of dollars, FRB; (10) index of department store sales, 1947–49 = 100, FRB; (11) average hours per week, manufacturing NICB; (12) business failure, liabilities, millions of dollars, Dun and Bradstreet. The series cover the period 1919–39, with following exceptions: items (5) and (6), 1925–39; item (7), 1923–29; and item (11), 1920–39.

Lines 10 and 13: Standard and Poor's index of current value, 1949 = 100. For its composition, see Appendix B.

Lines 11 and 12: Census Bureau series based on data from the Office of Business Economics (OBE), Department of Commerce.

Line 17: Compiled by the Bureau of the Census from data of the OBE and F. W. Dodge Corporation.

Line 18: Housing starts in thousands of new private nonfarm dwelling units; from Bureau of the Census.

Line 20: Change in business inventories, farm and nonfarm, after valuation adjustment, in billions of dollars, OBE; quarterly series.

Line 21: Total business expenditures on new plant and equipment, billions of dollars; Securities and Exchange Commission (SEC) and OBE; quarterly series.

Line 22: Includes the items identified in Source, line 9; the source for item (11) is now BLS, and the base of index (1) is 1947–49 = 100.

Line 23: Includes all twenty-six business cycle indicators from the 1960 list of the National Bureau of Economic Research except manufacturers' new orders. Averages computed from data given in Julius Shiskin, *Signals of Recession and Recovery,* Occasional Paper 7, New York, NBER, 1961, Table B-1, pp. 143–44. Among the twenty-five series, eleven are leading indicators, nine are coincident, and five are lagging indicators. The corresponding measures for these three subgroups are listed on lines 24–26. The series and their sources are identified in G. H. Moore, "Leading and Confirming Indicators of General Business Change," in Geoffrey H. Moore, ed., *Business Cycle Indicators,* Princeton for NBER, 1961, Vol. I, Table 3-7, pp. 106–107.

[a] ADR signifies average duration of run of seasonally adjusted series.
[b] MCD signifies months of cyclical dominance.
[c] Average for nineteen series.
[d] Average for nine series.
[e] Average for seven series.
[f] Average for three series.

As a broadly conceived scale of reference against which to compare our amplitude measures for new orders and related variables, Table 3-5 also presents the corresponding average figures for groups of selected aggregative series (lines 9 and 22–26). These are groups of "business cycle indicators," i.e., series chosen for their relatively high cyclical sensitivity. It is clear that new orders are both more "cyclical" and more erratic than are even these sensitive indicators, on the average (compare lines 1–3 and 9, and lines 10–12 and 22–26).

The leading indicators, those whose turning points tend to precede the peaks and troughs in business activity, are the most sensitive in terms of monthly cyclical and irregular amplitudes. The "coinciders," i.e., those series which tend to reach cyclical turns at about the same time as the economy in general, have much smaller cyclical and irregular movements and are much smoother. And the "laggers," whose turns usually follow business revivals and recessions, are the least irregular, although perhaps about as "cyclical" (according to their $\overline{Cy}$) as the coinciders. All this can be seen by comparing lines 24, 25, and 26 in Table 3-5. Presumably, the processes that are particularly sensitive to cyclical influences are also highly sensitive to other short-term disturbances; and the earliness of cyclical reaction, as expressed in the tendency to lead, may often be another manifestation of that general responsiveness. The group of leading indicators which includes new orders for durable manufactures is heavily weighted with series relating to investment and profits. The cyclical and irregular amplitudes of new orders are somewhat smaller than the corresponding averages for all the other leading indicators combined, but new orders are slightly more erratic in terms of the $\overline{I}/\overline{Cy}$ ratios and ADR (lines 10–12 and 24).

Finally, comparisons of the $\overline{I}/\overline{Cy}$ ratios for new orders, production, and the indicator groups show generally higher figures in the post-World War II period than in the interwar period. In addition, the ADR indexes were usually lower and the MCD indexes higher in the postwar than in the interwar years. Thus the cyclical component has decreased relative to the irregular component. It is well known, of course, that the cyclical movements have generally been milder since World War II than in the twenties and thirties. Our findings reflect this tendency but they show, too, that various economic processes contributing to it, such as ordering or production, have retained their characteristic differences in cyclical and other short-run variability.

Specific Cycles and Erratic Movements
in Individual Series, 1918–39

Data for various industries and products, covering different periods between 1918 and 1939 and subjected to the specific-cycle analysis of the National Bureau,[34] confirm the findings obtained by other methods for the more aggregative postwar series.

The figures in Table 3-6 cover three samples, each consisting of fourteen series: new orders (I), shipments and production (II), and selected aggregative indicators (III). Measures of the average amplitude of specific cycles for these series are shown in column 3 of the table and ranked in column 6. The product coverage of groups I and II is similar. Six of the fourteen items in the new-order sample are represented in group II by one series each (shipments only) and four by two series each (shipments and production). In contrast to these series, which are fairly narrow in scope, group III includes comprehensive indicators representing various activities: industrial production and employment.

The average of the ranks based on the amplitude figures (column 6) is 30.7 for the new-order series (group I), and 22.4 for the shipment and production series (group II). Ten of the group I ranks fall within the highest third of the total range, 29–42, three within the middle third, 15–28, and one within the lowest third, 1–14. For group II, the corresponding figures are four, seven, and three. The evidence of these measures is unequivocal: Cyclical swings in new orders are typically wider than their counterparts in shipments and production. Exceptions to this rule are exceedingly rare.[35]

In contrast to the figures of 30.7 for the individual new-order series and 22.4 for the activity series, the average rank of the amplitude measures for the comprehensive indicators (III) is only 11.4. This

[34] Specific cycles are broad swings in the seasonally adjusted series, of a duration roughly similar to that of business cycles (from over one year to ten or twelve years). Amplitudes of these movements are measured in "specific-cycle relatives," i.e., percentages of the average standing of the data during the given cycle. The rise from the initial trough to the peak is added to the fall from the peak to the terminal trough, disregarding the signs. Three-month averages centered on the trough and peak dates are used in these computations to diminish the influence of random factors. Measures for successive specific cycles covered by a series are averaged to obtain the presumably typical amplitude figure. For a detailed description of the method see Arthur F. Burns and Wesley C. Mitchell, *Measuring Business Cycles*, New York, NBER, 1946, pp. 131–41.

[35] The average amplitude of specific cycles is greater for shipments than for new orders in only one case of the ten in which data can be matched. There are no exceptions among the order-production comparisons. The systematic character of the amplitude differences can be traced back to the relative size of individual cycles matched in the corresponding order and activity series.

Table 3-6

Average Amplitude of Specific Cycles and Intensity of Irregular Movements, Forty-two Selected Series, 1918–38

Series [a]	Period Covered [b] (1)	No. of Complete Specific Cycles Covered (2)	Av. Amplitude of Specific Cycles [c] (rise + fall) (3)	Duration of Erratic Movements as % of Duration of Specific Cycles [d] (4)	Type of Erratic Movements [e] (5)	Ranks According to	
						Av. Amplitudes (col. 3) (6)	Durations (col. 4) (7)
I. NEW ORDERS OF INDIVIDUAL INDUSTRIES OR PRODUCTS [f]							
Machine tools and forging machinery (OR)	1919–38	5	265.0	2.7	mild	34	9
Fabricated structural steel (OR)	1919–39	7	140.1	2.8	mod.	15	10
Oak flooring (ST)	1918–37	6	206.5	4.5	mod.	31	19.5
Architectural terra cotta (ST)	1919–37	5	205.4	4.5	mod.	30	19.5
Fabricated steel plate (OR)	1924–38	3	190.0	7.7	g	26	30
Railroad locomotives (OR)	1919–37	7	537.6	7.8	mod.	39	31
Southern pine lumber (ST)	1918–37	6	104.9	9.7	mild	12	34
Merchant pig iron (OR)	1919–24	2	373.8	12.1	pron.	36	35
Railroad freight cars (OR)	1918–38	8	551.5	13.0	pron.	42	36
Railroad passenger cars (OR)	1919–37	7	498.0	13.6	pron.	38	37
Lavatories (ST)	1918–28	3	226.7	15.2	mod.	33	38
Bathtubs (ST)	1918–23	2	381.1	16.0	mod.	37	39
Steel sheets (OR)	1919–32	4	187.9	17.4	pron.	25	40
Sinks (ST)	1918–28	3	209.0	18.0	mod.	32	41.5

II. INDICATORS OF ACTIVITY FOR INDIVIDUAL PRODUCTS[f]

Shipments							
Lavatories (ST)	1919–24	2	160.4	0.0	mod.	20	3.5
Steel sheets (OR)	1919–32	4	130.4	3.1	mild	13	13
Railroad locomotives (OR)	1920–38	6	328.2	3.4	mod.	35	14.5
Oak flooring (ST)	1918–37	6	154.0	3.7	mod.	17	16
Railroad freight cars (OR)	1919–38	6	540.6	5.7	mod.	41	22
Bathtubs (ST)	1918–24	2	156.4	7.0	mod.	19	27
Southern pine lumber (ST)	1919–38	6	83.0	7.6	mild	10	29
Sinks (ST)	1919–24	2	148.2	8.8	mod.	16	32
Railroad passenger cars (OR)	1919–40	7	539.1	9.6	mod.	40	33
Merchant pig iron (OR)	1919–24	2	162.6	18.0	mod.	21	41.5
Production							
Merchant pig iron (OR)	1919–24	2	200.4	0.0	mild	29	3.5
Southern pine lumber (ST)	1918–38	5	84.0	3.0	mild	11	12
Oak flooring (ST)	1918–38	5	155.0	5.8	mod.	18	23.5
Steel sheets (OR)	1919–33	5	174.8	5.8	mod.	24	23.5
III. SELECTED COMPREHENSIVE INDICATOR SERIES[h]							
Wholesale price index, BLS	1922–39	4	34.0	0.0	mild	2	3.5
Index of factory employment, BLS	1919–36	5	49.2	0.0	mild	4	3.5
Business activity index, AT&T	1919–37	6	65.6	0.0	mild	7	3.5
Indus. common stock price index, Dow-Jones	1921–38	4	138.8	0.0	mild	14	3.5
Comm. and indus. bldg. contracts, fl. space, Dodge	1919–38	5	195.4	0.9	mod.	28	7
Indus. prod. index, FRB	1919–38	5	72.5	1.7	mild	8	8
Residential bldg. contracts, fl. space, Dodge	1918–37	6	169.9	2.9	mild	22.5	11
Av. hrs. of work, mfg., NICB-BLS	1921–38	5	31.0	3.4	mild	1	14.5
Freight car loadings, AAR	1918–38	5	49.4	3.9	mild	5	17
Bank debits outside NYC, FRB	1921–38	3	79.2	4.0	mild	9	18
New incorporations, no., Evans	1918–39	5	57.1	4.8	mild	6	21
Railroad operating income, ICC	1920–38	5	169.9	6.0	mod.	22.5	25
Dept. store sales index, FRB	1921–38	4	37.5	6.7	mild	3	26
Bus. failures, liabilities, indus. & comm., Dun's	1922–38	4	190.4	7.2	pron.	27	28

Notes to Table 3-6

ᵃ (ST) signifies goods made primarily to stock; (OR), goods made primarily to order.
ᵇ Identifies the complete specific cycles covered by the series.
ᶜ For explanation see footnote 34.
ᵈ See explanation in text.
ᵉ Mod. signifies moderate; pron., pronounced. See explanation in text.
ᶠ Corresponding data on new orders, shipments, and production are available for all the series included in groups I and II except machine tools and forging machinery, fabricated structural steel, architectural terra cotta, and fabricated steel plate.
ᵍ Erratic movements range from moderate to pronounced.
ʰ Group III includes eleven series selected from those listed and identified in Geoffrey H. Moore, *Statistical Indicators of Cyclical Revivals and Recessions*, New York, NBER, 1950, pp. 64–65. The factory employment index, the NICB segment of the average hours of work series, new incorporations, and the department store sales index are historical equivalents of current indicators.

The group also includes three series—the wholesale price index, the business activity index, and railroad operating income—taken from Wesley C. Mitchell and Arthur F. Burns, *Statistical Indicators of Cyclical Revivals*, New York, NBER, 1938, Table 2 and pp. 8–10.

illustrates the difference in the average size of cyclical fluctuations that is frequently observed between data of narrow scope and comprehensive aggregates. In view of the variety of the activities represented in group III, however, it is noteworthy that only four of these indicators have average cyclical amplitudes approaching the size of the *median* amplitude of the order group, 217.8 (others are all considerably smaller than the first quartile for that group).[36]

New orders show larger cyclical amplitudes than shipments or production not only for the goods classified as made primarily to order but also for those made primarily to stock (see column 8 for identification of these categories among the series included in groups I and II). On general grounds, one would expect that the amplitude reductions, in relative terms, will be on the average greater for items manufactured largely to order than for items manufactured largely to stock. On the whole, this expectation is not borne out by the data in Table 3-6,[37] but then we are dealing here with a small sample which does not represent strongly or sharply the distinction between the two types of manufac-

[36] The four are railroad operating income, liabilities of business failures, residential building contracts, and commercial and industrial building contracts. No comprehensive and continuous new-order series for the total interwar period is available for inclusion in group III, but it can be assumed on the basis of more recent records that such a series would show specific cycles of comparable size.

[37] Using averages weighted by the numbers of specific cycles covered (column 2) and including only the items for which matching series on new orders, etc., are available (as indicated by asterisks in column 8), the following results are obtained:

ture. What does come out clearly in these comparisons is that the amplitudes are generally larger for the goods made primarily to order than for the others, and this applies to new orders as well as to shipments or production.

Short movements that run counter to the specific-cycle phases are frequent in many monthly or quarterly time series adjusted for seasonal variation. Such "irregular" movements seldom last longer than a few months but may sometimes be quite large. It is often their duration rather than their amplitude that distinguishes them from the specific cycles. A simple and helpful, though indirect and rough, measure of their intensity has been developed as a by-product of the National Bureau method of tracing specific-cycle patterns. It is a percentage ratio relating the total duration of interstage intervals showing counter-cyclical movements to the total duration of all specific cycles covered.[38]

These measures of relative duration of countercyclical movements are entered in column 4 and (in the form of rankings) in column 7 of Table 3-6. They clearly indicate that series of new orders for manufactured products tend to have more pronounced irregular fluctuations than the corresponding shipment or production series. The comprehensive indicators are much less "irregular," as one would expect, since nonsynchronous erratic movements in the component series tend to cancel out in the aggregate. The average ranks of the duration percentages for groups I, II, and III are 30, 21, and 13.5, respectively. Of the ranks in the highest third of the total list (29–42), ten are in group I, four in group II, none in group III; the lowest ranks again are heavily concentrated in the set of the comprehensive series.

	Average Amplitude of Specific Cycles			Ratio of Amplitudes (per cent)	
	New Orders (1)	Shipments (2)	Production (3)	$\dfrac{Col.\,(2)}{Col.\,(1)}$	$\dfrac{Col.\,(3)}{Col.\,(1)}$
Items made to order (5)	459.3	393.3		85.6	
Items made to stock (5)	196.9	127.8		64.9	
Items made to order (2)	249.9	141.1	182.1	72.9	56.5
Items made to stock (2)	155.7	118.5	119.5	76.8	76.1

[38] Each specific cycle in a series is divided into nine stages covering the initial trough (I), the three successive thirds of the expansion (II, III, IV), the peak (V), the three successive thirds of the contraction (VI, VII, VIII), and the terminal trough (IX). Stages I, V, and IX are three-month periods centered on the turning points of the specific cycle. Nine-point patterns are computed, one for each cycle, by averaging the specific-cycle relatives for the months included in each stage. For a full discussion of the method see Burns and Mitchell, *Measuring Business Cycles*, pp. 144–60.

Furthermore, according to these measures, the irregular movements are more frequent in new orders than in shipments for both the goods made primarily to order and the goods made primarily to stock, while their frequency is least in production, again for either type of manufacture. The degree to which the erratic element in shipments is reduced vis-à-vis new orders should be greater for products manufactured largely to order, but this is not demonstrated here. The present data are too limited to provide conclusive evidence on this rather fine point. The measures do suggest strongly that new orders as well as shipments are more erratic for items produced chiefly to order than for items sold chiefly from stock.[39]

The duration percentages are crude estimates of the relative importance of the irregular factor. What is only a marked discrepancy in the basic (seasonally adjusted) data between the *rates of change* before and after a turning point may be translated into artificial irregularities in the averages of a specific-cycle pattern.[40] Conversely, considerable irregularities of the data can be smoothed out in the patterns. Therefore, the method of specific-cycle analysis calls for a reappraisal of the judgments based on the duration measures alone, by means of independent detailed examination of the series, aided by the data charts. The National Bureau rates the cycles of each of the series it analyzes as "mild," "moderate," or "pronounced," according to the relative intensity of erratic movements. For the forty-two series in Table 3-6 these ratings are given in column 5. In a number of cases these ratings differ from those which would be dictated by the duration percentages alone. However, they point to the same general conclusion as those

---

[39] The tabulation below shows weighted averages computed analogously to those listed in footnote 37 for the specific-cycle amplitudes; they are based on the entries in Table 3-6, column 4, which relate the duration of erratic movements to that of specific cycles.

	Average Relative Duration of Erratic Movements			Ratios of the Durations (per cent)	
	New Orders	Shipments	Production	Col. (2) / Col. (1)	Col. (3) / Col. (1)
	(1)	(2)	(3)		
Items made to order (5)	12.4	6.8		54.8	
Items made to stock (5)	10.8	5.8		53.2	
Items made to order (2)	15.6	8.1	4.1	51.9	26.3
Items made to stock (2)	7.1	5.6	4.4	78.9	62.0

[40] Thus, suppose the monthly values of a series are 7, 7.5, 8, and 8.3 in stage IV, and 8.5, 9, and 5 in stage V (around the peak). The average for stage IV (7.7) will be higher than that for stage V (7.5), even though the monthly figures show no changes bearing irregular signs.

percentages, namely, that data on new orders rank high among economic time series in the importance of the irregular factor.

Summary

Industrial companies generally manage to schedule production so as to make its flow over time substantially less variable than the flow of demand they face. Data for various industries and periods, on different levels of aggregation and in both nominal and "real" terms, testify that new orders (N) typically have larger relative amplitudes of cyclical movements than the corresponding series on output (Z) and shipments (S). Also, short irregular variations are generally more frequent and pronounced in N than in S and Z. Finally, the seasonal fluctuations are in most cases larger in N, though these differences seem more moderate. On a per month basis, the amplitude reductions that are observed in the transition from new orders to shipments tend to be larger for the irregular than for the cyclical movements.

The industries that face greater instability of demand, i.e., greater variability of cyclical and irregular movements in new orders received, show on the whole larger amplitude reductions in S as compared with N than do the industries that enjoy more stable demand for their products. The variability of new orders is reduced most in shipments of machinery, metal products, and, particularly, nonautomotive transportation equipment. Other major industries have N and S series that run much closer to each other. These include some industries that produce largely to stock and some that work with relatively short average delivery periods.[41]

According to the Census data for market categories, fluctuations of both new orders and shipments tend to be smallest for consumer goods, larger for materials (particularly those supplied by the cyclically sensitive metalworking industries), and by far the largest for producers' durable equipment. The groups with greater relative amplitudes are also, on the whole, the groups in which production to order is more important. However, production is largely to stock and demand is highly variable for the important *sui generis* category of motor vehicles. The

---

[41] Let us recall that in the official Commerce statistics most of the nondurable goods sector is assumed (not entirely convincingly) to produce to stock only, i.e., to have $N = S$.

differences between N and S are small and mostly irregular for this group and for consumer goods in general, while they are large and to a considerable extent systematic for producers' equipment. New orders for defense equipment have fluctuated widely and erratically, but the production smoothing process appears to be very effective for these products, which have large and variable backlogs (reflecting long and variable delivery periods).

4

TIMING COMPARISONS

TIMING RELATIONS can be examined by dating the fluctuations in the series concerned, identifying the movements that match, and measuring the leads and lags between the corresponding turning points. In this chapter, such measures are presented for the available data on new orders, production, and shipments. The analysis proceeds from series relating to individual products and industries, mostly in physical units, to value aggregates for the major divisions and some subdivisions of the manufacturing sector. The former group covers mainly the interwar period; the second group, the post-World War II period. Measures of relative timing in the recent years are also presented for several broadly defined market categories and for a set of deflated major-industry series on new orders and shipments as well as the corresponding production indexes.

Rules about the dating and matching of turning points have been developed and applied in the business cycle studies of the National Bureau. These rules, however, are merely designed to discipline the researcher's judgment, not substitute for it. In general, the turning points to be identified are the local maxima and minima in the series concerned, subject to certain constraints relating to the duration of the movements thus dated: very short peak-to-peak or trough-to-trough fluctuations do not qualify as "specific cycles." The presence of sufficiently marked and long movements must be established first; the precise dating of the turning points comes next. Occasionally, an extremely high or low standing of the series is so isolated that it seems to be the result of some random event or very short-term "irregularity" rather than the culmination of a longer cyclical process. In such cases, a less extreme value of the series, which is surrounded by similar values, would be selected instead; in other words, a "broader" peak or trough may be preferred to a higher or lower but "narrow" standing (say, a single-month high point occurring at a time when the series still shows a rising trend). Smoothing can help to identify the turns, and we do consult short-term averages (mostly of three to six months) as the need arises; but smoothing may also distort and bias the dating, and caution must be exercised not to let this happen. Whether or not moving averages were used as an aid in the dating process, the dates always refer to the unsmoothed series (after seasonal adjustment).[1]

Individual Industries or Products

Relative Timing of New Orders and Shipments

GOODS MADE TO ORDER. The first set of timing comparisons (Table 4-1) is based on eleven pairs of series for new orders and shipments, representing goods manufactured primarily to order. There are nine producer durable items equally divided between iron and steel products, machinery, and railway equipment; one consumer durable product (furniture); and one nondurable (paper). Seven of the comparisons are between physical series, and four employ current-value data (these are the machinery items — electric overhead cranes, machine tools, and woodworking machinery — and furniture).

Table 4-1 demonstrates that in manufacture of this type new orders lead shipments with a very high degree of regularity. This general finding can be viewed as a statistical reflection of a fairly obvious causal relation. Indeed, it is not the leading pattern of new orders itself but the few lapses from it that might need explanation. Of these, however, some are probably spurious, a result of the difficulty of marking a specific peak or trough in a jagged turning segment.

[1] On the dating of specific cycles, see Arthur F. Burns and Wesley C. Mitchell, *Measuring Business Cycles*, New York, NBER, 1946, pp. 56–66. The rules followed in matching the specific-cycle turns in two activities are analogous to those for the timing observations at business cycle turns (*ibid.*, pp. 116–28). The turns in the series to be compared were, as a general procedure, dated independently, with the aid of these rules. Individual timing comparisons based on such markings may well deviate from the expected patterns; but unless the results were clearly unsatisfactory and capable of reasonable improvement, we were careful not to modify the markings made according to the accepted rules. This insured against arbitrary decisions or inadvertent forcing of the evidence.

As another safeguard, the turning points in most of the series used in this book were dated independently by another member of the NBER staff. The consensus between the dates was very good, though some differences remained, of course, and were resolved by the author's decision. The assistance in this work by the late Miss Sophie Sakowitz is gratefully acknowledged.

The quantitative aspects of the data in Table 4-1 are of primary interest. The average leads of new orders at shipment turns (column 10) vary over a wide range of from eleven to less than two months. The items are ranked by the length of these leads, from longest to shortest. Railway equipment, heavy and specialized machinery, and structural steel (which includes some of the most elaborate steel products) constitute the upper part of the list, with mean leads of six months and more. Industries or groups of commodities that are presumably less heavily weighted with complex or specialized types of product—pig iron, steel sheets, paper products, furniture, and woodworking machinery—are characterized by shorter average leads (four months and less). Coincidences, lags, and short leads of three months or less are much more frequent, relative to all leads, at the bottom than at the top of the table (see columns 5–8). This is a suggestive array, although with the amount and type of data on hand we would not wish to push the matter beyond the broad observations offered.

The leads of orders vary substantially, not only between the different industries and products but also between successive observations for any single item in the table. The extent of their intercycle variability may be judged from the figures in columns 11 and 12, which ought to be read along with the corresponding entries in columns 9 and 10 (the former being average deviations of the individual timing comparisons, and the latter the mean leads from which they are measured). The average deviations vary from five to less than two months and tend to be larger in the upper than in the lower part of the table. They are thus positively associated with the corresponding mean leads, a relation that is probably not uncommon. However, other things aside, it takes a larger average deviation to cast doubt upon the nature of a timing relation when the mean lead is long than when it comes close to zero.[2]

[2] Thus, when the mean timing figure is −11.0, even an average deviation of five months will not disqualify it as an indication of leads of substantial duration (this is the situation for railroad passenger cars). On the other hand, an average deviation of five months associated with a mean of, say, −1.0 or less, would point to the presence of leads and lags of significant length at the individual turns; an average of such mutually offsetting observations would not be likely to represent any consistent timing patterns.

A comment should be added on the type of averages and variability measures used. For the data in this section, means and mean absolute deviations were computed some time ago, following the standard procedures then used by the business cycle unit of the National Bureau. Extension of the analysis to other measures such as medians and standard deviations appeared unwarranted. However, for the aggregative series discussed later in this chapter all four types of summary statistics are used.

Table 4-1
Timing of Turns in New Orders at Turns in Shipments, Eleven Industries or Products [a]
Representing Manufacture to Order, Various Periods, 1919–55

Period Covered [b] (1)	All Turns — No. of Order Turns Covered (2)	No. of Shipment Turns Covered (3)	Matched (4)	No. of Timing Observations[c] at Peaks or Troughs That Are: Leads (5)	Exact Coincidences (6)	Lags (7)	Rough Coincidences[d] (8)	Av. Lead (−) or Lag (+) (months) Peaks or Troughs[e] (9)	All Turns (10)	Av. Dev. from Av. Lead or Lag (months) Peaks or Troughs[e] (11)	All Turns (12)
RAILROAD PASSENGER CARS											
1919–55	26	22	22	11				−11.4	−11.0	4.6	5.0
				11			1	−10.6		5.3	
RAILROAD LOCOMOTIVES											
1920–38	15	13	13	5				−5.7	−7.3	3.2	3.9
				6	1	1	1	−8.7		4.2	
RAILROAD FREIGHT CARS											
1919–54	21	21	19	8		1		−9.1	−7.1	6.1	4.9
				9		1	2	−5.2		3.0	
ELECTRIC OVERHEAD CRANES											
1926–45	8	8	8	3	1	1	1	−6.5	−6.9	3.5	4.1
				4			1	−7.2		4.8	
FABRICATED STRUCTURAL STEEL											
1926–55	20	14	14	7			1	−6.9	−6.6	2.1	3.6
				6			3	−6.4		5.1	

132

	(1)	(2)	(3)	(4)	(5)	(6)	(7)	(8)	(9)	(10)	(11)	(12)
MACHINE TOOLS												
1927–55	11	9	9		4	1	1	1	−10.0	−6.0	6.5	4.7
					4			3	−2.8		3.0	
MERCHANT PIG IRON												
1919–24	5	5	5		2		1	1	−4.0	−4.0	3.0	2.4
					3			2	−4.0		2.0	
STEEL SHEETS												
1919–32	9	9	9		4		2	2	−5.8	−3.9	4.2	3.9
				2	3			4	−2.4		3.0	
PAPER, EXCLUDING BUILDING PAPER, NEWSPRINT, AND PAPERBOARD												
1937–52	10	8	8		4	1	1	1	−5.2	−2.6	2.2	2.8
				1	2			4	0		1.0	
FURNITURE (GRAND RAPIDS DISTRICT)												
1923–46	10	9	8		3	1	3	3	−2.0	−2.2	1.5	1.8
				1	3			2	−2.5		2.0	
WOODWORKING MACHINERY												
1923–39	10	10	10		5	2	3	3	−2.8	−1.6	1.4	1.7
				2	2			5	−0.4		1.3	
ALL ELEVEN ITEMS[e]												
	145	128	125		56	2	13	2	−7.2	−6.3	4.4	4.4
					53	7	28	5	−5.4		4.5	

[a] Ranked by the length of the average lead, all turns (column 10), from longest to shortest.

[b] Identifies the complete specific-cycle phases in the shipment series.

[c] For each item, the entry on the first line is for comparisons at peaks; the entry on the second line is for comparisons at troughs.

[d] Includes exact coincidences and leads or lags of one, two, or three months.

[e] Summary of the timing measures for the industries or products covered. Entries in columns 3–8 are totals, entries in columns 9–12 are averages weighted by the numbers of observations for each item.

133

The leads of new orders for the same group of products were on the whole longer at the peaks than at the troughs in shipments. The average of all peak observations for the eleven items covered in Table 4-1 is a lead of 7.2 months; the corresponding mean for the trough observations is 5.4 months. Since the capacity position of many firms at top levels of output and deliveries is presumably strained, longer average leads of orders at peaks conform to the economist's expectations.[3] However, in only seven components of this sample do the mean leads at peaks exceed those at troughs, in five of them by large margins. This is not a fully convincing record, but some additional evidence in support of the longer peak leads will be provided by timing comparisons for other groups of data.

GOODS MADE TO STOCK. Table 4-2 presents the timing measures for a sample of seven durable goods made primarily to stock. Of these, five are used principally by consumers (oil burners and the four items of enameled sanitary ware), and two are used principally by producers (oak flooring and southern pine lumber). This group of products contrasts with the sample of Table 4-1, representing manufactures to order. There we dealt mainly with producer goods: metal products and equipment for industry and transportation, including goods that are highly complex or specialized or large-unit and expensive. Here we have a small group of items that are much more standardized and closer to the needs of consumers, associated most of all with residential construction.

Tables 4-1 and 4-2 are arranged in the same manner, so that it is easy to compare them by corresponding columns. Together, the two tables include all but one of the individual industries or products for which we have matched series on new orders and shipments.[4]

---

[3] An extension of this argument leads to the presumption that "a good index of orders is likely to prove a better forecaster of business cycle recessions than of business cycle revivals" (Wesley C. Mitchell and Arthur F. Burns, *Statistical Indicators of Cyclical Revivals*, NBER Bulletin 69, 1938 (reprinted in Geoffrey H. Moore, ed., *Business Cycle Indicators*, Princeton for NBER, 1961, Vol. I, p. 182, n. 13).

[4] The one exception to this is foundry equipment, which proved particularly difficult to classify. For lack of data the test of the Q/U ratios could not be applied to it. According to information received from the Foundry Equipment Manufacturers' Association, this is a very heterogeneous group of products. Time lags of shipments against orders are reported to vary greatly among the different types of equipment, ranging from as low as 3 to 4 weeks to as high as 9 to 12 months. The proportion of short orders cannot be reliably estimated, although an inspection of the charts suggests that it might be large, since there is a good deal of parallelism between the cyclical fluctuations as well as the seasonal patterns in new orders and shipments.

The timing patterns of the two groups of data are distinctly different. The leads of new orders over shipments tend to be both shorter and less regular for the sample of goods made to stock than for that of goods made to order. The average of all the individual comparisons underlying the timing measures shown in Table 4-2 is a lead of 1.2 months. The corresponding over-all average in Table 4-1 is a lead of 6.3 months. None of the products sold mainly from stock shows a mean lead of orders of more than two months. The *longest* of these leads differs little from the shortest of the comparable leads for the group of items made to order: the last of the ranked entries in column 10 of Table 4-1 is −1.6; the first of the ranked entries in column 10 of Table 4-2 is −1.9. In other words, there appears to be little overlap between the two arrays: the one for made-to-order commodities stops descending (toward ever shorter leads) approximately where the other begins.

At troughs, the timing of orders and shipments is synchronous, or very nearly so, for each of the products covered in Table 4-2. Two order series lag, on average, and one is coincident (column 9). At peaks, the timing means, with one exception, are all leads. In each case these averages indicate that there is more of a tendency for new orders to lead shipments at peaks than at troughs. However, this tendency is weak; the timing of the two variables for this group of products is characterized by rough coincidence (including short leads or lags of three months or less, and "exact" coincidences). The weighted timing averages for the group as a whole are −2.0 months at peaks and −0.4 months at troughs. Even at peaks, then, the central tendency is toward a short lead within the roughly coincident range.

The variability of the timing observations for goods made to stock is large (columns 11 and 12). For all turns matched in this set of comparisons, the average deviation from the mean lead of only 1.2 months is 2.6 months.

SUMMARY. Table 4-3 presents distributions of all timing comparisons between new orders and shipments for the two groups of products. Here the nature of the differentiation among the recorded comparisons —whether it is due to intercycle or to interindustry variation—is disregarded. The figures provide further demonstration of the contrast between the two groups. For goods made to order the distributions

Table 4-2

Timing of Turns in New Orders at Turns in Shipments, Seven Products [a] Manufactured Primarily to Stock, Various Periods, 1913–55

| | | All Turns | | No. of Timing Observations [c] at Peaks or Troughs That Are: | | | | Av. Lead (−) or Lag (+) (months) | | Av. Dev. from Av. Lead or Lag (months) | |
| | | | No. of Shipment Turns | | | | | | | | |
Period Covered [b] (1)	No. of Order Turns Covered (2)	Covered (3)	Matched (4)	Leads (5)	Exact Coincidences (6)	Lags (7)	Rough Coincidences [d] (8)	Peaks or Troughs [d] (9)	All Turns (10)	Peaks or Troughs [c] (11)	All Turns (12)
OAK FLOORING 1913–55	25	23	23	9 5	1 5	2 1	7 9	−2.6 −1.2	−1.9	2.5 1.8	2.3
OIL BURNERS 1933–51	9	9	9	2 2	2 2	 1	3 5	−3.0 −0.4	−1.6	4.0 0.9	2.2
SOUTHERN PINE LUMBER 1919–53	23	23	23	6 6	5 5	 1	10 10	−2.1 −0.7	−1.3	2.2 1.3	1.7
KITCHEN SINKS 1919–25	6	6	6	1 2		2 1	2 1	−3.0 +0.7	−1.2	6.7 4.9	5.2

Table 4-2 (concluded)

Period Covered[b] (1)	No. of Order Turns Covered (2)	No. of Shipment Turns Covered (3)	No. of Shipment Turns Matched (4)	Leads (5)	Exact Coincidences (6)	Lags (7)	Rough Coincidences[d] (8)	Av. Lead (−) or Lag (+) (months) Peaks or Troughs[d] (9)	Av. Lead (−) or Lag (+) (months) All Turns (10)	Av. Dev. from Av. Lead or Lag (months) Peaks or Troughs[e] (11)	Av. Dev. from Av. Lead or Lag (months) All Turns (12)
BATHTUBS											
1918–25	6	6	4	1		1	2	−0.5	−0.5	2.5	1.5
				1	1		2	−0.5		0.5	
LAVATORIES											
1919–25	6	6	6	1		2	1	−0.3	−0.2	6.4	5.5
				2		1		0.0		4.7	
MISCELLANEOUS ENAMELED SANITARY WARE											
1919–24	4	4	4	1		1	1	+2.0	+2.8	3.0	3.8
				1		1	1	+3.5		4.5	
ALL SEVEN ITEMS[e]											
	79	75	75	21	8	8	25	−2.0	−1.2	3.2	2.6
				19	13	6	29	−0.4			

Note: For notes a through e, see Table 4-1.

137

Table 4-3
Distribution of Leads and Lags of New Orders at Shipment Turns in Monthly Data

Leads (−) or Lags (+), by Length in Months	Number of Timing Observations for				Percentage of Timing Observations for					
	11 Items Made Primarily to Order[a]		7 Items Made Primarily to Stock[b]		11 Items Made Primarily to Order[a]			7 Items Made Primarily to Stock[b]		
	Peaks (1)	Troughs (2)	Peaks (3)	Troughs (4)	Peaks (5)	Troughs (6)	All Turns (7)	Peaks (8)	Troughs (9)	All Turns (10)
−31 to −36	1				1.7		0.8			
−25 to −30		1				1.5	0.8			
−19 to −24	2				3.3		1.6			
−13 to −18	5	6			8.3	9.2	8.8			2.7
−7 to −12	17	16	2		28.3	24.3	26.4	5.4		5.3
−4 to −6	20	13	4	5	33.3	20.0	26.4	10.8	13.2	10.7
−1 to −3	11	17	3	14	18.3	26.2	22.4	8.1	36.8	34.7
0	2	7	12	13	3.3	10.8	7.2	32.5	34.2	28.0
+1 to +3	0	4	8	2	0	6.2	3.2	21.6	5.3	9.3
+4 to +6	1	1	5	1	1.7	1.5	1.6	13.5	2.6	5.3
+7 to +12	1	1	3	3	1.7		0.8	8.1	7.9	4.0
Total	60	65	37	38	100.0	100.0	100.0	100.0	100.0	100.0
Summary										
Long leads (−4 to −36)	45	36	9	5	74.9	55.3	64.8	24.3	13.2	18.7
Rough coincidences (−3 to +3)	13	28	25	29	21.7	43.2	32.8	67.6	76.3	72.0
Long lags (+4 to +12)	2	1	3	4	3.4	1.5	2.4	8.1	10.5	9.3
Total	60	65	37	38	100.0	100.0	100.0	100.0	100.0	100.0

[a] This sample consists of the industries and products covered in Table 4-1.
[b] This sample consists of the products covered in Table 4-2.

reach up into the classes of very long leads, show the highest frequencies
in the classes running from −4 to −12 months, and recede in the regions
of coincidences and lags. For goods made to stock the classes of very
long leads are empty, and those of short leads and coincidences most
heavily populated (compare columns 5–7 with columns 8–10). Approximately two-thirds of all observations for goods made to order are
intermediate and long leads of more than three months, while nearly
three-fourths of all observations for goods made to stock are rough
coincidences.

Relative Timing of New Orders and Output

The sample of individual industries for which we have matched
data on new orders and output (all in physical terms) is, regrettably,
very small. It includes three of the items that represented manufacturing to order in Table 4-1 (merchant pig iron, steel sheets, and paper),
two of the products made primarily to stock from Table 4-2 (oak flooring and southern pine lumber), and one commodity made primarily to
order, for which no comparisons with shipments could be made
(paperboard).

Timing comparisons between new orders and production based on
these data are summarized in Table 4-4. They demonstrate the tendency for the turns in new orders to anticipate the turns in output. All
of the timing averages in columns 9–10 are leads of new orders, although most of these leads are short, about 3 months or less. The mean
leads at troughs are shorter than those at peaks for all but one item. Of
the observations at peaks, somewhat more than half are rough coincidences; of the observations at troughs, over two-thirds.

For the four made-to-order items, the average lead at all turns is 2.6
months, and for the two made to stock, it happens to be the same.
There is no evidence here of any significant differentiation between
the timing patterns of the two groups. This is consistent with the notion that new orders guide and hence anticipate production even in
those industries in which they are customarily filled from stock shortly
after receipt.

However, it would be rash to make further generalizations from
this meager evidence. It would be unwise to infer that the lags of outputs, unlike those of shipments, are not likely to differ systematically
in length and regularity as between manufacture to order and manu-

Table 4-4
Timing of Turns in New Orders at Turns in Production, Six Industries or Products,[a] Various Periods, 1917–56

| | | All Turns | | | No. of Timing Observations at Peaks or Troughs[c] That Are | | | | Av. Lead (−) or Lag (+) (months) | | Av. Dev. from Av. Lead or Lag (months) | |
| | No. of Order Turns Covered (2) | No. of Production Turns | | | | | | | | | | |
Period Covered[b] (1)		Covered (3)	Matched (4)	Leads (5)	Exact Coinci-dences (6)	Lags (7)	Rough Coinci-dences[d] (8)	Peaks or Troughs[e] (9)	All Turns (10)	Peaks or Troughs[e] (11)	All Turns (12)
MERCHANT PIG IRON											
1 1919–24	5	5	5	2				−5.5	−5.4	1.5	1.7
2				3				−5.3		1.8	
PAPER, EXCLUDING BUILDING PAPER, NEWSPRINT, AND PAPERBOARD											
3 1937–52	10	8	8	4			1	−6.2	−3.0	2.3	3.5
4				1	2	1	4	+0.2		0.9	
OAK FLOORING											
5 1917–55	25	19	19	9	1		5	−3.1	−2.8	2.3	2.2
6				6	2	1	7	−2.4		2.2	
STEEL SHEETS											
7 1919–32	9	9	9	2	1	1	3	−3.5	−2.7	5.2	3.9
8				2	3		4	−2.0		2.8	
SOUTHERN PINE LUMBER											
9 1918–53	23	21	21	5	2	3	5	−1.1	−2.3	2.7	2.4
10				9	2		6	−3.5		2.0	

	Col 2	Col 3	Col 4	Col 5	Col 6	Col 7	Col 8	Col 9	Col 10	Col 11	Col 12
PAPERBOARD, TOTAL											
11 1926–56	19	17	17	8	1		7	−2.3	−1.5	1.5	1.3
12				4	3		8	−0.5		0.8	
ALL SIX ITEMS ABOVE [e]											
13	91	79	79	30	5	4	22	−2.9	−2.6	2.7	2.5
14				25	12	3	29	−2.2		2.3	
FOUR ITEMS MADE TO ORDER [f]											
15	43	39	39	16	2	1	11	−3.7	−2.6	3.0	2.7
16				10	8	2	16	−1.5		2.0	
TWO ITEMS MADE TO STOCK [g]											
17	48	40	40	14	3	3	11	−2.1	−2.6	2.0	2.3
18				15	4	1	13	−3.0			

[a] Ranked by the length of the average lead, all turns (column 10), from longest to shortest.

[b] Identified by the complete specific-cycle phases in the production series.

[c] For each item, the entry on the odd-numbered line is for comparisons at peaks; the entry on the even-numbered line, for comparisons at troughs.

[d] Includes exact coincidences and leads or lags of one, two, or three months.

[e] Summary of the timing measures for the six industries or products covered. Entries in columns 2–8 are totals; entries in columns 9–12 are averages weighted by the number of observations for each item.

[f] Summary of the timing measures for merchant pig iron; paper, excluding building paper, newsprint, and paperboard; steel sheets; and paperboard (lines 1–4, 7, 8, 11, and 12). Totals and weighted averages are explained in note e.

[g] Summary of the timing measures for oak flooring and southern pine lumber (lines 5, 6, 9, and 10). Totals and weighted averages are explained in note e.

facture to stock. The timing records of Table 4-4 cannot support such a generalization. The difficulty here is due not only to the smallness but to the character of the sample. That is, the items covered, in terms of the order-shipment comparisons, belong to the least differentiated segments of our two samples; those segments which show the contrast between the two types of manufacture most clearly are omitted (because corresponding production data are not available). Merchant pig iron, steel sheets, and paper are found in the *lower* part of Table 4-1, that is, among the made-to-order products that have short leads of orders relative to shipments. Oak flooring and southern pine lumber, again, are located in the *upper* part of Table 4-2; they rank first and third according to the length of their order leads among the components of the made-to-stock group. The accompanying tabulation compares the mean leads of orders relative to production with the mean leads of orders relative to shipments for *the same* groups of commodities. The to-order group therefore includes only three items: merchant pig iron; paper, excluding building paper, newsprint, and paperboard; and steel sheets. The to-stock group, however, includes both oak flooring and southern pine lumber, as in Table 4-4.

Average Lead of New Orders at:

	Peaks	*Troughs*	*All Turns*
	(*figures in parentheses are the corresponding average deviations*)		
Three items made to order			
Comparisons with production	−5.0 (3.8)	−2.1 (2.8)	−3.4 (3.5)
Comparisons with shipments	−5.2 (3.0)	−2.0 (2.3)	−3.5 (3.0)
Two items made to stock			
Comparisons with production	−2.1 (2.5)	−3.0 (2.0)	−2.6 (2.3)
Comparisons with shipments	−2.3 (2.4)	−0.9 (1.5)	−1.6 (2.0)

These figures do show the lead of new orders at all turns in output to be somewhat longer for goods made to order than for goods made to stock, but they make it clear that this is due entirely to the characteristics of the timing at peaks, not at troughs.[5] In the comparisons with shipments, on the other hand, order leads are shorter for goods

[5] The average leads in the first line of the tabulation above are longer than those in Table 4-4 because paperboard has been excluded from the group of goods made to order. We have no shipment data for paperboard, and wish to cover in the tabulation only those products for which we can compare new orders with *both* shipments and production.

made to stock, at both troughs and peaks. As a result, the difference in
the timing of orders for the two groups of goods at all turns is less for
the comparisons with production.

Small differences between averages based on small numbers of observations are, of course, of dubious statistical significance; they are
presented here as only mildly suggestive. But these observations do
seem sensible in view of our expectations: that output and shipments
would be closely synchronous in manufacture to order; that output
would lag behind orders, too, though probably only slightly, in manufacture to stock; and that even those manufacturers who ordinarily
work to stock would become more "order oriented" when their business was at its peak levels.

Major-Industry Aggregates

This section deals with the relative timing measures for the OBE-Census series on the value of manufacturers' new orders and shipments,
and also compares the timing of deflated series for N and S and the
corresponding production indexes. The major-industry data for these
comparisons were described in Chapter 3 and shown there in several
charts.

These charts will be referred to repeatedly and should be consulted.
They elucidate both the strengths and the weaknesses of the method of
analyzing cyclical timing relations. They show turning points that are
easily identified, along with others that are less certain and a few that
are rather problematic. They convey a strong impression of the (expected) parallelism between the matched series, allowing for the greater
amplitudes and earlier timing of new orders. But they also provide examples of shipments "skipping" certain cyclical turns and movements
in orders. They show both that which is continuous and that which is
episodic, and thus supplement effectively the timing observations at
turning points and the regression measures that summarize average
relationships over time.

New Orders vs. Shipments: Timing Comparisons
at Successive Peaks and Troughs

Table 4-5 lists the individual leads of new orders at successive turning points in shipments for each of the major industries and their group-

Table 4-5

Timing Relations Between Value Aggregates of New Orders and Shipments, by Business Cycle Turning Zones, Major Manufacturing Industries, 1948–62

Lead (−) or Lag (+), in Months of New Orders at Turns in Shipments in Turning Zone Associated with

Industry	1948 Recession: Peaks (1)	1949 Revival: Troughs (2)	Korean War[a] 1950–51: Peaks (3)	Korean War[a] 1951–52: Troughs (4)	1953 Recession: Peaks (5)	1954 Revival: Troughs (6)	1957 Recession: Peaks (7)	1958 Revival: Troughs (8)	1960 Recession: Peaks (9)	1961 Revival: Troughs (10)	Business Retardation 1962[a]: Peaks (11)	Business Retardation 1962[a]: Troughs (12)
All manufacturing	−1	−4	n.s.	n.s.	−6	−9	−2	−3	−1[b]	0	−2	−3
Durable goods, total	−5	−4	n.s.	n.s.	−6	−12	−14	−3	−2[b]	−1	−1	−3
Primary metals	−1	−3	−3	0	−1	−11	−12[c]	−2	−4[d]	−10	−3	−5
Blast furnaces, steel mills	n.a.	n.a.	n.a.	n.a.	n.i.	−11	−19[c]	−2	−4[d]	−11	−3	−3
Fabricated metal products	n.i.	−7	−1	−4	−6	−11	−2	−5	−2	0	0	0
Electrical machinery[e]	−5	−3	0[f]	+6[f]	−2	−5	−1	−4	−3[g]	+1[g]	−4	−2
Machinery except electrical[e]	−6	−1	n.s.	n.s.	−3	−5	−8[h]	−6	−12	−8	−3	−1
Transportation equipment	n.i.	n.i.	n.s.	n.s.	−7	−12	+1	−6	−3	0	n.t.	n.t.
Other durable goods[i]	+2	0	0	0	−4	−7	+1	0	−3	0	n.t.	n.t.
Nondurables, total	+1	−1	0	−9[j]	−9[j]	0	−2	0	0	0	n.t.	n.t.
Reporting unfilled orders[k]	−4	−5	−4	−5	−5	−1	+2	−3	−6	0	n.t.	n.t.

Notes to Table 4-5

n.s. = no turn in shipments.

n.i. = not identified (timing of new orders or shipments or both uncertain).

n.a. = data not available.

n.t. = no turning points.

Note: Measures for all manufacturing industries; durable goods industries, total; and nondurable goods industries, total; and measures on the other lines in columns 6–12 are based on the new Census data (1963 revision). The other measures are based on the earlier OBE data (the revised series for the component industries begin in 1953).

[a] These pairs of peaks or troughs represent "extra" turns, not related to any cyclical recession or revival recognized as such in the National Bureau chronology of U.S. business cycles. The timing comparisons in columns 11 and 12 refer for the most part to the dates marking the beginning and end of minor movements or retardations (see Charts 3-1 and 3-2).

[b] Based on peaks that occurred in April–June 1959, before the major steel strike in the second half of the year. After the strike, shipments rose again briefly to about the same peak levels in January 1960, while the increase in new orders was much smaller and still shorter (Chart 3-1).

[c] The length of these leads is partly a consequence of the 1956 steel strike. The peaks in new orders have on this occasion definitely preceded, and the peaks in shipments definitely followed, the strike (see Chart 3-2).

[d] Prestrike peaks in the first half of 1959 (Chart 3-2).

[e] The pre-1953 measures are based in part on unpublished data received from the U.S. Department of Commerce, Office of Business Economics.

[f] Shipments show only a short and small decline between January and July 1951. New orders, however, fell substantially between January 1951 and January 1952. These comparisons match major and minor turns (Chart 3-2).

[g] Refer to dates marking the beginning and end of a retardation in shipments (September 1959–February 1961). The former date is matched with the June 1959 peak in new orders, and the latter date with a minor trough in new orders in March 1961 (see Chart 3-2).

[h] Based on the secondary peak in new orders in December 1956, which matches the peak in shipments in August 1957. The comparisons between extra turns which occurred in these series in 1955–56 are not shown in this table (see Chart 3-2).

[i] Includes professional and scientific instruments; lumber; furniture; stone, clay, and glass; and miscellaneous industries.

[j] These measures may be questioned because they refer to movements with very small amplitudes which are particularly difficult to date (see Chart 3-1).

[k] Includes textiles, leather, paper, and printing and publishing.

ings. Eight of the twelve columns of the table refer to "turning zones" associated with the recessions and revivals in general economic activity. This arrangement is possible because the series covered conform well to business cycles, as suggested by Charts 3-1 and 3-2 and shown in detail later (Chapter 11). However, new orders also show widespread "extra" cycles associated with the Korean developments in

1950–52, which in some of the industries are matched by movements in shipments. Also, the slowdown of the economy in 1962 has been connected with retardations or declines (mostly mild and short) in new orders and shipments of several major industries. Thus Table 4-5 distinguishes twelve turning-point zones in the period covered by our data — eight corresponding to the recent business cycle chronology, as determined by the National Bureau, and four (columns 3–4 and 11–12) relating to two special episodes.

Most of the recorded comparisons for the durable goods industries in the Korean period are short leads and coincidences, but it would be wrong to conclude that the actual delivery periods were then generally short. One must stress the fact that no comparisons can be made in these turning zones for the machinery and transportation equipment industries and indeed for the most comprehensive aggregates — all manufacturing and total durables. The rapid expansion of new orders in 1950–51 left shipments far behind, resulting in a large-scale backlog accumulation. Even after their drastic decline in 1951, new orders still exceeded shipments; that is, the stock of unfilled orders kept on expanding through that period, though shipments continued their gradual rise. This implies that the delivery lags must have been very long and increasing in this period. The evidence of the backlog-shipment ratios bears out this presumption (Chapter 6). The method of turning-point comparisons obviously cannot provide the relevant measures where movements in new orders are not matched in shipments.

The rapid sequence of a buying surge and relapse in 1950–51 was followed in 1952–53 by a rather hesitant rise of new orders, with shipments now moving closely along. Only in the transportation equipment industry did new orders continue to exceed shipments in this phase; and then, when orders finally turned down decisively at the outset of 1953, shipments remained at high levels for seven more months before declining in July 1953 (Chart 3-2). Judging from the old OBE series for motor vehicles and nonautomotive transportation equipment separately, the lags of shipments behind new orders at the 1952–53 peaks were apparently long in both of these industries (see Chart 3-4). Elsewhere, the paired series nearly overlapped, and in some industries (primary metals and nonelectrical machinery) shipments in fact exceeded new orders most of the time in 1952–53; shipments were coincident with new orders or lagging by short intervals at the 1953 downturns.

On the whole, however, unfilled orders were still very high at the time, absolutely and relative to shipments, and the lags in the comprehensive aggregates were substantial (see Table 4-5, column 5, and the charts).

In 1953 new orders for durable goods dropped sharply, while output and shipments, cushioned by the still large backlogs, declined but slightly. At the end of the year, the decline in new orders was halted, but there was very little rise in the following eight months: Between September 1953 and May 1954, durables orders, after seasonal adjustment, remained virtually stable at monthly rates of about $10 billion (Chart 3-1). Most manufacturers apparently did not think this situation justified a prompt response of stepped-up activity. The mild business contraction then in process was dominated by the business objective of getting inventories under better control, i.e., closer to the desired balance with orders and sales. As long as new orders were still much lower in value than production and shipments, their slow recovery could be met by a retardation rather than by a reversal of such contractionary adjustment processes as the reduction of output schedules and inventory liquidation. Thus output and shipments continued to decline mildly through the first three quarters of 1954, and turned up only after incoming orders finally caught up with shipments, and backlogs stopped declining.

Inspection of charts for the component major industries confirms that the long leads of new orders at the 1954 troughs in shipments represent a real and widespread phenomenon.[6] As summarized in Table 4-5, column 6, new orders for each of the listed durable goods industries led shipments by intervals of considerable length (from 5–7 to 11–12 months). The 1954 episode contrasts in this respect with the other trough zones in which the lags of shipments were generally short. But then, consistent with the argument above, the declines in new orders tended to be much shallower on these other occasions, and the subsequent recoveries (whereby N regained the levels of S) were much more vigorous.

The dating of the peaks associated with the recessions of 1957 and

---

[6] For total durables, the trough in new orders is difficult to date because of the long flat bottom in 1953–54 (Chart 3-1). But the long lag of S relative to N in this period stands out clearly for total manufacturing. For the major durable goods industries, the existence of similar lags at the 1954 revival is definitely indicated, despite some difficulty in detail occasioned here and there by the erratic movements in the compared series. It may also be noted that the earlier OBE data for the durable goods industries leave no doubt about the long lag of shipments in 1954 (see Moore, ed., *Business Cycle Indicators*, Vol. I, Chart 14-1, p. 431).

1960 is made difficult by the "flattop" pattern of the series in 1955–56, with superimposed large erratic fluctuations, and by the effects of the steel strikes in 1956 and 1959. The long lag of shipments for total durables behind the December 1955 peak in new orders illustrates well the high sensitivity of relative timing measures to small differences in trends. While the movement of N tended to be downward and that of S upward in 1956 (Chart 3-1), these were both rather slow drifts interrupted by shorter irregular variations. It could be argued that a secondary (somewhat lower) peak in new orders occurred late in 1956, just a few months before the downturn in shipments, although the interpretation underlying the long lead specified in Table 4-5 (column 7) appears to be more consistent with our procedures and the data. On the other hand, the corresponding lead of N relative to S for all manufacturing is as short as two months, simply because new orders rose slightly during 1956 instead of declining slightly (otherwise, the series for total manufacturing and total durables can be seen, in the charts, to have followed a very similar course).

In 1959, new orders for both all manufacturing and total durables reached their peaks in April, before the steel strike; but shipments show in each case two peaks of about the same height, one in May or June 1959 and another in January 1960 (Chart 3-1). The prestrike downturns in S lagged the peaks in N by one or two months, as recorded in Table 4-6, column 9; the poststrike downturns in S lagged the peaks in N by eight months. Matching the former turns and treating the latter ones as secondary is the preferred alternative here. The other choice would appear to bias the results in the direction of overly long lags. It may also be noted that in primary metals, the industry principally affected by this disturbance, the prestrike peaks in both N and S were definitely higher than the poststrike ones (Chart 3-2). Buying and deliveries were undoubtedly strongly stimulated by anticipation of the work stoppage; after the strike was over, the need to replenish stocks caused a new rise in new orders, but one that was smaller and very short-lived; and shipments, though they increased more and ran higher than new orders, declined as promptly in 1960. The wide repercussions of these developments are of interest: The double-peak pattern in 1959–60 can be seen clearly in such diverse industries as transportation equipment (motor vehicles) and the group of "other durables."

Table 4-5 suggests that the leads of new orders may have become shorter in the more recent years. In the five turning zones 1958–62, long leads are few, while short leads and coincidences are relatively frequent (columns 8–12). Moreover, Charts 3-1 and 3-2 show that the paired series for N and S have tended to run closer together since the late 1950's than they did earlier in the postwar period. The ratios of unfilled orders to shipments (U/S) have been undergoing fluctuations with decreasing amplitudes around distinctly *downward* trends. The corresponding series on unfilled orders proper (in current dollars) show much weaker trends; some of them seem to show mild downward inclinations, but others have none.[7] From all this one can infer that, in the aggregate, producers in each of the major industries concerned must have acquired the capacity to handle the same volume of orders in less time.

Independent evidence suggests, in agreement with the above, that the impressive growth of manufacturing capacity in the decade following the war and immediate postwar readjustments may have come to exceed the growth of manufacturing output.[8] High average rates of investment in plant and equipment would indeed be expected in times of strong pressures of demand against capacity, such as prevailed in large areas of industry during those years (except only for the relatively brief recession periods). However, by the late 1950's, the demand pressures had apparently started to abate, and this at the very time when industry had acquired an unprecedented ability to meet them without undue strain. Later on, signs of excess capacities began to replace those of excess demand, as the 1957–58 recession gave way to a rather short and vigorless expansion, which was followed by another brief recession in 1960 and then again by a very gradual recovery, interrupted by temporary slowdowns, in 1961–62. Not until very recently, in 1964–65, did the extraordinarily long business expansion that started early in 1961 develop a symptom that was particularly characteristic of the previous upswings, namely, the outpacing of shipments by the faster-rising new orders in manufacturing (see Chart 3-1).

[7] Evidence on these points is presented in Chapter 6 (Charts 6-4 and 6-5 and the accompanying text).

[8] According to the estimates in *Business Plans for New Plants and Equipment, Annual Surveys*, prepared by the McGraw-Hill Department of Economics, the index of manufacturing capacity, 1948 = 100, stood at 167 by the end of 1957—an increase of two-thirds in nine years. Meanwhile, the FRB index of manufacturing output (also 1948 = 100) increased only to 141 in 1957.

Average Measures of Relative Timing

Table 4-6 is based on the 108 individual timing comparisons listed in Table 4-5, plus eight additional observations which cannot be assigned to any of the twelve turning zones identified in the latter table.[9] Ninety-four of these measures refer to pairs of turning points marking major movements that can definitely be classified as "specific cycles" under the NBER criteria; twenty-two refer to "minor" turns marking shorter but still distinct movements.

The total number of turns in shipments covered in Table 4-6 is 118, and all but two of these are matched by like turns in new orders (columns 2 and 3). There are more instances of unmatched turns in new orders mainly because of the already noted extra declines in these series during 1951–52 (columns 1 and 3).

The means of the timing comparisons are all negative (columns 8 and 9), that is, new orders lead shipments in each of the industries at both peaks and troughs by intervals long enough to be observable in monthly data. Leads account for about 77 per cent of the observations, coincidences for 15 per cent, and lags for nearly 8 per cent. The percentage of leads is larger at peaks than at troughs, while the reverse is true of the percentage of exact coincidences.[10] Most of the leads are short as are virtually all the lags; consequently, the proportion of "rough coincidences" is high (59 per cent), though still smaller than that of leads.

Individual long leads influence most means but in a fairly moderate degree. The medians are on the whole smaller than the means, but not by very large amounts, and the two statistics yield similar rankings of the industries. Our analysis here relies on the means, but elsewhere medians have been used as well for closely related data (Table 6-6).

Most of the mean absolute deviations listed in the last two columns of Table 4-6 vary between one and three months. In a normal distribution, 57.5 per cent of the observations would be within the range of plus and minus one average deviation on both sides of the mean; in a moderately skewed distribution, this would still be approximately

[9] These include the following (compare Chart 3-2): a lead of one month of N relative to S at the 1963 peak and the following 1963 trough in primary metals and in blast furnaces. The other four comparisons, all in transportation equipment, include a six-month lag at the 1955–56 peak in the series, a one-month lead at the trough in the same period, coincident timing at the 1959 trough, and a one-month lag at the 1960 peak.

[10] At peaks, the proportion of leads is approximately 81 per cent; of coincidences, 9 per cent; and of lags, 10 per cent. At troughs, the corresponding figures are 73, 22, and 5 per cent.

true. Thus with a mean lead of, say, three months, most of the comparisons would be expected to fall in the class of leads of six months or less; but the presumption of skewness means that among the observations outside that range long leads would be more frequent than short lags.[11]

The peak-trough differences among the average leads of new orders in column 8 seem to vary irregularly: for five industry groups, the peak figures are the larger ones, but in five others, they are the smaller ones. However, Table 4-5 suggests that the long leads of orders at the upturn were largely concentrated in one period, namely, in the zone of troughs associated with the business revival of 1954. When this particular episode is excluded, considerably smaller average leads at troughs are obtained, which tend to fall short of the corresponding measures for peaks, as illustrated by the following figures:

	Average Lead of Orders	
	Peaks (Table 4-5, col. 8)	*Troughs (excl. 1954)*
Durable goods, total	−5.6	−2.8
Primary metals	−3.6	−3.5
Blast furnaces, steel mills	−6.8	−4.2
Fabricated metals	−2.2	−3.2
Electrical machinery	−2.5	−0.4
Nonelectrical machinery	−5.0	−4.0
Transportation equipment	−2.2	−2.0
Other durable goods	−0.8	0.0
Nondurable goods, total	−2.0	−2.5
Reporting unfilled orders	−4.0	−3.5

Wide fluctuations in demand and production will often give rise to large variations in the degree of capacity utilization, from slack to

[11] A comment may be added on the use of mean absolute deviations vis-à-vis that of standard deviations, which have more convenient mathematical properties though a somewhat less simple meaning. Given a specific distribution, the two measures are proportional. The ratio of the average deviation to the standard deviation depends but slightly on the form of the distribution; for a variety of forms, the constant of proportionality was found to be approximately 0.8 (see Robert G. Brown, *Smoothing, Forecasting, and Prediction of Discrete Time Series*, Englewood Cliffs, N.J., 1962, pp. 282–90). This is also true for similar measures shown elsewhere in this book (Table 6-6): There the ratios of the average to standard deviations all exceed 0.7 and are heavily concentrated between 0.8 and 0.9.

Table 4-6

Summary Measures of Timing of Value of Manufacturers' New Orders at Turns in Value of Manufacturers' Shipments, Major Industries,[a] 1948–64

All Turns			No. of Timing Observations at Peaks or Troughs[c] That Are				Av. Lead (−) or Lag (+) (months)		Av. Dev. from Av. Lead or Lag (months)	
No. of Order Turns Covered[b] (1)	No. of Shipment Turns[b] Covered (2)	Matched (3)	Leads (4)	Exact Coincidences (5)	Lags (6)	Rough Coincidences[d] (7)	Peaks or Troughs[e] (8)	All Turns (9)	Peaks or Troughs[e] (10)	All Turns (11)
ALL MANUFACTURING INDUSTRIES										
12(2)	10(2)	10(2)	5			4	−2.4	−3.1	1.2	1.9
			4	1		3	−3.8		2.2	
DURABLE GOODS INDUSTRIES, TOTAL										
12(2)	10(2)	10(2)	5			2	−5.6	−5.1	3.5	3.3
			5			3	−4.6		3.0	
PRIMARY METALS										
14(4)	14(2)	14(2)	7			5	−3.6	−4.1	2.5	3.1
			6	1		4	−4.6		3.5	
BLAST FURNACES, STEEL MILLS										
9(2)	9(2)	9(2)	4			2	−6.8	−6.1	6.4	5.0
			5			3	−5.6		4.3	
FABRICATED METAL PRODUCTS										
11(0)	11(0)	11(0)	4	1		4	−2.2	−3.5	1.5	2.9
			4	2		2	−4.5		3.2	

ELECTRICAL MACHINERY[e]										
14(2)	12(6)	12(6)	5	1	4		-2.5	-1.8	1.5	2.2
			4		2	3	-1.2		3.1	
MACHINERY EXCEPT ELECTRICAL[e]										
12(2)	10(2)		5		3		-5.0	-4.6	3.2	2.8
			5		2		-4.2		2.6	
TRANSPORTATION EQUIPMENT										
13(4)	12(2)	10(2)	3	2	2	2	-2.2	-3.0	4.6	4.2
			3		0	3	-3.8		4.2	
OTHER DURABLE GOODS[f]										
10(0)	10(0)		2	1	2	4	-0.8	-1.1	2.2	2.1
			1	4		4	-1.4		2.2	
NONDURABLE GOODS INDUSTRIES, TOTAL										
10(4)	10(4)		2	2	1	4	-2.0	-2.0	2.8	2.8
			2	3		4	-2.0		2.8	
REPORTING UNFILLED ORDERS[g]										
12(2)	10(0)	10(0)	4	1	1	1	-3.4	-3.1	2.2	2.1
			4			3	-2.8		1.8	

[a] The series are those covered in Table 4-5. They all start in 1948 (or 1947) except blast furnaces and steel mills, which start in 1953. As in Table 4-5, the earlier OBE data are used for 1948–53 (including the determination of timing measures associated with the 1953 recession), and the new, revised Census data are used for the period since 1953.

[b] All turns covered are counted, except a few that could not be positively identified (such as some uncertain turns at the beginning or end of a series). The figures in parentheses give the number of minor turns included.

[c] For each item, the entry on the first line is for comparisons at peaks; the entry on the second line, for comparisons at troughs.

[d] Includes exact coincidences and leads or lags of one, two, or three months.

[e] The pre-1953 measures are based in part on unpublished data received from the U.S. Department of Commerce, Office of Business Economics.

[f] Includes professional and scientific instruments; lumber; furniture; stone, clay, and glass; and miscellaneous industries.

[g] Includes textiles, leather, paper, and printing and publishing.

strain, while small movements in the broad range of normal operations will have no comparable impact. Hence it would not be surprising to find that large swings in new orders and shipments are associated with greater discrepancies between these series than are observed in periods of stable trends. The lags of shipments behind new orders may accordingly also show a tendency to be longer for the major movements. These notions receive some broad support from our charts; as suggested before, the leads of new orders relative to shipments appear to have decreased in recent years while the cyclical movements in these series have become generally smaller. The tabulation below shows that larger average leads of new orders are in fact obtained when those observations that are associated with minor turns are excluded.[12]

Average Lead of New Orders Relative to Shipments (in months)

	Peaks		Troughs	
	All (Table 4-6, col. 8) (1)	Major Turns Only (2)	All (Table 4-6, col. 8) (3)	Major Turns Only (4)
All manufacturing industries	−2.4	−2.5	−3.8	−4.0
Durable goods industries	−5.6	−6.8	−4.6	−5.0
Primary metals	−3.6	−4.2	−4.6	−5.2
Blast furnaces, steel mills	−6.8	−11.5	−5.6	−8.0
Fabricated metal products	−2.2	−2.7	−4.5	−5.4
Electrical machinery	−2.5	−2.2	−1.2	0.0
Machinery except electrical	−5.0	−5.5	−4.2	−5.0
Transportation equipment	−2.2	−6.0	−3.8	−6.0

Timing Differences Among the Major Industries

The major industries in the Census-OBE compilation cannot be divided between goods made to order and goods made to stock, but can be grouped according to the durability of their products.[13] It will

[12] The excluded observations are those in columns 11 and 12 of Table 4-5 and those listed in note 9 above. For the group of other durable goods and the nondurable goods industries, all the comparisons made refer to major turns.

[13] See, however, the crude distinction, by the prevalent type of manufacture, drawn between the major industries in Table 2-5, columns 3 and 4.

be recalled that the durable goods industries as a whole have very low ratios of finished stocks to unfilled orders, and the total nondurables very high ratios. This indicates that manufacture to order prevails heavily among the former; and manufacture to stock, among the latter (Chapter 2). Hence, one would expect the leads of new orders to be substantially longer for the durable goods than for the nondurable goods sector of manufacturing. In fact, the difference between the respective averages is large, the typical lead being estimated as five months for the durables and as two months at most, but probably less, for the nondurables.[14] However, the assumption underlying the data is that all but four of the major nondurable goods industries produce to stock only. There is reason to think that this assumption is not quite valid (see Chapter 2, note 18 and the text to which the note applies). To the extent that this is so, the true lead in the nondurables sector may be understated, and, therefore, the difference between the averages is likely to be overstated. The industries in the nondurables sector for which the reported new orders and shipments differ show an average lead of incoming business of 3.1 months.

The averages for the major industries conceal wide differences in length among the leads for the smaller and more homogeneous component industries. Probably the most drastic example of this is provided by transportation equipment, which includes motor vehicles and parts made largely to stock and nonautomotive equipment made to order, typically with long delivery lags. According to the data shown in Chart 3-4 (which are of the pre-1963 vintage) the average lead of new orders for nonautomotive transportation equipment was 11.5 months—by far the largest one of the major-industry leads. This is understandable in view of the size and complexity of such items as ships, airplanes, or locomotives. It will be recalled that the longest average leads in Table 4-1, ranging from seven to eleven months, were those of the three principal types of railroad equipment. Corroborating evidence is also available for the aircraft industry. Chart 4-1 presents the quarterly series on the aggregate value of new orders and shipments of aircraft manufacturers, compiled by the Bureau of the Census and the Civil Aeronautics Administration for 1948–60. The similarity

[14] The average leads according to Standard and Poor's data for 1949–58 (Appendix B, Part 1) are similar: 4.3 months for durables and 1.7 months for nondurables. Exclusion of the questionable observations at the 1952–53 shipments turns (see Table 4-5, note j) would drastically reduce the average lead for the nondurable goods sector.

Chart 4-1
Value of New Orders and Shipments of Aircraft Manufacturers, Quarterly, 1948–60

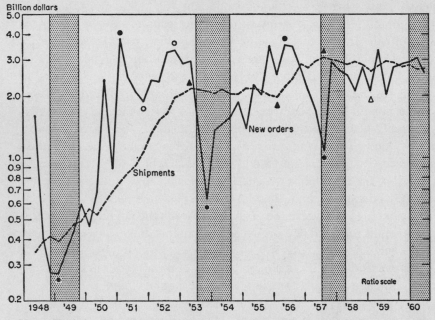

Note: Shaded areas represent business cycle contractions; unshaded areas, expansions. Dots identify peaks and troughs of specific cycles in new orders; black triangles, shipments. Circles and white triangles identify short cycles in new orders and shipments, respectively.

Source: Bureau of the Census and Civil Aeronautics Administration (seasonal adjustment by NBER). Data for the third and fourth quarters of 1950 and the first and second quarters of 1951 are not available. For shipments, linear interpolation was used over the period in question. New orders were estimated by adding to computed shipments the change, during the given quarter, in the backlog of aircraft orders (computed from the published Census-CAA figures on end-of-quarter backlogs). The resulting estimates for both shipments and new orders agree well with related evidence (Standard and Poor's monthly indexes of aircraft orders and sales; see App. C).

of the cyclical course of these series to that of the OBE series for total nonautomotive transportation equipment (cf. Charts 3-6 and 4-1) emphasizes the great importance of aircraft within that total. Aircraft orders led at the sales peaks in the second quarter of 1953 and the third quarter of 1957 by two and five quarters, respectively. No comparisons at troughs are available.

A very different picture is presented by motor vehicles and parts, where new orders moved ahead of shipments by much shorter and more variable intervals (Chart 3-6). Here the timing relation is blurred in the early 1950's, possibly reflecting the changes in the military-civilian mix of demand during the Korean period, but the two series are roughly coincident since 1955 (see the text accompanying Chart 3-6 on the corresponding contrast in relative amplitudes). In terms of aggregate shipments and new orders, the motor vehicle subgroup is, of course, much more important than the nonautomotive subgroup within total transportation equipment.[15] Accordingly, the timing measures for transportation equipment as a whole differ sharply from those for the nonautomotive group, and differ less from those for the motor vehicle division. The timing relation between new orders and shipments of total transportation equipment is difficult to establish, in large measure because of the dichotomy just discussed.

In the two metalworking industries—primary metals and fabricated metal products—new orders led shipments by about three to four months, while the average lead of orders received by blast furnaces and steel mills was as long as six months (Table 4-6). Electrical machinery shows short average delivery lags (two months), while the corresponding measures for nonelectrical machinery are in the 4–5 months' range. Aggregation is likely to suppress substantial differences among the lead times for the components of these major industries. The averages for machinery, for example, include figures for heavy and specialized equipment as well as for more standardized and less complex items. Data for individual types of equipment show considerable variation here: In Table 4-1 the average lag of shipments is seven months for electric overhead cranes and two months for woodworking machinery. These comparisons are merely suggestive because the data cover different periods. Timing measures based on the subdivisions of the major-industry series for the durable goods sector (Appendix E, Part 1) will shed more light on this subject.

At the other end of the scale from nonautomotive transportation equipment with its long delivery lags (averaging nearly one year) is the group of "other durable goods industries" for which the lags are very

[15] In terms of unfilled orders, on the other hand, motor vehicle manufacturers, who produce largely to stock, are much less important. The aircraft industry alone held 28 per cent of total manufacturers' unfilled orders in April 1956, while the motor vehicle industry held only 5 per cent of the total (see *Survey of Current Business*, June 1956, p. 3).

short (averaging about one month). The main components of this group are furniture; lumber; and stone, clay, and glass products. Furniture, according to industry reports, is manufactured largely to order but apparently at short notice; it has the second shortest shipment lag in Table 4-1. Clay and glass products and lumber are made predominantly to stock (Table 2-1), and the long records for oak flooring and southern pine suggest that lumber products typically have short order leads (Table 4-2).

Timing of Production Relative to New Orders and Shipments in Real Terms

Table 4-7 shows the timing comparisons between deflated new orders and production for each of the eight "turning zones" that can be identified from the data in the period 1948–58. These measures are based on the deflated series and indexes introduced in Chapter 3 (the pre-1963 OBE data); in reading the table and the comments below, it will be helpful to consult Charts 3-5 and 3-6.

The measures for total manufacturing and the durable goods sector indicate that outputs were quite slow to follow new orders at peaks associated with the recessions of 1953 and 1957 and at troughs of the intervening revival period of 1954. On these occasions, production and new orders in constant prices tended to move in opposite directions for as long as 7 to 15 months. These observations must be qualified by noting that such divergent movements in these aggregates were typically very gradual, sloping gently upward or downward in the vicinity of their turning points; also, that the developments were influenced by outside events, notably the 1956 steel strike. Nevertheless, the conclusion that production lags were relatively long in these periods is not really in doubt. In 1948 and again in 1949, production turned four months after new orders in constant prices for both total manufacturing and the durable goods sector as a whole; and at the 1958 upturns the lags of outputs were generally still shorter in the manufacturing industries (compare columns 1–2 and 5–8 in Table 4-7).

The volume of manufacturers' unfilled orders varied greatly over the period 1948–58, both absolutely and relative to production and shipments, and one would expect the lags of output to be longer when order backlogs are larger. Between 1952 and 1956, unfilled orders and their ratios to shipments were indeed much larger than in 1948–49 and in 1958. But other factors, in particular, autonomous expectations concerning future demand trends, undoubtedly also influence the relative timing of production.

The large waves of forward buying that marked the first year of the Korean War were not replicated in the flow of output, which instead was well maintained at high rates during that period. Aggregate production of durable goods underwent only a mild and brief decline at the end of this phase, in mid-1951, and gained slowly but steadily thereafter, while current ordering was hesitant and very erratic. Even if direct timing comparisons cannot be made here because there are no turns in output to match those in new orders, this should not obscure the substantial lag of production behind orders at that time, in the sense that the sustained strength of production reflected the great accumulation of unfilled orders in the months past. The vigor with which production rebounded after the interruption of the steel strike in mid-1952 must have still been due in large measure to that backlog factor, since new orders were not gaining much in the second half of 1952 and were weakening perceptibly in the first half of 1953.

An important observation that can be made with the aid of Table 4-7 and Charts 3-5 and 3-6 is that outputs lag significantly behind new orders in constant prices not only for durable goods but also for nondurable goods. As stressed before, production to order plays a much smaller role for nondurables than for durables. Production to stock, which prevails in industries manufacturing nondurable goods, is presumably scheduled largely according to market sales forecasts. The finding that outputs tend to follow new orders in these industries indicates, therefore, that new orders serve as an important basis for such forecasts (see section on "Sales Forecasts" near the end of Chapter 2). Since new orders are measures of *past* sales, this argument implies also that sales forecasts contain substantial "autoregressive" elements; that is, future sales (outputs needed) are predicted to a large extent by extrapolating past sales, a plausible though somewhat speculative inference.[16]

---

[16] That projections of past events are commonly used as tools of prediction requires little proof or elaboration; after all, there is often little else to go by. Autoregressive forecasts will earn a measure of success if applied to time series whose successive values are sufficiently correlated with each other. The relatively smooth series for nondurable goods producers suggest that this requirement may be satisfied by sales of many individual companies in this group (even though individual sales are probably often less well autocorrelated than the industry aggregates).

Table 4-7

Timing Relations Between Manufacturers' New Orders in Constant Prices and Production, by Business Cycle Turning Zones, Major Industries, 1948–58

| | Lead (−) or Lag (+) in Months of New Orders at Turns in Production in Turning Zone Associated with | | | | | | | | Av. Lead (−) or Lag (+) (months) | | |
| | 1948 Recession: Peaks | 1949 Revival: Troughs | Korean War 1950–51: Peaks a | Korean War 1951–52: Troughs a | 1953 Recession: Peaks | 1954 Revival: Troughs | 1957 Recession: Peaks | 1958 Revival: Troughs | Peaks | Troughs | All Turns |
Industry	(1)	(2)	(3)	(4)	(5)	(6)	(7)	(8)	(9)	(10)	(11)
All manufacturing	−4	−4	n.p.	n.p.	−7	−7	−12	−2	−7.7	−4.3	−6.0
Durable goods, total	−4	−4	n.p.	n.p.	−7	−7	−15	−3	−8.7	−4.7	−6.7
Primary metals	+1	−3	−10	−1	+2	−3	−9	−2	−4.0	−2.2	−3.1
Fabricated metal products	n.i.	0	+4	−11	−6	−6	−4 b	−1	−2.0	−4.5	−3.4
Machinery, total	n.p.	−5	n.p.	n.p.	−7 b	−2	−7	−4	−7.0	−3.7	−5.0
Electrical machinery e	n.i.	−2	−2	+5	−4	−2	−3	−3	−3.0	−0.5	−1.6
Machinery except electrical e	−1	0	n.p.	n.p.	−3	−7	−13 d	−3	−5.7	−3.3	−4.5
Motor vehicles and parts e	n.a.	n.i.	+5	0 b	−13 b	−10	−3	−1	−3.7	−3.7	−3.7
Nonautomotive transportation equipment e	n.a.	f	n.p.	n.p.	−10	−11	−8	−4	−9.0	−7.5	−8.2
Other durable goods g	−3	0	+3	+1	−6	−6	−12 h	−1	−4.5	−1.5	−3.0
Nondurables, total	n.i.	−6 b	−7	−4	−1 b	0 b	−7	0	−5.0	−2.5	−3.6
Reporting unfilled orders f	j	−3	−5	−4	−1	−1	−6 k	−3	−4.0	−2.8	−3.3
Textile mill products e	n.i.	−3	−5	−9	−1	−1	−7	−3	−4.3	−4.0	−4.1
Leather and leather products e	j	−7	−3	−2	−5	+3	−5	n.i.	−4.3	−2.0	−3.2
Paper and allied products e	n.i.	−3	−9	−4	n.p.	n.p.	−5	+1	−7.0	−2.0	−4.0

Notes to Table 4-7

n.i. = not identified (timing uncertain).

n.a. = data not available.

n.p. = no matching turn in production.

[a] These pairs of peaks and troughs represent "extra" turns, not related to any cyclical recession or revival recognized in the National Bureau chronology of U.S. business cycles.

[b] Based on turns in short cycles or retardations in deflated new orders or production. Although a few of these comparisons are somewhat doubtful, they are listed in the table and included in the averages of columns 9–11 (the more uncertain cases are mentioned in the notes below).

[c] Based in part on unpublished data received from the U.S. Department of Commerce, Office of Business Economics.

[d] A secondary peak in new orders occurred in October 1956, two months before the specific-cycle peak in production.

[e] Based on unpublished data received from the OBE and seasonally adjusted by the Census electronic computer method for the NBER.

[f] Timing of the trough in new orders is uncertain, but the low in this series occurred in July 1949, eight months before the trough in production.

[g] Includes professional and scientific instruments; lumber; furniture; stone, clay, and glass; and miscellaneous industries.

[h] In the period covered by this long lead, the decline in new orders and the rise in production were very gentle, but the direction of these movements is clear.

[i] Includes textiles, leather, paper, and printing and publishing.

[j] Timing of the high values in 1948 indicates that new orders led production by two months for the group of nondurable goods industries with unfilled orders and by one month for leather, but the comparisons are uncertain.

[k] Measured from the early peak of new orders in July 1955 to the *beginning* of a long movement of production along a high plateau (January 1956–September 1957). An uncertain but conservative estimate of the lead.

While the tendency for deflated new orders to anticipate outputs is distinct enough in the nondurable goods sector (both total and those industries reporting unfilled orders), the resulting leads are on the whole shorter than those observed for the durable goods industries (compare the aggregates in Table 4-7). Production of nondurables definitely declined in 1951, responding to the contraction of quantities newly ordered and shipped in the third quarter of 1950 and the first half of 1951 (Chart 3-5). This is unlike the concurrent developments in the durable goods sector, where production, reacting to similar but much larger relative movements of new orders, merely flattened off in 1951. Thus the distributed-lag process, whereby large fluctuations in the receipts of orders are smoothed out in the course of production, is strongly in evidence here for the durables, much less so for the non-durables.

The average leads of deflated new orders at turns in outputs suggest considerable differences among the industries, some of which may be recognized as familiar and reasonable (note, for example, the long leads recorded in Table 4-7 for nonautomotive transportation equipment). It is interesting to observe that the average leads tend to be longer at peaks than at troughs (columns 9 and 10).

In about 80 per cent of the observations listed in Table 4-7, deflated new orders lead output, demonstrating the regularity with which this behavior occurs. More than 90 per cent of the recorded turning points in production and orders can be matched with each other, which indicates that the correlation between the cyclical movements in these series is high indeed.

It remains to compare the timing of turning points in production and shipments in constant prices, on which the series for 1948–58 yielded 69 observations. The results may be summarized without being shown in tabulated form. As suggested by Charts 3-5 and 3-6, output and deflated shipments tend to rise and decline at about the same time. Indeed, nearly 70 per cent of the timing comparisons between these series are rough coincidences, that is, leads or lags of less than three months and exact coincidences (the latter alone account for slightly more than 20 per cent of the observations).

In the model of pure production to order, output should precede shipments, although by very short intervals, as a simple technical matter. In the model of pure production to stock, on the other hand, output could either anticipate or follow shipments, but the latter alternative is more likely because of uncertainty about future demand. The first of these statements is logically compelling, the second is persuasive, and both are already familiar; but it is difficult to demonstrate either of them empirically with the comprehensive series on hand. Nevertheless, it may be worth noting that lags of output relative to deflated shipments are much more frequent than leads for the nondurable goods industries and for the "other durable goods" group, where production to stock dominates (there are 19 lags, 4 leads, and 5 coincidences in this set of comparisons). For the remaining industries that account for most of the durable products manufactured in large part to order, leads of output vis-à-vis real shipments are as numerous as lags (the count here is 15 lags, 15 leads, and 11 coincidences). These differences may not be very sharp, but they do seem broadly reasonable.

Market Categories

Consumer Goods, Equipment, and Materials

The new Census series on new orders and shipments classified by market categories were described in Chapter 3 and are shown in Chart 3-3. Table 4-8 presents the measures of relative timing for these data.

In general, new orders and shipments of consumer goods move closely together and have synchronous timing. For the nondurable "consumer staples," the two series are dominated by trends and follow an identical upward course. No timing comparisons are made here, as there are no major fluctuations and turning points, but Chart 3-3 makes it clear that any deviations between N and S for this category are small and apparently random. The short series for consumer durables (other than automobiles), which begin in 1960, also contribute no observations to Table 4-8. They too show closely similar and coincident movements, consisting of a mild decline during the 1960–61 recession and a marked upward trend thereafter (Chart 3-3). Home goods and apparel, a group including nonautomotive household equipment and some nondurables, does provide several turning-point comparisons which clearly indicate coincident timing of new orders and shipments (Table 4-8).

In contrast, shipments of equipment for industrial and commercial uses fluctuate much less than, and definitely lag behind, new orders. The lags, as measured at the recent turning points, average about five months (fourth line). The longest delivery lags, as well as the largest differences in amplitude between new orders and shipments, are for the defense products: Defense orders lead shipments by 11 to 14 months.

The most variable, or least regular, of the timing relations appears to be that for automotive equipment (fifth line), but Chart 3-3 shows that substantial deviations between N and S have occurred here on only a few occasions in the early part of the period covered, notably in 1953–54. The two series fluctuated widely in the late 1950's but kept

Table 4-8

Timing Relations Between Value of New Orders and Shipments, by Business Cycle Turning Zones, Nine Market Categories, 1954–62

Market Category[a]	Lead (−) or Lag (+) in Months, New Orders at Turns in Shipments in Turning Zone Associated with					Av. Lead (−) or Lag (+) (months)			Av. Dev. from Av. Lead or Lag, All Turns (9)
	1954 Revival: Troughs (1)	1957 Recession: Peaks (2)	1958 Revival: Troughs (3)	1960 Recession: Peaks (4)	1961 Revival: Troughs (5)	Peaks (6)	Troughs (7)	All Turns (8)	
Home goods and apparel	0	0	−1	0	0	0	−0.3	−0.2	0.3
Nonautomotive equipment and defense[b]	−7	−9	−4	−1	−6	−5.0	−5.7	−5.4	2.3
Defense products	−11	−11	−17	−17	−6	−14.0	−11.3	−12.4	3.7
Other	[c]	−3	−2	−7	−7	−5.0	−4.5	−4.8	2.2
Automotive equipment	−10	+4	−5	0	0	−1.6[d]	−5.0[d]	−2.1[d]	3.9[d]
Machinery and equipment[b]	−7	−3	−5	−10	−4	−6.5	−5.3	−5.8	2.2
Materials, supplies, and intermediate products[b]	−10	−3	−3	−3	0	−3.0	−4.3	−3.8	2.5
Construction materials, etc.[b]	−1	0	0	−1	0	−0.5	−0.3	−0.4	0.5
Other materials, etc.[b]	−11	−5	−3	−3	0	−4.0	−4.7	−4.4	2.9

Notes to Table 4-8

^a For composition of these categories, see Chapter 3.

^b For these items, new orders and shipments show mild but distinct declines in 1962, corresponding to the retardation of the general business expansion in that year. The tabulation below show the timing comparisons between the resulting minor turns and the averages including these additional observations:

	Lead (−) or Lag (+) of Orders at 1962 Turning Points		Av. Lead (−) or Lag (+), 1954–62 (incl. 1962 comparisons)			Av. Dev. from Av. Lead, 1954–62,
	Peaks	Troughs	Peaks	Troughs	All Turns	All Turns
Nonautomotive equipment and defense products	0	−2	−3.3	−4.8	−4.1	2.7
Machinery and equipment industries	−4	−4	−5.7	−5.0	−5.3	1.8
Materials, supplies, and intermediate products	−2	−6	−2.7	−4.8	−3.9	2.4
Construction materials	0	0	−0.3	−0.3	−0.3	0.4
Other materials	−2	−4	−3.3	−4.5	−4.0	2.3

^c Timing of new orders is uncertain, but the lead appears to be at least 9 months. If this observation were included, the averages would read −6.0 for troughs and −5.4 (with an average deviation of 2.3) for all turns (compare the entries in columns 7–9 in this line).

^d The averages include two timing comparisons (−5 for troughs and +1 for peaks) in addition to those listed to the left. These observations relate to the extra rises in 1956–57 (see Chart 3-3).

much to the same course; and since 1959 they have followed even more closely similar paths, with simultaneous timing. This type of behavior would be expected in the light of the earlier discussion, since motor vehicles account for the bulk of the output in this market category.

Approximately coincident timing is characteristic of new orders and shipments in the construction materials group, while leads of orders prevail in the group of other materials, where they average about four months. Shipments in the latter category, which includes most of the output of the sensitive metalworking industries that produce typically to order, are about four to five times as large as in the former. Accordingly, the relative timing measures for total materials, supplies, and intermediate products reflect primarily the measures for "other materials, etc." rather than those for construction materials.

Before the official market-category data were first published, in 1963, an attempt was made to construct for this study series on the current value of new orders and shipments for materials, consumer durable goods, and equipment. The idea was simply to group the industries in the detailed OBE classification used in Table A-1 in Appendix A into categories representing primarily the production of the above types of goods. The resulting estimates, which cover 1948–61, are inevitably crude. Nevertheless, the summary measures based on these approximations do not seem altogether unreasonable.[17] In particular, the average timing measures obtained from the old data are broadly consistent with the presumably more reliable evidence of the recent market-category series as reported in Table 4-8 for 1954–62.[18]

Defense Products

While the bulk of orders received by manufacturers comes from the private business sector of the American economy, the amounts placed by the U.S. government and by foreign buyers are large, and their change over time is of much interest. Regrettably, comprehensive series on government and foreign orders have not been compiled for any extended length of time. Only some selected and fragmentary information is available, but it deserves attention.[19]

Special interest centers on military orders, both because of their size and the presumption that they may differ considerably from civilian orders and thus have a particular role as a major "exogenous" factor. Also, this is the only class of government orders on which there exists a significant amount of aggregative data.

The impact of the defense program on the economy results from fiscal measures that are expressed in two sets of data: obligations and ex-

[17] A summary of measures of cyclical conformity, timing, and amplitude for the grouped series and the constructed aggregates was published in *The Uses of Economic Research*, Forty-third Annual Report of the National Bureau of Economic Research, New York, 1963, pp. 66–68.

[18] The class of consumer durables based on the old data includes motor vehicles, which in the new classification are treated separately as part of "automotive equipment." The mean leads here are two months or a little more, which is probably not very different from what would be obtained by combining the new series for consumer durables and motor vehicles (as a rough approximation, consider a weighted aggregate of the items in the first and fifth lines of Table 4-8). Most of the estimates for equipment from the old data suggest an average lead of new orders of about five months, and a very similar timing is indicated by the measures for the new series on nonautomotive equipment other than defense products. For materials, the leads based on the 1948–61 estimates average somewhat less than what is indicated by the new series for 1954–62 in Table 4-8, but the estimates all lie in the relatively narrow range of two to four months.

[19] Data on export orders and shipments are particularly limited, and they refer to a rather special subject. For these reasons, the discussion of the export series is included in Appendix F.

penditures. Obligations measure the value of contract placements and other work undertaken during the given period. Expenditures represent the actual payments made in a given period against obligations made at earlier times. What the Defense Department defines as an "obligation" for hard goods is thus, as a rule, a "new order" to a durable goods manufacturer. On the other hand, "expenditures" on hard goods for defense are part of the payment for shipments from a durable goods manufacturer and are therefore roughly comparable to the value of manufacturers' shipments for the goods.[20]

Chart 4-2 shows two pairs of quarterly, seasonally adjusted series. The two curves in the lower part, covering the period 1950–62, represent Department of Defense obligations and net expenditures for procurement and research, development, and testing and evaluation.[21] The two upper curves trace the course of new orders and shipments for defense products according to the new Census data on "market categories," which begin in 1953.

The movements of expenditures, like those of shipments, are for the most part rather small, smooth, and gradual from quarter to quarter. In contrast, obligations, like new orders, show much greater short-term variability, both of the apparently "systematic" movements and the shorter "irregular" fluctuations. The largest deviations between the matched series occurred during the Korean War: Obligations greatly exceeded expenditures from mid-1950 to mid-1952, then fell precipitously below expenditures through 1953. In this period, the basic movements in the two series were so large and sustained that they agreed in direction most of the time, despite the long lag of expenditures visible at the 1952–53 peaks. At other times, however, when the fluctuations in obligations were shorter, the two series often moved in

---

[20] The foregoing explanation of the obligations and expenditure data is based on the testimony of Charles J. Hitch, Assistant Secretary of Defense, *Hearings on the Economic Report of the President, 1961*, Joint Economic Committee, 87th Cong., 1st sess., Washington, D.C., 1961, p. 616.

[21] The source of the fiscal-year totals for the entire period covered and of the quarterly data since III-1953 is the Department of Defense, *Monthly Report of the Status of Funds*. The figures for the period II-1950–IV-1960 are taken from Hitch, *Hearings*, pp. 667–68 (the data through II-1953 are estimated). The figures for the period since I-1961 are taken directly from the *Monthly Reports*. Seasonal adjustments were made for NBER by the Census electronic computer method.

The categories included are: (1) the purchase of major items of equipment such as aircraft, missiles, ships, tanks, vehicles, artillery, electronics, ammunition, etc.; and (2) the support of research, development of new weapons and equipment, procurement of items under development for evaluation, and the maintenance of laboratories and test facilities. The data cover "hard goods" and exclude "soft goods" such as subsistence, petroleum products, and clothing, and organization equipment and supplies.

Chart 4-2
Defense Products: New Orders and Shipments, 1953–65, and Obligations and Expenditures, 1950–62

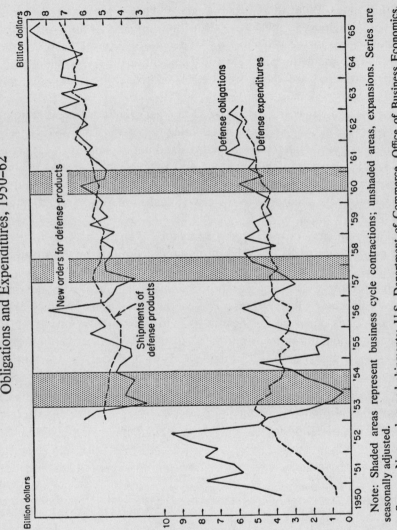

Note: Shaded areas represent business cycle contractions; unshaded areas, expansions. Series are seasonally adjusted.

Source: New orders and shipments: U.S. Department of Commerce, Office of Business Economics. Obligations and expenditures: Department of Defense, Fiscal Analysis Division; seasonal adjustment by NBER.

opposite directions.[22] From 1957–58 on, a substantial stabilization was achieved, with obligations showing the same slow upward trend as expenditures but much larger irregular movements around that trend.

The relationship of new orders for, and shipments of, defense products is similar to that of defense obligations and expenditures, and the trends in the two pairs of series have a broad resemblance over the period of overlap (1953–62). The shorter movements frequently diverge, as might be expected, but even they show at times a fair amount of correspondence.[23]

The Census series of new orders and shipments for defense-oriented products run at considerably higher levels than the Department of Defense series of obligations and expenditures. For example, Census shipments totaled $21.9 billion in 1960, while Defense expenditures totaled $17.9 billion, that is, about 18 per cent less. It seems likely that the Census figures are overstated because they include nondefense purchases of outputs of the industries classified as "defense-oriented" (communication equipment, aircraft and parts, and ordnance).[24]

The contrast between the large fluctuations of defense obligations and orders on the one hand, and the smooth and relatively mild movements of defense expenditures and shipments on the other hand, deserves to be stressed. The Defense Department series suggest that delivery periods for military hardware are on the whole quite long, though they may vary considerably for different items and perhaps also for different periods. (The Korean developments of the early 1950's were associated with a particularly large wave in obligations which could not help but cause severe strains on the industries affected.) Direct timing comparisons for the Census series, though they are few and difficult, certainly indicate that defense shipments lag behind new orders by long intervals (Table 4-7, third line). What the data suggest, then, is what would be expected, namely, that expenditures, like de-

---

[22] The double rise-and-fall sequence in obligations during the period from III-1953 to II-1957 is an example. Expenditures followed a gradual downward course between II-1953 and III-1956 (see Chart 4-2).

[23] Note in particular the similarity between the trough-peak-trough patterns of new orders and obligations in 1955–56–57. As an example of more divergent movements, compare the two series in 1953–55: The sharp peak of obligations in IV-1954 has no counterpart in new orders.

[24] There are other sources of divergence between the two sets of data, some of which would work in the opposite direction, but these are probably much less important. The Defense series of obligations are "gross" in the sense of including some interdepartmental transactions, but the amount of the resulting double counting (which cannot be eliminated) is said to be "relatively modest and fairly constant from year to year" (Hitch, *Hearings*, p. 616).

liveries and installations, follow orders with substantial distributed lags.[25]

By subtracting defense obligations or orders from total new orders of durable goods manufacturers and defense expenditures or shipments from total shipments of these manufacturers, a crude picture can be obtained of the recent changes in the corresponding "civilian" series. It is shown in Chart 4-3.[26]

After expanding vigorously in the first nine months of the Korean War period, business ceased gaining or started contracting in many sectors – primarily those industries whose sales depend in the main on household spending and residential construction. Industries related to defense, however, continued experiencing increases in activity.[27] Our graph shows that the aggregate of new durables orders from civilian buyers declined sharply in 1951, changed little during most of 1952, and recovered decisively only in 1953. In contrast, defense obligations had a strong upward trend in the first two years of the conflict, i.e., through mid-1952 (Chart 4-2). As a consequence, total new orders for durable goods showed considerably more strength in 1952 than did the civilian orders (Chart 4-3), which suggests that defense buying had a substantial stimulative effect in this period.

In the last months of 1952 and through 1953, new purchase commitments for defense declined sharply (Chart 4-2), thereby assuming temporarily the opposite role of a depressant. Manufacturers' new orders turned down in the first quarter of 1953, and shipments turned down in the second (Chart 4-3); one suspects that the cutbacks in military orders contributed significantly to these reversals. However, simple graphical comparisons are not sufficient to analyze such relationships. Since the levels of the defense series are low relative to the corresponding totals for durable manufactures, the civilian components must bulk

[25] It appears plausible that expenditures should be more evenly distributed over time than shipments or deliveries, particularly in the case of contracts concerning large and complex items or "jobs." This point is difficult to test with our fragmentary data. In Chart 4-2, expenditures seem a little more erratic than shipments, but this may be due to differences in aggregation. Expenditures did follow the upward course rather more consistently than shipments in the years 1956–62.

[26] Defense obligations and expenditures were used to compute the civilian series shown in the chart as broken curves for 1950–54; defense orders and shipments were used to compute the civilian series shown as solid curves for 1953–65. For 1953–62, the analysis was carried out in two alternative variants, based on the Defense and on the Census data. The two variables differ in some details but support about the same broad conclusions.

[27] These developments can be inferred from the behavior of the GNP components and other aggregative series. See Bert G. Hickman, *The Korean War and United States Economic Activity, 1950–1952,* Occasional Paper 49, New York, NBER, 1955, pp. 21–23.

Chart 4-3
New Orders and Shipments of Durable Manufactures and Their Estimated "Civilian" Components, Quarterly, 1950–65

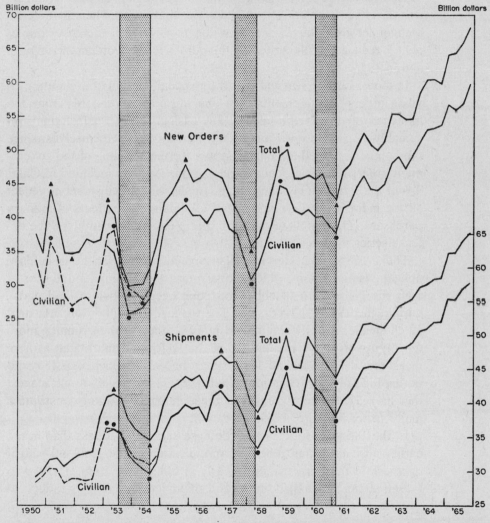

Note: Shaded areas represent business cycle contractions; unshaded areas, expansions. Dots identify peaks and troughs of specific cycles in the civilian series; black triangles, in the totals. Series are seasonally adjusted.

Source: Total new orders and shipments: Bureau of the Census. Civilian new orders and shipments: estimates based on Commerce and Defense Department data.

large in the totals; hence, these totals must be closely correlated with their civilian components. The general impression conveyed by Chart 4-3 is indeed that of a parallelism between the total and the civilian series for either variable. The paired series draw apart when the defense component grows larger and draw together when the defense component is reduced, as illustrated by the curves for new orders in 1951–52 and in 1953.

It should also be realized that the residual method of computing civilian orders and shipments is in one sense apt to underestimate the influence of defense purchases. Increasing defense obligations presumably give rise to new orders by the contractors themselves, since the contractors need to acquire inputs for the handling of the government orders. Durable goods orders of this kind are included in Chart 4-3 in the series on civilian orders. In short, the civilian series reflect all the indirect (positive and negative) "multiplier" effects of military purchases. They exclude only the direct effects measured by the defense series themselves.

The 1957–58 recession was also preceded by a decline in defense obligations and orders, which, however, was much milder and shorter than the contraction in obligations that occurred before (and partly during) the 1953–54 recession. The defense cutbacks were not only much smaller than those initiated in 1952, they were also much more quickly reversed.[28] Expenditures of the Defense Department, as here measured, did not decline significantly in 1957–58, whereas they did during the previous recession (Chart 4-3). These observations suggest that in 1957, unlike 1953, the defense cutbacks did not constitute a major factor in the recession.

In the 1958–60–61 cycle the defense series varied less than in the earlier postwar cycles. There is an indication of the 1959–60 budget tightness in these series, particularly in obligations from III-1959 to I-1960 after which expenditures and shipments rose fairly steadily and

[28] Defense obligations were allowed to fall to a nadir of $0.6 billion in IV-1953 and they were still low, though definitely gaining, in the first half of 1954 (Chart 4-2). As concern grew over the continuing recession, the government decided, in May, to allocate a larger portion of the funds budgeted for fiscal 1955 to the next few months (see Wilfred Lewis, Jr., *Federal Fiscal Policy in the Postwar Recessions*, Washington, D.C., Brookings Institution, 1962, pp. 165–87). The defense programs, particularly obligations, accounted for the great bulk of this intrafiscal shift. Most of the increase in the first half of the fiscal year appears to have been offset by reductions in the second half (compare Chart 4-2 for about 1954–55). In 1958, efforts to speed up government spending were again made, but this time defense procurement was to be excluded from that policy.

obligations and orders increased at a similar over-all pace, with some occasional spurts and falls. A large increase in military new orders and stepped-up deliveries began late in 1964 and continued in 1965–68, reflecting the steady intensification and painful persistence of the war in Vietnam (Chart 3-2). At the end of 1968, new orders of defense product industries reached an annual rate of $50 billion, and Depart-ment of Defense gross obligations incurred for procurement alone rose to a rate of $27 billion. Afterward, orders and obligations began to de-cline slowly from these peak levels, while shipments and expenditures were still a little lower than orders and still creeping upward. Finally, late in 1969, defense expenditures did turn gradually downward, but new orders and obligations gained again. In this period of war and in-flation, as in others before, there is little doubt about the inflationary effects of huge increases in military outlays (not offset by reduction in civilian demand).

In conclusion, new orders for defense products undergo large irreg-ular variations, which can be and sometimes are an important source of economic instability. But these movements have sometimes been stabilizing, too, and they are always strongly smoothed in the produc-tion process as well as in expenditures.

Summary

New orders systematically lead shipments of those individual indus-tries or products that represent goods manufactured primarily to order. Leads of N relative to S also prevail in the timing observations for a sample of goods made largely to stock, but they are both shorter and less regular. Similar distinctions can be made among the lags of output behind new orders in physical terms.

According to the postwar aggregate value data, the leads of new or-ders at turns in shipments are substantially larger for the durable goods sector of manufacturing than for the nondurables one: The respective average leads are about five months and two months or less. In general, the results conform to expectations in that the lags of shipments are longest for heavy, made-to-order equipment and the shortest for stand-ardized items.

Except for the particular episode of long lags of shipments at the upturns associated with the business revival of 1954, new orders have typically preceded deliveries by longer intervals at peaks than at troughs. This would be expected, since the capacity position of many firms is presumably strained at the top levels of aggregate output. The data also suggest that the delivery lags became on the whole shorter in the late fifties and early sixties as compared with their average duration in the earlier postwar years. This is attributed to both the relative easing of demand pressures and the completion of large build-ups of manufacturing capacity in the period between the end of the Korean War and the escalation of the war in Vietnam.

Production indexes for durable goods have lagged behind deflated new orders by substantial intervals, especially at peaks. Importantly, significant (although much shorter) lags of output are also observed for nondurable goods. Autoregressive sales forecasts based on recent order figures could help account for such lags in production to stock. The timing of production relative to shipments in constant prices is on the average roughly coincident for the comprehensive aggregates, with some tendency to lag in the stock-oriented nondurable goods industries.

Comparisons for the new market-category series show approximately coincident timing of N and S for consumer goods and construction materials. Shipments of metal products and equipment for commercial and industrial uses lagged by some 4 or 5 months, on the average. The longest delivery lags, of 11–14 months, are observed for the defense products.

5

REGRESSION ANALYSIS

IN WHAT FOLLOWS, regression models are first employed to answer these questions: How close are the relations between shipments and orders received currently and in the past? What lags characterize these relations? How sensitive are the results to differences in the methods used? The analysis proceeds from simple correlations for varying lags through multiple regressions with several lagged terms, to assumed forms of lag structure such as geometric and second-order distributions; a two-stage procedure using a linear combination of past orders as an "instrumental variable" is also applied. The lag estimates thus obtained are then compared with each other and with the results of the timing comparisons at turning points.

In the second part of the chapter, predictive equations are examined that use only past values of new orders, not the values concurrent with shipments. Here a model is estimated in which the lag coefficients of ·new orders are made to depend on the ratios of unfilled orders to shipments, so that when these ratios increase, indicating a rise in the rates of capacity utilization, the influence of recent orders decreases relative to that of orders of the more distant past. The performance of this model is compared with the results of regressions with fixed lag coefficients applied to the same series on shipments and new orders. This section also presents some estimates based on transformed variables that take account of observed autocorrelations in the residuals from a few selected distributed-lag equations.

The regressions are fitted to both monthly and quarterly data, seasonally adjusted, for total manufacturing, its durable and nondurable goods sectors, and seven major durable goods industries. The periods covered are 1947–65 for the sectoral aggregates and 1953–65 for the major-industry series. These are all the published data classified by industry groups that were available for such computations from the current statistics of the Bureau of the Census. Earlier, some rather fragmentary work with distributed-lag regressions was done on the pre-1963 major-industry series of new orders and shipments compiled by the Office of Business Economics (see Appendix G on the results of this exploration).

Because of aggregation problems, the variability of the lags, and the importance of production to stock, net new orders received by an industry must inevitably leave much to be desired as predictors of the industry's shipments. Nevertheless, new orders presumably provide the best available tool for prediction of shipments or sales in a large area of manufacturing.

The analysis does not cover regressions in which production rather than shipments appears as the dependent variable. While the values or volumes of production and shipments are highly correlated for industries working to order, the relations for production are interesting in their own right. Such relations, involving changes in output and in orders received or on hand, would provide tools for a study of short-term production scheduling. They receive some attention in Chapter 6.

Estimates of Average Distributed-Lag Relations Between New Orders and Shipments of Major Manufacturing Industries

Simple Correlations for Varying Lags

As the first step in analyzing the relations between new orders (N) and shipments (S) by means of regression and correlation measures, simple correlations between seasonally adjusted values of N_t and S_{t+i} were examined for different values of the lag i. The lags of shipments (= leads of new orders) are assumed to vary from zero to six months in this analysis. This range is in a broad sense consistent with the results of our earlier comparisons of turning-point dates in the aggregate current-value series for N and S (Chapter 4).[1]

The decision to use seasonally adjusted data in this regression analysis is motivated by our general intention to concentrate on nonseasonal and particularly on cyclical movements and the underlying relations.

---

[1] These comparisons occasionally yield long leads of orders, of nine to twelve months, or even more; but most of the leads are much shorter, and the postwar averages for all manufacturing and the total durable goods and nondurable goods sectors are −3.1, −5.1, and −2.0 months, respectively (see Table 4-7, column 9).

But the procedure could lead to considerable errors if the seasonal adjustments involved were seriously deficient and especially if a consistent seasonal pattern existed in the discrepancies between new orders and shipments. According to our tests, however, this is not the case. Regressions based on seasonally unadjusted data are not greatly improved when dummy variables are added to represent the seasonal components of the relations between N and S; the coefficients of these dummy terms are, for the most part, small relative to their standard errors. The results of these regressions are similar to those obtained by using the seasonally adjusted series for N and S (see below, p. 184).

For total manufacturing and total nondurables, simultaneous timing of new orders and shipments yields the highest correlation coefficient (r). The correlations decline steadily but very slowly as shipments are lagged by increasing intervals of from one to six months. This is summarized in Table 5-1, which gives the highest and lowest r coefficients and identifies the lags of shipments that are associated with these correlations (see columns 1–3, which relate to monthly series). For example, for all manufacturing, r varies merely from .984 (for $i = 0$) to .974 (for $i = 6$).

For the total durable goods sector, the coefficients first increase and then decrease steadily, reaching the highest value at $i = 2$ and the lowest at $i = 6$, but again differing little. Although very high, these correlations are lower than those for total nondurables and also somewhat below those for all manufacturing. This would be expected, since N_t and S_t are assumed to be equal for the greater part of the nondurable goods sector which consists of industries that do not report unfilled orders. Thus N_t and S_t have here a large common component, which biases their correlation toward unity.

This source of bias is removed when only the industries reporting unfilled orders are included in the all-manufacturing and all-nondurables aggregates. Such "advance orders" series can be computed from the currently available Census data for the period since 1953, and the correlations based on these estimates are summarized in Table 5-1. They are, of course, always lower than the correlations for the series that include the nondurable "shelf-goods" industries.[2]

---

[2] For comparability, calculations, limited to the 1953–65 period, were also made for the more comprehensive aggregates. These yield correlations that differ very little from the corresponding statistics for 1947–65 listed on the first six lines of Table 5-1. Thus, for all manufacturing, 1953–65, r^2 varies from .965 to .928 as i increases from 0 to 6 months; for total nondurables, the coefficient r^2 descends similarly from .998 to .980.

Table 5-1

Highest and Lowest Simple Correlations Between New Orders and Coincident or Lagged Shipments, Monthly and Quarterly, Major Manufacturing Industries, 1947–65 and 1953–65

Industry	Correlations of Monthly Series [a]			Correlations of Quarterly Series [a]		
	Lag of Shipments Behind New Orders [b] (months) (1)	Corr. Coeff. [c] (2)	Adj. Determination Coeff. [d] (3)	Lag of Shipments Behind New Orders [e] (quarters) (4)	Corr. Coeff. [f] (5)	Adj. Determination Coeff. [d] (6)
			1947–65 [g]			
All manufacturing	0	.984	.968	0	.986	.972
	6	.974	.948	2	.978	.957
Durable goods	2	.959	.919	0	.961	.923
	6	.946	.894	2	.955	.911
Nondurable goods	0	.998	.997	0	.999	.998
	6	.988	.976	2	.991	.980
			1953–65 [h]			
Reporting unfilled orders						
All industries [i]	2	.968	.937	1	.977	.954
	6	.937	.877	2	.952	.905
Nondurables industries [j]	0	.990	.981	1	.996	.991
	6	.980	.960	2	.989	.977

Primary metals	1	.812	.656	0	.809	.648
	6	.571	.322	2	.622	.426
Blast furnaces, steel mills	1	.675	.451	1	.753	.559
	6	.362	.125	2	.466	.201
Fabricated metal prod.	0	.929	.862	0	.960	.921
	5	.906	.820	2	.954	.909
Machinery exc. elect.	3	.969	.938	1	.977	.954
	0	.960	.920	0	.964	.929
Elect. machinery	0	.962	.924	0	.976	.951
	6	.927	.859	2	.948	.897
Transport. equip.	0	.865	.746	0	.925	.852
	6	.772	.593	2	.849	.715
Other durable goods[k]	0	.982	.964	0	.990	.981
	6	.932	.866	2	.952	.905

[a] For each industry, entry on first line is for the highest of the correlations, entry on second line is for the lowest.

[b] Zeros identify correlations between monthly values of new orders and shipments taken in the same month.

[c] Highest and lowest simple correlation coefficients observed when the lag of shipments behind new orders is varied from zero to six months.

[d] Adjusted for numbers of observations and constants according to the formula $r^2 = 1 - (1 - r^2)[(n - 1)/(n - m)]$, where n is the number of observations (see notes g and h) and m is the number of the parameter estimates in the equation (here, 2).

[e] Zeros identify correlations between values of new orders and shipments taken in the same quarter.

[f] Highest and lowest simple correlation coefficients observed when the lag of shipments behind new orders is varied from zero to two quarters.

[g] Effective sample size is 222 monthly observations (columns 1 and 2) and 74 quarterly observations (columns 3 and 4).

[h] Effective sample size is 150 monthly observations (columns 1 and 2) and 50 quarterly observations (columns 3 and 4).

[i] Includes all durable goods industries and the four nondurable goods industries reporting unfilled orders (see note j).

[j] Includes textiles, leather, paper, and printing and publishing.

[k] Includes professional and scientific instruments; lumber; furniture; stone, clay, and glass products; and miscellaneous industries.

179

Among the major components of the durable goods sector, nonelectrical machinery ranks first according to the average correlations between N and S (proceeding from the largest to the smallest). Here r increases steadily from .960 to .969 as i rises from 0 to 3, then decreases steadily to .963 as i is extended further to six months. For electrical machinery, the correlations are just slightly lower, but they decline from the beginning, i.e., r is largest at $i = 0$, and it gets smaller as the length of the lag increases. Similar patterns of declining r prevail also in fabricated metal products, the group of other durable goods, and transportation equipment including motor vehicles (where the range of the r values is relatively large). The lowest correlations and the largest differences among them are found in total primary metals and, particularly, in the blast furnaces and steel mills subdivision (Table 5-1).

The monthly regressions are affected, probably often strongly, by random effects, such as strikes, which would have their main impact upon both N and S at about the same time. This tends to produce a correlation between N_t and S_t even if no orders were filled in the same month as received.[3] It is not clear how this source of simultaneity bias could be removed; it is present in all the lagged regression models to be analyzed, but presumably in different degrees. Some models imply less emphasis upon the very short movements in the series than do other models, and more emphasis upon the longer movements; and the above argument gives a reason for preferring the models that do so.

It should be noted that the primary metals series are particularly vulnerable to strike-related disturbances. While approximately simultaneous, the reactions of N and S to such events often differ substantially in intensity. During the large steel strikes, shipments of primary metals dropped off suddenly and drastically, then recovered just as rapidly, while new orders showed much smaller dips that were occasionally, as in 1956, within the range of their usual month-to-month variations (see Chart 3-2, lines 1 and 2).

The smallness of the differences between the correlation coefficients that result from varying the lags i suggests that the series involved are highly autocorrelated. If S_t is almost as closely associated with N_{t-1} as with N_t, for example, then N_t and N_{t-1} are probably also closely correlated with each other. That this should be so is not surprising since, on this level of aggregation, expansions and contractions of new

[3] I am indebted to Geoffrey Moore for suggesting this point.

orders are cumulative movements, and shipments must reproduce or follow these movements in smoother form. As noted in Chapter 2, there are several reasons why the lags of shipments behind new orders are presumably distributed and variable rather than discrete and constant. In sum, the measures given in Table 5-1 portend major difficulties in properly identifying the structure of these lags. Where relations with several different lags are all very close, discrimination among various combinations of the lags is likely to be a troublesome problem.

Working with quarterly rather than monthly data may help to reduce these problems. First, there are then fewer possible specifications of the lag structure. Second, autocorrelation is often greater as the successive values of the series move closer together in time. Finally, it is likely that the erratic or "random noise" component will be smaller in the quarterly than in the monthly series.

Simple correlations between quarterly (seasonally adjusted) series on new orders and shipments were compared for (1) simultaneous timing of N and S; (2) a one-quarter lag of S; and (3) a two-quarter lag of S. For most of the industries, the highest correlations are obtained under timing assumption (1) and the lowest under (3): that is, the coefficients r decline as the lags in quarters increase (Table 5-1, columns 4–6). In some cases—the groups of industries reporting unfilled orders, and blast furnaces and nonelectrical machinery—the timing relationship that maximizes correlation is the one-quarter lag of shipments rather than simultaneity.[4] However, the differences between the correlations for varying lags tend to be quite small, just as for the monthly data. The largest differences are again those for the primary metals industry and its blast furnaces division.

The number of quarterly observations for any industry is, of course, only one-third of that of monthly observations. Table 5-1 presents, for both sets of series, coefficients of determination adjusted for numbers of observations and constants in the estimating equations, $\bar{r}^2$ (columns 3 and 6). Comparisons of these statistics suggest that the quarterly correlations are somewhat closer than the monthly ones for similar lags (that is, when coincident timing is used in both cases, or lags of three months and one quarter, or lags of six months and two quarters). Reflecting this rule, the coefficients in column 6 of the table all exceed their counterparts in column 3.

[4] Indeed, for nonelectrical machinery (Table 5-1, "machinery, except electrical"), coincident timing produces a lower correlation than either of the alternative assumptions about the delivery lag.

Multiple Regressions with Several Lagged Terms

Shipments in any unit period (month or quarter) conclude the process of filling orders received either in the same or in some previous period. Assume that a firm gets new orders for its xth product in each month and always produces and delivers exactly one-half of the number of units ordered in the same month (t), three-tenths in the next month ($t + 1$), and two-tenths in the following month ($t + 2$). The relation between new orders and shipments for X would then be expressed by an exact functional form:

$$s_t = 0.5n_t + 0.3n_{t-1} + 0.2n_{t-2}, \tag{1}$$

using the notation introduced in Chapter 2. Referring to equation (1) there, $\alpha_0 = 0.5$, $\alpha_1 = 0.3$, and $\alpha_2 = 0.2$; in this case then, $\Sigma\alpha_i = 1$, where the summation is over $i = 0$, 1, 2. The "relevant past" here includes only the two previous months. The lag is distributed, not discrete, but its structure is given and constant.

It is clear that this hypothetical case does not represent the way in which orders are actually translated into output and shipments. If it did, the time path of output and shipments would be completely determined by, and hence perfectly predictable from, the recent course of new orders. In the real world, except in the trivial case where new orders and shipments coincide so as to be for all practical purposes identical, the relations between these variables are not exact but stochastic. The coefficients α_i are not fixed but changing, and they are as a rule unknown. The changes in them may (though need not) be themselves partly systematic. Some of the reasons why this should be so have already been discussed.

Nevertheless, the unrealistic case exemplified by (1) above has some instructive aspects. It incorporates the valid concept of a basic distributed-lag relationship between shipments and new orders: in any reasonably defined (not excessively long) time period, the former may be taken to be a weighted sum of the past (and perhaps current) values of the latter. Since *all* of new orders received in any period must sooner or later result in output and shipments, except for cancellations, it is likewise true that *all* shipments made in any period must be traceable to orders that had at some time been accepted. In other words, the coefficients in an equation relating observed S_t to the terms N_{t-i} ($i = 0$, 1, . . . , m) should add up to unity, given that new orders are taken net of cancellations and for all relevant past periods up to the present.

Multiple regressions with S_t as the dependent variable and several terms N_{t-i} as the independent variables offer the most direct method of exploring these relationships. This approach, however, faces a major difficulty if the new-order series are highly autocorrelated. Close correlation among independent variables may preclude a reliable estimation of their separate influences upon the dependent variable.[5] For example, if N_t and N_{t-1} are highly correlated, then their joint use in a regression equation designed to "explain" S_t would result in very large standard errors of their regression coefficients. This so-called multicollinearity problem is, of course, quite familiar in relations among economic time series.

We proceed with the following experiment using monthly series: Regress S_t first on N_t and N_{t-1}, next on these two terms plus N_{t-2}, and so on, until seven terms are included (N_{t-i}; $i = 0, \ldots, 6$). This results, for each industry, in six successive least-square estimates of shipments, which have the form $(S_{jt})_{est} = a_j + \Sigma b_{ij} N_{t-1} = S_t - u_{jt}$, where the summation is from $i = 0$ to j ($j = 1, \ldots, 6$). The addition of another term typically reduces the regression coefficient of the preceding term but increases the sum of the coefficients (Σb_{ij}), as shown, for example, by the estimates for the total durable goods sector in the accompanying table.

$(S_{jt})_{est}$	Constant	N_t	N_{t-1}	N_{t-2}	N_{t-3}	N_{t-4}	N_{t-5}	N_{t-6}	Σb_{ij}	$\bar{R}^2$
				Regression Coefficients of						
$j = 1$	.738	.432	.513						.936	.923
	(.262)	(.090)	(.090)							
$j = 2$	.657	.341	.159	.445					.944	.931
	(.249)	(.086)	(.110)	(.087)						
$j = 3$	.614	.292	.137	.193	.328				.950	.936
	(.241)	(.085)	(.106)	(.107)	(.085)					
$j = 4$	.561	.349	.047	.170	.086	.304			.956	.939
	(.235)	(.084)	(.107)	(.104)	(.107)	(.084)				
$j = 5$	.520	.327	.117	.085	.070	.067	.291		.958	.942
	(.230)	(.082)	(.106)	(.104)	(.104)	(.106)	(.082)			
$j = 6$	.470	.350	.082	.153	−.020	.056	.055	.290	.966	.945
	(.224)	(.080)	(.104)	(.103)	(.104)	(.103)	(.104)	(.081)		

[5] This is a matter of degree. It is immediately clear that in the extreme case of perfect correlation between any two explanatory variables either one of them could be used just as well as the other, and there would be no reason to use both. In the much more likely case of high but not perfect correlation, the estimated parameters may or may not have an unsatisfactorily low level of accuracy.

In this case, the terms that definitely retain significance, as indicated by the size of their coefficients relative to the corresponding standard errors (which are given in parentheses), are the first and the last of the independent variables in each equation, that is N_t and N_{t-j}. Apparently because of the autocorrelation of new orders, the effects on S_t of the intermediate terms cannot be neatly separated but are largely absorbed in the coefficients b_{ij} and b_{jj} of each jth equation ($j = 1, \ldots, 6$). The last coefficient may also include the influence of the omitted terms with lags greater than j. These results are consistent with the plausible condition that the correlation between N_t and N_{t-i} weakens as i increases.

The sum of the regression coefficients, already high in the first equation with two terms only, increases by small steps but steadily as the number of the N_{t-i} variables is increased. The constant terms a_j decline greatly, in absolute size and relative to their standard errors, but even in the last equation ($j = 6$), a_j is still more than twice as large as its error and hence probably significant.[6] The ratio of a_6 to the average level of new orders in the sample period is $0.470/13.705 = 0.0343$, which, when added to 0.9659, totals approximately 1.000.

Although some of the N_{t-i} terms have coefficients that appear to lack statistical significance, the determination coefficients adjusted for the number of degrees of freedom increase steadily as the variables representing longer lags are added. There seems to be no plausible reason why the degree of intercorrelation among the explanatory variables should have any systematic or biasing effects on the estimates of the over-all multiple correlation.[7]

When seasonally unadjusted data (denoted by the superscript u) are used, the following estimate is obtained with three new-order terms:

$$(S_{2t}^u)_{est} = .919 + .593N_t^u + .033N_{t-1}^u + .301N_{t-2}^u; \ \Sigma b_i = .926; \ \bar{R}^2 = .938$$
$$\phantom{(S_{2t}^u)_{est} = .919 + }(.060) \quad\ (.071) \quad\quad\ (.060)$$

where the summation of the b's is over $i = 0, 1, 2$. This equation may be compared with that for $(S_{2t})_{est}$ in seasonally adjusted values (see data, p. 183, above). Some similarities will be noted; e.g., in each case, the coefficient of the second N term (for $t - 1$) is not significant. The

---

[6] With as many as 222 observations, the ratio $t = 0.4696/0.2240 = 2.096$ would be exceeded by chance only about once in thirty trials (3–4 per cent significance level).

[7] J. Johnston, *Econometric Methods*, New York, 1963, pp. 204–206. A related point is that "if forecasting is a primary objective, then intercorrelation of explanatory variables may not be too serious, provided it may reasonably be expected to continue in the future" (*ibid.*, p. 207).

sum of the b coefficients is here somewhat lower, the value of $\bar{R}^2$ slightly higher. When eleven monthly dummy variables (D_k) are included along with the N^u_{t-2} terms, $\bar{R}^2$ is raised just a little. The coefficients (d_k) of five of the eleven dummy terms are lower than their standard errors, and two of the others are of doubtful significance. It is well to observe that the results of the regression with the dummy seasonals (with the summation of dD taken over $k = 1, 2, 3, \ldots, 11$; and of b over $i = 0, 1, 2$)

$$(S^{ud}_{2t})_{\text{est}} = .916 + .398N^u_t + .142N^u_{t-1} + .384N^u_{t-2} + \Sigma d_k D_k;$$

$$\Sigma b_i = .909; \quad \bar{R}^2 = .946$$

are quite similar to those reported for the seasonally adjusted data in the table above. These tests suggest that working with series corrected for seasonal variations gives satisfactory results, at least for our present purposes.

Applications to Monthly Series

The results of fitting the six estimating equations to the monthly Census data for each of the major manufacturing industries are summarized in Table 5-2. The sums of the regression coefficients, Σb_{ij}, taken from $i = 0$ to j, typically continue to increase with i until all seven terms N_{t-i} $(i = 0, \ldots, 6)$ are included. That is, the lowest of these estimates is for $j = 1$ and the highest for $j = 6$ (column 1). These cumulative increases are interrupted only in a few isolated instances as all but four of the coefficients in the range considered are positive (see column 2 and note i). The corresponding $\bar{R}^2$ coefficients similarly increase in this range, with two exceptions (see column 3 and note l).

The outcome for all manufacturing (1947–65) is much like that for the durable goods sector: again, the most significant terms are N_t and N_{t-j}, where j denotes the largest lag, associated with the last term in each of the six equations (column 4). The Σb and $\bar{R}^2$ estimates are somewhat higher. The fits for the nondurable goods sector are, to be sure, still closer; the constant terms are not significant here, and the shorter lag terms are dominant (column 4). The totals in column 2, the sums of the b's, approximate unity for all manufacturing and total nondurables and are only slightly smaller for total durables (first six lines of Table 5-2).

Table 5-2

Relations Between Shipments and New Orders Received in the Current Month and in Each of Six Preceding Months, Multiple Correlation and Regression Measures, Major Manufacturing Industries, 1947–65 and 1953–65

Industry	Range of Estimates[a]			Regression[c] That Maximizes $\bar{R}^2$							
				Most Significant Lags[b]	Constant Term[d]	i	Regression Coefficients[e]				Av. Lag[f] (mos.)
	j	Sum of b's	$\bar{R}^2$				Largest	Second Largest	Third Largest	Sum of Three Largest	
	(1)	(2)	(3)	(4)	(5)	(6)	(7)	(8)	(9)	(10)	(11)
					1947–65 (222)[g]						
All manufacturing	1	0.976	.973	0,j	0.262 (0.255)	0, 6, 2	.438 (.069)	.245 (.070)	.125 (.094)	.809	2.3
	6	0.996	.981								
Durable goods	1	0.936	.923	0,j	0.470 (0.224)	0, 6, 2	.350 (.080)	.290 (.081)	.153 (.103)	.792	2.6
	6	0.966[h]	.945								
Nondurable goods	1	0.996	.9976	0, 1, 3	0.039 (0.039)	0, 1, 3	.635 (.029)	.148 (.038)	.111 (.038)	.894	1.0
	6	1.002	.9982								
					1953–65 (150)[g]						
Reporting unfilled orders All industries[i]	1	0.839	.941	0,j	3.146 (0.317)	0, 6, 1	.311 (.073)	.192 (.075)	.129 (.093)	.631	2.0
	6	0.886[h]	.959								

Industry										
Nondurables industries[j]	1	0.983	.985	0, 3, 5, j	0.075 (0.038)	0, 3, 5	.402 (.044)	.167 (.052)	.142 (.052)	.711	2.3
	6	1.022	.992								
Primary metals	1	0.660	.657	1, j	0.784 (0.107)	3, 1, 0	.268 (.080)	.258 (.111)	.117 (.079)	.643	1.45[l]
	3, 6[k]	0.747	.712								
Blast furnaces, steel mills	1	0.555	.451	1, 3	0.571 (0.083)	3, 1, 0	.258 (.084)	.243 (.114)	.096 (.084)	.597	1.21[l]
	3, 6[k]	0.660	.515								
Fabricated metal products	1	0.797	.902	0, 1, 2, j	0.274 (0.029)	0, 6, 1	.251 (.044)	.204 (.044)	.140 (.046)	.594	2.0
	6	0.846	.941								
Machinery exc. elect.	1	0.812	.934	0, j	0.292 (0.031)	6, 0, 1	.270 (.068)	.167 (.071)	.141 (.083)	.578	2.9
	6	0.876	.963								
Elect. machinery	1	0.834	.943	0, 1, j	0.249 (0.030)	0, 1, 6	.297 (.050)	.158 (.056)	.128 (.050)	.582	1.9
	6	0.882	.961								
Transport. equip.	1	0.683	.800	0, 1, j	1.024 (0.117)	0, 1, 6	.256 (.048)	.148 (.052)	.111 (.049)	.516	1.65
	6	0.765	.839								
Other durable goods[m]	1	0.941	.970	1, 2, j	0.078 (0.037)	0, 2, 6	.503 (.047)	.127 (.054)	.111 (.047)	.741	1.69
	6	0.982	.981								

Notes to Table 5-2

[a] The form of the estimating equation is

$$S_t = a_j + \Sigma_{i=0}^{j} b_{ij} N_{t-1} + u_{jt}.$$

The index j identifies the number of terms of N_{t-i} $(i = 0, \ldots, j)$ included in the given regression. The number varies from two $(i = 0, 1)$ to seven $(i = 0, \ldots, 6)$. See text.

The values of j in column 1 refer to the equations with the lowest (first line of entries for the industry) and highest (second line) estimated sums of regression coefficients $(\Sigma_{i=0}^{j} b_{ij})$ shown in column 2, and adjusted coefficients of multiple determination $(\bar{R}^2)$, in column 3.

[b] Identifies the time subscripts i of those terms of N_{t-i} $(i = 0, \ldots, 6)$ with t ratios of substantial statistical significance (generally, t ratios of 2.0 and more, values which always exceed those at the 0.05 probability level and often exceed the 0.01 level).

[c] Selected for each industry from the six estimating equations $(S_{jt})_{est} = a_j + \Sigma_{i=0}^{j} b_{ij} N_{t-i}$ obtained by varying j from 1 to 6 (see columns 1-4 and notes above). For all but two industries, these regressions include all seven terms N_{t-i} $(i = 0, 1, \ldots, 6)$, that is, $j = 6$. For primary metals and blast furnaces, etc., the highest $\bar{R}^2$ is observed when four terms of N_{t-i} $(i = 0, \ldots, 3)$ are used as independent variables, that is, $j = 3$. The values of j that maximize $\bar{R}^2$ are listed in column 1; the corresponding values of $\bar{R}^2$, in column 3.

[d] The standard error of the constant term (a_j) is given underneath in parentheses.

[e] In each regression, there are $j + 1$ regression coefficients b_i $(i = 0, 1, \ldots, j)$. Column 6 identifies the subscripts of i of the largest, second largest, and third largest of the regression coefficients, in that order. The values of these coefficients are given in columns 7, 8, and 9; their standard errors are given underneath in parentheses. Column 10 shows the sums of the three largest coefficients (i.e., the totals of the corresponding entries in columns 7-9, except for slight differences due to rounding of these entries). These sums may be compared with the second line of entries for each industry in column 2 (see text).

[f] Computed by multiplying the lags i by the corresponding regression coefficients b_i and adding the product. Based on regressions of S_t on N_{t-i} $(i = 0, 1, \ldots, 6)$. See text and note 7.

[g] The number of monthly observations, given in parentheses, represents the effective sample size for each of the industries covered in the section that follows.

[h] Includes one coefficient with negative sign.

[i] Includes all durable goods industries and the four nondurable goods industries reporting unfilled orders (see note j).

[j] Includes textiles, leather, paper, and printing and publishing.

[k] The first of the j values identifies the equation with the highest observed $\bar{R}^2$; the second, the equation with the largest observed $\Sigma_{i=0}^{j} b_i$. (Elsewhere, only one entry for j is given, indicating that the same equation produces the minimum or maximum observed values of both Σb_i and $\bar{R}^2$.)

[l] Based on equations with $j = 6$ (see preceding footnote). The estimated average lags for $j = 3$ are 1.23 for total primary metals and 1.13 months for blast furnaces.

[m] Includes professional and scientific instruments; lumber; furniture; stone, clay, and glass products; and miscellaneous industries.

For the nondurable goods industries reporting unfilled orders (1953–65), the regression coefficients also add up to about 1.000, and $\bar{R}^2$ is very high, but for all industries reporting, the results are less satisfactory. Substantial differences among the major durable goods industries are indicated. Thus the $\Sigma_i^6 b_i$ estimates fall in the ranges 0.84–0.88 (fabricated metals, machinery) and 0.74–0.80 (transportation equipment and total primary metals; for the blast furnaces component of the latter, however, the total is as low as 0.66). In contrast, the corresponding sum for the other durables group comes close to unity (column 2).

In total primary metals and in its blast furnaces and steel mills division, lags of three months and (less so) of one and two months seem to be primarily important; the partial effects of current new orders (N_t) are smaller here than for the other industries, but the influence of new orders received four to six months ago is also smaller (column 4). In fact, the highest $\bar{R}^2$ is observed for these industries when four terms $(N_{t-i}, i = 0, \ldots, 3)$ are used as independent variables,[8] whereas in all other cases seven terms $(i = 0, \ldots, 6)$ are needed to produce this result. Only about 52 per cent of the variance of shipments can be explained in this way for blast furnaces, etc., and 71 per cent for total primary metals. Elsewhere in the durable goods sector, the $\bar{R}^2$ coefficients all exceed .80, and are as high as .94 to .98 for fabricated metals, the two machinery-producing industries, and the residual group of "other durable goods" (column 3).

New orders received currently and in the last month or two are most significant for fabricated metal products and also for electrical machinery and total transportation equipment (dominated by motor vehicles), though the last terms N_{t-j} tend to be important, too. For non-electrical machinery, the long lags are of principal significance, in particular N_{t-6} in the last equation, which yields the highest $\bar{R}^2$. In the equations for the "other durable goods," the coefficients of N_t are particularly large, exceeding somewhat the coefficients of all earlier terms N_{t-i} $(i = 1, 2, \ldots, 6)$ combined. This presumably reflects the large importance of production to stock in this group.

The three largest regression coefficients in each of the equations that yield the highest observed $\bar{R}^2$ are identified in columns 6–9 of the table.

---

[8] The addition of N_{t-4}, N_{t-5}, and N_{t-6} makes $\bar{R}^2$ decline gradually from .7119 to .7089 for total primary metals and from .5153 to .5067 for the blast furnaces component.

Their sums represent from about 66 to 96 per cent of $\Sigma_{i=0}^{6}b_i$ (compare the figures in column 10 with the corresponding entries in column 2).

Average lags of S_t behind the terms N_{t-i} can be computed as weighted sums of the lags i, with the corresponding regression coefficients b_i being used as the weights.[9] Since the coefficients are generally positive, the resulting measures tend to increase as additional new orders terms are included. The estimates in column 11 of the table are based on the equations which contain all seven terms N_{t-i}, $i = 0, 1, \ldots, 6$. They seem to be both implausibly small when compared with other evidence and not sufficiently discriminating among the industries: They differ considerably less than those average delivery-lag estimates that are derived either from turning-point comparisons or from regressions that do not arbitrarily limit the number of the N_{t-i} terms.[10]

The values of the Durbin-Watson test statistic, $d = \Sigma(u_t - u_{t-1})/\Sigma u_t^2$, are generally very low for the residuals u from the regressions summarized in Table 5-2: None exceeds 1.3, and most are less than 1.0. This suggests that these residuals or error terms are positively autocorrelated.[11]

Chart 5-1 confirms that the fit of estimates obtained from these regressions leaves much to be desired. Two industries are covered in these illustrations, the total durable goods sector and machinery ex-

[9] For example, applying this procedure to the last equation for total durables as given in the tabulation shown above, one gets $.350(0) + .082(-1) + .153(-2) - .020(-3) + .056(-4) + .055(-5) + .290(-6) = -2.5660$, that is, an average lead of N relative to S of about 2.6 months.

[10] On casual reading, it might seem puzzling that the average lag is greater for "all manufacturing" than for "all industries reporting unfilled orders" (compare the entries for these in column 11), since the exclusion of those nondurables for which N_t and S_t are taken to be equal (i.e., the assumed lag is zero) ought to increase the lag. But there is no inconsistency, only a difference in the periods covered. The lags of S decreased in recent years. For 1953–65, the average lag for all manufacturing was 2.0 when rounded (it is a fraction of a month smaller than the corresponding figure for all industries reporting). For total nondurables, the average lag, analogously computed, was negligible (about 0.6 months).

[11] See J. Durbin and G. S. Watson, "Testing for Serial Correlation in the Least-Squares Regression, I and II," *Biometrika*, December 1950 and June 1951. The second article includes tables of significance points for the d statistics. For n, the number of observations, equal to 100, and for m, the number of independent variables, equal to 4 and 5 (these are the largest values of n and m in the tables), the lower and upper points, d_L and d_u, are as follows:

Level of Significance	$m = 4$		$m = 5$	
	d_L	d_u	d_L	d_u
5.0%	1.59	1.76	1.57	1.78
1.0%	1.46	1.63	1.44	1.65

If the calculated d is less than d_L, the residuals are probably positively autocorrelated; if d is greater than d_u, they are probably not; and if d falls between d_L and d_u, the test is inconclusive. A two-sided test may be performed by applying these rules to both d and $(4 - d)$.

cept electrical, and two estimates are presented for each, one derived by relating S_t to three and the other to seven N_{t-i} terms. The computed series [denoted as $(S_{2m})_{est}$ and $(S_{6m})_{est}$, respectively] clearly resemble new orders too much in that they show considerably larger cyclical movements and earlier timing than estimated shipments should. The fits are particularly poor in times of the greatest discrepancies between new orders and shipments: the Korean period from mid-1950 to mid-1952 and the recessions of 1953–54 and 1957–58. Adding more of the N_{t-i} terms (that is, introducing the longer delivery lags) definitely does improve the fits: The fluctuations of $(S_{6m})_{est}$ have smaller amplitudes and later timing than those of $(S_{2m})_{est}$, hence resemble the actual shipments better. However, the improvements are not large and cannot be considered adequate for either total durables or nonelectrical machinery.

Applications to Quarterly Series

In Table 5-3, shipments are related to new orders received in the same quarter and in each of the two preceding quarters. Seasonally adjusted data are used throughout, as before.

If the true unit period of adjustment were one month but, instead of months, quarters were used in an otherwise identical distributed-lag equation, the results could be seriously distorted by a systematic aggregation error. However, the basic unit period is typically unknown, and there is no exception from this rule in the present case. Moreover, these quarterly equations include fewer terms than the monthly ones, so as to cover the same lag range (six months when measured between the midpoints of the intervals). In this situation, the choice between the monthly and the quarterly units must depend on the verdict of the data. If the true structure of the lagged adjustment process is not substantially obscured by the use of the longer units, the latter should be preferable, since aggregation over time reduces the magnitude of measurement errors relative to the true values of the data.[12]

Comparisons of the corresponding estimates in Tables 5-2 and 5-3 do, in fact, suggest that some gains are made when quarterly rather than monthly series are used. The highest adjusted determination

[12] See Yair Mundlak, "Aggregation Over Time in Distributed Lag Models," *International Economic Review*, May 1961, pp. 154–63. Also, see Lester G. Telser, "Discrete Samples and Moving Sums in Stationary Stochastic Processes," *Journal of the American Statistical Association*, June 1967, pp. 484–99.

Chart 5-1
Regressions for Shipments of Durable Goods Industries and Nonelectrical Machinery, Based on Three and Seven Lagged Terms in New Orders, Monthly, 1947–65

PART A

$$(S_t)_{est} = a + b_1 N_t + b_2 N_{t-1} + b_3 N_{t-2}$$

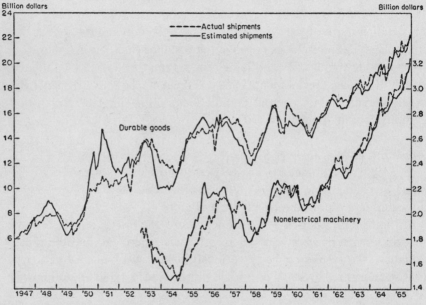

coefficients in Table 5-3 (columns 6 and 10)[13] exceed the highest $\bar{R}^2$ values in Table 5-2 for each industry. More importantly, the Durbin-Watson statistics give much less evidence of residual autocorrelation for the quarterly than for the monthly regressions. For several industries, these tests (Table 5-3, columns 7 and 11) either suggest that there is no autocorrelation (primary metals, blast furnaces) or are inconclusive on the 0.05 level (fabricated metals, other durables).

The average lags estimated from the two sets of regressions are closely similar. More figures in Table 5-3, column 8, exceed than fall short of their counterparts in Table 5-2, column 11, but the margins of

[13] The highest observed $\bar{R}^2$ values for primary metals and blast furnaces, etc., are those in column 10, which result from relating S_t to the two terms N_t and N_{t-1}; for all other industries, the highest $\bar{R}^2$ in the table are those in column 6, which result from relating S_t to three terms, N_t, N_{t-1}, and N_{t-2} (the subscripts referring to quarterly intervals).

Chart 5-1 (continued)

PART B

$$(S_t)_{est} = a + b_1 N_t + b_2 N_{t-1} + b_3 N_{t-2} + b_4 N_{t-3} + b_5 N_{t-4} + b_6 N_{t-5} + b_7 N_{t-6}$$

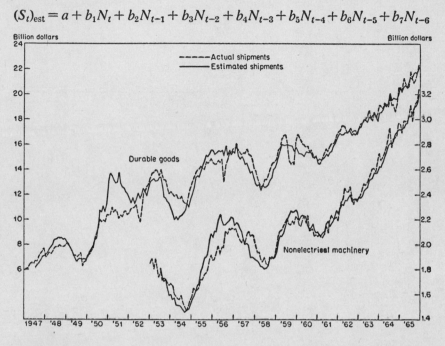

difference are very small fractions, sometimes as little as hundredths, of a month.

The influence on S_t of the same-quarter orders N_t is dominant in all but two cases, but particularly large for nondurables and the other durables group, as would be expected of industries that sell a large proportion of their output from stock (Table 5-3, column 2). The effects of N_{t-1} are dominant in primary metals and blast furnaces, significant for total nondurables and other durable goods, and quite weak elsewhere (column 3). The coefficients of N_{t-2}, conversely, are statistically not different from zero in the nondurables and primary metals regressions, but relatively large (mostly three to four times the size of their standard errors; see column 4) for all other industries.

The three regression coefficients add up to approximately 1.0 for the comprehensive aggregates (first three lines, column 5) and the group of nondurable goods industries reporting unfilled orders (fifth line, column 5). The constant terms in these regressions are probably not

Table 5-3

Relations Between Shipments and New Orders Received in the Current and in the Preceding One or Two Quarters, Multiple Correlation and Regression Measures, Major Manufacturing Industries, 1947–65 and 1953–65

Industry	Constant Term[b] (1)	Regression Coefficients[b] b_{20} (2)	b_{21} (3)	b_{22} (4)	Regression[a] Based on N_t, N_{t-1}, and N_{t-2} — Sum[c] of b's (5)	$\bar{R}^2$ (6)	Durbin-Watson Statistic[d] (7)	Av. Lag[e] (mos.) (8)	Regression[f] Based on N_t and N_{t-1} — Sum[g] of b's (9)	$\bar{R}^2$ (10)	Durbin-Watson Statistic[d] (11)
1947–65 (74)[h]											
All manufacturing	.242 (.412)	.527 (.080)	.138 (.118)	.330 (.081)	0.995	.984	0.567	2.4	0.986	.980	0.507
Durable goods	.434 (.369)	.480 (.104)	.092 (.157)	.397 (.104)	0.969	.951	0.488	2.7	0.953	.941	0.437
Nondurable goods	.042 (.051)	.738 (.032)	.209 (.040)	.055 (.032)	1.001	.999	1.296	0.95	0.9996	.9989	1.333
1953–65 (50)[h]											
Reporting unfilled orders											
All industries[i]	2.344 (.098)	.454 (.164)	.132 (.164)	.305 (.102)	0.892	.968	0.935	2.2	0.885	.954	1.126
Nondurables industries[j]	−.056 (.034)	.450 (.054)	.311 (.081)	.265 (.056)	1.027	.997	1.851	2.2	1.043	.992	1.683
Primary metals	.755 (.172)	.266 (.092)	.448 (.129)	.025 (.093)	0.740	.772	1.827	1.50	0.733	.777	1.794
Blast furnaces, steel mills	.593 (.137)	.209 (.103)	.458 (.135)	−.030 (.103)	0.638	.584	1.949	1.20	0.649	.592	1.977
Fabricated metal prod.	.258 (.037)	.419 (.062)	.052 (.086)	.386 (.063)	0.857	.9695	1.412	2.5	0.831	.946	1.197

Machinery exc. elect.	.282	.258	.199	.424	0.882	.9688	0.539	3.1	0.850	.956	0.501
	(.051)	(.092)	(.138)	(.096)							
Elect. machinery	.236	.489	.164	.236	0.888	.9694	0.650	1.9	0.867	.965	0.506
	(.046)	(.079)	(.115)	(.083)							
Transport. equip.	.980	.460	.121	.194	0.775	.881	0.791	1.53	0.740	.872	0.827
	(.174)	(.082)	(.107)	(.089)							
Other durable goods[k]	.078	.627	.163	.191	0.981	.991	1.488	1.64	0.966	.988	1.186
	(.045)	(.058)	(.088)	(.056)							

[a] The estimating equation is

$$S_t = a_2 + b_{20}N_t + b_{21}N_{t-1} + b_{22}N_{t-2} + u_{2t}.$$

[b] Standard errors of the parameter estimates are given underneath in parentheses.

[c] Sum of columns 2–4 ($b_{20} + b_{21} + b_{22}$).

[d] Durbin-Watson Statistic (d) = $\Sigma(u_t - u_{t-1})^2/\Sigma u_t^2$. Shown below are the exact upper and lower bounds for critical values of d for n, the number of observations (75 or 50) and for m, the number of independent variables in the regression (2 or 3). On the interpretation and source of these significance points, see note 11 in this chapter.

n	Level of Significance	$m = 2$		$m = 3$	
		d_L	d_u	d_L	d_u
50	5.0%	1.46	1.63	1.42	1.67
50	1.0	1.28	1.45	1.24	1.49
75	5.0	1.57	1.68	1.54	1.71
75	1.0	1.42	1.53	1.39	1.56

[e] Computed as the sum $b_{21}(-3) + b_{22}(-6)$, analogously to the estimates in Table 5-2, column 11 (cf. note f to that table and text).

[f] The estimating equation is

$$S_t = a_1 + b_{10}N_t + b_{11}N_{t-1} + u_{1t}.$$

[g] Sum of two regression coefficients ($b_{10} + b_{11}$).

[h] The figure in parentheses is the number of quarterly observations. It is the effective sample size for each of the industries covered in the section that follows.

[i] Includes all durable goods industries and the four nondurable goods industries reporting unfilled orders (see note j).

[j] Includes textile, leather, paper, and printing and publishing.

[k] Includes professional and scientific instruments; lumber; furniture; stone, clay, and glass products; and miscellaneous industries.

different from zero, being either smaller or not much larger than their standard errors (column 1). The results for the group of other durable goods (tenth line) are similar in these respects. However, for each of the remaining industries, the sums of the b coefficients fall appreciably short of unity. The constant terms in these equations are all several times larger than their standard errors, and hence presumably significant.

Graphs of the quarterly shipment estimates computed from regressions that include from one to three terms N_{t-i} ($i = 0, 1, 2$ quarters) show them to suffer from the same basic deficiency as that observed in Chart 5-1 for the analogously derived monthly estimates. The computed values resemble new orders too much, moving earlier than the actual shipments S and in wider swings—like the monthly estimates. Here too, adding additional lagged terms improves the fit. But even the estimates that incorporate the full range of the lags used, from zero to two quarters, still retain too much similarity to the path of new orders to be really satisfactory. Chart 5-2 illustrates this fact for total durables and machinery except electrical. Of course, the quarterly series are much smoother than the monthly series shown for the same industries in Chart 5-1.

Assumed Forms of Time-Lag Structure

The direct method of adding the lagged terms successively as long as their coefficients do not show "wrong" signs or erratic behavior provided the earliest approach to the estimation of distributed lags.[14] The main difficulty with it is that the lagged terms employed as independent variables are often highly intercorrelated, so that their coefficients cannot be reliably estimated. By imposing upon the data a specific form of lag distribution, this multicollinearity problem can be largely overcome, but not without cost. In general, the proper specification of the time-lag structure is unknown and cannot be readily inferred from either theory or data. Statistical difficulties of estimation are encountered in using the models, and the results based on them may admit of different interpretations.

[14] Irving Fisher and C. F. Roos both used the concept of a distributed lag first in 1925, and G. C. Evans used it in 1930. For a summary and references, see Franz L. Alt, "Distributed Lags," *Econometrica*, April 1942, pp. 113–28.

Chart 5-2
Regressions for Shipments of Durable Goods Industries and Nonelectrical Machinery, Based on Three Lagged Terms in New Orders, Quarterly, 1947–65

$$(S_t)_{est} = a + b_1 N_t + b_2 N_{t-1} + b_3 N_{t-2}$$

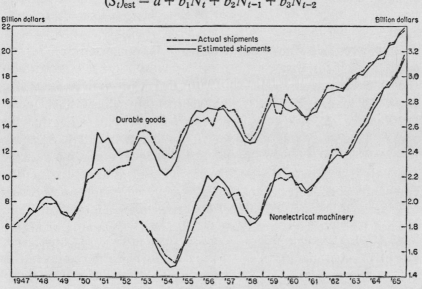

Suppose that the influence on S_t of N_{t-i} steadily declines as i increases; the more remote values of N have less effect than the more recent ones. A very simple form of this hypothesis is that the coefficients α in

$$S_t = \alpha_0 N_t + \alpha_1 N_{t-1} + \alpha_2 N_{t-2} + \cdots + u_t \tag{2}$$

(where u_t is the disturbance term) decline exponentially, so that $\alpha_i = \alpha \beta^i$ ($i = 0, 1, 2, \ldots$), and

$$S_t = \alpha \Sigma_{i=0}^{\infty} \beta^i N_{t-i} + u_t, \tag{3}$$

where both α and β are natural fractions (i.e., $0 < \alpha, \beta < 1$). As shown by Koyck,[15] (3) reduces to

$$S_t = \alpha N_t + \beta S_{t-1} + \epsilon_t, \tag{4}$$

[15] L. M. Koyck, *Distributed Lags and Investment Analysis*, Amsterdam, 1954.

where $\epsilon_t = u_t - \beta u_{t-1}$.[16] Equation (4) includes only two explanatory variables, and thus appears to be quite manageable and probably not subject to a serious multicollinearity problem. But the presence in the regression of lagged values of the dependent variable on the right-hand side may lead to a serious bias of the least-square estimates in small samples (in sufficiently large samples this defect is likely to be substantially reduced).[17] Moreover, if the original disturbance terms u_t in (3) were serially independent, then ϵ_t in (4) would not be; in other words, if the lag structure was properly specified in (3), then estimation by means of (4) will produce autocorrelated residuals. The latter can be particularly troublesome when combined with the complication of lagged variables (autoregressive schemes).[18]

In the present context, there is no strong presumption that the process whereby past new orders are translated into shipments is so well approximated by the geometric lag distribution (3) as to leave the residuals u free of autocorrelation. In some industries, production to stock is of major importance, which would make the coefficient of N_t much greater relative to those of the other terms than is here implied. (In the extreme case of pure production to stock, $\alpha = 1$ and $\beta = 0$.) In other industries, production to order may be so dominant and the delivery lags so long that, for short unit periods, the influence of N_t and perhaps of N_{t-i} would actually be relatively weak—again

[16] Equation (4) is derived from (3) as follows. From

$$S_t = \alpha N_t + \alpha\beta N_{t-1} + \alpha\beta^2 N_{t-2} + \cdots + u_t$$

subtract

$$\beta S_{t-1} = \alpha\beta N_{t-1} + \alpha\beta^2 N_{t-2} + \cdots + \beta u_{t-1}$$

to get

$$S_t - \beta S_{t-1} = \alpha N_t + \cdots + u_t - \beta u_{t-1}$$

or

$$S_t = \alpha N_t + \beta S_{t-1} + \epsilon_t.$$

[17] This is because the assumption that the disturbance term is distributed independently of the explanatory variables does not hold for autoregressive schemes. The least-squares estimates, however, will have the desirable asymptotic (large-sample) properties of consistency and efficiency. See Johnston, *Econometric Methods*, pp. 211–14.

[18] The estimates may be inconsistent in this case. Furthermore, if the autocorrelation of the residuals is positive, the estimated coefficients of the lagged dependent variables (such as that of S_{t-1} in equation (4) would be biased upward, which, as will be shown later, implies overestimation of the average lags involved. See Johnston, *Econometric Methods*, pp. 215–16, and references there; also, Zvi Griliches, "Distributed Lags: A Survey," *Econometrica*, January 1967, pp. 16–49 (particularly pp. 33–42).

unlike (3).[19] Moreover, aggregation over industries with very different types of orders-shipments relations could result in "multimodal" lag distributions.[20] If only for these reasons, one may well doubt the applicability of a fixed lag structure, such as (3), to the diverse industry processes under consideration. On the other hand, if the disturbances u are autocorrelated, then ϵ_t *may* be serially independent with a constant variance, in which case (4) would at least yield consistent estimates of α and β.[21] In any event, model (4) is easy to apply and potentially instructive in suggesting modified and different approaches; hence, considerable use was made of it in the course of this exploration and a report on the results is in order.

Estimates of Geometric Lag Distributions

Table 5-4 presents regressions of the form

$$S_t = k + aN_t + bS_{t-1} + v_t, \tag{5}$$

which follow Koyck's model of equation (4), except that a nonzero intercept k is admitted [a, b, and v_t correspond to α, β, and ϵ_t in (4), respectively]. If a is small and b large, then a slow lagged response (long distributed lag) is indicated; if, on the contrary, a is large and b small, then the response is prompt (i.e., the average and the dispersion of the lag distribution are both small). The sum of the regression coefficients implied in (5) is $a + ab + ab^2 + \cdots = a/(1 - b)$. It should ideally show the complete ultimate response of S to a unit change in N maintained forever, and hence should equal unity (in which case, of course, $a + b = 1$, also).

This estimated "total effect," $\Sigma = a/(1 - b)$, is indeed close to 1.000

[19] In pure production to order, the index i in (3) would start, not from zero, but from some positive value j representing the minimum period needed for production and delivery. The derived form analogous to (4) would then read

$$S_t = \alpha_1 N_{t-j} + \beta_1 S_{t-1} + \epsilon_{1t}; \quad j > 0,$$

thus embodying the assumption that this interval j also represents the "normal" or most frequent delivery lag. On some early experiments in applying this derived form to the 1948–58 OBE figures for N and S, see Appendix G.

[20] For example, if the aggregate consisted of an industry working largely to stock and of another industry, about as large, with a typical delivery lag of four months, then the coefficients of N_t and N_{t-4} would tend to dominate the others in the equation for the combined two-industry totals. Our data are, of course, very comprehensive and they undoubtedly combine much larger numbers of different patterns with varying weights; hence the outcomes are not nearly as simple.

[21] This will be so if u follows the first-order autoregressive (Markov) scheme in which $u_t = \beta u_{t-1} + \epsilon_t$.

Table 5-4
Regressions of Shipments on New Orders, Based on Geometric Lag Distribution, Major Manufacturing Industries, Quarterly, 1947–65 and 1953–65

| Industry | Constant Term [a] (1) | Regression Coefficients [a] | | Sum of Implicit Coefficients [b] (4) | $\bar{R}^2$ (5) | Lag [c] (mos.) Needed to Account for of Column 4 | | | Av. Lag [d] (mos.) (9) |
		a (2)	b (3)			50% (6)	70% (7)	90% (8)	
				1947–65 (74) [e]					
All manufacturing	−.008 (.245)	.397 (.035)	.608 (.036)	1.014	.994	4.2	7.3	13.9	4.7
Durable goods	.047 (.199)	.311 (.037)	.692 (.039)	1.009	.986	5.6	9.8	18.7	6.7
Nondurable goods	.027 (.048)	.736 (.028)	.265 (.029)	1.002	.999	1.6	2.7	5.2	1.1
				1953–65 (50) [e]					
Reporting unfilled orders									
All industries [f]	.825 (.425)	.417 (.044)	.548 (.055)	0.922	.981	3.5	6.0	11.5	3.6
Nondurables industries [g]	−.045 (.036)	.504 (.048)	.514 (.051)	1.036	.996	3.1	5.4	10.4	3.2

200

Primary metals	.403 (.216)	.495 (.064)	.367 (.084)	0.783	.745	2.1	3.6	6.9	1.7
Blast furnaces, steel mills	.380 (.183)	.471 (.079)	.298 (.102)	0.671	.513	1.7	3.0	5.7	1.3
Fabricated metal products	.105 (.042)	.401 (.047)	.542 (.057)	0.876	.972	3.4	5.9	11.3	3.5
Machinery exc. elect.	.031 (.027)	.278 (.025)	.715 (.031)	0.976	.994	6.2	10.8	20.6	7.5
Elect. machinery	.047 (.032)	.330 (.039)	.655 (.048)	0.956	.990	4.9	8.5	16.3	5.7
Transport. equip.	.391 (.183)	.353 (.061)	.562 (.085)	0.806	.922	3.6	6.3	12.0	3.8
Other durable goods [h]	.036 (.042)	.588 (.042)	.405 (.047)	0.988	.992	2.3	4.0	7.6	2.0

[a] The form of the estimates is given by equation (5) in the text. The figures in parentheses are standard errors.
[b] The sum equals $a/(1 - b)$.
[c] Computed according to equation (7); see text and note 23.
[d] The average length of the lag equals $3b/(1 - b)$.
[e] The figure in parentheses is number of quarterly observations. It is the effective sample size for each of the industries covered in the section that follows.
[f] Includes all durable goods industries and the four nondurable goods industries reporting unfilled orders (see note g).
[g] Includes textiles, leather, paper, and printing and publishing.
[h] Includes professional and scientific instruments; lumber; furniture; stone, clay, and glass products; and miscellaneous industries.

for all of the comprehensive aggregates, the two machinery industries, and the group of other durable goods industries (column 4). The constant terms k are in these cases apparently not significantly different from zero, except for the industries reporting unfilled orders in 1953–65 (column 1). For the metalworking industries and transportation equipment, however, Σ is considerably lower (varying from 0.67 for blast furnaces to 0.88 for fabricated metal products) and k is positive and significant.[22]

The estimated values of a and b are roughly 0.4 and 0.6, respectively, for total manufacturing, and 0.3 and 0.7 for the durable goods sector (columns 2 and 3). Conversely, a is larger than 0.7 and b smaller than 0.3 for the total nondurable goods sector. The part of that sector that reports unfilled orders illustrates the intermediate situation where a and b differ little, each being close to 0.5. Among the major industries, nonelectrical machinery has the lowest a and the highest b, and electrical machinery comes next, with coefficients similar to those for all durables. In contrast, the other durables group shows the highest a (nearly 0.6) and a correspondingly low b (0.4). In terms of broad interindustry comparisons, these results appear sensible and consistent with other relevant information. The equations for total primary metals and the blast furnaces subdivision, however, are much less satisfactory. They yield not only relatively low Σ statistics but also relatively low values of $\bar{R}^2$ (column 5). The a's are high and the b's are lower than for any of the component industries.

It is clear that b is inversely related to the speed with which the orders are filled, that is, translated into shipments. Let q represent the proportion of the "total effect" of new orders on shipments [i.e., of $a/(1 - b)$] that is accounted for by an interval of n unit periods. Then

$$q = [a(1 - b^n)/(1 - b)] \div [a/(1 - b)] = 1 - b^n \qquad (6)$$

or

$$n = \log (1 - q)/\log b. \qquad (7)$$

Columns 6–8 in Table 5-4 show, according to equation (7), the length of time necessary to account for 50, 70, and 90 per cent of the total

[22] Multiplying a and $a/(1 - b)$ by $\bar{N}/\bar{S}$, the ratio of the average values of new orders and shipments, gives elasticity expressions evaluated at the means. Over a sufficiently long period of time, the means $\bar{N}$ and $\bar{S}$ will tend to be equal. The true long-run elasticity of S relative to $N(\epsilon_L = (\bar{N}/\bar{S})\Sigma)$ is 1, as is the true value of Σ. Actually, the estimates for ϵ_L corresponding to those for Σ in column 4 are very close to the latter. Where $\Sigma \simeq 1$, $\epsilon_L \simeq 1$ also; and for the three industries with estimated Σ of less than 1, ϵ_L is likewise significantly smaller than unity.

long-run reaction, Σ.[23] Most of the impact of orders spends itself within the first few months, while the remainder tapers off very slowly. This, of course, is implicit in the adopted lag structure. But the speed of the process varies greatly among the industries. Thus, according to column 6, the "half-life" of the process is 5.6 months for the durable goods sector but only 1.6 months for the nondurables (1947–65). When the manufacturers not reporting unfilled orders are excluded, however, the estimate for all industries is only slightly larger than that for the non-durable goods industries (the figures for 1953–65 are a little in excess of 3 months). The half-life lags come to 5–6 months in the machinery industries and 2–3 months in the metalworking industries.

On the assumption that the distributed-lag coefficients are nonnegative weights that sum to unity (so that $0 < b > 1$ and $a = 1 - b$), it is possible to identify the mean lag of the geometric lag distribution here used as $b/(1 - b)$.[24] For the metalworking industries and transportation equipment the sums of the estimated coefficients actually fall short of unity (column 4), but this is disregarded and the average lags are computed uniformly according to the above formula.[25]

The resulting figures (Table 5-4, column 9) exceed in each case the average lags calculated from the regressions of shipments on new orders received in the current and in the preceding two quarters (Table 5-3, column 8). The differences are negligible (0.1 to 0.4 of one month) for the industries with the shortest estimated lags: primary metals, blast furnaces, other durable goods, and total nondurables all have average lags of one to two months according to either set of measures.

---

[23] These estimates are computed by inserting into (7) the values 0.5, 0.7, and 0.9 for q, and multiplying the resulting values of n by 3 (it is convenient for comparisons with other findings to translate n from quarters into months).

[24] The lag structure is in this case formally identical to the geometric probability distribution. If $a = 1 - b$ and $c = 0$, (5) can be written as

$$S_t = (1 - b)(1 + bL + b^2L^2 + \cdots)N_t = f(L)N_t,$$

where L is a lag operator; then $L(N)_t = N_{t-1}$; $L^2(N_{t-1}) = N_{t-2}$; etc. The mean lag is obtained as the first derivative of the "generating function" $f(L)$ evaluated at $N_t = 1$, which equals $b(1 - b)(1 - b)^{-2} = b/(1 - b)$. See William Feller, *An Introduction to Probability Theory and Its Applications*, New York, 1950, Vol. I, pp. 210 and 252–53.

[25] In those cases where the sums $(a + b)$ are significantly less than 1.0, the ratios b/a have been computed for comparison with $b/(1 - b)$. The values of $3(b/a)$ are as follows: primary metals, 2.2 (months); blast furnaces, 1.9; fabricated metal products, 4.1; and transportation equipment, 4.8. These figures, of course, exceed the corresponding entries for $3b/(1 - b)$ in column 9 of Table 5-4, since $a < (1 - b)$ for these industries.

Under the assumptions specified above, with the mean lag equal to $b/(1 - b)$, the variance of the geometric lag distribution is given by $b/(1 - b)^2$. The variance, then, is an increasing function of b, being $1/(1 - b)$ times as large as the mean (which is itself increasing with b). For example, if $b = 0.5$, the mean lag is 1.0 and the variance is 2.0; if $b = 0.8$, the mean lag is 4.0 and the variance is 20.0.

Elsewhere, however, the differences are large, varying from about one month for fabricated metals and the two aggregates with advance orders, to 2.3 months for transportation equipment and all manufacturing, to about 4 months for the two remaining items (total durables and the machinery industries).

The average lags estimated from regressions of shipments on a few recent values of new orders are generally small, varying in the range of approximately 1 to 3 months (Tables 5-2 and 5-3). They are probably too small in some cases, thus understating the timing differences among the industries (see above, page 190). If this is correctly recognized as a defect, the estimates in Table 5-4 are free of it. Their large range (from 1.0 to 7.5 months) is similar to the interindustry variation of the average leads derived in Chapter 4 from turning-point comparisons. The present estimates may have an advantage in that they are based on distributed-lag models which in a sense include the entire history of the explanatory variable rather than just its most recent past. However, they could err in the opposite direction, that is, toward overstatement of the lags. Positive autocorrelation of the residuals in (5) could be a source of such bias (see note 18, above). The use of a quarterly instead of monthly unit period might also work in this direction, and some evidence bearing on this point will be presented shortly.

Clearly, it is important to know whether the residuals in the model underlying equation (5) are really free of serial correlation. The Durbin-Watson statistic (d) is itself biased in equations with lagged dependent variables and hence provides no reliable test of the residual autocorrelation in these cases.[26] The d figures have been routinely computed and, as descriptive statistics, they show that the *estimated* disturbance terms contain no detectable correlation, but this gives no assurance that the "true" disturbances are likewise not autocorrelated.[27]

[26] When lagged values of the dependent variable are used as an explanatory factor, a downward bias in the autocorrelation of the estimated residuals is created along with an upward bias in the coefficient of the lagged variable, and for the same reason (see note 18, above). Durbin and Watson warn against the use of their statistic in such cases in their 1951 *Biometrika* article, p. 159 (see note 11, above). See also Zvi Griliches, "A Note on Serial Correlation Bias in Estimates of Distributed Lags," *Econometrica*, January 1961, pp. 65–73; and Marc Nerlove and Kenneth F. Wallis, "Use of the Durbin-Watson Statistic in Inappropriate Situations," *Econometrica*, January 1966, pp. 235–38.

[27] The computed Durbin-Watson statistics vary between 1.720 and 1.830 for the 1947–65 regressions ($n = 74$; see Table 5-4, first three lines), and between 1.573 and 2.386 for the 1953–65 regressions, excluding transportation equipment and other durable goods ($n = 50$). The observed values of d are generally greater than the upper bounds d_u (see Table 5-3, note d), which, taken at its face value, would suggest that the residuals are not positively autocorrelated. In two cases with the highest d values (primary and fabricated metals), the tests against negative serial correlation would be inconclusive at the 5 per cent level (that is, the value of $4 - d$ falls between d_L and d_u or the 5 per cent test, though it exceeds d_u for the 1 per cent test).

As shown in Chart 5-3 for the quarterly data on total durables and nonelectrical machinery, the use of the Koyck equation (5) can produce rather good results when applied to the orders-shipments relations. Certainly, much better fits are obtained here than with the regressions of S_t on the three terms N_{t-i} ($i = 0, 1, 2$ quarters), as will be seen by comparing Charts 5-3 and 5-2. The computed shipments series (S_{est}) fluctuate with amplitudes close to those of actual shipments (S) in Chart 5-3; they do not overstate greatly the cyclical movements of S in 1947–58 as do the S_{est} estimates in Chart 5-2. Furthermore, the timing of S_{est} is much closer to that of S in Chart 5-3 than in Chart 5-2. In the latter, S_{est} shares some of the earliness of N and often leads S at turning points. Here the timing of S and S_{est} is on the average more nearly coincident. Autoregressive forms are known to produce a certain tendency to lag in the estimates, which is favorable for these relations since it helps to offset the leads imparted to the computed series by the use of the early-moving new orders as predictors.

Chart 5-3
Regressions for Shipments of Durable Goods Industries and
Nonelectrical Machinery, Based on Geometric Lag
Distribution, Quarterly, 1947–65

$$(S_t)_{est} = a + b_1 N_t + b_2 S_{t-1}$$

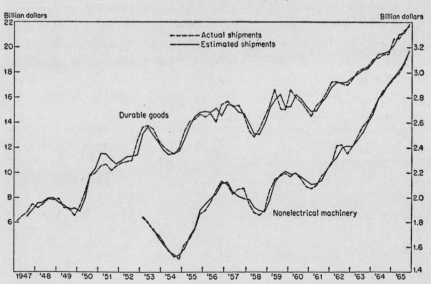

Further Results on Geometric Lag Models

Some earlier findings of this analysis favored the use of quarterly rather than monthly series in direct estimates of distributed lags of shipments behind new orders, but this does not in any way resolve the issue for the models now under consideration. Here the form of the lag distribution is given, and the choice of an inappropriate basic time period will lead to a misspecified model and overestimation of the average lags.[28] Accordingly, it is desirable to re-estimate model (5) using monthly data, and to compare the results (Table 5-5) with their counterparts for the quarterly regressions (Table 5-4). The regression takes the form $S_t = k' + a'N_t + b'S_{t-1} + v_t'$, again following Koyck.

Not surprisingly, the correlation measures offer little help in discriminating between the two sets of estimates: for most industries, the coefficients $\bar{R}^2$ are very high and very close in both tables (compare columns 5). However, substantial differences in favor of the monthly regressions can be seen for primary metals and blast furnaces (fourth and fifth lines). In these cases, too, the sums of implicit lag coefficients are definitely larger for the monthly data (i.e., $\Sigma' > \Sigma$; compare columns 4 in the two tables). For the other component industries and the sector reporting unfilled orders, $\Sigma > \Sigma'$ by margins varying within a narrow range. In the regressions for all manufacturing, for total durables, and for the two aggregates of nondurables, Σ and Σ' are approximately equal to unity.

The longer the period of reference, the larger will be the proportion of current shipments accounted for by new orders received during the same period; hence it is easy to see why the coefficients of N_t are always greater in the quarterly than in the monthly regressions (that is, $a > a'$; compare columns 2 in Tables 5-4 and 5-5). By the same token, the coefficients of S_{t-1} are in all cases smaller in the quarterly equations ($b < b'$; see columns 3).

More interesting are the differences, expressed in months, between the average lags based on the quarterly and on the monthly regressions [$\bar{n} = 3b/(1 - b)$ and $\bar{n}' = b'/(1 - b')$; see columns 9]. Only in transportation equipment does $\bar{n}'$ exceed $\bar{n}$ by a substantial margin (1.7 months). For both total primary metals and blast furnaces, $\bar{n}' > n$ too, but by minor fractions. Elsewhere $\bar{n} > \bar{n}'$, mostly by 1.0 to 1.5

---

[28] The latter is due to the positive correlation between the aggregated true disturbances and the lagged values of the aggregate dependent variable. See Mundlak, "Aggregation Over Time."

months (the difference is once more just a small fraction for total non-durables, and it is really large — 3.0 months — for nonelectrical machinery). Much larger differences are observed by comparing the lags necessary to account for 50 to 90 per cent of the total reaction of S to additional N (see columns 6–8 in the two tables). On balance, therefore, these results seem consistent with the hypothesis that the use of quarterly data tends to cause some overestimation of the lags, even though the evidence is somewhat mixed.

Inspection of graphs also suggests that in some cases marginal improvements result from the use of monthly rather than quarterly data in the geometric lag models. Because of the large discrepancy between $\bar{n}$ and $\bar{n}'$ observed for nonelectrical machinery, Chart 5-4 shows the estimates for this industry. The fit is indeed extremely close, with some tendency for S_{est} to lag S by one month at turning points.

It may not be correct, however, to assume that the lag coefficients decline from the very beginning of the adjustment process, particularly when the unit periods are very short. As one check on the possibility

Chart 5-4
Regressions for Shipments of Nonelectrical Machinery, Based on Geometric Lag Distribution, Monthly, 1953–65

$$(S_t)_{est} = a + b_1 N_t + b_2 S_{t-1}$$

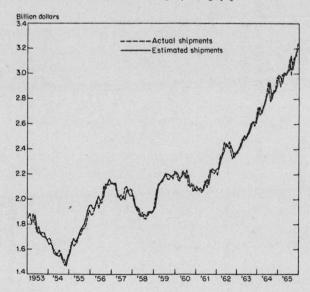

Table 5-5

Regressions of Shipments on New Orders, Based on Geometric Lag Distribution, Major Manufacturing Industries, Monthly, 1947–65 and 1953–65

Industry	Constant Term [a] (1)	Regression Coefficients [a] a' (2)	b' (3)	Sum of Implicit Weights [b] (4)	$\bar{R}^2$ (5)	Lag [c] (mos.) Needed to Account for of Column 4 — 50% (6)	70% (7)	90% (8)	Av. Lag [d] (mos.) (9)
				1947–65 (226) [e]					
All manufacturing	.029 (.125)	.222 (.022)	.779 (.022)	1.004	.995	2.8	4.8	9.2	3.5
Durable goods	.046 (.091)	.152 (.019)	.847 (.020)	0.994	.991	4.2	7.2	13.8	5.5
Nondurable goods	.030 (.036)	.598 (.026)	.401 (.026)	0.9995	.998	0.8	1.3	2.5	0.7
				1953–65 (154) [e]					
Reporting unfilled orders									
All industries [f]	.604 (.222)	.256 (.027)	.717 (.032)	0.904	.983	2.1	3.6	6.9	2.5
Nondurables industries [g]	.009 (.031)	.458 (.041)	.542 (.043)	1.000	.991	1.1	2.0	3.8	1.2

208

Primary metals	.200 (.099)	.291 (.034)	.642 (.043)	0.812	.821	1.6	2.7	5.2	1.8
Blast furnaces, steel mills	.149 (.080)	.290 (.040)	.621 (.050)	0.767	.680	1.5	2.5	4.8	1.6
Fabricated metal products	.097 (.031)	.266 (.032)	.679 (.040)	0.830	.952	1.8	3.1	6.0	2.1
Machinery, except electrical	.040 (.020)	.165 (.021)	.820 (.026)	0.913	.990	3.5	6.1	11.6	4.5
Electrical machinery	.031 (.020)	.176 (.025)	.809 (.031)	0.923	.986	3.3	5.7	10.9	4.2
Transportation equipment	.178 (.090)	.116 (.028)	.845 (.040)	0.750	.936	4.1	7.2	13.7	5.5
Other durable goods [h]	.070 (.037)	.481 (.039)	.499 (.043)	0.960	.980	0.8	1.3	2.6	1.0

[a] The form of the equation is

$$S_t = k' + a'N_t + b'S_{t-1} + v'_t$$

as discussed in the text. The figures in parentheses are standard errors of the statistics shown.

[b] The sum equals $a'/(1 - b')$.

[c] Computed according to equation (7); see text and note 23.

[d] The average length of the lag equals $b'/(1 - b')$.

[e] The number of monthly observations, given in parentheses, represents the effective sample size for each of the industries covered in the section that follows.

[f] Includes all durable goods industries and the four nondurable goods industries reporting unfilled orders (see note g).

[g] Includes textiles, leather, paper, and printing and publishing.

[h] Includes professional and scientific instruments; lumber; furniture; stone, clay, and glass products; and miscellaneous industries.

that the response does not reach its peak immediately or nearly so but rather builds up to it more gradually, N_{t-1} was added as the third independent variable to the regressions of S_t on N_t and S_{t-1} (in quarterly terms). The results suggest that the simple Koyck scheme does not apply to primary metals and blast furnaces. Here the coefficients of N_{t-1} are larger than those of N_t, while the coefficients of S_{t-1} are reduced to insignificance (being smaller than their standard errors and, for blast furnaces, negative).

Primary metals:

$$(S_t)_{est} = .655 + .291N_t + .389N_{t-1} + .095S_{t-1}; \bar{R}^2 = .775$$
$$(.220) \quad (.096) \qquad (.143) \qquad (.127)$$

Blast furnaces, steel mills:

$$(S_t)_{est} = .591 + .210N_t + .445N_{t-1} - .017S_{t-1}; \bar{R}^2 = .584$$
$$(.181) \quad (.112) \qquad (.148) \qquad (.140)$$

These estimates, then, along with some earlier ones (in Tables 5-2 and 5-3), indicate that in primary metals the lags are concentrated in the current and previous quarters, with the influence of N_{t-1} exceeding that of N_t.

Elsewhere, the coefficients of N_{t-1} are negative and small (for three industries, they are not significantly different from zero). The coefficients of N_t and S_{t-1} are highly significant whether or not N_{t-1} is added, and the values of $\bar{R}^2$ are either slightly lowered or not appreciably raised by the addition. This evidence contradicts the present hypothesis of a somewhat generalized Koyck model (with the added term N_{t-1}), but it is also unfavorable to the alternative hypothesis that S_t is a function of N_t with autocorrelated residuals.[29]

Also examined was the possibility that a trend factor enters the dis-

---

[29] Suppose that $S_t = \alpha N_t + u_t$ and $u_t = \rho u_{t-1} + \epsilon_t$; then, by substitution,

$$S_t = \alpha N_t + \rho u_{t-1} + \epsilon_t = \alpha N_t + \rho S_{t-1} - \alpha\rho N_{t-1} + \epsilon_t$$

(since $u_{t-1} = S_{t-1} - \alpha N_{t-1}$). In this case, the simple Koyck model, though inappropriate, would produce highly significant results since both N_t and S_{t-1} influence S_t positively. But the addition of N_{t-1} would in this case discredit this model by revealing that N_{t-1} has a negative coefficient approximately equal to the product of the coefficients of N_t and $S_{t-1}(\alpha\rho)$. See Griliches, "Distributed Lags."

In the situations here considered, the inclusion of N_{t-1} has no such implications, since the coefficients of N_{t-1}, whether positive or negative, are insignificant, or in any event much smaller than the products of the corresponding coefficients of N_t and S_{t-1}. Hence the hypothesis, which is implausible in the present context anyway, can be rejected by these tests.

tributed-lag relationship between new orders and shipments. A simple time trend, T (in the form of consecutive numbers for successive periods), was included as another independent variable in the monthly and quarterly regressions based on the Koyck equation (5).[30] The effects of this variable turned out to be either negligible or weak. Even in the most favorable cases—the 1947–65 equations for all manufacturing and all durables—the addition of T had little effect on the regression coefficients of N_t and S_{t-1} and even less effect on the $\bar{R}^2$ coefficients.[31]

Second-Order Distributed Lag Functions

In an attempt to evolve a model which will incorporate a more general and flexible form of lag distribution, another lagged value of the dependent variable was added to the Koyck scheme, that is, S_t was regressed on N_t and S_{t-1} and also on S_{t-2}. The equation

$$S_t = \alpha N_t + \beta S_{t-1} + \gamma S_{t-2} + e_t \tag{8}$$

is capable of producing rather different lag profiles depending on the magnitudes of β and γ. Under certain not too restrictive conditions, the implied lag coefficients or weights will all be nonnegative.[32] They will also often decline throughout, as in the simple geometric case, but at different rates. However, for certain combinations of values of β and γ, the decline of the implied weights will not be monotonic, i.e., occasionally N_{t-i} may have a smaller coefficient than N_{t-i-1}. Frequent

---

[30] As an alternative, the logarithmic trend expression, log e^t, was also tried, with almost entirely negative results.

[31] The following estimates may be compared with the corresponding entries in the first two lines of Tables 5-4 and 5-5:

	Regression Coefficients of			
	N_t	S_{t-1}	T	$\bar{R}^2$
All manufacturing				
Quarterly	.387	.526	.0029	.995
	(.034)	(.051)	(.0013)	
Monthly	.226	.705	.0075	.996
	(.021)	(.031)	(.0022)	
Durable goods industries				
Quarterly	.299	.613	.0016	.986
	(.038)	(.057)	(.0009)	
Monthly	.151	.788	.0038	.991
	(.019)	(.029)	(.0014)	

[32] The conditions are: (1) $0 < \beta < 2$; (2) $1 - \beta - \gamma > 0$; and (3) $\beta^2 \geq -4\gamma$. (They imply that $-1 < \gamma < 1$.) See Griliches, "Distributed Lags," pp. 27–29.

interruptions of this sort would result in an erratic lag form, which may be viewed as unsatisfactory. On the other hand, the *unimodal* pattern produced by certain particular paired values of β and γ has aroused considerable interest. In these distributions, the lag coefficients first increase (as a rule briefly) and then trail off slowly.[33]

While lag structures of the types implied by (8) may be applicable in many situations when the time units are appropriately chosen, the inclusion of the second lagged value of the dependent variable on the right-hand side of the equation again creates the problem of multicollinearity. If that variable is highly autocorrelated, this problem may frustrate estimation and render the model nonoperational.

In quarterly regressions, the addition of S_{t-2} actually fails to improve the results from the simple Koyck model for most of the industries. The coefficients of S_{t-2} are smaller than their standard errors, and in several cases $\bar{R}^2$ is decreased. Better results are obtained for only three industries: fabricated metal products, nonelectrical machinery, and "other durable goods."[34] In all regressions of this type, the coefficients of S_{t-2} are much smaller than those of S_{t-1} and not always positive. The lag distributions implied by these estimates are not unimodal—they would tend to decline from the beginning, though possibly not monotonically, and are in fact rather similar to the distributions produced by the geometric model. The average lag for these functions may be estimated as $\bar{n} = (b + 2c)/(1 - b - c)$. For most of the industries the figures thus obtained are larger than the average lags implied in the quarterly regressions with geometric distributions (Table 5-4, column 9), but the differences are small—typically about one month or less.

Second-order distributed lag regressions yield considerably better statistical results when applied to monthly data for some, but not all, industries. In the five equations shown in the tabulation below, all regression coefficients meet the conventional standards of significance, and the $\bar{R}^2$ slightly exceed their counterparts for the monthly Koyck

---

[33] Such distributions will be observed when β and γ assume values within the area bounded by $1 < \beta < 2$, $\beta + \gamma = 1$, and $\beta^2 = -4\gamma$. See Griliches, "Distributed Lags." For a discussion of unimodal lag profiles given by the Pascal distributions, see Robert M. Solow, "On a Family of Lag Distributions," *Econometrica*, April 1960, pp. 393–406.

[34] The best is the regression for fabricated metals, as follows:

$$(S_t)_{est} = .096 + .418N_t + .346S_{t-1} + .186S_{t-2}; \quad \bar{R}^2 = .974$$
$$\quad\quad (.041) \;\; (.046) \quad\; (.112) \quad\quad (.092)$$

equations (Table 5-5, column 5).[35] The average lags implied by these

Fabricated metal products:

$$(S_t)_{est} = .076 + .250N_t + .444S_{t-1} + .265S_{t-2}; \bar{R}^2 = .957; \bar{n} = 3.4$$
$$(.030) \quad (.031) \qquad (.069) \qquad (.065)$$

Machinery, except electrical:

$$(S_t)_{est} = .031 + .178N_t + .513S_{t-1} + .299S_{t-2}; \bar{R}^2 = .991; \bar{n} = 5.9$$
$$(.019) \quad (.020) \qquad (.072) \qquad (0.66)$$

Electrical machinery:

$$(S_t)_{est} = .027 + .184N_t + .529S_{t-1} + .278S_{t-2}; \bar{R}^2 = .988; \bar{n} = 5.6$$
$$(.020) \quad (.024) \qquad (.076) \qquad (.069)$$

Other durable goods:

$$(S_t)_{est} = .037 + .463N_t + .252S_{t-1} + .277S_{t-2}; \bar{R}^2 = .983; \bar{n} = 1.7$$
$$(.035) \quad (.036) \qquad (.063) \qquad (.055)$$

Nondurable goods industries:

$$(S_t)_{est} = .024 + .606N_t + .271S_{t-1} + .123S_{t-2}; \bar{R}^2 = .999; \bar{n} = 0.9$$
$$(.035) \quad (.025) \qquad (.046) \qquad (.036)$$

equations are larger than their counterparts in Table 5-5 (in fabricated metals and the machinery industries, by relatively large margins of more than one month). These estimates appear sensible by broad tests of consistency with other information and are actually preferable to the other figures obtained earlier for the same industries.

Patterns of lagged response implied by the second-order equations can be estimated by a stepwise method. They indicate declines in the effects on S_t of N_{t-i} as the lag i increases, but there are also some oscillations, e.g., the influence of N_{t-2} is in most cases larger than that of N_{t-1}.[36]

---

[35] The same is also true of the corresponding equations for primary metals and for blast furnaces and steel mills. Nevertheless, this model seems unsatisfactory for these two industries, since the coefficients of S_{t-2} are negative and the average lags are somewhat lower than those in Table 5-5, column 6. In the light of the earlier results, these lags would be judged too small.

[36] The effects of N_{t-i} on S_t are calculated as follows: for $i = 0$, the effect ("weight") of N_t is $w_0 = a$; for $i = 1$, $w_1 = ab$; for $i = 2$, $w_2 = a(b^2 + c)$; and, in general, $w_i = b(w_{i-1}) + c(w_{i-2})$. To illustrate, the results for fabricated metals are:

Lag (i):	0	1	2	3	4	5	6
Effect of N_{t-i} on S_t:	.250	.111	.116	.081	.066	.051	.040
Cumulative as % of total effect [= $a/(1 - b - c) = 0.859$]	29.1	42.0	55.0	65.0	72.6	78.6	83.2

Finally, N_{t-1} was added to the second-order lag regressions in tests analogous to those performed earlier on the Koyck equations, but the results were on the whole negative. In sum, the gains that can be made by the use of second-order lagged distributions are marginal and limited to monthly data for some industries. No graphs for the results of these calculations are reproduced, since it is generally difficult to establish meaningful differences between them and the graphs for the first-order equations.

Instrumental Variables

It is well known (cf. note 20) that the main difficulty with auto-regressive forms such as the Koyck model (equation 5) or the second-order functions (equation 8) is that, say, S_{t-1} is likely to be correlated with the disturbance terms (v_t or e_t) because of the association between these terms and S_t. Following an approach proposed in recent literature,[37] the variable S_{t-1} in (5) was replaced by $(S_{t-1})_{est}$ as estimated early in this chapter from

$$(S_{6t})_{est} = a_6 + \Sigma_{i=0}^6 b_i N_{t-i} = S_t - u_{6t}$$

for the monthly data and

$$(S_t)_{est} = a_2 + b_{20}N_t + b_{21}N_{t-1} + b_{22}N_{t-2} = S_t - u_{2t}$$

for the quarterly data. In this two-stage procedure, then, $(S_{t-1})_{est}$ is computed first and then substituted into (5) to give

$$S_t = k + aN_t + b(S_{t-1})_{est} + v_t + bu_t. \tag{9}$$

This amounts to using a linear combination of past new orders, that is, $(S_{t-1})_{est}$, as an "instrumental variable." By assumption, the terms N_{t-i} are uncorrelated with the disturbances and, by construction, $(S_{t-1})_{est}$ consists only of such terms; hence $(S_{t-1})_{est}$ may be hypothesized to be independent of the disturbances. Thus one may hope that (9) will provide a consistent estimate of b.

Table 5-6 presents the results of applying model (9) to the monthly and quarterly data. The monthly correlations are for the most part somewhat lower than their counterparts for the Koyck equations in Table 5-5; the average lags are larger for nondurable industries reporting unfilled orders and the three metalworking industries, and

---

[37] For discussion and references, see Griliches, "Distributed Lags," pp. 41–42.

about equal or smaller in the other cases. The quarterly regressions compare more favorably with the corresponding Koyck equations in Table 5-4. The correlations are larger in Table 5-6 for primary metals and blast furnaces, very similar elsewhere in the two sets. The average lags exceed those in Table 5-4 for the three metalworking industries. The quarterly estimates in Table 5-6 appear to be preferable to the others for primary metals and blast furnaces. In particular, the Durbin-Watson statistics d (column 6) show these regressions in a definitely favorable light.[38]

Quarterly estimates of shipments derived from equation (9) for total durables and nonelectrical machinery look very similar to the series for the underlying instrumental variable $(S_t)_{est}$ (see Chart 5-2) and are therefore not reproduced in graphical form. Like that series, these estimates still resemble too much the course of new orders, and they clearly have poorer fits with the observed shipments than do the corresponding estimates from the Koyck regressions in Chart 5-3.

Summary of the Average Distributed-Lag Relations

Different distributed-lag models produce estimates of timing relationships that vary considerably, often even where the models perform equally well according to the usual goodness-of-fit criteria. These timing estimates, which are scattered through several tables and the text, have been brought together so that the varied assortment may be appraised jointly and, if possible, reduced to a few preferred measures.

The result of this undertaking is Table 5-7, which shows first the ranges and then the medians of the average lag estimates for both the monthly and the quarterly regressions (columns 1–3). The lags (all expressed in months) are typically larger when based on quarterly data, though transportation equipment is a clear exception. Also for some industries, such as nondurables and the primary metals groups, the monthly-quarterly differences are small and not uniform in sign (compare the entries on the odd and even lines). The ranges are in most cases large, especially for the quarterly regression estimates (columns 1 and 2).

---

[38] These statistics are lower for the equations with the instrumental variables than for the corresponding Koyck equations. This would be expected, as the calculated d values for the latter equations are likely to be biased toward 2 (see note 26). The more relevant comparison is between the d statistics in Table 5-6 and those for the regressions in Tables 5-2 and 5-3 from which the S_{est} estimates are computed. Here the comparable d values are usually similar.

Table 5-6

Regressions of Shipments on New Orders and on Lagged Predicted Shipments, Major Manufacturing Industries, Monthly and Quarterly, 1947–65 and 1953–65

Industry	Constant Term[a] (1)	Regression Coefficients[a]		Sum of Implicit Coefficients[b] (4)	$\bar{R}^2$ (5)	Durbin-Watson Statistic[c] (6)	Av. Lag[d] (mos.) (7)
		a (2)	b (3)				
	MONTHLY DATA, 1947–65 (221)[e]						
All manufacturing	.046 (.256)	.320 (.051)	.679 (.052)	0.997	.982	0.344	2.11
Durable goods	.075 (.227)	.246 (.057)	.749 (.061)	0.979	.947	0.251	3.0
Nondurable goods	.036 (.041)	.622 (.030)	.377 (.030)	0.999	.998	1.156	0.6
	MONTHLY DATA, 1953–65 (149)[e]						
Reporting unfilled orders							
All industries[f]	.697 (.383)	.267 (.054)	.700 (.065)	0.890	.961	0.526	2.3
Nondurables industries[g]	−.016 (.030)	.379 (.043)	.627 (.045)	1.016	.992	1.706	1.7
Primary metals	.164 (.149)	.216 (.056)	.728 (.083)	0.781	.712	0.822	2.6
Blast furnaces, steel mills	.126 (.128)	.197 (.062)	.726 (.105)	0.721	.504	0.873	2.66
Fabricated metal products	.069 (.036)	.233 (.039)	.729 (.050)	0.858	.945	1.250	2.69
Machinery exc. elect.	.038 (.040)	.157 (.046)	.828 (.058)	0.914	.967	0.427	4.8
Elect. machinery	.082 (.036)	.284 (.044)	.678 (.055)	0.881	.963	0.504	2.10

Transport. equip.	.313 (.160)	.244 (.046)	.683 (.070)	0.772	.847	0.537	2.16
Other durable goods [h]	.058 (.039)	.488 (.043)	.496 (.047)	0.968	.979	1.417	1.0

QUARTERLY DATA, 1947–65 (73)[e]

All manufacturing	−.040 (.397)	.475 (.060)	.530 (.062)	1.011	.986	0.519	3.4
Durable goods	.095 (.364)	.402 (.074)	.592 (.078)	0.986	.955	0.468	4.4
Nondurable goods	.026 (.053)	.741 (.031)	.261 (.032)	1.002	.999	1.258	1.1

QUARTERLY DATA, 1953–65 (49)[e]

Reporting unfilled orders

All industries [f]	.786 (.535)	.429 (.064)	.537 (.078)	0.927	.973	0.960	3.5
Nondurables industries [g]	−.061 (.033)	.484 (.046)	.538 (.048)	1.047	.997	1.865	3.5
Primary metals	.282 (.229)	.426 (.075)	.477 (.108)	0.815	.755	2.097	2.7
Blast furnaces, steel mills	.275 (.203)	.396 (.089)	.435 (.147)	0.701	.528	2.139	2.3
Fabricated metal products	.088 (.045)	.364 (.053)	.589 (.065)	0.886	.970	1.649	4.3
Machinery exc. elect.	.043 (.055)	.291 (.054)	.697 (.068)	0.959	.977	0.506	6.9
Elect. machinery	.094 (.053)	.434 (.067)	.525 (.082)	0.913	.974	0.452	3.3
Transport. equip.	.536 (.248)	.481 (.086)	.395 (.125)	0.795	.888	0.872	1.96
Other durable goods [h]	.029 (.044)	.594 (.048)	.401 (.053)	0.991	.992	1.421	2.01

Notes to Table 5-6

ᵃ The form of the estimates is given by equation (9) in the text. The figures in parentheses are standard errors of the statistics shown.

ᵇ The sum equals $a/(1 - b)$.

ᶜ $d = \Sigma(z_t - z_{t-1})^2/\Sigma z_t^2$, where $z_t = v_t + bu_t$. For the significance points of d, see note 12 and Table 5-3, note d, above.

ᵈ The average lag equals $b(1 - b)$ for the monthly data and $3b(1 - b)$ for the quarterly data.

ᵉ The figure in parentheses is number of observations. It is the effective sample size for each of the industries covered in the section that follows.

ᶠ Includes all durable goods industries and the four nondurable goods industries reporting unfilled orders (see note g).

ᵍ Includes textiles, leather, paper, and printing and publishing.

ʰ Includes professional and scientific instruments; lumber; furniture; stone, clay, and glass products; and miscellaneous industries.

Table 5-7 incorporates four types of equations: the regressions of S_t on several lagged terms N_{t-i} (labeled "A"); the Koyck model relating S_t to N_t and S_{t-1} ("B"); the second-order equations, which include S_{t-2} on the right-hand side ("C"); and the two-stage model relating S_t to N_t and $(S_{t-1})_{est}$ ("D"). When these models are ranked according to the average lags they produce, from shortest to longest, A ranks first, followed in order by D, B, and C. These average ranks are the same for both the monthly and the quarterly regression estimates. However, there is considerable variation in the underlying ranks for the different industries.

The "best" estimates of the average lags (columns 4 and 5) for each industry are supplied by those equations which have the three largest values of the sums of calculated or implied coefficients of N_{t-i} (i.e., of the expressions $\Sigma'b$ or Σ in the preceding tables). Typically, but not always, these are also the equations with the highest adjusted determination coefficients $\bar{R}^2$. For the over-all aggregates (first six lines), the sums Σ are all approximately equal to one, so the "best" equations were selected primarily by the highest $\bar{R}^2$. The lowest and highest average lags thus estimated are listed in column 4. The regressions that produce average lags falling into these ranges are identified in column 5. They account for about half of the number of all estimated equations, but include only 4 applications of model A against 15 each of B and C and 14 of D. The average lags for A are generally smaller. Of the selected regressions, fewer are based on monthly than on quarterly data (20 vs. 28).

The "best" average lag estimates, then, point to rather long delivery periods in the machinery industries (6 to 7 months for nonelectrical machinery, 4 to 6 months for electrical machinery) and to short delivery periods (about 2 months or a little more) in primary metals. The midpoints of the selected ranges for fabricated metals and transportation equipment fall in between, at 4 and 3 months. The groups of industries reporting unfilled orders show average lags of about 3 months. For the other durables group, the typical lag is barely 2 months. The 5-month lag for all durable goods industries contrasts sharply with the 1-month lag for the nondurables.

Regression Estimates and Turning-Point Estimates

In Chapter 4, delivery lags were estimated by matching the dates of specific-cycle turns in new orders and shipments and measuring the intervals between them. This method appears to use only a small part of the evidence of monthly time series, but this impression is not correct. It is true that a cycle which may last several years yields only two additional timing comparisons, but the determination of the turning dates requires a thorough examination of the whole sequence of values that the series has assumed.[39] Problems arise because individual comparisons are often influenced by particular configurations of short movements in the vicinity of a turning point. One expects the resulting errors mostly to cancel each other in the average lag measures, but the probability of this is reduced when the available series are so short that the averages cover few observations.

The present approach based on regression and correlation measures avoids these difficulties but presents some problems of its own. It is more objective but also more mechanical. It uses all available information with about equal weights instead of concentrating on turning points, but a discrimination among the observations—e.g., in favor of major turns—may actually be desired for some purposes. The possibly systematic differences between lags at peaks and troughs, or between some other episodes or subperiods, are ignored.

Comparing the median estimates of the average delivery lags as

[39] This becomes clear when one attempts to substitute a mechanical operation for the judgmental process involved. Thus a computer program for selecting turning points that was recently developed by Gerhard Bry and Charlotte Boschan uses all observations for the given series in each of several computational steps; see their *Cyclical Analysis of Time Series: Selected Procedures and Programs*, Technical Paper 20, New York, NBER, 1971.

Table 5-7

Summary of Regression Estimates of Average Lags of Shipments Behind New Orders, Major Manufacturing Industries, Monthly and Quarterly, 1947–65 and 1953–65

| Industry | Estimates of Average Lags of Shipments Behind New Orders (months) | | | | | Av. Lag of Shipments Estimated from Turning Point Comparisons (months)[d] |
| | | | | "Best" Estimates[b] | | |
	Lowest[a] (1)	Highest[a] (2)	Median[a] (3)	Range of Av. Lags (4)	Regression Code[c] (5)	(6)
				1947–65		
All manufacturing	2.1	3.7	2.9	3.4–3.7	B1, C1, D2	3.1
	2.4	5.0	4.0			
Durable goods	2.6	5.6	4.2	4.4–5.6	B1, C1, D2	5.1
	2.7	7.0	5.6			
Nondurable goods	0.6	1.0	0.8	0.9–1.1	A1, A2, B2, C1, D2	2.0
	1.0	1.1	1.1			
				1953–65		
Reporting unfilled orders						
All industries[e]	2.0	2.6	2.4	2.5–3.6	B1, B2, C1, D2	4.1
	2.2	3.6	3.5			
Nondurables industries[f]	1.2	2.3	2.0	2.2–3.5	A1, A2, B2, C1, D2	2.2
	2.2	3.5	3.2			
Primary metals	1.3	2.6	1.6	1.7–2.7	B1, B2, C2, D1, D2	5.0
	1.5	2.7	1.8			
Blast furnaces, steel mills	1.1	2.7	1.4	1.6–2.7	B1, D1, D2	6.1
	1.2	2.3	1.3			

Industry					
Fabricated metal products	2.0	3.4	2.4	3.4–4.6	B2, C1, C2, D2	3.2
	2.5	4.6	3.9			
Machinery exc. elect.	2.9	5.9	4.6	5.9–7.5	B2, C1, C2, D2	4.9
	3.1	7.5	6.9			
Elect. machinery	1.9	5.6	3.2	4.2–6.0	B1, B2, C1, C2	2.5
	1.9	6.0	4.5			
Transport. equip.	1.6	5.6	3.8	2.0–3.8	B2, C2, D1, D2	3.0
	1.5	3.8	2.8			
Other durable goods [g]	1.0	1.7	1.3	1.7–2.4	B2, C1, C2, D2	2.2
	1.6	2.4	2.0			

[a] For each industry, entry on first line is for estimates from monthly regressions; entry on second line, for estimates from quarterly regressions.

[b] Based on the equations which provide the three highest values of the sums of calculated or implied coefficients of the new-order terms (i.e., the three highest values of Σb or Σ). For the 1947–65 aggregates, where the sums are all about equal to 1, the highest $\bar{R}^2$'s are used instead as criterion. See text.

[c] Identifies the equations referred to in note b and others that produce average lags in the range given in column 4. A refers to the regressions of S_t on N_{t-i}, where $i = 0, 1, \ldots, 6$ months (Table 5-2) or $i = 0, 1, 2$ quarters (Table 5-3); B, to the Koyck equations (Tables 5-4 and 5-5); C, to the second-order functions (see text with tabulations above); D, to the regressions of S_t on N_t and $(S_{t-1})_{est}$ (Table 5-6); 1, to monthly and 2 to quarterly regressions. For example, B1 denotes monthly Koyck equations, C2, quarterly second-order functions, etc.

[d] Based on the timing comparisons in Table 4-5 and note 9 in Chapter 4. For the over-all aggregates, the averages refer to the period 1948–65 and agree with the corresponding entries in Table 4-6, column 9. For the component durables industries, the averages refer to the period since 1953 and hence exclude the observations recorded in Table 4-5, columns 1–4.

[e] Includes all durable goods industries and the four nondurable goods industries reporting unfilled orders (see note f).

[f] Includes textiles, leather, paper, and printing and publishing.

[g] Includes professional and scientific instruments; lumber; furniture; stone, clay, and glass products; and miscellaneous industries.

221

derived from the monthly regressions with the averages of the turning-point measures for the same periods, one finds that the latter tend to exceed the former (Table 5-7, columns 3 and 6). The differences are very large for the primary metals industries, but elsewhere they are approximately equal to one month and are negligibly small in three cases. Reverse differences are found in only two instances: The median regression lags are somewhat longer than the turning-point lags for electrical machinery and transportation equipment.

The regression measures here considered largely reflect the association between fairly short movements in new orders and shipments, measured in months or quarters. For such movements, the maximum-correlation lags are evidently quite small: The highest correlations in Table 5-1 are typically those for the simultaneous timing of N and S. As noted earlier, it is plausible that many random events, e.g., strikes, affect both variables at about the same time. The correlations between the longer, cyclical movements, on the other hand, are likely to involve longer lags. Thus a transition from an expansion to a contraction in new orders, especially if it is gradual rather than abrupt, would require some time to be recognized as such and translated into a similar reversal in shipments. The intervening process is a cumulation of many short-lag effects, in which backlogs of unfilled orders act as a factor that cushions and delays the reaction on the supply side.

An important type of lag distribution in production to order contains a clustering of lags around some typical (modal) delivery period and also smaller frequencies of progressively longer lags. Such a distribution is skewed "to the left," i.e., in the direction of longer lags reaching further into the past. The skewness implies that the mean and median diverge from the mode in the direction of longer lags. The maximum-correlation timing probably often corresponds to the mode,[40] and it is indeed generally coincident or a shorter lag than the average derived from the estimated lag distributions (compare Table 5-1 with the subsequent tables). The average lags at the turning points correspond more nearly to the means than to the modes of the lag distributions, but they

[40] Let a_k be the highest of the coefficients a_i in $S_t = \Sigma a_i N_{t-i} + u_t$, where the summation is over $i = 0, \ldots, \infty$. Under certain conditions, the lag k will coincide with that lag of S relative to N which yields the highest simple correlation between the two variables. The assumptions here are that the autocorrelations of N are lower the longer the intervals over which they are taken (i.e., $r_{12} > r_{13} > r_{14}$, etc., for successive periods $t = 1, 2, 3, \ldots$) and that they are independent of t for a given interval ($r_{12} = r_{23} = r_{34}$, etc.). The variances of N_{t-i} are assumed equal for all values of i. I am indebted to Jacob Mincer for informing me of a proof of these propositions that he has recently developed.

are frequently still longer than the mean regression lags estimated from the monthly regressions.

In several cases, including all manufacturing and total durables (compare columns 4 and 6 in Table 5-7), the turning-point estimates fall within the ranges of our preferred regression estimates. The ranges, being based on quarterly as well as on monthly regressions, include longer lags, which actually exceed the turning-point lags in some instances (notably for the machinery industries). However, turning-point comparisons yield much longer lags than any of the regressions for the primary metals industries. This is due in large measure to particular developments, such as the major steel strike in 1956, which had effects of different intensities upon new orders and shipments (see Chart 3-2 and Table 4-5 with the accompanying text).[41]

Predictive Equations with Variable and Constant Lags

Variable Lag Coefficients

All preceding estimates are based on distributed-lag models with fixed coefficients. However, the lead time required to fill orders lengthens when the rates at which new orders are received are high relative to the desired or optimal levels of capacity utilization. At such times, as noted on earlier occasions, pressures of demand upon capacity are met in large part by backlog accumulation. The build-up of unfilled orders indicates that the average time-span between the receipt of an order and the start of production on it tends to increase. Conversely, when the demand pressures subside and the backlogs decline, this "waiting-period" part of the over-all delivery lag gets shorter. After the decline in the rates of new orders received and, possibly, an increase in the rates of past orders canceled (Chapter 2) had depleted the backlogs sufficiently, little if any waiting would be imposed on currently received orders, that is, work on them would tend to begin promptly after receipt and the delivery lag would be largely limited to the actual worktime required to fill the orders. This argument implies that the lags of shipments behind new orders vary systematically in the

[41] At most turning points, primary metals shipments followed orders by fairly short intervals, but their lags in 1953–54, 1956, and 1960–61 were long. Excluding these episodes leaves nine observations for total primary metals and five for blast furnaces; the average lags for these subsets are 2.4 and 3.0 months, respectively, which are already much closer to the regression estimates in Table 5-7.

course of the business cycle; hence it suggests that the coefficients in the distributed-lag relations between S and N should be variable rather than fixed and such as to make the average lag a positive function of some measure of the relative demand pressures.

A model with such variable lag coefficients was presented recently by Popkin.[42] In his original and very interesting article, Popkin starts from a predictive equation in which shipments are related only to the preceding, and not also to the current, values of new orders. The equation, designed to be applied to quarterly data, reads in our notation:

$$S_t = \alpha_{1,t}N_{t-1} + \alpha_{2,t}N_{t-2} + u_t. \tag{10}$$

The coefficients of the new-order terms in (10) are made to depend on the ratio of unfilled orders to shipments, U/S, and since this ratio varies over time so will these coefficients (it is because of this that time subscripts must be added to α_1 and α_2). In accordance with the preceding discussion, U/S can be viewed as an index of relative demand pressures, which provides the rationale for this approach. When U/S rises, the influence on S_t of orders received in the more distant past should increase, while the influence of the more recent orders should decrease, that is, α_2 is then to become more important relative to α_1. This is expected because when backlogs accumulate faster than output and shipments can be increased, newly received orders pile up and must presumably yield to the older orders which have priority in the production schedule. Thus current shipments would then consist in larger part of the older orders. By the reverse of the same argument, α_1 should gain relative to α_2 when the ratio U/S declines. Popkin assumes that these relations involve a one-period lag and are linear but not necessarily proportional; so

$$\alpha_{1,t} = \beta_0 + \beta_1(U/S)_{t-1}. \tag{11}$$

A further assumption is that all of each quarter's orders will result in shipments over the following two quarters, which implies the constraint $\alpha_{1,t} + \alpha_{2,t+1} = 1$. It follows that

$$\alpha_{2,t} = 1 - [\beta_0 + \beta_1(U/S)_{t-2}]. \tag{12}$$

---

[42] Joel Popkin, "The Relationship Between New Orders and Shipments: An Analysis of the Machinery and Equipment Industries," *Survey of Current Business*, March 1965, pp. 24–32.

Substituting (11) and (12) into (10) results in

$$S_t = [\beta_0 + \beta_1(U/S)_{t-1}]N_{t-1} + \{1 - [\beta_0 + \beta_1(U/S)_{t-2}]\}N_{t-2} + u_t. \quad (13)$$

Finally, by rewriting a little and dropping two constraints implicit in (13) so as to allow for departures from the hypothesis, one gets

$$S_t = \alpha_0 + \beta_0\Delta N_{t-1} + \beta_1\Delta[(U/S)N]_{t-1} + \beta_2 N_{t-2} + u_t, \quad (14)$$

which is the form to be estimated.[43]

Popkin applied equation (14) to shipments and new and unfilled orders for the market category of machinery and equipment. Since the data were deflated by the BLS wholesale price index for machinery and equipment, the variables are expressed in billions of 1957–59 dollars. For the period from III-1953 through III-1964 (45 quarters), Popkin reports the following result:

$$S_t = 2.409 + 1.205\Delta N_{t-1}$$
$$\quad (6.29) \quad (5.16)$$

$$- 0.390\Delta[(U/S)N]_{t-1} + 0.717N_{t-2}; \bar{R}^2 = .868 \quad (15)$$
$$\quad (3.70) \qquad\qquad (16.09)$$

The numbers in parentheses are the t statistics (ratios of the coefficients to their standard errors); they indicate that all the estimates (including the constant) are significant at the 1 per cent level. The equation provides a good fit to the sample data, but the residuals show a significant degree of autocorrelation.[44]

Equation (15) implies that $\alpha_{1t} = 1.035 - 0.390(U/S)_{t-1}$, which corresponds to (11), and that $\alpha_{2t} = 0.318 + 0.390(U/S)_{t-2}$, which corresponds to (12) when allowance is made for the fact that β_2 in (15) is not 1 but 0.717.[45] It is clear that α_1 varies inversely and α_2 varies directly with U/S. As expected, then, a rise in the ratio U/S is associated

[43]Note that (13) can be written as $\beta_0[N_{t-1} - N_{t-2}] + \beta[(U/S)_{t-1}N_{t-1} - (U/S)_{t-2}N_{t-2}] + N_{t-2} + u_t$. The two terms in brackets are changes over time for which the shorter notation ΔN_{t-1} and $\Delta[(U/S) N]_{t-1}$ is adopted. Allowing for the possibility of a nonzero constant term (α_0) and of a coefficient of N_{t-2} which differs from 1 (β_2), this equation is then translated directly into (14).

[44]The adjusted standard error of estimate is $0.271 billion, while the mean value of shipments during the period is $8.46 billion. The residual autocorrelation statistic is 1.292, significant at the 1 per cent level. When charted, the calculated shipments are seen to miss turning points by changing direction one quarter after actual shipments. See Popkin, "Relationship Between New Orders and Shipments," pp. 28–29 and Chart 16.

[45]Accordingly, the values of α_{1t} and α_{2t} always add up to 0.717 (not to 1). The ratio of the constant term in (15) to the average value of new orders is 0.289, which, when added to 0.717 totals approximately 1.

with an increase in the proportion of orders received during $t - 2$ and a decrease in the proportion of orders received during $t - 1$, within the aggregate of shipments for period t. Thus the higher (lower) the ratio, the longer (shorter) is the average lag of S relative to N.[46]

When production runs at virtually full capacity, increases in shipments may be constrained to smaller amounts than those predicted only by the recent levels and changes of new orders and backlog-shipment ratios. Severe shortages of materials due to strikes, etc., could likewise interfere with the performance of the model. Popkin notes these and some other possible shortcomings of his estimating equations. The other models of the N-S relationship that are considered in this chapter are subject to similar difficulties. However, the limitations to quarterly data and to orders of only two quarters $(t - 1)$ and $(t - 2)$ may well cause a misspecification of the lag structure, and other models not so restricted are possibly better in this respect. This is the cost paid for the presumably realistic and important feature of variable coefficients combined with the ease of estimation and the predictive nature of the model.[47]

In an effort to examine further the variable lag hypothesis in the context of orders-shipments relations, I have applied equation (14) to the OBE-Census major-industry data. The results are presented in Table 5-8.

For most of the industries, the directly estimated regression coefficients β are definitely significant statistically and have the expected signs. Typically, β_0 is large and positive, while β_1 is small and negative (columns 2 and 3). This means that $\alpha_{1,t}$, the implied coefficients of N_{t-1}, are likely to be large, except at high values of the backlog-shipment ratios [according to equation (11)]. It is not surprising that the effects

---

[46] The simple average of one-quarter and two-quarter lags is a lag of 4.5 months, which would apply if N_{t-1} and N_{t-2} had equal weights ($\alpha_{1,t} = \alpha_{2,t}$). The value of U/S associated with such a lag is about 1.735, as implied by equation (15). When U/S is as low as 0.815, α_1 and α_2 equal 0.717 and zero, respectively, giving an average lag of 3 months; when U/S is as high as 2.743, $\alpha_1 = 0$ and $\alpha_2 = 0.717$, and the average lag is 6 months. Actually, the ratio of unfilled orders to shipments (quarterly, seasonally adjusted, and deflated) fluctuated in 1953–64 within a narrower range, approximately between 1.0 and 2.0. This implies a low value of the average lag of about 3.3 months (with $\alpha_1 \simeq 0.645$ and $\alpha_2 \simeq 0.072$) and a high value of the average lag of about 4.9 months (with $\alpha_1 \simeq 0.255$ and $\alpha_2 \simeq 0.462$).

[47] Only a few small modifications of the assumed lag distribution were tried, with some success, in the machinery-and-equipment analysis under review. The contents of the quarterly terms N_{t-1} and N_{t-2} were redefined by one-month shifts forward or backward relative to the current quarter t to which S_t refers. The shift forward in time would cause a one-month "overlap" and a shortening of the imposed lag structure; the shift backward would cause a one-month "gap" and a lengthening of the lag. Popkin reports that the shortening worked better than the lengthening.

on S_t of N_{t-1} should be large, especially since they probably absorb much of the influence of the omitted N_t terms.

The β_2 coefficients are approximately equal to 1 for all manufacturing, the nondurables, and the other durables group, and are not much smaller than 1 for total durables and the machinery industries (column 4). In these cases, then, the total effect on S_{t-1} of N_{t-2} does come close to unity (the sums of the variable coefficients $\alpha_{1,t}$ and $\alpha_{2,t}$ equal β_2, up to rounding errors). For the other industries, the values of β_2 fall short of 1.0 by varying but at least appreciable margins. In these cases, the constant terms α_0 are also disturbingly large.

Once more the least satisfactory results are for total primary metals and for blast furnaces. Here the α_0 are very large and highly significant, and the β_2 are only 0.66 and 0.55. Moreover, the β_1 coefficients are either positive, which contradicts the hypothesis that α_1 varies inversely to U/S, or, more likely, are not different from zero, which contradicts the notion of variable lag coefficients.[48]

The determination coefficients, $\bar{R}^2$, like their counterparts for the other models, are very high (exceeding .9) for industries other than primary metals and transportation equipment (column 5). Not surprisingly, these correlations tend to be lower than those for the equations that include N_t (see Tables 5-3 and 5-4), but the differences involved are generally small.

The best feature of the regressions in Table 5-8 is the high Durbin-Watson statistics, d, which give no indications of significant autocorrelation in the residuals. This contrasts with the generally low d values for the quarterly regressions of S_t on N_t, N_{t-1}, and N_{t-2} (see Table 5-3, column 7 and note c).

The values of the variable coefficients $\alpha_{1,t}$ and $\alpha_{2,t}$ can be computed given the estimates of β_0, β_1, and β_2, and the reported figures for the backlog-shipment ratios U/S. The estimates for the mean values of U/S over the regression periods, $\bar{\alpha}_{1,t}$ and $\bar{\alpha}_{2,t}$, are shown in columns 7 and 8 of the table.

These measures are not apt to be satisfactory for interindustry comparisons of the lag structures, since each equation includes only two new-order terms with the same time subscripts ($t-1$, $t-2$). Estimates

---

[48] These results are not inconsistent with the earlier ones which suggest that shipments of primary metal products consist of orders received in the same and (perhaps to a larger extent) in the preceding quarter, while the longer lag terms are unimportant. See the regressions for these industries in Table 5-3.

Table 5-8
Regressions of Shipments on New Orders of Two Preceding Quarters, Variable Lag Coefficients, Major Manufacturing Industries, 1947–65 and 1953–65

Industry	Constant Term[a] (1)	Regression Coefficients[a] β_0 (2)	β_1 (3)	β_2 (4)	$\bar{R}^2$ (5)	Durbin-Watson Statistic[b] (6)	Estimates at Mean Values[c] $\bar{\alpha}_{1,t}$ (7)	$\bar{\alpha}_{2,t}$ (8)
				1947–65 (74)[d]				
All manufacturing	.164 (.404)	1.202 (0.104)	−.225 (.032)	1.001 (0.015)	.985	2.026	.762	.246
Durable goods	.358 (.314)	1.283 (0.123)	−.181 (.024)	0.976 (0.022)	.964	1.820	.626	.356
Nondurable goods	−.003 (.152)	0.856 (0.114)	−.095 (.109)	1.014 (0.011)	.991	1.872	.878	.187
				1953–65 (50)[d]				
Reporting unfilled orders								
All industries[e]	2.020 (.588)	1.043 (0.158)	−.085 (.038)	0.908 (0.030)	.958	1.631	.802	.110
Nondurables industries[f]	−.099 (.052)	0.975 (0.139)	−.090 (.064)	1.038 (0.014)	.992	1.864	.899	.140

Primary metals	.980 (.180)	0.662 (0.129)	.021 (.031)	0.660 (0.064)	.733	1.827	.710	-.051
Blast furnaces, steel mills	.732 (.130)	0.608 (0.119)	.013 (.022)	0.548 (0.082)	.550	1.981	.643	-.096
Fabricated metal products	.216 (.061)	0.760 (0.169)	-.093 (.043)	0.883 (0.036)	.945	1.955	.519	.367
Machinery, exc. elect.	.113 (.045)	1.379 (0.145)	-.226 (.033)	0.954 (0.020)	.982	1.849	.638	.326
Elect. machinery	.145 (.063)	1.283 (0.198)	-.158 (.046)	0.934 (0.031)	.955	1.520	.664	.279
Transport. equip.	.929 (.209)	0.953 (0.147)	-.067 (.021)	0.789 (0.051)	.836	1.720	.488	.307
Other durable goods[g]	.051 (.085)	1.103 (0.159)	-.105 (.077)	0.993 (0.027)	.968	2.018	.933	.062

[a] The estimates are based on equation (14) in the text. The figures in parentheses are standard errors of the statistics shown.

[b] The Durbin-Watson statistic (d) equals $\Sigma[(u_t) - (u_{t-1})]^2/\Sigma(u_t^2)$. For the significance points of d, see text note 11 and Table 5-3, note d.

[c] Computed from the equations for the mean values of the backlog-shipments ratios: $\bar\alpha_{1,t} = \beta_0 + \beta_1(\bar U/\bar S)_{-1}$ and $\bar\alpha_{2,t} = \beta_2 - [\beta_0 + \beta_1(\bar U/\bar S)_{t-2}]$.

[d] The figure in parentheses is number of quarterly observations. It is the effective sample size for each of the industries covered in the section that follows.

[e] Includes all durable goods industries and the four nondurable goods industries reporting unfilled orders (see note f).

[f] Includes textiles, leather, paper, and printing and publishing.

[g] Includes professional and scientific instruments; lumber; furniture; stone, clay, and glass products; and miscellaneous industries.

of average lags may be obtained by multiplying $\bar{\alpha}_{1,t}$ by 3 and $\bar{\alpha}_{2,t}$ by 6 and adding the products. When this is done, the results vary only from 3.2 to 4.0 months among industries other than total primary metals and blast furnaces. The actual differences between the average delivery lags in the industries compared are, in all likelihood, considerably larger, as indicated by the measures assembled in Table 5-7.

Variable vs. Fixed Lag Coefficients

Despite the weakness just noted, equation (14) turns out to be a useful model in dealing with the specific question of the variability of shipments lags over time. When compared with estimates which use the same quarterly data to link S_t to N_{t-1} and N_{t-2} by means of fixed lag coefficients (Table 5-9), the results obtained with variable coefficients are for the most part superior.

The implied average coefficients $\bar{\alpha}_{1,t}$ and $\bar{\alpha}_{2,t}$ in Table 5-8 are strikingly (and somewhat reassuringly) similar to the corresponding,

Chart 5-5

Regressions for Shipments of Durable Goods Industries and Nonelectrical Machinery, Based on Variable Lag Coefficients, Quarterly, 1947–65

PART A

$$(S_t)_{est} = a + b_1(N_{t-1} - N_{t-2}) + b_3[(U/S)_{t-1} - (U/S)_{t-2}] + b_3N_{t-2}$$

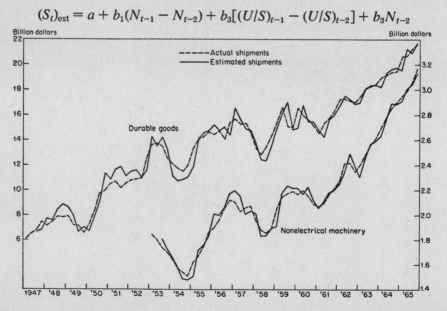

Chart 5-5 (continued)

PART B

$$(S_t)_{est} = a + b_1 N_{t-1} + b_2 N_{t-2}$$

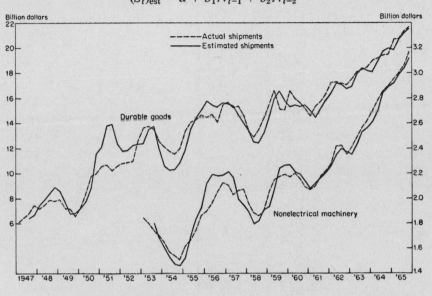

directly estimated coefficients in Table 5-9, that is, to b_{31} and b_{32}, respectively. But the sums of the variable coefficients are in several cases appreciably larger than the sums of the fixed coefficients (compare columns 4 in the two tables). The constant terms are often considerably smaller in the variable lag than in the fixed lag equations (columns 1). The differences between the values of $\bar{R}^2$, while small, also favor the variable lag regressions (column 5). And the Durbin-Watson statistics are low for most of the fixed lag equations, suggesting positive autocorrelations of the residuals, whereas the evidence from the d tests for the variable lag estimates is generally favorable (columns 6).

Only for total primary metals and for blast furnaces are the regressions with fixed coefficients somewhat better than those with variable coefficients, but neither type of equation works really well for these industries; in particular N_{t-2} does not emerge as a significant factor in either model (see sixth and seventh lines in the two tables).

Chart 5-5 compares the estimates of shipments of durable goods manufacturers and the nonelectrical machinery industry based on the

Table 5-9

Regressions of Shipments on New Orders of Two Preceding Quarters, Fixed Lag Coefficients, Major Manufacturing Industries, 1947–65 and 1953–65

Industry	Constant Term[a] (1)	Regression Coefficients[a] b_{31} (2)	b_{32} (3)	Sum of b's (4)	$\bar{R}^2$ (5)	Durbin-Watson Statistic[b] (6)
		1947–65 (74)[c]				
All manufacturing	0.521 (0.519)	.717 (.101)	.275 (.102)	0.992	.974	0.945
Durable goods	0.719 (0.412)	.641 (.116)	.313 (.117)	0.955	.937	0.664
Nondurable goods	0.011 (0.151)	.796 (.091)	.218 (.093)	1.014	.991	1.876
		1953–65 (50)[c]				
Reporting unfilled orders						
All industries[d]	2.535 (0.563)	.776 (.107)	.109 (.112)	0.885	.954	1.126
Nondurables industries[e]	-0.110 (0.052)	.817 (.084)	.226 (.088)	1.043	.992	1.683

Primary metals	0.942 (0.172)	.722 (.095)	−.050 (.096)	0.672	.736	1.989
Blast furnaces, steel mills	0.718 (0.127)	.643 (.102)	−.087 (.102)	0.556	.556	2.118
Fabricated metal products	0.294 (0.051)	.448 (.087)	.391 (.088)	0.840	.940	1.692
Machinery exc. elect.	0.281 (0.054)	.494 (.097)	.393 (.102)	0.885	.964	0.665
Elect. machinery	0.242 (0.062)	.690 (.105)	.203 (.111)	0.892	.945	0.900
Transport. equip.	1.076 (0.222)	.506 (.105)	.253 (.113)	0.819	.805	1.176
Other durable goods[f]	0.073 (0.084)	.928 (.095)	.060 (.100)	0.988	.968	1.761

[a] The estimating equation is

$$S_t = a_3 + b_{31}N_{t-1} + b_{32}N_{t-2} + u_{32}.$$

The figures in parentheses are the standard errors of the statistics shown.

[b] The Durbin-Watson statistic (d) equals $\Sigma(u_{3t} - u_{3t-1})^2/\Sigma(u_{3t})^2$. For the significance points of d, see note 11 and Table 5-3, note d, above.

[c] The figure in parentheses is the number of quarterly observations. It represents the effective sample size for each of the industries covered in the section that follows.

[d] Includes all durable goods industries and the four nondurable goods industries reporting unfilled orders (see note e).

[e] Includes textiles, leather, paper, and printing and publishing.

[f] Includes professional and scientific instruments; lumber; furniture; stone, clay, and glass products; and miscellaneous industries.

variable lag model (Part A) and the fixed lag model (Part B), and refer to the regressions shown in Tables 5-8 and 5-9. Here, as elsewhere, shipments estimated from new-order data (S_{est}) show larger variations than do actual shipments (S), but the use of variable instead of fixed coefficients reduces the amplitudes of S_{est} markedly, thus bringing S_{est} and S closer together. This is because in expansion, when the levels of "older" orders are low relative to those of the more recent orders, the former gain greater influence on the variable lag estimate of shipments, while in contraction, when the reverse is true, the relative influence of the older orders declines.[49]

Generalized Least-Squares Estimators

The disturbance terms are probably positively autocorrelated for several of the relationships in Table 5-9, and it is interesting to observe that this cannot be attributed to the omission of N_t from these regressions. (Actually, there is *more* evidence of autocorrelation in Table 5-3, where S_t is related to N_t as well as to N_{t-1} and N_{t-2}.)[50]

A very simple form of the dependence of disturbances over time is the first-order autoregressive scheme

$$u_t = \rho u_{t-1} + \epsilon_t. \tag{16}$$

This relation is often assumed, although it is actually rather special and may not apply, because knowledge about the true structure of the disturbances is usually lacking and ρ is easy to obtain from the least-squares regression of calculated residuals. The computed autocorrelation coefficient can then be used to transform the variables and re-estimate their relationship so as to get new residuals e_t, which are presumably not significantly autocorrelated.[51]

Applying this approach to the residuals u_{3t} from the regressions of Table 5-9, let us first estimate ρ_1 from

$$u_{3t} = \rho_1 u_{3t-1} + e_{it}, \tag{16a}$$

by least squares. In cases where the coefficients ρ_1 are definitely

---

[49] However, the systematic error of overestimating the fluctuations of shipments, while substantially reduced, is still quite evident in the variable coefficients case. It should be noted that no provision is made in any of the regressions for a capacity constraint that may limit the expansion of output and shipments at certain times. Limitations of this sort could be responsible for some of the discrepancies between S_{est} and S, particularly in 1951.

[50] Compare the Durbin-Watson statistics in Table 5-9, column 6, with those in Table 5-3, column 7.

[51] Inefficient predictions and underestimation of the sampling variances of the regression coefficients are among the costs of a direct application of the usual least-squares estimation formulas to situations involving autocorrelated disturbances. On the consequences and treatment of this problem, and in particular on the above approach as an implication of "generalized least squares," see Johnston, *Econometric Methods*, pp. 179–88, 193–94.

significant, the next step is to compute least-squares regressions for the transformed variables according to

$$S_t - \rho_1 S_{t-1} = a_3^*(1 - \rho_1) + b_{31}^*(N_{t-1} - \rho_1 N_{t-2})$$
$$+ b_{32}^*(N_{t-2} - \rho_1 N_{t-3}) + e_{1t}. \quad (17)$$

The regression coefficients b_{31}^* and b_{32}^* in (17) are new estimates of the effects on S_t of N_{t-1} and N_{t-2}, to be compared to b_{31} and b_{32} in Table 5-10.[52] The residuals e_{1t} are subject to tests for the presence of auto-correlation; if they are significantly autocorrelated, an iteration of the procedure would be indicated.

The same method was also applied to the relations that link S_t to N_t as well as to N_{t-1} and N_{t-2}, so as to learn more about the uses of this approach in the present context and in particular to check on the effects of the omission of N_t from (17). That is, using the residuals u_{2t} from the regressions of Table 5-3, the values of ρ_2 were estimated from

$$u_{2t} = \rho_2 u_{2t-1} + e_{2t} \quad (16b)$$

and used to compute the transformed variables for equations

$$S_t - \rho_2 S_{t-1} = a_2^*(1 - \rho_2) + b_{20}^*(N_t - \rho_2 N_{t-1})$$
$$+ b_{21}^*(N_{t-1} - \rho_2 N_{t-2}) + b_{22}^*(N_{t-2} - \rho_2 N_{t-3}) + e_{2t}. \quad (18)$$

The estimated autocorrelation coefficients ρ_1 range from 0.019 to 0.735; the values of ρ_2 vary from 0.064 to 0.830. Both ρ_1 and ρ_2 are very small for the metalworking industries, and at least one of them is also small for the nondurables and the other durables group. The sectors or industries for which both ρ_1 and ρ_2 are large enough to appear significant include all manufacturing, total durables, the group of industries reporting unfilled orders, the two machinery industries, and transportation equipment.

[52] From

$$S_t = a_3 + b_{31} N_{t-1} + b_{32} N_{t-2} + u_{3t}$$

subtract

$$\rho_1 S_{t-1} = \rho_1 a_3 + \rho_1 b_{31} N_{t-2} + \rho_1 b_{32} N_{t-3} + \rho_1 u_{3-1}.$$

The result is

$$S_t - \rho_1 S_{t-1} = a_3(1 - \rho_1) + b_{31}(N_{t-1} - \rho N_{t-2}) + b_{32}(N_{t-2} - \rho_1 N_{t-3}) + e_{1t}.$$

This indicates the general relationship between the model used in Table 5-9 and equation (17). Of course, the estimated coefficients differ, since direct least-squares procedures are applied without any constraints in both cases: to the basic data on S and N in Table 5-9 and to the transformed variables $(S_t - \rho_1 S_{t-1})$, $(N_t - \rho_1 N_{t-1})$, etc., in (17).

Table 5-10

Lagged Relations Between Shipments and New Orders Estimated from Data Transformed to Account for Autocorrelated Disturbances, Selected Industries, Quarterly, 1947–65 and 1953–65

Industry	Autocorrelation Coefficient[a] (1)	Constant Term[b] (2)	Regression Coefficients[c] (3)	(4)	(5)	$\bar{R}^2$ (6)	Durbin-Watson Statistic[d] (7)
			I. EQUATION (17)[e]				
1. All manufacturing	.526	0.561 (0.437)		.568 (.079)	.401 (.080)	.924	1.693
2. Durable goods	.668	0.823 (0.295)		.492 (.083)	.337 (.083)	.725	1.684
3. All industries reporting unfilled orders[f]	.420	1.758 (0.479)		.699 (.105)	.164 (.110)	.904	1.804
4. Machinery except elect.	.658	0.147 (0.035)		.462 (.067)	.359 (.069)	.872	1.711
5. Elect. machinery	.526	0.172 (0.044)		.524 (.076)	.314 (.080)	.873	1.585
6. Transport. equip.	.508	0.766 (0.172)		.345 (.086)	.300 (.091)	.550	1.732

236

		II. EQUATION (18)[g]					
7. All manufacturing	.715	0.304 (0.262)	.541 (.051)	.256 (.052)	.164 (.052)	.929	1.697
8. Durable goods	.725	0.422 (0.217)	.476 (.063)	.230 (.068)	.179 (.064)	.803	1.657
9. All industries reporting unfilled orders[f]	.53	1.132 (0.358)	.532 (.090)	.201 (.113)	.151 (.083)	.923	1.779
10. Machinery exc. elect.	.735	0.106 (0.025)	.325 (.055)	.308 (.055)	.191 (.057)	.896	1.059
11. Elect. machinery	.647	0.116 (0.028)	.439 (.059)	.286 (.057)	.117 (.058)	.910	1.413
12. Transport. equip.	.601	0.391 (0.120)	.473 (.068)	.143 (.064)	.154 (.065)	.723	1.850

[a] On estimation, see equations 16a and 16b and text.

[b] Standard errors of the constant terms are given in parentheses.

[c] For equation 17, b_{31} is shown in column 4, and b_{32} in column 5. For equation 18, b_{20}, b_{21}, and b_{22} are shown in columns 3–5 in that order. The figures in parentheses are standard errors of the statistics shown.

[d] Durbin-Watson statistic (d) equals $\sum(e_t - e_{t-1})^2/e_t^2$, where e stands for e_1 in lines 1–5 and for e_2 in lines 6–10. For the significance points of d, see note 11 and Table 5-3, note d, above. There are 74 quarterly observations for the series on all manufacturing and durable goods industries and 50 for the others.

[e] See text and note 52.

[f] Includes all durable goods industries and four nondurable goods industries: textiles, leather, paper, and printing and publishing.

[g] See text.

Table 5-10 presents the estimates of equations (17) and (18) for these six industries. The Durbin-Watson statistics are considerably higher here than before the transformation of the variables (compare the figures in Table 5-10, column 7, lines 1–6, with the corresponding entries in Table 5-9, column 6). The d tests gave strong indications of positive residual autocorrelations in Table 5-9 (all manufacturing, durables, electrical and nonelectrical machinery, transportation equipment); they suggest that there is little if any residual autocorrelation in the equations of Table 5-10, lines 1–5.

Consistently with other findings (see note 52 and text above), $\rho_1 < \rho_2$ for each of the industries covered (Table 5-10, column 1). A few differences of the same kind still exist between the estimates from the transformed variables, that is, between equations 17, which do not, and equations 18, which do, include N_t. Unlike the former regressions in the first six lines [from equation (17)] the ones from (18) do, in some cases, give considerable evidence of autocorrelated residuals. This is shown by the values of d for the machinery industries, particularly non-electrical.

The regression coefficients in Table 5-10 are lower for the current and immediate past values of new orders and higher for the more distant past values, when compared with the corresponding coefficients in Tables 5-3 and 5-9. For illustrations of the statements in this paragraph, see the accompanying table. (Similar results can be obtained

	All Manufacturing, from Table				Durable Goods Industries, from Table			
	5-9	5-10 (Part I)	5-3	5-10 (Part II)	5-9	5-10 (Part I)	5-3	5-10 (Part II)
Coefficient of N_t			.527	.541			.480	.476
Coefficient of N_{t-1}	.717	.568	.138	.256	.641	.492	.092	.230
Coefficient of N_{t-2}	.275	.401	.330	.164	.313	.337	.397	.179
Sum of co-efficients	.992	.969	.995	.961	.954	.829	.969	.885
$\bar{R}^2$	.974	.924	.984	.929	.955	.725	.951	.803

Chart 5-6
Regressions for Shipments of Durable Goods Industries and Nonelectrical Machinery, Based on Transformed Variables, Quarterly, 1947–65

PART A

$$S_t - \rho_1 S_{t-1} = a + b_1(N_{t-1} - \rho_1 N_{t-2}) + b_2(N_{t-2} - \rho_1 N_{t-3})$$

PART B

$$S_t - \rho_2 S_{t-1} = a + b_1(N_t - \rho_2 N_{t-1}) + b_2(N_{t-1} - \rho_2 N_{t-2}) + b_3(N_{t-2} - \rho_2 N_{t-3})$$

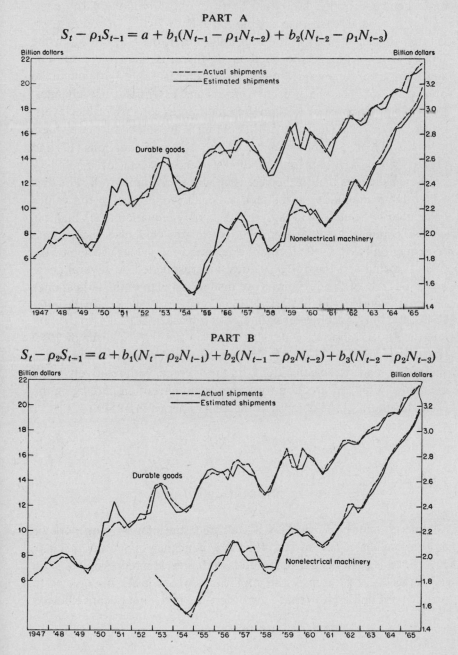

for the other industries from the same tables.) Moreover, the transformation of the variable results in "well-behaved" patterns of a monotonic decrease of the lag coefficients in the direction of the past: $b_{20}^* > b_{21}^* > b_{22}^*$ in each case (Table 5-10, lines 7–12). In contrast, b_{21} is often smaller than b_{22} in the regressions of Table 5-3, and b_{20}, while typically the largest of the coefficients there, is not always so. The sums of the coefficients are somewhat smaller in Table 5-10 than in the other tables. Since the present regressions essentially use changes, they also produce lower $\bar{R}^2$ than the other regressions which use levels, but the values of $\bar{R}^2$ in Table 5-10, column 6, are still comfortably high.

Finally, Chart 5-6 shows that the applications of equations (17) and (18) to the quarterly data for total durables and nonelectrical machinery produce estimates that fit the recorded shipments quite well. The bias of too large amplitudes is reduced to small proportions in the values calculated by relating S_t to N_{t-1} and N_{t-2} only [equation (17)], and it is almost eliminated in the improved estimates that also incorporate N_t [equation (18)]. In the former series, the peak values are somewhat overestimated and the trough values underestimated on several occasions, but few of the deviations are disturbingly large (the largest ones refer to the durables in the early Korean phase in 1950–51). In the latter series, the only sizable overestimates can be seen at peaks, in the first quarter of 1951 (for total durables) and in the third quarter of 1959 (for nonelectrical machinery). The timing of the computed and actual shipments tends to be coincident, on the average, with relatively small deviations in either direction (one significant exception here being the early downturn of the computed machinery series in 1959).

Summary

Shipments may be viewed as a weighted sum of past (and perhaps current) values of new orders, for the dependence of S_t on N_{t-i} ($i = 0$, $1, \ldots, m$) is basically a distributed-lag relation. In a regression of S_t on the terms N_{t-i}, the sum of the coefficients of the latter is expected to tend toward unity, given that new orders are taken net of cancellations and for all the relevant past periods m. Various distributed-lag regressions, including those that include up to seven monthly or three quarterly terms for N_{t-i} and those with assumed forms of time-lag structure (geometric, second-order), generally confirm this expectation and the implied view of the lagged production (order-filling) process.

Regressions with several lagged terms in new orders suffer from multicollinearity and positive autocorrelation of residuals. Typically, the $\bar{R}^2$ coefficients are already high for equations that contain only the shortest lags, but they do increase by small steps as successively earlier values of new orders are included to account for the longer delivery lags.

Geometrical lag distributions produce definitely better results. The constant terms in most of these regressions are not significant, the correlations are very high, and the fits, as shown by the graphs, are good. On the other hand, the second-order distributed-lag functions give no improvements except a few small ones for some of the monthly data.

Autoregressive equations using linear combinations of past new orders as "instrumental variables" compare favorably with the geometric lag equations in a few cases. In particular, good results were obtained for primary metal industries—just where the other regressions had been found least satisfactory.

Median estimates of the typical delivery lags as derived from the preferred regression models suggest rather long lags in the machinery industries and short ones in primary metals and the "other durables" group, with fabricated metals and total transportation equipment in intermediate positions. The five-month lag for the durable goods sector contrasts with the one-month lag for all nondurables. These estimates tend to be smaller than the average lags of shipments at the turning points in new orders, but, except for primary metals, the differences are minor. The two types of timing measures have different meanings and it is neither possible nor necessary to reconcile them precisely, but some plausible reasons for the observed differences are suggested. One of these is that the correlations between the short movements in N and S may involve smaller lags than those between the longer cyclical movements.

There is reason to believe that the lags of shipments behind new orders are subject to systematic variation during the business cycle; so the coefficients in these relations should be variable rather than fixed. A model embodying variable lag coefficients has been applied to the quarterly major-industry data and has been found in most cases to perform well — definitely better than the estimates applying fixed lag coefficients to the same data. The variable lag approach consists in making the lag coefficients depend on the value of the backlog-shipment (U/S) ratios, which serve as an index of the pressure of demand upon capacity.

PART II

CAUSES AND IMPLICATIONS OF CHANGES IN UNFILLED ORDERS AND INVENTORIES

6

UNFILLED ORDERS AND INDUSTRIAL ACTIVITY

THIS CHAPTER GIVES a description and interpretation of the behavior of unfilled orders in relation to shipments and other measures of industrial activity, beginning with a formulation of some expectations about these relations.

For goods made to order and subject to fluctuations in sales and delivery periods, new orders might be expected to lead unfilled orders. This hypothesis is based on a generalization of the following cyclical pattern: (1) In expansions, N first rises and then declines, moving throughout above the level of S, which increases steadily. (2) In contractions, symmetrically, N first declines and then rises, moving throughout below the level of S, which decreases steadily. It follows that U increases in expansions and decreases in contractions, since $N > S$ during the former and $N < S$ during the latter. This implies a lag of U behind N at both peaks and troughs, and suggests the likelihood of a roughly coincident timing of U and S.[1] This rests on two assumptions: that new orders have larger fluctuations than shipments, and that they turn ahead of shipments. These should be safe premises to make in the case of manufacture to order and, as already shown, the data bear them out for a variety of industries and products. However, they are not the only relevant facts. Backlog movements, especially when they are large, can themselves strongly influence the scheduling of production and hence the timing of output and shipments.

[1] Using the symbols introduced earlier, this typical turning-point sequence would be written as $N \to U, S$ (with the arrow pointing from the leader to the lagger and the comma denoting roughly coincident timing). If S turned down *before* N fell below the level of S, U would lag behind S at the peak; if S turned down *after* that happened, U would lead S (and an analogous statement applies, *mutatis mutandis*, at the trough). Unless the discrepancies between N and S are quite large, the timing differences between U and S are not likely to be very great either.

Where backlogs are small, either because the typical delivery periods are short or because production is largely to stock or both, they are also likely to behave less systematically, and their relation to shipments may be quite loose. S would then follow N with a short lag and might turn ahead of U (instead of together with or after U, as was assumed before). On the other hand, where delivery periods are long and backlogs large, production is to a large extent concerned with orders on hand and correspondingly less dependent on currently received (new) orders. Shipments and output are here closely correlated; therefore, S, too, would be relatively more responsive to U and less to N. Given a large backlog just accumulated, one would expect the lags of S relative to U to be pronounced on the downgrade, since an ample stock of orders can sustain production for some time, even when new orders are declining.

An Historical Survey of the Principal Evidence

Data for Steel, 1902–33

The earliest historical series on unfilled orders is that of the United States Steel Corporation. The published figures (1902–33) have been regarded as "accurate barometers of the trend of the steel industry and even of general business conditions." [2] In part, their prestige was undoubtedly derived from that of U.S. Steel as the industry leader and was aided by the paucity of available rival indicators. But, some overstated language aside, this series is indeed worthy of considerable attention as a tool of analysis; and it certainly could have been quite helpful to contemporaries as a smooth and highly sensitive cyclical indicator with roughly coincident or slightly leading timing characteristics.

No shipments series to match the U.S. Steel backlog data is available, but steel production has long been measured by the output of ingots as they come from the hearth or converter. Accordingly, Chart 6-1 presents the two series after seasonal adjustments and in the usual form suitable for cyclical comparisons: The dots denote the peaks and

[2] Quoted from a description in Bureau of the Census, *Record Book of Business Statistics, Part II*, Washington, D.C., 1928, p. 7.

Chart 6-1
Unfilled Orders of U.S. Steel Corporation and Steel Ingot Production, 1902–33

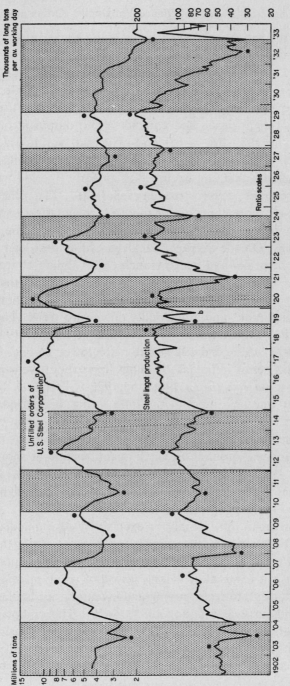

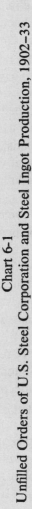

Note: Shaded areas represent business cycle contractions; unshaded areas, expansions. Dots identify peaks and troughs of specific cycles.
Series are seasonally adjusted.
  a Quarterly, 1902–10; monthly, 1910–33.
  b Labor strike.

troughs of the series; shadowed areas in the background denote general business recessions.

There is a one-to-one correspondence between the specific cycles in the two steel series; both unfilled orders and production rose in each business expansion and declined in each contraction. Steel backlogs led output at eight peaks and coincided with output at one. One of these leads, in 1917–18, at the end of World War I, was very long (19 months). This could have been a consequence of the massive backlog accumulation that had occurred at an earlier period when strong demand pressures caused capacity shortages. The other leads at peaks were all short: three of one month each and three of two to four months. At troughs, there were four coincidences, three leads, and two long lags. On the average, backlogs had a short lead relative to production at peaks and nearly synchronous timing at troughs: The means are −3.9 and +0.6; the medians, −1.5 and 0 months.

After the war, unfilled orders of steel had relatively short cycles of declining amplitudes and a decidedly downward trend. Their peak in 1920 was just a little lower than the all-time high of 1917, but the peaks of 1923, 1925, and 1929 were much lower; in fact, the *highest* values of this series in the late twenties lie at about the same level as the first postwar *troughs* in 1919 and 1923 (Chart 6-1). In contrast, steel output was high most of the time during this period and had a rising trend. The implication of a simultaneous decline in order backlogs and rise in output is that the average delivery periods were falling markedly. Indeed, ordering in small quantities and at short intervals, commonly known as "hand-to-mouth buying," was a widespread phenomenon in the 1920's, causing increased concern right up to the onslaught of the depression.

Buying in small lots, mainly or exclusively for immediate requirements, had been a business practice in earlier times. But in the twenties, many regarded it as a new and particularly worrisome problem, perhaps because it came after a long period of rising prices, and a few years of intensive forward buying and inventory accumulation during the war and postwar inflation of 1916–20.[3] The complaint of producers-sellers was that the "buyers' market" was imposing on them the higher costs of handling small orders, greater uncertainty, and more severe limitations on business planning. Actually, many prices were

[3] Cf. Leverett S. Lyon, *Hand-to-Mouth Buying*, Washington, D.C., 1929.

weak or declining in these years, particularly after 1925, and this, as on previous occasions, was a major cause of hand-to-mouth buying. At the same time, the amounts spent by business on plant and equipment were substantial and showed a moderately rising trend. Thus the productive capacities — for manufacturing, transportation, communication — were expanding and improving. Buyers, aware that suppliers could cover their requirements on short orders, appear to have taken liberal advantage of this situation.

Aggregative Indexes, 1920–33 and 1935–44

For the years 1920–33, a monthly index of unfilled orders based on seventeen commodities has been compiled by the Department of Commerce.[4] The U.S. Steel Corporation series accounts for nearly 40 per cent of the total weight in this index, which helps to explain the similarity of the two series (compare the upper curves in Charts 6-1 and 6-2). However, the general trend and cyclical characteristics of steel backlogs were shared broadly by other components of the Commerce unfilled orders index. Chart 6-2 shows the latter along with the Federal Reserve index of manufacturing production. The divergent trends in the two indexes during the twenties are of the same kind as those found in the steel series, which suggests that the tendency to place short orders was common to buyers of a wide variety of manufactured products. The cyclical timing comparisons again indicate a lead of unfilled orders at output peaks and a more irregular, on the average roughly coincident, timing at troughs.[5]

Not surprisingly, unfilled orders fell more rapidly than production during the Great Depression. Between 1929 and 1938, the Commerce index of backlogs declined from approximately 90 to 26 points, or by 71 per cent. The index of manufacturing production went down from 40 to 18 points, or by 55 per cent. This may perhaps exaggerate the

[4] See *Survey of Current Business*, January 1928, pp. 22–23, for a description of this index and data for 1920–27. The composition of the index and the percentage weights of the groups are: textiles (cotton finishing, hosiery, knit underwear, pyroxylin-coated textiles), 16; iron and steel (pig iron, steel, sanitary enamelware), 47; transportation equipment (freight cars, ships, locomotives), 10; lumber products (flooring, furniture), 20; paper (boxboard), 2; brick and glass (common brick, face brick, paving brick, illuminating glassware), 5.

All these series, as well as the combined index, were seasonally adjusted for the National Bureau by the Census electronic computer method.

[5] Backlogs led at the three successive peaks in production by 2, 9, and 3 months (on the average, by 4.7 months). They lagged by 10 months at the 1921 trough in production, but turned up at about the same time as production in the following three recoveries; the mean here is a short lag of unfilled orders (of 1.8 months), the median a short lead (of 0.5 months). Cf. Chart 6-2.

Chart 6-2

Indexes of Unfilled Orders and Manufacturing Production, 1920–33

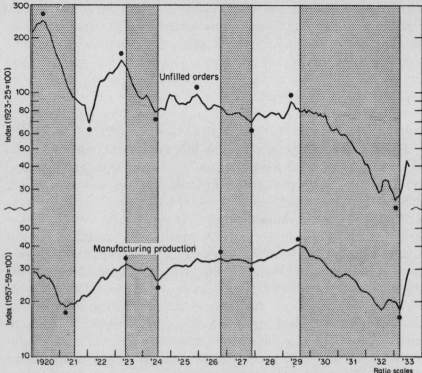

Note: Shaded areas represent business cycle contractions; unshaded areas, expansions. Dots identify peaks and troughs of specific cycles. Series are seasonally adjusted.

contrast; the production index is a much more comprehensive aggregate than the unfilled orders index. However, the result makes good sense, at least qualitatively. A dwindling of advance orders was inevitable since prices were falling, pessimistic expectations were spreading, and investment goods, which are primarily produced to order, were being hit harder than any other category by the slump in demand.

Most of the new and unfilled order series published by trade associations were discontinued in the early 1930's, and so were the Commerce indexes based on a cross section of these statistics. A new index of the value of manufacturers' backlogs, compiled by the National

Industrial Conference Board, begins in 1935. These figures, introduced in May 1941, refer to three aggregates: (1) durable goods manufacturers (said to cover ten industries); (2) nondurable goods manufacturers (seven industries); and (3) the combined index (all seventeen industries). Chart 6-3 shows the NICB indexes for the durable and nondurable goods sectors separately, and the corresponding NICB shipments indexes.[6]

At the time of the 1937 downturn, industry on the whole was still operating considerably below capacity. The peaks in unfilled orders for both durable and nondurable goods occurred in April 1937, coinciding with the peaks in the corresponding shipments series (Chart 6-3). At these peaks, backlogs were still rather small, absolutely and relative to shipments, even though they had increased substantially during the slow recovery of the thirties, because they had risen from painfully low levels. In January 1935, the ratio of backlogs to shipments was 0.7 for all durable goods; in April 1937, the ratio was 1.3. This is still a low figure compared to the ratio of more than 3.0 in March 1941, when backlogs were said to average from three to eight times more than monthly shipments of the various durable goods industries.[7]

Because they were so low, unfilled orders could provide very little support to production in 1937. Once new orders turned down, which according to the NICB estimates occurred in December 1936 or March 1937,[8] output and shipments had to turn down very soon. There was simply no reserve of unfinished advance commitments to stem or even cushion the fall, and the downturns in both shipments and order backlogs were, as the chart shows, abrupt.

After declining steeply during the recession, the two durables series unmistakably turned up in June 1938 (the month of the general business trough). Through the third quarter of 1939 their recovery pro-

---

[6] The unfilled orders indexes include the following industries: Durable goods – automobile equipment, building equipment, electrical equipment, iron and steel, machinery, metal products, nonferrous metals, office equipment, railroad equipment, and household furnishings; nondurable goods – boots and shoes, chemicals and drugs, clothing, leather, paper manufactures, and textiles.

The shipments indexes cover the same industries plus two durable goods industries (cement and glass) and one nondurable goods industry (rubber goods).

See National Industrial Conference Board, *Conference Board Economic Record*, New York, May 24, 1941, pp. 223–24, for a description of the unfilled orders indexes and data for 1935–41. For a description of the value-of-shipments indexes and the corresponding data for 1929–40, see *ibid.*, December 26, 1940, pp. 1–11.

[7] Cf. *Conference Board Economic Record*, May 24, 1941, p. 223.

[8] The level in March was only slightly lower than that in December. See Chart 10-1.

Chart 6-3
Value of Manufacturers' Unfilled Orders and Shipments, 1935–44 and 1939–49

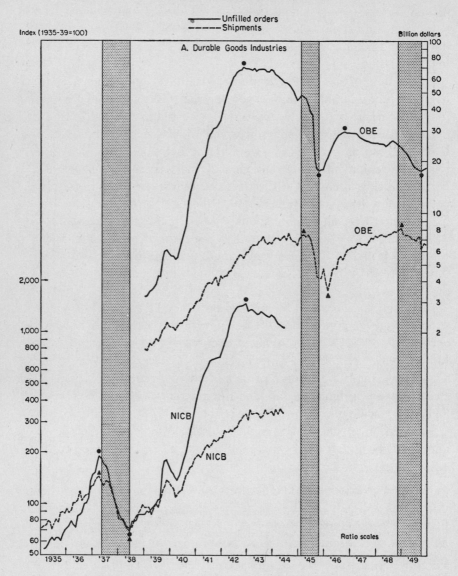

Chart 6-3 (concluded)

——————Unfilled orders
– – – – – Shipments

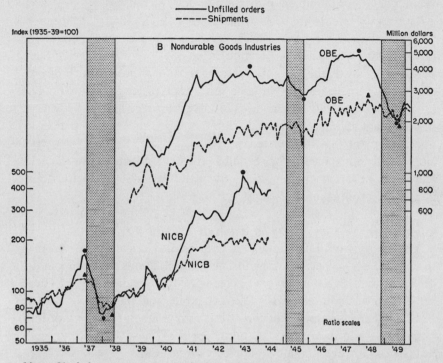

Index (1935-39=100)   Million dollars

B Nondurable Goods Industries

Note: Shaded areas represent business cycle contractions; unshaded areas, expansions. Dots identify peaks and troughs of specific cycles in unfilled orders; triangles, sales (value of shipments). Series are seasonally adjusted.

Source: National Industrial Conference Board (NICB) and U.S. Department of Commerce, Office of Business Economics (OBE).

ceeded at similar rates. But then, with the outbreak of the war in Europe and the beginning of the great armament program in the United States, aggregate demand began to outstrip supply, despite fuller utilization of the existing productive resources and the addition of new ones. This is clearly apparent in the chart, which shows that during the period of approximately forty months from mid-1939 through 1942, shipments increased from 100 to about 350 but unfilled orders increased from 100 to nearly 1,500! For nondurables, the levels and increases were of course much smaller throughout, but even here the rise in backlogs was very marked (from 100 in 1939 to a peak of over 450 in mid-1943) and was much larger than the rise in the rate of deliveries (which just about doubled in the same period).

These movements are easy to understand qualitatively. Production, though expanding greatly, was nevertheless lagging well behind the rapidly rising demand, causing large extensions of the average delivery periods. This was the time of a vast shift in the whole pattern of production as required by the armament program of the government. The creation of complex war industries involved unprecedented investment in new plant and machinery and related equipment. Despite the heavy unemployment that still existed in 1939, shortages soon developed of skilled and semiskilled labor needed in the new industries. Bottlenecks were also reported in some key raw materials, steel capacities, machine-tool production, and shipping.[9]

Comprehensive Current-Dollar Estimates, 1939–49

The aggregative Department of Commerce series on the value of manufacturers' order backlogs for all durable goods industries and a group of reporting nondurable goods industries begin in 1939. These are the most comprehensive data available, and they correspond to the Commerce estimates of the value of manufacturers' new orders, shipments, and inventories. A breakdown of these figures by major industries, however, is not available before 1948.

Chart 6-3 shows the Commerce series on unfilled orders and shipments for 1939–49. During 1939–44, the period covered by both the NICB indexes and the Commerce aggregates, the behavior of the corresponding series in the two sets is very similar, especially for durables (for nondurables there are some more significant differences in 1942–43).

In addition to confirming broadly the findings on the relative changes provided by the NICB indexes, the Commerce figures offer some interesting level comparisons. They show that unfilled orders of all manufacturers underwent an enormous rise in the four years from 1939 to 1942: from $4 billion to about $74 billion. All but $2 billion or $3 billion of these backlogs were in durable goods. At the same time, shipments increased greatly but in far less spectacular manner; sales of durable goods, for example, rose from $1.6 billion to $5.9 billion.

---

[9] See the annual reviews for 1940 and 1941 in *Survey of Current Business,* February 1941 and February 1942. Also see *Conference Board Economic Record,* May 24, 1941, pp. 225–28.

The first, relatively small wave in backlogs occurred between August 1939 and March 1940 and reflected protective buying against anticipated wartime scarcities and rising prices. New orders fell back to the level of shipments as soon as it became evident that the expected shortages were not about to materialize. Comparing these developments with those observed during the first year of the Korean War strongly suggests that situations of this sort will produce similar reactions (see Charts 3-1 and 3-2 and accompanying text, above).

The next and far greater rise in backlogs, which started in the spring of 1940, mostly represented the excess of new orders for defense products placed by government agencies (mainly with durable goods manufacturers) over the outputs that the producers could supply on relatively short notice. However, orders for civilian goods also increased substantially in this period as a result of rising incomes and, probably, of renewed fears of shortages. After a slowdown in the second half of 1941, unfilled orders for durables rose rapidly in 1942, the first year of active war for the United States, despite impressive increases in production and shipments. The bulk of these orders called for the delivery of war goods by companies converting to war production; the backlogs of nondurables stayed high but increased just a little and erratically. In 1943, unfilled orders leveled off and started declining. The flows of critical materials for war production were by then generally controlled by priorities and allocations, which most likely made "forward buying" more difficult and less needed. Industry was now geared to war needs, and new orders conformed well on the whole to actual requirements, as did the production schedules.

To the extent that the price ceilings imposed upon most categories of goods and services in April 1942 were effective, prices were prevented from rising in counteraction to excess demands. This in itself would tend to contribute to backlog accumulation of purchase orders.[10] But a large part of the output of durable goods manufacturers was actually excluded from the general price-ceiling legislation. The exemption applied to "distinctively military" goods and to products made largely to order at prices determined in individual contracts.[11]

[10] On the relation between price changes and backlog changes, see Chapter 7.

[11] Harvey C. Mansfield and Associates, *A Short History of OPA*, Office of Price Administration, Washington, D.C., 1947, pp. 46–47. Soon after the General Maximum Price Regulation (GMPR) was issued, another regulation (MPR 136) provided a pricing formula for machinery of all sorts. This held a manufacturer to his own price-determining method as of the base period (spring 1942) but did

New orders for durable goods ceased expanding in March and unfilled orders in November 1942; but shipments maintained their rate of growth through the summer of 1943, then oscillated around a high and slightly rising level for about 18 months, and did not turn down decisively until after March 1945 (see the OBE series in Chart 6-3). Presumably, the huge accumulation of backlogs in the early phase of the war helped to keep up production and shipments for a considerable time in the subsequent phase. However, one must add that the downward drift of the backlogs was, according to the Commerce estimates, very mild initially; so no significant decline resulted before 1944. In contrast to the abrupt downturn in 1937 (when backlogs were still low), the big wartime wave in durable unfilled orders was gently rounded off at its peak late in 1942.[12]

At the end of the war, order backlogs dropped sharply under the impact of cancellations of military contracts, but they rose again in 1946. Shipments turned upward only four months after backlogs, in February 1946.

The expansion in backlogs of durable goods that began late in 1945 lasted only one year, and at its end the aggregate value of the accumulated orders was much smaller than it had been during the war. However, the increase in the rate of output was in this phase limited by the difficulties of conversion from wartime to peacetime production, and backlogs were, in effect, still very large relative to shipments (see Chart 6-3). Hence, shipments could again continue to rise gradually for a long time after backlogs ceased growing. The lags of shipments on this occasion were as long as 23 to 26 months for total manufacturing and all durables.[13]

In nondurables, which account for a minor proportion (about 5 to 7 per cent) of total order backlogs of manufacturers, the wartime expan-

not effectively control the labor time and quantities of materials entering into his computation. The decision not to attempt to establish ceilings for military goods was taken tentatively when the GMPR was issued, then confirmed officially in the autumn of 1942. However, large volumes of raw and semifabricated materials used in the production of such goods were left under the general price control of the OPA.

[12] A late version of the NICB figures shows a more pronounced decline of durable backlogs in 1943 (see Chart 6-3), but this series, which was shortly afterward discontinued, is believed to give less reliable evidence here than the Commerce series.

[13] However, among the major component industries, electrical and nonelectrical machinery are the only groups to which lags of this magnitude can be traced (see below, Table 6-1, column 1). Also note the mildness of the 1947–48 decline in durable backlogs and a secondary peak in this series in August 1948 (Chart 6-3).

sion was, of course, much smaller in percentage terms than it was in durables. In contrast, the first postwar wave (1945–49) was relatively larger in nondurable backlogs, reflecting the shifts in demand and the difficulties of reconverting the industries in the period of transition to a peacetime economy.

Major-Industry Series Since 1948

Charts 6-4 and 6-5 present the major-industry series on unfilled orders and their ratios to the value of shipments.[14] The prevalence of horizontal or downward trends is a common characteristic of these series in the decade 1952–62 which followed the great backlog accumulations of the Korean War period. Later in the 1960's, however, rising tendencies are again strongly in evidence for unfilled orders of most component industries and the over-all aggregates.

Another feature of these series is the dominance of large cyclical movements during most of the postwar period and the drastic reduction in their amplitudes in the late fifties and the sixties. Unfilled orders of durable goods manufacturers increased vastly in the first phase of the Korean War, 1950–52, then declined much less in the second phase and during the recession of 1953–54. Between 1954 and 1962, three increases in total and durables backlogs occurred which were progressively smaller and shorter; of the three corresponding decreases, each was about equal to the preceding rise in size and duration. As this implies, the successive peak levels of backlogs declined, while the successive trough levels differed little. In other words, the fluctuations in unfilled orders had a downward drift and became at the same time shallower in amplitude.

The aggregates resumed a rather steady upward movement at the end of 1962 (Chart 6-4). After four years, this long climb brought them back to the top levels of 1952, and by mid-1969 most of these series had risen to new all-time heights.[15] This, however, refers to current-dollar values; in constant dollars, the backlogs of the mid-1960's would be smaller than those of the early 1950's. Furthermore, the re-

[14] Data on unfilled orders in the post-World War II period correspond to the data on shipments, inventories, and new orders and come from the same source: The monthly Industry Survey of the OBE before the 1963 revision, and the current Census Bureau compilation thereafter. The OBE industry series begin in 1948; the Census series in 1953. The published data relate to the two-digit industries and (after the revision) to broad market categories.

[15] Unfilled orders for durable goods reached a level of $76 billion in October 1966, just a little above their standing in November 1962. In May 1969, their new peak level was nearly $87 billion.

Chart 6-4
Value of Unfilled Orders and Ratios of Unfilled Orders to
Shipments, Total Manufacturing, Total Durable Goods
Industries, and Nondurable Goods Industries
Reporting Unfilled Orders, 1947–65

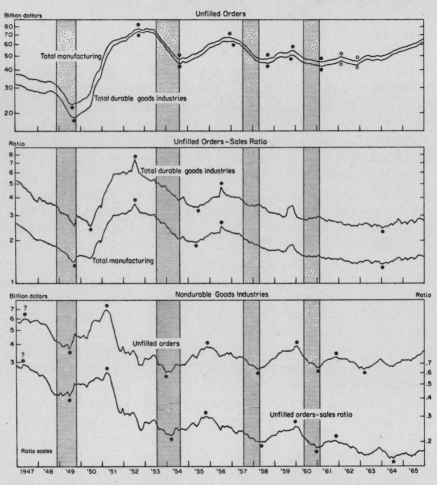

Note: Shaded areas represent business cycle contractions; unshaded areas, expansions. Dots identify peaks and troughs of specific cycles; circles, short cycles or retardations. Series are seasonally adjusted.

Source: U.S. Department of Commerce, Office of Business Economics and Bureau of the Census.

Chart 6-5
Value of Unfilled Orders and Ratios of Unfilled Orders to Shipments, Seven Major Durable Goods Industries, Quarterly, 1953–65

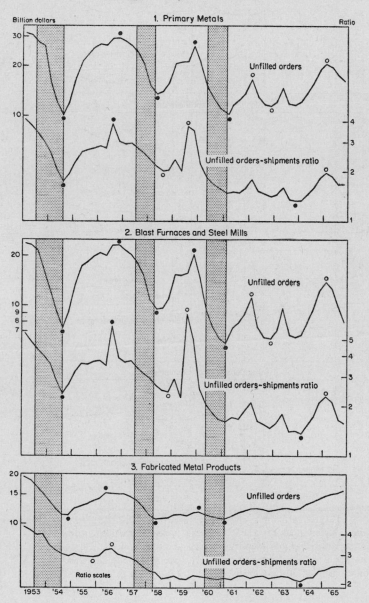

Chart 6-5 (concluded)

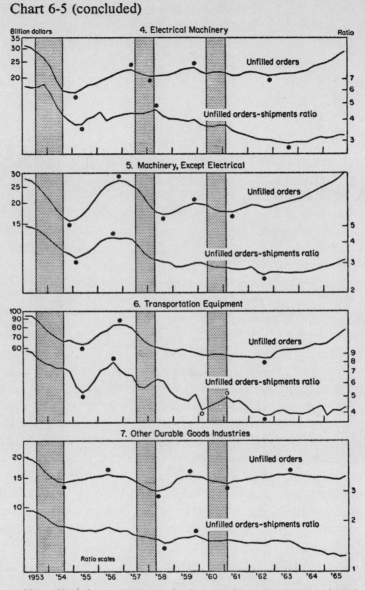

Note: Shaded areas represent business cycle contractions; unshaded areas, expansions. Dots identify peaks and troughs of specific cycles; circles, short cycles or retardations. Series are seasonally adjusted.

Source: Bureau of the Census.

cent over-all ratios of unfilled orders to sales are much smaller than they were during the earlier postwar booms.

While this seems to describe the over-all picture fairly, there were differences among the major component industries. Thus the machinery industries show relatively mild fluctuations and more rising trends in their order backlogs; the primary metals series show huge fluctuations and declining trends (Chart 6-5).

Total Backlogs and Backlog-Shipment Ratios

Over long stretches of time, industrial capacities are kept large enough by past and continuing capital formation to accommodate demand at moderate growth rates. Thus, output and shipments had upward trends in 1921–29, but unfilled orders show little of any trend (or some slight downward drift) in the same period (Chart 6-2). This implies that the backlog-shipment (U/S) ratios, an indicator of relative demand pressures, declined in the 1920's. A similar situation prevailed during much of the decade following the Korean War (Charts 6-4 and 6-5).

Cyclically, unfilled orders and shipments move in the same direction much of the time, but the fluctuations of unfilled orders are much larger.[16] Hence, the cyclical course of the backlog-shipment ratios is influenced more strongly by the major movements of U than of S, and in fact tends to reflect closely the course of U for each industry. By the same token, however, the cyclical movements of the ratios tend to be smaller in relative amplitude than the corresponding movements of the backlog series. On the other hand, the U/S ratios are subject to much more frequent and larger irregular month-to-month variations than are the U series, which are remarkably smooth. This reflects not only the much greater smoothness of the backlog values, which are "stock" variables, compared to the shipments values, which represent "flows," but also any cumulation of the errors of observation of U and S in the ratios that combine both.

Strike effects deserve to be specially noted as one type of the major sporadic disturbances that are conspicuous in some U/S ratio series. The industry principally affected is, of course, primary metals. Since its shipments fall drastically during major steel strikes and its backlogs are not much affected, its U/S ratios show needlelike rises and falls

[16] Charts 3-1 and 3-2 show value-of-shipments aggregates comparable to the unfilled orders series in Charts 6-4 and 6-5.

during the strikes in 1949, 1952, 1956, and 1959 (Chart 6-5). Moreover, intensified buying in anticipation of a strike can cause a temporary valley in the ratio series immediately preceding the rise in the strike months (such developments are strongly in evidence in 1949 and 1959). The strike effects cause a certain amount of difficulty in dating some of the turning points in the series.[17]

The backlog-shipment ratio often lags behind troughs in total backlogs but not peaks (Charts 6-4 and 6-5). As already noted, the peaks of large backlog expansions led the downturns of shipments by long intervals. The ratio should begin to decline at least as soon as U does, if S is still rising; indeed, it should turn down earlier if the expansion of U in its terminal phase is slowed down to rates lower than those at which S is expanding. Actually, our charts show that leads of U/S relative to U at peaks are not uncommon, although they tend to be short.

At troughs, in contrast, the timing of unfilled orders and shipments is in most cases roughly coincident. When the two start rising together, the percentage increase of U will often initially be less than that of S, which implies that the upturn of the U/S ratio will lag. For the ratio to turn upward at once, in fact, new orders should increase rapidly in the early expansion phase, overshooting shipments by large amounts and thereby giving rise to sufficiently large positive ΔU. Apparently, this does not occur frequently. Moreover, backlogs have often lagged shipments at troughs since 1954, though usually not by long intervals (see below, Table 6-1). Where this happens, the upturn in U is likely to come at a time when the rise in S is already well on its way, which would accentuate the lag of the U/S ratio.

Market-Category Series Since 1953

The new series on unfilled orders classified by market categories, and their ratios to shipments, are presented in Chart 6-6. These data

[17] The strike peak in 1949 came shortly after the trough in the U/S series for primary metals and can thus be ignored. (That trough was presumably accented, but was certainly not caused, by prestrike buying; compare, for example, the behavior of U and U/S during this episode in Chart 6-5.) In contrast, the strike peak in 1952 came at the time when the ratio series reached its highest levels; it therefore can be regarded as approximately coincident with the "true" specific-cycle peak in this series. The situation was similar in 1956, though here there was still a slight rise in the ratio in the first quarter of 1957. Finally, in 1959 the deep prestrike valley must be disregarded in dating the troughs; but the long strike brought such a pronounced increase in the ratio that the existence of a peak here is not seriously in doubt (cf. also the movement of total backlogs in this period).

It may be added that measures of peak and trough levels and cyclical amplitudes are very strongly affected in these cases, even where the timing measures are not. In an analysis of the peak and trough values of the U/S ratios later in this chapter, we shall in effect smooth out the extreme effects of the strikes (see Table 6-4).

correspond to the series on new orders and shipments analyzed in Chapters 3 and 4.[18]

The recorded course of these aggregates begins from top levels attained early in 1953 and describes steep declines in 1953–54, followed by large expansions in 1955–56 and contractions in 1957–58. After that, the series generally drift downward through 1962, with only very small cyclical variations. Finally, there are the long upward movements after 1963, initially somewhat hesitant but later proceeding at very impressive and sustained rates. Late in 1966 most of these series had already regained their peak levels of 1953.

This is the "typical profile" against which one might consider the differences among the market categories. Thus, the movements of 1955–58 add up to large and almost symmetrical trough-to-trough waves in equipment industries and in the larger part of the category of materials, supplies, and intermediate products. For construction materials, the expansion phase of this cycle was longer but less pronounced, and the contraction phase was more accentuated. The rise in order backlogs for defense products came late (in the last quarter of 1955) and was relatively short (about one year). The ensuing decline in this series lasted, with minor interruptions, through 1962.

The diminution of cyclical movements after the 1957–58 recession was most drastic for the equipment-producing group of industries and for construction materials, and least for home goods and apparel and consumer staples. The expansions of the 1960's have been very large in unfilled orders for equipment, defense products, and materials. The rise in consumer goods backlogs has been much more modest (Chart 6-6).

In the consumer goods category, it is interesting to observe that its total unfilled orders show a succession of clearly outlined specific cycles, even though the corresponding series on new orders and shipments differ by very small amounts (see Chart 3-3). This cyclical pattern is probably largely due to the consumer durables component of this market category. Unfilled orders for consumer durables, available

[18] See in particular Chart 3-3 and Table 4-9 and the accompanying text. For two categories, consumer staples and automotive equipment, no separate figures on unfilled orders are published, though the series on new orders and shipments are available. As shown in Chart 3-3, new orders and shipments run very close to each other for consumer staples and, after 1955, for automotive equipment. This implies that at least the reported *changes* in unfilled orders are small for these products. The *levels* of these backlogs are probably low, too, and the random elements in the changes are likely to be relatively large.

Chart 6-6
Value of Unfilled Orders and Ratios of Unfilled Orders to
Shipments, Seven Market Categories,
Monthly, 1953–66

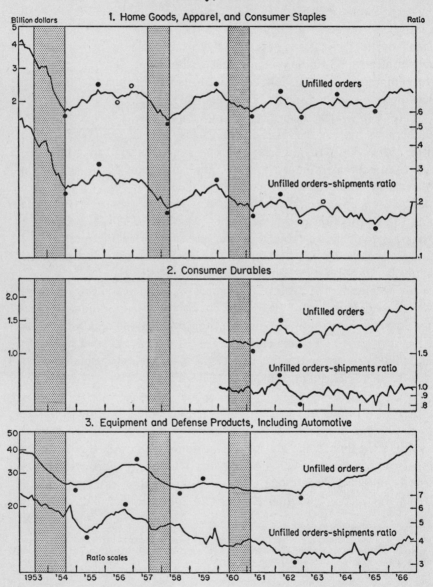

Chart 6-6 (concluded)

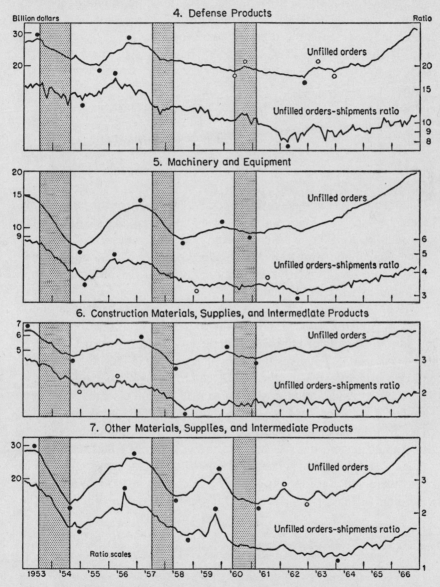

4. Defense Products

5. Machinery and Equipment

6. Construction Materials, Supplies, and Intermediate Products

7. Other Materials, Supplies, and Intermediate Products

Note: Shaded areas represent business cycle contractions; unshaded areas, expansions. Dots identify peaks and troughs of specific cycles; circles, minor turns and retardations.

Source: Bureau of the Census.

since 1960, show broad movements parallel to those of unfilled orders for the total category of home goods, etc., and the timing of the two series in the early 1960's is virtually identical.[19]

Unfilled orders for the different market categories vary greatly in size. Their end-of-month stock values, in billions of current dollars, range as follows in the period 1953–69:

Home goods, etc.	1.6–4.2	Machinery and equipment industries	7.8–25.1
Equipment and defense	23.8–48.9	Construction materials, etc.	4.2–10.9
Defense products	17.4–34.0	Other materials, etc.	14.7–29.0

Thus equipment and defense products accounted for the largest part of the backlog of orders and consumer goods for the smallest, with materials ranking in between. Defense orders represented a larger proportion of the aggregate backlog of commitments to supply machinery and nonautomotive equipment than did the orders on other predominantly private accounts.[20]

The general characteristics of the U/S series for the market categories compiled through 1966 are much like those of the corresponding data for the major industries. The ratios show downward trends in the decade 1953–62, interrupted by rises in 1955–56 and 1958–59, and upward movements in the last three or four years that are covered. The longer trends and the short irregular variations are more pronounced and the cyclical fluctuations are less pronounced, in the U/S ratios than in backlogs proper. By the end of 1966, unfilled orders for the equipment and defense and materials categories had regained or slightly exceeded their highest 1953 levels, but the backlog-shipment ratios were still considerably lower in 1966 than in 1953. Where turning points in the ratios series can be identified and matched with the

[19] Consumer durables include household furniture, fixtures, and appliances, and various other items such as kitchen articles, hand tools, watches, and personal goods. Home goods, etc., includes knitting and floor covering, apparel, and leather products, additional consumer staples such as food and beverages, tobacco, paper and printed products, drugs, etc. See section on "Market Categories" in Chapter 3 for more detail. In 1960–63, consumer durables accounted on the average for approximately two-thirds of total unfilled orders of the category of home goods, apparel, and consumer staples.

[20] This is in part due to the much longer average delivery periods for the defense products, as indicated by the high U/S ratios for this category (see text below). Within total *shipments* of machinery and equipment except automotive, the shares of defense products and of all other items tend to be more nearly equal.

turning points in the corresponding backlog series, rough coincidences or short leads of the ratios are often found at peaks, and lags at troughs.

The U/S ratios for the different market categories also vary greatly in their average size and in the amplitudes of their movements. Thus the ratios for home goods, etc., range from 0.15 to 0.56; and those for defense products, from 8.0 to 17.3. Between these extremes are the figures for machinery and equipment (3.1 to 7.2), construction materials (1.6 to 3.1), and other materials (1.2 to 2.9).

Measures of Relative Timing

Major-Industry Series

Turning points in unfilled orders and shipments can be compared in each of the zones associated with postwar recessions and revivals in business activity, with a few exceptions in the nonautomotive transportation equipment and the nondurable goods industries (Table 6-1). No "extra" movements and additional timing observations are recorded here for the Korean War period, unlike the comparisons with new orders in Chapter 4.[21] On the other hand, unfilled orders did undergo minor declines in connection with the business retardation in 1962, which give rise to extra comparisons with shipments in this period (columns 9 and 10).

The leads of unfilled orders at peaks in shipments of durable goods show a definite and strong tendency to get shorter, as can be seen by comparing the odd-numbered columns 1, . . . , 9 in the table. From the measures for the six component industries, the average leads or lags for the five successive peak zones are $-9.2, -7.3, -3.5, +1.8,$ and -1.0 months. However, there are indications of longer leads of U relative to S at the most recent (1969) peaks in these aggregates (-5 for total durables). It will be recalled that the downward trend of un-

---

[21] The contractions in unfilled orders of durable goods start generally in 1952 and continue through the 1953–54 recession; their beginning dates match the peaks in shipments that can be associated with the 1953 business downturn. The declines in 1951 did not carry new orders below the levels of shipments; hence backlogs continued to increase and had no "extra" movements and turns in this period.

Backlogs of nondurables turned down early in 1951, and so did shipments. These turns cannot be associated directly with the 1953 recession, and the recording of their comparison in column 3 of Table 6-1 is merely a matter of convenience. However, here too, backlogs show no substantial extra movements; their decline lasted well into the 1953–54 recession (while shipments increased in 1952 and early 1953; see Chart 3-1).

Table 6-1

Timing of Value of Unfilled Orders at Turns in Shipments, by Business Cycle Turning Zones, Major Manufacturing Industries, 1948–62

| | Lead (−) or Lag (+) in Months of Unfilled Orders at Turns in Shipments in Turning Zone Associated with | | | | | | | | | | Av. Lead (−) or Lag (+) (months) | | | |
| | 1948 Recession: Peak (1) | 1949 Revival: Trough (2) | 1953 Recession: Peak (3) | 1954 Revival: Trough (4) | 1957 Recession: Peak (5) | 1958 Revival: Trough (6) | 1960 Recession: Peak (7) | 1961 Revival: Trough (8) | 1962 Business Retardation Peak[a] (9) | 1962 Business Retardation Trough[a] (10) | Peaks 1948–53[b] (11) | Peaks 1957–62[c] (12) | Peaks All (13) | Troughs All (14) |
Industry														
All manufacturing	−23	−2	−10	−1	−2	+5	+6[d]	+2	−2	−1	−16.5	+0.7	−6.2	+0.6
Durable goods, total	−26	−1	−10	−1	0	+5	+4[d]	+1	−1	−1	−18.0	+1.0	−6.6	+0.6
Primary metals	0	−1	−11	0	−3[e]	+2	+5[d]	+1	−1	+3	−5.5	+0.3	−2.0	+1.0
Blast furnaces, steel mills	n.a.	n.a.	n.a.	0	−3[e]	+2	+5[d]	0	−1	+5	n.a.	+0.3	+0.3	+1.7
Fabricated metal products	n.i.	0	−10	+1	−12	+1	+8	0	+2	0	−10.0	−0.7	−3.0	+0.4
Elect. machinery[f]	−23	−2	+1	+5	+2	−3	+1	+4[g]	−3	+2	−11.0	0.0	−4.4	+1.2
Machinery exc. elect.[f]	−22	0	−14	+1	0	−1	−5	+1	−2	−1	−18.0	−2.3	−8.6	0.0
Transport. equip.[h]	−3	−2	−8	−3	−13	n.u.	n.u.	n.u.	n.u.	n.t.	−5.5	−13.0	−8.0	−2.0
Other durable goods[i]	+2	+1	−2	+2	+5	+1	0	+1	n.t.	n.t.	0.0	+2.5	+1.2	+1.2
Nondurables industries reporting unfilled orders[j]	−12	−1	−2[k]	+2	−16	0	−6	−1	n.s.	n.s.	−7.0	−11.0	−9.0	0.0

Notes to Table 6-1

Note: All measures for all manufacturing, total durables, and nondurables and measures for the component industries in columns 6–12, are based on the new Census data (1963 revision). The other measures are based on the earlier OBE data (the revised series for the component industries begin in 1953).

n.a. = data not available.

n.i. = not identified (timing uncertain).

n.u. = no turn in unfilled orders.

n.s. = no turn in shipments.

n.t. = no turning points.

[a] These pairs of peaks or troughs represent "extra" turns, not related to a cyclical recession or revival recognized in the National Bureau chronology. All of the comparisons in column 9 and some of those in column 10 refer to dates marking the beginning and end of minor movements or retardations rather than to specific-cycle turns.

[b] Averages of entries in columns 1 and 3.

[c] Averages of entries in columns 5, 7, and 9.

[d] Based on peaks in shipments that occurred in May–June 1959, before the major steel strike in the second half of the year (Charts 3-1 and 3-2).

[e] Based on poststrike peaks in shipments (Chart 3-2).

[f] The pre-1953 measures are based in part on unpublished data received from the Department of Commerce, Office of Business Economics.

[g] Based on secondary troughs in unfilled orders and shipments.

[h] Unfilled orders are compared with shipments excluding motor vehicles and parts.

[i] Includes professional and scientific instruments; lumber; furniture; stone, clay, and glass; and miscellaneous industries.

[j] Includes textiles, leather, paper, and printing and publishing.

[k] Relates to turning points in March and May of 1951. See note 21 in this chapter.

filled orders in 1952–61 was followed by an upward movement of somewhat larger over-all amplitude in 1962–69.

The comparison for nondurables does not show any regular tendency of this sort, but here, too, leads of U relative to S are dominant at peaks and occasionally are long (as before the 1948 and the 1957 recessions).

Short leads and lags prevail throughout at troughs, as shown by a comparison of the even-numbered columns 2, . . . , 10. The averages for the six component durable goods industries at the successive trough zones are −0.7, +1.0, 0, +1.4, and +0.6 months. The averages by industry are also of the same type, mostly short lags of shipments (column 14).

A plausible interpretation of these findings is that they indicate an important link between the size of order backlogs during the expansion and the timing of the downturns of shipments. The evidence supports the hypothesis that the rise of shipments is prolonged (the downturns lag more) when backlogs are large. However, the output-supporting potential of unfilled orders may vary with changes in productive capacities, relative strength of current demand, and expectations.[22]

The roughly coincident timing of unfilled orders at troughs in shipments contrasts with the lead at peaks, especially the long lead in the first part of the period. Since the upturn in unfilled orders, as we date it, would sometimes come at the end of a "bottoming-up" phase, short lags are not inconsistent here with some active role for the backlog factor. Even a stabilization of unfilled orders following a period of decline may help end the contraction in production and deliveries; and an upturn in unfilled orders, signaling an influx of new business above the current rates of manufacturing operations, is likely to have a definite stimulating effect.

It is clear that the leads and lags in Table 6-1 vary greatly over time for most industries, and cannot therefore be adequately described by the means in columns 11–14.[23] The purpose of the means is merely to highlight the broad tendencies just discussed.

Average Measures for Subdivisions of the Durables Sector

Measures of the relative timing of unfilled orders and shipments are summarized in Table 6-2 for the detailed industry categories of the pre-1963 OBE compilation. (The underlying data correspond to those used in Appendix E.)

The recorded observations are grouped into (1) those relating to the early postwar peaks, 1948–53; (2) those relating to the more recent peaks, 1957–60; and (3) those at all covered troughs, 1949–61. There were two peak zones in the earlier and two in the later period, and four trough zones. For some industries, however, fewer observations are available, particularly for the early postwar peaks.

In those durable goods industries where manufacture to order is

---

[22] Note, e.g., that the lags of S at the 1952 peaks of U, although still long, were on the whole significantly shorter than the lags in the 1940's. The U/S ratios were higher in 1952–53 than in 1947–48, but their reduction required more time in the earlier than in the later period. (The ratio for the durable goods industries declined from 5 to 3 in approximately two years during the late forties; it declined from 7 to 5 – in terms of generally higher monthly sales rates – in about seventeen months during the mid-fifties.) This may reflect the growth of industrial capacity and efficiency of production; later, when the demand pressures generally subsided, the same forces manifested themselves more directly in the downward trends of the U/S ratios.

[23] The average deviations from these means vary from 2 to 12 months for the 1948–53 peaks, from 1.8 to 7.6 months for the 1957–62 peaks, and from 0.4 to 2.3 months for the troughs.

Table 6-2

Average Timing of Unfilled Orders at Turns in Shipments, by
Subperiods and Type of Turn, Thirty Manufacturing Industries,
1948–61

| | Average Lead (−) or Lag (+) of Unfilled Orders at Turns in Shipments [a] (months) | | | |
| | Peaks [b] | | | Troughs, |
Industry	1948–53 (1)	1957–60 (2)	All Covered (3)	All Covered (4)
Primary metals				
Iron and steel	−6.0	−3.0	−4.5	−0.2
Primary nonferrous metals	−10.5	+0.5	−5.0	+3.5
Other primary metals	−5.5	+1.5	−2.0	0
Fabricated metal products				
Heating and plumbing [c]	n.a.	+6.0	+6.0	0
Structural metal work [c]	n.a.	−3.5	−3.5	+2.5
Tin cans and other [c]	n.a.	−5.5	−5.5	+0.5
Electrical machinery				
Electrical generator apparatus	−9	+10 [d]	+0.5	+10.3
Radio, TV, and equipment	+1	+5 [d]	+3.0	+2.7
Other electrical equipment	−4	+1.5 [e]	−0.3	−3.2
Machinery exc. electrical				
Metalworking machinery	+10	−4 [d]	−7.0	+0.7
General industrial machinery	−18	−4.5	−9.0	+1.5
Special machinery	+1	−13 [d]	−6.0	−2.3
Engines and turbines	−15	−6.5	−9.3	+1.5
Construction machinery	+1	−7.0	−4.3	+3.5
Office and store machines	0	−11 [e]	−5.5	+3.0
Agricultural implements	+1.5	+0.5	+1.0	+8.7
Household and service appliances	+0.5	+4.0	+2.2	+4.8
Other machinery and parts	−15	+1.0	−4.3	+1.2
Transportation equipment				
Motor vehicles	−7	−1.5	−3.3	+0.5
Motor vehicle parts and accessories	−4.5	0	−2.2	+0.5
Aircraft	−4	−13 [d]	−5.5	−7
Other nonautomotive equipment	−5	−6.5	−6.0	−2.2
Other durable goods				
Lumber	+1	−2.0	−1.0	−0.3
Furniture	+5	+1.5	+2.7	+0.7
Stone, clay, and glass products	−1.0	−1.0	−1.0	+4.5
Professional and scientific instruments	−1	−3.0	−2.3	+0.7
Miscellaneous incl. ordnance	−2.0	n.a.	−2.0	+5.0
Nondurable goods industries				
Textile-mill products	−2.3	−2.0	−2.2	+0.6
Leather and leather products	−2.0	−19.5	−9.0	−2.0
Paper and allied products	−8.0	0 [d]	−6.0	+2.2

Notes to Table 6-2

n.a. = not available.

a Numbers with decimals represent averages. Negative or positive integers refer to cases in which only one observation was available for the given period and type of turn. (In column 1, such figures refer to the 1953 peak zone, i.e., no observations were available in these cases for the 1948 peak zone.)

b Column 1 covers the turning zones associated with the recessions of 1948 and 1953; column 2, those associated with the recessions of 1957 and 1960.

c The series begin in 1955, and their first turning points are peaks associated with the 1957 recession.

d Single observation; no comparison could be made in the 1960 peak zone.

e Single observation; no comparison could be made in the 1957 peak zone.

strongly represented, the tendency for the average leads of U relative to S to be longer at the earlier than at the later postwar downturns shows up clearly in Table 6-2. Of the nineteen industries in this sector for which comparisons can be made (all those in primary metals, electrical machinery, machinery other than electrical, and transportation equipment), eleven show reductions in the backlog leads and five show increases (columns 1 and 2).[24] On the other hand, the results for the group of "other durable goods" show roughly coincident timing of U and S at both the early and the late postwar peaks. There are also no apparent systematic differences between the two subperiods in the observations for the nondurable goods industries.

At troughs, rough coincidences are predominant throughout, with a tendency toward short lags of U and S. This finding, too, is consistent with the results based on the previously introduced data for the major industries.

Market Categories

One-to-one correspondence exists between the cyclical movements of U and S for each of the three groups, machinery and equipment, construction materials, and other materials, despite their divergent trends in the decade starting in 1953 (Charts 3-3 and 6-6). The series for defense products show similar agreement, except in 1959–62 when unfilled orders for defense kept declining almost without interruption while shipments underwent sizable fluctuations. The series for consumer goods also have matching turns except in the early 1960's.

Of the thirteen timing comparisons at peaks identified in Table 6-3,

[24] In three cases, the averages are short lags at the early, and longer lags at the late, peaks.

Table 6-3

Timing of Value of Unfilled Orders at Turns in Shipments, by Business Cycle Turning Zones, Six Market Categories, 1954–62

Lead (−) or Lag (+) in Months of Unfilled Orders at Turns in Shipments in Turning Zone Associated with

Industry	1954 Revival: Troughs (1)	1957 Recession: Peaks (2)	1958 Revival: Troughs (3)	1960 Recession: Peaks (4)	1961 Revival: Troughs (5)	1962 Business Retardation Peaks[a] (6)	1962 Business Retardation Troughs[a] (7)	Av. Lead (−) or Lag (+) (months) Peaks (8)	Av. Lead (−) or Lag (+) (months) Troughs (9)
Home goods, apparel, and consumer staples	+8	0	+5	n.m.	n.m.	n.s.	n.s.	b	+6.5
Equip. and defense prod.									
Total incl. automotive	+2	−6	+1	−6	n.u.	n.u.	−1[c]	−6.0	+0.7
Defense prod.	−7	−10	n.u.	n.u.	n.u.	n.u.	−4	b	−5.5
Machinery and equip.	+2	0	+1	−7	−4	−4	−2	−3.7	−0.8
Materials, supplies, and intermediate products									
Construc. materials, etc.	+10	0	+2	+8	0	+2	+1	+3.2	+3.3
Other materials, etc.	0	−2	+2	+6	+2	−1	0	+1.0	+1.0

n.m. = not matched.

n.s. = no turn in shipments.

n.u. = no turn in unfilled orders.

[a] These pairs of peaks or troughs represent "extra" turns not related to a cyclical recession or revival recognized in the National Bureau chronology. Except in nonautomotive equipment and defense, the declines of shipments during this period qualify as minor movements rather than specific-cycles contractions.

[b] Only one comparison at peaks is available (see column 2).

[c] Based on the December 1962 upturn in shipments of nonautomotive equipment and defense products. Shipments of automotive equipment expanded throughout in 1961–63. Unfilled orders are much more important in the nonautomotive than in the automotive equipment category.

Table 6-4
Timing of Unfilled Orders at Turns in Production and Shipments, Ten Individual Industries or Products,[a] Various Periods, 1919–63

Period Covered[b] (1)	All Turns			No. of Timing Observations at Peaks or Troughs[d] That Are				Av. Lead (−) or Lag (+) (months)	
	No. of Unfilled Order Turns Covered[c] (2)	No. of Shipment or Production Turns		Leads (5)	Exact Coincidences (6)	Lags (7)	Rough Coincidences[e] (8)	Peaks or Troughs[d] (9)	All Turns (10)
		Covered[c] (3)	Matched (4)						

I. TIMING AT TURNS IN SHIPMENTS

STEEL SHEETS

1919–32	9[f]	9	9	2	1	1	3	−1.0	+1.5
					2	3	3	+3.6	

ELECTRIC OVERHEAD CRANES

1928–45	7	7	7	2	1		3	−0.7	−2.3
					3	1	2	−3.5	

FOUNDRY EQUIPMENT

1925–38	6	6	6	2	1		3	−1.3	+1.5
				1		2	1	+4.3	

WOODWORKING MACHINERY

1921–38	11	11	11	4	1		4	−1.4	−1.0
				4	1	1	6	−0.7	

274

FURNITURE 1927–38	9	9[a]	9	2	1	1		1	4	−0.8	+1.0
				1	2	2		2	3	+2.4	
RAILROAD FREIGHT CARS 1925–54	14	16	14	7	1	1		2	2	−6.0	−3.1
				5					5	−0.1	
MACHINE TOOLS 1950–63	10	9	9	4						−10.0	−7.1
				5			1		1	−4.8	
OIL BURNERS 1933–51	13	9	8	2		1		3	3	−1.0	+1.9
				1		4		2	2	+3.6	
OAK FLOORING 1920–55	23[g]	25[h]	23	3	4	5		11	11	+0.8	+1.3
				2	1	8		4	4	+2.0	

II. TIMING AT TURNS IN PRODUCTION

STEEL SHEETS 1919–32	9[f]	9	9	2	2	1			1	+1.2	+2.8
					5	3			3	+4.0	
PAPERBOARD 1926–56	21[i]	19[g]	18	8	1	2		8	8	−1.7	−1.3
				4	3				8	−1.0	
OAK FLOORING 1920–55	23[g]	19[g]	17	4	3	2		9	9	−0.4	−1.1
				4	2	2		6	6	−1.8	

275

Notes to Table 6-4

^a Data are in current dollars except for the following: steel sheets, paperboard—tons; freight cars, oil burners—numbers; oak flooring—board feet.

^b The dates identify the years of the first and the last turn in shipments or production at which the timing of the series can be determined.

^c Includes some minor but well-established turns (see notes f–i). Comparisons based on these turns are included in the figures in columns 4–10. All numbers refer to the periods listed in column 1.

^d For each item, the entry on the first line is for comparisons at peaks; the entry on the second line, for comparisons at troughs.

^e Includes exact coincidences and leads or lags of one, two, or three months.

^f Includes one turn that may be regarded as a minor rather than a specific-cycle turn.

^g Includes two minor turns.

^h Includes six minor turns.

ⁱ Includes four minor turns.

seven are leads and three are lags of U relative to S; of the nineteen comparisons at troughs, five are leads and thirteen are lags. Most of the leads are relatively long (4 months or more), while most of the lags are short (1 or 2 months). Rough coincidences (observations in the range of ±3 months) account for less than half of the comparisons at peaks and for about two-thirds of those at troughs.

Backlogs appear to lead shipments for defense products and to lag shipments for consumer goods, but these results rest on an extremely slender basis and might at best have some suggestive value. For the total equipment category and its nondefense component, the evidence is stronger that U led S at peaks and that the two variables were approximately coincident at troughs. Lags and coincidences prevail among the observations for the two materials categories, and the timing averages here are short lags at both peaks and troughs (see Table 6-3, columns 8 and 9).

Individual Industries or Products

Table 6-4 summarizes the timing comparisons between unfilled orders and shipments or output for ten different products or groups of products. Those items are from the sample used in Chapters 3 and 4 for the analysis of the relationships with new orders. Most of the series go back to the 1920's; in several cases, they extend to the post-World War II years.

The products include some items of equipment which definitely represent manufacture to order and have substantial average delivery periods, some materials made mainly to order but with short delivery periods, and some staples made typically to stock. Railroad freight cars and machine tools exemplify the first, steel sheets the second, and oak flooring the third category. However, the sample gives a rather weak representation to goods made to order and having long delivery lags. This may help to explain the preponderance among these observations of rough coincidences, including many short lags of backlogs, particularly at troughs. For goods made to stock or on very short notice, new orders and shipments usually run closely together and whether N exceeds S or vice versa is often governed by random influences. Where this is true, unfilled orders should show relatively little systematic movement over stretches of time but many small and short irregular variations. These variations in the backlog series should cease and the series should begin expanding only after cyclical or other forces that can cause long systematic runs of positive N-S differences have become dominant. While this argument, *mutatis mutandis,* also applies in principle to runs of negative differences and the beginning of backlog contraction, the two situations are actually not symmetrical, or at least need not be. This is because of delivery delays and backlog accumulations during a business boom; these may occur in any industry and when they do, output and shipments can "feed" on unfilled orders and are likely to lag behind the latter on the downgrade.

A related fact to which the observed timing patterns can be attributed is that unfilled orders were generally small in the interwar years except in the immediate aftermath of World War I; in the depressed thirties, of course, their levels were extremely low. While many time series may be used to illustrate the great economic upheaval that marked the transition to the wartime economy of the 1940's, there can be only a few that showed the contrast as sharply as did the order backlogs, especially for durable goods. From the comparisons underlying Table 6-4, it appears that the timing relations between unfilled orders and shipments changed markedly with the advent of the war. (For example, in the period before 1941, the mean lags of S behind U for railroad freight cars, in months, were 3.8 at peaks and 1.2 at all turns; in the period after 1941, the corresponding figures were 9.0 and 5.5. For electric overhead cranes, the over-all lags were 0.8 months before 1941 and 6 months after.

Backlog-Shipment Ratios

Peak and Trough Values

Table 6-5 lists the successive high and low standings of the U/S ratios for the major manufacturing industries and the averages of these values classified by industry and type of turn. The ratios are based on the Census data shown in Charts 6-4 and 6-5, and on the old OBE data for component industries and some of their groupings, which permit coverage of the earlier postwar years, 1948–53.[25]

The backlog-shipment ratios are throughout much higher for the durable goods than for the nondurable goods industries. Even the lowest of the individual ratio series for the durables exceed on most occasions the highest of the ratio series for the nondurables.[26]

In the durable goods sector, transportation equipment has the highest mean ratios; electrical machinery is second; nonelectrical machinery, third; fabricated metals, fourth; and primary metals, fifth. Other durable goods shows the lowest ratios. The ranking is the same for the peak, trough, and "all turns" measures. Among the nondurables, the ranking is also the same at either turn: textiles, leather, printing, and paper, proceeding from the highest to the lowest ratio (Table 6-5, columns 12–14).

The ranks of the industries according to the U/S ratios in the different peak and trough zones are highly correlated. This is shown by the "coefficient of concordance," W, which measures the degree of agreement among any number of rankings on a scale ranging from zero (complete randomness) to one (perfect consistency, i.e., preservation of the same ranks).[27] For a subset of observations relating to durable

---

[25] An analysis of the U/S ratios based on the OBE data for 1948–61 was completed before the new series became available in 1963. It shows good agreement with the results which incorporate the revised data.

[26] Compare other durable goods with textile-mill products in Table 6-5.

[27] Let m be the number of rankings and n, that of the items to be ranked. The total of ranks in each of the m arrays is $n(n + 1)/2$ and the grand total is $mn(n + 1)/2$. (In the present case, it is the industry components of a sector that are ranked and there is a ranking for each period; that is, m refers to the columns and n to the lines of Table 6-5.) If the ranks were randomly allocated, one would expect their sum for each item to be the same, namely $1/n$th of the grand total or $m(n + 1)/2$. On the other hand, if the rankings were in perfect agreement, the sums of the ranks for the different items would be $m, 2m, 3m, \ldots, nm$ (in some order not identifiable in advance). The sum of squares of the deviations of these rank totals from $m(n + 1)/2$ is $S_{max} = m^2(n^3 - n)/12$; and the ratio of the sum of squares of the actual deviations (S) to S_{max} is

$$W = S/S_{max} = 12S/m^2(n^3 - n).$$

For a complete statement of the theory underlying the measurement of concordance, see Maurice G. Kendall, *Rank Correlation Methods*, London, 1948, Chap. 6.

goods industries, $W = .702$. A few columns are not included in this measure because of gaps caused by the "no turns" entries in the table, but the correlations among the ranks in these columns are even higher.[28] For the subset of the four nondurable goods industries, $W = .916$. These values (calculated with adjustments for tied ranks) are highly significant according to the usual statistical tests.[29]

In short, I find that relatively high backlog-shipment ratios are consistently characteristic of some industries, while low ratios are typical of others, although all these series are subject to trends and fluctuations which are often pronounced. This parallels the results presented early in this book for the stock-backlog ratios (Chapter 2).

Compared with orders and shipments, the U/S series show much less variability over time. Most of the variability is contributed by the peak values whose average deviations from the mean range from 0.1 to 2.1; the range of the corresponding dispersion measures for the trough values is from zero to 0.9.[30] The largest deviations are associated with the largest mean ratios, notably those in blast furnaces, electrical machinery, and transportation equipment.

The figures for the three peak periods in the 1950's reflect the general decline of the backlog-shipment ratios in that decade. For most industries, the U/S values were lower in 1958–60 than in 1955–56 and lower in 1955–56 than in 1951–52 (cf. columns 3, 5, and 7).

Backlog-Shipment Ratios and the Delivery Lags

As ratios of a stock (measured in dollars) to a flow (in dollars per unit period), the variable U/S has a time dimension. For example, if ship-

---

[28] The computation of W requires that the rankings be complete in each case. The reported value of W refers to the six major durable goods industries listed, and to the periods covered in columns 1–4, 7, 10, and 11. The ranks in columns 5 and 6 (with no entries for nonelectrical machinery) are similar, and they show a correlation of 0.9; the ranks in columns 8 and 9 are identical, and they, too, correspond closely to the others, except that here no measures are recorded for either of the machinery industries.

The concordance coefficients provide a convenient formula for deriving the average of all rank correlation coefficients (Spearman's) that can be computed for the m rankings. Such average correlation equals $\bar{R} = (mW - 1)/(m - 1)$.

[29] The calculated F values are 13.98 for the durables and 56.61 for the nondurables. The test is applied to W after a continuity correction (in which S is decreased by 1 and S_{max} increased by 2). The value of F is computed as $F = (m - 1)W/(1 - W)$, and tables of F are consulted, using the degrees of freedom $n_1 = (n - 1 - 2)/m$ and $n_2 = (m - 1)[n - 1 - 2)/m]$. The 1 per cent significance points ($F_{.99}$) thus found are of the order of 5.0 and 10.0, respectively; the observed F exceeds even the $F_{.999}$ points.

For more detail on this test, see Helen M. Walker and Joseph Lev, *Statistical Inference*, New York, 1953, pp. 283–86.

[30] Standard deviations exceed the average deviations by very small, often very trivial, fractions and are also small relative to the corresponding means.

Table 6-5

Ratios of Unfilled Orders to Shipments, Successive Peak and Trough Values and Averages by Type of Turn, Major Manufacturing Industries, 1948–66

| | Peak and Trough Values of Unfilled Orders-Shipments (U/S) Ratios [a] | | | | | | | | | | | Average U/S Ratio at | | |
Industry	Peak 1947–48 [b] (1)	Trough 1949–50 (2)	Peak 1951–52 (3)	Trough 1954–55 (4)	Peak 1955–56 (5)	Trough 1957–59 (6)	Peak 1958–60 (7)	Trough 1960–61 [c] (8)	Peak 1961–63 [c] (9)	Trough 1962–64 (10)	Peak 1965–66 [d] (11)	Peaks (12)	Troughs (13)	All Turns (14)
All manufacturing [e]	3.1	2.1	5.7[f]	3.0	4.0	n.t.	n.t.	n.t.	n.t.	2.1	2.7	3.9	2.4	3.5
Durable goods	5.3	2.5	6.8[f]	3.4	4.7	n.t.	n.t.	2.8	3.0	2.5	3.3	4.6	2.8	3.8
Primary metals	3.3	2.4[g]	4.5[h]	1.8	3.8[i]	2.0	3.9[j]	1.5	1.9	1.3	2.0	3.2	1.8	2.6
Blast furnaces, steel mills	n.a.	n.a.	5.6[k]	2.4	6.5[i]	2.3	8.1[i]	1.6	2.2	1.4	2.4	5.0	1.9	3.6
Fabricated metal products	4.5	2.7	5.7	2.9	3.3	2.1[m]	2.4[m]	2.0	2.3	2.0	2.9	3.5	2.3	3.0
Elect. machinery [n]	4.5	3.4	9.7	3.6	n.t.	n.t.	4.7	n.t.	n.t.	2.8	3.5	5.6	3.3	4.6
Machinery exc. elect. [n]	4.8	2.7	7.2	3.2	4.4	2.8[m]	3.0[m]	n.t.	n.t.	2.5	3.7	4.6	2.8	3.8
Transport. equip.	4.2	2.2	11.0[n]	5.2	8.2	5.4[m]	6.5[m]	4.1	5.1	3.8	5.5	6.8	4.1	5.6
Other durable goods [o]	1.9	1.3	2.8	1.7[m]	1.9[m]	1.5	1.7	1.4	1.5	1.2	n.t.	2.0	1.4	1.7
Nondurable goods [p]	1.9	1.0	2.0	0.9	1.2	0.8	1.0	0.7	0.8	0.6	0.7	1.3	0.8	1.1
Textile-mill products [q]	2.5	1.1	3.1	1.2	1.9	1.2	1.6	1.1				2.3	1.2	1.7
Leather and leather products [q]	1.5	1.1	1.6	0.8	1.6	0.9	1.5	1.1				1.6	1.0	1.3
Paper and allied products [q]	0.9	0.6	1.1	0.6	0.6	0.4	0.5	0.4				0.8	0.5	0.6
Printing and publishing [q]	1.9	0.7	1.2	0.6	0.8	0.5	0.9	n.i.				1.2	0.6	0.9

Notes to Table 6-5

n.a. = not available.

n.i. = not identified.

n.t. = no turning point.

[a] Each of the successive peak and trough zones is identified by the annual dates of the earliest and latest turns in the U/S ratios.

[b] The highest ratios in 1947–48 (data for 1947 are available only for the three most comprehensive series). These are not necessarily the specific-cycle peak values of these ratios. (Since unfilled orders of the durable goods sector declined through 1947 while shipments rose—see Chart 6-3—the ratios for 1948 must be lower than the earlier peak ratios for a number of industries.) Earlier data required to establish the peak ratios for several industries are not available.

[c] These observations refer to minor turns in the U/S ratios. Similar observations in other periods are identified in note m.

[d] The highest ratios reached by the time this analysis was completed (the latest available figure refers to November 1966). For the industries in which the U/S ratios continued to grow, these values underestimate the true peak ratios.

[e] Industries reporting unfilled orders include the durable goods industries and the four major nondurable goods industries listed on the last four lines.

[f] Average of four monthly values, June–September 1952; used to reduce the reliance on individual ratios, which were strongly affected by a steel strike (Chart 6-4). Averages elsewhere in this table (see notes g–j and l below) were used for the same reason.

[g] Average of three monthly values, July–September 1949.

[h] Average of three monthly values, April, May, and September 1952.

[i] Average of four monthly values, June–September 1952.

[j] Averages of six monthly values, July–December 1959.

[k] Highest value in 1953, the first year covered by this series; probably somewhat lower than the peak ratios in 1952 (judging from the total primary metals data; see Chart 6-5).

[l] Average of six monthly values, June–November 1956.

[m] Refer to minor turns in the U/S ratios.

[n] Based in part on unpublished data received from the U.S. Department of Commerce, Office of Business Economics.

[o] Includes professional and scientific instruments; lumber; furniture; stone, clay, and glass; and miscellaneous industries.

[p] Includes textiles, leather, paper, and printing and publishing.

[q] Based on unpublished OBE data for 1948–61.

ments per month are $10 billion and unfilled orders equal $30 billion, the ratio $U/S = 3$ means that the backlog equals three months' worth of current shipments. Alternatively, the ratio indicates that the backlog could be eliminated in three months at the current rate of operation—provided that no new orders were received. Under the more realistic assumption that new orders continue to add to the backlog, even while shipments continue to reduce it, the current value of U/S does not tell how U is going to change or at what rate. These developments depend on the future time paths of N and S.

In this connection, it is instructive to consider a recent suggestion that such ratio measures can be improved by using the rates of shipments in later periods instead of the current rate.[31] The procedure rests on the assumptions that customers are served on a first-in first-out basis (orders keep their chronological places in the queue) and that new orders and deliveries are evenly distributed over the periods of observation. Given the backlog U_t at the end of month t, one then asks how many months of the *subsequently* observed shipments would have been needed to liquidate that backlog. That is, one cumulatively adds $S_{t+1}, S_{t+2}, \ldots, S_{t+k}$, and determines the value of k for which $\Sigma_{i=1}^{k} S_{t+i} = U_t$. Like the ordinary ratio U_t/S_t, k can be interpreted as a "number of months." In each case, a stock variable, U_t, is related to flow magnitudes, S_{t+i}, although U_t/S_t uses a single rate of shipments (for the current month, $i = 0$), while k incorporates different, future rates.

Variations in shipments could have such patterns and be large enough to make the estimates of U/S and k significantly different. However, for U.S. durable goods industries, our calculations show that this is not the case. Chart 6-7 compares two estimates of the "average delivery periods" for these industries: the current ratio of unfilled orders to shipments, U/S, and the Steuer-Ball-Eaton measure of "waiting time" defined above as k. The two series are closely similar, although k is somewhat smoother than U/S and considerably less affected by occasional large shocks such as the 1952 strike. While k is indeed conceptually preferable to the ratio of U_t to S_t, it takes more time to compute, and the return on these extra costs seems small. Hence only U/S ratios are used elsewhere in this book. The results of the experiment presented in Chart 6-7 are encouraging, since they suggest that much the same broad conclusions are obtained from an analysis of the current ratios as from a different and presumably better estimation method.

The observed backlog-shipment ratio clearly tells us nothing definite about the magnitude of the lead of new orders relative to shipments. Nevertheless, one might expect a positive association between the size of the ratio and the average length of time that buyers have to wait for delivery on orders currently placed. At least, changes in U/S over

[31] See M. D. Steuer, R. J. Ball and J. R. Eaton, "The Effect of Waiting Times on Foreign Orders for Machine Tools," *Economica*, November 1966, pp. 389–90.

Chart 6-7
Two Estimates of Delivery Periods, Durable Goods Industries, 1947–65

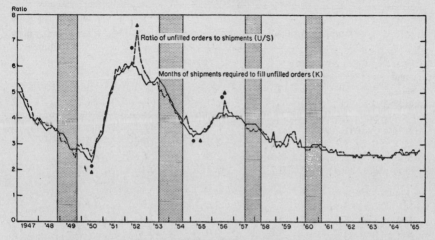

Note: Shaded areas represent business cycle contractions; unshaded areas, expansions. Dots identify peaks and troughs of specific cycles in the K index; triangles, the U/S ratio. Series are seasonally adjusted.

Source: Bureau of the Census.

time may serve as an approximation to changes in the average waiting or delivery periods. Also, there is some reason to believe that a cross-sectional relationship may exist: An industry that has a backlog of unfilled orders that is large relative to output and shipments is presumably an industry in which production to order is important and delivery periods are substantial. By the same token, an industry with low U/S ratios is likely to have only a small proportion of its output made to order.

Industry Averages for the Ratios and Lags

Comparisons of the average U/S ratios and the average leads of N relative to S for the major manufacturing industries (Table 6-6) do show some correspondence between the two sets of measures. Transportation equipment has the highest ratios and the longest leads, while the "other durables" group has the lowest ratios and the shortest leads among the major components of the durable goods sector. Leather, paper, and printing have very low U/S ratios and also, on the average,

Table 6-6
Means, Medians, and Standard Deviations of Backlog-Shipment Ratios and of Leads of New Orders at Turns in Shipments, Major Manufacturing Industries, 1948–64

Industry and Statistic [a]	Backlog-Shipment Ratios [b] at Turns in				Timing [c] of New Orders at Turns in Shipments (mos.)	
	New Orders		Shipments			
	P (1)	T (2)	P (3)	T (4)	P (5)	T (6)
ALL MANUFACTURING [d]						
M	3.2	2.8	2.9	2.7	2.4	3.8
Md	2.9	2.5	2.8	2.5	2	3
SD	0.9	0.7	0.7	0.4	1.9	2.9
DURABLE GOODS						
M	3.8	3.4	3.6	3.2	5.6	4.6
Md	3.7	3.0	3.1	3.0	5	3
SD	1.0	0.8	0.9	0.5	4.6	3.8
PRIMARY METALS [e]						
M	2.9	2.7	2.8	2.5	3.6	4.6
Md	2.8	2.6	2.9	2.0	3	3
SD	0.7	1.0	0.8	1.1	3.6	4.0
BLAST FURNACES, STEEL MILLS [f]						
M	2.9	2.8	2.6	2.1	6.8	5.6
Md	3.0	2.6	2.0	2.0	3.5	3
SD	0.6	1.0	0.9	1.6	7.2	4.4
FABRICATED METAL PRODUCTS						
M	3.3	3.3	3.1	3.1	2.2	4.5
Md	2.9	3.1	2.8	2.7	2	4.5
SD	1.1	1.1	1.2	1.2	2.0	3.0
ELECT. MACHINERY [g]						
M	4.5	4.8	4.4	4.9	2.5	1.2
Md	4.2	4.4	4.0	4.2	2.5	2.5
SD	1.0	1.6	1.1	2.0	1.7	3.7
MACHINERY EXC. ELECT. [g]						
M	3.7	3.2	3.5	3.1	5.0	4.2
Md	3.7	3.1	3.5	3.1	3	5
SD	0.8	0.4	0.8	0.3	3.8	2.8
TRANSPORT. EQUIP.						
M	6.5	6.4	5.6	6.0	2.2	3.8
Md	6.0	5.9	5.2	6.5	3	1
SD	2.1	1.1	1.6	1.1	5.2	4.7

(continued)

Table 6-6 (concluded)

| Industry and Statistic [a] | Backlog-Shipment Ratios [b] at Turns in | | | | Timing [c] of New Orders at Turns in Shipments (mos.) | |
| | New Orders | | Shipments | | | |
	P (1)	T (2)	P (3)	T (4)	P (5)	T (6)
OTHER DURABLE GOODS [h]						
M	2.0	1.9	1.9	1.9	0.8	1.4
Md	1.9	1.8	1.8	1.8	0	0
SD	0.3	0.5	0.3	0.5	2.3	2.8
NONDURABLE GOODS [i]						
M	1.4	1.0	1.3	0.9	3.4	2.8
Md	1.1	0.9	1.1	0.9	4	3
SD	0.4	0.3	0.4	0.2	2.8	2.0
TEXTILE-MILL PRODUCTS [j]						
M	2.0	1.4	1.8	1.3	3.6	4.2
Md	1.7	1.3	1.7	1.2	4	5
SD	0.5	0.4	0.5	0.2	1.9	2.3
LEATHER AND LEATHER PRODUCTS [j]						
M	1.2	1.1	1.1	1.2	0.6	4.0
Md	1.2	1.0	1.2	1.2	0	4
SD	0.1	0.1	0.2	0.1	1.2	1.0
PAPER AND ALLIED PRODUCTS [j]						
M	0.8	0.6	0.7	0.6	3.5	(0.5)
Md	0.8	0.6	0.6	0.6	3.5	(0.5)
SD	0.2	0.1	0.1	0.1	2.5	2.5
PRINTING AND PUBLISHING [j]						
M	1.0	0.7	0.8	0.8	0.0	(0.5)
Md	0.8	0.8	0.7	0.8	k	k
SD	0.5	0.1	0.4	0.0	0.7	0.5

P = troughs.
T = peaks.
Note: The entries for the individual durable goods industries are based on the older (pre-1963) OBE data for the period 1948–52 and on the new Census data (1963 revision) for 1953–62. The entries for all manufacturing and for the durable goods aggregate are based on the new data. The entries for the four individual nondurable goods industries are based on the older data for 1948–61 only. The same series were used earlier in this chapter for unfilled orders and shipments (see, e.g., Tables 6-1 and 6-2); the series for new orders are of the same vintage and cover the same years.

[a] M = arithmetic mean; Md = median; SD = standard deviation.

Notes to Table 6-6 (continued)

ᵇ The dates of the turns are those used in the measures of the leads of new orders relative to shipments (the leads included in the averages of columns 5 and 6).

ᶜ All the figures denote average leads of new orders relative to shipments, except those in parentheses, which are lags. The means (M) are the same as the corresponding entries in Table 4-6, column 8, and in Appendix E, Table E-1, columns 11 and 12, lines 28–31, written without sign. See Tables 4-5 and E-1 for the full record of timing underlying these measures. The medians and standard deviations (Md, SD) are based on the same observations as the means.

ᵈ All industries reporting unfilled orders; includes the durable goods industries and the four major nondurable goods industries covered in the last twelve lines.

ᵉ The values of the U/S ratios at the 1952 troughs in new orders and shipments were estimated by averaging over selected months (April, May, and September for the new orders chronology and June–December for that of shipments) to dampen the effects of the steel strike. In 1959, prestrike turns were used.

ᶠ Data begin in 1953. In 1959, prestrike turns in N and S were used.

ᵍ Based in part on unpublished data received from the U.S. Department of Commerce, Office of Business Economics.

ʰ Includes professional and scientific instruments; lumber; furniture; stone, clay, and glass; and miscellaneous industries.

ⁱ Includes textiles, leather, paper, and printing and publishing.

ʲ Based on unpublished OBE data for the period 1948–61.

ᵏ Only two observations are available.

very short leads. These results do not depend greatly on whether the U/S ratios are measured at their own turning points or at those of new orders or shipments. In Table 6-6, ratios at turns in both new orders and shipments are presented. Typically, the values of U/S are higher at the turning points of N than at those of S but the differences are small (compare columns 1 and 3, and columns 2 and 4).

It appears in several instances that the average leads show haphazard interindustry differences, while the average U/S ratios yield more systematic and meaningful results. The leads provide a fair basis for discrimination only in the extreme cases. The correspondence between the industry ranks according to the two measures is also limited to these cases.

General considerations suggest that no more than a loose association may be expected between these two quite different and independently derived sets of estimates. One major reason lies in aggregation over industries with different types of manufacture and different incidence and lags of delivery. The observable timing relations between N and S can be quite sensitive to the characteristics of the resulting compositions.[32] For example a major industry as diversified as electrical machinery has large order backlogs for many products and thus relatively high U/S ratios. At the same time, the lags of S behind N are typically rather short in this industry, which may be caused by offsetting effects of aggregation.

Further complications may arise because of vagaries in the course of sales or new orders and the effects of the resulting uncertainty and errors of prediction. In manufacture to stock, scheduling production depends on expectations of market sales. When these turn bearish early, production may well be curtailed with little delay, even if total order backlogs for the industry's other products are still large. In fact, it should be clear that large backlogs do not *insure* long lags of output at peaks in new orders even in manufacture to order, except in the probably rare cases where suppliers are committed to rigid production schedules under large long-term contracts. Large backlogs do *enable* firms to continue producing at high rates in the face of declines in current demand, but when such declines are expected to be severe and persistent enough, the costs of maintaining the high rates of output will appear greater than the costs of changing the rates. Production cutbacks will then be made. Thus the short lags of the electrical machinery shipments may also occasionally or in part reflect prompt reactions to early changes in expectations of market sales.

The peak-trough differences in the ratios are generally small, often inappreciable, and sometimes "perverse" in the sense that the peak values are smaller than the trough ones (columns 1–2 and 3–4). Much of this is due to discrepancies in timing between the ratios and either new orders or shipments. The average lags of shipments show large but by no means uniform or systematic differences between peaks and troughs. For example, as noted in Chapter 4, some of the lags at troughs were unusually long for particular reasons.

[32] Suppose that industry A sells all but one of its products from stock; the single item it makes to order accounts for a small proportion of the value of its output but requires a long delivery period. On the other hand, suppose industry B produces only to order, with sizable delivery periods for its individual products; but the time patterns involved are such that the over-all average delivery period for the value aggregates of all its products is short. Then industry A would have low U/S ratios, in terms of values of total backlogs and shipments, and substantial lags of S behind N. This is because for most of A's output $N = S$, but for a small part of it, which alone determines the lag, the two variables differ and N precedes S by long intervals. Industry B would, on the contrary, have relatively high U/S ratios and short lags of S behind N. This is because, by assumption, B has at any time a large volume of advance orders to be processed but the delivery lags on its products largely cancel each other out, leaving short average lags only in the relation between its aggregate new orders and shipments.

Because of the limitations of data and measures, it seems inadvisable to go into the detail of the comparisons by industry and type of turn.[33] On the whole, the U/S ratios are far more stable and well-behaved than the timing comparisons, which are particularly sensitive to irregular and episodic influences. The ratios show much less dispersion than the timing measures, as can be seen by comparing the respective standard deviations and averages in Table 6-6. Hence the averages of the U/S values are more representative of their distributions than are the averages of the N-S leads of theirs.

Table 6-7 presents measures of the same type for twenty-seven subdivisions of the durable goods sector. It was hoped that the difficulties arising from aggregation would be somewhat reduced in these comparisons, which apply to more narrowly defined industrial categories. The table is based on the older OBE data and has a simplified format.[34]

Both the average backlog-shipment ratios and the average leads of new orders indicate substantial and apparently systematic differences between the subdivisions of several major industries, namely, nonelectrical machinery, transportation equipment, and the other durables group. It is significant that in each of these cases the two measures identify the same component industries as having extreme ranks. Thus metalworking machinery and engines and turbines have the highest U/S ratios and the largest N-S leads, while office and store machines, agricultural implements, and household appliances are at the other end in either ranking. Aircraft ranks high and motor vehicles low according to either measure. Among the "other durables," only one subdivision has high average U/S values—professional and scientific investments—and this is also the only industry in the group that shows long lags of shipments behind new orders.

The main counterexample is electrical machinery, where the relatively high backlog-shipment ratios observed before for the group as a whole appear to be common to all three subdivisions, while the order leads are on the average short.

---

[33] There is little doubt that errors of measurement adversely affect the present results. In particular, the combination of low U/S ratios and relatively long lags of S behind N may arise partly from overestimation of the lags at turning points.

[34] For the U/S ratios, only the values at turns in shipments are used (the corresponding measures at new-order turns are very similar). The means and the medians of the ratios differ little, too, and only the former are included.

The Relations Over Time

The cross-sectional hypothesis—that those industries which have high (low) average U/S ratios would also tend to have relatively long (short) average leads of new orders relative to shipments—turned out to have some limited support in the data. Its counterpart for time series is that, over the cycle, long leads of N relative to S would occur when the U/S ratio for the given industry is high, and short leads when the ratio is low. This, too, is unlikely to be a regularly observable relationship for several reasons, some already noted, and others noted below.

The vagaries of individual observations are particularly troublesome here, since the analysis is concerned directly with comparisons at successive turns rather than with averages. But more is involved than technical difficulties of estimation. The relative timing of new orders, output, and shipments depends on other systematic factors in addition to the rates of capacity utilization and the size of backlogs. Expectations influence the speed and strength of reactions to changes in demand, while being themselves affected by the size and other characteristics of current and earlier changes.

The greater and the more sustained the change in demand, the more definite the expectations and the stronger the response. This point seems reasonable on a priori grounds and also consistent with the evidence. Thus the reaction of the industry to a sluggish and hesitant reversal in new orders would tend to be slower or weaker than the reaction to a more decisive and visible reversal. A related influence is the size of the changes before the turn. Consider a recovery preceded by large declines in new orders and much smaller declines in shipments (which implies a sizable backlog decumulation). In this case, new orders have relatively low levels at the upturn and for some time thereafter, and backlogs continue to be reduced; whether or not incoming business will regain its strength is still uncertain, and as long as this is so, output and delivery rates are more likely just to be stabilized than appreciably increased. The developments in 1953–54 illustrate this. At the 1953 peaks, the lags of shipments behind new orders were generally shorter than at the 1954 troughs. Backlogs were ample, absolutely and relative to shipments, throughout this period, but they were larger in 1953 than in 1954. In 1953, the declines of new orders were large and steep, from levels about equal to those of shipments. In

Table 6-7
Average Ratios of Unfilled Orders to Shipments and Average Leads of New Orders at Peaks and Troughs of Shipments, by Subdivisions of Durable Manufactures, 1948–61

| | Value of U/S Ratios at Turns in Shipments [b] | | Timing [c] of New Orders at Turns in Shipments [b] | | |
| | Mean (1) | Standard Deviation (2) | Mean [d] (3) | Median (4) | Standard Deviation (5) |
Industry [a]					
Primary metals					
Iron and steel (5, 5)	3.2	0.8	2.2	2	1.6
	3.2	1.3	4.4	1	4.6
Primary nonferrous metals (5, 5)	1.5	0.2	1.2	1	1.7
	1.7	0.4	(0.8)	0	1.2
Other primary metals (5, 5)	2.6	0.8	3.4	3	2.7
	2.5	1.2	3.4	3	2.2
Fabricated metal products [e]					
Heating and plumbing (2, 2)	3.6	0.4	(0.5)	f	1.5
	5.0	0.4	6.0	f	2.0
Structural metal work (2, 2)	2.4	0.9	2.0	f	5.0
	1.9	0.4	5.0	f	1.0
Tin cans and other (2, 2)	1.6	0.2	2.5	f	0.5
	1.4	0.2	1.5	f	0.5
Electrical machinery					
Electrical generator apparatus (4, 4)	5.5	1.3	0.2	1	3.3
	5.7	0.4	0.8	1.5	5.0
Radio, TV, and equipment (5, 5)	5.5	2.1	(0.8)	0	1.9
	7.2	2.5	1.8	2	3.2
Other electrical equipment (5, 5)	4.3	1.5	1.2	0	1.9
	4.9	0.7	6.5	7.5	4.0
Machinery except electrical					
Metalworking machinery (2, 3)	6.8	2.0	14.0	14	1.0
	3.4	0.7	8.0	6	6.7
General machinery (5, 5)	5.4	1.3	4.0	5	3.9
	5.6	1.3	4.6	4	1.7
Special machinery (4, 4)	4.4	1.1	5.5	5.5	0.5
	4.0	2.1	5.3	7	3.9
Engines and turbines (4, 3)	5.7	0.5	16.3	20	7.4
	7.4	1.4	3.5	2.5	2.7
Construction machinery (4, 5)	3.5	1.2	6.5	8	3.8
	3.1	1.1	2.8	1	3.1

(continued)

Table 6-7 (concluded)

Industry [a]	Value of U/S Ratios at Turns in Shipments [b]		Timing [c] of New Orders at Turns in Shipments [b]		
	Mean (1)	Standard Deviation (2)	Mean [d] (3)	Median (4)	Standard Deviation (5)
Machinery except electrical (cont.)					
Office and store machines (4, 5)	1.8	0.3	3.3	4	0.9
	1.9	0.3	0.8	−0.5	3.8
Agricultural implements (4, 4)	2.8	0.7	1.0	1	0.7
	3.1	0.8	1.3	1	1.2
Household and service appliances (6, 6)	2.6	0.5	2.7	4	2.6
	3.1	0.9	3.5	1.5	4.4
Other machinery and parts (3, 4)	4.3	0.9	4.7	5	3.7
	3.8	0.6	4.5	5	1.5
Transportation equipment					
Motor vehicles (6, 6)	1.0	1.0	3.8	2	6.5
	1.9	1.8	3.4	2.5	4.1
Motor vehicle parts and accessories (6, 6)	3.8	1.3	4.6	4	2.7
	3.6	1.4	3.0	1	3.8
Aircraft (3, 3)	14.7	3.4	12.0	[f]	2.0
	17.5	4.3	11.0	[g]	[g]
Other nonautomotive transportation equipment (3, 4)	6.5	2.0	6.5	[f]	1.5
	6.6	1.5	9.0	12	4.2
Other durable goods industries					
Lumber (2, 3) [h]	0.7	0.2	2.0	[f]	2.0
	0.8	0.5	0.7	1	0.5
Furniture (2, 3) [h]	0.8	0.2	1.0	[f]	1.0
	0.9	0.2	0.3	0	0.5
Stone, clay, and glass products (5, 5)	1.4	0.3	1.2	3	2.7
	1.5	0.3	0.4	0	3.2
Professional and scientific instruments (3, 3) [h]	5.8	0.9	7.0	[f]	1.0
	5.7	0.2	7.7	7	2.5
Miscellaneous including ordnance (3, 3) [h]	1.4	0.7	0	[f]	2.0
	1.2	0.3	0.3	−1	1.9

Notes to Table 6-7

ᵃ The first figure in parentheses gives the number of observations on the U/S ratios at peaks; the second, the number at troughs.

ᵇ For each item, the entry on the first line is for peaks; the entry on the second line, for troughs.

ᶜ All the figures in columns 3 and 4 denote average leads of new orders relative to shipments, except those in parentheses, which are lags.

ᵈ Same as the corresponding entries in Appendix E, Table E-1, columns 11 and 12, written without sign. See that table for the full record of timing underlying these measures. The medians and standard deviations in columns 4 and 5 are based on the same observations as the means.

ᵉ The series on unfilled orders for the components of the fabricated metals industry begin in 1955.

ᶠ Only two observations are available.

ᵍ Only one observation is available.

ʰ The series on unfilled orders for these industries begin in 1953.

1954, new orders moved up hesitantly from levels well below those of shipments.

All possible obstacles notwithstanding, rank correlations between the successively observed lags of shipments behind new orders and the corresponding U/S ratios are positive for most of the durable goods industries. For the durables aggregates, Spearman's correlation coefficients, adjusted for tied ranks, are .648 and .836, depending on whether the ratios are measured at turns in new orders or at turns in shipments. For transportation equipment, the corresponding coefficients are .607 and .621; for fabricated matals, .548 and .388; and for blast furnaces and steel mills (since 1953), .603 and .230. In the first two cases, both figures are significant; in the others, at least the larger figure in each pair is.[35] However, the rank correlations for the other major components of the durable goods sector are low enough to be of doubtful or no significance.[36]

Evidence supporting the relationship is provided by data for individual industries, which go back to the years before World War II. Table

[35] Predominantly positive results were also obtained in earlier calculations based on the older (pre-1963) data. For the averages of seven major industries, the rank correlation is .64; for the averages of twenty-seven industrial subdivisions, it is .60. These measures use U/S ratios taken at turns in new orders; when the ratios at the turns in shipments are used instead, somewhat lower correlations (of .57 and .52, respectively) are obtained.

[36] The significance points for rankings of ten or fewer items are given in *Biometrika Tables for Statisticians*, Vol. I, ed. E. S. Pearson and H. O. Hartley, Cambridge, 1958, Table 44, p. 211.

Table 6-8

Rank Correlations Between Leads of New Orders, Backlog-Shipment
Ratios, and Related Measures, Five Industries, 1919–56

Industry	Timing Measures		Number of Paired Observations [b] (3)	Coefficients of Rank Correlation [c] Between Timing Measures and	
	New Orders Relative to Shipments (S) or Production (Z) (1)	Period Covered [a] (2)		Ratio: U/S or U/Z (4)	Production as Per Cent of Capacity (5)
Steel sheets	S	1919–32	9	0.50	0.63
Woodworking machinery	S	1923–38	10	0.44	
Furniture	S	1926–45	8		0.33
Paperboard	Z	1926–56	17	0.31 [d]	0.52
Oak flooring	S	1918–54	19	0.11	

[a] Identifies the dates of the first and of the last turning point in shipments or production.

[b] Equals the number of ranks used in the correlations; refers to the periods listed in column 2.

[c] Spearman's coefficient adjusted for the presence of "ties" or duplicated rank standings. The underlying data are three-month averages centered on the month of turn in shipments or production, as indicated in column 1. Backlogs $= U$.

[d] Correlation between the leads of new orders relative to output (see column 1) and ratios of backlogs to output (U/Z).

6-8 shows that the correlations between the leads of new orders and the corresponding U/S ratios are all positive for these limited materials. For one industry, paperboard, production rather than shipment figures were used, with similar results.

The leads of new orders are also positively correlated with the rates of capacity utilization in the given industry at the turning points. These correlations are somewhat higher than those with the backlog-shipment (or backlog-output) ratios (cf. cols. 4 and 5).

While none of these associations is close, their consensus in sign is not likely to be accidental. It supports the presumption that the lags of production behind orders tend to be longer, the larger the relative size of backlogs and the higher the capacity utilization.

Summary

Unfilled orders (U) would be expected to move in the same direction as the business cycle, since there is a tendency for new orders (N) to exceed shipments (S) in expansions and for $N < S$ in contractions; also, U should lag behind N, whereas its timing relative to S would probably be roughly coincident. However, this scheme is partly oversimplified because of the implicit treatment of the order backlogs as merely a product of the past history of N and S without any active influence of its own. Actually, backlog movements can themselves strongly affect the scheduling of production and the timing of shipments. Where the backlogs are large and the delivery periods are long, production and shipments are concerned in a large measure with old orders on hand rather than with current orders; that is, they then depend relatively more on U and less on N. At high peak levels of U, the lags of S would often be long, since an ample stock of orders can sustain production for some time, even when the current order receipts are declining (witness the wartime and postwar developments in 1917–18 and 1942–48).

Where backlogs are small, either because the typical delivery periods are short or because production is largely to stock, they are likely to behave less systematically and their relation to shipments may be rather loose. In the decade 1952–62, following the build-up of the Korean War period, backlogs had horizontal or downward trends and drastically reduced cyclical movements. At both the peaks and troughs of this period, unfilled orders have for the most part had either rough coincidences or lags relative to the corresponding shipments series. Afterward, long upward movements have reasserted themselves in the order backlogs of durable goods industries, and shipments show again a sizable lag at the recent peak of these backlogs in 1969.

The U/S ratios have a time dimension and provide some indications of the changing average duration of delivery lags. The ratios for the durable goods sector have been declining most of the time in the years 1953–63 (from levels of 6.0 or more to about 2.5). Afterward, through 1969, they were generally larger (mostly close to 3.0, with a high of 3.5 in October 1967), but still much lower than in the 1950's. For most of the industries, cyclical fluctuations of U/S resemble those of U but are smaller. The U/S ratios often lag behind total backlogs at troughs, but coincide with or lead backlogs at peaks. This conforms to expectations: Demand pressures reach their greatest intensity before aggregate output peaks, but revival of production at low levels of capacity utilization does not imply an immediate lengthening of the average delivery or waiting times.

The average size of backlogs differs greatly among the industries: It is, of course, large for durable goods and small for nondurables (the latter account for no more than 5–7 per cent of total unfilled orders of manufacturers). The U/S ratios show similar interindustry differences. In the durable goods sector, transportation equipment has the highest average ratios; electrical and nonelectrical machinery rank second and third; fabricated and primary metals, fourth and fifth; and other durables show the lowest ratios. In terms of market categories, defense products show the highest U/S figures, followed in descending order by machinery and equipment, materials, and consumer goods.

An industry with a high (low) average U/S ratio is probably an industry with a large (small) proportion of output accounted for by advance orders that have long delivery periods. This, however, does not imply that a close relation must exist between these ratios and the average lags of S relative to N at turning points, because of the disturbing effects of uncertainty about the future course of sales, of aggregation, of other measurement errors, etc. Actually the hypothesis of a positive association between these two quite different and independently derived sets of estimates does receive a modest degree of support from the data. Also, rank correlations between the successively observed lags of shipments at turns in new orders and the corresponding U/S ratios are typically positive although not high.

7

UNFILLED ORDERS, DELIVERY PERIODS, AND PRICE CHANGES

AN INDUSTRY whose unfilled orders continue for some time to expand, both absolutely and relative to shipments, may be assumed to be experiencing "excess demand" for at least a large proportion of its output. This suggests that price adjustments ought to be related to such systematic backlog movements. My primary concern will be with these short-term price adjustments to demand pressures. Why does excess demand in some industries result in an accumulation of unfilled orders and queuing of buyers instead of its being absorbed by price increases as in other industries?

Consideration of the problem requires an analysis of variable delivery periods. Following a general discussion of their role and a brief discussion of the data used, the major part of this chapter develops measures of the relations between price changes and changes in backlogs and delivery periods (the last are indirectly represented by the backlog-shipment ratios). The consistency of these measures with some of my theoretical arguments is examined. Also, the principal factors presumed to influence the relationships concerned are reviewed, and some additional evidence is presented.[1]

Economics of Variable Delivery Periods

Media and Models of Adjustments to Business Change

Rises and falls in demand, reflected in fluctuations in the volume of orders received at given prices, can be met by: (1) increases and de-

[1] This chapter utilizes, but also expands and elaborates upon, parts of my article, "Unfilled Orders, Price Changes, and Business Fluctuations," *Review of Economics and Statistics*, November 1962 (reprinted as Occasional Paper 84, New York, NBER, 1962).

creases in current output and/or price; (2) depletions and replenishments of the inventory of the product; and (3) accumulations and decumulations of the order backlog.

In the limiting case of instantaneous reactions (1), finished stock is always nil and so is the backlog. The smaller the flexibility of inputs (the steeper the rise in marginal costs), the more the shifts of demand are absorbed by price changes and the less by output changes. It is well known that the marginal calculus of cost and revenue assures, within this pure model relying on (1) only, a continuous or period-by-period maximization of profit; also, that the model excludes some of the basic ingredients of economic life—uncertainty, lags of adjustments, and cost of change as a function of size and frequency of change. In manufacturing, particularly, the importance of these elements is accentuated, since demand for many industrial products is highly volatile in the short run and subject to large and varying cyclical movements. Rapid and frequent fluctuations in production rates are undesirable, since they are a proximate cause of increased costs and reduced operational efficiency.[2] Thus, the interaction of demand and cost factors in an unstable and uncertain envirohment often favors the role of stocks and backlogs as adjustment instruments or shock absorbers.

The relative importance of these forms of adjustment depends in part on business conditions in the given industry. A model showing this strongly, and providing at the same time a sharp contrast to the pure model of price-output adjustments (1), would employ (2) and (3) in the following cyclical sequence. Assume that new orders move cyclically in such a way that their rate exceeds that of capacity production in the latter part of an expansion. Then, in the first part of the contraction in buying, the level of production is sustained by drawing upon the backlog of orders carried over from the expansion. As the backlog is exhausted and the contraction of new orders continues, production is supported by working up a surplus inventory of the product. During the first half of the subsequent buying expansion, that surplus finished stock is sold first (in addition to the current output); in the second half, a backlog of unfilled orders is again accumulated.

In making maximum use of (2) and (3), this cyclical model dispro-

---

[2] Changes in the output rate will be accompanied by changes in the size and/or the rate of utilization of the work force, which are expensive in various ways, for example, through terminal payments, training outlays, overtime premiums, idle time, and possible impairments of good labor relations, morale, or productivity.

portionately magnifies certain elements of reality. It implies that order backlogs originate only in a strong boom and disappear in a slump, and vice versa for finished stock. Although a tendency toward such behavior probably does exist for certain products, it is too weak to show up in the aggregates or even in the more narrowly defined series in our sample. The model also treats backlog and stock accumulations in a strictly parallel fashion, whereas in fact the two have some implications that are quite different. The risk that some of the unfilled orders may be canceled varies among industries and with business conditions but on the whole appears to be much less prevalent and much less effective or serious than risk associated with the accumulation of unsold finished stock. Needless to say, new orders do not behave in the neat symmetrical manner assumed in the model. Instead they are for the most part notoriously difficult to predict, and this uncertainty factor favors the use of (3) rather than (2). But, however important for cost considerations, production stabilization is presumably not itself the primary objective, as the pure model of (3) implies. It should thus be treated as a means subordinate to, not as a goal commensurate with, profit maximization.

Furthermore, the type of short-run response mechanism in use frequently depends upon certain structural industry or market characteristics. It is not only in the advanced stages of vigorous business expansions and in the early stages of contractions that backlogs of unfilled orders appear, since it is common practice for firms in many lines of manufacturing to produce in response to demand ("to order") rather than in anticipation of demand ("to stock"). Pure production to stock allows adjustments of current output, price, and stock, but obviously not of unfilled order backlogs. In pure production to order, price adjustments are available for a firm that can influence price. The rates of output reflect those of new orders, with lags; the greater the input flexibility, the closer the relationship. However, while the volume of output under contract is determined by past orders, the short-period rate of output is not, since it depends also on delivery dates, over which the producer often has considerable discretion. It is these delivery-period adjustments (and the closely associated backlog changes) that are potentially of great importance here, while the stock adjustments are, of course, not feasible.

Differentiation of Delivery Periods and Competition

Lead times allowed the supplier are a source of costs to the customer. As a rule, the longer and more variable the leads, the higher are these costs. In the absence of major imperfections in the market, therefore, a supplier whose deliveries lag behind those of other manufacturers of the same product would not be able to maintain his sales for long, assuming equality of other trade terms.

However, a buyer may agree to accept a longer delivery period in return for a price concession; and, correspondingly, a premium may be paid for a reduction in the delivery period. Except in the special model of a market in which prompt delivery is insisted upon as a standard of product quality, differences in the delivery periods are perfectly compatible with competitive equilibrium if they are compensated for by price differentials acceptable to the buyer and seller. Thus, given sufficient information, competition would tend to equalize not just the selling price but the price for the item with a given delivery period (as well as other terms of sale disregarded in this analysis); there would be no discrimination in terms of compensatory price and delivery period combinations.[3]

The above argument counters the notion that the very existence of unfilled order backlogs is proof of a noncompetitive industry structure.[4] Actually, order backlogs are no more necessarily a symptom of departures from competition than are product stocks. Empirical evidence supports this view. We have matched up a number of the average stock-backlog (Q/U) ratios with concentration data for the same industries. The available comparisons indicate that there is little difference in competitiveness between those that manufacture to order and

[3] It is true that differentiation by delivery period (like that by customer specification of the desired product characteristics, which is probably more important) would lead to a segmentation of markets; but the resulting markets need not be small, and they would often be closely connected. The expert knowledge of industrial purchasers reduces the possibility that sellers will promote *artificial* product differentiation in the markets for equipment and materials and is generally a force supporting competition.

[4] The following (from Murray Brown, "Ex Ante and Ex Post Data in Inventory Investment," *Journal of the American Statistical Association,* September 1961, p. 526) is a more radical statement of this position than others I have found but it is representative: "The unfilled order variable applies only to an oligopolistic or imperfectly competitive firm and cannot be interpreted as a proxy for future demand for a firm in perfect competition. To show this, assume an increase in demand facing an industry; if each firm chooses to add to its order books and not raise [its] price, the market price remains constant; this violates an assumption of perfect competition that no firm can influence price."

those that manufacture to stock.[5] However, these tests use indicators of average conditions over relatively extended periods of time. It is still important to consider the role of competition in the context of short-run *changes* in backlogs, delivery periods, and prices. This topic will be taken up later in this analysis.

Interaction of Changes in Delivery Period and Price

The preceding suggests that the quantity demanded of a product is likely to be a decreasing function of the length of the delivery period, given the price and other terms of sale. Also, the average cost of producing a certain output often depends positively on the delivery period; so producers may ask for price premiums in return for speedier delivery and allow price discounts on longer-term orders. Thus both the buyer and the seller have schedules of equivalent combinations of delivery period and price, the former for a given quantity demanded, the latter for a quantity supplied. In the market there is an equilibrium process of weighing and reconciling these preferences of buyers and sellers.

A theoretical analysis of some basic aspects of this situation is given in Appendix H. There, a simple criterion is defined for a choice by the firm of a unique profit-maximizing combination of price (p) and delivery period (k). The position is such that no alteration of p and k by the firm can increase profit because the associated changes in sales and costs would offset each other.[6]

[5] The concentration ratios are substantial or high for some of the goods made largely to order (e.g., steel barrels, sheet and strip, pig iron) and low for others (e.g., most types of machine tools). For products made primarily to stock, the ratios vary similarly from extremely high (e.g., electric bulbs) to low (e.g., hosiery, hardwood flooring). Low concentration here means that the four leading firms produce less than 40 per cent of the industry's shipments in dollars; high, that they produce more than 60 per cent; substantial, 40 to 60 per cent. (The observations are based on data given in *Concentration in American Industry*, Report of the Senate Subcommittee on Antitrust and Monopoly to the Committee on the Judiciary, 85th Cong., 1st sess., Washington, D.C., 1957.) The limitations of concentration ratios as measures of competitiveness are well known but so also is the fact that in general no better summary measures are available.

Examination of the data for major industries (where our criterion is the proportion of total value of shipments accounted for by component industries with high or low concentration ratios) leads to similar negative results. For example, the electrical machinery industry is much more concentrated than the nonelectrical, and the weight of production to order in it is almost certainly considerably lower (note the importance of standardized electrical appliances for household use). A similar situation is found in transportation equipment, where the automobile industry, which is working to stock, is far more concentrated than the rest of the group in which production to order predominates (aircraft, shipbuilding, railroad equipment).

[6] It is a "joint optimum" of p and k, graphically a point determined by two sets of indifference curves for each given quantity demanded and supplied. These sets consist of: (1) the pairs of k and p associated with each given volume of demand, according to the preferences of buyers; (2) the pairs of k and c (average costs) associated with each given volume of supply, as seen by the producer-seller. See Appendix H, Figure H-1, and related text.

Changes in demand or the cost function or both would shift the equilibrium combination and bring about changes in p and k.[7] Given sufficient substitutability and variability of p and k, one would expect an expansion (contraction) of demand to be associated with increases (decreases) in both p and k. If substitutability or variability are low, however, the main burden of adjustment would presumably be shifted to one of the two variables and away from the other. What happens in any particular case depends on the pertinent demand and cost elasticities with respect to p and k and on the "shifts" on the demand and supply side; hence, ultimately it depends upon the host of factors that determine these parameters. For example, if sales are regarded as much more sensitive to price increases than to delivery-period increases, this in itself would favor the latter over the former as a means of reacting to actual and expected increases in demand.

It will be shown later that changes in U/S and changes in P (price indexes) for several major manufacturing industries are positively correlated. These findings support the notion that p and k tend to move in the same direction cyclically. However, in some cases the brunt of adjustment is borne to a much larger extent by price changes, in others by delivery-period changes. Either mode of adjustment results in some degree of production stabilization in the face of cyclically fluctuating demand, but the behavior over time of prices and orders can differ sharply between the two situations.

Uncertainty and Related Considerations

The future time path of sales (orders received) is, of course, uncertain; even the probabilities of the various possible paths are unknown to the firm, let alone the actual outcome. Knowledge of the present — the properties of the relevant cost and demand functions — is also quite imperfect. To reduce the area of ignorance in these matters is costly, and the costs of obtaining the information must be weighed against the returns expected from it.[8]

The hazards of uncertainty and the requirements of information are very large indeed for a manufacturer who would rely only on pricing policy to meet cyclical demand fluctuations in the manner described

---

[7] See Appendix H, Figure H-2, and related text.

[8] The returns depend essentially on the quality of the information, and they are themselves uncertain. See George J. Stigler, "Economics of Information," *Journal of Political Economy*, June 1961, pp. 213–25.

in the first part of this chapter. He would have to undertake much more than the difficult task of projecting sales at the existing price structure, for his forecasts need to incorporate the response of his customers and competitors to the changes in that structure due to his own active price policy. These reactions may depend on changing business conditions and may involve substantial and variable lags. Furthermore, the "sunk" costs of publicizing a new price may be a significant deterrent to frequent price adjustments in a fluctuating market.

The policy of letting backlogs accumulate and decumulate cyclically requires no such heroic efforts. The seller adopts the relatively passive attitude of accepting the fluctuations of demand instead of trying to minimize them and the corresponding output variation by sharply cyclical pricing. He need only keep more or less in step with his competitors in the price and delivery terms quoted.[9] This behavior implies that the firm acquires unfilled orders on a large scale at the same time as the rest of the industry, i.e., when the demand for their output is strong and diffused so that firms throughout the industry are working at or near capacity. In this phase, the bargaining position of the seller tends to be strong, and extensions of delivery periods will be an industrywide phenomenon and generally acceptable to the buyers. Thus, while it is true that the sensitivity of sales to the relative delivery period (D_k; see Appendix H) is not necessarily easier to estimate than the sensitivity of sales to relative price (D_p), the firm has much less need to know D_k under the policy of backlog accumulation than to know D_p under the policy of relying on price adjustments.

Concentrated ordering associated with widespread delays in delivery is often seen as current "overbuying" and an indication of probable "underbuying" sometime in the future. But when such a slack comes, it again will be recognized as an industrywide phenomenon. It is precisely in those industries where demand is generally expected to fluctuate that producers would have good reason to appreciate the advantage of increased production stability offered by backlog accumulation. In fact, various expressions of business opinion leave little doubt that manufacturers in many cyclically sensitive durable goods industries regard large order backlogs as highly desirable.[10]

---

[9] It seems probable that the delivery period or "lead time" is often less formally or strictly established than the price.

[10] This discussion of the costs and benefits of backlog accumulation points out the inadequacy of the view of cost adopted in Appendix H (equation 5), which can serve only as a simple first approxi-

The fact that it is durable goods that are mainly produced to order provides some support for the hypothesis that backlog adjustments are most important in industries in which demand is more unstable. Moreover, as shown in Chapter 3, industries with greater variability of cyclical and irregular movements in demand (larger averages of monthly percentage changes in cycle-trend components of new orders, $\overline{CyI_n}$) achieved a higher degree of stabilization of shipments vs. new orders (higher ratios of $\overline{CyI_n}/\overline{CyI_s}$, $\overline{Cy_n}/\overline{Cy_s}$, $\overline{Se_n}/\overline{Se_s}$, and $\overline{I_n}/\overline{I_s}$) than did the industries with smaller variability. The correlations among the ranks of the industries according to $\overline{CyI_n}$, and their ranks according to the ratios $\overline{CyI_n}/\overline{CyI_s}$, etc., are all significantly positive.

Competitive and Noncompetitive Behavior

The model of a perfectly competitive market has been interpreted in dynamic terms to mean that excess demand is corrected instantaneously by price adjustments, so that equilibrium is, in effect, continuous. Strictly speaking, this implies simultaneity of demand and supply or a zero delivery period. Price adjustments still retain their exclusive role as the equilibrating medium if the model is slightly relaxed, in which case the delivery period (k) is assumed to be positive but is treated as a constant. But it is not satisfactory to postulate this point; rather, the possibility of variable k's must be recognized. Variations over time in the average k for a given industry are compatible with a stable structure of the k-p relations, which may be enforced by competition (i.e., with stability of the contour maps in Appendix H, Figure H-1, for the different firms in the industry). If buyers are willing to wait for delivery but not willing to pay higher prices (i.e., if demand is elastic with respect to p, inelastic with respect to k), then backlogs are likely to appear or increase as demand rises. In the opposite case, price rather than backlog reactions would be dominant.

There is no necessary presumption, therefore, that the competitive

mation. The reduction of current costs due to a marginal extension of the delivery period (C_k) will presumably become larger with the transition to higher-capacity utilization levels—with increasingly less flexible inputs. But when the firm begins to accept orders for future delivery *beyond its capacity output*, it lengthens the average delivery period on its aggregate unfilled orders. Its average production costs *of the current period* (C) need not be affected thereby. But the change in the time profile of the stream of output and shipments, which is involved in this expansion of the backlog, certainly does have the effect of reducing the firm's operating costs over a longer stretch of time, as brought out in the text. A promising approach to a generalization of the cost function, which is pertinent here, has been offered in Armen Alchian, "Costs and Outputs," in Moses Abramovitz et al., *The Allocation of Economic Resources*, Stanford, 1959, pp. 23–40.

nature of the market will prevent sizable increases of delivery periods and backlogs in an industrywide boom. Such increases may and apparently do occur in industries in which the degree of competition is high, but there they are essentially market-determined, that is, they are due to short-run excess demand rather than to any policies of the individual seller (paralleling, in this respect, the cyclical increases in price levels).

Lags of price adjustments due, for example, to contractual arrangements must also be considered. And if the demand curve rose steadily, rather than by separate shifts, more persistent lags would be likely because price, though increasing, would then lag behind the rising equilibrium or clear-the-market level and would thus continue below it.[11]

In an industry in which prices are set by firms with considerable "monopoly power," the process of large-scale backlog expansion, besides feeding on a sustained pressure of demand on capacity, may also be aided by deliberate policies of "conservative" pricing. Sellers may see a conflict between higher pricing and large backlog accumulation, and may believe that the best strategy is to proceed cautiously on the former so as not to jeopardize the latter. Such price policy is not justified by the immediate situation during a boom; hence the hypothesis presumably applies only to firms that look well ahead. But in some markets the effects of a firm's current action often extend far into the future.[12] Awareness of this leads firms to longer-term policies, and these may well counsel restraint in pricing. This applies particularly to noncollusive oligopoly where aggressive price policy, which must include undercutting in the slack period, is risky, because of the uncertain reactions of the rivals, and will often be inhibited by fear of retaliation or of costly warfare. Letting the delivery periods vary may appear far less hazardous.

If competition in factor markets is also restricted, the interrelation of product and factor markets may provide an additional deterrent to a policy that would rely principally on price adjustments. Higher-wage demands by labor unions may be prompted by price increases and may be hard to resist. If wage increases are viewed as virtually irreversible, then raising the price now and lowering it in an ensuing slump would

[11] See, e.g., Kenneth J. Arrow and William M. Capron, "Dynamic Shortages and Price Rises: The Engineer-Scientist Case," *Quarterly Journal of Economics*, May 1959, pp. 299–301.

[12] In contrast effects would be limited to the present under conditions of perfect competition. See George J. Stigler, *The Theory of Price*, New York, 1952, pp. 168–69.

seem an imprudent course to follow. On the other hand, delivery periods are subject to changes that are definitely reversible—no more than the cessation of the boom is needed to reduce them again to a more nearly "normal" length.

The Effects of Changes in Buying Policies

An increase in unfilled orders may be due primarily to earlier ordering by customers rather than to the postponement of deliveries by suppliers. It may be contended that the resulting extension of the delivery periods does not increase costs to the customers since it reflects their voluntary behavior. This is a valid argument, but one must ask next to what extent the earlier ordering really represents a "voluntary" action. The ordering of materials well in advance of the time they will be needed is often prompted by the buyers' expectations of price increases or shortages. It is likely to mean that customers, in anticipation of tight supplies, are anxious to protect themselves by early, and perhaps duplicative, ordering. It is then an expression of their concern about possible delivery delays, not of their indifference to such delays. The extreme form of this behavior is a scramble for materials in times of a (current or impending) boom.

However, if efforts to cover requirements for longer periods ahead coincide in time for many buyers, the result must inevitably be an increase of orders in suppliers' books and delivery lags. Buyers will have to accept the fact that supplies have indeed tightened generally — what they feared came to pass through the working of another mechanism of collectively self-justifying expectations. If sufficiently strong, the demand pressures will have generated major price increases along with the lead-time extensions.

This period of long-range buying is likely to be followed by a phase of short-range ("hand-to-mouth") buying. Together, these phases add up to much instability over time on the demand side. But even here, where materials rather than finished goods are most important, backlog accumulation will have some stabilizing effect on output, assuming that to work off the temporary backlog of advance orders takes some time during which higher levels of production can be supported.

In contraction, a customer whose own business is doing poorly may actually have little interest in getting his orders executed promptly. He may wish to cancel some orders placed when the business outlook was better or, if this is too costly, to postpone the execution of these orders by his suppliers. To the extent the latter is done, the buyer may benefit from the deferred costs of acquiring the ordered goods and/or from the deferred or reduced costs of storing them. But this would, by the same token, impose costs on the producer-seller.

One would expect such postponements to increase the delivery periods over what they otherwise would be. The aggregative backlog-shipment ratios, U/S, which might be used as rough measures of the average delivery periods, will increase because the postponements reduce S relative to U. The effect here is one of slowing down the liquidation of a given stock of unfilled orders, of spreading the backlog U, as it were, over a longer period of time.

Some developments of this kind are likely to occur when business conditions deteriorate, and they probably help to explain why shipments decrease at a time when unfilled orders are still high. The U/S ratios kept declining through the 1948–49 and 1953–54 business contractions, but they were fairly stable for most of the durable goods industries during the 1957–58 recession and even increased a little in the recession of 1960–61 (see Charts 6-4 and 6-5). Still, judging from our data, the scope of the postponements appears rather limited.

Information on unfilled orders classified according to their time of receipt and time of scheduled shipment would help to disclose how delivery periods vary during the business cycle, reflecting buyers' policies as well as changing conditions of supply. In the absence of such data, the issues raised in this section must remain largely unresolved, at least in their quantitative aspects. However, an important qualitative inference can be drawn from the preceding discussion: The notion that longer delivery periods are burdensome to buyers and welcome to sellers does not apply in all situations. In particular, when a sudden slump occurs in the demand for their own output, buyers may actually wish to delay delivery of the orders they have placed before the disappointing development occurred, and this is certainly not a favorable development for the sellers.

The Data and Their Limitations

The Industrial Price Series

The principal body of U.S. statistics on prices in the primary (i.e., nonretail) markets is the Wholesale Price Index of the Bureau of Labor Statistics. The BLS collects prices as quoted by the sellers. Preannounced sellers' prices (list prices) are often kept unchanged for considerable periods of time, while actual transaction prices are varied by means of special discounts, sales rebates, or other concessions to the buyers.[13] List prices are therefore biased toward inflexibility and are known to understate seriously the short-term price changes. Although the BLS asks the reporting companies for actual prices received, allowing for discounts and other departures from the sellers' quotations, recent studies cast considerable doubt upon the validity of WPI data for measuring short-term fluctuations in prices. There are various reasons for, and methods of, concealing the actual transaction prices, and many sellers apparently report prices which differ little from, or tend toward, the list quotations.[14] Therefore the short-term price reactions are probably often significantly understated, although the magnitude of this bias is difficult to ascertain.

Gaps caused by the difficulty of pricing individual custom-made goods are another shortcoming of the WPI data (as already noted in Chapter 3). This has adverse effects for those industries in which the made-to-order goods not priced by the BLS are important.[15]

Finally, the need to match the price and backlog series imposes various problems and limitations on the statistical work for this chapter. In addition to individual difficulties in matching the data, there is the aggregation problem, which may be particularly troublesome in a study of price behavior. Comprehensive group price indexes had to be used, however, to produce agreement in coverage with the available aggregates of unfilled orders.[16]

Backlog Changes and Price Changes: Graphical Comparisons

Monthly changes in the price indexes for several major manufacturing industries or industry groups are shown in Chart 7-1. Along with

[13] While list prices usually represent the upper bound of the transaction prices, "extras" over the quoted price may also be imposed upon special-quality or small-quantity purchases.

[14] See Harry E. McAllister, "Statistical Factors Affecting the Stability of the Wholesale and Consumers' Price Indexes," and John Flueck, "A Study in Validity: BLS Wholesale Price Quotations," in *The Price Statistics of the Federal Government,* Report of Price Statistics Review Committee, New York, NBER, 1961, pp. 373–412 and 419–31.

[15] See Appendix C for some detail on the problems involved and on sources of price data, other than BLS, used in construction of the major-industry price indexes used in this study. It should be added that the industries here concerned (in particular transportation equipment) are also those in which military orders play a large role. It would be highly desirable to have a breakdown between military and civilian orders for these industries, but the available information is very fragmentary.

[16] The regression analysis in the next part of this chapter was completed at an early stage of this study and included only the major-industry series on unfilled orders which were then available (these are the OBE data prior to the 1963 revision). Some replications using recent Census data will also be presented below.

Chart 7-1
Monthly Changes in Deflated Unfilled Orders (Backlogs) and in Price Indexes, Nine Major Manufacturing Industries, 1948–58

(change in backlogs: millions of dollars in average 1947–49 prices; change in prices: index, 1947–49 = 100)

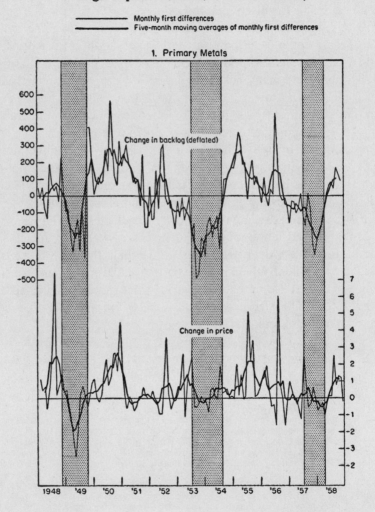

Chart 7-1 (continued)

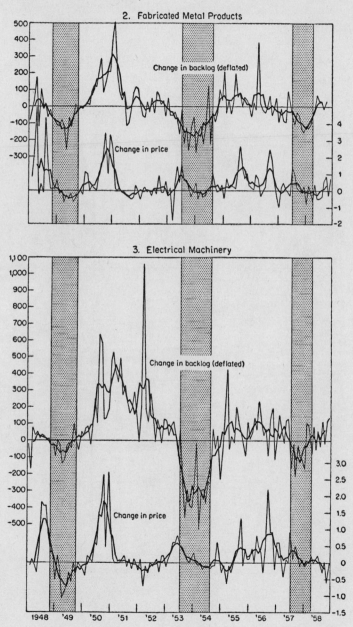

2. Fabricated Metal Products

Change in backlog (deflated)

Change in price

3. Electrical Machinery

Change in backlog (deflated)

Change in price

1948   '49   '50   '51   '52   '53   '54   '55   '56   '57   '58

Chart 7-1 (continued)

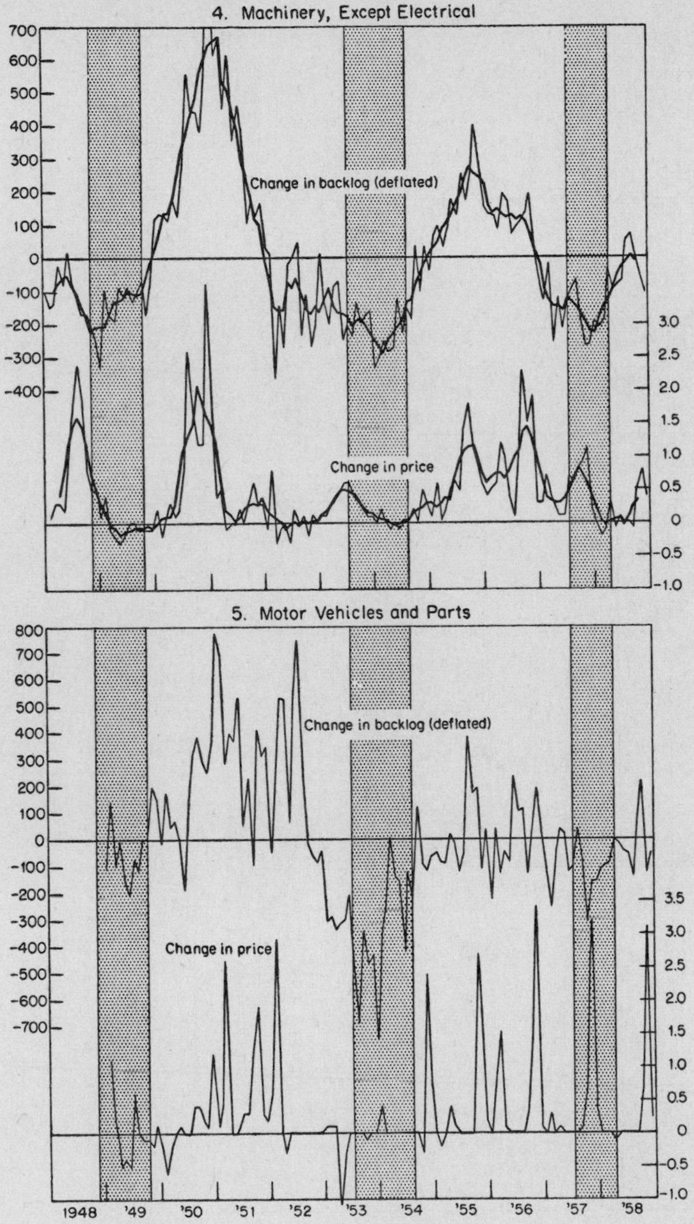
4. Machinery, Except Electrical
700
600
500
400
300
200
100
0
-100
-200
-300
-400
Change in backlog (deflated)
Change in price
3.0
2.5
2.0
1.5
1.0
0.5
0
-0.5
-1.0
5. Motor Vehicles and Parts
800
700
600
500
400
300
200
100
0
-100
-200
-300
-400
-500
-600
-700
Change in backlog (deflated)
Change in price
3.5
3.0
2.5
2.0
1.5
1.0
0.5
0
-0.5
-1.0
1948
'49
'50
'51
'52
'53
'54
'55
'56
'57
'58

Chart 7-1 (continued)

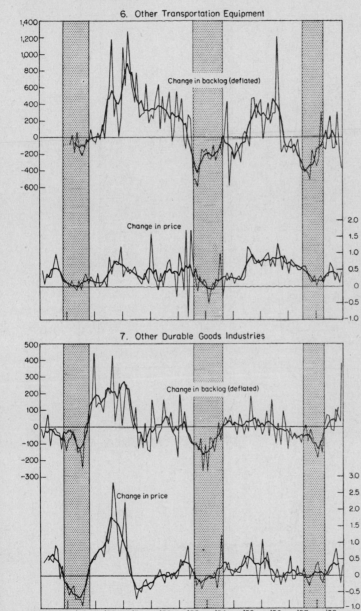

6. Other Transportation Equipment

Change in backlog (deflated)

Change in price

7. Other Durable Goods Industries

Change in backlog (deflated)

Change in price

Chart 7-1 (concluded)

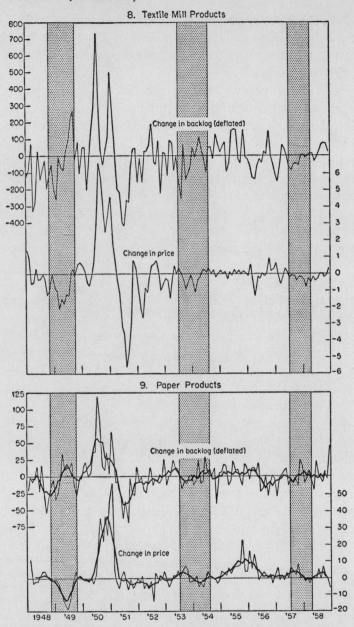

8. Textile Mill Products

Change in backlog (deflated)

Change in price

9. Paper Products

Change in backlog (deflated)

Change in price

1948 '49 '50 '51 '52 '53 '54 '55 '56 '57 '58

Note: Shaded areas represent business cycle contractions; unshaded areas, expansions.

Source: U.S. Department of Commerce, Office of Business Economics, and U.S. Department of Labor, Bureau of Labor Statistics.

these data, the chart shows the corresponding series of monthly first differences in deflated unfilled orders. The regression analysis in the next part of this chapter is based on these series of short-period price and backlog changes.

The deflation procedure, analogous to that applied to the series of new orders and shipments (see Chapter 3 and Appendix C), had little effect on the short-term movements of the series concerned because the month-to-month changes in measured prices are very small relative to those in backlogs. It must be recognized that deflation procedures are usually crude and risky. Their application to stock magnitudes such as unfilled orders or inventories is particularly difficult, since the prices used for items included in such aggregates were obtained at various points of time.[17]

It is evident from the graphs that the series of monthly changes in prices and unfilled orders of the major manufacturing industries are highly erratic; to be sure, this is often the case for economic indicators cast in short-unit periods and in a first-difference form. In the backlog series, however, the cyclical movements are pronounced, while in the price series they are much weaker and often obscured by short irregular variations. Among the backlog changes, negative as well as positive values are common, whereas the price changes are overwhelmingly positive, reflecting the dominance of upward trends in the postwar records of industrial price indexes proper.

The first-difference series of Chart 7-1 probably contain relatively large errors of observation. This is so because short-term changes in price and backlog (ΔP and ΔU) are typically small in comparison with the corresponding "totals," i.e., the prices and backlogs proper (P and U); thus, even errors that are small relative to P and U are likely to be large relative to ΔP and ΔU.[18] If only because of the influence of large random errors, then, one would not expect the monthly ΔP and ΔU series to show high correlations. There is indication in the graphs,

---

[17] This problem cannot be solved in any satisfactory manner with the limited information on hand. Our backlog-change estimates in constant dollars were derived simply by taking monthly differences between deflated values of new orders and deflated shipments.

[18] For example, assume (rather optimistically) that the accuracy of a price index is within ±0.1 of one index point. Let the lowest observed standing of the index be 80 and the highest, 140 points. Then the error in the price proper varies between 0.07 and 0.125 per cent. But the average monthly first difference may well be slightly less or slightly more than one index point. Even if it were as large as two points, errors of observation would equal up to 10 per cent of $\Delta P(2.0 \pm 0.2)$. Actually, it is more likely that the errors are more disturbing still, perhaps accounting for 20–25 per cent of the total variance in ΔP.

however, that significant positive correlations do exist between the longer and more systematic — predominantly cyclical — movements in these series for a number of industries. (Note the moving averages superimposed on the monthly series in Chart 7-1).

The ΔU series typically expand in the early stages of business expansions, and contract in the later stages. This is also true of the ΔP series, though with less regularity. The ΔP series often do not descend below zero even in recession. The downward inflexibility of industrial prices was particularly marked in the business contraction of 1953–54, somewhat less so in that of 1957–58. In the 1947–48 recession, on the other hand, the ΔP series did fall below zero in most cases.

Marked interindustry differences in the behavior of the paired series shown in Chart 7-1 must also be noted. In some cases, the data do not appear sufficiently meaningful to warrant their use in further tests.[19]

Some Tests, Estimates, and Interpretations

Price Change vs. Backlog Change, by Broad Industry Groups

The first hypothesis to be tested is that the greater the importance of production to order and the longer the delivery lags, the greater will be the role of backlog reactions relative to that of price reactions. This is borne out strongly by the available evidence for major manufacturing industries.

In Table 7-1, column 7 lists the regression coefficients b computed by least squares from the equation

$$(\Delta P)_t = a + b(\Delta U)_{t-j} + u_t, \tag{1}$$

where ΔP is the change in the price index for the output of the corresponding industry and ΔU is the change in the backlog of the industry's unfilled orders (in millions of dollars, deflated). Quarterly data

---

[19] Consider the motor vehicle industry, where the price index proper, based on rigid quotations, assumes the form of a step curve. In terms of ΔP, this means zero values and sharp up-and-down movements to and from the zero level, as shown in the chart (the seasonal element is evident in the timing of these shifts in recent years). It may well be questioned to what extent this picture is representative of the behavior of actual transaction prices. Moreover, there are also problems with the unfilled orders data for this industry. It would clearly be futile to relate reported ΔP to ΔU in this case.

In no other instance does ΔP behave in a similarly extreme fashion. However, the series for the leather and printing and publishing industries were also excluded because of their particularly erratic behavior and questionable quality.

are used, and ΔU is taken either with simultaneous timing or with a lead of one quarter relative to ΔP, whichever gives a higher correlation. The regression coefficients are all significantly positive, and their ranks (column 8) show a very high inverse correlation with the ranks of the average U/S ratios ($-.976$). These rankings appear to make good sense in terms of the relevant differential characteristics of the industries included.[20]

Table 7-1, column 9, shows the ratios of the standard deviations of ΔP and ΔU. These ratios represent another measure of the relative role of price and backlog adjustments in that they compare the average size of variations in ΔP and ΔU for different industries. Again, correlation between the ranks of the average U/S values and of the standard deviations is high and inverse ($-.881$).

There is some danger of spurious correlation in these tests. Larger absolute U/S ratios may be associated with larger absolute values of U, and thus also with ΔU that are larger absolutely and relative to ΔP. However, while U and S depend on industry size, U/S and P do not. Column 11 lists the regression coefficients b' computed by least squares from the equation

$$(\Delta P)_t = a' + b'\Delta(U/S)_{t-j} + u'_t. \tag{2}$$

The correlation between the ranks of the average U/S values and the ranks of the b' coefficients is also negative and high.

Column 13 gives the ratios of the standard deviations of ΔP and $\Delta(U/S)$. The ranks of these ratios show a perfect negative correlation with the ranks of the average U/S values.

Further tests based on the average leads of new orders in relation to shipments (column 2) are free from all possibility of spurious correlation. The correlations between the ranks of these leads and the ranks of the regression coefficients and standard deviation ratios are all negative and substantial (last line of table).

The ranks of the average U/S ratios and of the regression and dispersion measures used in Table 7-1 would not be very sensitive to data

---

[20] For example, the paper industry not only has small backlogs but its finished inventory is even smaller (Table 2-1). Hence current price and output adjustments are, as expected, very important here. The weight of manufacture to stock is probably larger in textiles, other durables, and electrical machinery than in the other industries, but this could not be inferred from our gross measures, perhaps because the role of backlog adjustments is much greater than that of product stock adjustments in all these industries.

Table
Average Backlog-Shipment Ratios, Average Leads of New Orders,
Measures, Eight Major

Industry	Average Monthly U/S Ratio[a] (1)	Average Lead of New Orders at Turns in Shipments		Standard Deviation[d] of		
		Months[b] (2)	Rank[c] (3)	Price Change (index points) (4)	Backlog Change (mill. dol.) (5)	Change in U/S Ratio (6)
Paper and allied products	0.65	1.7(6)	2	2.46	51.35	.069
Textile-mill products	1.63	3.3(6)	3	3.52	362.39	.358
Other durable goods[i]	1.92	0.9(8)	1	1.46	324.55	.145
Primary metals	2.99	3.5(8)	4.5	3.29	498.66	.364
Fabricated metal products	3.55	3.9(7)	6	2.10	308.11	.356
Nonelectrical machinery	4.20	4.0(6)	7	1.64	677.53	.428
Electrical machinery	6.04	3.5(6)	4.5	1.53	529.67	.550
Nonautomotive transportation equipment[j]	16.85	11.5(4)	8	0.87	951.59	.982
Rank correlations (Spearman coefficients):						
With average U/S ratios (col. 1)						
With average lead of orders (col. 3)[k]						

Source: Unfilled and new orders and shipments: Based on data from the U.S. Department of Commerce, Office of Business Economics; Prices (i.e., components of the WPI index, 1947–49 average = 100): U.S. Department of Labor, Bureau of Labor Statistics. The OBE data are of the pre-1963 vintage.

[a] Listed from the lowest to the highest. Covers 1948–58 (132 observations), except for nonautomotive transportation equipment for which data cover 1949–58 (120 observations).

[b] Covers 1948–58. The figure in parentheses gives the number of observations for each industry. See also text and footnote 21.

[c] Ranked from the shortest to the longest.

[d] Based on quarterly data.

[e] Coefficient b from the regression $\Delta P_t = a + b(\Delta U)_{t-j} + u_t$. Quarterly series (converted from monthly) used throughout. Leads of one quarter ($j = 3$) used for paper, nonautomotive transportation equipment, and fabricated metal products; simultaneous relationships ($j = 0$) used for the remaining industries. These timing relations maximize simple correlations between ΔP and ΔU in quarterly terms.

7-1

Regressions of Price Change on Backlog Change, and Related Manufacturing Industries, 1948–58

Av. Change^d in ΔP Per Mill. Dollars of Change in ΔU		Ratio of Standard Deviations^d of ΔP and ΔU		Av. Change^d in ΔP Per Unit Change in $\Delta(U/S)$		Ratio of Standard Deviations^d of ΔP and $\Delta(U/S)$	
Index Points[e] (7)	Rank[c] (8)	Per Cent[f] (9)	Rank[c] (10)	Index Points[g] (11)	Rank[c] (12)	Ratio[h] (13)	Rank[c] (14)
.03190	8	4.790	8	23.85	8	36.72	8
.00664	7	.972	7	6.39	7	11.57	7
.00308	6	.450	4	4.30	6	10.25	6
.00277	4	.661	5	1.12	3	8.39	5
.00305	5	.682	6	1.40	4	5.79	4
.00110	3	.243	2	1.67	5	3.57	3
.00049	2	.287	3	0.41	2	2.56	2
.00037	1	.092	1	0.25	1	0.90	1
−.976		−.881		−.905		−1.000	
−.786		−.643		−.697		−0.816	

[f] Equals the ratio of $\sigma(\Delta P)$ in column 4 to $\sigma(\Delta U)$ in column 5 multiplied by 100. Also equals the ratio of the regression coefficient b in column 7 to the corresponding correlation coefficient r in column 5 of Table 7-2, multiplied by 100.

[g] Coefficient b' from the regression $\Delta P_t = a' + b'\Delta(U/S)_{t-j} + u'_t$. Leads of one quarter ($j = 3$) used for paper and fabricated metal products; simultaneous relationships ($j = 0$) assumed for the remaining industries. These timing relations maximize simple correlations between ΔP and $\Delta(U/S)$ in quarterly terms.

[h] Equals the ratio of ΔP to $\Delta(U/S)$ for the periods covered by the appropriate data. (These ratios differ slightly from those obtained by dividing column 4 by column 6 because of differences in time coverage between the figures in these columns.) Also equals the ratio of the regression coefficients b' in column 11 to the corresponding correlation coefficients r in column 1 of Table 7-5, multiplied by 100.

[i] Includes professional and scientific instruments; lumber; furniture; stone, clay, and glass; and miscellaneous industries.

[j] Backlog data are not available before 1949.

[k] The coefficients in this line are all adjusted for the tie in the ranks of the average order leads of primary metals and electrical machinery (column 3).

sions and errors of observation, but the timing measures and their
tive size could be strongly affected. The tabulated results are based
on the analysis of the old OBE data. In an effort to see whether they
are validated by the new Census series, average leads of N relative to
S, estimated from the revised (1963) data, were substituted for the
averages shown in column 2 of the table. The ranks of these new timing
measures (for the same period, 1948–58) are found to be in each case
negatively correlated with the ranks of the regression coefficients and
standard deviation ratios, though these correlations are lower than their
counterparts in Table 7-1 (last line).[21]

Further Implications

The analysis in the first part of this chapter implies that, given the
amplitude of fluctuation in demand, the more the average delivery period fluctuates the less does the average price, and vice versa. This
proposition is difficult to test with the available data, but Table 7-1
provides some evidence that seems at least consistent with it. Thus, in
addition to the negative correlations listed in the last two lines of the
table, there are also negative rank correlations between the standard
deviations of ΔP and ΔU and between those of ΔP and $\Delta(U/S)$. The
Spearman coefficients here are $-.452$ and $-.405$, respectively.

These comparisons, however, make no explicit allowance for interindustry differences in the amplitudes of demand fluctuations. As
argued before, greater variability of demand may signify greater uncertainty, which is likely to be associated with more backlog variation
and less price variation. In fact, the standard deviations of both the
deflated new orders and the first differences in new orders are found to
be negatively correlated with $\sigma(\Delta P)$ and positively correlated with
$\sigma(\Delta U)$ and $\sigma\Delta(U/S)$.[22] The rank correlations (Spearman coefficients)
for the eight industries included in Table 7-1 are shown below.

	$\sigma(\Delta P)$	$\sigma(\Delta U)$	$\sigma\Delta(U/S)$
$\sigma(N)$	$-.667$	$+.857$	$+.667$
$\sigma(\Delta N)$	$-.381$	$+.500$	$+.381$

[21] The new average lead figures, which are based on the observations listed in Tables 4-6 and 4-8,
are, in months: paper, 1.5; textiles, 3.5; other durable goods, 1.0; primary metals, 4.1; fabricated
metal products, 5.1; nonelectrical machinery, 3.7; electrical machinery, 1.8; and nonautomotive
transportation equipment, 11.5. The correlation between the ranks listed in Table 7-1, column 3,
and the ranks based on the above figures is .874. When the new data are used, the following rank
correlations corresponding to those shown in the last line of Table 7-1 are obtained: with b (column
8), $-.571$; with $\sigma(\Delta P)/\sigma(\Delta U)$ (column 10), $-.357$; with b' (column 12), $-.643$; and with $\sigma(\Delta P)/$
$\sigma[\Delta(U/S)]$ (column 14), $-.595$.

[22] Deflated new orders can be regarded as an index of demand—of the indifference curves in Ap-

Among the implications of the analysis is that, within a given industry, delivery periods and prices should be negatively correlated at any one time. The cross-sectional tests needed to confirm this cannot be made because data for firms grouped by homogeneity of product are lacking.[23]

A Regression Analysis of Lagged Price Adjustments

It is plausible to assume that prices react mainly to the more systematic and persistent variations in the demand-delivery conditions. Pursuing this notion, we have applied to the data two types of *distributed-lag* relation. The simpler of these is a regression of ΔP for the current quarter on ΔU's for the current and previous quarters. The resulting multiple correlation coefficients are substantially higher in some cases than the maximum simple correlations of quarterly data (Table 7-2, columns 5 and 6).[24]

For the second distributed-lag approach, equations of the Koyck form

$$(\Delta P)_t = a_1(\Delta U)_{t-j} + b_1(\Delta P)_{t-1} + c_1 + u_t \tag{3}$$

were fitted to the monthly data. The timing $(t - j)$ here is the lead that maximizes the simple correlation between monthly ΔP and $\Delta U (j \geqslant 0)$. The results are presented in Table 7-2, columns 2-4. The regression coefficients a_1 and b_1 all have the anticipated positive sign. All but one of them are highly significant, in the sense of being different from zero at least at the .01 level.[25]

Although significant, the a_1 coefficients are very small throughout, being measured in thousandths of a price-index point per \$1 million

pendix H, Figure H-2. Our theoretical argument suggests that variations in this index are met partly by price and delivery-period adjustments. Thus, the indicated association is between P and U/S on the one hand and N on the other, or between the changes in each of these variables. Actually we find that ΔP and $\Delta(U/S)$, as well as ΔU, are positively associated with both ΔN and N.

[23] In the absence of such information, it may be noted that descriptions of trade practices offer examples of price discounts granted the advance buyer (see, e.g., Temporary National Economic Committee, *Geographical Differentials in Prices of Building Materials*, 76th Cong., 2nd sess., Washington, D.C., 1940, pp. 66 and 288).

[24] In turn, the simple correlations with quarterly series are for the most part appreciably higher than those with monthly series (see Table 7-2, columns 1 and 5). This may be due to a reduction in the influence of measurement errors and to the smoothing obtained by conversion to quarterly data.

[25] The exception is the b_1 for nonautomotive transportation equipment. Presumably the distributed-lag scheme does not apply in this case. The R coefficient also is very low for this industry, considerably less than even the simple r obtained for the quarterly series (Table 7-2, columns 2 and 5). In two other industries, fabricated metal products and paper, similar, though weaker, inferences are indicated. For the remaining four industries, the Koyck-type distributed-lag approach does result in correlations that exceed significantly the R's computed by relating ΔP_t to ΔU_t and ΔU_{t-1} in quarterly terms (Table 7-2, columns 2 and 6).

Table 7-2
Relations Between Price Changes and Backlog Changes, with Simple and Distributed Lags, Seven Major Industries, 1948–58

Industry [a]	r: Simple Lag [b] (monthly) (1)	Distributed Lags [c] (monthly) R (2)	Regression Coefficient of ΔU_{t-j} (3)	Regression Coefficient of ΔP_{t-1} (4)	r: Simple Lag [d] (quarterly) (5)	R: Lags of 1 and 2 Quarters [e] (6)
Paper and allied products	.549(5)	.747(5)	.0119 (.0029)	.5723 (.0695)	.666(3)	.824
Textile-mill products	.656(1)	.872(0)	.0032 (.0004)	.7075 (.0427)	.683(0)	.786
Other durable goods [f]	.558(0)	.742(0)	.0012 (.0002)	.5577 (.0595)	.685(0)	.696
Fabricated metal products	.311(0)	.458(0)	.0018 (.0006)	.3475 (.0795)	.447(3)	.478
Nonelectrical machinery	n.a.	.681(0)	.0005 (.0002)	.5994 (.0628)	.453(0)	.455
Primary metals	.432(1)	.480(1)	.0028 (.0006)	.2152 (.0782)	.419(0)	.449
Nonautomotive transportation equipment [g]	n.a.	.245(0)	.0003 (.0001)	.0446 [h] (.0898)	.404(3)	.437

n.a. = not available.

Source: Same as Table 7-1.

[a] Ranked by the multiple correlation coefficients in column 6, from highest to lowest. Electrical machinery, one of the industries covered in Table 7-1, is omitted here. It shows correlations between ΔP and ΔU that are much lower than those for the other industries (e.g., a simple correlation in quarterly terms of .171).

[b] The lags of ΔP relative to ΔU (in months) are given in parentheses. These timing relations maximize simple correlations between ΔP and ΔU in monthly terms.

[c] Based on regressions of ΔP_t on ΔU_{t-j} and ΔP_{t-1} (see text). Parenthetical figures in column 2 indicate the lags of ΔP relative to ΔU (the j's): those in column 3 indicate calculated standard errors.

[d] The lags of ΔP relative to ΔU, converted from quarters to months, are given in parentheses (0 = simultaneous timing; 3 = one-quarter lag). These correlation coefficients correspond to the regression coefficients in Table 7-1, column 7.

[e] Based on regressions of ΔP_t on ΔU_t and ΔU_{t-3}. The number of observations (number of quarterly intervals covered by all three series) is 43 for each industry, except textiles (42) and nonautomotive transportation equipment (38). The same number of observations applies to the corresponding simple correlations in column 5.

[f] Includes professional and scientific instruments; lumber; furniture; stone, clay, and glass; and miscellaneous industries.

[g] Measures refer to 1949–58 because backlog data are not available before 1949.

[h] Not significant.

change in the constant-dollar value of ΔU_{t-j}. The b_1 coefficients are of the order of tenths of an index point per index point. If accepted at their face value,[26] these results suggest that the price reactions measured here are small and rapid; their speed is inversely related to the value of b_1. Indeed, the sums of the implicit lag coefficients, $\Sigma = a_1/ (1 - b_1)$, which may be taken to reflect the cumulative effect upon ΔP_t of all past changes in ΔU, are not more than 1.3 to 2.3 times the value of the corresponding a_1 coefficients in Table 7-2, which measure the impact of the single initial change in ΔU_{t-j} (except for textiles, where the ratio is about 5). This indicates that the processes involved are relatively short for most of the industries. The "half-life" estimates of the number of months (n) needed to account for 50 per cent of Σ range from 0.5 for primary metals to 2.0 for textiles; the figures for 70 per cent absorption range from 0.8 to 3.5 months; those for 90 per cent absorption, from 1.5 to 6.7 months.[27]

Our measures suggest that the price reactions are particularly weak in those durable goods industries in which backlogs are typically large and widely fluctuating (metalworking, machinery, and nonautomotive transportation equipment). For textiles, paper, and the other durables group, where average levels of and changes in backlogs are much smaller, the prevalence of stronger price adjustments is indicated.

A Comovement Analysis

Inspection of the graphs in Chart 7-1 suggests that it might be of interest to separate the *direction* from the *magnitude* of change in studying the relations between ΔU and ΔP. The correlation analysis takes both elements into account, but it may deny the existence of a significant relation between two series which move consistently in the same direction, because of large changes in the relative size of such "comovements." The analysis may also testify to a strong positive relation between series that often move in opposite directions if such countermovements are sufficiently small relative to the fewer but larger comovements. Nonparametric tests of the degree of agreement

---

[26] The pitfalls of least-squares estimation of models in which lagged values of the dependent variable occur as independent variables have been noted before in Chapter 5.

[27] These measures are computed from the formulas $q = 1 - b_1^n$ and $n = \log (1 - q)/\log b_1$, where q is set to equal 0.5, 0.7, and 0.9, alternately. They are analogous to the estimates presented in Chapter 5 for the N-S relations (see Tables 5-4 and 5-5 and the accompanying text).

in the direction of movements are available.[28] The results of applying such tests to quarterly backlog and price changes are summarized in Table 7-3.

For example, for textiles, ΔU increased twenty-one times in a total of forty-three comparisons, and ΔP increased eighteen times in the same number of comparisons. If the two variables were independent, the expected number of instances in which both ΔU and ΔP were rising would be $(21/43)(18/43)43 = 8.8$, and the expected number of instances in which both were falling would be $(22/43)(25/43)43 = 12.8$. Hence the expected total of all comovements would be $8.8 + 12.8 = 21.6$. But actually the number of all observed comovements of the two textile series was substantially larger, namely, 28. A comparison of the observed and the expected comovements shows that, for each of the seven industries covered, the number of observed comovements exceeded the figure that would be expected on the assumption of independence.

A further step can be taken by computation of the statistic K (Table 7-3, last line, and defined in note d). This is simply an application of the chi-square procedure to the 2 by 2 table describing the joint distribution of n pairs of signs of ΔU and ΔP. For one degree of freedom, the values of chi are normally distributed. Under the null hypothesis of independence between the sign series, then, the distribution of K would be approximately normal with zero mean and unit variance. The appropriate probabilities of the observed K values, taken from the table of areas under one tail of the normal curve, are given in parentheses under the values of K. These probabilities turn out to be quite low, indicating significance on the levels of 1 to 4 per cent in all industries except nonelectrical machinery and primary metals.[29]

---

[28] See Geoffrey H. Moore and W. Allen Wallis, "Time Series Significance Tests Based on Signs of Differences," *Journal of the American Statistical Association*, June 1943, pp. 153–64; and Leo A. Goodman and Yehuda Grunfeld, "Some Nonparametric Tests for Comovements Between Time Series," *ibid.*, March 1961, pp. 11–26 (see the latter paper for other references). A test of the type described in the next paragraph of the text has been applied by Grunfeld in "The Determinants of Corporate Investment," in Arnold C. Harberger, ed., *The Demand for Durable Goods*, Chicago, 1960, pp. 221–32.

[29] It should be noted that K as given in Table 7-3 includes no correction for continuity of the normal curve or for the fact that the signs of first differences in a purely random series are negatively autocorrelated. Had such corrections been made, K would have been lowered and the associated probability would have been increased. But it was found that the adjustment for autocorrelation (as proposed by Goodman and Grunfeld, "Some Nonparametric Tests") reduced the K figures only slightly. Thus, the K for nonautomotive transportation equipment, a suitably low-ranking statistic, is reduced by such an adjustment from 1.802 to 1.796.

Table 7-3
Analysis of Comovements in Quarterly Changes of Backlogs and Prices,
Seven Major Industries, 1948–58

Direction of Movement[a] in ΔU and ΔP	Number of Observations (quarter-to-quarter comparisons)						
	Textile-Mill Products (1)	Paper and Allied Products (2)	Other Durable Goods (3)	Fab. Metal Products (4)	Non-elect. Mach. (5)	Primary Metals (6)	Nonautomotive Transport. Equip. (7)
Both series rise (RR)	12	15	14	13	16	9	13
Both series fall (FF)	16	14	14	17	10	14	11
Rise in ΔU, fall in ΔP (RF)	9	8	7	4	10	9	7
Fall in ΔU, rise in ΔP (FR)	6	6	7	8	7	11	6
Total number of comparisons (n)[b]	43	43	42	42	43	43	37
Observed comovements ($RR + FF$)	28	29	28	30	26	23	24
Expected comovements[c]	21.6	21.5	21.0	21.0	21.8	21.7	18.5
K (probability of K in parentheses)[d]	1.98 (0.024)	2.30 (0.011)	2.16 (0.015)	2.83 (0.002)	1.31 (0.095)	0.39 (0.348)	1.80 (0.036)

[a] For textiles, other durables, nonelectrical machinery, and primary metals, ΔP_t is compared with ΔU_t. For the other industries, the comparisons are between ΔP_t and ΔU_{t-1}. This choice of the timing relations follows the results of Table 7-2, column 5.

[b] $n = RR + FF + RF + FR$.

[c] See text.

[d] $K = (RR \times FF - RF \times FR)\sqrt{n}/\sqrt{[(RR + RF)(RR + FR)(FF + RF)(FF + FR)]}$. See text for further explanation of K and the associated probabilities.

The industry with the lowest correlations in Table 7-2, nonautomotive transportation equipment, scores fairly well on the evidence of the comovement test of Table 7-3. This industry shows a particularly strong contrast between the huge backlog changes and the minuscule price changes (Chart 7-1 and Table 7-1). There is no reason to doubt that this reflects a real phenomenon: in this case, the great relative importance of backlog and delivery-period adjustments. The comovement test confirms the existence of a positive association between ΔP

and ΔU. The correlation measures may have understated this association because the values of ΔP are frequently understated, though correct in sign (note the virtual absence of negative values in this series in Chart 7-1).

Models with Finished Stocks and Unfilled Orders

Like the divergence between new orders and shipments in production to order, the divergence between shipments and output in production to stock gives expression to the changing demand and supply conditions that influence price. A sufficiently systematic or persistent increase (decrease) in the orders backlog may indicate positive (negative) excess demand; by an analogous argument, corresponding indications might be obtained from a similar decrease (increase) in finished-goods inventories for nonperishable commodities made to stock.[30]

The main difficulty of price adjustment models that incorporate changes in finished stock is that the change may be desired by the seller. If slackening sales leave a producer with undesired inventory of unsold output on his hands, he may offer or accept a lower price. But if the stock increase does not represent excess supply, but rather the firm's planned investment in its own product, there is clearly no reason for a price reduction. The problem, then, is how to distinguish the planned from the unplanned component in the stock variable.[31]

The first approach to this problem on the theoretical level was to assume that the change in price is a negative function of the difference between the actual and some "normal" value of the product inventory.[32] In practice, the difficulty of ascertaining what constitutes a

[30] As $U = N - S$, systematic movements in this variable may be regarded as indicative of systematic changes in quantities demanded relative to quantities supplied. In this view, the distributed-lag regressions of Table 7-2 show that increases and decreases in "excess demand" tend to be associated with increases and decreases, respectively, in ΔP (both variables being taken with regard to sign). This, of course, assumes production to order where S and N differ substantially and S and Z are closely correlated (indeed, for not too short a period, approximately equal). In production to stock, where $S \simeq N$ represents quantities demanded, i.e., ordered and shipped from stock, it is the change in finished stock, ΔQ and $Z - S$, which could perhaps be used similarly as an indication of movements in excess demand.

[31] In dealing with production to order, it is also possible that backlog changes may be wanted; the producer's desire to attract more orders for future delivery may have a braking effect upon the tendency of price to increase in times of rising demand. But the time-path of the backlog depends primarily upon the course of sales (new orders), over which the producer ordinarily has only a limited degree of indirect influence. On the other hand, attempts to alter the stock level, which involve increases or decreases in the output rate, are within the power of the firm. There is both more of the volitional element here and more difficulty in allowing for it than in the case of backlog change.

[32] An assumption to this effect by Francis Dresch was given early consideration by Paul A. Samuelson in "The Stability of Equilibrium: Comparative Statics and Dynamics," *Econometrica*, April 1941, pp. 107 ff.

normal level of stock in any particular case is formidable. In a more general theoretical model, the current price of a durable good is viewed as determined not by the current flow functions of demand and supply but by demand for and supply of the existing aggregate stock of the good.[33]

For a single-product firm producing to stock but accepting advance orders in periods of exceptionally brisk demand, the change in price may depend on backlog change (Δu) during the boom and on stock change (Δq) the rest of the time. Thus, the price adjustment model should incorporate both Δu and Δq as determinants of Δp and should involve some "switching rule" for the transition from one of the estimators to the other. In practice, data refer to multifirm, multiproduct industries, where there may be some alternation between the two types of production, but probably some products would typically be made to stock and others to order most of the time. For such an industry, one can only expect that the aggregative data would show a positive association between ΔP and ΔU and a negative association between ΔP and ΔQ, both holding continuously over time. In order to secure material on the relative merits of different types of price adjustment equations, a number of computations were made for data on the paper industry.[34]

The results of these experiments are listed in Table 7-4. The first part of the table shows the simple correlations computed from monthly data, with ΔP assumed to lag behind either ΔU or ΔQ by intervals varying from 0 to 6 months. The coefficients for the ΔP vs. ΔQ relation are all negative, as expected, but they are much lower absolutely than the (positive) coefficients for the relation between ΔP and ΔU.

The correlations between the quarterly series (middle part) are much

[33] R. W. Clower, "An Investigation into the Dynamics of Investment," *American Economic Review*, March 1954, pp. 64–81. This is price determination for a very short period. Over time, current flows of production and consumption will add to and subtract from the stock, and the stationary as distinguished from the momentary equilibrium requires that excess demand be zero for the flow as well as for the stock functions. The stock-flow model provides a useful reminder that the influence of the current flows upon the price of a durable good is limited by the existence of an accumulated stock of that good. However, if the flows are measured over longer periods than those assumed in Clower's analysis, their short-run influence on price will not be negligible for many durable goods; for many durable and especially nonstaple goods, accumulated stocks would not be overwhelmingly large relative to outputs. Also, it may be argued that the stock influence will be less for durables made to order than for other durable goods because the former are held principally by buyer-users, whereas the latter are held also by producer-sellers.

[34] The paper industry was selected because data on U and Q were available; because both production to order and production to stock are well represented, although there is evidence that the overall share of the former is larger; and because the simple regressions for paper showed relatively long lags of price change, a pattern promising more scope for experimentation.

Table 7-4
Prices vs. Unfilled Orders and Finished Inventory, Regressions with Various Lags, Paper and Allied Products Industry, Monthly and Quarterly Changes, 1948–58

	Assumed Lead of Independent Variable Relative to ΔP (mos.)						
	0	1	2	3	4	5	6
	COEFFICIENTS OF SIMPLE CORRELATION						
1. ΔU	.366	.350	.401	.416	.467	.549 [a]	.450
2. ΔQ	−.070	−.194	−.226	−.195	−.232	−.235 [a]	−.105

	Simple Regressions,[b] Quarterly; One-Quarter Lags of ΔP				
	Regression Coefficients		Standard Error of		
	Intercept	Slope	Estimate	r	r^2
3. ΔU	−.145	.031	1.59	.717	.514
4. ΔQ	.582	−.126	4.50	−.424	.180

	Multiple Regressions, Monthly; Distributed Lags[c]					
		Regression Coefficients of				
	Intercept	$\Delta U(-5)$	$\Delta Q(-1)$	$\Delta P(-1)$	R	R^2
5. $\Delta U(-5)$, $\Delta P(-1)$	.095	.0119 (.0029)		.5723 (.0695)	.747	.558
6. $\Delta Q(-1)$, $\Delta P(-1)$	.135		−.0362 (.0159)	.6936 (.0644)	.719	.517

[a] Highest correlation coefficients, denoting the lead that maximizes correspondence between ΔP and ΔU or between ΔP and ΔQ.

[b] Change in trend-adjusted price series was used as dependent variable in these regressions, which led to some slight improvements in correlation as compared with the use of the trend-unadjusted data.

[c] ΔU used with a five-month lead, ΔQ with a one-month lead, over ΔP. These are the leads that maximize the multiple correlations with ΔP, given $\Delta P(-1)$ as the second independent variable. Figures in parentheses are calculated standard errors of the regression coefficients.

higher in each case than the best correlations based on monthly data. Here, too, ΔP is considerably better correlated with ΔU than with ΔQ.

The bottom part of the table shows the results obtained by application to these relations of the distributed-lag approach of the Koyck type. The relations with ΔU have a small advantage over those with ΔQ in the multiple correlations, and they yield more significant regression coefficients.

I have also experimented with a multiple regression model in which both ΔU and ΔQ are included as determinants of price change. Taking ΔU with a five-month and ΔQ with a two-month lead over ΔP, a correlation of .557 is obtained, which is only a trifle higher than the simple correlation with ΔU_{t-5} alone. When ΔP_{t-1} is included as another independent variable, i.e., assuming a distributed lag, the result is an R of .750, which is again only a little higher than the best of the distributed-lag equations with ΔU alone (compare the first and fifth lines). It may be objected that the application of a distributed lag to each of the two partial relationships involved should result in a more complex form with several lagged terms, but high intercorrelations of the independent variables thwart efforts to estimate the equations that would be yielded by this approach.[35]

Responses to Changes in New Orders

Since new orders are generally more variable than shipments (Chapter 3), fluctuation in ΔU often strongly reflects the fluctuations in N. This is not merely a matter of arithmetic: The underlying fact is that short-term changes in demand meet with lagged and partial adaptations of supply. Sufficiently large and long imbalances resulting from this process should give rise to adjustments of prices and delivery periods. Actually, price changes are positively associated with both levels and changes of deflated new orders, and so are the changes in the U/S ratio, which serve here as rough indicators of movements in average delivery periods.

[35] Assume that ΔP_t is a function of ΔU_{t-i} and of ΔQ_{t-j}; then, the use of the Koyck scheme would give here, in effect, two component lag distributions that result in a relationship in which ΔP depends on six terms: ΔU with leads of i and $(i + 1)$; ΔQ with leads of j and $(j + 1)$; and ΔP with leads of one and two periods. This is a "reduced equation" type of lag distribution obtained by a method worked out by Marc Nerlove, "Distributed Lags and Demand Analysis," *Agricultural Handbook No. 141*, U.S. Department of Agriculture, June 1958, pp. 25–31. An application of this form to the paper industry data gave coefficients with the expected signs (minus for the ΔQ terms, plus for the others), but also gave very large standard errors.

Table 7-5 lists the results of correlating ΔP_t with current or recent levels and changes of new orders (N, ΔN) and also of correlating $\Delta(U/S)_t$ with the same variables (columns 1 and 2). Multiple regressions with values of either N or ΔN for the current and previous quarters produce only small or even trivial improvements over the optimal simple correlations. There are substantial positive autocorrelations in the N series, much lower and generally negative autocorrelations in the ΔN series. The associations between the terms N and ΔN vary in sign and are rather weak. There are some gains from combining these terms, though they are quite modest. The most common timing in these equations is such as to imply positive effects upon ΔP_t of N_t and N_{t-1}, and negative effects of N_{t-2}.[36] In most cases, ΔP and $\Delta(U/S)$ are somewhat better correlated with N than with ΔN, which may appear surprising (see note 22, above). The explanation may lie partly in the relative measurement errors, which are presumably larger in ΔN than in N, and partly in the asymmetrical feature of the recent behavior of measured prices: The dominance of upward price movements is intensified in times of high demand, but comparable downward movements in times of low demand do not occur.

Comparatively high correlations between ΔP and the new-order variables are found in industries that face highly cyclical demand and produce either predominantly or in large part to order: nonelectrical machinery, transportation equipment (other than passenger automobiles), textile mills, and metalworking. The same industries also have relatively high correlations between $\Delta(U/S)$ and new orders. This suggests that there is considerable room for both price and backlog reactions in those areas of manufacturing where the flows of demand are particularly variable.

At the other extreme is the paper industry, with relatively stable flows of new orders and prompt output adjustments (see note 20). The average values of U/S are very low here, and price variations are large relative to backlog variations (Table 7-1).

The correlation statistics in Table 7-5, columns 1 and 2, yield very similar rankings of the industries: The Spearman coefficient is +.929.

We expect positive correlations between changes over time in prices and delivery period adjustments because p and k respond in the same direction to fluctuations in demand. However, such correlations would

---

[36] This is the implication of positive influences on ΔP_t of N_t and of $\Delta N_{t-1} = N_{t-1} - N_{t-2}$.

Table 7-5

Changes in Price and in Backlog-Shipment Ratios Correlated with
Each Other and with Changes and Levels of New Orders,
Quarterly, 1948–58

	Multiple Correlation Coefficients [b]		
Industry [a]	ΔP on N and ΔN (1)	$\Delta(U/S)$ on N and ΔN (2)	ΔP on $\Delta(U/S)$ (3)
Textile-mill products	.734	.762	.599
Nonelectrical machinery	.713	.665	.467
Primary metals	.580	.326	.163
Nonautomotive transport. equip.	.565	.631	.310
Fabricated metal products	.562	.403	.274
Other durable goods [c]	.483	.244	.443
Electrical machinery	.407	.239 [d]	.162
Paper and allied products	.238	.061	.723

Source: Same as Table 7-1.

[a] Ranked by the correlations listed in column 1, from highest to lowest.

[b] In column 1, $\Delta P = P_t - P_{t-1}$ is used throughout; N_{t-1} is used for fabricated metals, electrical machinery, and paper; N_t, for the other industries. $\Delta N_t = N_t - N_{t-1}$ is used for other durable goods; $\Delta N_{t-1} = N_{t-1} - N_{t-2}$, for the other industries.

In column 2, N_t and $\Delta(U/S) = (U/S)_t - (U/S)_{t-1}$ are used throughout. ΔN_t is used for textiles, nonautomotive transportation equipment, and other durable goods.

In column 3, correlations of ΔP with $\Delta(U/S)_t$ and $\Delta(U/S)_{t-1}$ (changes in backlog-shipment ratios in the current and previous quarter) are used.

[c] Includes professional and scientific instruments; lumber; furniture; stone, clay, and glass; and miscellaneous industries.

[d] Coefficient of simple correlation between $\Delta(U/S)_t$ and N_t. Multiple correlation with ΔN added is not available, but it is not likely to be much higher. (Simple correlation between $\Delta(U/S)_t$ and ΔN_{t-1} is .176.)

be low if, say, price adjustments were sporadic and backlog adjustments were regular—or vice versa. They may be low, too, for those industries in which both types of reactions are weak because input flexibility is high and short-term fluctuations in quantities ordered can be met promptly by changes in the rates of output. Where changes in prices and delivery periods are generally small, it may be particularly difficult to separate their systematic components, which could still be well correlated, from the irregular components, which are not.

Consistent with this argument, the correlations between ΔP_t and current and preceding changes in the U/S ratios are all positive but not high (Table 7-5, column 3). In all but one case, these correlations are lower than those between ΔP_t and new orders, and they give a quite different ranking of the industries.[37] They also tend to be lower than the corresponding measures of the association between ΔP and ΔU (see Table 7-2, column 6), but the ranking of the industries in terms of these two sets of coefficients is similar.[38]

Buyers' Prices and Delivery Periods: Evidence from Diffusion Data

Data compiled by the Purchasing Agents Association (PAA) of Chicago provide at least a partial remedy for the two major short-comings of our statistical results: (1) the reliance on seller-reported prices, which are unduly rigid in the short run, and (2) the reliance on indirect indicators of changes in the average delivery periods rather than on any direct measures.

The "vendor performance" index (D^*) is a monthly series of differences between the percentage of PAA survey members reporting slower and the percentage reporting faster deliveries to their companies by the suppliers (vendors).

The price series (P^*) is also a net diffusion index. It shows the differences between the percentage of PAA members reporting higher and the percentage reporting lower buying prices each month. While primary-market sellers tend to quote list prices, primary-market buyers would presumably use actual transaction prices or close approximations to such figures.[39] Hence, there is ground to expect that estimates based on purchasing agents' data will go far toward avoiding understatement of short-run price flexibility, an error that is likely to mar the results obtained from the BLS data.

Chart 7-2 shows that the P^* index is, in fact, very sensitive to cyclical and other short-run influences. Certainly the index displays more

[37] Rankings based on the entries in columns 1 and 3 of Table 7-5 show a very low correlation (.119). The rank correlation coefficient for columns 2 and 3 is similar (.190).

[38] The rank correlation coefficient here is +.750. Statistically, the observed differences between these results in Tables 7-5 and 7-2 probably occur mainly because the U/S ratio series is much more erratic and much less cyclical than the corresponding U series. Measurement errors are likely to affect the ratio series more, and they could be quite troublesome when first differences in these series are used. For this reason, the measured correlations between ΔP and $\Delta(U/S)$ may significantly understate the actual association between changes in the average prices and delivery periods.

[39] See Harry E. McAllister, "Statistical Factors Affecting the Stability of the Wholesale and Consumers' Price Indexes," and Flueck, "A Study in Validity," both in *Price Statistics of the Federal Government.*

Chart 7-2
Diffusion Indexes of Delivery Periods, Order Backlogs, and Prices Paid, and Change in Manufacturers' Unfilled Orders and Prices, 1946–60

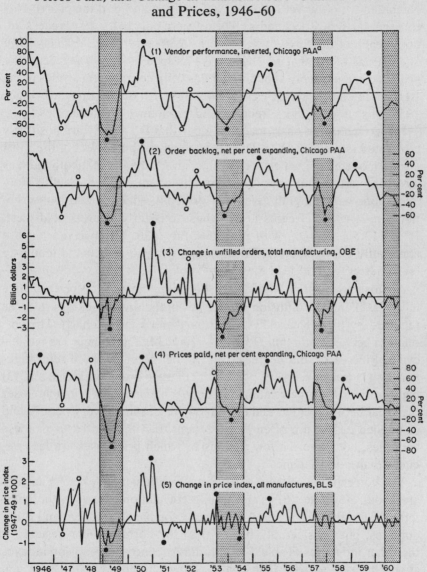

Note: Shaded areas represent business cycle contractions; unshaded areas, expansions. Dots identify peaks and troughs of specific cycles; circles, minor turns.

^a Percentage reporting slower deliveries minus percentage reporting faster deliveries. See text.

cyclical flexibility than does the all-manufactures price change series computed from the WPI figures (see series 4 and 5 in the chart). It is true that the index declined well below zero only in the 1949 recession, but in each of the three cycles before 1958 there were relatively large fluctuations of P^* that reached peaks as high as 80–90 per cent (the peak in 1958 was only about 50 per cent). In contrast, the cycles in the BLS price change series were relatively small and, particularly since 1952, obscured by more frequent and pronounced irregularities.

Inspection of the chart makes it clear that D^* and P^* are positively correlated (series 1 and 4). To reduce the disturbing effect of the short erratic movements, which are stronger in P^* than in D^*, both indexes were converted into quarterly form (by averaging the monthly data over nonoverlapping three-month periods), yielding sixty observations in 1946–60. Regression of these quarterly figures yields: est. $P_t^* = 113.5 + .544D_t^*$, with $r^2 = (.660)^2 = .436$. The two indexes are apparently approximately synchronous, with no systematic tendency for either of them to lead the other.[40]

A close association was found between the vendor performance index (D^*) and the diffusion of changes in the order backlogs (U^*), as reported by the Chicago PAA (series 1 and 2 in the chart). The correlation between monthly D^* and U^* is .934. Thus, there are parallel cyclical increases and decreases in the net percentages of returns reporting (1) longer delivery periods, (2) larger order backlogs, and (3) higher prices; but the relationship between (1) and (2) is much closer than that between either and (3). The increases in delivery periods and in unfilled orders are often less frequent than the decreases in these variables, but there are few periods in which price rises are less frequent than price declines.

The correlations between the quarterly diffusion indexes P^* and D^* are about the same (.6) as the simple correlations between the quarterly first-difference series ΔP and ΔU for paper, textiles, and other durables, but considerably higher than the corresponding results for the other industries (Table 7-2, column 5). Since the diffusion indexes appear to have a broad industrial coverage and to give large represen-

---

[40] When a lead of D^* relative to P^* of one quarter is assumed, a somewhat lower correlation (.611) results. But the former series is highly autocorrelated: The coefficient of correlation between D_t^* and D_{t-3}^* is .811. Correlating P_t^* with both D_t^* and D_{t-1}^* yields very little improvement [$R^2 = (.664)^2 = .441$]; the contribution of D_{t-1}^* is of low statistical significance.

tation to products of industries for which the correlations between ΔP and ΔU are low (e.g., metal products), there is some indication here that the measures based on the major-industry (OBE and BLS) series do understate price flexibility.[41]

It will be noted in Chart 7-2 that P^* is not only distinctly more cyclical but also less irregular than ΔP. The Chicago indexes, of course, may deviate considerably from the corresponding national series because of their regional origin. Moreover, even for the same aggregates, diffusion indexes and rates of change can differ significantly.[42] When all this is considered, the similarity in the cyclical change in the PAA backlog index and the first differences in the Commerce estimates of unfilled orders seems rather pronounced (series 2 and 3 in the chart). Most of the divergences between these series are due to the intensity of the irregular movements in backlogs. The coefficient of correlation between the PAA vendor performance index and the quarterly change in unfilled orders (series 1 and 3) is .692.

Wage Changes as an Additional Variable

Recent studies provide some examples of extreme emphasis on the dependence of short-run price behavior upon changes in costs. Sometimes, the influence of demand is excluded from explicit consideration.[43] This implies that changes in demand are met largely by backlog or stock adjustments. However, our regressions suggest that current or past changes in unfilled orders can account for a significant proportion of the variance of current changes in some industrial price indexes. Yet, It is also true that much of the price change remains "unexplained"

[41] However, this inference rests on the assumption that the PAA price index includes only fabricated or semifabricated items sold by manufacturers. (The BLS series presumably does satisfy this requirement.) Unfortunately, little information is available about the coverage of the PAA sample, and it was not possible to ascertain to what extent the price diffusion index (P^*) is indeed free of raw materials. We do know that the PAA series cover a broad range of industries but that they are, at least in one respect, more restricted than the OBE series. The former data cover manufacturers who supply industrial concerns; the latter, all manufacturers regardless of their role as suppliers.

[42] See Geoffrey H. Moore in Moore, ed., *Business Cycle Indicators*, Princeton for NBER, 1961, Vol. 1, pp. 282–93.

[43] See, e.g., Joseph V. Yance, "A Model of Price Flexibility," *American Economic Review*, June 1960, pp. 401–18. Applied to U.S. tanning and shoe manufacturing industries, 1947–56, Yance's model incorporates a distributed lag of price change relative to changes in the cost of materials and average hourly earnings. The resulting R^2 coefficients vary between .41 and .75, with better fits being obtained from bimonthly or quarterly than from monthly data. The residuals of these regressions are generally autocorrelated, and Yance notes that "the autocorrelation may represent, in part, the effect of demand on profit margins . . ." and that "these demand effects are likely to persist from one month to the next . . ." (*ibid.*, pp. 411–12).

in these calculations. Let us ask, therefore, how much improvement can be achieved by allowing for the direct cost effects on price.

If a single cost variable is to be used, the best available choice appears to be the change in average hourly earnings as an approximation to the change in wages. The figures are easily derived from the monthly BLS data for five of the seven industries examined in Table 7-2. Let us denote the quarterly change in these gross hourly earnings by ΔW and assign to it the subscript "3" (ΔP and ΔU are the variables "1" and "2," respectively). Table 7-6 presents measures obtained from regressions of ΔP_t on (1) ΔU_t or ΔU_{t-1}, and (2) ΔW_t or ΔW_{t-1}. The measures are based on quarterly data for 1948–58.

I find that the inclusion of ΔW, while important in all cases, does not eliminate the influence of ΔU. In fact, price changes in paper and textiles are apparently more strongly affected by demand pressures as measured by ΔU than by the direct "cost push" (ΔW). The partial correlations of ΔP and ΔU, holding ΔW constant, exceed the simple correlations of the same variables and are considerably higher than the partials between ΔP and ΔW, holding ΔU constant (that is, $r_{12.3} > r_{12} > r_{13.2}$; also, $r_{12} > r_{13}$).[44] Compared with the distributed-lag regressions employing the ΔU's alone (monthly or quarterly), the present equations that include ΔW yield lower correlation coefficients for both textiles and paper (cf. the first two lines in Tables 7-2 and 7-6).

The influence of wage changes is relatively stronger in the regressions for the other industries. Thus, in nonelectrical machinery and in primary and fabricated metals, $r_{12} < r_{13}$ and $r_{12.3} < r_{13.2}$.[45] But the contributions of the ΔW's are not much more impressive here than those of the ΔU's; both variables together still do not explain more than between 40 and 50 per cent of the variation in ΔP. For nonelectrical machinery, the distributed-lag equation with monthly ΔU performs somewhat better than the present regression using quarterly ΔU and ΔW (the respective R^2 coefficients are .463 and .420).

It may perhaps be questioned whether the factors ΔU and ΔW should really be treated equally as potential determinants of price change. Since labor costs are an important part of price, it is only natural for the simultaneous changes in the two to be positively correlated. While

---

[44] The values of r_{12} and r_{13} are .714 and .463, respectively, for the paper industry and .679 and .481 for the textile industry.

[45] The values of r_{12} and r_{13} are .418 and .644, respectively, for primary metals; .471 and .612 for nonelectrical machinery; and .450 and .567 for fabricated metal products.

Table 7-6
Regressions of Price Changes on Changes in Backlogs and Wages, Five Major Industries, Quarterly, 1948–58

Industry [a]	Independent Variables [b] (1)	Regression Constants (2)	Regression Coefficients [c] of		Partial Correlation Coefficients [d]		
			ΔU (3)	ΔW (4)	$r_{12.3}$ (5)	$r_{13.2}$ (6)	$R_{1.23}$ (7)
Paper and allied products	$\Delta U_{t-1}, \Delta W_{t-1}$	−0.609	.0314 (.0043)	58.826 (14.468)	.737	.518	.801
Textile-mill products	$\Delta U_t, \Delta W_t$	−0.615	.0061 (.0009)	76.768 (19.454)	.697	.525	.781
Primary metals	$\Delta U_t, \Delta W_t$	0.316	.0018 (.0007)	41.452 (7.733)	.348	.613	.696
Nonelectrical machinery	$\Delta U_t, \Delta W_t$	1.301	.0061 (.00038)	45.711 (10.525)	.271	.505	.648
Fabricated metal products	$\Delta U_{t-1}, \Delta W_t$	−0.287	.00213 (.00025)	58.508 (14.408)	.360	.510	.640

[a] Ranked according to the value of R in column 7, from highest to lowest.

[b] The subscripts identify the timing of ΔU and ΔW relative to the dependent variable, ΔP_t. The timing of ΔU follows the indication of Table 7-2, column 5. The regressions cover 43 quarters for textiles and fabricated metals, 44 quarters for each of the other industries.

[c] Figures in parentheses are calculated standard errors of the regression coefficients.

[d] ΔP, ΔU, and ΔW are variables 1, 2, and 3, respectively.

it is true that, at least in the framework of our short unit periods, it is easier to think of ΔW influencing ΔP than vice versa, the simultaneous relationship between the two variables must be presumed to contain some elements of a feedback. Thus, when prices rise because profit margins do, owing to strong and increasing demand for the product, wage increases may be demanded and rather promptly gained. Moreover, such demand pressures will often cause overtime work, and our wage-cost variable is computed from data which include overtime earnings. To avoid feedback difficulty, one could take the wage change with a lead relative to the price change, i.e., use ΔW_{t-1}, but this would drastically reduce the importance of the wage variable as a determinant of ΔP_t. Graphical analysis suggests strongly that the relation between ΔP and ΔW is simultaneous rather than lagged; this is confirmed in further computations.[46]

On the other hand, any feedback effect of ΔP upon ΔU is probably small. To be sure, actual price rises may induce expectations of further rises which stimulate advance buying. This would result in larger increases in both ΔU and ΔP, but it is consistent with the view that the increase in unfilled orders anticipates measured price increases rather than vice versa. A lag of ΔU relative to ΔP would imply that prices are often raised or lowered in anticipation of demand increases or decreases. But this does not appear to be common in the industries and periods considered here. Analysis of monthly data suggests that ΔU often precedes ΔP by short intervals, while the reverse sequence seems rather infrequent. Even when simultaneous quarterly values of the two variables are used, the treatment of ΔU as "given" or independent seems unlikely to be a source of any major errors.

Some Replications and Additions

Regressions of price change on deflated backlog change, analogous to those discussed above with the aid of Tables 7-1 and 7-2, have also been computed for some of the new Census series on unfilled orders and the current BLS wholesale price indexes. This analysis covers three industries—nonelectrical machinery, electrical machinery, and fabricated metal products—and employs monthly and quarterly data for 1953–64.

Such recalculations do not have the power of independent predictive tests, but they are certainly useful means of organizing additional evidence and of evaluating the closeness and stability of the relationships involved. The new data are, of course, akin to the old but are based on larger and presumably better samples (see Chapter 3, first section).

---

[46] Consider, e.g., the lowest-ranking industry in Table 7-6, fabricated metal products. Denote ΔW_{t-1} as variable "4" (ΔP_t, ΔU_{t-1}, and ΔW_t being represented by subscripts 1, 2, and 3, as before). Then $r_{14}^2 = (.266)^2 = .051$; $r_{14.2}^2 = (.045)^2 = .002$; $r_{12.4}^2 = (.402)^2 = .162$. These results make it clear that ΔW_{t-1} bears virtually no relation to ΔP_t, especially when the effect of ΔU_{t-1} is taken into account. In contrast, the influence upon ΔP_t of ΔW_t was found to be significant, whether or not ΔU_{t-1} was included (see Table 7-6, last line, and note 45). The substitution of ΔW_{t-1} for ΔW_t also cuts in half the multiple correlation coefficient: $R_{1.23}^2 = .410$, while $R_{1.24}^2 = .205$. The only industry in our set in which ΔW_{t-1}, as distinguished from ΔW_t, seems to be of importance as a determinant of ΔP_t is paper (see Table 7-6, first line, and note 44).

Price changes in the current quarter (month) are positively correlated with backlog changes in each of the two preceding quarters (in each of the six preceding months). When ΔP and ΔU are taken with coincident timing (in quarterly or monthly terms), their correlations turn out to be positive for nonelectrical machinery and negative, but very low, for the other two industries. The simple correlations are generally lower than those reported in Table 7-2, which may be due to the greater stability of prices in the more recent period. The r coefficients for quarterly changes tend to be larger than those for monthly changes, probably because errors of measurement are reduced when the volatile monthly data are transformed into the smoother quarterly data.

In quarterly distributed-lag equations of Koyck form, the effects of ΔU are not suppressed by the generally strong influence of the autoregressive term ΔP_{t-1}, which is mildly encouraging. The regression results are as follows:

Fabricated metal products:

$$\Delta P_t = .256 + .0268\Delta U_{t-1} + .315\Delta P_{t-1}; R = .463$$
$$(.122)\ (.0099)\qquad\quad (.136)$$

Electrical machinery:

$$\Delta P_t = .064 + .0082\Delta U_{t-1} + .522\Delta P_{t-1}; R = .593$$
$$(.102)\ (.0056)\qquad\quad (.123)$$

Machinery, except electrical:

$$\Delta P_t = .305 + .0298\Delta U_t + .555\Delta P_{t-1}; R = .608$$
$$(.120)\ (.0196)\qquad\quad (.121)$$

The coefficients of the backlog terms, although small (fractions of index points per million dollars of change in ΔU), exceed their standard errors 1.5 to 3 times and are therefore probably significant. The addition of ΔP_{t-1} produces a relatively small increase in the correlation for fabricated metals but a large increase in the correlations for the two machinery industries.

The estimates suggest that reaction periods of 1.5 to 3.5 months are sufficient to account for about half or slightly more of the implied distributed-lag effects (fabricated metals would be close to the lower figure, the machinery industries close to the upper one). These are longer lags than those obtained for the Koyck equations of Table 7-2, but the use of quarterly rather than monthly data could work in this direction, and the differences in the implied lags seem of rather small importance. According to the replications, price changes are related to prior backlog changes, but the adjustments are small and the lags are rather short. The measures based on the older data, for the 1948–58 period, can be said to support the same general conclusions.

To what extent do these relations reflect the trends and fluctuations of the industrial sector of the economy as a whole and to what extent do they reflect developments that are specific to the particular industries concerned? In each of our equations, the dependent variable is an index showing changes in money prices rather than changes in relative prices. These indexes pertain to major industries and are therefore broad in coverage, but much less comprehensive than the over-all price-level indicators. General price movements depend on forces influencing the general level of economic activity, such as monetary changes and the over-all rate of capacity utilization or the relation between aggregate expenditures and supply, and relative prices depend on the conditions of particular markets and production processes. However, individual money price movements may reflect changes in the economy at large as well as more narrowly defined or local conditions. It seems plausible that the more comprehensive the money price index the greater should be the influence on it of general economic factors rather than particular ones.

The industry price indexes are indeed closely correlated with the price index for all manufacturing: the adjusted determination coefficients $\bar{r}^2$ are .973, .835, and .955 for fabricated metals, electrical machinery, and other machinery, respectively.[47] The industry backlog series show lower correlations with the unfilled orders series for total manufacturing: the $\bar{r}^2$ estimates here range from .752 to .881 for nonelectrical machinery and fabricated metal products, but are no larger than .118 to .308 for electrical machinery (the $\bar{r}^2$ coefficients are here larger for the monthly than for the quarterly series).

Positive but very low correlations exist in most cases between the residuals from these regressions (that is, between $u_t = P_{it} - a - bP_{mt}$ and $v_t = U_{it} - a' - b'U_{mt}$, where the subscript i denotes the industry series and m, the all-manufacturing one). The correlation coefficients

---

[47] These measures refer to quarterly data. For the monthly series, the $\bar{r}^2$ values are very similar: .972, .853, and .959.

for nonelectrical machinery and fabricated metals fall in the range of .3 to .4 for both the simultaneous relations between u_t and v_t and the lagged relations between u_t and v_{t-j}, $j = 0, \ldots, 3$ months. For electrical machinery, no significant associations are found between the corresponding residuals. Similarly, changes in relative prices $[\Delta(P_i/P_m)]$ show positive but low correlations with the changes in "relative backlogs" $[\Delta(U_i/U_m)]$. Only about one-tenth of the variance of $\Delta(P_i/P_m)$ can be accounted for in these regressions. The weakness of these relations suggests that any associations that can be found between the price and backlog changes (ΔP_t and ΔU_{t-j}) for the industries concerned must be attributed primarily to general developments in the economy rather than in the particular industry. These general developments, as defined by this analysis, are apt to be widely diffused and to account for a large proportion of changes in the major-industry series.

Quarterly data for 1953–64 also show that the lagged backlog changes ΔU_{t-1} still have net positive effects on P_t when the current wage changes, ΔW_t, are included in the regressions (as illustrated by the estimates below). In fact, the significance of the ΔU_{t-1} terms, as indicated by the t ratios, remains about the same or improves when the wage variable is added, except for nonelectrical machinery.

Fabricated metal products:

$$\Delta P_t = -.086 + .0241\Delta U_{t-1} + 24.640\Delta W_t; \; \bar{R}^2 = .254$$
$$ (.180) \; (.0094) (7.671)$$

$$\Delta P_t = -.181 + .0259\Delta U_{t-1} + 23.461\Delta W_t + .288\Delta P_{t-1}; \; \bar{R}^2 = .324$$
$$ (.176) \; (.0089) (7.320) (.123)$$

Electrical machinery:

$$\Delta P_t = -.389 + .0138\Delta U_{t-1} + 32.448\Delta W_t; \; \bar{R}^2 = .228$$
$$ (.203) \; (.0059) (9.942)$$

$$\Delta P_t = -.367 + .0097\Delta U_{t-1} + 25.514\Delta W_t + .455\Delta P_{t-1}; \; \bar{R}^2 = .422$$
$$ (.176) \; (.0052) (8.784) (.116)$$

Machinery, except electrical:

$$\Delta P_t = .078 + .0077\Delta U_{t-1} + 26.442\Delta W_t; \; \bar{R}^2 = .250$$
$$ (.173) \; (.0054) (7.013)$$

$$\Delta P_t = -.054 + .0051\Delta U_{t-1} + 18.970\Delta W_t + .449\Delta P_{t-1}; \; \bar{R}^2 = .424$$
$$ (.156) \; (.0048) (6.461) (.120)$$

There are indications that ΔP is related to ΔU with lags: ΔU_{t-1} performs much better in these equations than does ΔU_t.[48] On the other hand, the relationships between ΔP and ΔW are mainly simultaneous ones, that is, the influence upon ΔP_t of ΔW_t is stronger than that of ΔW_{t-1}. However, even when both the wage changes and the autoregressive factor ΔP_{t-1} are included in the equations along with the lagged backlog changes, the over-all results, as judged from the $\bar{R}^2$ statistics, are only fair.[49]

Related Studies

To my knowledge, Thomas A. Wilson and I, independently, were the first to use unfilled orders in price adjustment models.[50] Wilson's informative paper deals with quarterly prices of machinery and steel in the period III-1953–II-1959. In addition to orders variables, $[(N - S)/S]_{t-1}$ and $(U/S)_{t-1}$, Wilson used changes in the wage index ΔW (based on average hourly earnings figures) and the deviations of GNP from its estimated trend values. For machinery, the regression coefficients were positive for all terms and significant for all except U/S. For steel, the coefficients of both order variables turned out to be negative and lacking significance.[51]

In his recent quarterly model of the U.S. economy,[52] Lawrence R. Klein related the price indexes for consumer durables and nondurables (p_d and p_n) to the general price level (p) and to manufacturers' unfilled orders of durable and nondurable goods in billions of 1954 dollars (U_d and U_n). The price indexes are implicit deflators for GNP and selected

[48] For nonelectrical machinery, ΔU_t appears to work somewhat better than ΔU_{t-1} in simple correlations with ΔP_{t-1} and also when taken along with ΔP_{t-1} (as in the equation at the beginning of the section, "Some Replications and Additions"). Yet here, too, ΔU_{t-1} is preferable to ΔU_t in regressions that include ΔW_t. However, in this case the net effects of backlog changes on price changes are quite weak.

[49] It would probably be easy to improve the correlations by adding, as another determinant of price movements, the changes in raw materials. Where materials have sensitive prices and are an important component of total costs, changes in their prices are likely to exert a strong influence upon the product price. It may be, too, that prices significantly lag costs but that the lengths are too short to be revealed by quarterly data. However, it must be recognized that the effect of changes in product demand upon input prices and the joint dependency of input and output prices can be just as important to material costs as to labor costs.

[50] Wilson, "An Analysis of the Inflation in Machinery Prices," Study Paper No. 3, Joint Economic Committee, 86th Cong., 1st sess., Washington, D.C., 1959. My first report on this work can be found in "Cyclical Behavior of Manufacturers' Orders," in *Investing in Economic Knowledge*, Thirty-eighth Annual Report of the National Bureau, New York, NBER, May 1958, p. 38.

[51] See Wilson, "An Analysis," App. Table 1, p. 67.

[52] "A Postwar Quarterly Model: Description and Applications," in *Models of Income Determination*, Studies in Income and Wealth, Vol. 28, Princeton for NBER, 1964, p. 18.

components, $1954 = 100$. They are endogenous variables, while the unfilled orders for the two sectors of manufacturing are not.[53] Klein reports the following results:

$$p_d = .548 + .422p + .00067(U_d)_{-1}; \bar{R} = 0.94$$
$$\quad (.034) \quad (.039) \quad (.00017)$$

$$p_n = .346 + .618p + .00946(U_n)_{-1}; \bar{R} = 0.97$$
$$\quad (.027) \quad (.024) \quad (.0021)$$

In a recent article Eckstein and Fromm seek to explain changes in wholesale price indexes for all manufacturing and durable and nondurable manufacturing by combining cost variables—standard and actual unit labor costs and materials input prices—with demand variables, namely, the U/S ratio, deviations of the actual inventory-sales ratio from a twelve-quarter moving average of it, and rates of capacity utilization.[54] These specifications are intended to test both the competitive price determination model and the target-return pricing hypothesis.[55] Regression equations for quarterly first differences are shown to be preferable to those for levels and percentage changes. They show, for 1954–65, that the demand variables were nearly as important as the cost variables.[56] The industrial operating rate was more influential and significant than the backlog-shipment ratio, which Eckstein and Fromm found surprising, and which they attributed to the crude estimation of lags from quarterly data and the available price statistics; the inventory variable had no effect independent of the operating rate. The adjustment of prices to changes in demand and cost conditions appears to be rather prompt, the greatest part of it being completed within a few months.

Finally, in another recent paper,[57] T. H. Courchene, using Canadian data, finds quarterly changes in price indexes to be positively associ-

[53] However, *total* unfilled orders are endogenous in Klein's model. For a discussion of his equation for U_t, see below, Chapter 8, in section "The Supporting Equations for Orders in Recent Models of the Economy."

[54] Otto Eckstein and Gary Fromm, "The Price Equation," *American Economic Review*, December 1968, pp. 1159–83.

[55] *Ibid.*, pp. 1159–66; also, Otto Eckstein, "A Theory of the Wage-Price Process in Modern Industry," *Review of Economic Studies*, October 1964, pp. 267–86.

[56] This evaluation is based on sums of beta coefficients. Three to five cost variables (standard and actual, current and lagged) are included in these equations, as against two demand variables (the current capacity utilization rate and the lagged U/S ratio).

[57] "An Analysis of the Price-Inventory Nexus with Empirical Application to the Canadian Manufacturing Sector," *International Economic Review*, October 1969, pp. 315–36.

ated with new and unfilled orders for several major manufacturing industries that produce largely to order. He uses unlagged levels, rather than changes in orders, which may be the reason he gets better results with another proxy for "excess demand," namely, deviations of actual from equilibrium inventories (where the latter are regression estimates which do incorporate the effects of current and lagged orders).

Summary

Changes in unfilled orders are associated with planned and unplanned changes in delivery periods. Speedups of delivery often raise costs to the producer; delays, costs to the buyer. Other things being equal, therefore, an inverse relation between price and delivery period is to be expected. However, if demand increases give rise to pressures upon the industry's capacity to produce, the result may be both backlog accumulation associated with a lengthening of the average delivery lags and an increase in prices of the affected products.

Unpredictable fluctuation in demand is probably a central phenomenon behind the large volume and wide swings in unfilled orders. The hazards of uncertainty are large for a manufacturer who would rely only on pricing policy to meet such changes, and so are the requirements of information. Letting backlogs accumulate and decumulate would often be seen as less risky and less demanding. However, noncompetitive behavior or restrictions on the competition in product and factor markets may act in the same direction, as reinforcing forces.

The assembled evidence is generally consistent with the hypotheses presented. Changes in the price index for a given industry's products (ΔP) are positively correlated with changes in that industry's unfilled orders (ΔU). Since $\Delta U = N - S$, systematic movements in this variable (expressed in constant prices) may be viewed as indicative of systematic changes in quantities demanded relative to quantities supplied. It seems plausible that prices should react primarily to the more persistent variations in the demand-delivery conditions, and this is partly confirmed, e.g., quarterly regressions of ΔP on ΔU give better results than monthly regressions. However, the gains from replacing discrete lags by distributed lags in these models often proved to be small.

Both price changes and average delivery-period changes [represented by $\Delta(U/S)$] are positively correlated with fluctuations in quantities demanded (new orders in real terms). Relatively high correlations of N and ΔN with both ΔP and $\Delta(U/S)$ are observed for several industries with highly variable flows of new orders. In contrast, the correlations are very low for products which face relatively stable flows of demand and which are subject to prompt output adjustments. Positive correlations also exist between ΔP and $\Delta(U/S)$, but they are generally quite weak, partly for economic and partly for statistical reasons.

The greater the importance of production to order and the longer the average delivery lag, the greater the role of backlog reactions compared to price reactions. Thus, when the industries are ranked according to the coefficients of ΔU in the regressions of ΔP on ΔU, a high inverse correlation is obtained between these ranks and rankings by average U/S ratios for the same industries.

Changes in wages (average hourly earnings), ΔW, are positively correlated with changes in prices when quarterly series with simultaneous timing are used. This would be expected, of course, since labor cost is typically an important component of price; the relationship between these variables may contain substantial elements of interdependence rather than being limited to one-way causation from ΔW to ΔP. On the other hand, there are indications that ΔU leads ΔP; and there are still significant net effects of ΔU upon ΔP in regressions that also include ΔW.

Diffusion indexes based on surveys of purchasing agents provide independent, confirming evidence that changes in unfilled orders and delivery periods are directly and closely associated and that both tend to agree in direction with changes in transaction prices.

8

ORDERS, PRODUCTION, AND INVENTORY INVESTMENT

THERE ARE THREE major sections in this chapter. The first is a theoretical discussion of the major determinants of purchasing and inventory behavior. The second, a critical survey of recent work in inventory analysis, concentrates on the role of orders and related factors and on the importance of disaggregation by type of production and stage of fabrication. The third assembles and evaluates additional evidence on the relations that underlie the cyclical fluctuations of inventories.

Determinants and Patterns of Inventory Behavior

Relations with Sales and Orders Placed and Outstanding

We will consider orders relating to goods that are to be resold by the buyer in unchanged physical form, e.g., orders for a consumer good received by the producer from the distributor.[1] Let us suppose that we have data for the *purchasing firm* on (1) the sales of the product in each consecutive planning period ("month"); (2) the orders for the product placed by the firm each month with its suppliers; (3) the volume of such orders outstanding at the end of each month; and (4) the stock of the product in possession of the firm at the end of each month. To abstract from problems of measurement and aggregation, assume that all these series are in homogeneous physical units of the given

---

[1] Some of what follows can, with modifications, be applied to the buying of goods to be resold after processing, e.g., to materials purchasing by the manufacturer. The restriction adopted above will help to keep the analysis simple. Investment in purchased materials will be taken up in the following section.

good. A number of different models based on such data can be devised, embodying certain more or less simple assumptions about the relations among the four variables. The few such models presented here, while no doubt highly oversimplified, are nevertheless instructive (see Chart 8-1 and Table 8-1).

The simplest inventory objective for the firm is to maintain a constant stock of the item in each period, say $\bar{F} = 200$ units. This assumption underlies the four models designated I, Ia, Ib, and Ic in Chart 8-1. In the second group of models, labeled II through IIc, the assumed objective is a constant stock-to-sales ratio with $\bar{F}/\bar{S}$ equal to 2. The models start in each case from a given cyclical time-path of sales (S). In all models except Ia and IIa, this path is identical and embodies retardations of sales at the peaks and troughs. In models Ia and IIa sales paths show sharp downturns and upturns not preceded by retardations.

In models I, Ia, II, and IIa, the delivery period and outstanding orders are zero. The firm places all its orders at the end of the month after having determined the amount of the product it has sold and the inventory it has left. All these orders are supplied at the beginning of the next month. The actual change in inventory in month t equals new orders placed (OP) in $(t-1)$ minus sales in t: $\Delta F_t = OP_{t-1} - S_t$. Hence, the actual inventory $F_t = F_{t-1} + OP_{t-1} - S_t$.

In the other models a positive delivery lag is introduced, resulting in the appearance of positive outstanding orders. It is assumed that $\Delta F_t = OP_{t-2} - S_t$. The delivery lag is constant, and outstanding orders simply equal the total of new orders issued in the month just ending and the month preceding: $OU_t = OP_t + OP_{t-1}$.

Orders placed equal the sum of current sales and a correction element C: $OP_t = S_t + C_t$. The corrective component C equals the inventory error, i.e., the discrepancy between desired and actual inventory, which is, in each of the models, a function of changes in sales (ΔS). In the simplest case, C_t just equals ΔS_t (models I and Ia); elsewhere, it may be the sum of current and past sales changes (Ic), a multiple of the current change (II), or some more complicated function.[2]

---

[2] In model I we have $C_t = \bar{F} - F_t$; hence $\Delta C_t = \Delta F_t$. But $\Delta F_t = OP_{t-1} - S_t$, and $OP_{t-1} = S_{t-1} + C_{t-1}$. Therefore, by substitution, $\Delta C_t = S_t - S_{t-1} - C_{t-1}$, which reduces to $C_t = \Delta S_t$.

In Ic, analogously, $\Delta C_t + \Delta C_{t-1} = -\Delta F_t = S_t - OP_{t-2} = S_t - S_{t-2} - C_{t-2}$, which reduces to $C_t = \Delta S_t + \Delta S_{t-1}$. In Ib, the relation is somewhat more complicated. It can be shown that $C_t = \Delta S_t + \Delta S_{t-1} + \Delta C_{t-1}$. The counterpart of this for type II models is shown in the text and note 3, below.

It follows that orders placed depend on the level of sales and on changes in sales. The latter corrective component imparts to the behavior of orders (in relation to sales) the well-known characteristics of acceleration and magnification. For cyclically fluctuating series such as sales, levels and changes are positively correlated. Hence orders, being directly related to both the level of and the first differences in sales, exceed sales in amplitude of fluctuation (compare the curves S and OP in the upper panels of Chart 8-1). But there are differences. The magnification of the movement of orders in comparison with product sales is greater in the models with a delivery lag than in those

Chart 8-1

Cyclical Time-Paths of Sales, Orders Placed and Outstanding, and Product Inventory in Eight Hypothetical Models

S = sales
Op = new orders placed
Ou = outstanding purchase orders
F = product inventory

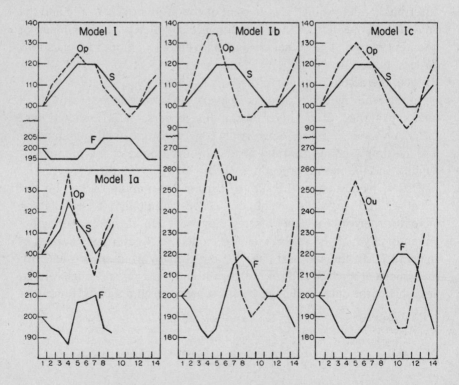

Chart 8-1 (concluded)

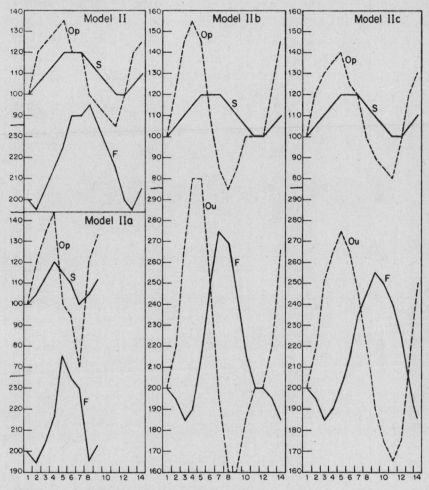

Note: For explanation of models, see text.

without it (compare models Ib and Ic with I; and IIb and IIc with II). This is reasonable. The interval between the ordering of a good and its delivery and sale has lengthened, while the firm's buying is still based on a simple extrapolation of (unchanged) sales and on the correction factor. The range of the inventory error to be reversed by the corrective orders has increased, and this alone amplifies the movement of orders placed.

Table 8-1
Data Input and Output for Eight Models of Sales-Orders-Inventory Relations

Variable and Model [a]	Period [b]													
	1	2	3	4	5	6	7	8	9	10	11	12	13	14
SALES (S) [c]														
I, Ib, Ic; II, IIb, IIc	100T	105	110	115	120	120	120P	115	110	105	100	100T	105	110
Ia	100T	105	112	125P	115	110	100T	105	112					
IIa	100	105	112	120P	115	110	100T	105	112					
NEW ORDERS PLACED (OP)														
I	100	110	115	120	125P	120	120	110	105	100	95T	100	100	115
Ib	100	110	125	135	135P	120	105	95	95T	100	100	100	110	125
Ic	100	110	120	125	130P	125	120	110	100	95	90T	95	110	120
II	100	120	125	130	135P	120	120	100	95	90	85T	100	120	125
IIb	100	120	145	155P	145	110	85	75T	85	100	100	100	120	145
IIc	100	120	130	135	140P	125	120	100	90	85	80T	95	120	130
Ia	100	110	119	138P	111	102	90T	110	119					
IIa	100	120	133	144P	100	95	70T	120	133					
INVENTORY (F) [d]														
I	200	195	195	195	195T	200	200	205	205	205	205P	200	195	195
Ib	200	195	185	180T	185	200	215	220P	215	205	200	200	195	185
Ic	200	195	185	180	180T	185	195	205	215	220	220P	215	200	185
II	200	195T	205	215	225	240	240	245P	235	225	215	200	195T	205
IIb	200	195	185T	190	215	250	275P	270	245	215	200	200	195	185T
IIc	200	195	185T	190	200	215	235	245	255P	250	240	225	200	185T
Ia	200	195	193	187T	207	208	210P	195	193					
IIa	200	195T	203	216	245P	235	230	195T	203					
OUTSTANDING ORDERS (OU) [d]														
Ib	200	210	235	260	270P	255	225	200	190T	195	200	200	210	235
Ic	200	210	230	245	255	255P	245	230	210	195	185	185T	205	230
IIb	200	220	265	300	300P	255	195	160	160T	185	200	200	220	265
IIc	200	220	250	265	275P	265	245	220	190	175	165T	175	215	250

Notes to Table 8-1

P = peak; T = trough. In the case of high or low plateaus of equal value, the last standing is taken to be the peak or trough.

[a] The models are divided into three groups: (1) models I, Ib, and Ic; (2) models II, IIb, and IIc; and (3) models Ia and IIa. For definition and explanation of the relationships involved, see text.

[b] In each line, the series is carried through a sufficient number of periods to complete a full trough-to-trough or peak-to-peak cycle. Trends are not assumed, and the cycles (which are not necessarily symmetrical) are supposed to recur periodically without change. The series are shown for two periods after they regain their initial values. For the graphs of these series, see Chart 8-1.

[c] The sales variable is exogenous—a given input to each model. The other variables all depend on the levels and rates of change of sales in various combinations and with various lags.

[d] End of month.

The amplitude of the corrective orders, and therefore (given the course of sales) of total orders placed, will also be greater for a firm that chooses to have stocks change in proportion to sales than for a firm that wishes to keep stocks at a constant level. This is so because the former plans its ordering so as to provide not only for the replacement of what was sold last month but also for the replenishment or reduction of the stock to the desired ratio $\overline{F/S} = \mu$. In model II, the corrective factor C_t is equal, not to ΔS_t as in model I, but to $(\mu + 1)$ ΔS_t, or in our illustrative case, $3\Delta S_t$.[3] The multiplier $(\mu + 1)$ is necessarily positive and larger than unity; therefore, the excess of the amplitude of OP over that of S must be greater in model II than in model I.

Orders placed will lead sales if the latter show retardations, i.e., ΔS turning earlier than S, for then C will show the same early timing as ΔS, causing OP to lead S. Accordingly, Chart 8-1 shows that new orders lead sales at either turn in each of the models, except in Ia and IIa where there is no sales retardation and therefore OP and S have coincident timing.

In models Ib and IIb, the attempts to adjust the inventory to the

[3] From

$$F_t = F_{t-1} + OP_{t-1} + S_t$$

and

$$OP_{t-1} = S_{t-1} + C_{t-1} = S_{t-1} + \mu S_{t-1} - F_{t-1},$$

we obtain by substitution $F_t = (1 + \mu)S_{t-1} - S_t$; and

$$C_t = \mu S_t - (1 + \mu)S_{t-1} + S_t = (1 + \mu)(S_t - S_{t-1}).$$

desired level are made only through current corrective orders without regard to the effect of orders that have already been issued and are still to be delivered. But Ruth Mack's study of the practices in the shoe trade supports the view that businessmen will not order in any given month the whole amount by which the actual stock fell short of the desired stock (or cancel outstanding orders to the extent of the full excess of the desired over the actual stock). Instead, they will take account of those outstanding orders that they have placed previously, with the intention of raising or reducing inventory to the desired level.[4] For example, C_t will then no longer be just $200 - F_t$ as in models I, Ia, and Ib, but will instead equal $(200 - F_t) - C_{t-1}$. This is the assumption embodied in model Ic. Similarly, in IIc the inventory error $(2S - F_t)$ is offset, not by C_t (as in II, IIa, and IIb), but rather by $C_t + C_{t-1}$.

As a result of this allowance for outstanding orders, the movement of OP is somewhat smoothed and its amplitude reduced. The lead of OP at turns in S may also be shortened a little (compare models Ic and IIc with Ib and IIb, respectively).

The only substantial body of direct data on orders placed and outstanding is found in the Federal Reserve Board reports on merchandizing activities of department stores. A comparison of new orders issued by the department stores (OP) with sales of the same stores (S) shows that: (1) The short-term fluctuations in OP are always much larger than those in S; and (2) the timing of OP and S is roughly synchronous but OP sometimes leads S by short intervals.[5] These findings are broadly consistent with what the model relationships would lead one to expect.

Stocks (F) definitely lag behind sales in all our models. Where constant inventory is desired (I–Ic), the lags are so long that F and S frequently move in opposite directions. Where planned inventory is proportional to sales (II–IIc), the lags are shorter, and the relation is more positive. The relations between stocks and outstanding (and new) orders are essentially inverted (see Chart 8-1).

[4] See Ruth P. Mack, *Consumption and Business Fluctuations: A Case Study of the Shoe, Leather, Hide Sequence*, New York, NBER, 1956.

[5] See Ruth P. Mack and Victor Zarnowitz, "Cause and Consequence of Changes in Retailers' Buying," *American Economic Review*, March 1958, Table 1, p. 26. Some more up-to-date charts of the department store series can be found in Ruth P. Mack, "Changes in Ownership of Purchased Materials," in Joint Economic Committee, *Inventory Fluctuations and Economic Stabilization*, 87th Cong., 1st sess., 1961, Part II, pp. 77 and 81.

Stocks undoubtedly lag behind sales in the department store data: They lagged at each of the six turns in sales in 1941–54. But the lags were not long (they averaged 2.3 months), and the relation was basically positive rather than inverted.[6] Relative to orders placed and outstanding, stocks show longer lags and correspondingly somewhat stronger inverted characteristics. Here the evidence is less favorable to our models but on the whole still not inconsistent with them.

Factors Influencing Purchases and Stocks of Materials

Consider now the purchase of goods for use in production rather than resale. Inventory of purchased materials (M) increases when orders for materials placed by the firm (OM) are filled, that is, are translated into deliveries to the firm (DM). Inventory M decreases when materials are withdrawn as input for production (IN). Therefore,

$$M_t = M_{t-1} + DM_t - IN_t. \tag{1}$$

If the materials are supplied with delivery lag k, then $OM_{t-k} = DM_t$; so

$$M_t = M_{t-1} + OM_{t-k} - IN_t. \tag{1a}$$

Outstanding orders for materials (OUM) increase (decrease) when orders placed exceed (fall short of) receipts, that is,

$$OUM_t = OUM_{t-1} + OM_t - DM_t. \tag{2}$$

Substituting the order terms from (2) for DM_t in (1), one gets

$$M_t = M_{t-1} + OUM_{t-1} - OUM_t + OM_t - IN_t. \tag{3}$$

Following Ruth Mack, the sum of inventory and outstanding orders for materials will be called the "ownership" of purchased materials. Let this aggregate of stocks on hand and on order be denoted as $OWM_t = M_t + OUM_t$. Then (3) can be rewritten as

$$OWM_t = OWM_{t-1} + OM_t - IN_t. \tag{3a}$$

Definitional equations such as these of course tell us nothing directly about human behavior or testable economic relationships, but they can help to identify the roles of the variables concerned and to avoid some omissions and inconsistencies. Thus (3) and (3a) suggest that it is not

---

[6] Mack and Zarnowitz, "Cause and Consequence."

only the levels and changes of stocks on hand that matter in the analysis of investment in purchased-materials inventories, but also the levels and changes of stocks on order (outstanding purchase orders).[7]

The models of the preceding section suggest that sales-related goals and variables have a central role in shaping the changes in inventories. While sales have been treated as exogenous, this is clearly not necessary; for example, sales expectations based on past sales behavior could well be explicitly introduced.[8] In the equations for materials, it is the productive inputs (IN) that have a role analogous to that of sales (S) in the earlier models. The materials stock (M) here corresponds to the "product inventory" (F) there, and the orders variables, OM and OUM, correspond to OP and OU, respectively. By substituting M for F, etc., the models could, *mutatis mutandis*, be adapted to reflect the relations among materials stocks, inputs, and orders. The magnification and acceleration effects would then be observed in the comparison of movements in IN and OM; also, stocks on order would again be found to move ahead of stocks on hand.

The rates of utilization for materials (IN) depend primarily on the planned production and its requirements. In manufacture to order, the scheduling of production is geared to orders received, their terms of delivery, and the progress of work on them: in other words, to the relevant dimensions of the firm's unfilled commitments to its customers. Manufacturers' shipments are closely correlated with output, and they can be fairly well estimated as weighted totals of past, and perhaps also current, inflows of new orders (Chapter 5). Hence, these order receipts, N_{t-i}, along with the distribution of the product delivery lags i, provide the main guide to the estimates of future output and of the associated materials inputs (IN).

In production to stock, sales anticipations S^a are presumably the main factor in short-term production planning. While "autonomous" expectations based on some "inside knowledge," guesswork, hopes, and the like, are probably often involved in the formation of S^a, the major observable determinant here is past sales experience. That is,

[7] This point received early and strong recognition in the writings of Ruth P. Mack (see notes 4 and 5, above).

[8] In a "complete" macro model, sales would be taken to depend on total output or income, and a feedback effect of inventory investment on sales and income would be included. Such models have been developed in the basic and influential articles by Lloyd A. Metzler, "The Nature and Stability of Inventory Cycles," *Review of Economic Statistics*, August 1941, and "Factors Governing the Length of Inventory Cycles," *ibid.*, February 1947; and Ragnar Nurkse, "The Cyclical Pattern of Inventory Investment," *Quarterly Journal of Economics*, August 1952.

S^a is likely to be, in large part, some extrapolation of actual sales, that is, of the value of new orders received and shipped ($S_{t-i} = N_{t-i}$). Once more, then, IN is seen as a function of N_{t-i}; but new orders clearly make a much less dependable guide here, where they are filled from stock rather than from future output.[9] In production to stock, errors of sales forecasts will inevitably occur and they imply the existence of a passive or unintended component of the investment in materials (which, in turn, may give rise to corrective elements in materials purchasing). In contrast, errors of sales forecasts are nonexistent in the extreme case of pure production to order.

Given the state of technology in the broad sense (involving business organization as well as physical production and transportation constraints), the aggregate stock of materials on hand and on order can be viewed as being in the first place a positive function of the rates of scheduled output. Thus a certain level of materials "ownership," say $\overline{OWM}$, will be necessary to maintain a certain rate of production, say $\bar{Z}_t$. In this hypothetical stable state, purchase orders would be placed at a rate, $\overline{OM}_t$, that balances IN_t, the required rate for the input of materials into production or, more strictly, the transformation of materials into "goods in process" [see equation (3a), above]. The positive association between the desired levels of OWM and Z implies that net investment in materials stocks on hand and on order is similarly related to the rate of change in output.

Even in this rudimentary form, the above argument is not simply equivalent to the accelerator hypothesis that links inventory investment to output changes. It is consistent with a lag of materials stocks behind the level of output and with a lag of investment in these stocks behind the change in output. Such lags may occur because of delays in the recognition of changes in the demand for output (in production to stock) or because of delays in filling the purchase orders by the suppliers of materials (in production to stock or to order). Stocks on order would not be expected to show the same lagging tendencies, since they can probably be adjusted more easily and promptly than stocks on hand.

Moreover, there are other important aspects and motivations of inventory investment. The observed changes of inventory in successive short periods may represent only partial adjustments toward the "de-

[9] Compare the discussion of sales anticipations and the predictive properties of new orders in the last section of Chapter 2.

sired" inventory level because of the effects of uncertainty and the costs involved in making larger and more abrupt changes. This notion, when combined with the view of the desired inventory as essentially a function of sales or output, leads to the "flexible accelerator" models that have been widely used in recent aggregative studies of inventory behavior. But intended inventory can be related to other variables as well, notably the expected changes in prices and availability of the goods to be purchased and the cost of financing and holding the inventory (usually represented by short-term interest rates).

To sum up, what happens to the stocks of materials on hand and on order (M and OUM) depends upon: (1) the demand for the outputs of the firms that purchase M; this can be represented by some weighted function of the N_{t-i} terms; (2) the reactions of the purchasing firms to changes in N; these are expressed in OM, the flow of orders placed by the firms with the suppliers of materials; (3) the performance of the suppliers, as reflected in the relation between OM and the deliveries of materials (= materials orders received, DM); the delivery lags involved (k) may vary with business conditions. Of the variables listed, OM is the most readily controlled. Consequently, it reflects best the intentions of the firms that invest in materials.

A firm needs to hold some inventory of materials to be competitively efficient in production; to keep the delivery periods (i) for its products reasonably short; to handle discontinuities in the flow of demand and output; and to be protected against irregularities in the performance of the suppliers (such as delays in delivery, i.e., increases in k). Our understanding of how each of these motives works would be greatly enhanced by knowledge of the relations between sales orders received and purchase orders placed. Unfortunately, data that are essential for the study of these relations are lacking, since statistics on orders placed and outstanding, by industries or product categories, are generally not available.[10]

The Role of Changes in Supply Conditions

Unfilled orders for the market categories of "materials, supplies, and intermediate products" equaled from one to three months' worth of current shipments in the period 1953–66 (see Chart 6-6 and related

[10] The argument that purchase orders data are greatly needed for a more fruitful analysis and better understanding of inventory fluctuations has been made repeatedly and forcefully by Ruth Mack. For the most recent formulation, see Ruth P. Mack, *Information, Expectations, and Inventory Fluctuation: A Study of Materials Stock on Hand and on Order*, New York, NBER, 1967, p. 293.

text). Evidence based on timing comparisons of new orders and shipments (Chapter 4) supports these indications of generally prompt availability of materials supplied by the domestic factories. Raw materials from domestic nonmanufacturing sources can apparently also in large part be procured without major delay.[11] Imported goods and commodities of agricultural origin have on the whole larger or more variable delivery lags, but these categories carry much less weight than the materials from domestic and industrial sources.

It appears, therefore, that purchases of goods to be processed involve for the most part relatively short delivery periods; to a large extent, they are serviced promptly from the seller's stock. This is not surprising, since such goods are as a rule highly standardized. Similar statements can also be made about most of the goods purchased to be resold. The U/S ratios are indeed extremely low (less than 1) for the market category of "home goods, apparel, and consumer staples" (Chapter 6). Consistent evidence of the shortness of the average delivery periods on goods bought by retailers is provided by department-store data.[12]

Moreover, timely delivery of standardized goods bought to be processed or resold is enforced by competitive conditions. Efficient operation of the buyer's business will often require that he be assured of prompt supplies. There is, therefore, strong demand for these goods to be available when needed. If that demand cannot be satisfied by a seller, he may well lose the order to a competitor who can.

An important implication is that purchasing for inventory is likely to be significantly influenced by the conditions of supply as viewed and anticipated by the buyer. He will endeavor to avoid any unusually long delivery delays for his inputs, as well as price increases, which he knows are often associated with tightened supply conditions. If delays and difficulties in getting supplies should arise, this is likely to be signalized by an accumulation of unfilled orders on the suppliers' books. Buyers may watch for such signs, and try to place additional orders in time to protect themselves against the possibility of shortages and price increases in the near future. But in the aggregate, the process can become cumulative and self-defeating. In a full-grown expansion, as

[11] On this and the following statement, see Moses Abramovitz, *Inventories and Business Cycles with Special Reference to Manufacturers' Inventories,* New York, NBER, 1950, Chap. 9.

[12] On the average, in 1941–54, receipts of (deliveries of merchandise to) department stores lagged behind new orders placed by these stores by a little less than one month. See Mack and Zarnowitz, "Cause and Consequence," Table 1, p. 26.

suppliers approach capacity operations they begin to quote longer "lead times" to their customers. To the extent that the latter respond by placing more orders in an attempt to increase their stocks on order, their actions, designed to alleviate the problem for the individual firm, are apt to aggravate the total problem. As the additional orders only succeed in swelling the suppliers' backlogs, they actually result in an intensified excess demand situation of which the increases in backlogs, delivery lags, and prices are primary symptoms.

However, some stabilizing forces are also at work in this process. Buyers basically prefer shorter delivery periods, and the competition among producer-sellers works toward satisfying this preference. Price increases may deter some buying. Moreover, just as the buyers watch the backlogs of the suppliers, so may the latter watch the materials stocks of the buyers. When these stocks run low, suppliers are likely to expect an expansion of customer orders and might prepare for it in various ways. Production to stock, in anticipation of the rise in orders, would be one such way, and would have a stabilizing effect.[13]

During contractions, conversely, sales decrease and with them the desired levels of stocks on hand and on order. Firms accordingly reduce their current purchases, thereby gradually liquidating their outstanding orders, which are also the unfilled commitments of their suppliers. The delivery periods are thus cut back to their normal levels, which for much of inventory buying means immediate availability or very short lead times. As the downward adjustment of stocks is completed, there is no more reason for further reduction of purchases, unless sales continue declining. But in the early stages of contraction, the cessation of advance buying will have motivated some inventory disinvestment and contributed to the business decline.

The interaction of changes in buyers' anticipations and ordering and of changes in supply conditions has long been neglected by the inventory theory. The theme has, however, received considerable attention in some recent studies.[14]

---

[13] It should be noted, however, that large customer stocks are a phenomenon associated with production to order. (The major example is steel products, which are largely manufactured to order and the inventories of which are heavily concentrated in user hands.) In industries that are predominantly engaged in manufacture to order, low levels of customer-held stocks may not be a sufficient inducement for the producers to switch, on a large scale, to production to stock.

[14] In addition to the previously cited books by Mack and the article by Mack and Zarnowitz, see Thomas M. Stanback, Jr., *Postwar Cycles in Manufacturers' Inventories*, New York, NBER, 1962.

The Effects of Backlog Changes

The preceding discussion of the effect of changes in supply conditions and anticipations on buying of materials and stocks in trade would
lead one to predict a positive association between backlog changes and
inventory investment. Such a relation has indeed been repeatedly observed, but in a form which admits (or even demands) a different interpretation.

Manufacturers who accumulate unfilled orders can look forward to
increased sales and, to the extent that the backlogs represent firm
commitments, will indeed feel assured of a growing amount of business
in hand. It may therefore be expected that a rise in their backlogs will
induce producers working to order to step up their buying of materials
as input requirements increase with higher output and sales rates
ahead.

It is necessary to distinguish between this "backlog effect" proper
and the "supply conditions effect" discussed previously. The former
refers to inventory investment by manufacturers working to order;
the latter to inventory investment by those who buy from such manufacturers (including, of course, some manufacturers who fall into the
same class, inasmuch as they purchase materials from one another).
The hypothesis that inventory investment is a positive function of the
rate of change in backlogs is really an extension of the hypothesis that
inventory investment is a positive function of the rate of change in
sales. This becomes clear when the backlog is conceived as representing future sales. The sales-to-inventory relationship, however, may be
rather loose for manufacturers who receive orders in advance of production, precisely because of the particular importance here of the
backlog-to-inventory relationship. On the other hand, the proposition
that inventory investment depends on supply conditions as viewed by
the buyer is clearly quite different in nature from an accelerator-type
approach, whether this implies the central role of sales changes or
emphasizes backlog changes.

In regressions based on highly aggregative data, e.g., for all manufacturing or manufacturing and trade, the presence of a substantial
reaction of inventory investment to changes in unfilled orders can reflect either the backlog effect, the supply conditions effect, or—most
likely—some combination of both. The two effects work in the same
direction, since the unfilled sales orders of the suppliers are, of course,

the outstanding purchase orders of their customers, and the aggregative figures reflect actions of suppliers and customers alike.

Disaggregation can help to clarify the situation. For example, when inventory investment of the primary metals producers is regressed on the change in backlogs for primary metals products, it is the backlog effect that is directly represented. On the other hand, when inventory investment by merchants is regressed on the change in backlogs held by the manufacturers from whom the merchants buy, it is the supply conditions effect that is directly aimed at. It must be realized, however, that this approach is unlikely to reduce the difficulty altogether. This is true not only because little is known about orders, sales, and inventories by vertical stages of production; even with more and better data, a formidable problem would remain because inventory and backlog changes for buyers and sellers (i.e., at the adjoining vertical production stages) appear to be highly intercorrelated.[15]

Goods in Process and Finished Stocks, by Type of Production

Goods-in-process inventories (G) increase when materials are absorbed into the productive process, which occurs at the rate IN_t, and when labor and capital inputs are combined with the materials input, which results in the value-added rate VA_t. The stock G decreases when goods in process are transformed into finished goods, which occurs at the output rate Z_t. Hence,

$$G_t = G_{t-1} + IN_t + VA_t - Z_t. \tag{4}$$

As suggested earlier, the rates of utilization of materials (IN_t) depend on the rates of output presently planned, which, in production to order, can be estimated from new orders received (N_{t-i}). In production to stock, the main determinant will be sales anticipations (S^a), but these may themselves be strongly influenced by the flow of orders received and shipped in the recent past. It seems reasonable to assume that VA_t would also depend to a large extent on the same output and proxy variables.

In production to order, the values of current output and of shipments can be taken to be equal. It follows that $\Delta G_t (= G_t - G_{t-1})$ should de-

---

[15] Thus, as noted in Chapter 7, the high correlation of the Chicago PAA indexes of backlog diffusion and vendor performance suggests a close association between unfilled orders of the buying and selling companies.

pend positively on new orders received and about to be processed and negatively on $S_t \simeq Z_t$, according to (4) and the preceding considerations.

In production to stock, ΔG_t is presumably a positive function of S^a, which in turn may be approximated by $S_{t-1} = N_{t-1}$. It does not seem likely that a negative net relation will be found between ΔG_t and S_t. In industries working to stock, the time required for production is often short, and it may be less than the unit period of the analysis. Stocks of goods in process are then likely to be small relative to the rates per unit period of output and shipments, that is, their turnover would be high. The observed net effect upon ΔG_t of S_t would in such cases probably be positive, though possibly weak.

Passive inventory investment due to unforeseen changes in demand is presumably a component of net changes in goods-in-process stocks as well as in materials stocks. When $S_t < S_t^a$ this unintended investment is positive, i.e., actual inventory is greater than planned. When $S_t > S_t^a$, unintended investment is negative. Full and prompt adjustments of output could conceivably avert such deviations of actual from planned inventory, but production may not be flexible enough to permit this. Even if it were, such adjustments may be too costly. In these cases, some unplanned inventory changes will be tolerated in preference to unduly large or abrupt output changes.

It is probably quite common for firms to attempt to correct excessive deviations of actual from planned inventories by adjustments in the rate of their purchase orders. Corrective action of this type is clearly restricted to the stage of materials. It appears that the opportunities for stock adjustments in the goods-in-process stage are much more limited. To a large extent (though not completely), the size and composition of goods-in-process inventories are determined by production needs.

To the firm that produces in anticipation of a certain level of market demand, the passive component of inventory investment is most clearly visible in the finished-goods stage: When sales exceed (fall short of) the firm's expectations, the actual stock of finished products (Q) must be correspondingly smaller (greater) than the stock that was expected or planned. At the same time, it is also here that the implications for inventory behavior of the distinction between production to stock and production to order are most evident. In pure production to order, no finished goods are held for sale; here Q consists only of sold products in transit — temporarily stored by the producer-seller or on the way to the buyer. Such stocks exist merely as a by-product of the activity of the firms concerned; the latter do not *plan* investment in finished-goods inventory. For an expanding industry working to order, these stocks are likely to be growing, too, but their movements, apart from such trends, would probably be random or irregular.

In contrast, firms that produce for expected market demand would have, as a rational goal, a *desired* finished-goods inventory consistent with their sales anticipations (although, in any short unit period, the adjustment of actual Q toward the intended level may be only partial). In addition, investment in finished stocks (ΔQ) would here probably contain a passive component reflecting unforeseen changes in sales, as already noted.

To conclude this part of the chapter, analytical considerations suggest strongly that distinctions by type of production (to stock or to order) and by stage of fabrication (materials, goods-in-process, finished goods) are associated with important differences in patterns and determinants of inventory behavior. Different models of inventory investment are therefore appropriate for several different categories of stocks that are defined by this double classification. In much of the recent work on inventory behavior, however, the need for such disaggregation is not fully recognized, and attention focuses directly on aggregate inventories. A summary review of this work follows.

Recent Work on Inventory Investment:
A Survey of Findings

Regression Studies of Aggregate Inventories

The apparently large role of inventories in postwar business cycles stimulated much research in this area. The output of this work consists in large part of quarterly regressions based on comprehensive aggregates, and Table 8-2 assembles a large number of such estimates from several published studies.[16]

[16] Because the authors worked independently, the equations often overlap in various ways. Although one could argue that some coordination of the effort would have substantially increased the net value of the work, inferences to this effect based solely on the collected statistical results can be exaggerated: It may be more fruitful to have differing interpretations of similar relationships.

The table indicates a remarkable degree of consensus among the different studies in the selection of the explanatory variables: The most commonly used are levels and changes of sales and unfilled orders. Their treatment varies mainly in that they are taken either with coincident timing or with different leads. Lagged inventory levels and changes are also often included. Most of the studies are based on deflated data but a few use current-dollar series. As a rule the data are seasonally adjusted.

Most of the equations incorporate the flexible-accelerator and buffer-stock concepts developed in earlier literature.[17] Thus, common to the models of Darling and Lovell is the basic assumption that the desired (equilibrium) inventories are a function of sales and that deviations between desired and actual stocks determine, with a lag, the rate of inventory investment. The adjustment of inventories toward the equilibrium level is partial in any period. However, the desired inventory usually depends also on other variables, notably unfilled orders.

The actual stock that is compared with the desired one refers to the time at which the decision regarding inventory investment is made; it is usually taken as of the end of the preceding (or the beginning of the current) period. On this approach, the lagged inventory term will appear with a negative coefficient in the inventory investment equation, but with a positive coefficient in the inventory level equation.[18]

In Table 8-2, the signs of the coefficients of lagged inventory are indeed consistent with this expectation in every case (Table 8-2, part I, column 4, and parts III and IV, column 7). The coefficients are

---

[17] The main references here are to the work of Metzler (see note 8, above) and Richard M. Goodwin, "Secular and Cyclical Aspects of the Multiplier and Accelerator," in *Income, Employment, and Public Policy: Essays in Honor of Alvin H. Hansen*, New York, 1948.

[18] Suppose that firms, on the average, plan to eliminate in each period a fraction (δ) of the difference between the actual stock (H) and the anticipated desired stock (H_t^a). The latter is a function of anticipated sales (S_t^a), which will as a rule deviate from actual sales by a forecasting error ($S_t^a - S_t$). Then the intended inventory investment would depend on the discrepancy between the desired and the actual stock, and the unintended or passive inventory investment would depend on the error of sales anticipations:

$$\Delta H_t = \delta(H_t^a - H_{t-1}) + \lambda(S_t^a - S_t) + u_t.$$

The coefficient of the previous level of stock (H_{t-1}) should thus be negative ($-\delta$) in the inventory investment equation, and positive ($1 - \delta$) in the corresponding equation for the level of inventory. Cf. Michael C. Lovell, "Factors Determining Manufacturing Inventory Investment," in Joint Economic Committee, *Inventory Fluctuations*, Part I, p. 127; and Lovell, "Determinants of Inventory Investment," in *Models of Income Determination*, Studies in Income and Wealth, Vol. 28, Princeton for NBER, 1964, pp. 179 and 194.

Table 8-2
Regressions of Inventory Levels and Changes on Selected Variables, Total Nonfarm, Manufacturing, and Trade Inventories, Quarterly, 1947–61

Regression[a]	Dependent Variable[b]	Constant Term (1)	(2)	(3)	(4)	(5)	(6)	(7)	(8)	R² (9)	Stand. Error of Est. (10)	Durbin Watson Statistic (11)	Period[c] (12)
			— Regression Coefficients[b]										
I. TOTAL NONFARM INVENTORY INVESTMENT			S_G^*	ΔU^*	H_{-1}^*	ΔP	ΔS_G^*	U_{-1}^*	ΔH_{-1}^*				
Fromm (F)	ΔH^*	−29.4	.460 (.137)	.166 (.051)	−.731 (.224)					.781	1.912[d]	1.48	1953–60
Klein (K)[e]	ΔH^*	−48.4 (13.5)	.268 (.071)	.203 (.047)	−.300 (.06)	269.3 (75)							1948–58
Duesenberry-Eckstein-Fromm (DEF)[f]	ΔH^*	8.5	.295 (.078)	.771 (.139)	−.947 (.267)		−.333 (.107)	.115 (.054)	.341 (.115)	.81	1.74	2.27	1948–57
Lovell (L)[g]	ΔH^*	2.5 (2.9)	GNP^* .328 (.040)		H_{-1}^* −.407 (.048)		ΔGNP^* −.137 (.092)	U^* .043 (.007)		.736			1947–59
II. MANUFACTURING AND TRADE			$(H/S)_{-1/2}^b$	$(N/S)_{-1}$	$(U/S)_{-1/2}^b$	X_n	$\Delta \bar{P}/\bar{P}$	$\bar{L}_{-1}$					
Terleckyj T1	$(\Delta H/H)^i$	−121.13	−18.48 (3.84)	72.51 (9.73)		−.028 (.461)	.788 (.111)	−.026 (.310)		.91			1948–60
T2	$(\Delta H/H)^i$	−17.64	−25.26 (3.07)	55.31 (7.18)	2.88 (0.74)					.89	1.12[k]		1948–60
T3	$(\Delta H/H)^j$	−14.59	−11.26 (2.33)	30.75 (5.52)	1.88 (0.57)					.78	.87[k]		1948–60

362

III. MANUFACTURING

Smith-Paradiso

Model	Dep.	const	S	S_{-1}	S_{-2}	S_{-3}	ΔU_{-1}	H_{-2}	R^2	Period
SP1	H	.760			1.811	.770			.96	1948–61
SP2	H	.801	.465	.367	.270				.98	1948–61
SP3	ΔH	.381		.327			.233		.64	1948–61
SP4	ΔH	−.038					.149	−.173	.80	1948–61

Lovell

Model	Dep.	const	S^*	ΔS^*	U^*	ΔU^*	$\Delta P/P$	H^*_{-1}	R^2	DW	Period
L1	H^*	3066.	−.167 (.033)	−.170 (.047)	.062 (.008)		−1.685 (.410)	.570 (.051)	.993	1.98	1948–55
L2	ΔH^*	−1.47 (0.62)	.122 (.024)	−.012 (.038)	.014 (.005)	−.002 (.024)		−.165 (.035)	.53	1.30	1948–55

Darling

Model	Dep.	const	S^*_{-1}	U^*_{-1}	ΔU^*_{-1}	ΔH^*_{-1}	H^*_{-1}	T	R^2		DW	Period
D1	ΔH^*	−0.432	.136 (.030)				−.190 (.041)		.310	.723		1948–60
D2	ΔH^*	6.297	.040 (.020)	.035 (.011)	.055 (.028)	.383 (.086)	−.265 (.076)	.062 (.022)	.811	.373	2.105	1948–60
D3	ΔH^*	6.850	.060 (.020)	.038 (.010)	.061 (.018)	.373 (.129)	−.313 (.059)	.067 (.019)	.955	.145	2.199	1952–58

Model	Dep.	const	S_{-1}	ΔU_{-1}	H_{-2}	R^2	DW	Period
D4[l]	ΔH	−0.387	.415 (.044)	.324 (.054)	−.212 (.022)	.945	1.85	1947–58

Kareken-Solow (K-S)[m]

Model	Dep.	const	S	H_{-1}	i_{-1}	R^2	Period
	H	−1.192	.224 (.027)	.762 (.048)	−1.155 (.405)	.994	1947–60

IV. TRADE

Darling[n]

Model	Dep.	const	S^*	CP	i	$\Delta P/P_{+1}$	H^*_{-1}	ΔH^*_{-1}	R^2		Period
D5	ΔH^*	.268	.096 (.026)	.018 (.010)	−.279 (.202)	12.9 (7.8)	−.243 (.065)	.142 (.146)	.510	.261	1951–60
D6	ΔH^*	.190	.073 (.016)	.025 (.009)		15.4 (7.6)	−.241 (.065)		.466	.273	1951–60

Notes to Table 8-2

ᵃ All regression equations, except the six identified in notes e, f, g, m, n, and o, are from the following articles in Joint Economic Committee, *Inventory Fluctuations and Economic Stabilization,* 87th Cong., 1st sess., 1961:

"Analysis of Business Inventory Movements in the Postwar Period," prepared under the general direction of Louis J. Paradiso (Part I by Mabel A. Smith), *ibid.,* Part I, p. 158, Table 2.

Michael C. Lovell, "Factors Determining Manufacturing Inventory Investment," *ibid.,* Part II, pp. 129–30, 143 (Table I), and 145 (Table III).

Paul G. Darling, "Inventory Fluctuations and Economic Instability: An Analysis Based on the Postwar Economy," *ibid.,* Part III, pp. 27 (Table 3) and 37 (Table 5).

Nestor E. Terleckyj assisted by Alfred Tella, "Measures of Inventory Conditions," *ibid.,* Part II, pp. 189–90.

Gary Fromm, "Inventories, Business Cycles, and Economic Stabilization," *ibid.,* Part IV, p. 71.

ᵇ Wherever available, standard errors are given beneath regression coefficients. Symbols for variables are as follows:

Time subscripts: -1 and -2 indicate leads of one or two quarters ($t-1$, $t-2$). Variables that refer to the current quarter t (timing simultaneous with that of the dependent variable) carry no time subscripts. An asterisk identifies deflated variable (price deflators, 1954 = 100, are used in most cases).

H = inventories at end of quarter.

Δ = change (first difference) in the given variable; e.g.,

ΔH = change in inventories during quarter, $H_t - H_{t-1}$.

S = sales during quarter.

U = unfilled orders.

GNP = GNP in billions of 1954 dollars.

ΔP = change in the implicit GNP deflator, 1954 = 100.

$\Delta \bar{P}/\bar{P}$ = percentage change in the index of industrial wholesale prices, $(\bar{P}_t - \bar{P}_{t-1})/\bar{P}_t$.

$\Delta H/H$ = percentage change of manufacturing and trade inventories less inventory valuation adjustments.

H/S = ratio of inventories to sales.

N/S = ratio of new orders to sales. (In trade, new orders are assumed to equal sales.)

U/S = ratio of unfilled orders to sales.

X_H = percentage change in inventories attributable to changing mix (composition of business).

S_G = final sales of goods (GNP accounts in 1954 dollars).

$\bar{i}$ = interest rate on four-to-six-month prime commercial paper; average for the first quarter of the six-month unit period.

i = bank rate of interest on short-term business loans, average for nineteen large cities (per cent).

CP = percentage of capacity output utilized in manufacturing (McGraw-Hill).

$\Delta P/P(\ )$ = percentage change in the wholesale price index during quarter $t(0)$ or $t + 1(+1)$.

T = time trend.

ᶜ Identifies the first and last year for which data were used. These years are not necessarily completely covered.

ᵈ Billions of current dollars at annual rates.

ᵉ See Lawrence R. Klein, "A Postwar Quarterly Model: Description and Applications," *Models of Income Determination*, Studies in Income and Wealth, Vol. 28, Princeton for NBER, 1964, e.g., (6), p. 16. This equation is part of a large interdependent system. The method of estimation is limited information, maximum likelihood. The correlation coefficient $\bar{R} = .99$ (stock form); it is computed as

$$\sqrt{1 - \frac{\Sigma Z^2}{T - m} \frac{T - 1}{\Sigma x^2}},$$

where Z is the residual, x is the dependent variable, and m is the number of parameters in the equation. Unlike elsewhere in this section, farm inventories are not excluded here.

[f] See James S. Duesenberry, Otto Eckstein, and Gary Fromm, "A Simulation of the United States Economy in Recession," *Econometrica*, October 1960, p. 798.

[g] See Michael C. Lovell, "Determinants of Inventory Investment," in *Models of Income Determination* (see note e, above), equation (2.15), p. 186.

[h] Ratio at the beginning of the period.

[i] Six-month changes.

[j] Three-month changes.

[k] Percentage points. Unbiased estimates.

[l] See Paul G. Darling, "Manufacturers' Inventory Investment, 1947–1958," *American Economic Review*, December 1959, pp. 950–63.

[m] See John Kareken and Robert M. Solow, "Lags in Fiscal and Monetary Policy," in Commission on Money and Credit, *Stabilization Policies*, Research Study One, Part I, Englewood Cliffs, N.J., 1963, equation (7), p. 43.

[n] See Paul G. Darling and Michael C. Lovell, "Factors Influencing Investment in Inventories," in Duesenberry et al., eds., *Brookings Quarterly Econometric Model of the United States*, equations (4.12) and (4.13), p. 151.

generally rather small in absolute terms, varying from −.165 to −.407 in the investment equations.[19]

Reaction coefficients of 0.2 to 0.4 suggest that from about one-fifth to two-fifths of the discrepancy between desired and actual inventory would be eliminated each quarter if no further change occurred in sales (or, generally, in the determinants of the desired stocks). This raises a doubt and a question: Why should the adjustments of inventories to the desired levels be so painfully slow, resulting in such inordinately large unintended stocks?[20] It should be remembered that

[19] The two apparent exceptions are in equations F and DEF, where the estimated coefficients of lagged inventory are as large as −.731 and −.947, respectively. However, the flows are measured at annual rates here, not as absolute quarterly changes as in the other regressions; hence, these figures should be divided by 4 for comparability, which results in estimates of −.185 and −.195, respectively. Cf. James S. Duesenberry, Otto Eckstein, and Gary Fromm, "A Simulation of the United States Economy in Recession," *Econometrica*, October 1960, p. 796.

[20] See the calculated "surplus inventory" series in Lovell, "Determinants," pp. 187–88, for equation L in Part I of Table 8-2. Here, the coefficient of H_{t-1}^* is on the high side of the estimates (0.407), but the surplus inventory figures are still relatively very large (most often absolutely greater than the corresponding values of actual inventory investment).

the estimates refer to aggregates that include not only the typically lagging finished-goods inventories of firms selling from stock but also purchased materials and goods-in-process stocks, which should be geared much more closely to sales and production. These results, then, seem to me rather suspect: They could be underestimating the speed of adjustment because of a misspecification of the determinants of the "desired" inventory.

The principal factors used as such determinants are sales and unfilled orders. They are sometimes assigned leads relative to the dependent inventory variable but are often taken as simultaneous with the latter (compare equations D1–D3 with equations L1–L2). But actual sales are not yet known at the time when the firm decides upon the level of its output and any desired inventory change, except in production to order (where the known sales should be represented not by the current shipments, but by advance orders received). Hence, in principle, anticipated or ex-ante sales (S_t^a) should be used as the main determinant of the desired inventory, not the actual or ex-post sales (S_t). In short, unless sales are made in advance of production, they must be predicted. Usually, forecasts of sales will contain errors, and these are likely to result in some unintended or passive inventory investment.

If the forecasts were unbiased and their errors were random, a rationale would exist for the use of S_t as a surrogate measure of S_t^a for analytical purposes; and in this case the "passive" inventory component could itself be treated as random and incorporated in the residuals of the inventory equation.[21] But there is no firm theoretical or empirical basis for this approach. According to Nurkse, "if the cyclical variation in aggregate demand is not treated as a random perturbation, the passive component of inventory investment cannot be either." [22] Observations on sales anticipations are scanty, and studies based on them are on the whole rather inconclusive. However, even

[21] This approach is implicit in the inventory equation of the early aggregate model by Lawrence R. Klein (see his *Economic Fluctuations in the United States, 1921–41*, New York, 1950). Its logic and implications have been worked out by Edwin S. Mills in "Expectations, Uncertainty, and Inventory Fluctuations," *Review of Economic Studies*, No. 1, 1954–55, pp. 15–23, and in "The Theory of Inventory Decisions," *Econometrica*, April 1957.

[22] "Cyclical Pattern," p. 396. Nurkse recognizes that random shifts in demand from one product to another may make the passive inventory investment a random variable for individual firms or industries. But such changes "will be in opposite directions, tending in the aggregate to cancel out. In dealing with total inventory investment, the unintended change that remains cannot be due to such random intercommodity shifts, but can only stem from the expansion and contraction of demand in the aggregate. . . ."

the most favorable of the results obtained do not show anticipations to be so unbiased and efficient as to justify any confident use of realized sales as a proxy for expected sales.[23]

Under certain assumptions, the effect of errors in sales anticipations could be inferred approximately from the coefficient of the change in sales (ΔS_t) in the inventory equation.[24] In the simple case of naive expectations, $S_t^a = S_{t-1}$, that coefficient would measure directly the fraction of the forecasting error that results in inventory change.[25] More generally, if systematic expectational errors exist and give rise to passive inventory investment, then ΔS_t is likely to have a significant negative effect in inventory equations.

In Table 8-2, change-of-sales variables are included in five regressions; their coefficients are all negative but two are not significant (see in Part I, DEF and L; in Part III, L1, L2, and K-S). It must be remembered that these estimates refer to total inventories, aggregated across categories with different behavioral characteristics. The hypothesized relation between sales anticipation errors and buffer stocks seems primarily and directly applicable to finished-goods inventories; it can be extended by analogy and implication to goods-in-process and purchased materials, but there it may well be much less pertinent. More important, the hypothesis is definitely limited to industries working to stock, in anticipation of market demand.

The measured effects of the backlog factor are in general strong, ranking with those of sales. For example, according to the current-

[23] The new quarterly OBE series on manufacturers' sales expectations apparently work better than some of the old (and notoriously weak) anticipations data. However, for some industries, these series mainly reflect information conveyed by orders received and unfilled. Generally, their effective forecast span is short, and their contribution to estimated models of inventory generation is neither large nor well established. (See the last section of Chapter 2; also, M. C. Lovell, "Sales Anticipations, Planned Inventory Investment, and Realizations," and comments by M. Hastay and R. Eisner in *Determinants of Investment Behavior,* Universities–National Bureau Conference 18, New York, NBER, 1967.) I believe the conclusion I draw in the foregoing text is a fair inference from the materials presented in Albert A. Hirsch and Michael C. Lovell, *Sales Anticipations and Inventory Behavior,* New York, 1961.

[24] This will be so, for example, if the anticipated sales change represents a fraction of the actual change and the effects of current output and price adjustments are separately estimated or assumed to be negligible. See Lovell, "Determinants," pp. 203–204.

[25] Suppose that $H_t^a = \alpha + \beta S_t^a$. By substitution into the equation shown in note 18, above, one gets

$$\Delta H_t = \delta\alpha + (\delta\beta + \lambda)S_t^a - \lambda S_t - \delta H_{t-1} + u_t.$$

If $S_t^a = S_{t-1}$, this is equivalent to

$$\Delta H_t = \delta\alpha + \delta\beta S_{t-1} - \lambda(S_t - S_{t-1}) - \delta H_{t-1} + u_t.$$

If $S_t^a = S_t + v_t$, where v_t is random (as in the studies referred to in note 21), then

$$\Delta H_t = \delta\alpha + \delta\beta S_t - \delta H_{t-1} + (\delta\beta + \lambda)v_t + u_t.$$

dollar estimates SP3 and SP4, the change in manufacturers' unfilled orders alone accounts for 64 per cent of the variance in manufacturers' inventory investment in 1948–61; the addition of the prior sales change and inventory level raises this proportion to 80 per cent. In another study using deflated variables, a regression of inventory investment on prior sales change and inventory level yielded an R^2 of only .310, and the addition of the unfilled orders variables U^* and ΔU^*_{-1}, plus a ratchet term and trend factor, raised R^2 to .811 (equations D1 and D2). The role of unfilled orders is also important in the regressions for total or nonfarm inventory investment and for manufacturing and trade inventories combined (all the equations in Part I of Table 8-2 and, also, equations T2 and T3).[26]

The aggregative backlog-inventory relationship, although highly significant statistically, does not lend itself to a straightforward analytical interpretation. Since unfilled orders of sellers are also outstanding orders of buyers, their rise may stimulate inventory investment of buyers as well as sellers in two different ways. Aggregation over the stages of fabrication provides still another source of difficulty. An increase in unfilled orders is likely to stimulate buying of *materials* by those who are to fill the orders, but it will hardly be associated with an increase in the finished stocks of these producers. On the contrary, where backlogs accumulate so that production may be order-oriented, the need for finished inventory is reduced.

Other variables received considerably less attention and yielded results that seem partly negative but should probably be regarded rather as inconclusive. Lovell found no support for the hypothesis that actual price increases, by creating expectations of price rises, stimulate inventory investment; actually, the coefficient of $\Delta P/P$ in his equation L1 is negative. Darling did obtain positive coefficients for his proxy for price expectations (the proportionate change in the wholesale price index during the *approaching* quarter) in his study of trade inventories (equations D5 and D6).[27] One possible explanation for the negative results in the manufacturing equations is that the effect of the

---

[26] In the T equations, unfilled orders are used in the form of a ratio to sales. Also included is the ratio of new orders to sales, which is highly correlated with the *change* in unfilled orders. Terleckyj assumes that unfilled orders in trade are nil. His results raise a difficulty concerning the influence of sales (see Lovell, "Determinants," p. 185).

[27] Terleckyj also reports a significant positive coefficient for the concurrent relative change in the industrial price index, but not for the prior change. The use of undeflated data in his study might be an appreciable drawback in this context.

price change could not be separated from that of the change in unfilled orders. However, Klein reports significant positive associations between aggregate inventory investment and changes in both the GNP price deflator and unfilled orders (the price variable being taken without and the backlog variable with a lead; see equation K).

The Kareken-Solow equation based on undeflated data for manufacturing includes the interest rate on short-term bank loans to business with a significant coefficient that has the expected negative sign and denotes a small (−0.4) elasticity at the point of the means. The evidence on the effects of interest rates and liquidity factors assembled by McGouldrick is mixed and not encouraging.[28] In contrast to these studies, more promising indications of the role of financial variables in inventory determination are reported by Ta-Chung Liu[29] and Paul W. Kuznets.[30]

Major-Industry and Stage-of-Fabrication Estimates

Disaggregation by industry and stage of fabrication is not a frequent feature of regression studies of inventory behavior. Furthermore, disaggregation has for the most part been used in a very limited sense, with the same or very similar models being applied to the different sectors or categories of stocks.

Table 8-3 shows some further results of Lovell's 1961 study.[31] These

[28] See Paul F. McGouldrick, "The Impact of Credit Cost and Availability on Inventory Investment," in Joint Economic Committee, *Inventory Fluctuations*, Part II, pp. 89–117.

[29] "An Exploratory Quarterly Econometric Model of Effective Demand in the Postwar U.S. Economy," *Econometrica*, July 1963, pp. 301–48. Liu uses a real-interest variable, defined as the difference between the average rate on prime commercial paper (4–6 months) and the lagged rate of change in the GNP price deflator, both in per cent per year. Its coefficient is about −0.3, with a standard error half as large. Interestingly, Liu's equation also includes, among others, money and time deposits held by nonfarm nonfinancial business (in constant dollars). This variable has a positive coefficient, which, however, is small relative to its standard error, according to simple least squares (the two-stage estimate is more significant).

[30] "Financial Determinants of Manufacturing Inventory Behavior: A Quarterly Study Based on United States Estimates, 1947–1961," *Yale Economic Essays*, Fall 1964, pp. 331–69. The equation that presents the financial variables in the best light reads:

$$(H_t)_{est} = -953.3 + .088S_t + .042U_t + 1.071IF_{t-1} + .114XF_{t-1} - 15.6i_{t-1} + .737H_{t-1},$$
$$\quad\quad\quad (.018) \quad (.010) \quad (0.253) \quad (.028) \quad\quad (7.2) \quad (.049)$$

where the data are for all manufacturers, in constant (1954) dollars. IF and XF denote internal and external finance, respectively, and i is the average interest rate for short-term business loans. Each of the three financial variables is here transformed according to a moving average formula with triangular weights that implies rather extended (seven-quarter) adjustment periods. When these variables are entered with simple one-period lags (in an equation which contains the same nonfinancial variables, including H_{t-1}), the coefficients of i_{t-1} and IF_{t-1} are apparently not significant. On the other hand, the other variables require no transformation, and their effectiveness seems to be relatively independent of the different specifications of the financial factors (*ibid.*, Table 1, p. 352).

[31] In *Inventory Fluctuations*, Part II. This is also the source of equations L1 and L2 in Table 8-2.

Table 8-3

Regressions of Inventory Levels and Changes on Selected Variables, Total Inventories, Purchased Materials and Goods in Process, and Finished-Goods Inventories, All Manufacturing and Major-Industry Groups, 1948–55 and 1948–60

Industry	Dependent Variable	Constant Term	Regression Coefficients					R^2	Durbin-Watson Statistic
			PURCHASED MATERIALS AND GOODS IN PROCESS						
			Z^*	ΔZ^*	U^*	$\Delta P/P$	$(M+G)^*_{-1}$		
1. All mfg.	$(M+G)^*$	4004	.062 (.016)	−.100 (.030)	.061 (.005)	−.320 (.206)	.542 (.046)	.993	2.27
2. Durables	$(M+G)^*$	1412	.053 (.019)	−.080 (.030)	.038 (.004)	.038 (.173)	.637 (.034)	.994	1.82
3. Nondurables	$(M+G)^*$	−356	.023 (.021)	−.037 (.056)	.221 (.051)	.148 (.121)	.903 (.067)	.970	2.02
			FINISHED-GOODS INVENTORIES						
			S^*	ΔS^*			Q^*_{-1}		
4. All mfg.	Q^*	−258	.042 (.020)	.132 (.042)			.848 (.065)	.958	1.39
5. Durables	Q^*	−326	.055 (.014)	.097 (.028)			.817 (.052)	.966	1.33
6. Nondurables	Q^*	419	.006 (.029)	.170 (.068)			.935 (.086)	.947	1.57

TOTAL INVENTORIES (LEVEL OR CHANGES)

			S^*	ΔS^*	U^*	ΔU^*	$\Delta P/P$	H^*_{-1}		
7. Durables	H^*	1032.	.126 (.037)	.104 (.054)	.037 (.006)		-.499 (.331)	.676 (.045)	.991	1.46
8. Durables	ΔH^*	-1.55 (0.55)	.127 (.033)	-.002 (.044)	.009 (.005)	.047 (.021)		-.115 (.033)	.57	1.23
9. Nondurables	H^*	-661.	.036 (.038)	.171 (.075)	.329 (.083)		-.618 (.185)	.926 (.065)	.981	2.23
10. Nondurables	ΔH^*	-0.508 (0.409)	.043 (.016)	-.029 (.033)	.254 (.046)	-.356 (.058)		-.082 (.039)	.66	1.93
11. Primary metals	H^*	-172.8	.063 (.031)	.043 (.032)	.018 (.012)		-.036 (.035)	.945 (.053)	.939	1.72
12. Machinery	H^*	751.9	.035 (.039)	.070 (.065)	.059 (.007)		.029 (.067)	.701 (.043)	.991	1.49
13. Transport. equip.	H^*	266.0	.083 (.032)	.031 (.046)	.032 (.005)		.006 (.084)	.684 (.054)	.990	1.13
14. Stone, clay, and glass	H^*	27.4	.108 (.020)	.234 (.050)	a		.002 (.020)	.733 (.051)	.978	1.29
15. Other durables	H^*	32.8	.122 (.030)	.135 (.048)	a		a	.806 (.050)	.960	0.92

Note: See Table 8-2, note b, for explanation of all symbols except the following:

M = purchased material inventories.

G = goods-in-process inventories.

Q = finished-goods inventories.

$Z = S + \Delta Q$ = value of output estimated by adding change in finished-goods inventory to sales.

Source: Michael C. Lovell, "Factors Determining Manufacturing Inventory Investment," in Joint Economic Committee, *Inventory Fluctuations and Economic Stabilization*, 87th Cong., 1st sess., 1961, Part II. Entries on lines 1–3 are from Table I, p. 143; lines 4–6, from Table II, p. 144; and lines 7, 9, and 11–15, from Table III, p. 145. All these regressions are based on deflated, seasonally adjusted, quarterly series for 1948–55. Entries on lines 8 and 10 are from equations given in *ibid.*, pp. 129–30; they refer to quarterly deflated and deseasonalized data for 1948–60.

a Lack of data is cited as the reason for absence of estimates in these cells.

371

regressions use largely simultaneous relationships between constant-dollar series. Only one of the explanatory variables is taken with a lead: the inventory level as of the end of the previous quarter, H_{t-1}^*. However, no account is taken of the possible feedback effects of inventory investment on sales, unfilled orders, etc., that could impose a simultaneous equation bias on the estimates.

One model, based on the flexible or partial-adjustment version of the acceleration principle, is adopted for both the purchased-materials and goods-in-process inventories (first three lines). The desired level of the combined inventory for these two stages is assumed to be a linear function of the level of output, the change in output, unfilled orders, and the relative change in the wholesale price index. Realized inventory investment, $\Delta(M + G)_t^*$, is viewed as a fraction, δ, of the difference between the desired and the available stock. Since the dependent variable is the *level* of inventory, its previous value, $(M + G)_{t-1}^*$, has the coefficient $(1 - \delta)$.

The sign of the coefficient of the change in output ΔZ_t^*, is not clearly prespecified. "When output is increasing, orders may be placed with suppliers in an attempt to build up stocks, but considerable delays may be involved in obtaining delivery." [32] On this reasoning, the effect of ΔZ_t^* would be positive if the attempt succeeded. Negative estimated coefficients would then be attributed to long delivery lags for materials. But the evidence reviewed earlier in this chapter suggests that the delivery lags for materials are on the whole rather short. A different explanation of the negative effect of ΔZ_t^* is that this term, being well correlated with ΔS_t^*, reflects the influence of sales anticipation errors in production to stock: After all, passive or unintended changes due to such errors can occur in purchased-materials and goods-in-process inventories as well as in finished-goods stocks. Of course, unexpected delivery delays may here and there also contribute to the observed results.

The model appears to work poorly for the nondurable goods sector, where the estimates are unsatisfactory or implausible. The coefficients of Z^*, ΔZ^*, and $\Delta P/P$ are all small relative to their standard errors, and the reaction coefficient δ, computed as 1 minus the coefficient of lagged inventory, is very small indeed (0.097). Of the causal variables,

[32] *Ibid.*, p. 140.

only unfilled orders, which in this sector are assumed to be nil for most industries and of modest size for a few (according to the statistics used), have a significantly large positive coefficient (Table 8-3, third line). The results for all manufacturing and the durable goods sector are considerably better, since Z^* and ΔZ^*, as well as U^*, show significant effects, while the estimates for δ are much larger and more reasonable (0.458 and 0.363, respectively). However, the evidence on the influence of price changes $\Delta P/P$ is again negative.

In the finished-goods inventory equations, a simple form of the "buffer-stock motive" is adopted and neither U^* nor $\Delta P/P$ is included. Deflated sales, not output, are now used. The influence of S_i^* is positive and significant for all manufacturing and the durable goods industries, but it is not significant for the nondurables. The coefficients of ΔS_i^* are large relative to their standard errors in each case, but they are positive. If these coefficients were to represent the effects of sales anticipation errors that result in passive or unintended inventory changes, their signs ought to be negative. On Lovell's more complex interpretation, however, these estimates must be "unscrambled" to reveal the implicit "anticipation coefficient," ρ.[33]

One would expect the adjustments of finished-goods inventories to be slower than those of the materials and goods-in-process inventories. The coefficients of Q_{t-1}^* are much higher than those of $(M + G)_{t-1}^*$ in Table 8-3, which is, in terms of the model applied here, consistent with this expectation. But the implied reaction coefficients of 0.152 for all manufacturing, 0.183 for the durables, and 0.065 for the nondurables seem uncomfortably low. The large coefficients of Q_{t-1}^* reflect the high autocorrelations of the smooth series on aggregate finished-goods stocks, and probably also reflect the limitation of these equations to two causal variables (S^* and ΔS^*) only; it is not at all clear that they can be safely used to infer extremely low reaction coefficients, i.e., extremely slow inventory adjustments.

---

[33] Defining $S_t^a = \rho S_{t-1} + (1 - \rho)S_t$ implies that $\rho = 1$ for naive or static expectations ($S_t^a = S_{t-1}$) and $\rho = 0$ for unbiased expectations ($S_t^a = S_t$). On this definition, the coefficient of ΔS_t equals $(\delta\beta + \lambda)\rho$ (see notes 18 and 25, above, on the meaning of δ, β, and λ). The model does not provide sufficient information to permit unconstrained simultaneous estimation of both λ and ρ. If one assumes that $\lambda = 1$ (complete inflexibility of production plans), ρ varies from 0.092 for the durables to 0.168 for the nondurables. The implication would be that manufacturers' sales forecasts are rather good, particularly in the durable goods sector. If moderately large output adjustments were assumed, the estimates of ρ would be larger, but still not very high (given $\lambda = 0.5$, for example, ρ for all manufacturing would be 0.243, instead of 0.126, obtained when $\lambda = 1$).

The equations for total inventories (Table 8-3) use a combination of the stage-of-fabrication models. It is interesting that the coefficients of both S_i^* and ΔS_i^* are not significant for machinery, an industry with a large proportion of output produced to order. On the other hand, the coefficients of both S_i^* and ΔS_i^* are highly significant for two industry groups in which production to stock is very definitely the rule: stone, clay, and glass products and "other durables." However, the coefficients of ΔS_t are here again positive.[34]

The coefficients of unfilled orders are all positive and are generally large relative to their standard errors. It may be worth noting that the largest t ratios for U_i^* are in the equations for machinery and transportation equipment, while the lowest recorded ratio is in the equation for primary metals. In the inventory-investment regressions, ΔU_i^*, which is included along with U_i^*, appears to have a positive effect in durables but a negative effect in nondurables. These results suggest that the influence of unfilled orders on inventory behavior is greater in industries where production to order is important, but the evidence is far from conclusive.

The assumption that unfilled orders affect the inventories of materials and goods in process, but not those of finished goods, receives some support from the estimates in Table 8-3. The coefficients of U_i^* in the durable goods regression for $(M + G)_i^*$ and for H_i^* are almost identical.

The evidence on the influence of price changes is entirely negative for the total-inventory equations, as it was for the materials and goods-in-process equations. The coefficients of $\Delta P/P$ have minus signs as often as plus signs but are in any event typically quite small when compared with their standard errors.

In their critique of Lovell's two models (one for materials and goods-in-process inventories, the other for finished-goods inventories), Eisner and Strotz conclude that "we cannot really distinguish between them (identify them) on the basis of the statistical results."[35] They are

---

[34] The coefficient of ΔS_i^* is also positive and fairly significant in the total-inventory regression for the durables, but it is negative and not significant in the inventory investment regression. In the total-inventory equation for nondurables, S_i^* is not effective, but ΔS_i^* is; in the corresponding inventory-investment equation, the opposite applies. These estimates for the comprehensive industry groups, then, seem rather ambiguous, as if they were adversely affected by aggregation (in addition to any basic specification errors).

[35] R. Eisner and R. H. Strotz, "Determinants of Business Investment," in Commission on Money and Credit, *Impacts of Monetary Policy*, Englewood Cliffs, N.J., 1963, p. 220.

not persuaded that inventories should be disaggregated by stage of fabrication and state their preference to "disaggregate by motive" (*ibid.*, p. 106). But motivations, here as elsewhere, must be analyzed within the context of the relevant technological and institutional constraints.[36] If my observations are correct, Lovell's results suffer from insufficient rather than from excessive disaggregation (as well as from some errors of specification). It is important for the analysis of inventory behavior to distinguish between production to stock and production to order, and among the stages of fabrication, and to combine these distinctions.

Disaggregation by Type of Production

Thomas J. Courchene has recently made a very interesting examination of several hypotheses relating to the central proposition that inventory behavior differs significantly between industries producing largely to stock and industries producing largely to order, depending at the same time also on the stage of fabrication at which the stocks are held.[37] Courchene computed inventory investment regressions for ten divisions of Canadian manufacturing that are broadly similar to the U.S. data for the "market categories." Particularly interesting, and emphasized, are his estimates for two sectors in which inventory policies are governed by demand rather than supply conditions: (1) heavy transportation equipment (HTE), where production is almost exclusively to order; and (2) semidurable consumer goods (SDCG), where production to stock definitely predominates.[38]

Courchene's main results for these two sectors are reproduced in Table 8-4. Application to extremes should bring out the hypothesized

---

[36] The motives for investment and their implications certainly form an important subject to be studied with the aid of economic theory, whether it is investment in inventories or in other capital goods such as structures and equipment; but so are the above-noted "constraints." Now, in the case of inventories, these underlying conditions are quite different for, say, investment in materials (which are inputs into the production process) and finished goods (which, for the investing firm, are the outputs). Such distinctions, therefore, may be as important as those by motives, even from a purely theoretical point of view.

[37] Courchene, "Inventory Behaviour and the Stock-Order Distinction: An Analysis by Industry and Stage of Fabrication with Empirical Application to the Canadian Manufacturing Sector," *Canadian Journal of Economics and Political Science*, August 1967, pp. 325–57.

[38] Applying the criterion of the stock-backlog ratios Q/U (as discussed in Chapter 2 above), Courchene presents a "ranking of sectors along [a] stock-order spectrum." Classified as producing primarily to order are heavy transportation, other capital goods, and construction goods, while intermediate goods and supplies, motor vehicles, "largely export producing," and semidurable and perishable consumer goods, are found to represent primarily manufacture to stock. The durable consumer goods sector is treated as mixed.

Table
Regressions for Inventory Investment by Stage of Fabrication,

Stage of Fabri- cation[a]	Dep. Var.	Con- stant Term (1)	New and Unfilled Orders U_t; N_{t-1} (2)	N_t (3)	U_{t-2}; U_{t-1} (4)	Shipments S_t (5)	S_t; $(S_t - N_{t-1})$ (6)
							Regression
						HEAVY TRANSPORTATION	
1. PM	ΔM_t	2.765 (2.91)	$0.037\Delta U_t$ (3.90)		$0.038U_{t-1}$ (3.52)		
2. GIP	ΔG_t	5.363 (2.15)	$0.241N_{t-1}$ (7.83)	0.142 (5.41)	$0.295U_{t-2}$ (8.19)	−0.307 (3.75)	
3. FG	ΔQ_t	0.170 (0.65)				−0.0075 (0.73)	$0.0074\Delta S_t$ (0.87)
4. All	ΔH_t	10.62 (3.03)	$0.266N_{t-1}$ (6.17)	0.151 (4.35)	$0.317U_{t-2}$ (5.97)	−0.280 (2.59)	
						SEMIDURABLE CONSUMER	
5. PM	ΔM_t	−1.266 (0.80)		0.165 (3.98)	$0.159U_{t-1}$ (2.84)		$-0.193(S_t - N_t)$ (4.06)
6. GIP	ΔG_t	0.401 (0.78)			$0.066U_{t-1}$ (3.81)	0.063 (4.39)	$-0.047\Delta S_t$ (3.03)
7. FG	ΔQ_t	0.202 (0.33)				0.130 (3.66)	$-0.176\Delta S_t$ (4.18)
8. All	ΔH_t	−2.291 (0.86)		0.264 (4.41)	$0.217U_{t-1}$ (2.36)		$-0.381(S_t - N_{t-1})$ (5.18)

Note: For explanation of symbols see Table 8-2, note b, and Table 8-3, Note. The series are seasonally adjusted and undeflated and are for I-1955–IV-1962. Most of the data are from the Dominion Bureau of Statistics, *Inventories Shipments and Orders in Manufacturing Industries* ("Economic Use Classification" of Canadian industries). Monthly observations are converted to quarterly observations by summing for the flows and by using the values for the last month of the quarter for the stocks. Figures in parentheses below the coefficients are t values.

Source: Thomas J. Courchene, "Inventory Behaviour and the Stock-Order Distinc-

8-4
Two Sectors of Canadian Manufacturing, Quarterly, 1955–62

Coefficients

| Inventories | | | | | | Dur-bin-Wat-son |
| Lagged, Same Stage (7) | Other | | Inter-est Rate[b] (10) | Time Trend (11) | R (12) | Sta-tistic (13) |
	(8)	(9)				
EQUIPMENT (HTE)						
$-0.181M_{t-1}$	$0.609\Delta M_{t-1}$	$-0.078G_t$	-0.239		.70	2.32
(2.31)	(3.49)	(2.95)	(1.99)			
$-0.549G_{t-1}$			-2.434	0.278	.91	2.39
(6.55)			(4.50)	(5.26)		
$-0.061Q_{t-1}$	$-0.203\Delta Q_{t-1}$	$.002\Delta G_t$		0.003	.40[c]	1.80
(0.37)	(1.02)	(.017)		(0.68)		
$-0.601H_{t-1}$			-2.387	0.210	.84	1.70
(5.04)			(3.34)	(3.14)		
GOODS (SDCG)						
$-0.392M_{t-1}$					.67	1.73
(3.40)						
$-0.244G_{t-1}$	$-0.138M_{t-1}$				.76	2.24
(2.98)	(3.69)					
$-0.379Q_{t-1}$	$1.480\Delta G_t$	$0.345\Delta M_t$			.78	2.29
(4.50)	(3.52)	(2.70)				
$-0.275H_{t-1}$					.75	1.50
(3.42)						

tion: An Analysis by Industry and Stage of Fabrication with Empirical Application to the Canadian Manufacturing Sector," *Canadian Journal of Economics and Political Science*, August 1967, pp. 325–57.

[a] PM = purchased materials; GIP = goods in process; FG = finished-goods inventory; All = total inventory (all stages combined).

[b] Corporate bond rate, taken with a one-quarter lag.

[c] Refers to the regression which includes, in addition to the terms listed in this table, ΔM_t, whose coefficient is not significant (-0.012 with a t ratio of 0.19).

differences in inventory behavior most forcefully, but comparisons between other sectors in which either type of production prevails should also show such differences, although in a more attenuated form. The evidence confirms this expectation in large part. Limitations of the available data, however, seriously impede the analysis and also its evaluation.[39]

The basic approach is once more guided by the familiar flexible-accelerator hypothesis. Intended inventory investment is a fraction of the difference between the desired and the available stock. A negative coefficient of the lagged inventory term is therefore expected. Its absolute magnitude is viewed as an estimate of the above fraction. These coefficients are shown in column 7 of Table 8-4; they are all negative and significant, except for the coefficient of Q_{t-1} in the finished-goods equation for the HTE sector, which is not significant.

The main differences in inventory behavior between production to stock and production to order derive from differences in (1) the roles of new orders and shipments as determinants of planned output and inventories; (2) the significance of passive or unintended inventory investment; and (3) the nature and function of finished-goods inventories.

1. In the HTE sector, representing manufacture to order, previous values of unfilled orders (U_{t-2}) are important factors in the purchased-materials and goods-in-process equations (Table 8-4). Large backlogs indicate high levels of future output, hence greater materials requirements for production. It is also possible that, when backlogs of order accumulate, buying of materials would be accelerated because of expected delays on the suppliers' deliveries.[40] Goods-in-process stocks tend to be closely related to the role of production, which is here largely determined by the amount of new orders received in the past; but output is made less volatile than new orders because backlogs act as a buffer. Hence ΔG_t depends positively on prior values of new and

---

[39] The quarterly series used cover only eight years, 1955–62. Corresponding price data are not available, and the series are not deflated. Sales anticipations are not directly measured but are equated to the preceding values of shipments or new orders, thus implying that a naive model of current-level extrapolation adequately represents the expectational process involved. The validity of the concept of materials ownership and the need for data on orders placed are recognized, but the manufacturing statistics for Canada (like those for the United States) refer only to orders received and unfilled, not to orders placed and outstanding.

[40] Here it would be more appropriate to use the unfilled orders of the materials suppliers as an indicator, rather than the unfilled orders of the purchasers, but data are available only for the latter.

unfilled orders, with some sizable lags reflecting the time-consuming nature of the production process involved (second line).

Stocks of materials are increased through deliveries on purchase orders and decreased through transformation into stocks of goods in process [see equation (1), above]. The regression for ΔM_t in the first line includes the stock of goods in process, G_t, which has a significant negative coefficient, thus roughly isolating the effect of the rate of this transformation (i.e., of the use of materials as productive inputs, IN_t).

Stocks of goods in process are increased through inflow of materials and decreased through outflow into the finished-goods stocks [equation (4), above]. The rate of this outflow is measured by the rate of output or (in production to order) of shipments. Hence, ΔG_t should be negatively related to S_t, and it is (second line).[41]

In the SDCG sector, representing manufacture to stock, elements of production to order nevertheless exist, as indicated by the presence of unfilled orders which, although relatively small, have significant effects on ΔM_t and ΔG_t (see fifth and sixth lines, column 4). However, the lags are shorter, and the importance of the backlog factor (as indicated by the t ratios) is smaller for the SDCG sector than for the HTE one.

Since the production process is typically short for SDCG, it is not possible here to distinguish between the inflow and outflow factors in the purchased-materials and goods-in-process regressions. The turnover ratios of quarterly shipments to product inventory are high — greater than 1 — in this as in other sectors producing primarily to stock. New orders or shipments (the two do not differ much) appear with positive signs in the SDCG equations for ΔM_t and ΔG_t (fifth and sixth lines, columns 3 and 5).

2. Sales anticipations that guide production in industries working to stock inevitably generate errors, and so passive inventory investment due to these errors is a feature of these industries. As an illustration, the coefficients (column 6) of ΔS_t or of $(S_t - N_{t-1})$ are all negative and highly significant for the SDCG sector. Where production is undertaken in response to demand (past orders from customers), rather than

---

[41] Note that the coefficient of S_t is also negative in the total inventory investment equation for HTE (column 5). This can only be explained in production to order; in production to stock, the effect of S_t is positive (see text below), and it is usually presumed to be so in aggregate inventory analyses. Courchene also reports that for total Canadian manufacturing, the coefficient of S_t in the equation for ΔG_t is insignificant, because of offsetting effects in the two types of production (*ibid.*, pp. 343–44).

in anticipation of demand (future market sales), there is clearly no basis for such an association between forecasting errors and inventory changes. The coefficient of ΔS_t in the finished-goods equation for the HTE sector is therefore not significant, as would be expected (third line). Sales forecast errors may influence purchases of materials by industries producing to order, but it is difficult to isolate this effect in regressions for *net change* in materials stocks (where purchase orders for materials are not separately observed or analyzed).

3. Stocks of finished goods are small in the HTE sector, representing mainly sold output in transit to the buyer. Changes in such stocks should be largely random, due to occasional shipping delays and perhaps cancellations (but the latter are not likely to be very frequent in this late stage of production), although some upward trend could arise here for a growing industry. In fact, the flexible-accelerator hypothesis that seems to work rather well elsewhere fails entirely in the HTE equation for finished-goods inventories (Table 8-4). None of the regression coefficients here is unambiguously significant, and the signs of some (those of S_t and ΔS_t) are contrary to expectations. Only 16 per cent of the variance of ΔQ_t is accounted for by the equation.

In contrast, the behavior of finished-goods inventories in the production-to-stock sector SDCG conforms well to the hypothesis in terms of the signs and significance of the coefficients of S_t, ΔS_t, and Q_{t-1}. In particular, the coefficient of ΔS_t is here negative and larger absolutely than the (positive) coefficient of S_t. This indicates that passive inventory investment plays a large role in this case and that there are important elements of an inverse relation in the movements of Q_t and S_t.

To conclude this review, the evidence presented does indeed confirm the existence of systematic and important differences in inventory behavior between production to stock and production to order. The differences between stages of fabrication also become more significant when the distinction between the two types of operation is taken into account. These results are not altered by the inclusion in the analysis of some other factors that are apparently much less important as determinants of inventory investment than the orders and shipments variables.[42]

[42] Interest rates are the most important of these factors in Courchene's study. The expected negative effects of interest rates are reported in several of his regressions. In addition to the short-term rates more commonly used in inventory analysis, long-term (corporate bond) rates were used with similar results.

The Supporting Equations for Orders in Recent
Models of the Economy

To the extent that new and unfilled orders are included in the comprehensive econometric models, their main function is to contribute to the explanation of inventory changes. Their treatment here is typically rather *ad hoc* and cursory; they are presumptive tools, not objects of interest in their own right. Nevertheless, as endogenous variables in systems of simultaneous equations, orders must themselves be "explained," which introduces a source of potentially important errors (the more so, the greater the role of orders in determining inventory investment and the greater the effects of inventory investment on the short-run fluctuations of the economy at large).

Gary Fromm's quarterly model (1962) includes the following estimated unfilled orders function: [43]

$$\Delta U_t = 111.4 - .388 S_t^a + .523 \Delta S_{t-1}^G - .554 U_{t-1} + .810 \Delta U_{t-1}.$$
$$\quad\quad (.109)\quad\quad (.332)\quad\quad\quad (.104)\quad\quad\quad (.101)$$

Fromm proceeds from the identity $\Delta U_t \equiv N_t - S_t$, but his use of GNP final sales, S_t^G, as if it were substitutable for S_t (the much smaller manufacturers' shipments) is at least doubtful. He also uses the definition of ΔU to argue that the coefficient of S_t^G should be negative, but this again is questionable for the same reason. (Moreover, one could maintain that the effect of S_t^G in the above equation is actually positive, though small.) [44]

In the 1964 model by Lawrence Klein, unfilled orders are a function of new orders and the rate of capacity utilization computed from GNP data. The equation,[45] estimated by two-stage least squares, reads

$$U_t = -101 + 2.12 N_t + 111 (X/X_c)_t,$$
$$\quad\quad (44)\quad (0.84)\quad\quad (55)$$

[43] "Inventories, Business Cycles, and Economic Stabilization," in Joint Economic Committee, *Inventory Fluctuations*, Part IV. Some symbols have been changed to conform to the notations used elsewhere in this book: S_t^a denotes final sales of goods in period t (GNP component), and U_t denotes manufacturers' unfilled orders at the end of period t, both in 1954 dollars; Δ stands for quarterly changes.

[44] Fromm lets $N_t = \alpha + \beta S_t^G$, with $\beta < 1$, then states that, since $\Delta U_t \equiv N_t - S_t^G$, $\Delta U_t = \alpha + (\beta - 1) S_t^G$ (*ibid.*, p. 73, n. 38). But ΔU_t is *not* identically equal to $(N_t - S_t^G)$; it equals $(N_t - S_t)$, and S_t certainly differs from S_t^G. As for the estimates reproduced in the text, note that the terms $-.388 S_t^G + .523 \Delta S_{t-1}^G$ may be rewritten as $.135 S_t^G - .523 S_{t-1}^G$.

[45] Lawrence R. Klein, "A Postwar Quarterly Model" in *Models of Income Determination* (see also Table 8-2, equation K).

where X is private gross national product, X_c is estimated private GNP at full capacity, and all variables are expressed in billions of 1964 dollars. Since changes in backlogs reflect the varying pressure of demand upon capacity, it is well to find that U is positively related to an independent measure of such pressures, namely, the ratio X/X_c. Relating the simultaneous values of U and N, however, does not result in a very adequate or interesting specification.[46]

An additional equation is then required to explain new orders, and the variables employed by Klein for this purpose are recent "sales of private GNP" (i.e., $X - I_i$, where I_i is inventory investment in billions of 1954 dollars) and recent change in prices (more precisely, in p, the implicit GNP deflator, 1954 = 1.00). The equation, estimated by the limited-information maximum-likelihood method, reads

$$N_t = 2.56 + .059(X - I_i)_{t-1} + 0.387(p_t - p_{t-1}).$$
$$(3.2) \quad (.010) \qquad\qquad (72.0)$$

The dependence of new orders on recent price changes is certainly of considerable interest. It could mean that price expectations are formed by projecting past changes, and that attempts to "beat the price hike" and to "wait for better buys" lead to increased ordering after a rise in p and to decreased ordering after a fall in p. But another argument that is relevant at this point was developed in Chapter 7. Price changes are correlated with backlog changes, and the latter lead new orders.[47]

The relationship between new orders and recent "sales," defined broadly as $X - I_i$, may represent an important link in the propagation of demand. However, new orders turn earlier than GNP; so this connection is not likely to be of much help in explaining the tendency of new orders to lead at recessions and revivals in aggregate economic activity. The exclusion of the government component from the "sales" variable could be questioned, since N_t includes defense and other government orders.

The Brookings model in its first version (1965) is similar to others in basing the inventory investment equations on a stock adjustment

[46] Since U, by definition, equals the cumulated total of past differences between N and S, it should be positively associated with N_{t-i} and negatively associated with S_{t-i}, presumably with weights declining with the increasing lags i.

[47] The relation between prices and unfilled orders is actually used in some of the equations designed to explain specific price levels in Klein's model. See Chapter 7, note 52, above and the text discussion thereto.

process, with GNP "final sales" components and manufacturers' un-filled orders cast as the principal explanatory variables.[48] Lagged values of levels and changes in unfilled orders are used, but in most cases the GNP sales terms coincide in timing with the inventory variables. There is disaggregation by production sector (durable manufacturing, non-durable manufacturing, trade, and other), and orders are included in the manufacturing relations only. The model accordingly contains functions for new and unfilled orders in each of the two manufacturing sectors, which adds up to four equations.

Disaggregation in the form used in the Brookings model hurts rather than helps some of these equations when orders and sales are taken with simultaneous timing, because of the interaction between these variables. For example, new orders for durable goods are regressed on the GNP component representing final sales of durables plus new construction. But expenditures follow orders; when the two are taken for the same quarter, it is presumably more appropriate to say that orders determine expenditures than to specify the reverse. A similar form is used for nondurables, where the delivery periods tend to be so short that orders are likely to reflect transactions which are also contained in the nondurable goods component of GNP. Some of the underlying industry equations developed for the Brookings project by Manoranjan Dutta[49] similarly include the gross product originating in the given industry, which again is more a consequence than a source of new orders received by the same group of firms in the same quarter. These specifications seem to have been devised for orders *placed,* not for orders *received,* by the given industry; yet, except for the economy as a whole, the two concepts differ and the available series refer to orders received only.[50]

In short, final sales of durables and nondurables can hardly be viewed

[48] Gary Fromm and Lawrence R. Klein, "The Complete Model: A First Approximation," in J. S. Duesenberry, G. Fromm, L. R. Klein, and E. Kuh, eds., *The Brookings Quarterly Econometric Model of the United States,* Chicago-Amsterdam, 1965, pp. 688–89 and 723.

[49] "Business Anticipatory Demand: An Analysis of Business Orders, 1948–1962," in Duesenberry et al. (eds.), *The Brookings Model,* pp. 162–75.

[50] As Dutta states: "Taking an aggregative view of the production sectors of the economy, orders received and orders placed reduce to the same economic magnitude. This generalization has been a maintained hypothesis of this study" (*ibid.,* p. 175). Dutta's equations for the following industries are open to the criticism given in the text above: electrical machinery (one of the alternative forms offered); transportation equipment, total; motor vehicles and parts; and lumber, furniture, and fix-tures. His equations for other industries are not so vulnerable, being based on relations with broad components of GNP.

as determining new orders for these goods received in the same quarter: They are expenditures originating in these or earlier orders. However, where the relations involve lags of new orders behind some suitable comprehensive sales aggregates, the latter may have a valid role to play as causal factors affecting the purchases of industrial products.[51]

Further discussion of the treatment of the orders-inventory relations in econometric models is relegated to Appendix I. This concerns mainly an alternative approach in which, with sales given, inventory accumulation is viewed as a residual from the production operation and is motivated by the objectives of minimizing cost over a time period in the face of fluctuating demand.

Cyclical Fluctuations in Orders and Inventories

Production Requirements and the Timing of Investment in Materials

Abramovitz regarded the inventories of goods "purchased by manufacturers . . . but not yet manipulated by their owners" as being essentially a function of the manufacturers' output.[52] Investment in these stocks, correspondingly, should be primarily a function of the rate of change in output. It would lag behind output changes because of delays in the placement of orders or in the receipt of deliveries. Lags in placing orders occur because changes in the demand for output are not foreseen promptly enough. The availability of materials depends upon the nature and source of supplies but varies over time as well.

Abramovitz had to rely on data with substantial limitations (ten individual commodities for raw materials stocks), but his suggestion that most purchased materials are available with relatively short lags is to some extent confirmed by much more comprehensive recent statistics.

---

[51] In the Fromm-Klein equations for new orders in the Brookings model, lagged as well as simultaneous values of GNP final sales are used for durable goods, but simultaneous values only are used for nondurables. Relative changes in price indexes from the previous quarter also appear in these estimates with positive coefficients. The unfilled orders equations are again derived from the definition of ΔU as the difference between N and S in any period t, but they use the values of gross product originating in durable and nondurable manufacturing rather than the corresponding values of shipments. This necessitates certain adjustments involving inventory changes in the two sectors. See Fromm and Klein, "The Complete Model," p. 689.

[52] Abramovitz, *Inventories*, p. 178, and Chap. 9.

A piece of direct evidence is provided in monthly surveys of the national and regional associations of purchasing agents, in which members report on their buying policy, answering such questions as "How far in advance must you buy in order to have principal materials on hand when needed?" The categories distinguished in these reports have varied somewhat.[53] The results indicate that ordering for 60 days or less is often taken to denote coverage of known requirements rather than buying ahead for future needs (which would presumably be but vaguely recognized or unknown). However, in the immediate postwar period of strong demand pressures and serious supply shortages, the range of 30 to 90 days was sometimes implicitly treated as the period for normal purchasing commitments. As shown in Chart 8-2 (curve 2), an index of the percentage of firms reporting advance commitments for 60 days or more shows wide fluctuations, declining very markedly in each recession. But except in the early postwar period 1946–47, the Korean boom of 1950–51, and a few months late in 1955, most of the participating firms were buying materials for no longer than two months in advance, or less.[54] This evidence is consistent with the observation made earlier that the bulk of purchases for inventory probably involve short delivery periods.

The lags obtained by comparing turning points are often a good deal longer than would be indicated by the above measures. Turns of purchased-material investment lagged behind those of the change in output by quite variable intervals averaging nearly four months for total manufacturing in 1946–61 (Table 8-5, column 3). At peaks, these lags were somewhat longer than at troughs. The irregularity of these measures as well as the duration of the lags do not accord well with the hypothesis that purchased-stock movements are altogether dominated by output changes. The greatest irregularity is in the nondurable goods industries. This may be partly due to the relatively strong influence of independent changes in agricultural supply conditions. However, the

---

[53] Thus, right after the war the Chicago survey categories were: hand to mouth, 30 days, 60 days, 90 days, 4 to 6 months, and longer. Later, a better-defined classification was used: 0 to 30 days, 30 to 60 days, 60 to 90 days, and 90 days or longer.

[54] In Chart 8-2, the Chicago purchasing policy data are used because they can be compared with the vendor performance index, which is available only from this regional survey, and because the Chicago series could be extended back to 1946. As far as can be established, the Chicago figures relate consistently to principal materials needed by the highly diversified industry of the region. The cyclical movements of the Chicago index and the national index based on the surveys of the National Purchasing Agents Association are quite similar. The NPAA index begins in 1950; it is shown through 1958 in Stanback, *Postwar Cycles*, Chart 9.

Chart 8-2
Vendor Performance, Purchasing Policy, Purchased-Materials Investment, and Changes in Manufacturers' Output, Unfilled Orders, and Prices, 1946–61

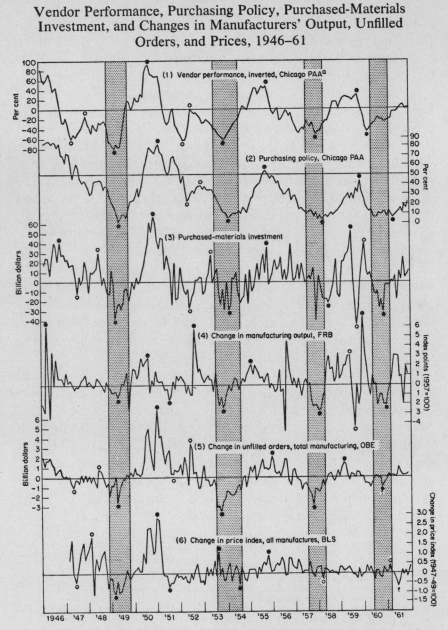

Note: Shaded areas represent business cycle contractions; unshaded areas, expansions. Dots identify peaks and troughs of specific cycles; circles, minor turns or retardations.

a Percentage reporting slower deliveries minus percentage reporting faster deliveries. See text.

duration of the lags certainly cannot be explained by technical factors such as time required for transportation and production of materials. One must consider the factors bearing on the manufacturer's decision to buy more or less material at a particular time.

Expectations, Sales Terms, and Purchasing Policy

In the real business environment, which is one of changing trends and fluctuations and of pervasive uncertainty, cyclical turns in sales are seldom very promptly *recognized,* let alone correctly *predicted.* The inability to forecast sales correctly with sufficient lead time can help explain the lags of materials inventories at cyclical turns in sales and production. But changes in backlogs of unfilled orders and in conditions of availability of materials also are instrumental here.

Chart 8-2 and Table 8-5 provide some evidence bearing on these relations. The vendor performance series has already been introduced as a diffusion index of changes in the delivery period—the excess of the percentage of purchasing agents reporting slower deliveries over the percentage reporting faster deliveries. Comparison of series 1 and 3 in Chart 8-2 suggest a substantial correlation between the cyclical movements in vendor performance and in purchased-materials investment (allowing for the much greater strength of the erratic component in the latter than in the former series). But the vendor performance index moves up and down earlier than materials investment (Table 8-5, column 1). In 1946–61, the index led investment nine times, and the two series coincided twice. Most of the leads were in the range of two to six months, and the average was about four months.

The purchasing policy index, showing the proportion of firms in the Chicago PAA survey that buy for 60 days ahead or more, is also positively correlated with materials investment with respect to cyclical movements, although it too is much less erratic than the investment series (compare curves 2 and 3 in Chart 8-2). But this index does not systematically lead (or lag behind) investment in purchased commodities; rather, the two series tend toward roughly coincident timing (see Table 8-5, column 2).

As implied by these observations, purchasing policy lags behind vendor performance. Direct comparisons show that these lags have been quite persistent and mostly, but not always, short. They varied

Table 8-5

Timing of Selected Series at Turning Points in Manufacturers' Investment in Purchased Materials, 1947–60

	Lead (−) or Lag (+), in Months				
Date of Turn in Purchased Materials Investment	Vendor Per- formance (1)	Pur- chasing Policy (2)	Change in Mfg. Output (3)	Change in Mfrs. Unfilled Orders (4)	Change in Mfg. Price Index (5)
Trough July 1947 [a]	−2 [b]	c	d	−2 [b]	−3 [b]
Peak June 1948 [a]	−6 [b]	c	d	0 [b]	−5 [b]
Trough March 1949	0	+2	+1	+1	−1
Peak Nov. 1950	−2	+3	−3	+2	+1
Trough June 1952 [a]	−3 [b]	−1 [b]	−11	−9 [b]	−12
Peak May 1953 [a]	−10 [b]	−5 [b]	−9	−11 [b]	+2
Trough Feb. 1954	−2	+1	−3	−4	+4
Peak Oct. 1955	0	−1	−9	+2	−1
Trough June 1958	−6	−3	−5	−8	e
Peak June 1959	f	g	−1	−4	n.t.
Trough Sept. 1959 [a]	n.t.	n.t.	−1 [b]	n.t.	n.t.
Peak Jan. 1960 [a]	−3 [f]	−2 [g]	−1 [b]	n.t.	n.t.
Trough Nov. 1960	−8	+5	+1	−1	n.t.
Average timing [h]					
Peaks	−4.2	−1.2	−4.6	−2.2	−0.8
	(3.0)	(2.2)	(3.5)	(4.2)	(2.2)
Troughs	−3.5	+0.8	−3.0	−3.8	−3.0
	(2.3)	(2.2)	(3.3)	(3.2)	(4.5)
All Turns	−3.8	−0.1	−3.7	−3.1	−1.9
	(2.7)	(2.5)	(3.5)	(3.7)	(3.6)

n.t. = no turn.

[a] Minor rather than cyclical turn in purchased materials investment.

[b] The turning point in the series compared with purchased materials investment is minor rather than cyclical.

[c] The July 1947–June 1948 rise in purchased materials investment cannot be matched with a corresponding movement in purchasing policy. Note, however, the weak increase in the latter series between February and July 1948 and compare the rise in materials investment between January and June 1948 (Chart 8-2).

[d] Change in manufacturing output shows only a small increase between May and November 1947, i.e., shortly prior to and partly overlapping with the early part of the rise in investment (Chart 8-2). No turning point comparisons are made.

[e] No cyclical turning points in the price-change series are distinguished in the period 1957–60 (cf. Chart 8-2 and text with note below).

[f] The peak in vendor performance lags behind the June 1959 peak in investment by

four months but it would be more appropriate to match it with the secondary January 1960 peak in investment, which yields a lead of three months (Chart 8-2).

ᵍ The peak in purchasing policy lags behind the June 1959 peak in investment by five months, but it would be more appropriate to match it with the secondary January 1960 peak in investment, which yields a lead of two months.

ʰ Average deviations, in months, are given in parentheses.

from two to five months, with three exceptions, and averaged 3.7 months.[55]

The difference in relative timing between the vendor performance and the purchasing policy index is interesting because of its consistency with the presence of what was called earlier the supply conditions effect; that is, when industrial buyers perceive a lengthening of the average delivery periods quoted by their suppliers, they will soon attempt to place more long-term orders to protect themselves against possible shortages in the future. Conversely, when sellers start quoting shorter delivery periods again, buyers will relax and begin reducing the average length of their purchasing commitments. Of course, the relation is really a good deal more complicated, for it is definitely one of mutual dependence and reinforcement rather than unidirectional. An extension of quoted delivery periods may induce more long-term buying, but it also means in itself an enforced increase of the share of advance orders in total purchases.

When more than 50 per cent of suppliers are reported to make slower deliveries, this is usually a symptom of increased pressures of demand upon capacity, and so is an accelerated expansion of unfilled orders. When the pressure subsides, the net percentage of slower deliveries begins to decline, and a retardation occurs in the backlog accumulation. Investment in purchased-materials inventories is positively correlated with the backlog change (curves 3 and 5), in part because the desired volume of these stocks increases with unfilled orders for the firm's products and in part because of the effects on buyers' behavior of changes in availability as reflected in the vendor performance index. Backlog change leads purchased-materials investment irregularly by approximately three months on the average (Table 8-5, column 4).

[55] Altogether, in the 1947–60 period, these comparisons include two lags of 2 months each, two of 3 months, and two of 5 months, one of 1 month, and one of 13 months; and one lead of 1 month. The averages at peaks and troughs are lags of 2.5 and 4.6 months, respectively.

Investment in purchased materials appears to be more loosely associated with the change in the price index for all manufactures than with any of the other series plotted in Chart 8-2. This is consistent with the results frequently obtained in the regression studies, but much doubt remains. It must be reiterated that the wholesale price data commonly used in this work probably understate considerably the cyclical price flexibility. The one period in which investment in materials and the change-of-price index moved in markedly similar fashion was the early phase of the Korean War (1950–51).[56]

The relationship that emerges from this analysis is a rather complex one in which fluctuations in materials inventories depend on a number of factors such as the changes in output, availability of materials, backlogs, and prices. One can identify some periods (e.g., during most of 1955) in which purchased-materials investment moved contrary to output change and apparently in consonance with changes in order backlogs, availability, and prices. At other times, for example, in the last half of 1959 under the impact of the steel strike (see Chart 8-2), investment in materials and the change in output paralleled each other, while the other series behaved quite differently.

Estimates for Materials Stocks on Hand and on Order

There are no direct estimates of outstanding purchase orders for materials, but the new Census data available for the period since 1953 provide a usable approximation: the series on unfilled sales orders held by manufacturers, classified into the market categories "construction materials and supplies" and "other materials and supplies." Consequently, the sum of these two series will be taken to represent the "stock on order" of the purchasers of materials, i.e., their outstanding orders, OUM. The stage-of-fabrication breakdown of total manufacturers' inventories gives direct estimates of the "stock on hand," i.e., the inventories of materials and supplies actually held by users, M. Estimates of total "ownership" of materials, OWM, can be obtained by simple addition of the identically dated, consecutive values of M and OUM.

---

[56] Our investment series reflects quantity as well as price changes, of course, and the latter were exceptionally large at the time. The same circumstance helps to explain the relative weakness in this period of the association between materials investment and the output change; the use of deflated figures would make the bulge in investment smaller and more similar to the 1950 contour of the output-change series. See Stanback, *Postwar Cycles,* Chart 6.

Changes in stocks on hand and in stocks on order should occur in response to a set of common factors, but the elasticities and the lags involved could well be different for the two components of materials ownership. For example, outstanding orders may be subject to prompter changes and more effective control than materials inventories on hand. Several questions in this context can be addressed to the new data, and the following analysis marks a limited effort in this direction.

Table 8-6, based on quarterly, seasonally adjusted data, presents regressions of M_t, OUM_t, and OWM_t on the following independent variables: current shipments or lagged new orders of all manufacturers (S_t or N_{t-1}, used as alternatives); unfilled orders, also for total manufacturing, as of the end of the preceding quarter, U_{t-1}; bank rate on short-term business loans, similarly dated, i_{t-1}; change from the previous quarter in the price index of intermediate materials and supplies, ΔPM_t; and the lagged value of the dependent variable (M_{t-1} or OUM_{t-1} or OWM_{t-1}).[57] Negative coefficients are expected for the interest rate, positive coefficients for the other factors. The signs of the estimated coefficients agree with these expectations in each case, except that the impact of i_{t-1} in the inventory regressions is significantly positive.

The positive dependence of M_t on N_{t-1} in an equation that also includes U_{t-1} and M_{t-1}, among others, confirms that an increase in the demand for outputs that require materials results on the average in a rise of the desired relative to the actual stock of materials. When S_t is used to replace N_{t-1}, it acquires a similar positive (and highly significant) coefficient that reflects essentially the same relationship.[58] An advantage of using N_{t-1} is that a predictive lead is gained that is absent in the application of S_t. Moreover, in the estimates for outstanding orders and for total stocks on hand and on order, it is the equations with N_{t-1} rather than S_t that produce the better statistical results, although

[57] The stock variables (M, OUM, OWM, U) and the price variables (PM, i) are last-month values in each calendar quarter; the flow variables (S, N) are quarterly averages of monthly data. The interest rate, i, is a weighted average for a selected sample of banks in nineteen cities (Federal Reserve). The price series, PM, covers intermediate materials, supplies, and components purchased by manufacturers; it is a wholesale price index for one stage of processing, $1957–59 = 100$ (U.S. Department of Labor, Bureau of Labor Statistics). The other data are taken from U.S. Department of Commerce, Bureau of the Census, *Manufacturers' Shipments, Inventories, and Orders: 1947–1963 (Revised)*, Washington, D.C., 1963, and the recent issues of the *Survey of Current Business;* all are in millions of dollars.

[58] S_t and N_{t-1} are, of course, highly correlated ($r = .992$). The regression with S_t yields a higher $\bar{R}^2$ than that with N_{t-1}, but the difference is quite small (Table 8-6, columns 1 and 2).

Table 8-6
Regressions for Inventories, Outstanding Orders, and Total Inventories on Hand and on Order of Materials Purchased from Manufacturers, Quarterly, 1954–66

Constant Term (1)	S_t (2)	N_{t-1} (3)	U_{t-1} (4)	i_{t-1} (5)	ΔPM_t° (6)	Lagged Dependent Variable [a] (7)	$\bar{R}^2$ (8)
			Regression Coefficients				
			ESTIMATES FOR INVENTORIES (M_t) [b]				
1,746.5	.109		.026	5.566	2.561	.532	.982
(600.1)	(.019)		(.007)	(1.694)	(0.910)	(.088)	
1,785.3		.097	.022	5.103	2.417	.574	.980
(673.5)		(.020)	(.007)	(1.785)	(0.988)	(.092)	
			ESTIMATES FOR OUTSTANDING ORDERS (OUM_t) [c]				
1,304.9	.182		.271	−14.461	7.600	.382	.940
(1,816.2)	(.055)		(.141)	(5.008)	(3.800)	(.272)	
2,218.5		.204	.251	−16.524	6.354	.405	.945
(1,809.2)		(.052)	(.135)	(4.856)	(3.708)	(.258)	
			ESTIMATES FOR INVENTORIES ON HAND AND ON ORDER (OWM_t) [d]				
3,992.0	.322		.347	−5.428	9.914	.307	.964
(1,651.7)	(.054)		(.134)	(6.470) *	(3.697)	(.235)	
5,326.1		.341	.366	−6.337	8.420	.251	.967
(1,626.6)		(.051)	(.126)	(6.107)	(3.533)	(.223)	

Note: Standard errors of the coefficients are given underneath in parentheses. S, N, and U denote, respectively, the current-dollar values of shipments, new orders, and unfilled orders, for total manufacturing; i is the bank rate of interest on business loans in nineteen cities; ΔPM is the change in the wholesale price index for intermediate materials, supplies, etc. ($\Delta PM_t^\circ = \Delta PM_t \times 100$; see text and note 70).

[a] M_{t-1} for the equations in the first two lines; OUM_{t-1} for third and fourth lines; and OWM_{t-1} for last two lines. See notes b, c, and d, following.

[b] The dependent variable M_t = purchased-materials inventories, total manufacturing.

[c] The dependent variable OUM_t = unfilled orders of the market category "materials, supplies, and intermediate products" (see text).

[d] The dependent variable $OWM_t = M_t + OUM_t$.

again the differences are marginal. Outstanding orders for materials appear to be generally more sensitive than the inventories to changes in demand, which is consistent with the notion that firms can adjust OUM considerably better than M.[59]

[59] The short-run elasticities at the point of the means with respect to S_t, N_{t-1}, and U_{t-1}, respectively, are: for M_t, 0.177, 0.157, and 0.072 or 0.060; for OUM_t, 0.240, 0.266, and 0.600 or 0.555;

Unfilled orders of manufacturers at the end of the preceding quarter have in each case a significant positive effect on the current inventories and/or outstanding orders of materials (column 4). It should be noted, however, that the partial correlations for U_{t-1} are not high and are smaller throughout than those for either S_t or N_{t-1}.[60]

The net impact of changes in the bank rate on business loans on materials stocks on hand is quite significant but positive, according to both the first and the second equation in Table 8-6. However, stronger negative effects are obtained for i_{t-1} in the regressions for outstanding orders (particularly in the estimates with N_{t-1}).[61] Since negative co-efficients are expected, this finding, if valid, would again suggest that adjustments are made more promptly and with greater success in outstanding orders than in the physical stock of materials. For the aggregate of stocks on hand and on order, the results are mixed: The co-efficients of i_{t-1} are negative but very low relative to their standard errors.

If price expectations have large extrapolative components, so that rises in the level of materials prices are associated with forecasts of further rises, at least some of the firms would probably attempt to hedge against or beat the price hike by accelerating their purchases in periods of inflationary developments. The evidence on the presence of such "speculative" behavior is mixed, as reported before (see text and Tables 8-2 and 8-3). Our estimates in Table 8-6, column 6, show fairly significant coefficients of the price-change variable ΔPM_t, with the expected positive signs. Since the measured price index changes are very small, their coefficients in absolute value are large, and it seemed advisable to apply a scale factor to this variable.[62] It is pos-

---

for OWM_t, 0.234, 0.246, and 0.425 or 0.448. (The first of the estimates for U_{t-1} refers to the equations with S_t, the second to those with N_{t-1}.) The elasticity of OUM_t to U_{t-1} is relatively high, but this must be discounted because total backlogs represent a massive aggregate that includes outstanding orders for materials. (The simple correlation between OUM_t and U_{t-1} is 0.953. The average value of U in the regression period was $55.3 billion; of OUM, $24.7 billion.)

[60] The highest of these partials with U_{t-1} are .499, .281, and .404 for M_t, OUM_t, and OWM_t, respectively, whereas the corresponding partials with S_t are .659, .450, and .672, and those with N_{t-1} are .604, .514, and .716.

[61] The partial correlations of i_{t-1} with M_t and OUM_t are .400 and −.461, respectively (this is for the equations with N_{t-1}; the estimates for the equations with S_t are .448 and −.403). The corresponding elasticity figures are .122 and −.318 (or .133 and −.278).

[62] That is, the estimates in Table 8-6 refer to $\Delta PM_t^* = 100 \times \Delta PM_t$. Had the observed changes been used without this adjustment, the coefficients in column 6 would have been 100 times larger, ranging from 241.74 to 991.36. A casual glance at such large values could be misleading — suggestive of stronger effects than are actually involved. The partial correlations, for example, are rather low, varying from .253 to .394.

sible that this factor operates with longer and more complex lags, but the evidence on this point is fragmentary and at best only suggestive.[63]

In the first equation of Table 8-6, subtracting the coefficient of M_{t-1} from 1.000 gives 0.468, which, when interpreted in accordance with the flexible-accelerator model, means that a little less than one-half of the discrepancy between the available and desired stock of materials would on the average be targeted for correction within one quarter of a year. The corresponding fraction is somewhat lower (0.426) for the second equation, which includes N_{t-1} instead of S_t. Some other inventory studies estimate the adjustments to be much slower than that, but the sluggishness thus implied seems to me rather implausible.[64]

One would expect the adjustments to be speedier for outstanding orders than for stocks on hand, and the estimates in column 7 of Table 8-6 are consistent with this hypothesis in that the coefficients of OUM_{t-1} are lower than those of M_{t-1}. The regression results suggest that about 0.6, or a slightly higher fraction, of the gap between the actual and the planned level of outstanding orders would on the average over time be corrected in any one quarter. (However, unlike the coefficients of M_{t-1} in the estimates for inventories, the coefficients of OUM_{t-1} have relatively large standard errors; they are significantly different from zero at the 10 per cent but not at the 5 per cent level, according to one-sided t tests. In the equations for total stocks on hand and on order, the coefficients of OWM_{t-1} are still lower absolutely and relative to their standard errors.)

Chart 8-3 compares the actual values of inventories, outstanding orders, and stocks on hand and on order of materials and supplies with the corresponding estimates based on the equations from Table 8-6, lines 2, 4, and 6 (these are the regressions that include the new orders variable N_{t-1}). It is clear that the fits, which are somewhat better for M and OWM than for OUM, are generally close. Relatively large residuals and differing patterns in actuals and estimates are observed in 1959. However, the major steel strike then in progress created unusually severe disturbances. Even so, the calculated values tend to lag behind by a quarter at the turns in the recorded values and to under-

---

[63] The effects of ΔPM_{t-1} approximate those of ΔPM_t in the equations for outstanding orders, but they are considerably weaker and of low or doubtful significance in the equations for stocks on hand.

[64] The result here is similar to that obtained by Lovell in his all-manufacturing regression for materials and goods in process (see Table 8-3, first line).

Chart 8-3
Actual and Estimated Values of Inventories, Outstanding Orders, and Total Stocks on Hand and on Order of Materials and Supplies, Quarterly, 1954–66

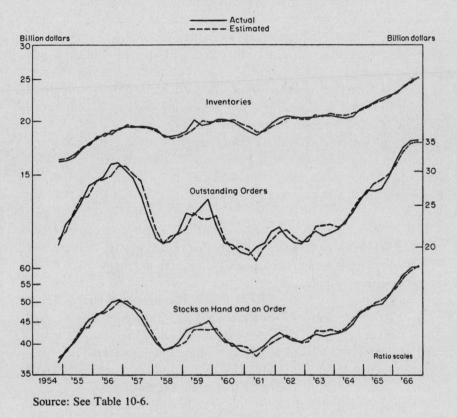

Source: See Table 10-6.

(over-) estimate the actual levels in periods of rise (decline). It should be recalled again that errors of this type are common in estimates from regression equations that include lagged values of the dependent variable.

The graphs of the compiled series are interesting in their own right, and their main features conform to expectations rather reassuringly. Thus, there is considerable similarity between the cyclical movements of inventories and those of outstanding orders, but the latter have a marked tendency to lead the former and also have much larger relative amplitudes. This presumably reflects the greater adaptability of stocks on order, which results in their being much more sensitive than stocks on hand to cyclical changes in the demand for output and other factors.

Additional Variables and Investment Equations for Materials

Conceivably, errors that the firms are making in forecasting their sales could affect their inventories or outstanding orders of materials or both, although the importance of this factor has been established only for finished stocks. The difference between current shipments and previous new orders of manufacturers may provide a simple estimate of such errors, that is, $E_t = S_t - N_{t-1}$. When included as an additional variable in such inventory equations as those used in Table 8-6, E_t shows positive coefficients; its effect appears to be statistically significant in the model with N_{t-1} but not in that with S_t. In regressions for outstanding orders analogous to those reported in the table, the coefficients of E_t are negative and significant at least at the 5 per cent level.[65]

If the coefficient of E_t in an equation for M_t is viewed as an estimate of that fraction of the forecasting error that results in passive inventory investment, its sign should be negative: When shipments exceed expectations, for example, the rate of production would be increased and the stock of materials somewhat depleted. The import of such a development on outstanding orders for materials is, however, not clear: If faster delivery on these orders is requested and provided, this would tend to reduce OUM_t, but at the same time the unexpected improvement in their sales might induce the firms to place more orders with their suppliers, which would tend to increase OUM_t.

On this reading, therefore, the observed coefficients of E_t in the inventory equations have the wrong sign, and those in the outstanding orders equations describe net balance effects of opposite tendencies. In any event, E_t contributes little to the over-all correlations ($\bar{R}^2$) and, generally, little seems to be lost when it is omitted. It may be, of course, that E_t is an overly crude or inappropriate measure of sales anticipation errors.[66]

---

[65] The coefficient of E_t in the inventory regression with S_t is .031 ($\pm$.057); the corresponding estimate in the regression with N_{t-1} is .139 ($\pm$.059). For outstanding orders, the coefficients of E_t are −.583 ($\pm$.223) and −.398 ($\pm$.228) in the regressions with S_t and with N_{t-1}, respectively. (The figures in parentheses are the standard errors of the coefficients.)

[66] In particular, E_t as defined is bound to interact with S_t (or N_{t-1}). Let a be the directly estimated coefficient of S_t and b that of E_t in an equation that includes these variables along with others. Then the implicit net coefficients are $a + b$ for S_t and $-b$ for N_{t-1}. If one starts from an equation that in-

Significant changes in the prevailing delivery periods for materials and supplies are certainly likely to influence outstanding orders for these goods. For example, the immediate impact of an over-all lengthening of these lags should be to reduce the rate of deliveries, which tends to increase the amount of orders outstanding. This effect may later be reinforced if users place more orders for materials to protect themselves against possible shortages. The influence of changes in the average delivery period for materials on inventories M is more indirect and should be weaker; moreover, here reactions in the opposite direction can be more readily envisaged.[67]

The average delivery lag for materials may be approximated by the ratio of unfilled orders to shipments for the industries that produce materials, that is, $DL_t = OUM_{t-1}/DM_t$. A quarterly series of such ratios can be computed from the new Census market-category data.[68] When DL_t is included along with the other variables from Table 8-6 in the inventory equations, it has in each case a negative coefficient, which, however, is definitely not significant, since the coefficient is smaller than its standard error. Since no strong effect of this factor on M had been expected, this result is not implausible. When DL_{t-1} is similarly added to the equations for outstanding orders, the results are not meaningful; indeed, the relationships estimated in Table 8-6 for OUM_t are then thoroughly disrupted (the coefficients of S_t and N_{t-1} become negative!). This is apparently because of the interaction of DL_{t-1} with the lagged value of the dependent variable, OUM_{t-1}, and the backlog of unfilled orders of manufacturers, U_{t-1}. When these two factors are omitted, DL_{t-1} enters the regression with a highly significant positive coefficient, and the remaining variables also have relatively large coefficients with the expected signs. When either U_{t-1} or OUM_{t-1} is

cludes N_{t-1} and E_t, their measured effects will be a and $a + b$, respectively, which implies the same net coefficients as before for S_t and N_{t-1}. The coefficient of S_t (or N_{t-1}) in the regression for inventories that includes E_t is .108 ($\pm.019$); the corresponding estimate in the regression for outstanding orders is .185 ($\pm.052$). These figures are extremely close to the coefficients for S_t in the first and third lines of Table 8-6. The coefficients of the other variables are only very slightly affected by the inclusion of E_t.

[67] The same demand pressures that generate an increase in the delivery lags may also cause the rates of utilization of materials to rise. The latter factor would work to reduce the stocks of materials on hand.

[68] The series combines data for two categories, as identified early in the previous section. The unfilled (= outstanding) orders, OUM, are as of the last month of the quarter ($t - 1$) when the shipments (deliveries) of materials, DM, refer to the tth quarter. Most of the time, the delivery periods for materials and supplies are relatively short; they average 1.607 months, with a standard deviation of 0.297.

readmitted, the coefficient of DL_{t-1} becomes negative. This suggests that the backlog variables (and perhaps also the price change, ΔPM) act in part as proxies for the variation in delivery periods. Lags in delivery of materials probably do have some positive influence on materials orders outstanding, but it is difficult to separate that influence from the effects of the other variables.

When net changes (investment) in stocks of materials (ΔM_t, ΔOUM_t, ΔOWM_t) are used as dependent variables instead of the stocks proper (M_t, OUM_t, OWM_t), with the independent variables the same as in the equations of Table 8-6, the regression estimates in columns 1–6 of that table remain unchanged. If the coefficient of the lagged stock term (Table 8-6, column 7) is set equal to $1 - b$, the coefficient of the same variable in the corresponding investment equation is $-b$ (see note 18 above). The correlation coefficients are, of course, considerably lower for the investment regressions than for the stock regressions. Thus, those versions of the former that include N_{t-1} give R^2 coefficients of .609, .520, and .636, which may be compared to R^2 values of .982, .951, and .971 for the regressions in Table 8-6, in the second, fourth, and sixth lines, respectively.

It is interesting to examine the consequences of adding to each of the investment equations the lagged value of its dependent variable.[69] Table 8-7 shows that they are minor for inventory investment: The coefficient of ΔM_{t-1} is not much larger than its standard error, and the inclusion of ΔM_{t-1} raises $\bar{R}^2$ from .564 to .574 only. The coefficients of the other variables are virtually unaffected (compare the corresponding entries in Table 8-7, first line, and Table 8-6, second line). On the other hand, the estimates for investment in stocks on order are strongly influenced by the addition of ΔOUM_{t-1}: $\bar{R}^2$ is raised from .465 to .598; the coefficients of U_{t-1} and OUM_{t-1} are increased, while those of the other variables are substantially reduced; and the statistical significance of N_{t-1} and ΔPM_t° is now in doubt (see Table 8-7, second line, and Table 8-6, fourth line). Thus the model used previously is shown to be quite vulnerable in this case. This is disturbing, but it may well be that the revealed weakness is due mainly to inadequate specification of the lag structure in the model.

---

[69] Flexible-accelerator models that include both lagged capital stock and lagged investment have been considered in John R. Meyer and Robert R. Glauber, *Investment Decisions, Economic Forecasting and Public Policy*, Boston, 1964 (cf. note 27 in Chapter 10 below).

Table 8-7
Regressions for Investment in Materials Inventories, Outstanding
Orders, and Inventories on Hand and on Order,
Quarterly, 1954–66

					Regression Coefficients			
Dependent Variable	Constant Term (1)	N_{t-1} (2)	U_{t-1} (3)	I_{t-1} (4)	ΔPM_t° (5)	Lagged Stock Level [a] (6)	Lagged Dependent Variable [b] (7)	$\bar{R}^2$ (8)
ΔM_t	1,964.1 (677.2)	.093 (.020)	.019 (.007)	5.377 (1.774)	2.412 (0.976)	−.430 (.091)	.158 (.111)	.574
ΔOUM_t	1,094.7 (1,594.5)	.077 (.056)	.428 (.126)	−8.552 (4.679)	3.679 (3.286)	−.937 (.240)	.520 (.133)	.598
ΔOWM_t	5,845.3 (1,407.7)	.242 (.050)	.365 (.109)	1.878 (5.510)	5.193 (3.150)	−.760 (.192)	.450 (.113)	.698

Note: Standard errors of the coefficients are given underneath in parentheses. For an explanation of the symbols, see the note to Table 8-6.

[a] M_{t-1} for the equation in the first line; OUM_{t-1} for the second line; and OWM_{t-1} for the last line.

[b] ΔM_{t-1} for the equation in the first line; ΔOUM_{t-1} for the second line; and ΔOWM_{t-1} for the last line. See Table 8-6, notes a, b, and c. Quarter-to-quarter change is denoted by Δ.

The results for investment in total materials stocks on hand and on order are more satisfactory. The over-all correlation is here fairly high for an equation with first differences ($R^2 = .736$), and all but two of the regression coefficients are more than three times larger than their standard errors. However, ΔPM_t° is considerably less effective here than in the equation without ΔOWM_{t-1}, and the coeffcient of i_{t-1} becomes positive and is reduced to a fraction of its standard error (compare Tables 8-7 and 8-6).

Estimates in Real Terms

At least some of the aspects of inventory behavior require in principle an analysis in terms of physical quantities or price-deflated values, a notable example being the possible price-change effects on inventory policies. An attempt was therefore made to discover what may be expected in the present context from the use of series expressed in constant dollars. The very limited scope and purpose of this effort must be emphasized, along with the need to recognize that deflation of aggregative data on stocks and orders presents particularly difficult estimation problems and may result in large measurement errors.

The price index PM for materials has been used as a deflator for the dependent variables, to produce the series in constant $(1957–59 = 100)$ dollars, M^*, OUM^*, and OWM^*. The all-manufacturing series have been deflated by means of the wholesale price index for manufactured products.[70]

The models underlying Table 8-6 were then re-estimated with the constant-dollar series replacing the current-dollar ones. Table 8-8, lines 1–3, shows the results for the equations that include N_{t-1} (cf. with Table 8-6). The coefficients of N^*_{t-1}, U^*_{t-1}, and the lagged values of the dependent variables are very close indeed to the coefficients of N_{t-1}, U_{t-1}, etc., in Table 8-6. The coefficients of i_{t-1} are also similar in the two sets of regressions. However, the significance of the coefficients of ΔPM°_i is considerably reduced in the estimates with price-deflated data, suggesting that some (but by no means all) of the previously observed effects of this variable must be attributed to the purely nominal movements of the value aggregates for stocks on hand and/or on order. The values of $\bar{R}^2$ in the two tables differ very little.

Rising prices may offset some of the increase in the cost of borrowing (and gains from lending) that result from rising interest rates. To the extent that inflationary expectations existed in the period surveyed, the deterrent effect of increasing interest costs was presumably blunted. It seemed advisable, therefore, to examine the effectiveness in the constant-dollar equations of the *real* interest rate i^*; but since this variable involves the *expected* changes in the general price level, it is not directly observable. The measure of i adopted here is the nominal rate minus the last actual change in prices, both expressed in percentages per year, but this proxy may be a poor one.[71]

As shown in the last three lines of Table 8-8, the coefficients of i^*_{t-1} are all negative, but the one in the inventory regression is not significantly different from zero. The coefficient of ΔPM°_i in the same regres-

---

[70] Asterisks denote the deflated series. That is, $M^*_i = 100 \ (M_i/PM_i)$, $N^*_i = 100 \ (N_i/P_i)$, etc. (where PM is the price index for materials and P the index for all manufactured products).

[71] The price series used in this computation of i^* is the all-manufacturing price index P. While not as comprehensive as might be desired, this index was deemed representative enough for our purpose.

Table 8-8
Regressions for Inventories, Outstanding Orders, and Inventories on Hand and on Order of Materials, Based on Data in Constant Dollars, Quarterly, 1954–66

				Regression Coefficients					
Line	Dependent Variable	Constant Term (1)	N^*_{t-1} (2)	U^*_{t-1} (3)	i_{t-1} (4)	i^*_{t-1} (5)	ΔPM^p_t (6)	Lagged Dependent Variable [a] (7)	$\bar{R}^2$ (8)
1	M^*_t	29.451 (8.111)	.091 (.015)	.024 (.007)	4.756 (1.348)		1.046 (0.899)	.526 (.090)	.967
2	OUM^*_t	4.579 (20.275)	.218 (.053)	.282 (.142)	−13.458 (4.542)		4.185 (3.764)	.331 (.277)	.939
3	OWM^*_t	52.625 (16.454)	.348 (.039)	.377 (.116)	−4.602 (4.466)		6.498 (3.074)	.212 (.209)	.968
4	M^*_t	24.097 (9.665)	.099 (.022)	.011 (.008)		−0.108 (0.235)	−0.176 (0.992)	.696 (.089)	.959
5	OUM^*_t	−13.163 (16.073)	.130 (.033)	.413 (.129)		−2.606 (0.754)	9.222 (3.016)	−.005 (.252)	.943
6	OWM^*_t	71.945 (18.039)	.359 (.049)	.399 (.099)		−2.061 (0.714)	5.673 (2.909)	.104 (.175)	.965

Note: Standard errors of the coefficients are given underneath in parentheses. For an explanation of the symbols, see the note to Table 8-6, the accompanying text, and also text notes 70 and 85.

[a] M^*_{t-1} for the equations in lines 1 and 4; OUM^*_{t-1} for those in lines 2 and 5; and OWM^*_{t-1} for those in lines 3 and 6.

sion is also negative and smaller than its standard error. In the equations for OUM^* and OWM^*, however, both i^*_{t-1} and ΔPM^p_t appear with significantly large and properly signed coefficients. These estimates appear quite reasonable and so, once more, the results for stocks on hand and on order are more satisfactory than those for stocks on hand alone. In other respects, the substitution of i^*_{t-1} for i_{t-1} apparently makes little difference.[72]

[72] The lagged values of the dependent variables are entirely ineffective in the equations with the real interest rate for OUM^* and OWM^*; their coefficients in the corresponding equations with i_{t-1} are larger, but they barely exceed their standard errors (compare the appropriate entries in column 7). The coefficients of N^*_{t-1} and U^*_{t-1} are not affected substantially or systematically. The substitution yields a slightly higher $\bar{R}^2$ in the regression for OUM^*, and a slightly lower $\bar{R}^2$ in the regressions for M^* and OWM^* (column 8).

Composition and Behavior of Inventories

For the durable goods sector of manufacturing, inventories of work in process have been, at least since 1953, consistently larger than those of materials and supplies, which in turn have been consistently larger than those of finished goods. These facts reflect the distribution of inventories in the large part of this sector where production to order is very important; in the more stock-oriented part, the proportion of finished goods in the inventories was much greater.[73] For the nondurable goods sector, goods-in-process stocks are the smallest; finished goods added up to smaller values than materials and supplies in the fifties but rose to exceed them in the sixties. Again, as is expected, the high proportion of finished goods is due to that large part of this sector representing manufacture to stock. For other component nondurable goods industries, the weight of finished stocks is considerably smaller.[74]

In short, there are strong indications that inventories in those industries that produce largely to order consist principally of materials and work in process, while in industries that produce mainly to stock a much larger proportion of the inventory is in finished form. It can also be said that the former industries account for a major part of total manufacturers' inventories of materials and goods in process, while the latter industries account for the bulk of total manufacturers' inventories of finished goods.

These findings confirm the argument that the finished stocks of goods made to order should be small, since such goods are usually shipped promptly. Accordingly, materials and goods in process ought to make up the bulk of inventories in industries that produce largely to order. The purpose of these stocks is to keep the delivery periods for the products into which they are processed competitively short. In production

[73] Finished stocks were particularly small relative to either of the other categories in the transportation equipment industry, due only in part to the prevalence of production to order in the nonautomotive division of this industry, since large inventories of cars are held by dealers. But finished stocks were also much smaller than materials stocks in primary metals and much smaller than work-in-process stocks in machinery. On the other hand, finished stocks were larger than either the materials or the in-process stocks in the stone, clay, and glass products industry, and they were not consistently smaller than either in the combined remaining durable goods industries. For evidence, see U.S. Department of Commerce, Bureau of the Census, *Chart Book, Manufacturers' Shipments, Inventories, and Orders: 1953–1963 Revised,* Supplement, Washington, D.C., 1964, Charts 98 and 100–104, pp. 99, 101–105.

[74] In chemicals, petroleum and coal, and rubber and plastic products, finished stocks are definitely dominant, but in the group of all other nondurable goods industries, where the weight of production to order is greater, materials stocks exceed finished stocks. See *ibid.,* Charts 99 and 105–108, pp. 100, 106–109.

to stock, where immediate delivery is expected, this can be accomplished only by holding adequate inventories of *finished* goods.

These results yield some interesting implications on the plausible assumption that the behavior of an aggregate series for inventory or inventory investment depends on the composition of the aggregate. One expectation is that changes in the demand indicators for industries engaged in production to order should have important direct effects on the stocks of goods in process as well as on those of purchased materials. On the other hand, changes in unfilled orders should have no such effects on finished-goods inventories in the same industries.

The similarity of movements in aggregate purchased-materials and goods-in-process inventories has been recognized in regression studies that combine the two categories into one aggregate or treat them separately but use nearly the same specification for each.[75] However, these approaches disregard important differences that are revealed through disaggregation by both industry and stage of fabrication. For an industry producing to order, investment in goods in process has been shown to depend positively on lagged values of orders received but negatively on current shipments (Table 8-4, second line). This result at first seems puzzling. It is attributable to production processes that typically take a long time to complete and are presumably also discontinuous.[76] The net impact of current shipments on investment in goods in process was also found to be negative for the motor vehicles sector, where output consists largely of standardized mass-produced goods but the production processes are classified as predominantly discontinuous. In other industries that work largely to stock, the estimated effects of

[75] In Lovell's equations, materials and goods in process are combined (see Table 8-3, first three lines). The estimates by Smith and Paradiso in Joint Economic Committee, *Inventory Fluctuations*, Part I, are based on separate regressions for each stage of fabrication, all of which include sales and the change in unfilled orders for the preceding quarter, as well as a lagged stock variable.

[76] Following Abramovitz, *Inventories*, pp. 160–71, stocks of goods in process can be classified into those held between and those held within stages of manufacture. In some industries, production processes are discontinuous, i.e., they combine two or more operations of making and assembling parts into a finished product, and firms can store semifinished goods between such operations or "stages." Production increases may then be accompanied by a conversion of some of these stocks into actively processed "within-stage" stocks, instead of requiring prompt and commensurate increases in total work-in-process inventories. In other industries, however, keeping surplus stocks of partly fabricated goods between stages may be either technically impossible or economically impractical, because of the prevalence of continuous (single- or multistage) processes. The proportions of aggregate inventories accounted for by the discontinuous-process industries are apparently substantial in most divisions of durable goods manufacturing, and especially for machinery and transportation equipment (see Abramovitz, *Inventories*, App. D, pp. 557–60, and Stanback, *Postwar Cycles*, pp. 96–97).

shipments are on balance positive. The new orders and backlog variables have generally positive and significant coefficients. These results appear broadly consistent with, and supplementary to, the conclusions of the studies of cyclical behavior of inventories by Abramovitz and Stanback.

Also interesting in this context is the sluggishness of finished-goods inventories, shown in the lower panel of Chart 8-4.[77] It is clear, particularly for the durables, that these aggregates tend to lag, i.e., continue to rise in the first half of contraction and to decline in the initial stage of expansion. Furthermore, stocks of finished goods tend to lag behind the other inventory investment series. Product inventories also typically continue to increase (decrease) well after the downturn (upturn) in shipments.[78]

The lags and the corresponding inverted movements in these comprehensive series can be traced to staple, nonperishable, made-to-stock goods whose production fluctuates mainly with changes in demand. The cyclical movement that is characteristic of a sample of inventory investment series for commodities in this class resembles quite well the movement observed for aggregate finished-goods investment.[79] To the extent that the inventories of these goods rise (fall) with the irregularly timed decreases (increases) in sales, they act as short-period "buffers," i.e., output stabilizers.

In accordance with these considerations, one finds that finished-goods inventories of industries working predominantly to stock, e.g., chemicals and allied products and stone, clay, and glass products, show much the same trends and cyclical fluctuations as shipments, allowing for the definitely lagging and smoother time-path of the inventories.[80] Similar, although somewhat less regular, associations are observed between the comprehensive series. In the nondurable goods sector, finished stocks followed shipments at each major turn of the period 1948–61, with lags averaging eight months. In the durable goods sector, the behavior of product inventories shows similar conformity and slug-

[77] The inventory series in book value are Department of Commerce end-of-month estimates. The deflated series, in 1947 prices, have been compiled by Thomas Stanback and are available through mid-1956 (see Stanback, *Postwar Cycles*, App. B).

[78] For evidence, see *ibid.*, Chap. 5, with reference to Abramovitz's earlier work.

[79] See *ibid.*, pp. 74–75.

[80] This is evident from the graphs in Census, *Chart Book*, pp. 14, 41, 101, and 106.

Chart 8-4
Unfilled Order Backlogs and Finished-Goods Inventories in
Current and Constant Prices, Durable and Nondurable
Goods Industries, 1948–61

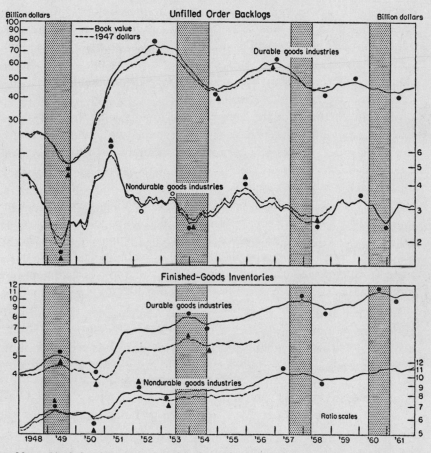

Note: Shaded areas represent business cycle contractions; unshaded areas, expansions. Triangles identify peaks and troughs in the deflated series; dots, undeflated series; circles, retardations.

Source: See note 76, in this chapter.

gishness (the average lag is about six months), with a little less consistency.[81]

I conclude that there is little doubt about the dominant role of unsold made-to-stock products in the recorded cyclical fluctuations of the finished-inventory series, and about the dependence of the latter on past values of shipments, as incorporated in many regression studies. The evidence suggests that the adjustments of finished stocks are as a rule partial and gradual, and at times too slow to prevent inverse and probably unintended movements. This may be due to predictive errors, inertia, high costs of abrupt and large changes in production rates, or some combinations of these factors.

While finished stocks are larger for the nondurables than for durables and most of the time behave similarly in the two sectors, backlogs of unfilled orders are far smaller for the nondurables than for durables and often behave very differently in the two sectors. To show these contrasts, Chart 8-4 includes, in the upper panel, the unfilled orders aggregates for both the durable and nondurable goods industries.[82] The marked differences between the series in the two panels may serve as a reminder that there is no ground for expecting finished goods to have the type of relationship with unfilled order backlogs that can be expected for purchased materials and probably also to a large extent for goods in process. Finished inventories and unfilled orders of manufacturers differ drastically in their composition. In 1954, for example, 41.9 per cent of total manufacturers' backlogs were held by the transportation equipment industry and 5.9 per cent by the entire nondurables sector; the corresponding shares in total finished-goods stocks were 6.0 per cent for transportation equipment and 52.8 per cent for nondurables. There is no simple cause-and-effect or mutual-dependence relation between the heterogeneous industry aggregates involved.

[81] The last two sentences of the text refer to the inventory series shown in Chart 8-4 for 1948–61 and to the corresponding value-of-shipments series in Chart 3-3.

[82] The deflated backlog series are calculated by cumulation of monthly differences between new orders and shipments expressed in constant (average 1947–49) prices, starting from the initial levels of unfilled orders in 1948. The differences due to the adjustments for price changes are, on the whole, not large.

Summary

Materials are acquired to be used in production; hence, their stock depends on the demand for output. Changes in purchase orders for materials express reactions of the purchasing firms to the changes in sales orders received by them. Stocks on hand and stocks on order perform closely related functions, and their sum, the total "ownership" of materials, represents a meaningful decision variable.

Buying for inventory may be significantly influenced by supply conditions. Expectations of higher prices and longer delivery lags, for example, can be destabilizing if they cause intensified ordering ahead; rises in suppliers' backlogs would then both signalize such a development and result from it. In time, however, increases of prices and delivery periods will likely begin to deter buying, and competition among suppliers will tend to counteract such increases.

Firms that accumulate unfilled orders for their products have a growing amount of business in hand and are expected to increase their buying of materials. Since the orders backlog represents future sales, this hypothesis is really an extension of the general accelerator concept of the inventory-sales relationship.

Stocks of materials increase through deliveries on purchase orders and decrease through transformation into stocks of goods in process, which in turn decrease through transformation into finished-goods stocks. Where the production processes are sufficiently long and responsive to past orders, it is possible to distinguish between the inflow and outflow factors in estimating inventories classified by stage of fabrication. Where the processes are typically short, as in many industries working to stock, such distinctions are not operational.

In production to stock, unintended changes in inventories of finished goods occur because of errors in sales forecasts. In production to order, which follows revealed rather than anticipated demand, this component of inventory investment is of minor or no importance. Inventories of products made to order consist of presold goods in transit, and their changes are largely random, apart from any long-term trends reflecting the industry's growth or the like.

The analysis indicates that one should expect inventory behavior to show systematic differences both between stages of fabrication and between industries producing mainly to stock and industries producing mainly to order. A review of literature brings out evidence that is generally consistent with this position but is rather severely limited by (1) frequent neglect of the required distinctions and (2) inadequacy of the data.

Census series for the period since 1953 permit the construction of estimates of outstanding purchase orders for materials (OUM). Quarterly regressions show OUM to be positively associated with the previous values of new and unfilled orders of all manufacturers and with the change in the price index for materials, and negatively associated with the lagged interest rate on short-term bank loans to business. These signs of the estimated coefficients agree with expectations. Purchased-material inventories (M) are less sensitive than OUM to changes in demand (the lagged order variables). The results are consistent with the view that firms can and do adjust their orders for materials considerably better than their inventories of materials. Typically, OUM are larger than M and have cyclical fluctuations of greater amplitude and earlier timing. The adjustments of M and, particularly, OUM toward desired levels do not involve very long lags. (Some recent studies of inventory behavior produced estimates that imply rather implausibly sluggish adjustments.)

Postwar data are in accord with expectations in indicating that inventories in those industries that produce largely to order consist principally of materials and goods in process, while inventories in industries that produce mainly to stock are held in much larger proportions in finished form. Stocks of finished goods tend to lag behind materials and work in process, and also behind shipments. These lags are attributable to nonperishable made-to-stock goods, which constitute the largest component category of finished stocks.

PART III

THE BEHAVIOR OF INVESTMENT
COMMITMENTS AND EXPENDITURES

9

INDICATORS AND STAGES OF INVESTMENT IN PLANT AND EQUIPMENT

Introduction: Some Important Aspects of the Investment Process

The process of capital formation in durable producer goods consists of two sets of lagged reactions: (1) Investment decisions respond, presumably with varying delays, to changes in a number of determining factors. (2) The implementation of these decisions requires time, hence expenditures lag appropriations, contracts, etc.

The lags in the implementation of investment decisions (2) are in a sense more tangible than the lags in the formation of decisions (1), and probably easier to establish. It is necessary to draw a clear distinction between the two lagged relations, both of which are of major importance in the analysis of the investment process and in theories of business cycles and the effects of stabilization policies.

Plant and equipment is a generic term denoting a vast variety of capital goods needed to satisfy the demand for capital services. The investment process is set in motion as this demand changes and the need to acquire the capital goods is recognized. The initial stages of technical and economic planning and cost estimation may be long and important, but they apparently are not directly represented in the data available for measuring aspects of the investment process. In time, the decision to invest becomes firmer, with respect to both the details of the project and the time it is to be initiated; and funds to finance it are budgeted, appropriated, and contractually committed. These latter stages can be measured by the current aggregative series on capital appropriations and investment orders and contracts.

It is at this point that orders data may find their first application to investment analysis. As the orders for equipment and contracts for plant are filled, payments are made on their account. Meanwhile, the capital goods, which are to be the end product of the process, as far as their sellers are concerned, assume their material form and economic function. That is, they are produced, built, shipped, and installed—in short, acquired in some way to render services to the user.

The demand for capital services is a function of the demand for the output which these services help to produce. The demand for outputs of manufacturing industries is measured by manufacturers' orders. This is the second point at which orders data appear as potentially useful for investment analysis. The two applications are certainly different in concept and in their data requirements.

On the Role and Timing of Investment Decisions

The view that investment expenditures play a central role in business cycles is an old one, held by many economists. Its main sources are the following notions or observations: (1) that these expenditures are neither constrained nor required by prior receipts, and are not closely related to the latter; (2) that they fluctuate during business cycles with wider relative amplitudes than other major expenditure categories; (3) that they lag, often by long intervals, the *decisions* to invest; and (4) that the investment decisions themselves have a cyclical pattern and a tendency to lead at peaks and troughs in aggregate economic activity.

Point (1) has been particularly emphasized in those Keynesian models where investment is treated as an important category of "autonomous" expenditures that set in motion the multiplier process; but it is also found, *mutatis mutandis,* in some older theories in which much weight is attached to investment. The other points concern empirical observations: (2) can be said to have long been well established; (3) is plausible enough and was often assumed, but the relevant measurements have until recently been few and quite crude—which is not surprising, as it is not easy to measure investment "decisions"; and (4) is even more difficult to establish for the same reason, and is much more in need of being documented since it is far from obvious.

A cyclical model of the economy can be constructed on the basis of (1), (3), and (4); (2) is neither a necessary nor a sufficient condition here. However, positing (1), interpreted to mean that investment is independent of income, cannot be simply taken for granted. It is a hypothesis which, far from being established empirically, is widely viewed as dubious and unsatisfactory. The situation for (3) and (4) is very different: There is already much evidence to validate and quantify these statements, owing largely to recent gains in assembling data that reflect investment decisions, such as orders and appropriations.

The existence of (4) is particularly important because it appears to be a necessary condition for the validity of any hypothesis that ascribes to investment the prime causal role in business cycles. It is difficult to see how any hypothesis in this class could be successfully defended if the decisions to invest and the resulting commitments did not tend to move ahead of aggregate production and income. Expenditures on plant and equipment actually lag at business cycle turns, which was deemed by some to be the major argument against the investment hypothesis of the cycle. But this is not convincing, since it ignores the possibility that investment commitments may lead and have important influences of their own.

In fact, the early cyclical timing of commitments can be well documented, as will be shown in this chapter. But it must be recognized that acceptance of both (3) and (4) is still *not* sufficient for a demonstration that investment is indeed the prime mover in major fluctuations of the economy. As elsewhere, one must guard here against the *post hoc, ergo propter hoc* fallacy. Even if the amounts of investment decided upon begin to swell and shrink ahead of the troughs and peaks of the economy at large, this does not necessarily mean that these early changes in investment commitments are "the cause" and the later changes in general business activity "the effect." Investment decisions are necessarily the antecedent and can be treated as the proximate "cause" of investment spending [as stated in (3)]. There are also further propagation effects to the extent that increases in this spending stimulate and decreases discourage other types of expenditure. But it is conceivable that other factors, more "autonomous" than investment, determine first the investment decisions and then spending.[1]

---

[1] Cf. Milton Friedman and Anna J. Schwartz, "Money and Business Cycles," *Review of Economics and Statistics, Supplement,* February 1963, p. 48, n. 21.

Issues Relating to the Cyclical Behavior of Investment

The lag of investment expenditures behind investment decisions is an essential element in several otherwise quite different theories of business cycles. Consider the hypothesis that downturns of investment are attributable to the stresses of advanced expansion in aggregate income and output. It could be used to explain why investment decisions (or commitments) begin to decline. But investment expenditures can hardly be assumed to decline simultaneously in a degree sufficient to bring about a general business downturn, for this would at once cut off the rise in income, whereas income must be permitted to rise if the changes that are unfavorable to investment are to develop. Introduction of an expenditure lag removes this logical difficulty by reminding us that investment undertakings can already be declining while investment expenditures and income are still rising. The undertakings determine future spending on investment, but current income is associated with current spending. Thus it can be argued that the lag in the execution of investment projects (contracts or orders) plays a critical role in explaining business cycle reversals in theories that link investment decisions to elements of current and recent incomes and their distribution.

An argument along the above lines was made by Milton Friedman in his interpretation of Wesley Mitchell's view of the investment process and its role in business cycles.[2] To recall its salient points, Mitchell's analysis (first developed in his 1913 *Business Cycles*) relates investment decisions to profits expectations and the latter to current profits and their distribution. As a business expansion unfolds, aggregate income rises and so do both the volume of sales and average profit margins; hence, total profits must increase. Later in the expansion, however, profit margins begin to decline because of rising cost schedules and the tendency for many buying prices to increase faster than selling prices. When the decline in margins eventually outweighs the continuing increase in sales, total profits turn down. These developments influence strongly the timing of decisions to implement investment projects. New investment commitments begin to decline, which is an early factor of great importance in the process leading to the gen-

[2] Milton Friedman, "Wesley C. Mitchell as an Economic Theorist," *Journal of Political Economy*, December 1950; reprinted in Arthur F. Burns, ed., *Wesley Clair Mitchell, The Economic Scientist*, New York, NBER, 1952; see in particular pp. 263–66.

eral business downturn. Investment expenditures, on the other hand, lag in this process, reflecting the long periods of time that are required for completion of many undertakings to build and equip productive plant.

An early appearance of the distinction between orders and deliveries of capital goods marks a business cycle model by Kalecki (1933). In this system, deliveries lag behind orders for capital goods by a given "gestation period," θ. Gross saving or "accumulation" equals production of capital goods, which proceeds at a rate measured by the average volume of unfilled investment orders over the interval θ. Net investment, or the change in capital stock, equals capital goods deliveries minus depreciation of capital equipment due to wear and tear and obsolescence. The ratio of new investment orders to capital stock is a function of the rate of profit, and real gross profit itself is related to gross accumulation. The model implies that new investment orders are an increasing function of capital goods production and a decreasing function of the existing capital stock. It produces a cyclical movement by letting the capital stock itself fluctuate, that is, capital goods deliveries periodically fall short of replacement requirements.[3]

In models based on the interaction of savings and investment functions, fluctuations can come about by assumption either of certain time-lags or of certain nonlinearities or both. In his 1940 model, Nicholas Kaldor employs nonlinear functions and deliberately abstracts from lags.[4]

The familiar business cycle model of J. R. Hicks (1950) represents a theory which employs both lags and nonlinearities. For investment in plant and equipment, Hicks suspends the accelerator over a part of the cycle (because of surplus capacity), making it operative only in the later stages of expansion and at the beginning of the contraction. Dis-

[3] M. Kalecki, "A Macrodynamic Theory of Business Cycles," *Econometrica*, 1935, pp. 327–44 (paper presented in 1933). This business cycle model underwent several changes in Kalecki's later works, but the feature of the orders-delivery lag for capital goods has been retained throughout this development. Given the structural coefficients of these models, the length of that lag determines the duration of the implicit cycles and whether or not they are damped (in the absence of erratic shocks).
[4] N. Kaldor, "A Model of the Trade Cycle," *Economic Journal*, March 1940, pp. 78–92. Kaldor regards it as a virtue of his model that it does not depend on particular parameters, lags, or initial "shocks." But a theory of business cycles may also suffer from being overly self-contained (endogenous) and too dependent on particular nonlinearities. The virtual disregard of lags can hardly be a merit if the theory is to retain contact with fluctuations in the real world, which surely include certain lags as one of their foremost features. And it is not established at all that lags *should* be important only "in determining the *period* of the cycle" and have no part "in explaining its existence" (*ibid.*, p. 92).

tributed lags are worked into the consumption function and are also included, somewhat cursorily, in the discussion of induced investment. The main effect of replacing a simple discrete lag by a longer lag, which spreads the response of investment to changes in output over several periods, is to prolong the expansion (for any given combination of values for the coefficients of the consumption and induced investment functions).[5]

Whether simple or distributed, the lags are assumed to remain unchanged over the cycle, as are the coefficients of the system. Yet in the case of the fixed investment function, one can expect the lags to increase late in expansion, when, due to the strain on capacities of capital goods producers, more time is likely to be required, on the average, for investment contracts to materialize in deliveries and installations. Such a development would be accompanied in part by price increases and in part by unfilled orders accumulations, which may temporarily provide some further stimulation of investment demand. It seems improbable that the latter would then be kept in check by the current and recent increases in output or for that matter that it would bear any fixed relation to these increases.

The extension of the lag, however, may tend to prolong the expansion (in analogy to Hicks's comparison of simple and distributed lags). The resulting increase in the orders backlog may also tend to make the downturn more gradual and the early stages of contraction less severe, for old unfilled contracts can provide a reserve of work to be carried out long after new investment has been curtailed.[6] Gestation periods for various types of investment projects vary widely. Also, the peaks of orders for different categories of capital goods usually fall on dates that are scattered over a substantial period rather than being heavily concentrated at one time. These facts make for a less sharp decline in aggregate investment orders and for a more gradual and lagged decline

[5] J. R. Hicks, *A Contribution to the Theory of the Trade Cycle*, Oxford, England, 1950, pp. 113–15.

[6] On the other hand, depletion of the backlog may worsen the economic situation in the midst of a downswing. Expenditures on, and presumably also completions of, investment projects tend to reach their peaks when a business decline is already in progress. Burns draws attention to a suggestive fact when he notes that "it appears that the crop of newly completed factories reaches its maximum when contraction is well under way—or just in time to intensify the competitive struggle then in progress." Cf. Arthur F. Burns, "Economic Research and the Keynesian Thinking of Our Times," *Twenty-Sixth Annual Report of the National Bureau of Economic Research*, New York, June 1946; reprinted in Burns, *The Frontiers of Economic Knowledge*, New York, NBER, 1954; see p. 23.

in investment expenditure than could be hypothesized in disregard of them. They create a presumption against the concept of abrupt downturns in general economic activity being caused by a recurring collapse of confidence in the profitability of investment undertakings and a consequent collapse of "aggregate investment" as such.[7]

It is indeed likely that the demand for new plant and equipment will weaken and eventually fall off when capacity increases begin to overtake output increases, or when most firms come to hold the expectation that this is imminent. But the concepts involved are extremely difficult to handle. Short-term changes in the demand for its products currently appear to a firm as erratic in a large degree. It is not easy to distinguish with sufficient confidence a change that is just transitory from one that is more lasting and less risky to use for extrapolation. Measurement of existing capacities is difficult, and estimation of required capacities even more so. The analyst also faces formidable problems of aggregation.

As shown by this brief and selective survey, important issues in business cycle analysis relate to the internal lag structure and the cyclical timing of investment stages. These matters require much further study before the lagged relations involved can be adequately specified, estimated, and tested. This chapter and the next will report merely on a few small steps in this direction.

Investment Plans, Commitments, and Outlays

New Orders for Producer Equipment and Construction Contracts for Plant

The aggregate of new orders received by durable goods manufacturers contains not only some that correspond to the "equipment" component of business fixed investment outlays, but also a large variety of other kinds. These include orders placed by domestic intermediate (nonfinal) users for resale purposes, those placed by foreigners, and those placed by the government.[8]

---

[7] This idea, found in many recent writings, goes back to Keynes and his, certainly understandable, preoccupation with the rapid business contraction of the early 1930's. Cf. Burns, *Frontiers*, pp. 18–19.

[8] All orders for consumer durable goods must, of course, be excluded in deriving the business investment order series. But these would typically be "resale" orders, received from the trade sectors, as consumers do not ordinarily place direct orders with manufacturers.

The breakdown by major industries used in the published Commerce figures on new orders permits only a very crude approximation to what is needed here: a series on commitments for the purchase of equipment by business enterprise. However, much better estimates of new orders for industrial and other productive equipment were made available in 1961 by the Department of Commerce on the basis of a more detailed classification of their orders data.[9]

The series of new orders for machinery and equipment in its present form includes new orders received by the following thirteen durable goods industries: steam engines and turbines; internal combustion engines; construction, mining, and materials-handling machinery; metalworking machinery; miscellaneous equipment; special industrial machinery; general industrial machinery; office and store machines; service industry machinery; electrical transmission, distribution equipment; electrical industrial apparatus; other electrical machinery; and shipbuilding and railroad equipment. Orders for other industries do not, for the most part, represent business purchases of equipment. The exclusion of these industries, however, does mean omitting such important items as trucks and commercial aircraft.[10] On the other hand, inclusion of all *orders* received by the machinery and equipment industries results in overstatement, since some of these orders are placed by government and foreign buyers.

The information needed to correct for these elements of under- and overestimation is essentially lacking because the statistics are reported by the receiving industry rather than by product and user categories. Also, like the output of multiproduct companies that are included in an industry according to the definition of their main productive activity, orders received by an industry are highly diversified. However, a significant improvement in the latter respect has probably resulted from

[9] These estimates were introduced in Victor Zarnowitz, "The Timing of Manufacturers' Orders During Business Cycles," in Geoffrey H. Moore, ed., *Business Cycle Indicators*, Princeton for NBER, 1961, Vol. I, pp. 475 ff. The data were published in *ibid.*, Vol. II, series 6.1, p. 90. Since autumn 1961, the monthly figures have been reported regularly in U.S. Department of Commerce, *Business Cycle Developments*, as series 24, "Value of manufacturers' new orders, machinery and equipment industries." Since December 1963, this series has been published in revised form to reflect the 1963 revision of the Industry Survey data and to exclude fabricated metal products.

[10] Most of the output of the motor vehicle industry consists of consumer durables (civilian passenger automobiles). Military purchases are also important here, but even more so in the nonautomotive transportation equipment industry, particularly aircraft. This explains the decision to omit these industries from the aggregate of private orders for capital equipment.

the 1963 revision that put the data on a divisional instead of company basis (see the description of the current Census data at the beginning of Chapter 3, above).

Before 1963, the series of new orders for machinery and equipment included fabricated metal products. The selection of this industry seems to have been largely an error, since fabricated metals represent mainly materials to be further processed rather than capital goods bought by first users. However, since we have used the old data in the part of the subsequent analysis that predated the 1963 changes in the orders series, Chart 9-1 presents these data in two versions: with and without new orders for fabricated metal products (see curves 2 and 3). The two series run a closely similar course, although their levels differ substantially, since the fabricated metal orders add up to rather large monthly amounts.

The "plant" component of business capital formation is not directly represented in the new-order aggregate. The best counterpart to it among the commitments data is the series of contracts awarded to building contractors for industrial and commercial construction, plus contracts for privately owned public works and public utilities, as compiled by the F. W. Dodge Corporation. This series is plotted as curve 4 in Chart 9-1.[11]

The aggregate of current commitments to invest in plant and equipment combines series 2 and 4. Since the data on construction contracts as well as those on new orders are in current-dollar values, the series can be combined by simple addition. In the resulting totals, the component categories are weighted by the transaction volumes they represent. The estimated totals of equipment orders and plant contracts are shown as curve 1 in Chart 9-1.

The chart makes it clear that the construction contract values form a highly volatile series with large month-to-month variations, especially in the period before 1954. New orders are much less erratic and have a considerably clearer cyclical pattern. It is also evident that the total

[11] The Dodge data cover private projects of $10,000 minimum valuation (previously, lower valuations were included). The data available for our purpose cover thirty-seven eastern and southern states in 1948–56 and forty-eight states since then. They include contracts for commercial buildings such as banks, offices, stores, garages, etc., and for manufacturing buildings (e.g., processing, mechanical). Adjustments for cancellations, additions, and corrections are made when ascertained. For more detail, see the description and references in Moore, ed., *Business Cycle Indicators*, Vol. II, series 6.0, pp. 12–14.

Chart 9-1
Manufacturers' New Orders for Machinery and Equipment and Contracts for Plant Construction, 1949–61

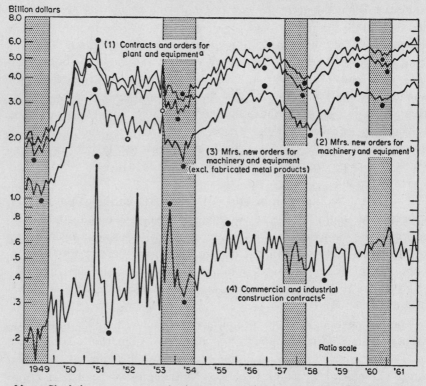

Note: Shaded areas represent business contractions; unshaded areas, expansions. Dots identify peaks and troughs of specific cycles; circles identify minor turns and retardations.

Source: U.S. Department of Commerce, Office of Business Economics; F. W. Dodge Corporation.

[a] This series is the sum of series 2 and 4 in this chart.
[b] Includes new orders for fabricated metal products.
[c] Includes contracts for privately owned public works and utilities.

investment orders-and-contracts series reflects the behavior of new orders much more than contracts, because orders are a large, and contracts a relatively small, component of the total.

In fact, the new-order data overstate investment in equipment and the contracts data understate investment in plant greatly. For example, the value of new orders received by industries producing machinery and equipment averaged $52 billion (annual rate) in 1956–58 if fabricated metal products are included, and $35 billion if they are excluded. In the same period, the producer durable equipment component of gross national product had an average annual value of $27 billion. There is no doubt that the new orders aggregates include products that should be regarded as "materials" rather than "final" capital goods. Elimination of fabricated metals appears to remedy much but not all of this overstatement. Materials can of course be counted repeatedly at successive production stages. The orders figures are gross, while the investment expenditure data on the GNP basis are net, of such duplications. (The latter are presumably "gross" only in the sense of covering outlays for replacements as well as new net additions to the stock of real capital held by business.)

For the construction contracts component of our investment commitments series, the annual average value for 1956–58 was somewhat less than $7 billion. The corresponding figure for the value of industrial and commercial construction and other private nonfarm nonresidential construction was somewhat more than $14 billion. In part, this large difference in levels reflects conceptual divergencies, but it does indicate the amount of undercoverage of construction projects in the contracts data.[12]

An approximate correction for the overstatement of equipment orders (EO) and understatement of plant contracts (PC) in the simple aggregate of orders and contracts (OC) was made by constructing a reweighted aggregate, OC^r, according to the formula $OC^r = (1.6/4.9)$ $(EO) + PC$. Here new orders for producer equipment (excluding fabricated metal products) are given only about one-third of their former weight relative to plant contracts. This is done because the average ratio for 1957–59 of producer durable equipment to nonresidential structures was approximately 1.6, according to the national income accounts of the Department of Commerce, while the corresponding average ratio of equipment orders to plant contracts was about 4.9.

In Chart 9-2, the first curve shows OC and the second shows the re-

[12] Commercial and industrial building contracts accounted for about 78 per cent of the value of this type of construction completed in 1956–58; other private nonfarm nonresidential construction contracts (of which not all are included in our series) accounted for only 42 per cent of the value put-in-place. The proportion for both categories combined was approximately 59 per cent. (See Moore, ed., *Business Cycle Indicators*, Vol. II, p. 14.) Before 1956, the coverage of the Dodge statistics was considerably lower because eleven western states were excluded. It is estimated that construction in these states amounted to 20 per cent or more of the national total in the period 1926–56.

Chart 9-2
Commitments and Expenditures for Plant and Equipment,
Quarterly, 1953–65

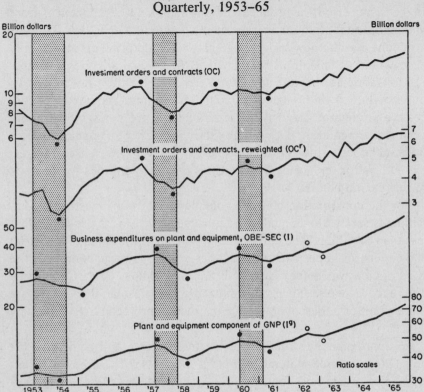

Note: Shaded areas represent business cycle contractions; unshaded areas, expansions. Dots identify peaks and troughs of specific cycles; circles, minor turns and retardations.

Source: U.S. Department of Commerce; Securities and Exchange Commission; F. W. Dodge Corporation.

weighted series OC^r, each in quarterly, seasonally adjusted form, for 1953–65. These graphs are based on the most recent Census data on new orders of the machinery and equipment industries and also the latest Dodge data on commercial and industrial contracts. The relative movements of the two series are on the whole quite similar; the effects of the reweighting are thus fairly small. The short variations in OC^r are often a little larger than those in OC (see the curves for 1953 and 1962–64), which reflects the relatively large erratic movements in the

PC series, which is given greater weight in OC^r than in OC. The cyclical turning points in the two series coincide, except for the peaks in 1959–60, where OC seems to have an earlier major turn; but even here the difference is marginal.[13]

Fixed-Investment Orders and Expenditures

The investment orders-and-contracts series – both the simple (OC) and the reweighted (OC^r) aggregates – can be used as indicators of business expenditures on plant and equipment. The investment commitments and expenditures data are compared in quarterly form in Chart 9-2.

The capital outlay estimates denoted as I (curve 3) are compiled by the Office of Business Economics, U.S. Department of Commerce (OBE), and the Securities and Exchange Commission (SEC). They are derived from reports by corporations registered with the SEC, by unincorporated and incorporated companies reporting to the OBE, and by a group of transportation firms under the jurisdiction of the Interstate Commerce Commission. The total sample accounts for over 60 per cent of aggregate new investment in plant and equipment, but coverage varies among the industries.[14] These figures, then, reflect the actual quarterly costs that are charged to capital accounts. Ordinarily, depreciation accounts are maintained for such outlays. The data come from the reports of those who, having placed the investment orders and contracts, incur the costs as measured by the expenditure. On the other hand, the value of investment commitments is estimated in large part from the reports of firms in the machinery and equipment industries, i.e., those who have received the orders.

The OBE-SEC business capital outlays series (I) is not as comprehensive as the plant-and-equipment component of GNP (I^g) (curve 4 in Chart 9-2). The OBE-SEC data exclude, while the GNP data include, investment by professionals, nonprofit institutions, real estate firms, and insurance companies; expenditures for petroleum and natural gas well drilling; and capital outlays charged to current expense (e.g., hand tools). The average annual value of business expenditures

---

[13] A double-peak configuration will be noted in each of the two series during this period. In OC, the 1959 peak is a little higher than the 1960 one, while the reverse applies to OC^r (see Chart 9-2).

[14] It is high in railroad transportation, public utilities, and some manufacturing industries, and low in real estate and parts of the financial sector. See description and references in Moore, ed., *Business Cycle Indicators*, Vol. II, series 22.0, pp. 54–55.

on plant and equipment in 1956–58 was $34 billion according to the OBE-SEC estimates, but $41 billion in the GNP accounts.[15] Despite these differences in coverage between I and I^g, the relative movements in the two series resemble each other closely most of the time (the only significant divergence shown on the chart is in the second half of 1954).

The orders-contracts figures are more nearly comparable to I than to I^g, and the OBE-SEC data will be used more intensively in the analysis to follow than the GNP data. However, only the latter provide a division of the expenditures into those for producer durable equipment (PDE) and those for plant or nonresidential structures (Str), which makes it possible to set up separate investment realization functions for the two types of capital goods. In the OBE-SEC data, outlays on equipment and construction are not available separately.

Chart 9-2 accords with general expectations of what the relation between investment commitments and expenditures should be. The time-path of outlays on investment goods resembles the course of new orders and contracts for such goods, but the fluctuations in outlays lag behind those in orders and have smaller relative amplitudes. Two-quarter lags of expenditures are observed at the I-1957 peaks and again at the I-1958 troughs of commitments (regardless of whether orders are represented by OC or by OC^r and whether expenditures are measured by I or by I^g). Three-quarter lags of I are recorded at the II-1954 trough and at the III-1959 peak of OC.[16] However, the upturns of investment orders and expenditures coincide in the second quarter of 1961.

Chart 9-3 demonstrates a very similar relationship between the equipment components of fixed-investment commitments and outlays. In the period from I-1953 to II-1954, new orders for machinery and equipment (EO) declined strongly, while the PDE expenditures rose a little in the first two quarters of this interval and decreased gently in the next three. Then EO turned up sharply between II-1954 and I-1955, while PDE barely increased, describing a "flat-bottom" movement that

[15] This is approximately the sum of $27 billion of producer durable equipment and $14 billion of private nonresidential nonfarm construction. (Of course, this aggregate, like that for business capital outlays compiled by the OBE-SEC, excludes expenditures by farmers and on all residential housing.)

[16] The 1954 trough in I^g falls in the second quarter, just like the troughs in OC and OC^r, but actually I^g did not start rising significantly until after I-1955, i.e., three quarters later (see the text below about the underlying behavior of expenditures on producer durable equipment). The use of the late peak of OC^r in 1960 could also lead to a misleading timing comparison (see note 13, above).

Chart 9-3
Commitments and Expenditures for Producers' Durable Equipment and for Structures, Quarterly, 1953–65

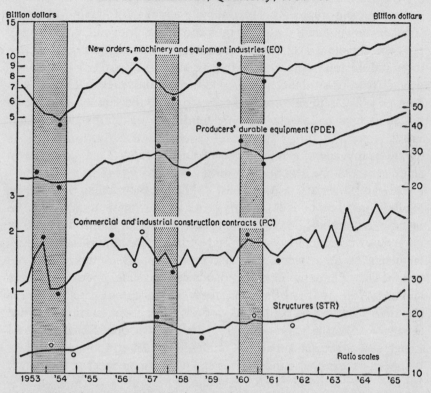

Note: Shaded areas represent business cycle contractions; unshaded areas, expansions. Dots identify peaks and troughs of specific cycles; circles, minor turns and retardations.

Source: U.S. Department of Commerce; F. W. Dodge Corporation.

only in 1955 ended in a decisive upswing. Thus, although the troughs or lowest standings of the two series technically coincide in II-1954, the actual recovery of *PDE* lagged behind the upturn in *EO* by three quarters. At the peaks of 1956–57 and 1959–60, two lags of *PDE* relative to *EO* of three quarters each are clearly seen on the chart. The 1958 troughs are separated by a two-quarter lag. Again, only the II-1961 troughs appear to be really coincident.

Contracts for commercial and industrial plant construction (*PC*) and outlays for the nonresidential structures component of fixed investment (*Str*) differ much more. *PC* shows large erratic variations, but *Str* follows a generally quite smooth course (Chart 9-3). The erratic appearance of *PC* is no doubt in considerable measure due to the limited sample coverage of this series, but a marked differentiation of this sort between commitments and realizations would be expected in this area and is believed to represent a real and basic phenomenon. Structures presumably require substantially longer gestation or "delivery" periods than does equipment; hence there is more room here for stabilization of the flow of funds spent relative to the flow of funds committed — which reflects the stabilization of production relative to demand.

As a result, the two series for investment in plant show particularly sharp contrasts on several occasions. Thus in 1954 *PC* first declined steeply and then rose substantially, while *Str* merely flattened off. In 1960–61, *Str* responded similarly, with a prolonged sideward movement, to a marked contraction and recovery in *PC*. In 1963–65, short up-and-down movements in *PC* were transformed into a smooth upward drift in *Str*. Such strong smoothing suppresses turning points, and thus few direct timing comparisons can be made, but the estimates leave little doubt about the pronounced tendency of expenditures for plant construction to lag behind contracts. These retardations in *Str* lag behind the contractions in *PC* by intervals of one to two quarters. Longer lags — six quarters at the 1956–57 peaks and four quarters at the 1958–59 troughs in the two series — can also be observed, although there is some uncertainty about these observations because of double-turn configurations in *PC*.[17]

Older data covering the earlier postwar years show the same type of relationship between new investment orders and contracts and business expenditures on plant and equipment. Curve 1 from Chart 9-1 is reproduced in quarterly form in Chart 9-4 (the OBE-Dodge series including fabricated metals orders). With it are shown the OBE-SEC series for fixed-investment outlays of all industries and all manufacturing, 1948–61 (curves 3 and 4). Again, it is evident that the cyclical movements in outlays follow with substantial lags and smaller relative amplitudes the corresponding fluctuations in new orders. The one con-

---

[17] Thus, when measured from the secondary peak of *PC* in I-1957, the lag of *Str* is two quarters, but such a comparison would ignore the fact that *PC* declined strongly in 1956, while *Str* kept increasing.

Chart 9-4
Investment Orders and Contracts, Actual and Anticipated Business Expenditures on Plant and Equipment, and New Capital Appropriations and Outlays by Manufacturing Companies, 1948–61

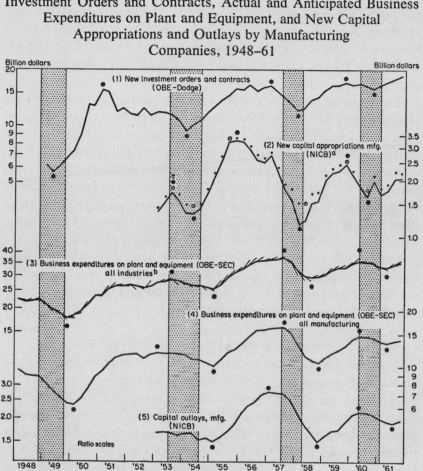

Note: Shaded areas represent business cycle contractions; unshaded areas, expansions. Dots identify specific peaks and troughs of specific cycles.

Source: U.S. Department of Commerce, Office of Business Economics; Securities and Exchange Commission; F. W. Dodge Corporation; National Industrial Conference Board.

[a] Net of cancellations. Computed by addition of series for component industries, seasonally adjusted by NBER. The gross appropriations figures, seasonally adjusted by NICB, are shown as points lying above the net appropriations curve. (The encircled points represent the specific-cycle turns in the gross appropriations series.)

[b] The solid curve shows actual expenditures. The points linked with the curve are "first anticipations" of the expenditures converted to the present levels. They are obtained by taking the first anticipated changes $(A_1 - A_2)$ and adding these changes, observing signs, to the present levels. The links connect actual expenditures of any given quarter with the anticipated expenditures of the next quarter; the former is the quarter in which the projection was made; the latter is the quarter to which the projected figure refers. The anticipations data are seasonally adjusted by the source since 1953; for the earlier years, they were adjusted by means of the average seasonal factors for 1953–58.

spicuous difference between these series is that the short but pronounced "Korean" cycle in investment orders, with a high peak in the first quarter of 1951, is largely smoothed out in the series on expenditures for plant and equipment (as it is in the corresponding production and shipments series).

On five occasions, two-quarter lags of business capital outlays are recorded at cyclical turns of new investment orders in Chart 9-4 (compare curves 1 and 3). At the 1954 trough, the lag is four quarters, and at the 1951 peak it is as long as ten quarters. That peak, of course, was associated with the heavy accumulation of unfilled order backlogs during the first year of the Korean War. The average lag of outlays in the period since 1949 turns out to be 10.3 months according to these data. For the period since 1954, it is 7.2 months, similar to the average lag of 6 months obtained by using the new data from Chart 9-2.

To conclude, it is reassuring to find that the main results of the analysis in this section show a certain degree of robustness in that they do not depend critically on which of the different sets of data for fixed-investment orders and expenditures are used.

Capital Appropriations, Commitments, and Spending

Chart 9-4 includes quarterly series on new capital appropriations and capital expenditures of several hundred large manufacturing companies reporting to the National Industrial Conference Board.[18] An "approved capital appropriation" is an authorization by top management (typically the board of directors or president) of a future capital expenditure. Appropriations cover new plants and buildings, additions to or improvements of plants and buildings, new machinery, office machines, storage equipment, and motor vehicles for business use. Ex-

[18] The number of reporting companies has increased over time. Data for 1953–54 from a 353-company subsample were linked to the 1955–58 data from a 507-company subsample; the latter again were linked to the 1958–60 data for the currently responding 602-company sample. The series have recently been adjusted for seasonal variation. (The NICB publishes the figures in unadjusted form in the *Conference Board Business Record* but provides the user with some charts of the adjusted series.) In addition to statistics of newly approved capital appropriations, cancellations, and expenditures, the NICB compiles data on volume ("backlog") of appropriations outstanding, amounts committed and spent, and the percentage of companies reporting increases in appropriations. All these measures are based on a continuing quarterly survey among the nation's largest manufacturing companies. For a description of statistical procedures, the survey coverage, and limitations of the data, see *Conference Board Business Record*, October 1956 and July 1960; and Morris Cohen, "The National Industrial Conference Board Survey of Capital Appropriations," in *The Quality and Economic Significance of Anticipations Data*, Universities–National Bureau Conference 10, Princeton for NBER, 1960.

cluded are funds earmarked for land purchase, maintenance and repair, acquisition of existing companies, used equipment and buildings, and capital spending outside the United States.

The approval of a capital appropriation confirms or changes the annual capital budget of the company. In setting up the budget, the first stage is to complete the process of planning and executing capital outlays; the second stage is the appropriations procedure in which the budget is disaggregated and "tested" by individual projects.[19] The third stage, logically, would be the commitment of the money, i.e., placing of the order or contract for equipment or plant. Actual outlays may begin as construction work takes place and machinery and equipment are produced, shipped, and installed. In the last stage the payment for the capital goods acquired is completed and the expenditure is recorded.

In this sequence, appropriations lead commitments (investment orders). In fact, for those companies in the NICB sample which report commitments as distinguished from expenditures, commitments of appropriated funds do show some lag vis-à-vis the approvals of such funds, though the lag appears to be relatively short and irregular.[20] The amplitudes of appropriations exceed those of commitments. These observations, however, are highly tentative as they are based on slender evidence. Only about 35 per cent of the companies in the NICB sample are able to report their commitments.[21]

New authorizations made during a quarter add to the backlog of appropriations outstanding at the beginning of the quarter; commitment or spending, as well as cancellation, of the appropriations reduce the backlog. Hence the change in the appropriations backlog during a given quarter equals the difference between new approvals and the sum of the appropriations committed, spent, or cancelled. For the companies unable to report commitments—the majority of the sample—outstanding appropriations are taken to expire only when spent or cancelled. The fact that the appropriation backlog series is largely on an expended rather than "committed" basis makes it less forward looking than it

[19] Cohen, "Capital Appropriations," p. 300.

[20] Thus, for 117 durable goods manufacturers, a downturn in appropriations occurred in IV-1955 and a downturn in commitments in II-1956; but both series moved briefly down together in III-1956, whereupon commitments reached a secondary peak in IV-1956 and appropriations in I-1957. In 1958, both appropriations and commitments turned up together in the third quarter. See Conference Board Business Record, July 1960, p. 7.

[21] Cohen, "Capital Appropriations," p. 307.

would be otherwise. Since the placement of orders precedes spending, uncommitted appropriations backlogs should be an earlier anticipatory series than the unexpended backlogs.[22]

For comparisons with orders and expenditures, appropriations are best taken net of cancellations. The latter, however, are apparently not large enough to create major discrepancies between the time-paths of gross and net appropriations; the two series tend to move closely together and turn at the same time, as shown in Chart 9-4.[23]

Relating the Aggregative Data on Investment Stages

Even if manufacturers' new capital appropriations (App) should lead investment orders placed by the same companies, they need not lead our investment orders-contracts series (OC), which has a different and broader scope. The investment orders are reported by the firms that receive them; the appropriations, by those that place the orders. The former data relate to orders to be processed by manufacturers and to contracts for plant construction to be put in place by builders. These orders and contracts originate in many sectors of the U.S. economy as well as abroad; but appropriations all originate with large domestic manufacturing corporations.[24]

Nevertheless, it would not be implausible if appropriations actually did have a definite tendency to lead new orders for capital goods. It cannot be firmly established that this is actually so, since the timing of these series appears to have been more nearly coincident on a few occasions, notably at troughs in 1954, 1958, and 1967; but on the average a short lag of orders is indicated, at least at the peaks. At the height

---

[22] Let B_t be the appropriations backlog *at the end* of the quarter; A_t^g, gross new appropriations; C_t, cancellations; $A_t^n = A_t^g - C_t$, net new appropriations; O_t^*, capital commitments for those companies that report them; E_t^*, capital expenditures for the other companies; $E_t = O_t^* + E_t^*$, appropriations committed or spent. (All these variables, except B, which is a stock, are flows *during* the quarter.) Then, $B_{t-1} + A_t^g - C_t - O_t^* - E_t^* = B_t$ or $B_t - B_{t-1} = \Delta B_t = A_t^n - E_t$.

For those companies which report appropriations on a commitment basis, B_t represents capital appropriations outstanding that have yet to be committed, i.e., the backlog of capital goods orders yet to be placed. This should be a foreshadowing series for unfilled orders recorded by the receiving companies in the capital-goods-producing industries: However, for all those firms that do not report commitments, outstanding totals of appropriations represent unexpended, rather than uncommitted, backlogs. Here the orders may have been placed earlier; all that the totals tell us is that a certain sum of money is yet to be spent. It is important to note that this distinction applies to the meaning of the appropriations backlogs, not to the newly approved appropriations which, unless cancelled, do represent investment orders to be placed. See *Conference Board Business Record*, October 1956, p. 425.

[23] Cancellations did increase in the vicinity of troughs in appropriations, particularly in 1958 and less so in 1954. Compare gross and net appropriations in Chart 9-4.

[24] Recently, the NICB has also begun reporting appropriation figures for electrical and gas utilities.

of the investment boom of the mid-1950's, appropriations did in fact lead orders by a long interval (compare curves 1 and 2 in Chart 9-4). For the 1959 peaks, the comparison is somewhat inconclusive, depending as it does on which of the orders-contracts series is used (compare the OC curves in Charts 9-2 and 9-4), but the best indication is one of roughly coincident timing. However, it is particularly notable here that OC declined initially very little in 1960, lingering at high levels well after App dropped off sharply. In 1966, App reached a peak in the second quarter, OC in September (or third quarter); and most recently App had its highest value in the third quarter of 1969, OC in January 1970.[25]

Manufacturers' appropriations have considerably larger percentage amplitudes of cyclical movement than the total investment orders (compare curves 1 and 2 in Chart 9-4). Similarly, the NICB capital outlays of manufacturers move in larger cycles, measured in percentages, than do total business expenditures on plant and equipment (cf. curves 3 and 5). These results may in part be due to technical reasons such as differences in sample size, but they also reflect the fact that investment by manufacturers is more cyclical than investment by nonmanufacturing business—perhaps because of the greater cyclical sensitivity of manufacturing output compared with that of other sectors of the economy. Evidence of that behavior is provided by the OBE-SEC series on plant and equipment expenditures, which show larger relative fluctuations for manufacturers alone than for business as a whole (cf. curves 3 and 4). The NICB capital outlays series resembles the OBE-SEC figures for manufacturing rather well, those for all business appreciably less (cf. curve 5 with curves 3 and 4).

New capital appropriations very definitely lead plant and equipment expenditures, not only as estimated by the NICB for the same sample of large manufacturers, but also total business and the total manufacturing outlays on fixed investment as estimated by OBE-SEC (see Chart 9-4). These are all leads of either 2 or 3 quarters, except for a few longer leads (4–7 quarters) that are associated mainly with the IV-1955 peak in appropriations. On the average, expenditures lagged appropriations by 10 to 11 months at the five turning points of the

---

[25] See charts and figures in the latest issue of the *Business Conditions Digest* (*BCD*) available at the time of this writing: the April 1970 issue, pp. 23–24 and 72, series 10 and 11. (My charts were prepared much earlier and have not been updated.)

1954–60 period. This may be compared with average lags of 6 to 8 months obtained by comparing the corresponding turns in expenditures and new investment orders. There is no indication of a systematic difference in timing between the different capital expenditure series compared here.

As would be expected, the association between the two NICB series is much closer than that between manufacturers' appropriations and the comprehensive investment outlays. The latter bear more resemblance to new investment orders than to the appropriations series, allowing for the lags. This is suggested by graphical comparison (see Chart 9-4) and confirmed by Table 9-1, which shows that business expenditures on plant and equipment (I) are more closely correlated with investment orders and contracts (OC) than with appropriations (App). The regressions use lags of I of one to three quarters (see lines 1e and 1f and 3a–3c in the table). The best result for the orders-contracts series was obtained with a two-quarter lag of I. In this relationship (Table 9-1, line 1f), where the data are expressed in billions of dollars,

$$I_t = 11.1 + 1.48 OC_{t-2} + u_t.$$

About seven-eighths of the variance of the investment expenditures are statistically explained ($\bar{r}^2 = .871$) and the standard error of estimate (SE) is $1.3 billion. The best result for appropriations (Table 9-1, line 3c) was obtained with a three-quarter lag of I:

$$I_t = 20.3 + 1.57 App_{t-3} + v_t.$$

But here $\bar{r}^2$ is smaller (.786) and SE is higher ($2.5 billion). Note also that the intercept in (3c) is more than 80 per cent larger than the intercept in (1f).[26]

Regressions based on the new data for 1953–65 yield results consistent with the above. Close correlations exist between expenditures on plant and equipment and prior values of new investment orders and contracts, and it matters relatively little whether OC or OC^r and whether I or I_g are used (the distinctions between these series were discussed earlier; see Chart 9-2 and text). Again, higher correlations are obtained with a two-quarter lag of expenditures than with a one-quarter

---

[26] In these equations, gross appropriations seasonally adjusted directly by the NICB were used, rather than the net appropriations series with the NBER adjustment (the latter is plotted as curve 2 in Chart 9-4). In later work, however, regressions with the net appropriations series were computed, and the results were not improved. In fact, the determination coefficient for the relation between I_t and App_{t-3} (net) is $(.742)^2 = .551$, i.e., significantly lower than for the corresponding relation with gross appropriations (3c in Table 9-1).

Table 9-1
Simple Correlations of Plant and Equipment Expenditures on Each of Three Symptomatic Variables, 1949–61 and 1954–61

Ind. Var. Corr. with Plant and Equip. Expend. (I)	Lag of I Relative to Ind. Var. (qrs.) (1)	r (2)	$\bar{r}^2$ (3)	Stand. Error of Est. (bill. dol.) (4)	Period[a] (5)
1. NEW INVESTMENT ORDERS AND CONTRACTS (OC)					
a.	0	.776	.594	3.3	1949–61
b.	1	.870	.752	2.5	1949–61
c.	2	.918	.843	2.1	1949–61
d.	3	.910	.824	2.1	1949–61
e.	1	.868	.745	1.8	1954–61
f.	2	.936	.871	1.3	1954–61
g.	3	.924	.849	1.4	1954–61
2. FIRST ANTICIPATIONS OF PLANT AND EQUIPMENT EXPENDITURES (A_1)	b	.979	.957	1.1	1949–61
3. NEW CAPITAL APPROPRIATIONS, MANUFACTURING (App)					
a.	1	.686	.454	2.7	1954–61
b.	2	.850	.714	1.9	1954–61
c.	3	.891	.786	2.5	1954–61
4. LAGGED PLANT AND EQUIPMENT EXPENDITURES (I_{t-1})	1	.975	.950	1.2	1949–61

Source: Variable 1, Office of Business Economics–Dodge Corporation; variables 2 and 4, OBE–Securities and Exchange Commission; variable 3, National Industrial Conference Board.

[a] Regressions for 1949–61 are based on series of 50–52 quarterly observations; those for 1954–61, on 33 quarterly observations.

[b] Released two and a half to three months before the middle of the quarter to which they refer (see text).

or zero lag; the r coefficients between I_t and OC_t, OC_{t-1}, and OC_{t-2}, respectively, are .929, .958, and .971. Moreover, when all three OC terms are included simultaneously, OC_t proves redundant.

Short-Term Anticipations of Capital Outlays

Their Nature and Predictive Value

The OBE-SEC quarterly data on capital outlays are accompanied by data on *anticipated* capital outlays compiled from reports of the same sample of companies. About 4–6 weeks after the beginning of each quarter, the firms are asked to provide figures on their plant and equipment expenditures for the quarter just passed and on expected expenditures for the current and succeeding quarter. Both the current-quarter and the next-quarter expectations (called "second anticipations," A_2 and "first anticipations," A_1, respectively) are released in the third month of the quarter. Thus A_1 becomes available less than four months prior to the end of the quarter to which it refers, and nearly six months ahead of the date of release of the preliminary actual data. The reported A_2 figure, which of course utilizes more current information, has only about half as long a lead over the date of release of the first estimate of the actual outlay and a lead of less than one month relative to the end of the quarter concerned.

Anticipations do not represent a "stage" of the investment process in the sense in which this term was applied to capital appropriations, contracts and orders, and outlays. They are not a measure of early planning of investment expenditures that is to be followed by the above operational stages. Investment projects typically take much more time to gestate than the three or (at most) six months that separate the dates when anticipations are collected and the *end* of the period to which they refer. These figures, therefore, express not planned but expected expenditures. More specifically, they imply forecasts of how the outlays, which typically will have already been determined by previous appropriations and orders or contracts, would be allocated between the current and next quarters and the further future.

The forecasters are in this case highly qualified, since they represent the companies that incur the outlays. Coming from this source, and at a rather late point in the time scale of the investment process, when pertinent information should already be ample, the anticipations data promise to serve as a useful tool for forecasting plant and equipment outlays. However, the distribution over time of investment expenditures depends in part on the progress of the work underway, and hence must be related to the developments on the supply as well as on the demand side, including such factors as changes in prices and availability of capital goods. These considerations suggest that the relation between anticipated and actual investment may be subject to influences of major analytical interest.

A series made up of anticipated expenditures levels alone cannot be taken to show at what points of time the actual expenditures were expected to experience upturns or downturns. Such a series would show changes from a *previously anticipated* level to the next anticipated level, whereas, in fact, at any given time the anticipated change is from the latest available estimate of the *actual* level to the next anticipated level. To take this into account and, at the same time, to avoid the difficulties due to revisions of the expenditure series, the following mode of presenting the anticipations was adopted in Chart 9-4: (1) The anticipated *change* in expenditures between the current quarter (t) and the next quarter ($t + 1$) is computed as the algebraic difference $\Delta A_{t+1} = A_{1,t+1} - A_{2,t}$. The base is the second anticipation rather than the actual outlay for the period t, because the latter figure is still unavailable when the first anticipation for $t + 1$ is made. (2) The anticipated change is added to the present version of the actual expenditures series (I_t) to obtain the *levels* of first anticipations, adjusted for the effects of the revisions in the basic data: $A_{1t}^* = I_t + \Delta A_t$. (3) Points representing the levels of A_{1t}^* are plotted in Chart 9-4 to the common scale with the actual business outlays on plant and equipment, that is, along with the series I_t (curve 3). The points do not form a continuous series, but rather each is linked with the value of I in the preceding quarter. Thus the vertical differences between the points and the curve indicate the level errors of the adjusted first anticipations, and the differences between the slopes of the links and of the curve indicate the change errors (all in relative terms, since the chart uses vertical logarithmic scales).

This presentation puts the anticipations in a better light than would others of a more ex-ante character, for several reasons. First, revised actual data are used in a way implying elimination of those errors of measurement that are assumed to be corrected by the revisions. Second, the anticipations figures have been adjusted for seasonal variation. The official adjustment starts in the second half of 1952, but I have carried it back to the beginning of the anticipations series. Third, the anticipations figures have also been adjusted for the bias of underestimating, on the average, the changes in actual expenditures. Again, the bias adjustment by the source goes back to 1953 only, but I have carried it back through the earlier years covered by the data.

The improved processing of the reported figures since August 1952 caused a marked reduction in the aggregate anticipation errors. In particular, the correction for seasonal variations resulted in a decisive improvement.[27] Even after the adjustments, however, relatively large dispersion and errors are found in the anticipations figures for individual industries. Individual-company deviations from planned investment are often very substantial, but they tend to cancel out in industry projections; and, similarly, the errors in the latter tend to cancel out in the record for all industries combined.[28]

This may seem disappointing. It is easy to think of some factors that should enhance the predictive value of short-term investment anticipations. Certain projects involving outlays on plant and equipment are "autonomous" in the sense of being very little affected by current considerations. When such projects reach the point of being included in the anticipated outlay reports for the next quarter, one would assume them to be largely independent of such momentary fluctuations as may then be occurring in sales, profits, interest rates, etc. The influence of current changes in the business situation would be significant here only on those occasions where a current development causes the firm to revise the long-range expectations governing the given investment project. Another consideration that favors the projectability of investment by the firm is that capital outlays, unlike sales or profits, are to a large extent controllable. The rate at which the expenditures are made depends substantially on the firm's past planning and decisions. However, these arguments should not be pushed too hard. Plant and equipment outlays, viewed over short spans of time, are autonomous and controllable only in a limited sense and degree.

To the extent that bias is absent or effectively eliminated by data processing, it is certainly reasonable to expect that the larger the sample

[27] Before the correction, the anticipated changes in expenditures (A_1) averaged -3.1 per cent and the actual changes $+1.2$ per cent in the period 1953–58, yielding a bias of -4.3 per cent per quarter. After the correction, the mean relative changes were only 0.7 for first anticipations and 0.5 per cent for actual expenditures, which gives a bias of merely 0.2 per cent. As a result of both the regular seasonal adjustment and a separate residual bias correction, the directional errors of the anticipations of change and the dispersion of the anticipated about the actual changes were also drastically reduced. See "An Appraisal of OBE-SEC Estimates of Plant and Equipment Expenditures, 1947–1958," *Statistical Evaluation Reports,* Report No. 1, Office of Statistical Standards, Bureau of the Budget, October 1959, p. 40. This report was prepared by Raymond Nassimbene and Benjamin T. Teeter.

[28] *Ibid.,* Part IV, pp. 46 ff. Analyses of individual-company anticipations for selected years are given in Irwin Friend and Jean Bronfenbrenner, "Plant and Equipment Programs and Their Realizations," in *Short-Term Economic Forecasting,* Studies in Income and Wealth, Vol. 17, Princeton for NBER, 1955, pp. 65–68; and also in articles by Murray F. Foss and Vito Natrella, *Survey of Current Business,* January and March 1957.

the smaller will be the error of the aggregate. This explains in part the better showing of the all-industry anticipations in comparison to the individual-industry figures. But the collection of companies and investment projects covered by the anticipations aggregates is far from homogeneous, and offsetting biases among the component groups also contribute to the net error-reducing effect of aggregation. While relatively small firms tend to underpredict, the larger firms show a slight inclination to overpredict the levels of their actual capital outlays (but the latter are on the whole significantly better predictors than the former).[29]

The discrepancies between anticipated and realized capital outlays can in some periods be related to unexpected changes in prices and the availability of capital goods. Another factor is the errors in sales anticipations. Data on the latter are also collected by the SEC and the Commerce Department. The ex-ante approach of relating the errors of investment anticipations to the errors of sales expectations met with considerable success. When actual sales exceed (fall short of) expectations, investment plans generally are revised upward (downward) so that actual capital expenditures exceed (fall short of) anticipations. For example, annual data for all manufacturing show a positive correlation of .88 between the relative sales and investment deviations in 1948–56. This relationship, however, is much closer on the aggregate than on the company level.[30]

Eisner estimated quarterly "realization functions" by regressing the current errors of anticipations expressed as ratios $(I - A_1)/A_1$ on two

[29] See Murray F. Foss and Vito Natrella, "Business Anticipations of Capital Expenditures and Sales," Survey of Current Business, March 1957, p. 8; Friend and Bronfenbrenner, "Plant and Equipment," pp. 69–70; Robert A. Levine, "Capital Expenditure Forecasts by Individual Firms," in Quality and Economic Significance of Anticipations Data, pp. 361–62; and Murray F. Foss and Vito Natrella, "The Structure and Realization of Business Investment Anticipations," ibid., pp. 391–95.

It may be noted that outlays for major investment projects (large percentage additions to the firm's fixed assets) tend to be forecast more accurately than those for small projects. The former are often slightly overstated, the latter considerably understated. The scale-of-investment factor reinforces the size-of-firm factors but each has some independent influence.

[30] See Murray F. Foss and Vito Natrella, "Investment Plans and Realizations," Survey of Current Business, June 1957, pp. 16–17. Compare also Arthur M. Okun, "The Value of Anticipations Data in Forecasting National Product," in Quality and Economic Significance of Anticipations Data, pp. 439–42, and "The Predictive Value of Surveys of Business Intentions," American Economic Review, May 1962, p. 222. Interestingly, sales expectations are valuable in explaining investment deviations even though their record in predicting actual sales is poor. Sales errors are more systematic and investment errors are more volatile and random; so the former cancel out much less in the aggregate than the latter. Hence, "sales errors may explain only a trivial portion of the investment errors at the microeconomic level and yet explain a substantial fraction of aggregative investment errors" (Okun, "Anticipations Data," p. 441).

terms involving deviations for anticipations of I_{t-1} and on lagged relative changes in sales, in profits after taxes, and in unfilled orders for machinery.[31] In most cases, the resulting coefficients show the expected signs (positive for all the relative change variables), but are generally small relative to their standard errors, except for the terms that include the lagged values of the dependent variables. The record is admittedly "sufficiently mixed to call for careful attention to difficulties underlying this approach and to possible modifications in its application."[32]

Investment Anticipations, Orders, and Expenditures

As shown above, new orders and contracts for capital goods lead expenditures on plant and equipment consistently by substantial intervals. Production of equipment or construction of plant comes between ordering or contracting and payments. There may also be additional delays due to demand pressures and shortages on the supply side. For first anticipations, no such built-in leading scheme exists, other than that they are reported about one quarter earlier than the actual outlays. Indeed, when plotted in the quarter to which they refer, the anticipations, for optimal timing, should obviously have turning points exactly coincident with those for actual expenditures. The purpose of this index of investment intentions is not to give an intermediate-range prediction of turns in expenditures, but to forecast the levels of expenditures over a short range.

Chart 9-4 shows that the agreement in sign between the actual investment outlays and the corresponding first anticipations was indeed

---

[31] "Realization of Investment Anticipations," in J. S. Duesenberry, G. Fromm, L. R. Klein, and E. Kuh, eds., *The Brookings Quarterly Econometric Model of the United States*, Chicago-Amsterdam, 1965, pp. 95–128.

[32] *Ibid.*, p. 128. For a critique and countercritique, see also Zvi Griliches, "The Brookings Model Volume: A Review Article," *Review of Economics and Statistics*, May 1968, pp. 217–18; and Gary Fromm and Lawrence R. Klein, " 'The Brookings Model Volume: A Review Article:' A Comment," *ibid.*, pp. 236–37.

It should be noted that Eisner earlier adopted a different, stepwise approach to the same general problem, by separately relating (1) the actual investment expenditures and (2) the anticipated investment expenditures to a common group of causal variables (several lagged sales changes, profits, and depreciation), then (3) making the actual values depend on the same variables plus the anticipations. See R. Eisner, "Investment: Fact and Fancy," *American Economic Review*, May 1963, pp. 237–46. In this and related papers ("A Distributed Lag Function," *Econometrica*, January 1960, pp. 1–29; "Capital Expenditures, Profits, and the Acceleration Principle," in *Models of Income Determination*, Studies in Income and Wealth, Vol. 28, Princeton for NBER, 1964, pp. 137–65), Eisner used data from the annual McGraw-Hill surveys of capital expenditures instituted in 1954.

very good (compare the slopes of curve 3 and of the attached projections in each successive quarter). A few directional errors (divergent slopes) did, of course, occur. At the seven major cyclical turns in expenditures, two such errors can be spotted. Realized investment reached a trough in the last quarter of 1949, but the anticipated change from that quarter to the next was negative. Again, actual outlays show a peak in II-1960, but the anticipated change at the mid-year was still positive. However, it should be noted that it takes only slight differences in levels to produce such timing discrepancies.

Quarterly percentage changes in first anticipations, computed as $100[(A_{1,t+1} - A_{2,t})/A_{2,t}]$, are plotted in Chart 9-5 along with the corresponding changes in actual plant and equipment outlays and in new investment orders and contracts.[33] The use of first differences, which reduces sharply the influence of common trends, provides a strong test for the short movements in the series and their possible association. The erratic elements are emphasized but the cyclical ones, if sufficiently valid to begin with, will not be suppressed. They are well in evidence in each of the series here considered.

It is evident that the changes in orders-contracts are often considerably larger than those in expenditures. They are also more erratic and show more frequent sign reversals. Due to the adjustments noted before, there is little difference in the average size between the actual and the anticipated expenditure changes (but underestimation is still more frequent than overestimation).

Chart 9-5 gives additional evidence of the early timing of the orders-contracts series relative to investment expenditures. The leads relating to the aggregates themselves are shown here by the sequence of baseline crossings, which mark the transition from positive to negative changes, or vice versa. The turning points in the plotted quarterly rates of change (which, of course, correspond to the inflection points in the level series) typically follow the same sequence. Either type of measurement suggests that on the average expenditures lag behind orders by some 6 to 7 months.

---

[33] A similar chart appears in my article in Moore, ed., *Business Cycle Indicators*, Vol. I, p. 478, but the relative changes in first anticipations shown there for 1953–59 were computed differently. The figures used here are the correct ones in that they allow for the rate of second anticipations and for all available adjustments of the data.

Chart 9-5

Quarter-to-quarter Percentage Change in Investment Orders and
Contracts and in Actual and Anticipated Plant and Equipment
Expenditures, 1948–61

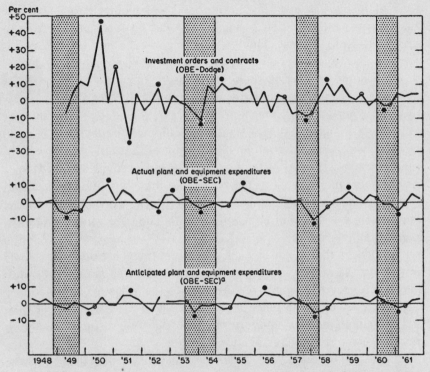

Note: Shaded areas represent business cycle contractions; unshaded areas, expansions. Dots identify peaks and troughs of specific cycles. Circles identify the timing of the turns in the corresponding aggregates (see Chart 9-4).

Source: See Chart 9-4.

[a] Anticipated changes are differences between the first anticipations for quarter $t + 1$ and the second anticipations for the current quarter (t). They are plotted in the center of the second quarter ($t + 1$). The anticipations data have been seasonally adjusted by the source since 1953; for earlier years, they were adjusted by means of the average seasonal factors for 1953–58.

Chart 9-5 also confirms the essential agreement in sign between anticipated and the actual capital outlay changes relating to the same time periods. Except in a few quarters, both curves representing these changes lie either in the positive or in the negative region (above or

below these base lines, respectively). This can be interpreted as meaning that the two variables are basically synchronous.

There is much less agreement in size between the expected and the
realized changes. The local maxima and minima of the two curves fall
in most instances into different quarters, but without any systematic
lags of either variable; consequently, the patterns involved are on the
whole roughly coincident.[34]

The investment-orders estimates can be constructed with a lag of
1 to 2 months. Assume they predicted correctly the turn of investment
expenditures with a lead of six months, as they did on several recent
occasions. Then their net effective forecasting lead would be about four
to five months to the middle of the quarter in which the turn occurred
(defining the net lead as the measured lead minus the publication lag).
Now the first anticipations figures are released about two months before the middle of the quarter to which they refer, and their expected
timing relative to actual expenditures is coincident; thus two months
is the net effective lead with which they can correctly predict a turn
in expenditures. It follows that the lead of orders is two to three months
longer than the lead of anticipations. This advantage of earlier signals
offsets, in some degree, the advantage of greater predictive reliability
held by the anticipations figures. Investment orders would probably
yield more false leads (signals of turns that do not materialize) than
would anticipations. As so often happens, the price of earlier forecasts
is their larger average error.

A correlation analysis leads to the same general conclusion (see
Table 9-1, line 2). Not surprisingly, first anticipations (A_1) are closely
correlated with the investment expenditures (I) to which they directly
refer. Over the period 1949–61 (series of 50 quarterly observations),
correlating I and A_1 results in $r^2 = (.979)^2 = .958$, with a standard error
of estimate of $1.1 billion. This is significantly better than the highest
correlation between the OBE-Dodge investment orders and contracts
(OC) and I, which is obtained for OC taken with a lead of two quarters
(Table 9-1, line 1c): here $r^2 = (.918)^2 = .843$ and $SE = $2.1 billion.
However, OC taken with a three-quarter lead is still almost as good a
predictor of I as is OC taken with a two-quarter lead, judging from the

[34] Although it is difficult to identify the "turning points" in the anticipated changes, a close comparison of the two curves in Chart 9-5 shows a perceptible similarity between their longer fluctuations, which is probably all one could reasonably hope for.

correlation measures alone (Table 9-1, lines 1c and 1d). The net effective lead for this relation between I_t and OC_{t-3} is 7 to 8 months, which is more than three times that for the relation between I and A_1. Again one finds that for earlier availability of forecast OC is preferable to A_1, while for greater reliability of forecast A_1 is preferable.[35]

Distributed Lags of Expenditures

Regressions on Several Lagged Values of Commitments

Replications of the work done with the older data for 1949–61 were performed on the currently available quarterly series for 1953–65: the new Census-Dodge data for fixed-investment orders and contracts and the OBE-SEC or Commerce (National Income Division) data on expenditures for plant and equipment. These calculations confirm that the highest correlations between I_t and OC_{t-i} (or between I_t and OC_{t-i}^r) are obtained with two-quarter lags of expenditures ($i = 2$). Three-quarter lags give somewhat lower r's, and one-quarter and four-quarter lags rank third and fourth in this respect. All these correlations are high, usually exceeding the correlations obtained with the older data for 1949–61.

There is an indication that the association between outlays and commitments is closer and that it involves shorter lags for producer durable equipment than for the structures component of GNP. In the former case, correlation between PDE_t and EO_{t-i} is maximized when $i = 1$; in the latter, correlation between Str_t and PC_{t-i} is maximized when $i = 2$. However, the second-highest r's are just a little lower; in each case, because of high autocorrelations in the time series, the results associated with the different lags fall into relatively narrow ranges.[36]

---

[35] Compare Okun, "Predictive Value of Surveys," pp. 221–24. For 48 quarters from 1949-III to 1961-II, Okun obtained results similar to mine by regressing I on A_1. He reports that A_1 explained nearly 97 per cent of the variance of predicted quarterly outlays and yielded a standard error of $0.95 billion (at annual rates). He comments on the relation between the OBE-Dodge investment orders and contracts series (here denoted OC) and the plant and equipment expenditures one (I), lagged by one to three quarters, saying that OC taken alone "does not nearly match the first anticipations series; taken with anticipations, [it] does not add significantly to the accuracy of the explanation" (p. 224). However, Okun does not present his numerical results on this point, does not allow for the length of the lead involved, and does not mention the trade-off between the gain in timeliness and the loss in accuracy.

[36] When the lag i is varied from zero to four quarters, the following values of r are obtained: (1) for I_t vs. OC_{t-i}, .925 to .970; (2) for I_t vs. OC_{t-i}^r, .920 to .961; (3) for PDE_t vs. EO_{t-i}, .886 to .963; and (4) for Str vs. PC_{t-i}, .812 to .844. The correlations with OC^r are slightly lower than those with OC, apparently because of the larger weight of structures in the former.

When included along with the values of OC for each of the two preceding quarters, the current value (OC_t) has no significant influence upon I_t; also OC_{t-2} then has a much stronger effect than OC_{t-1}.[37] Indeed, it seems reasonable to assume that some minimum gestation periods prevail so that the shortest-lag terms of OC have no significant effects of their own, although this assumption could well result in some error. In other words, the distributed-lag influence on I_t of OC_{t-i} starts essentially with $i = 2$ and extends to larger lags $(i > 2)$.[38] For the equipment component of fixed investment, however, the one-quarter lag term, OC_{t-1}, will also be included.

In Table 9-2, investment expenditures in the period t are related to commitments in periods $t - j$, $t - j - 1$, and $t - j - 2$, where j is the lag that maximizes the simple correlation between expenditures and commitments. The best results for total fixed-investment outlays by business are obtained with lags of two and three quarters, that is, with two terms, OC_{t-j} and OC_{t-j-1}. The addition of the four-quarter lag term fails to improve the fit in any significant manner. Application of the reweighted orders-contracts series, OC^r, yields again very similar, though slightly lower, correlations (see lines 1–3 and 4–6).

When the longer lags in commitments are included in the separate equations for the equipment component, more systematic improvements are observed. Here $j = 1$ and the addition of two- and three-quarter lag terms results in higher $\bar{R}^2$'s and lower SE's although the gains are small (lines 7–9). Larger relative improvements are achieved in the regressions for the plant component, where $j = 2$ and the three- as well as four-quarter lag terms are also definitely significant (lines 10–12). Again, however, the correlations for plant (structures) are appreciably lower than those for equipment (which in turn are slightly lower than those for total fixed investment). The Durbin-Watson statistics are low throughout in Table 9-2, indicating positive autocorre-

---

[37] Consider the regressions

$$I_t = 3.147 - .035OC_t + .979OC_{t-1} + 2.266OC_{t-2} + u_t; \bar{R}^2 = .945$$
$$(1.155)\ (.420) (.591)\phantom{OC_{t-1}} (0.435)$$

and

$$I_t = 3.146 + .944OC_{t-i} + 2.265OC_{t-2} + v_t; \bar{R}^2 = .946$$
$$(1.143) (.410)\phantom{OC_{t-i}} (0.430)$$

[38] Regressions based on earlier data for 1949–61 also support this hypothesis. According to Table 9-1, OC_{t-2} and OC_{t-3} represent the choice of best simple leads relative to I_t. Using both terms,

$$(I_t)_{est} = 9.19 + .831OC_{t-2} + .739OC_{t-3}; \bar{R}^2 = .859; SE = \$1.97 \text{ billion.}$$
$$\phantom{(I_t)_{est} = 9.19 + }(.224)\phantom{OC_{t-2} + }(.217)$$

Table 9-2
Regressions of Business Expenditures on Plant, Equipment, and Total Fixed Investment and Commitments Incurred One to Four Quarters Earlier, 1953–65

Depen. Var.[a] (1)	Independent Variables and Regression Coefficients [b]			Constant Term[c] (5)	$\bar{R}^2$ (6)	Standard Error of Estimate (bill. dol.) (7)	Durbin-Watson Statistic (8)
	(2)	(3)	(4)				
REGRESSIONS FOR EXPENDITURES ON PLANT AND EQUIPMENT							
	OC_{t-2}	OC_{t-3}	OC_{t-4}				
1. I_t	3.215 (0.120)			3.243 (1.247)	.939	1.695	0.924
2. I_t	2.010 (0.406)	1.304 (0.423)		2.407 (1.178)	.948	1.557	0.421
3. I_t	2.009 (0.410)	1.179 (1.576)	.138 (.424)	2.311 (1.225)	.947	1.573	0.428
4. I_t	7.288 (0.311)			2.917 (1.443)	.921	1.925	1.539
5. I_t	4.218 (0.704)	3.427 (0.731)		1.521 (1.233)	.946	1.596	0.712
6. I_t	3.926 (0.733)	2.820 (0.862)	.995 (.762)	1.168 (1.252)	.947	1.583	0.650
REGRESSIONS FOR EXPENDITURES ON EQUIPMENT							
	EO_{t-1}	EO_{t-2}	EO_{t-3}				
7. PDE_t	3.565 (0.147)			−0.244 (1.285)	.926	1.826	0.651
8. PDE_t	2.137 (0.541)	1.528 (0.560)		−0.880 (1.226)	.935	1.710	0.412
9. PDE_t	2.226 (0.528)	0.502 (0.763)	1.017 (0.531)	−1.446 (1.227)	.939	1.661	0.432
REGRESSIONS FOR EXPENDITURES ON PLANT							
	PC_{t-2}	PC_{t-3}	PC_{t-4}				
10. Str_t	6.780 (0.635)			5.857 (1.169)	.706	1.621	1.277
11. Str_t	4.348 (0.718)	3.588 (0.733)		3.874 (1.037)	.804	1.324	0.876
12. Str_t	3.334 (0.659)	2.384 (0.688)	2.808 (0.667)	2.938 (0.913)	.857	1.130	0.905

Notes to Table 9-2

ᵃ As in the text, *I* denotes business capital outlays (OBE-SEC); *PDE*, expenditures for producer durable equipment; *Str*, expenditures for plant or nonresidential structures. Time subscripts, here as elsewhere, refer to quarters. All the variables are in quarterly totals at annual rates, in billions of dollars.

ᵇ *EO* denotes new orders for machinery and equipment (Census); *PC*, contracts for industrial and commercial construction (Dodge); *OC*, estimated total fixed-investment commitments (sum of *EO* and *PC*). In lines 4, 5, and 6, the reweighted orders-contracts series, OC^r is used, with the timing subscripts corresponding to those of *OC* in lines 1, 2, and 3. These variables are expressed in quarterly totals at quarterly rates, in billions of dollars. Standard errors of the regression coefficients are given underneath in parentheses.

ᶜ Standard errors of the constant terms are given underneath in parentheses.

lation of the residuals, and are not improved by the addition of longer lags (column 9).

Estimates of average lags can be obtained by multiplying the lags *i* by the corresponding regression coefficient and adding the products. Here, however, each coefficient must first be divided by 4, because the investment expenditure data used in the regressions are at annual rates, while the investment commitments data are at quarterly rates. The calculations yield average lags of about 2 to 2.5 quarters for the equations relating to total fixed investment and to equipment (lines 2, 8, and 9) and of about 5 to 6 quarters for the equations relating to plant (lines 11 and 12). In the light of other evidence to be discussed, these are in all likelihood substantial underestimates, and the presumed reason for this is that the method admits only two or at most three significant OC_{t-i} terms because of multicollinearity. Each additional term with a positive coefficient makes for an increase in the estimated average lag.

Chart 9-6 compares the estimates of total business capital outlays based on the regression that includes OC_{t-2} and OC_{t-3} (Table 9-2, line 2) with actual outlays. The fit is fairly good in that the estimated series has no systematic lead or lag relative to the actuals. Significant underestimation errors, however, can be seen at the 1954–55 trough and again at the end of the sample period in 1965, while overestimates prevail between mid-1959 and mid-1963. At other times, including the turning points of 1957–58, the estimated and observed values show a close agreement.

The lower part of Chart 9-6 presents a corresponding comparison

Chart 9-6
Regression Estimates for Business Equipment Expenditures and
Total Fixed Investment Outlays, Based on Two Lagged
Commitment Terms, Quarterly, 1953–65

$$(I_t)_{est} = 2.407 + 2.010(OC)_{t-2} + 1.304(OC)_{t-3}$$
$$(PDE_t)_{est} = -0.880 + 2.137(EO)_{t-1} + 1.528(EO)_{t-2}$$

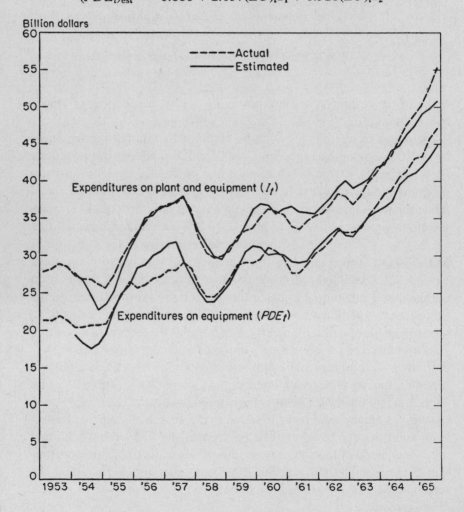

for equipment expenditures estimated from lagged orders, EO_{t-1} and EO_{t-2} (Table 9-2, line 8). Here again there are no persistent timing differences between the estimates and the actual values, but there are substantial underestimates at the trough of 1954 and in 1964–65 and overestimates before the peaks of 1957 and 1960.

Variable Lag Coefficients

The argument developed in Chapter 5 in favor of variable, rather than fixed, lag coefficients in functions expressing the dependence of shipments on new orders applies, *mutatis mutandis*, also to the relations between investment commitments and expenditures. The method of allowing for the variability of the coefficients by making them depend on the backlog-shipment ratios, U/S, worked rather well in the analysis of the orders-shipments (N-S) relations, where matching data on N, S, and U was available. Its application to the investment functions now under study, however, is severely impeded because the data on hand at best permit only a crude approximation to the U/S ratios that are needed. Ratios can be constructed from series for the machinery and equipment industries, but no usable backlog statistics could be found for the plant component of business fixed investment. Furthermore, the method involves only two lagged terms in orders or commitments (say, for the periods $t - 2$ and $t - 3$), permitting the relative influence of the more distant term to rise when U/S, as a proxy for capacity utilization, increases. This limitation to shifts between two lag coefficients or weights is probably more detrimental here, where the lags are longer and more complex, than it was in the case of the simpler N-S relations.

Applied to total fixed investment, the variable-lag equation is

$$I_t = \alpha_{1,t}(OC)_{t-j} + \alpha_{2,t}(OC)_{t-j-1} + v_t, \tag{1}$$

where, $\alpha_{1,t} = \beta_0 + \beta_1(U/S)_{t-j}$ and $\alpha_{2,t} = \beta_2 - [\beta_0 + \beta_1(U/S)_{t-j-1}]$. The form actually used for calculations [39] is

$$I_t = \alpha + \beta_0\Delta(OC)_{t-j} + \beta_1\Delta[(U/S)(OC)]_{t-j} + \beta_2(OC)_{t-j-1} + u_t. \tag{2}$$

The estimates for both β_0 and β_1 turned out to be smaller than their standard errors. Better results were obtained in the separate regressions for equipment and for plant, which are, respectively:

---

[39] These formulations are analogous to equations 10–14 in Chapter 5.

$(PDE_t)_{\text{est}} = 0.883 + 8.586\Delta(EO)_{t-1} - 1.644\Delta[(U/S)(EO)]_{t-1}$
$\quad\quad\quad (1.208)\ \ (4.252) \quad\quad\quad\quad (1.075)$

$\quad\quad\quad\quad\quad\quad\quad + 3.655(EO)_{t-2};\ \bar{R}^2 = .937;\ SE = 1.685;\ d = .546;$
$\quad\quad\quad\quad\quad\quad\quad (0.140)$

and

$(Str_t)_{\text{est}} = 4.061 + 13.491\Delta(PC)_{t-2} - 2.463\Delta[(U/S)(PC)]_{t-2}$
$\quad\quad\quad (1.026)\ \ \ (5.753) \quad\quad\quad\quad (1.538)$

$\quad\quad\quad\quad\quad\quad\quad + 7.843(PC)_{t-3};\ \bar{R}^2 = .810;\ SE = 1.301;\ d = 1.063.$
$\quad\quad\quad\quad\quad\quad\quad (0.564)$

In each case, the estimates of α_1 and α_2 at the mean values of the U/S ratios come quite close to the values of the corresponding coefficients in the fixed-lag equations, as reported in Table 9-2.[40] Hence, approximately the same *average* lags are implied by both types of regressions, as should be expected. The backlog-shipment ratios for machinery and equipment came close to the high value of 6 early in 1953, but varied between 3 and 5 in the years 1954–66 (see Chart 6-6). According to the model, α_1 would be going from about 1 toward zero and α_2 would be going in exactly the opposite direction, as the U/S ratio in the equation for equipment increased from 3 to 6. Hence the implied lag for investment in equipment at $U/S = 6$ would be twice the lag at $U/S = 3$.

Geometric and Second-Order Lag Distributions

The model examined next is a form of geometric lag distribution which implicitly includes all lags equal to j and more quarters and excludes the lags shorter than j. For example, using the symbols for total business investment in plant and equipment, the equation reads

$$I_t = k + a(OC)_{t-j} + bI_{t-1} + u_t, \tag{3}$$

[40] These estimates are computed from the formulas $\tilde{\alpha}_1 = \beta_0 + \beta_1(\bar{U}/\bar{S})_{t-j}$ and $\tilde{\alpha}_2 = \beta_2 - [\beta_0 + \beta_1(\bar{U}/\bar{S})_{t-j-1}]$. When each coefficient is divided by 4 (see text above), the results are as follows:

	Avg. Variable-Lag Coefficients			Fixed-Lag Coefficients		
Investment Commitments	Plant and Equip- ment	Equip- ment	Plant	Plant and Equip- ment	Equip- ment	Plant
For $t-j$	.506	.567	1.005	.503	.534	1.087
For $t-j-1$	.321	.365	0.982	.326	.382	0.897

where u_t is supposed to have the usual assumed properties of the random disturbance. This form will be recognized as a variant of the familiar Koyck distributed-lag transformation. The results of its application are presented in Table 9-3, odd lines.

The regression coefficients of the lagged dependent variable, that is, of I_{t-1} or PDE_{t-1} or Str_{t-1}, are all highly significant (column 4). This, to be sure, could merely reflect the fact that investment expenditures, like most comprehensive economic aggregates, show a substantial degree of autocorrelation. But the investment commitments variables — OC_{t-2}, EO_{t-1}, and PC_{t-2} — retain in each case a strong effect upon expenditures having coefficients that are comfortably large relative to their standard errors (column 3). The regression constants do not appear to differ significantly from zero, except perhaps in the case of equipment (column 6). The values of $\bar{R}^2$ are appreciably higher and those of SE appreciably lower than the best corresponding figures in Table 9-2 (columns 7 and 8). The improvement here is particularly substantial for the estimates of investment in structures. On the other hand, the Durbin-Watson statistics are still mostly low in these equations, even though they are typically biased upward in such autoregressive forms (column 9).

The estimates listed on the even lines of Table 9-3 represent second-order lag distributions that use two autoregressive terms. For example, the equation for total business outlays on fixed investment contains I_{t-2} in addition to the factors included in (3), to read:

$$I_t = k' + a'(OC)_{t-j} + b'I_{t-1} + c'I_{t-2} + u'_t. \tag{4}$$

The coefficients of I_{t-2} are negative, and so is the coefficient of the corresponding term PDE_{t-2} in the regression for outlays on equipment; but the contribution of Str_{t-2} in the equation for expenditures on plant is effectively zero (column 5). Where the second lagged dependent variable turns out to be significant, its inclusion results in reductions of the coefficients of investment commitments and increases of the coefficients of the first autoregressive term, I_{t-1} or PDE_{t-1} (compare lines 2, 4, and 6 with lines 1, 3, and 5, respectively). The values of $\bar{R}^2$ are increased but slightly, while the standard errors of estimate are of course reduced; the values of d, the Durbin-Watson ratios, are raised considerably.

Most of the estimates in Table 9-3 seem quite respectable by con-

Table 9-3
Regressions of Fixed-Investment Expenditures on Commitments, Based on Alternative Assumptions of Geometric and Second-Order Distributed Lags, Quarterly, 1953–65

Line (1)	Investment Commitments Variable (2)	Investment Commitments [a] (3)	Lagged Dependent Variable [b] For $t-1$ (4)	For $t-2$ (5)	Constant Term (6)	$\bar{R}^2$ (7)	Stand. Error of Est. (bill. dol.) (8)	Durbin-Watson Statistic (9)
\multicolumn{9}{c}{REGRESSIONS FOR EXPENDITURES ON PLANT AND EQUIPMENT (I_t)}
1	OC_{t-2}	1.154 (0.247)	0.706 (0.081)		−.772 (.895)	.977	1.044	0.961
2	OC_{t-2}	0.786 (0.228)	1.291 (0.155)	−.518 (.122)	.312 (.805)	.983	0.890	1.498
3	OC_{t-2}^r	2.075 (0.576)	0.784 (0.082)		−1.219 (.946)	.973	1.121	1.068
4	OC_{t-2}^r	1.416 (0.493)	1.402 (0.146)	−.581 (.123)	.179 (.830)	.982	0.921	1.659
\multicolumn{9}{c}{REGRESSIONS FOR EXPENDITURES ON EQUIPMENT (PDE_t)}
5	EO_{t-1}	0.991 (0.223)	0.775 (0.064)		−1.250 (.633)	.982	0.891	1.363
6	EO_{t-1}	0.870 (0.229)	1.026 (0.157)	−.235 (.134)	−.818 (.666)	.983	0.872	1.740
\multicolumn{9}{c}{REGRESSIONS FOR EXPENDITURES ON PLANT (Str_t)}
7	PC_{t-2}	.988 (.387)	0.942 (0.052)		−.469 (.535)	.964	0.565	1.698
8	PC_{t-2}	.990 (.405)	0.940 (0.182)	.003 (.171)	−.470 (.548)	.963	0.572	1.695

Note: For identification of symbols, see Table 9-2, notes a and b. Standard errors of the regression coefficients and constant terms are shown in parentheses underneath each statistic.

[a] As identified in column 2.

[b] I, PDE, or Str, as indicated in the heading, with the subscripts $t-1$ or $t-2$ as indicated in columns 4 and 5.

ventional statistical standards. The regression coefficients are several times larger than their standard errors and, hence, appear to be highly significant. The values of $\bar{R}^2$ are very high, too. However, a far more difficult and sensitive test for such equations is provided by the reasonableness and definiteness of what they imply about the lag structure of the investment processes.

It is helpful at this point to consider the long-run equilibrium aspects of these relations. If the orders-contracts series referred strictly and exclusively to new plant and equipment and were net of cancellations and duplications, and if expenditures covered exactly the same items and no others, then a unit increase in orders, indefinitely maintained, should be associated with a unit increase in expenditures. Briefly, a permanent rise in OC of, say, $1 billion would result in an equal rise in I. This is the case of perfect measurement, which of course cannot be assumed. Actually, the equations for total fixed investment and for equipment in Table 9-3, lines 1–2 and 5–6, imply that a maintained change in commitments of one unit does induce a parallel long-run change in expenditures of approximately one unit. For example, for the regression on line 1 of the table, the estimated "total response" of I to a persistent unit rise in OC equals $0.2885/(1 - 0.7055) = 0.9695$. The corresponding value for the equation on line 2 is $0.1964/(1 - 1.2914 + 0.5177) = 0.8680$.[41] Similarly, estimates of 1.0996 and 1.0414 are obtained for the total long-run response of expenditures on PDE in the equations on lines 5 and 6 on Table 9-3, respectively.

The regressions for business investment in plant, however, imply a maintained increase of $4,290 billion in expenditures (Str). This clearly reflects the large discrepancy in coverage between the series of nonresidential building contracts on the one hand and the series of capital outlays on structures on the other. The equations for total plant and equipment investment that use the reweighted orders-contracts data, i.e., OC^r, also yield long-run response estimates that exceed unity. The figures obtained here are 2.403 for the geometric and 1.979 for the second-order lag distribution (Table 9-3, lines 3 and 4). They are at least

---

[41] The figure for line 1 equals $(1/4)[a/(1 - b)]$, using the symbols from equation (3); the figure for line 2 equals $(1/4)[a'/(1 - b' - c')]$, using the symbols from equation (4). The formulas allow for the use of data at quarterly and annual rates but are otherwise familiar and equivalent to those used in Chapters 5 and 7, above.

twice as large as they should be because the scaling-down of the equipment orders component, designed to bring it into better relation with plant contracts, also reduces the average level of OC^r to less than half that of OC.

The tabulation below lists the average lags for the investment functions identified by their principal variables.[42] Except in the case of structures, investment expenditures taken with a two-quarter lead have significant negative coefficients (Table 9-3, column 5). This implies that the average lags calculated from the second-order functions are here preferable to those calculated from the geometric lag distributions that tend to be overestimates. The second-order model suggests mean lags of expenditures of three to four quarters for total fixed investment and equipment. For plant, however, the estimated average lag is as long as eighteen quarters.[43]

| | | Average Lag in Quarters | |
| | | | |
Investment Function for	Line No., Table 9-3	Geometric Model (odd lines)	Second-Order Model (even lines)
Plant and equipment (I, OC)	1, 2	4.4	3.1
Plant and equipment (I, OC^r)	3, 4	5.6	3.3
Equipment (PDE, EO)	5, 6	4.4	3.7
Plant (Str, PC)	7, 8	18.4	18.4

The patterns of lagged response implied by the second-order equations can be computed by the stepwise method used before (see Table 5-6 for description and illustrations). For example, the results for the

[42] The averages are computed with the aid of the formulas $b/(1 - b)$ for the geometric and $(b' + 2c')/(1 - b' - c')$ for the second-order lag distribution. Since the investment commitments variables bear the subscript $t - 2$ for total fixed-investment and plant and $t - 1$ for equipment, 2 and 1, respectively, must be added to the values calculated from the formulas. Compare the discussion of the corresponding measures in Chapter 5.

[43] It will be noted that the second-order models give a longer average lag for equipment alone than for plant and equipment combined. This is certainly unsatisfactory, since the lag for equipment must be presumed shorter. It is generally recognized that the lags for structures are much longer than those for equipment, and our results show this contrast very strongly. But let us recall that the dependent variable in the total fixed-investment regressions is represented by the OBE-SEC business capital outlays series (I), which is not equal to the sum of the two dependent variables in the separate regressions for equipment and for plant, where the GNP investment components (PDE and Str) are used. Hence the reported results are not internally inconsistent.

equipment regression from Table 9-3, line 6, which are tabulated below, suggest that the modal effect of equipment orders (EO) on outlays for producer durables (PDE) involves a lag of two quarters (the one-quarter effect is a little smaller). Nearly 60 per cent of the total long-run reaction would be accomplished within a three-quarter interval, but seven quarters are needed to reach the 90 per cent mark.

Length of Lag (i) (quarters)	Effect of EO_{t-i} on PDE_t	Cumulative Effect as Per Cent of Total Effect
1	0.218	20.9
2	0.223	42.3
3	0.178	59.4
4	0.130	71.9
5	0.092	80.8
6	0.064	86.9
7	0.044	91.1
Cumulative, 1–4	0.749	
Cumulative, 1–7	0.949	
Total effect $\{= (1/4)[a'/(1 - b' - c')]\}$	1.041	

The estimates from the second-order equations for total business capital outlays and equipment expenditures (Table 9-3, lines 2 and 6, respectively) are presented in Chart 9-7 for comparison with the observed values. The fits are very good indeed and appreciably closer than those in Chart 9-6. The estimates, however, lag slightly at some turning points and tend to understate somewhat the actual levels on the upgrade and overstate them somewhat on the downgrade. Such results are frequently observed for models with lagged dependent variables.

Additional Tests and Models

To test for possible misspecification of these models, it is desirable to include in the regressions additional lagged terms of the independent variable (compare note 29 and text in Chapter 5, above). This procedure also could conceivably result in improved estimates of the time structure of the investment process. Thus I_t was related stepwise to

Chart 9-7

Regression Estimates for Business Equipment Expenditures and
Total Fixed Investment Outlays, Based on Second-Order
Distributed Lags, Quarterly, 1953–65

$$(I_t)_{est} = .312 + .786(OC)_{t-2} + 1.291I_{t-1} - .518I_{t-2}$$

$$(PDE_t)_{est} = -.818 + .870(EO)_{t-1} + 1.026(PDE)_{t-1} - .235(PDE)_{t-2}$$

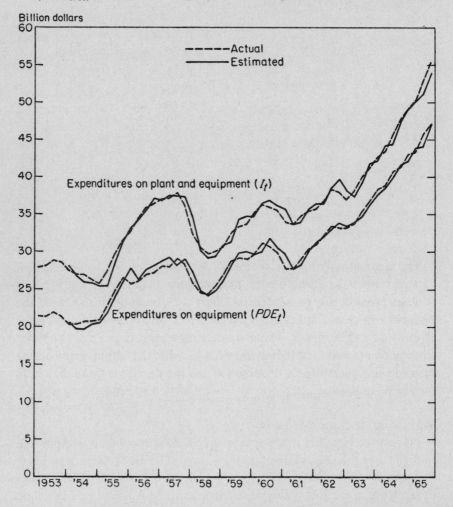

the terms of OC_{t-2}, OC_{t-3}, and OC_{t-4}, plus I_{t-1} and I_{t-2}, and similarly for the regressions that refer to the equipment and plant components of investment separately. In each case, then, three values of the commitments variable were included (for the lags j, $j + 1$, and $j + 2$), as well as two lagged values of the dependent variable. Corresponding forms are found in some recent empirical work on distributed-lag investment functions.[44] The possibility of comparing these estimates with the results of those studies was an additional motive for these experiments.

The tests refute the (a priori doubtful) hypothesis that capital outlays are simply a function of a single term in prior investment commitments with autocorrelated residuals. The addition of OC_{t-3}, for example, contributes little if anything to the regression of I_t on OC_{t-2} and I_{t-1}. However, multicollinearity presents a difficult problem for the equations considered here, as it probably does in other applications of models that include several lagged terms in both the independent and the dependent variables.[45] The coefficients of I_{t-1} retain values close to those listed in Table 9-3, but the coefficients of I_{t-2}, while still negative, tend to be considerably smaller and are not always significant by conventional standards. No gains at all result from adding the earlier values of investment commitments to the separate regressions for equipment and for plant; the coefficients of these terms are not significant.[46]

In equations (3) and (4) estimated in the preceding section, I_{t-1} is used as an explanatory variable and should be independent of u_t or of u_t'; but this desideratum may not be satisfied, since the assumed process makes I_{t-1} a weighted average of past disturbances. In one approach for dealing with this problem, the actual value of the lagged dependent variable is replaced (as in the section on "Instrumental Variables" in

[44] See Dale W. Jorgenson and James A. Stephenson, "The Time Structure of Investment Behavior in United States Manufacturing, 1947–1960," *Review of Economics and Statistics*, February 1967, pp. 16–27.

[45] In some cases, it is difficult to verify this supposition because the necessary information is lacking; for example, the Jorgenson-Stephenson article fails to list the standard errors of the regression coefficients presented there.

[46] To illustrate, the "best" of the equations of this type, that for total fixed investment using the reweighted commitments data, reads

$$(I_t)_{est} = .192 + 1.295(OC^r)_{t-2} + .765(OC^r)_{t-3} - .513(OC^r)_{t-4} + 1.357I_{t-1} - .553I_{t-2},$$
$$\quad\;\;(.858)\;(0.510)\qquad\quad(.571)\qquad\quad(.594)\qquad\quad(0.151)\qquad(.137)$$

and yields $\bar{R}^2 = .982$, $SE = .916$, and $d = 1.448$. The implied average lag is 3.3 quarters, the same as for the second-order model with one OC^r term only (see the tabulation on page 452, above).

Chapter 5) by an estimated value. In the present case, I_{t-1} estimated from past values of OC, as in Table 9-2, could be substituted for I_{t-1}. Accordingly, the regression

$$I_t = k^* + a^*(OC)_{t-j} + b^*I_{t-1} + c^*I_{t-2} + u_t^* \qquad (4a)$$

was computed for total business capital outlays, with $j = 2$ and $I_t = 2.010(OC)_{t-2} + 1.304(OC)_{t-3}$, as in Table 9-2, line 2. Analogously, estimates from the equations shown on lines 8 and 11 of Table 9-2 were used to calculate regressions for PDE_t and Str_t, respectively.

The results thus obtained proved disappointing. The estimated coefficients of (4a), with their standard errors in brackets, are: $a^* = 1.994\ (\pm 0.470)$; $b^* = 0.522\ (\pm 0.306)$; and $c^* = -0.122\ (\pm 0.218)$. It appears, therefore, that OC_{t-2} carries the brunt of such explanation as is offered here, since the effect of I_{t-1} is relatively weak and that of I_{t-2} insignificant. The fit ($\bar{R}^2 = .942$, $SE = 1.616$) is somewhat worse than in the regression of I_t on OC_{t-2} and OC_{t-3} (see Table 9-2, line 2). Apparently, the estimates I_{t-i} are not good enough for the role assigned them in equation (4a), even though they are certainly quite closely associated with the lagged values of the actual expenditures they replace (see Table 9-2, column 7). Corresponding calculations for equipment and for plant yield $\bar{R}^2$ coefficients that are somewhat higher than their counterparts in Table 9-2 but also significantly lower than those in Table 9-3. Such estimates of lag structure as can be derived from these equations are unsatisfactory.[47]

Another approach assumes a specific form of serial dependence among the disturbances, such as the simplest autoregressive scheme $u_t = \rho u_{t-1} + t$. Applying this to the residuals u from the regression $I_t = a + b(OC)_{t-2} + c(OC)_{t-3} + u_t$ (Table 9-2, line 2), ρ is estimated to be .6924. The relation between the transformed variables (compare equation 21 in Chapter 5) is

$$I_t - \rho I_{t-1} = a(1 - \rho) + b[OC_{t-2} - \rho(OC)_{t-3}]$$
$$+ c[OC_{t-3} - \rho(OC)_{t-4}] + \epsilon_t, \qquad (5)$$

and the least-square estimates for this equation (with standard errors) are: $a(1 - \rho) = -0.597\ (\pm 0.738)$; $b = 1.900\ (\pm 0.225)$; and $c = 1.816$

---

[47] The coefficients of the lagged values of estimated expenditures are low, and calculations based on them result in implausibly short average lags [e.g., little more than three quarters for the equation (4a)].

(±0.223). Considering the usual effects of a transition from levels to differences, the correlation obtained is quite good ($\bar{R}^2 = .871$). The Durbin-Watson statistic is 1.394, a sharp increase from the value observed for the level regression ($d = 0.421$ in Table 9-2, line 2). The equation implies positive coefficients for OC_{t-2} and OC_{t-3}, and an average lag of about 5.2 quarters.

Chart 9-8 compares the estimates of business fixed-investment expenditures based on regression (5) with actual expenditures. The fit is very close indeed in the period from 1955 through the first half of 1958 and in the years 1963–65. The deviations of the estimates from the actual values are occasionally larger in the intervening period 1958–62, but even here the fit is on the whole good. The timing of estimated expenditures coincides with that of actual expenditures at most of the recorded turns: the peaks in 1957 and the troughs in 1958, 1961, and 1963. The behavior of I_t in the vicinity of its peak in the second quarter of 1960 is not well reproduced in the estimates, which were somewhat too low at the time but too high in the preceding and subsequent intervals, that is, in IV-1959 and IV-1960 and I-1961. There is also a one-quarter lag of $(I)_{est}$ behind I at the minor peak of I in 1962.

Comparisons with Other Estimates

Kareken and Solow estimate by least squares the equation

$$B_t = -7.330 + .314N_t + .955B_{t-1}; \qquad R^2 = .9927 \qquad \text{(KS)}$$
$$(.040) \qquad (.009)$$

where B_t is the FRB index of production of business equipment (1957 = 100) and N_t is the OBE series on new orders for nonelectrical machinery, deflated by the BLS index of wholesale prices for machinery and motive products (1947–49 = 100). Both series are monthly and seasonally adjusted and cover the period from April 1947 to April 1960.[48]

To approximate the period covered by Kareken and Solow, their results are compared with a similar distributed-lag regression based on estimated fixed-investment commitments and outlays of business

---

[48] See John Kareken and Robert M. Solow, "Lags in Fiscal and Monetary Policy," Research Study One for the Commission on Money and Banking, in Albert Ando et al., *Stabilization Policies*, Englewood Cliffs, N.J., 1963, Part I, pp. 25–30.

Chart 9-8

Regression Estimates for Business Total Fixed Investment Outlays,
Based on Transformed Variables, Quarterly, 1954–65

$$(I_t)_{est} = -.597 + 1.900[OC_{t-2} - .692(OC)_{t-3}]$$
$$+ 1.816[OC_{t-3} - .692(OC)_{t-4}] + .692I_{t-1}$$

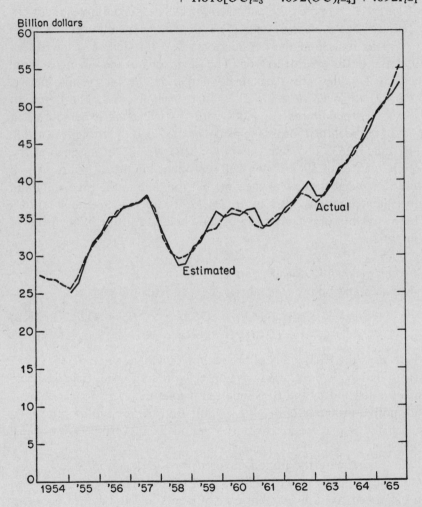

in 1949–61. Here the older data on orders must be used, which alone are available before 1953 (as in the simple regressions of Table 9-1). My Koyck-type equation is

$$I_t = 2.452 + .422OC_{t-2} + .738I_{t-1}; \ R^2 = .964; \ SE = 1.03 \quad \text{(Z)}$$
$$(0.828) \ (.101) \qquad\qquad (.058)$$

Using the symbols a for the first and b for the second of the slope coefficients, let us compute for each of these two regressions:

$$q = \frac{a(1 - b^n)}{1 - b} \Big/ \frac{a}{1 - b} = 1 - b^n \text{ or } n = \frac{\log (1 - q)}{\log b}.$$

It will be recalled from Chapters 5 and 7 that q is the proportion of the "total effect" $[a/(1 - b)]$ accounted for by an interval of n unit periods.

For five selected proportions, ranging from 30 to 90 per cent of the total response of investment expenditures to a unit change in commitments, the resulting lag distributions are as follows:

	Value of q				
n	0.3	0.5	0.7	0.8	0.9
For (KS)	2.6	5.0	8.7	11.6	16.7
For (Z)	2.2	4.3	6.0	7.3	9.6

These figures suggest a slower reaction for the Kareken-Solow equation than for my equation involving I and OC. In the first year, no significant difference appears: for $n = 4$, $q = .425$ in the former case and $q = .455$ in the latter (where allowance is made for the initial two-quarter lead of OC relative to I). But widening discrepancies can be observed in comparing the times required to absorb more than 50 per cent of the total response.

The meaning of such comparisons is, to be sure, rather uncertain, if only because the different explorations use very different data. There are, for example, these four sources of discrepancies between my results and those of Kareken-Solow: (1) their use of output rather than expenditures; (2) their use of the equipment component only, excluding plant; (3) their use of nonelectrical machinery orders only, rather than a more comprehensive orders aggregate; and (4) their reliance on series in "real" terms. General knowledge of the data suggests that (2) and

(3) are the most important of these sources, while (4) makes probably less of a difference and (1) perhaps still less. The OC series or rather its orders component should, despite its weakness, be definitely preferable to N. It is a much more comprehensive indicator of investment orders and therefore more suitable for use in connection with investment realization for equipment, whether the latter are measured by output or expenditures.

Kareken and Solow also estimated some distributed-lag relationships of a higher order by including additional lagged values of the dependent variable (B_{t-2} and B_{t-3}) in the regressions of B_t on N_t and B_{t-1}. This leads from the geometrically declining to unimodal lag distributions. The resulting lag structures are more concentrated; e.g., within the span of five quarters, one half of the total response is accounted for when only one lagged term is used, but with two terms the proportion rises to 56 per cent, and with three terms to 65 per cent. Shifts in the same direction are implied by my estimates in Table 9-3.

The relation between new capital appropriations and investment expenditures has recently been estimated for total manufacturing and seventeen subdivisions by Shirley Almon.[49] This study, based on the NICB large-company data for 1953–61, presents a new method of estimating distributed lags that employs polynomial interpolations between a few points obtained from regressions. Almon selects an eight-quarter lag distribution for "all manufacturing" as yielding the best fit and the most stable weights. The proportions of appropriations spent, according to this model, are 15 per cent within the first half year, 45 per cent in a year, 77 per cent during the first six quarters, and 92 per cent by the end of two years. The distribution is roughly symmetric, with the half-way point in spending being reached just after the fourth quarter.

The geometric and second-order models used previously yield, of course, highly skewed lag distributions that tail off slowly in an asymptotic fashion in the direction of long lags; this is quite unlike Almon's diversified but in general much more symmetrical patterns, with finite numbers of periods (mostly seven to nine quarters) in each distribution. The choice of the model of the lag distribution usually has to be made on empirical rather than theoretical grounds, and the statistical results

[49] "The Distributed Lag Between Capital Appropriations and Expenditures," *Econometrica*, January 1965, pp. 178–96.

as well as criteria are far from clear-cut. Hence, in practice, lag structures are commonly estimated by some more or less arbitrary and intuitive procedures, used partly because of computational convenience. Relatively small differences in the calculated regression coefficients can result in large differences between the associated lag patterns.[50] Consequently, it is very difficult to establish such patterns with any substantial precision. The more modest objective of estimating the average and perhaps also the variance of a lag distribution has a much greater chance of being reasonably well attained. Different models that inevitably yield very divergent lag patterns may well be in essential agreement on the length of the average lag. Thus the average lags of three to five quarters reported for the investment functions in the two preceding sections are approximately consistent with the average lag of somewhat more than four quarters that is implied by the all-manufacturing equation of Almon.[51]

Other equations for investment in plant and equipment that were examined employ "causal" variables, such as sales, profits, capital stock, and interest rates, either alone or in combination with "symptomatic" variables, such as appropriations, commitments, and anticipations. The lag patterns suggested by such functions are discussed and compared in the next chapter.

Summary

Series on new investment commitments—capital appropriations, orders, and contracts—reflect the change in the demand for services of capital goods that is embodied in the "investment decision." On the other hand, business expenditures on plant and equipment are typically concentrated in later stages of the investment process and also depend on the developments on the supply side—along with production, deliveries, and installations. A hypothesis that assigns to investment the major causal role in business cycles does not require that capital outlays lead aggregate production and income (actually, they tend to lag), but it presumably does require, among other conditions, that investment commitments lead, which they do.

[50] See Zvi Griliches, "Distributed Lags: A Survey," *Econometrica*, January 1967, pp. 29–31.
[51] If the contracting stage is thought of as following upon the appropriations stage, the lags using appropriations ought to be the longer ones, but the differences on this account may not be large (also, orders may sometimes precede appropriations).

Estimates of aggregate investment commitments can be obtained by adding the value of new orders received by industries mainly producing machinery and equipment to the value of new contracts for industrial and commercial construction. The resulting series (OC) has various shortcomings — most particularly, its equipment component is too large relative to its plant component — but this appears to affect chiefly the level of, not the relative changes in, these data. The time-path of business capital expenditures (I) resembles the course of new investment orders and contracts, but the fluctuations in I lag behind those in OC and have smaller percentage amplitudes. Most of the lags recorded at the cyclical turning points in these series are two- or three-quarter lags.

New capital appropriations of large manufacturing corporations (App) are roughly coincident with OC. The highest simple correlations with I are observed when App is taken with a lead of three quarters relative to I ($r = .89$) and when OC is taken with a lead of two quarters ($r = .94$).

The so-called first anticipations of plant and equipment expenditures (A_1) show a higher correlation with actual expenditures (I) than any other investment indicator. The close association between the two series is not surprising, since they have the same source and coverage and, importantly, since A_1 predicts I in the next quarter, that is, with a very short lead. Investment products typically take more time to gestate; consequently, the quarterly anticipations express not planned but expected expenditures. In other words, at this late stage, outlays are already largely known from previous commitments; remaining to be "anticipated" is how they will be allocated between the current and next quarters and the further future. The commitments series OC and App, when taken with subscripts ($t - 3$), have effective forecasting leads relative to I_t that are much longer than the lead of A_1. These series can give early signals of turning points in expenditures, while anticipations can only give current recognition of these turning points.

The estimates of business capital outlays improve when distributed lags are used. For example, when I_t is regressed on OC_{t-2} and OC_{t-3}, the calculated series coincides with the actual one at turning points and, on the whole, the observed discrepancies are not large. Autocorrelated disturbances present a problem, but this can be handled rather well by using modified first differences of the variables. Higher correlations are obtained with equations that include, in addition to the selected terms in earlier commitments, the previous values of the dependent variable, i.e., of expenditures. However, although the residual errors are then on the whole very small, they contain systematic elements, as manifested in short lags of the estimates at several turning points.

The distributed-lag regressions suggest that the average lags of I behind OC vary between three and five quarters. At least half of the expenditures are made within one year after commitment; two-thirds or more, within the first six quarters. There are some indications supporting the hypothesis that the lags vary directly with the degree of capacity utilization in the capital-goods-producing industries. Thus when the coefficients in the equation for expenditures on equipment are assumed to depend on the backlog-shipments ratio for equipment manufacturers, rises (falls) in that ratio produce relatively large increases (decreases) in the estimated lag of expenditures.

10

FACTORS INFLUENCING INVESTMENT COMMITMENTS AND REALIZATIONS

THE distributed-lag relation between investment commitments and realizations suggests the following procedure: Study the dependence of commitments on the economic factors that are believed to be important determinants of fixed-investment demand, and link the estimates of commitments thus obtained to subsequent realizations by the appropriate distributed-lag functions. However, although this is an elegant approach, it is not necessarily the most informative; it bypasses some antecedent questions and presupposes knowledge that is as yet lacking.

The procedure followed here consists of successive approximations; it is more tentative but is also less pretentious and potentially more instructive than the approach outlined above. It recognizes that the available measures of new investment commitments, such as the OC series, may not be adequate; tests are needed to see if these measures still significantly influence the realizations (such as I) in equations that also contain those "causal" factors that are supposed to codetermine investment. Since there is no general agreement based on tested knowledge about what precisely these factors are and how they are to be measured, it would seem prudent not to rely on a single specification of some particular type. To be helpful, data on investment commitments must have substantial *net* effects upon realizations; they must absorb most of the combined influence of the determinants of investment decisions and leave "unexplained" the elements that are due to later modifications of these decisions or to changes in the rate of their implementation. Of course, such data must therefore themselves be meaningfully related to the variables that are presumably shaping the decisions to invest.

A Regression Analysis of Investment Expenditures

Symptomatic and Causal Factors

Investment anticipations, like appropriations or orders and contracts for capital goods, are "symptomatic" factors—reflections of the firm's decisions to make the outlays—rather than "causal" factors which shape these decisions. Symptomatic relationships predict the behavior of the dependent variable but do not "explain" it analytically; causal relationships are supposed to explain as well as predict. For this reason, causal factors are generally viewed as superior to symptomatic ones. But the best equation using only causal variables may not provide the optimal forecast; symptomatic variables may improve the forecast and, if so, they should be used.[1]

The plans and expectations that govern business decisions are based on current and past values of some causal variables, but they typically include additional elements of judgment, which are supplied by the decision makers themselves and not by the available data. Hence, the causal variables, even if correctly specified, may fail to predict the outcome of economic decisions adequately, because the information they provide contains only projections of past values and misses the judgments about the future. The symptomatic or anticipatory data will presumably reflect this extra ingredient of "judgment."

Expectational variables may, however, fail to include some of the relevant information contained in the past and contemporaneous values of the causal factors. But this applies primarily to anticipations of events or processes which are largely beyond the control of the anticipator (e.g., to forecasts of sales of a competitive industry or firm or of GNP). It is not an important source of major difficulties for variables that reflect decisions over whose implementation the decision maker has considerable control and which are embodied in bona fide contracts that look into the future; and new investment orders, as well as capital appropriations, have essentially the characteristics of such variables. The forecasting errors may, in fact, be much less important in this case than errors of measurement. As noted before, perfect measures of investment orders and contracts, and of the temporal pattern of their

---

[1] See Arthur M. Okun, "The Predictive Value of Surveys of Business Intentions," *American Economic Review*, May 1962, p. 218.

execution, should in principle go far indeed to insure good predictions of investment realizations.

The subsequent course of events may, of course, diverge from the expectations which prevailed at the time a decision or action found expression in the symptomatic data. Firms would presumably modify their plans in response to such divergencies. Forecasts with both anticipated and realized values of causal variables may be able to allow for these reactions more or less efficiently. Ideally, one would want to specify and estimate the appropriate "realization functions" in Modigliani's sense.[2] However, little is known yet about how to integrate (rather than just combine) the two categories of factors in prediction.

It is often difficult to determine what is properly to be viewed as causal and what as symptomatic. One familiar difficulty is that a factor that seems causal may really stand in a derived rather than fundamental relation to the dependent variable.[3] Then, too, a variable that is symptomatic in one context may well be causal in another. For example, new orders received by producers of industrial machinery are symptomatically related to expenditures on investment in industrial machinery, but may be causally related to investment outlays of the machinery manufacturers.

Two sets of relationship are examined in this chapter with a view to evaluating the performance of both types of variables as determinants of investment in plant and equipment. The first employs series in current dollar values, the second uses data adjusted for price change, where appropriate.

Gross Relations with Selected Variables

Table 10-1 relates investment to several variables treated as independent and taken here one at a time. The regressions of investment expenditures (*I*) on the first three variables (which are excerpted from Table 9-1) illustrate symptomatic relationships. The others are presumably causal; they are broadly associated with the following hypotheses regarding the motivation of spending on plant and equipment:

[2] Cf. Franco Modigliani and Kalman J. Cohen, *The Role of Anticipations and Plans in Economic Behavior and Their Use in Economic Analysis and Forecasting*, Urbana, Ill., 1961.
[3] This is a basic distinction for economic relations, though its treatment in literature varies. The terms "derived" and "fundamental" are used as in James S. Duesenberry, "Income-Consumption Relations and Their Implications," in *Income, Employment, and Public Policy; Essays in Honor of Alvin H. Hansen*, New York, 1948, pp. 56–61.

Table 10-1
Simple Correlations of Plant and Equipment Expenditures on Selected Variables, 1949–61 and 1954–61

Indep. Var. Correlated with Plant and Equip. Expend. (I) and Period [a]	Lag of I Relative to Indep. Var. (qrs.) (1)	r (2)	$\bar{r}^2$ (3)	Stand. Error of Est. (bill. dol.) (4)
1. New investment orders and contracts (OC)				
1949–61	2	.918	.840	2.1
1954–61	2	.936	.871	1.3
2. First anticipations (A_1), 1949–61		.979	.957	1.1
3. New capital appropriations, manufacturing (App), 1954–61	3	.891	.789	2.5
4. Final sales, GNP minus net change in inventories (FS)				
1949–61	1	.887	.783	2.5
1954–61	1	.667	.427	2.7
5. Corporate profits after taxes (R)				
1949–61	1	.586	.331	4.3
1954–61	1	.748	.546	2.4
6. Corporate cash flow (retained earnings plus depreciation) (CF)				
1949–61	2	.919	.841	2.1
1954–61	2	.830	.678	2.0
7. Rate of capacity utilization in manufacturing (CP)				
1949–61	1	.071	.005	5.3
1954–61	1	.190	.036	3.6
8. Ratio of unfilled orders to sales, mfr. (U/S)				
1949–61	1	−.072	.005	5.3
1954–61	1	−.383	.147	3.4
9. Change in final sales (ΔFS)				
1949–61	1	.172	.030	5.1
1954–61	1	.337	.114	4.4
10. Change in corporate profits after taxes (ΔR)				
1949–61	1	.081	.007	5.4
1954–61	1	.116	.013	3.6

Source: Variable 1, Office of Business Economics–Dodge Corporation; variable 2, OBE–Securities and Exchange Commission; variable 3, National Industrial Conference Board; variables 4–6 and 8–10, OBE; variable 7, Frank de Leeuw, Federal Reserve Board.

[a] Regressions for 1949–61 are based on series of 50–52 quarterly observations; those for 1954–61, on 33 quarterly observations.

1. These outlays vary with the demand pressures on available productive capacities, according to the acceleration principle in its more flexible or the simplest rigid version. This accounts for the inclusion of the level and change of final sales $(FS, \Delta FS)$, the rate of capacity utilization (CP), and (U/S), the backlog-shipment ratio.

2. Business capital expenditures depend on internal funds of corporations (CF), which are preferred because of the risks attached to rising debt-earnings ratios or imperfections in the capital market.

3. Profits (R) are important because they generate profit expectations and may be usable as a proxy for the latter.[4] Changes in profits (ΔR) also reflect the changing cyclical relations between costs and selling prices, which are believed to influence the timing aspect of investment decisions. Moreover, profit changes are related to changes in the distribution of total profits between different industries and firms; that is, ΔR may serve as a proxy for the diffusion index of profits. A fall in the latter signifies that an increasing proportion of companies experience declining profits; when this happens in the late phase of expansion, investment may well be discouraged even though aggregate profits are still rising.[5]

Since these hypotheses are not necessarily mutually exclusive, the different variables will be tested jointly. At this point, however, we are concerned merely with the comparative performance of the anticipatory data as predictors of investment, not with the causal relationships as such; hence, no effort is made here to specify these relations in a more integrated and refined form. Some of the variables were chosen in part because the estimates for them were conveniently available or

[4] What undoubtedly counts most are the expected profits from contemplated investment projects, not expected profits from sales at large; and the two need not be related in any simple way.

[5] See Arthur F. Burns, *New Facts on Business Cycles*, Thirtieth Annual Report of the National Bureau of Economic Research, New York, May 1950; reprinted in Burns, *The Frontiers of Economic Knowledge*, Princeton for NBER, 1954, pp. 125–29. On the fluctuations in the diffusion of profits, see Thor Hultgren, *Cyclical Diversities in the Fortunes of Industrial Corporations* Occasional Paper 32, New York, NBER, 1950.

These are believed to be the most convincing arguments for inclusion of R and ΔR in the investment function, but others that have been offered should also be noted, partly because they complicate the situation. Thus R has aspects of a financial variable and is likely to be well correlated with CF. Kalecki used ΔR, arguing that "a rise in profits from the beginning to the end of the period considered renders attractive certain projects which were previously considered unprofitable and thus permits an extension of the boundaries of investment plans in the course of the period" (*Theory of Economic Dynamics*, London, 1954, p. 97). To the extent that profit change and output change are intercorrelated, the use of this factor also "corresponds roughly to the so-called acceleration principle" (*ibid.*, p. 100).

because they have been used by others in related work. Not represented here is the hypothesis that capital outlays depend on long-term interest rates, but these rates will be included later in regressions that use data adjusted for price changes.

Some clues as to which lags to use were found in recent reports that contain regressions of plant and equipment expenditures (I) on assorted variables. The calculations suggest that it is not difficult to obtain rather high correlations with I in various ways.[6]

It seemed desirable to include in the analysis some representation of capital utilization, but the available measures of capacity show major discrepancies. The selected series (CP) is an index of percentage capacity utilization for manufacturing, constructed by Frank de Leeuw. This is a seasonally adjusted series of quarterly ratios of the Federal Reserve Board index of manufacturing production to related estimates of manufacturing capacity.[7] Also included is the quarterly series of ratios of manufacturers' unfilled orders to sales (U/S), which was considered a proxy measure reflecting the relation of demand to capacity.

In terms of the gross measures of Table 10-1, I_t shows the closest correlations with corporate cash flow (CF_{t-2}) and final sales (FS_{t-2}), a weaker association with after-tax profits (R_{t-1}), and positive but quite low correlations with ΔFS and CP. For the relations between I_t and $(U/S)_{t-1}$ and between I_t and ΔR_{t-1}, the r's are both very low and negative. However, as shown later, when these variables are used jointly rather than individually their effectiveness as factors influencing I_t is considerably different. What Table 10-1 does bring out clearly is that the anticipatory data (lines 1–3) are in general better predictors of capital outlays than the causal variables (lines 4–10); and this finding will not be refuted by the multiple-regression tests to follow.

Fixed-investment expenditures show a high degree of inertia over

---

[6] See, e.g., Jack Robinson and Albert T. Sommers, "How Good Is the Capital Goods Market?," *Conference Board Business Record*, March 1960, pp. 12–17. The authors report that correlations of I_t with new orders of all manufacturers, N_{t-i}, range from .82 (for $i = 0$) to .94 (for $i = 2, 3$). The correlations of I_t with corporate cash flow, C_{t-i}, range from .83 (for $i = 0$) to .91 (for $i = 2$). The lags considered vary from zero to four quarters. The correlation figures were read off a graph and are therefore approximate.

[7] Three series are used to develop these estimates: (1) the Commerce estimates of manufacturers' fixed capital stock in 1954 dollars; (2) the McGraw-Hill index of manufacturing capacity; and (3) McGraw-Hill "rate-of-operations" figures (available since 1955). Since it is judged that the sources of error in these measures are sufficiently different in each, a less biased estimate can be obtained by combining them. See *Measures of Productive Capacity*, Subcommittee on Economic Statistics of the Joint Economic Committee, 87th Cong., 2nd sess., May 1962, pp. 127–29.

the short run, in the sense that the value of I in the current quarter is closely associated with its value in the preceding quarter. The coefficient of autocorrelation for the quarterly seasonally adjusted values of I is .975. This is a higher r than any other in the table except that for A_1.

Multiple Regressions with Symptomatic and Causal Factors

Multiple regression studies of economic time series encounter certain typical problems because of the presence of common trends and cycles. Chart 10-1 helps to uncover some probable sources of such problems in the data used here. The correlation between I and FS appears to be accounted for largely by the common upward trend in these series. The relative cyclical movements in FS are much milder than those in I, which is a well-known phenomenon; they are also quite different in other respects, e.g., the contractions of FS are much shorter and end earlier. Both trend and cyclical movements are pronounced in CF, and they combine to produce the marked correlation between this series and I. The cyclical movements in R parallel those in CF and are even stronger, but R does not drift upward significantly in the period covered and so its correlation with I is lower. To keep the multicollinearity problem down to manageable size, these two variables are used as alternatives in our regressions, that is, they do not appear together in any single equation. Finally, by definition, the capacity utilization factor (CP) can have no rising secular trend, while investment in a growing economy must have it. A given level of the CP series, therefore, would correspond over time to increasing levels of I, and this difference in trends may be a real stumbling block if CP is used as a factor in our regressions.[8]

The use of single-equation models implies that the chain of influence runs only from the series used to represent the independent variables to the dependent variable, in this case I. The presence of significant influences running in the opposite direction would raise the question of the single-equation bias. The present exploration tries to steer clear of this issue mainly by avoiding the simultaneous relations and using only the lagged or "predictive" ones.

Regressions of mixed (symptomatic-causal) type are assembled in Table 10-2. Here sets of two or three causal variables are used and

---

[8] This difficulty is avoided by the use of a "capital requirements" series instead of the (related) capacity utilization figures. This point will be taken up in the next section of this chapter.

Chart 10-1
Selected Series Used in Regression Analysis of Orders and Outlays for Capital Goods, Quarterly, 1948–61

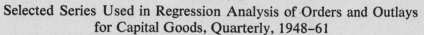

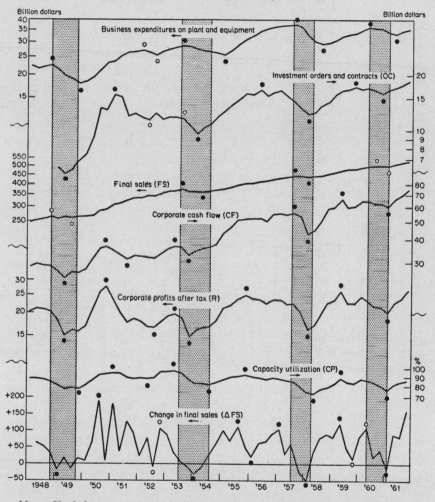

Note: Shaded areas represent business cycle contractions; unshaded areas, expansions. Dots identify peaks and troughs of specific cycles; circles, minor turns or retardations. All but the bottom curve are plotted against ratio scales.

Source: See Table 10-1.

Table 10-2

Regressions for Plant and Equipment Expenditures, Quarterly Data, 1949–61 and 1954–61

Regress. No.[a]	Con-stant Term	Regression Coefficients[b]								R	$\bar{R}^2$	Stand. Error[c]
		OC_{t-2}	A_1	App_{t-3}	FS_{t-1}	R_{t-1}	CF_{t-2}	CP_{t-1}	$(U/S)_{t-1}$			
Ia	−6.203 (5.553)	0.705 (0.185)			.040 (.008)	.043[d] (.101)		.118 (.061)		.953	.899	1.700
Ib	−2.157 (2.310)		.687 (.045)		.007 (.004)	.213 (.045)		.051 (.027)		.990	.978	.782
Ic	−3.773 (5.764)			3.527 (0.355)	.044 (.006)	.099[d] (.118)		.092[d] (.063)		.965	.926	1.013
IIa	−1.437 (3.231)	0.620 (0.207)			.039 (.007)	.258 (.121)			0.603 (0.298)	.953	.900	1.694
IIb	−0.450 (1.113)		.665 (.044)		.007 (.003)	.306 (.040)			0.328 (0.114)	.991	.980	.748
IIc	−13.972 (4.268)			2.808 (0.329)	.055 (.005)	.389 (.075)			2.230 (0.498)	.979	.954	.801
IIIa	−7.551 (5.391)	0.526 (0.206)			.026 (.011)		.198 (.111)	.142 (.056)		.956	.905	1.646
IIIb	−4.483 (2.459)		.614 (.052)		.0007[d] (.006)		.159 (.052)	.109 (.025)		.988	.974	.869
IIIc	−5.672 (5.064)			3.482 (0.433)	.042 (.013)		.056[d] (.115)	.121 (.048)		.965	.925	1.021
IVa	0.711 (2.087)	0.344[d] (0.235)			.002[d] (.011)		.485 (.323)		0.939 (0.323)	.957	.910	1.612
IVb	3.838 (1.168)		.619 (.069)		−.012[e] (.006)		.271 (.072)		0.345 (0.072)	.984 (.168)	.966	.986
IVc	−3.336 (4.719)			3.189 (0.482)	.032 (.012)		.236 (.114)		1.305 (0.588)	.963	.922	1.044

	OC_{t-2}	A_t	App_{t-3}	ΔFS_{t-1}	ΔR_{t-1}	CP_{t-1}	$(U/S)_{t-1}$			
Va	14.900 (4.989)			−.244[d,e] (.682)		−.069[d,e] (.059)		.922	.840	2.138
Vb	0.745 (2.400)	.816 (.022)		.060 (.031)		.053 (.028)		.984	.967	0.999
Vc	38.737 (7.135)		4.918 (0.703)	.282 (.093)		−.208[e] (.092)		.820	.651	2.190
VIa	10.634 (1.674)			−.057[d,e] (.061)			−0.329[d,e] (0.260)	.922	.841	2.133
VIb	5.438 (0.854)	.814 (.022)		.089 (.029)			−0.059[d,e] (0.126)	.983	.964	1.036
VIc	32.392 (2.501)		4.640 (0.551)	.060[d] (.081)			−2.565[e] (0.597)	.874	.749	1.857
VIIa	15.518 (4.415)				.261 (.147)	−.083[e] (.052)		.927	.850	2.072
VIIb	−0.948 (2.111)	.824 (.021)			.197 (.067)	.073 (.023)		.985	.968	0.950
VIIc	32.628 (7.658)		5.088 (0.835)		.246[d] (.245)	−.124[d,e] (.098)		.764	.556	2.467

[a] Roman numerals refer to sets of independent variables other than the symptomatic ones (OC, A_t, and App), as follows: Set I − FS, R, CP; set II − FS, R, U/S; set III − FS, CF, CP; set IV − FS, CF, U/S; set V − ΔFS, CP; set VI − ΔFS, U/S; and set VII − ΔR, CP. In addition, letter a denotes regressions containing the variable OC; b, variable A_t; and c, variable App (in addition to the above sets of the other variables). Regressions with OC and A_t cover 1949–61 (50–51 quarterly observations); those with App cover 1954–61 (33 quarterly observations).

[b] See Table 10-1 for explanation of the symbols. Subscripts ($t − i$) identify the lead of i quarters with which the given series is taken relative to the dependent variable, I_t. Standard errors of the coefficients are given underneath in parentheses.

[c] Adjusted for degrees of freedom (unbiased); in billions of dollars.

[d] Not significant at the 5 per cent level. Coefficient less than 1.7 times its standard error. (One-sided t test is applied because the signs expected of the regression coefficients are stated beforehand.)

[e] Sign is "wrong," i.e., contrary to expectation.

each set is combined alternatively with OC_{t-2} or A_1. This results in pairs of comparable equations for 1949–61 such as Ia-Ib, IIa-IIb, etc. We review also the combinations of the same variables with App_{t-3}, but these regressions (Ic, IIc, etc.) apply to the period 1954–61 and thus are favored by the fact that the period since 1954 yields generally better statistical explanations of I than the longer period since 1949.

Consistent with Okun's findings, the regressions featuring A_1 yield in each case a higher $\bar{R}^2$ and a lower SE than the corresponding equations with OC_{t-2} or App_{t-3}. In most instances, the same criteria also suggest that better results are obtained with App than with OC, but this is not a conclusive comparison because of the difference, noted above, between the periods covered.[9]

Except for cash flow (CF), which is taken with a two-quarter lead, the causal variables are all applied with a one-quarter lead relative to I. (The leads chosen are those that maximize the simple correlations with I, see Table 10-1.) CF is important in all but one of the six regressions in which it appears. However, this series is highly correlated with some of the other independent variables, notably with final sales (FS), which fails whenever it is included along with CF. The profits variable (R) is less closely associated with the other factors, and it works somewhat better than CF in combination with several of them.[10]

The capacity utilization and the backlog-shipment ratios (CP and U/S) are used as alternates only (like CF and R). U/S proves significant in each case and CP in each except one; their coefficients are all positive. It is worth recalling that neither factor, when taken alone, shows significant positive correlations with I (Table 10-1). All in all, U/S appears to have a certain advantage over CP (compare Table 10-2, regressions Ia-IIa, IIa-IIIa, IIIa-IVa, etc.).

The regressions which use the variables ΔFS or ΔR (sets V and VII) are on the whole worse than those which use FS and R or CF (sets I–IV; note that the other factors are common to both groups). The former equations yield lower values of $\bar{R}^2$ and higher SE's, and the regression coefficients are more frequently insignificant or "wrong" in

---

[9] It may be recalled that, for 1954–61, the simple correlations between I and OC are substantially higher than those between I and App (see Table 10-1).

[10] For R, the highest correlations are with OC (.626), A_1 (.471), and FS (.448); for CF, those with FS (.952), A_1 (907), and OC (.883). Note that CF is used in equation sets I and II of Table 10-2 and P in sets III and IV; otherwise the pairs of equations Ia-IIIa, Ib-IIIb, . . . , IIa-IVa, IIb-IVb, etc., contain the same variables, so the roles of CF and R can be directly compared.

sign. However, the weakness of these equations may reflect errors of omission more than of commission. The coefficients of ΔFS are positive and significant, except in the equations with OC (Va and VIa). The coefficients of ΔR are positive and significant in all cases. It is possible that a different lag structure would considerably improve the performance of these variables. Even with simple lags, their use in combination with A_1 and CP gives good results (Vb and VIIb).

In general, the symptomatic variables contribute much more than the causal ones to the over-all correlations. It is possible that a better selection of the causal factors would reverse this result. But there is considerable evidence here that this is unlikely, and the same is indicated by the analysis to follow, which is an effort to improve the data inputs and specifications used. This conclusion is also supported by other exploratory work in the area.[11]

Data Related to Investment in Real Terms

In another round of trial regressions for plant and equipment expenditures, series expressed in dollars of constant purchasing power were used instead of the series in current prices. Asterisks denote deflated variables. The investment orders series was adjusted by means of the implicit deflator for producer durable equipment (one of the price series used to deflate the GNP components). The construction contracts series was adjusted separately by means of the deflator for nonresidential, nonfarm construction. The deflated series were added to obtain OC^*. A weighted combination of the two price deflators was also used to adjust the plant and equipment expenditures and the cash flow and profit series.[12]

Fabricated metal products were this time excluded from the aggregate of investment orders. The net result should be a better approximation to a measure of such orders, as noted in Chapter 9.

[11] Okun ("Predictive Value of Surveys," pp. 223–24) finds that the predictive value of first anticipations is "significantly enhanced" by the addition of either the change in GNP or the change in corporate profits (SE is $0.95 billion when A_1 alone is used, $0.85 billion when either ΔGNP or ΔR is used as well in the regression for I). Even "a shameless amount of data mining," Okun reports, failed to produce a "causal explanation" of plant and equipment outlays that would match these regressions.

[12] The weights (0.59 for the producer durables equipment index and 0.41 for the nonresidential construction index) were determined from the 1951–59 quarterly data.

The price indexes used as deflators are based on prices of inputs to the equipment or construction industries rather than on prices of the outputs of these industries. The latter would be preferable but are in general not available.

Three new variables were added to the others in these experiments: the "capital requirements" (CR^*); the real capital stock (K^*); and the interest rate (i). The data on capital stock relate to manufacturing and are net of depreciation. They were computed by Jorgenson, using the end-of-year figures for 1948 and 1960 from the OBE "Capital Goods Study" (unpublished).[13] Interest rates are represented by Moody's composite average of yields on corporate bonds (Baa through Aaa ratings).[14]

A "capital requirements" series designed to estimate "the constant-dollar volume of projects which will bring capacity into an optimum relationship to output" has been compiled by de Leeuw.[15] Capital requirements were conceived as consisting of projects needed to: (1) adjust capacity optimally to present output; (2) take account of expected changes in output; and (3) replace the worn-out capital stock. Component (1) was estimated on the assumption that manufacturers prefer a rate of operations of 90 per cent. Our CR^* series was computed according to the procedure described by de Leeuw, but with some modifications in the estimation of (2) and a different measure of (3).[16]

The deflated series are shown in Chart 10-2. They resemble the corresponding series in current dollars with strongly reduced trends (Chart 10-1). The division by the rising price indexes shifts some of the peaks to later dates and some of the troughs to earlier ones. Of the

---

[13] The method of computation is described in Dale W. Jorgenson, "Capital Theory and Investment Behavior: Statistical Supplement," mimeographed, pp. 55–61. The data have been adjusted for seasonal variation by Jorgenson (*ibid.*, pp. 148 ff. and pp. 176 ff.).

[14] No attempt was made to cope with the problem of measuring price expectations and their effects in the present context; hence a *real-interest* variable was not used (see Table 8-8 and the accompanying text).

[15] Frank de Leeuw, "The Demand for Capital Goods by Manufacturers: A Study of Quarterly Time Series," *Econometrica*, July 1962, pp. 407–23.

[16] De Leeuw computes (2) under the assumption that the expected rate of increase in output is 4 per cent per year. He thus adds $C_2 = 0.04$ to $C_1 = (1.111Z - CP)/CP$, where Z is the output index and CP the capacity index (note that a rate of operations of 90 per cent implies that capacity is equal to 111.1 per cent of output). The total ($C_1 + C_2$) is then multiplied by the constant-dollar value of the capital stock for each quarter. De Leeuw uses Commerce estimates of the constant-dollar value of capital stock, interpolated quarterly; I use the related estimates by Jorgenson (see note 13). Also, I find that the assumption of a projected growth rate of 4 per cent would imply an average gestation period of about four years, if CR^* is to be positive throughout 1949–62. A shorter gestation period, perhaps three years, seems more appropriate; this, however, would imply a higher expected rate of growth in output of about 5.12 per cent. The higher rate (or shorter gestation period) results in a higher *level* of the CR^* series, but it does not affect its pattern of changes. As for replacement (3), I again use Jorgenson's estimates based on his capital-stock figures and the assumption that the rate of the wearing-out of capital is proportional to the rate of output. De Leeuw uses his own estimates. See *ibid.*, pp. 412–13.

Chart 10-2
Selected Series Relating to Investment in Constant Dollars,
Quarterly, 1949–62

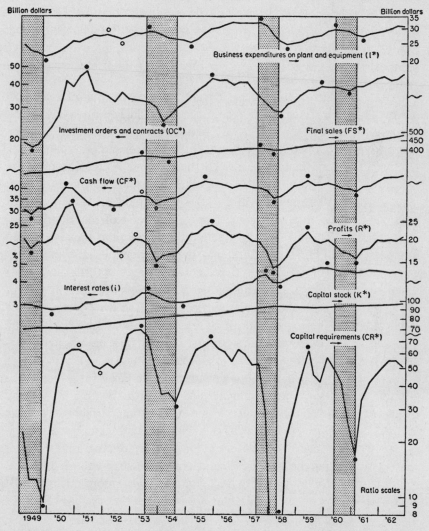

Note: Shaded areas represent business cycle contractions; unshaded areas, expansions. Dots identify peaks and troughs of specific cycles; circles, minor turns or retardations.

Source: See Table 10-1 and text.

new variables, i shows a marked trend in the fifties, but also considerable declines in 1953–54, 1957–58, and in the early sixties. Plotted on the logarithmic scale, K^* shows an almost linear trend through 1957 (with a retardation in 1950), and a definite slowdown in 1958–62. CR^* is dominated by very large cyclical fluctuations; its trend is, if anything, downward in the decade since 1953.

Regressions with Constant-Dollar Series

Deflated orders-contracts (OC^*) taken alone "explain" nearly 50 per cent of the variance of real capital outlays lagged one quarter and nearly 60 per cent when a lag of two quarters is applied. The best result ($\bar{R}^2 = .626$) is obtained with a three-quarter lag of expenditures relative to orders, in real terms. In the multiple regression of I^* on OC^*_{t-i} ($i = 1, 2, 3$), only OC^*_{t-3} is significant at least on the 5 per cent level. The contribution to $\bar{R}^2$ of OC^*_{t-4} is very small, and it is clear that multicollinearity precludes gains from extensions of this distributed-lag approach. These results are generally worse than those obtained for the series in current dollars, and the same applies to the Koyck-type equations, in which the coefficients of the OC^* terms are rather uncomfortably low relative to those of I^*_{t-1} (though they are significant for OC^* terms with short leads). Not only are the fits poorer, but the implications of the regression estimates are rather awkward, since the effect on expenditures of orders-contracts would here appear to be considerably smaller yet also substantially more sluggish.

It is quite possible that the deflation procedures introduce large additional errors of measurement that affect our estimates. In any event, there is no reason to attach much importance to measurements in constant-dollar terms as far as the relations with symptomatic variables only are concerned. These relations are interesting from the forecasting rather than the analytical point of view. Use of values in current prices is more convenient here and apparently also more rewarding. It is only when some causal variables are included that the use of values in base-year prices is indicated.

It may be added that the correlogram of I^* shows a steep decline: I^*_t is highly correlated with I^*_{t-1}, considerably less with I^*_{t-2}, and but weakly with I^*_{t-3}. While OC^* performs worse than the autoregressive factor in investment outlays over a period as short as one quarter, it performs better than that factor over longer spans, say, of two or three quarters. In a regression of I_t^* on OC_{t-3}^* and I_{t-3}^*, for example, the statistical significance of the former factor is high, that of the latter very low or doubtful.

Taken either with a two-quarter or a three-quarter lead, OC^* proves likewise highly significant when used in combination with the presumed causal determinants of I^*, whether or not the autoregressive factor is also included. This is shown by the six regression equations in Table 10-3 and the corresponding simple and partial correlation coefficients in Table 10-4. OC_{t-3}^* comes out somewhat better than OC_{t-2}^* in these estimates.

Of the causal variables, which are all once-lagged, "capital requirements" (CR^*) definitely stands out, judging by the t tests and partial r's (Tables 10-3, column 5, and 10-4, column 4). However, capital stock (K^*) retains significance in four of the regressions shown (Table 10-3, column 6), even though CR^*, which involves a comparison of the available with the required capacity, should incorporate a substantial part of the influence of K^*. The effect of the latter factor remains positive and significant when FS^*, a proxy for the "demand-for-output" variable, is added. Demand for investment to expand capacity would be expected to depend negatively on the capital stock and positively on the demand for output. But this "flexible accelerator" or general "capacity effect" should be largely captured by the factor CR^*. The coefficient of K^*, therefore, presumably represents in the main the effect of the size of the capital stock upon the replacement component of gross investment, and perhaps also some residual trend influences.[17]

The interest variable, i_{t-1}, has throughout the expected negative sign and is in most cases significant (Table 10-3, column 7). It is worth pointing out that the simple correlations between the interest rate and lagged investment expenditures are positive (Table 10-4, column 6). The contributions of cash flow (CF_{t-1}^*) are small or of doubtful significance. The partial correlations are here decidedly lower than the simple ones (Table 10-4, column 7).

The Durbin-Watson statistics indicate a strongly positive autocorrelation of the residuals in those cases where no autoregressive term

---

[17] The replacement demand for capital goods should vary positively with the capital stock (given its composition by age of equipment, etc.). Nevertheless, for total gross investment, the negative effect can be expected to prevail. As will be seen later, the coefficient of K^* is indeed negative when calculated for what must be the more appropriate relationships, namely, those with OC^* rather than I^* as the dependent variable. See below, in the section "Estimates for Constant-Dollar Data."

Table 10-3
Regressions for Plant and Equipment Expenditures in Constant Dollars, 1949–62

Regression No.[a]	Constant Term (1)	Regression Coefficients[b]							$\bar{R}^2$ (9)	Stand. Error of Estimate (bill. dol.) (10)	Durbin-Watson Statistic[c] (11)
		OC^*_{t-2} (2)	OC^*_{t-3} (3)	I^*_{t-1} (4)	CR^*_{t-1} (5)	K^*_{t-1} (6)	i_{t-1} (7)	CF^*_{t-1} (8)			
1a	5.190 (1.958)	.173 (.033)			.064 (.011)	.230 (.041)	−1.577 (0.532)		.833	1.077	0.781[d]
1b	5.374 (1.766)		.188 (.024)		.069 (.008)	.220 (.036)	−1.582 (0.582)		.865	0.911	0.747[d]
2a	2.502 (1.312)	.065 (.025)		.544 (.067)	.044 (.007)	.098 (.031)	−0.641 (0.364)		.930	0.699	1.618[e]
2b	3.221 (1.390)		.075 (.027)	.476 (.080)	.049 (.007)	.108 (.033)	−0.705 (0.372)		.922	0.692	1.184[e]
3a	2.166 (1.307)	.053 (.026)		.597 (.073)	.034 (.004)	.056[f] (.040)	−0.526[f] (0.364)	.076[f] (.047)	.932	0.688	1.791[e]
3b	2.970 (1.314)		.076 (.025)	.528 (.078)	.033 (.009)	.048[f] (.039)	−0.611 (0.353)	.111 (.043)	.931	0.653	1.508[e]

[a] Set 1 excludes and sets 2 and 3 include the autoregressive factor I^*_{t-1}. Set 2 excludes and set 3 includes CF^*_{t-1}. Regressions 1a, 2a, and 3a contain OC^*_{t-2}; regressions 1b, 2b, and 3b contain OC^*_{t-3}. The former are based on series of 53, the latter on series of 52, quarterly observations.

[b] See text for explanation of the symbols. Subscripts identify the lead, in quarters, with which the given series is taken relative to the dependent variable, I^*. Standard errors of the coefficients are given beneath in parentheses.

[c] $d = \Sigma(u_t - u_{t-1})^2 / \Sigma u_t^2$, where u_t is the estimated least-squares residual for the given regression.

[d] Indicates strongly positive autocorrelation of the residuals.

[e] See text on the limitations of the Durbin-Watson statistic in these cases.

[f] Not significant at the 5 per cent level. Coefficient is less than 1.7 times its standard error. (One-sided t test is applied because the signs expected of the regression coefficients are stated beforehand.)

Table 10-4
Simple and Partial Correlation Coefficients for Regressions for Plant and Equipment Expenditures in Constant Dollars, 1949–62

Regression No.[a]	Coefficients of Correlation[b] Between I_t^* and						
	OC_{t-2}^* (1)	OC_{t-3}^* (2)	I_{t-1}^* (3)	CR_{t-1}^* (4)	K_{t-1}^* (5)	i_{t-1} (6)	CF_{t-1}^* (7)
	PARTIAL CORRELATION COEFFICIENTS						
1a	.606			.653	.629	−.393	
1b		.746		.772	.669	−.456	
2a	.354		.766	.651	.419	−.249	
2b		.383	.659	.712	.437	−.269	
3a	.292		.770	.480	.199	−.208	.232
3b		.409	.710	.477	.182	−.250	.361
	SIMPLE CORRELATION COEFFICIENTS						
	.807[c]	.796[d]	.925[c]	.608[c]	.485[c]	.397[c]	.628[c]

[a] For identification, see Table 10-3, note a.

[b] See text for explanation of symbols. Subscripts identify the lead, in quarters, with which the given series is taken relative to the dependent variable, I_t^*.

[c] Based on the 53 observations used in the regressions with OC_{t-2}^* (1a, 2a, 3a).

[d] Based on the 52 observations used in the regressions with OC_{t-3}^* (1b, 2b, 3b).

is included (Table 10-3, column 11). Where such terms (here I_{t-1}^*) are used, they appear to absorb most of that autocorrelation but the d test is then known to be biased and therefore inapplicable in any strict sense (see Chapter 5).

The other factors considered, that is, FS^*, ΔFS^*, R^*, and ΔR^*, add virtually nothing to the goodness of the fit when taken together with the other variables.

To sum up, these results indicate again that the constructed series on fixed-investment commitments, for all its undoubted weaknesses, is significant in the regression analysis of investment expenditures, even when other factors are put into the equations. Its effect is decidedly weaker than that of the autoregressive term I_{t-1}^*, but the serial dependence of expenditures may itself be mainly the reflection of a distributed-lag process linking the later stages of investment to previous commitments.

The effects on investment expenditures of causal variables should be relatively weak in equations that include investment commitments.

The regressions in constant dollars, which are probably better specified than the preceding current-dollar regressions and are also less affected by the common-trends difficulty, show that these effects are indeed generally weak. Nevertheless, the significant contribution of some variables, notably CR^*, may leave one uneasy: They can well be understood as influencing investment decisions but hardly as intervening in the period after the contracts have been placed with only a short lead over expenditures.

I suspect that technical factors are mainly responsible for this intervention, namely, the various proxy and echo effects due to the autocorrelation and intercorrelation of the independent variables. These are difficult to eliminate. Ideally, one would wish to distinguish two groups of factors in an equation for plant and equipment expenditures: (1) those influencing decisions; and (2) those influencing the transformation of orders into expenditures. The joint impact of (1) would presumably in large part be reflected in the behavior of orders. The impact of (2) should mainly show up in changes in the rate at which the investment projects are implemented. Yet it is uncertain how well these two sets can be separated and quantified. Factors which influence capital outlays with relatively long lags, by shaping investment decisions, may also be affecting the process by which the decisions are carried out. In this role, they would then also be influencing outlays with shorter lags.

An Approach to Investment-Order Analysis

Selected Factors Relating to New Investment Commitments

The causal variables suggested by the theory of the demand for capital goods apply primarily to investment commitments rather than to expenditures. This is because the theory concerns the decisions that set the process in motion, and these are expressed relatively promptly and directly in orders and contracts which commit money capital. Outlays, however, trail investment decisions and orders, often by long and possibly complex lags.

Realized investment, of course, depends not only on demand but also on supply conditions for capital goods. On the demand side, the volume of planned additions to the stock of machinery and structures is subject in a high degree to the control of the firms which decide upon the new investment projects. However, these firms can generally only influence, not directly control, the supply flow of the goods they demand. In a boom, for example, they may order in the aggregate a larger volume of capital equipment than can be supplied with the available resources within the periods normally required for production and delivery or installation. In this case, prices of the goods and services involved are likely to rise, thereby discouraging some new investment demand in its early, controllable phase. For the projects already under way, however, the main effect will be to slow down their execution. New investment orders and contracts will run at peak rates during a relatively short period (as, e.g., early in the Korean War, 1950–51), but production in response to these orders will only gradually attain high levels and may continue rising slowly at high rates of capacity utilization for a considerable time (as in 1951–53). Capital outlays will then follow a course similar to that of production. The general phenomena of order-backlog accumulation and production smoothing are most pertinent in the present context, since it is the capital goods that are typically produced to advance orders, often in time-consuming multiphase operations.[18]

These considerations suggest that in principle it should be better to use new capital appropriations or orders in statistical demand functions for capital goods than to use expenditures. Commitments data should help to deal with the identification problem, since they are more nearly representative of investment demand, while outlays bear a closer relationship to production or supply. In practice, to be sure, caution is needed in the application of these data because of their considerable limitations. Accordingly, the question now asked is simply whether the

[18] James Duesenberry notes that "investment moves as though it were being backlogged in the years in which investment opportunities are very large and released in later years" (*Business Cycles and Economic Growth,* New York, 1958, pp. 87–89). He attributes this behavior largely to limitations on the supply of money capital that force some firms to restrict or delay their investment and believes that other factors such as shortages of capital goods and engineering staffs are on the whole less important. In particular, referring to the 1953–54 recession, Duesenberry argues that "investment continued at high levels" and that this cannot be due to "the completion of projects undertaken in earlier years." But the figures he himself quotes show that investment expenditures declined only 12 per cent, while orders and contracts declined about 23 per cent or nearly twice as much, which surely suggests that work on orders accumulated in the recent past played a considerable stabilizing role in this episode. Of course, it could still be true that the financial factors stressed by Duesenberry are important in the determination of investment decisions and that they help to maintain these decisions at high levels during recessions. To test this, the appropriate relations for study would be those between measures of these factors and investment appropriations or commitments.

factors already introduced in the analysis of expenditures could, when taken with different timing, make significant contributions to a statistical explanation of the composite of investment orders and contracts.

Table 10-5 shows the results of correlating OC with each of several series in current dollars, without lags and with lags of one to three quarters. The highest of these correlations are with CF, FS, and R. Those with App and ΔFS are considerably lower, and the others are very low and in a few instances negative.

The correlation between OC_t and OC_{t-1} ($r^2 = .88$) is the highest in the table. It should be noted, though, that the corresponding autocorrelation coefficient for investment expenditures is significantly higher still ($r^2 = .951$).

Investment orders and contracts move early in the business cycle, leading rather than lagging behind most of the related processes. In Table 10-5, the assumption of simultaneous timing yields higher correlations than the assumption of quarterly lags of OC, and lengthening the lag works systematically to reduce the correlations. However, the differences between the results for simultaneous relations and one-quarter lags tend to be small. Perhaps monthly regressions would provide more convincing evidence of short lags if the data were available and workable in this form.

In Tables 10-1 and 10-2, lags of one quarter were assumed for investment expenditures relative to most of the "causal" variables. The present results suggest longer lags, at least of the order of those separating expenditures from investment commitments (which, as shown earlier, equal probably two to three quarters, on the average).

In multiple regressions with discrete lags, corporate profits, and cash flow (not used simultaneously) have apparently strong effects upon OC (Table 10-6, regressions A1–A8). The backlog-sales ratios show surprising strength when combined with profits. The coefficients of final sales are (as in the equations for expenditures) either not significant or "wrong" in sign when cash flow is included.

The multiple correlation coefficients all exceed .9 and, when squared, suggest that from 84 to 92 per cent of the variance of OC can be "explained" with the aid of the few selected variables. According to the standard errors of estimate and the $\bar{R}^2$ coefficients, the best equation in this group is A6 [with FS_{t-2}, R_t and $(U/S)_t$]. Of the subgroup of regressions using lagged variables only, the best ones are A4 [with CF_{t-1} and $(U/S)_{t-1}$] and A2 [with R_{t-1}, $(U/S)_{t-1}$, and FS_{t-2}].

Table 10-5
Simple Correlations [a] of Investment Orders and Contracts (OC)
with Selected Variables, 1949–61

Indepen. Var. Correlated with OC	Lag of OC Relative to Indepen. Var. (qrs.) (1)	r (2)	$\bar{r}^2$ (3)	Stand. Error of Est. (bill. dol.) (4)
1. FINAL SALES (FS)				
a	0	.828	.679	1.810
b	1	.805	.641	1.913
c	2	.782	.603	2.010
d	3	.765	.577	2.078
2. CORPORATE PROFITS AFTER TAXES (R)				
a	0	.777	.595	2.029
b	1	.761	.572	2.090
c	2	.644	.403	2.465
d	3	.478	.193	2.866
3. CORPORATE CASH FLOW (CF)				
a	0	.894	.795	1.444
b	1	.889	.786	1.477
c	2	.850	.717	1.697
d	3	.795	.625	1.955
4. RATE OF CAPACITY UTILIZATION, MANUFACTURING (CP)				
a	0	.216	.027	3.147
b	1	.142	.020 [b]	3.191
5. RATE OF UNFILLED ORDERS TO SALES, MANUFACTURING (U/S)				
a	0	−.102	.010 [b]	3.207
b	1	−.158	.005	3.183
6. CHANGE IN FINAL SALES (ΔFS)				
a	0	.425	.165	2.847
b	1	.398	.142	2.957
c	2	.286	.064	3.089
d	3	.199	.021	3.159
7. CHANGE IN CORPORATE PROFITS AFTER TAXES (ΔR)	0	−.076	.006 [b]	3.086
8. NEW CAPITAL APPROPRIATIONS (App)				
a	0	.549	.287	2.007
b	1	.536	.273	2.018
9. INVESTMENT ORDERS AND CONTRACTS	1	.940	.881	1.059

Source: Variables 1–3 and 5–7, Office of Business Economics; variable 4, Frank de Leeuw, Federal Reserve Board; variable 8, National Industrial Conference Board; variable 9, OBE–Dodge Corporation.

[a] All regressions are based on series of 52 quarterly observations, except the one involving OC_{t-1} (variable 9) which uses 51 observations.

[b] Unadjusted (r^2); these correlations are too low to give meaningful adjusted coefficients ($\bar{r}^2$).

Table 10-6

Regressions for Investment Orders and Contracts, Quarterly Data, 1949–61

Regression No.	Constant Term	Regression Coefficients [a]									R	$\bar{R}^2$	Stand. Error [b]
		FS_{t-2}	R_t	R_{t-1}	CF_t	CF_{t-1}	CP_t	CP_{t-1}	$(U/S)_t$	$(U/S)_{t-1}$			
A1	−10.935 (3.317)	.025 (.003)		.462 (.074)				.060[c] (.039)			.919	.834	1.323
A2	−8.988 (1.625)	.024 (.002)		.568 (.063)						.416 (.163)	.925	.847	1.272
A3	−8.460 (3.496)	−.010[c,d] (.008)				.416 (.068)		.101 (.037)			.917	.831	1.339
A4	−2.475 (1.253)	−.028[c] (.007)				.592 (.065)				.063 (.017)	.925	.847	1.271
A5	−17.746 (2.863)	.028 (.003)	.376 (.061)				.146 (.034)				.944	.884	1.107
A6	−11.473 (1.270)	.024 (.002)	.603 (.047)						.778 (.127)		.956	.909	0.981
A7	−15.206 (3.112)	.002[d] (.006)			.320 (.055)		.172 (.033)				.941	.879	1.135
A8	−4.389 (1.051)	−.024[c] (.005)			.569 (.048)				.091 (.014)		.952	.900	1.031

486

		FS_t	FS_{t-2}	R_t	CF_t	CF_{t-1}	ΔFS_t	ΔR_t	App_t	OC_{t-1}			
B1	1.007 (0.779)		.0025 [d] (.0032)							.870 (.079)	.940	.879	1.085
B2	1.138 (n.a.)		−.014 [c] (.005)			.227 (.062)				.631 (.096)	.954	.904	0.968
B3	−2.890 (0.807)		.006 (.002)	.296 (.044)						.605 (.069)	.970	.937	0.783
B4	0.924 (0.582)		−.017 [c] (.004)		.252 (.040)					.656 (.068)	.968	.933	0.810
B5	0.733 (0.784)	.005 [d] (.003)								.823 (.085)	.942	.882	1.072
B6	1.317 (0.573)						.103 (.027)			.877 (.043)	.954	.907	0.953
B7	0.675 (0.522)							.198 (.060)		.960 (.038)	.965	.928	0.840
B8	0.508 (0.784)								.524 (.250)	.905 (.061)	.953	.905	0.758

n.a. = not available.

[a] See Table 10-5 for explanation of symbols. Subscripts identify the lead of i quarters with which the given series is taken relative to the dependent variable OC. Standard errors are given in parentheses below the coefficients.

[b] Standard error of estimate is adjusted for degrees of freedom; in billions of dollars.

[c] Sign is "wrong," i.e., contrary to expectation.

[d] Not significant at the 5 per cent level. Coefficient is less than 1.7 times its standard error. (One-sided t test is applied because the signs expected of the regression coefficients are stated beforehand.)

When the lagged value of investment orders is included as an independent variable, still higher $\bar{R}^2$ coefficients and lower standard errors of estimate are generally obtained (Table 10-6, regressions B1–B8). FS (with or without lag) is redundant when coupled with OC_{t-1} alone, and its lagged effects are small and negative in equations that include CF. However, in combination with profits, FS again has a small but positive and significant coefficient. The inclusion of OC_{t-1} reduces but does not eliminate the significance of the other variables: $CF, R, \Delta FS$, ΔR, and App.

The one inference we are prepared to draw from these results is that apparently rather close associations exist between the estimates of new investment commitments (OC) and several factors that may be considered as potentially important determinants of investment decisions. This is worth knowing despite the obvious limitations of the statement. The calculations admittedly raise many questions and answer few. Again, improvements are sought mainly through different specifications, adjustments for price level changes, and assumptions about the lags involved.

Estimates for Constant-Dollar Data

Table 10-7 presents regressions of deflated investment commitments (OC^*) on several deflated variables and on the interest rate. To reduce the risk of bias due to joint dependencies, only those predictive equations are included in which the exogenous variables lead OC_t^* by intervals of one quarter. The explanatory factors can be placed in three groups:

1. Deflated final sales and capital stock, FS^* and K^*: The "flexible accelerator" hypothesis suggests that net investment depends positively on the former and negatively on the latter.[19] However, investment designed to replace and maintain the capital stock should be positively related to the size of that stock. Since OC^* reflects gross

---

[19] FS^* performs here the role of output (X) in the basic formulation of this hypothesis by R. M. Goodwin ("The Nonlinear Accelerator and the Persistence of Business Cycles," *Econometrica*, January 1951, pp. 1–17) and Hollis Chenery ("Overcapacity and the Acceleration Principle," *ibid.*, January 1952, pp. 1–28). A simple version of this model is given by the equation $I_t = b(\beta X_t - K_{t-1})$, where β is the desired capital-output ratio and b is the "reaction coefficient," or fraction of the difference between the desired and the available capital stock that is acquired during the current period. This model implies that X_t is equated to the expected output and that no excess capacity is carried or wanted by business firms.

rather than net investment commitments (that is, it includes orders and contracts for reinvestment as well as new investment), the sign of the coefficient of K^* might seem uncertain. But recent studies by Jorgenson and associates indicate that replacement investment per quarter represents on the average a small proportion of the capital stock, about 0.025 or 0.03.[20] My estimates of the coefficient of K_{t-1}^* in equations for OC_t^* fall mainly in the range from -0.45 to -0.48.[21] This coefficient may be viewed as the sum $(\mu + \delta)$, where μ denotes the marginal effect of capital stock on *net* investment commitments. If $(\mu + \delta) = -0.48$ and $\delta = 0.03, \mu = -0.51$. The negative component definitely outweighs the positive one in these estimates, which seems entirely plausible.[22]

The "capital requirements" series (CR^*) represents a synthetic variable to be used in alternative tests of the accelerator hypothesis. Similarly, the change in final sales (ΔFS^*), when included as a single lagged term, may be viewed as representing yet another version (the early and rigid one) of the acceleration principle. This version has well-known implications for the dynamics of growth and cycles (owing mainly to the 1939 work by Paul A. Samuelson), but it is now widely recognized as a rather crude concept and decidedly inferior to the more recent flexible- and distributed-lag accelerator models.

2. Deflated corporate cash flow (CF^*) stands for the "financial" influences, and deflated profits (R^*) share partly in this role, but may also reflect the effects of changing cost-price relations and expectations. First differences in these variables are used partly to examine somewhat more complex lag patterns and partly to capture the possible expectational contents of these terms; also, as noted earlier, changes in profits may act as a proxy for profits diffusion.

3. The interest rate (i) measures, no doubt quite imperfectly, the costs of capital. It is included in each equation. Its effect on investment demand is expected to be negative, of course.

[20] See Dale W. Jorgenson and James A. Stephenson, "Investment Behavior in U.S. Manufacturing, 1947–1960," *Econometrica*, April 1967, pp. 178–79, 192, 211–12.

[21] These are the estimates from the regressions that use "causal" variables only—that do not include the term OC_{t-1}^*. When the latter is included, the coefficient of K_{t-1}^*, while still negative, is sharply reduced and appears not to be significant; see text below for some thoughts on this result.

[22] In the words of Carl F. Christ, ". . . if firms desire to make up in one year more than about 4 per cent of the difference between desired and actual capital, as seems highly reasonable, the coefficient [of K_{t-1}^*] can be expected to be negative in a gross investment equation, but it is not expected to exceed or even to equal 1 in absolute value" (*Econometric Models and Methods*, New York, 1966, p. 583). Christ assumes that δ is about .04.

Table 10-7

Regressions for Investment Orders and Contracts in Constant Dollars, One-Quarter Lags, 1949–62

Re-gres-sion No.	Con-stant Term (1)	FS* (2)	K* (3)	CR* (4)	ΔFS* (5)	R* (6)	ΔR* (7)	CF* (8)	i (9)	OC* (10)	Adj. Coeff. of Det. ($\bar{R}^2$) (11)	Stand. Error of Est. (bill. dol.) (12)	Dur-bin-Wat-son Sta-tistic[b] (13)
					Regression Coefficients[a]								
C1	−20.704 (7.560)	.227 (.039)	−0.484 (0.212)			1.200 (0.170)			−3.530 (1.686)		.742	3.429	1.002
C2	−14.122 (6.369)	.086 (.043)	−0.078[c] (0.193)			0.695 (0.173)			−2.272[c] (1.412)	.523 (.105)	.825	2.826	1.782
C3	17.246 (n.a.)	.312 (.051)	−1.028 (0.276)				.398[c] (.324)		−3.858[c] (2.374)		.500	4.770	0.514
C4	4.357 (n.a.)	.032[c] (.044)	−0.063[c] (0.202)				.656 (.203)		−1.058[c] (1.504)	.812 (.090)	.808	2.957	2.196
C5	−7.908 (4.705)			.069 (.035)				1.198 (0.200)	−1.526[c] (1.205)		.650	3.994	0.699

	1	2	3	4	5	6	7	8	9	10	11	12	13
C6	-4.246[c] (3.318)			-.046[c,d] (.029)				0.688 (0.156)	-2.525 (0.651)	.710 (.096)	.830	2.786	1.956
C7	-8.025 (4.752)				.223 (.131)			1343 (0.170)	-2.335 (1.074)		.643	4.030	0.698
C8	-3.470[c] (3.360)				.127[c] (.092)			0.605 (0.154)	-1.635 (0.752)	.612 (.082)	.828	2.803	1.865
C9	-31.856 (15.543)	.308 (.073)	-0.483 (0.315)	-.044[c,d] (.040)		1.843 (0.683)		-0.620[c,d] (0.744)	-5.289 (2.216)		.741	3.435	1.088
C10	-24.391 (8.208)	.209 (.042)	-0.357 (0.236)		.131[c,e] (.131)	1.237 (0.183)	-.308[c,e] (.272)		-3.900 (1.720)		.740	3.441	0.999
C11	5.513 (2.514)				.042[c] (.106)		.661 (.217)		0.016[c,d] (0.632)	.854 (.067)	.810	2.945	2.268
C12	-22.975 (n.a.)	.225 (.039)	-0.452 (0.216)			1.253 (0.183)	-.205[c,e] (.250)		-3.745 (1.712)		.740	3.440	0.962
C13	-9.464 (n.a.)	.068[c] (.044)	-0.068[c] (0.191)			0.535 (0.204)	.332[c] (.228)		-1.737[c] (1.445)	.601 (.117)	.829	2.794	2.074

n.a. = not available.

[a] See text for explanation of the symbols. Each of the variables identified in columns 2–10 is taken with a lead of one quarter relative to the dependent variable OC_t^*. Standard errors of the coefficients are given underneath in parentheses.

[b] On the meaning and limitations of the Durbin-Watson statistic, see text, above.

[c] Not significant at the 5 per cent level according to the one-sided t test.

[d] Sign is "wrong," i.e., contrary to expectations.

[e] On the signs of the coefficients in these cases, see text, note 25.

491

On the whole, the signs of estimated regression coefficients seem rather sensible. All equations with final sales and capital stock are consistent with expectations based on the capacity-accelerator hypothesis in that FS_{t-1}^* appears with positive and K_{t-1}^* with negative coefficients. However, the addition of the autoregressive factor OC_{t-1}^* reduces strongly or eliminates the significance of these variables, particularly of K^*. To see what this may mean, let us recall that the coefficient of K_{t-1}^* can be viewed as a "reaction coefficient" that is positively related to the rate of speed of these adjustments.[23] But then, if a geometric lag distribution is assumed, the coefficient of OC_{t-1}^* measures inversely the speed of adjustment of new investment commitments to changes in the causal variables. There is an ambiguity here and probably a partial redundancy, with OC_{t-1}^* proving the strongest proxy variable.

The distributed lags involved may be attributable in large part to the continuity aspects of the investment process. If drastic changes in OC^* are seen as associated with large cost, the immediately past rate of real investment commitments would, as a visible result, exercise a substantial influence upon the current rate. The lagged adjustments may then depend more on the gap between the desired and the previously achieved rates of investment commitments and realizations than on the gap between the desired and the initially available capital stock. In this situation, the "capacity accelerator" variables could still be conceived as codetermining investment along with the autoregressive factor, although their role would have to be redefined.[24] In my estimates, however, this possibility is not realized, since the effects of OC_{t-1}^* typically overwhelm those of FS_{t-1}^* and K_{t-1}^*, perhaps because of strong interactions between those variables and the resulting multicollinearity. Just to mention one source of such difficulties, the initial conditions of investment decisions, as embodied in such predetermined

---

[23] Assume, with L. M. Koyck, that $K_t = \alpha \Sigma_{i=0}^{\infty} \lambda^i X_{t-i}$, where $0 \leqslant \lambda < 1$ (*Distributed Lags and Investment Analysis*, Amsterdam, 1954, p. 22). This can be written as $K_t = \alpha X_t + \lambda K_{t-1}$ and $I_t = \Delta K_t = \alpha X_t - (1 - \lambda)K_{t-1}$. The latter form is equivalent to the equation given above in note 19, where $b\beta = \alpha$ and $b = 1 - \lambda$.

[24] Meyer and Glauber have derived the model $I_t = \alpha b S_t - b K_{t-1} + (1 - b)I_{t-1}$ from two simple assumptions: (1) that the desired capital is proportional to sales; and (2) that the delay in adjustment is proportional to the gap between the desired rate of investment and the last actual rate. If b is the reaction coefficient and the superscript d denotes the "desired" quantities, one can write (1) $K_t^d = \alpha S_t$; $I_t^d = \alpha S_t - K_{t-1}$, and (2) $\Delta I_t = b(I_t^d - I_{t-1}) = b(\alpha S_t - K_{t-1} - I_{t-1})$; from which the above formula follows directly. See J. R. Meyer and R. R. Glauber, *Investment Decisions, Economic Forecasting, and Public Policy*, Boston, 1964, pp. 26–27.

quantities as OC_{t-1}^* and K_{t-1}^*, could well be important both in their own right and as codeterminants of the relevant expectations.

In equations C5 and C6, the synthetic capital requirements variable CR_{t-1}^* is used to represent the "accelerator principle," as is ΔFS_{t-1}^* in C7 and C8. These variables, too, have the expected positive effects when OC_{t-1}^* is not included and lose significance when it is. However, when CR^* is included along with the combination of FS^* and K^*, its coefficients are either not significant or are, contrary to expectations, negative (see equation C9). Since these factors presumably represent the same or similar forces, one of them ought to be redundant, and it turns out to be CR^*. Similar tests for ΔFS^* show that the coefficients of this variable retain positive signs in equations with FS^* and K^* but that they have little or no significance.

Gratifyingly, the coefficients of the interest rate factor show the expected negative signs (Table 10-7, column 9), but their statistical significance is in some cases rather low.

Treated singly as alternatives, the profit or cash-flow variables, R_{t-1}^*, ΔR_{t-1}^*, and CF_{t-1}^*, show considerable strength, i.e., the coefficients are positive and tend to be large relative to their standard errors. However, the cash flow variable is not significant when it is included along with profits (see equation C9). Also, ΔR^* turns out to have negative and very weak effects (if any) when used jointly with P^* (see regressions C10, C11, and C12).[25]

While the effects of the accelerator variables (Table 10-7, columns 2–5) are strongly reduced by the inclusion of OC_{t-1}^*, those of the profit variables (columns 6–8) are affected much less. It is possible that this reflects a basic difference between the two sets of influences: The pressures of demand upon capacity work more as a longer-term factor in shaping the trends of capital commitments and outlays, while the profit variables are primarily effective as determinants of short-term-invest-ment timing decisions.

In particular, it is interesting to observe that in equation C3, which does not contain the autoregressive term OC_{t-1}, both FS_{t-1}^* and K_{t-1}^*

[25] Note that, if R_{t-1}^* has a positive coefficient (e.g., 1.2), then an absolutely smaller but significant *negative* coefficient of $\Delta R_{t-1}^* = R_{t-1}^* - R_{t-2}^*$ (e.g., −0.3) would imply positive coefficients for both R_{t-1}^* and R_{t-2}^* (of 0.9 and 0.3). Hence a negative sign associated with the change term need not in such cases be "wrong" or inconsistent with expectations. By the same token, if ΔR_{t-1}^* makes no significant contribution in addition to that of R_{t-1}^*, neither should R_{t-2}^*. In practice, to be sure, it is difficult to rely on such arguments because collinearities are often involved. *Mutatis mutandis,* the same applies also to the combination of FS^* and ΔFS^*.

show significant coefficients, while the effect of R_{t-1}^* is quite weak. When OC_{t-1}^* is added to these variables, in equation C4, the situation is reversed. Thus, the flexible-accelerator combination of final demand and capital stock appears to be "explaining" much the same component of OC_t^* as is determined by the previous values of that variable, only less effectively. This autoregressive component probably consists largely of the more persistent movements of OC^*, notably its growth. The deviations of OC^* from its trend thus defined might then be largely due to *changes* in such factors as sales and profits, which are believed to influence investment.

Some further tests were made to examine this hypothesis. They give it a modest degree of support inasmuch as they confirm that profit changes in the preceding quarter tend to have a measurable influence upon new investment commitments in equations that incorporate lagged values of OC^*, such as C11 in Table 10-7. At the same time, it is clear that ΔFS_{t-1}^*, when used jointly with ΔR_{t-1}^*, fails to exhibit such an influence. However, one must recognize that equations such as C11 are not satisfactory—in my view mainly because of the omission of the consistently significant profits variable R_{t-1}^*. The failure of the interest variable i_{t-1} to be effective in such models is also related to this omission.

The equations that do not contain the autoregressive factor OC_{t-1}^* account for up to 74 per cent of the variance of new investment commitments (column 11). The highest $\bar{R}^2$ in this category is produced by regression C1, which includes four causal variables (FS^*, K^*, R^*, and i), each of which is apparently significant. The addition of ΔFS^* and ΔR^* to this equation does not improve results, as shown by regressions C10 and C12. When OC_{t-1}^* is added, the proportion of variance "explained" rises to more than 80 per cent. These are fairly satisfactory results considering the limitations of the measurements used.[26] However, the Durbin-Watson statistics (column 13) are low for the equations without OC_{t-1}^*, suggesting the presence of substantial positive autocorrelations in the residuals.

The estimate OC_{est}^* from equation C1 is compared with the actual values of new investment orders and contracts, OC^*, in Chart 10-3.

---

[26] The correlations are in general lower here than for the current-dollar series in Table 9-6, which need not be surprising because the deflation procedure eliminates some of the common trends in the series included and may also introduce some additional measurement errors.

The fit leaves much to be desired in the first five years covered, when OC_{est} greatly underestimated first the rise of OC^* in 1949–51 and then the decline of OC^* in 1951–54. The two series move appreciably closer to each other in the later years, but the movements of OC_{est}^* exceed those of OC^* on the downgrade in 1957–58 and on the upgrade in 1961–62. The deviations of OC_{est}^* from OC^*, that is, the residuals from the regression C1, are shown as the bottom curve in panel B of Chart 10-3. They clearly retain elements of positive autocorrelation and are also similar to some of the systematic movements in investment commitments. The latter relationship is evident primarily in 1949–54; in later years, it is rather blurred, and at times negative. Over the period as a whole, a positive correlation between the residuals u_t and the lagged commitments OC_{t-1}^* is indicated. When OC_{t-1}^* is used jointly with the causal variables included in Chart 10-3 the new residuals have a substantially smaller variance and autocorrelation than the residuals shown in the chart (compare equations C1 and C2 in Table 10-7). It appears that new investment commitments are difficult to predict, particularly without the autoregressive factor, presumably because they move early and depend in large part on "autonomous" expectations for which we have no good proxy measures.

No systematic timing differences are observed in panel A of Chart 10-3: OC_{est}^* led OC^* in 1951 and 1960, lagged behind OC^* in 1956 and 1961, and turned upward coincidently with OC^* in 1954 and 1958. Such leads or lags as occurred at these turning points were typically short (one quarter), and the average timing is nearly coincident. Panel B of Chart 10-3 shows that the early turns in OC_{est}^* are attributable to two of its components: $1.200R_{t-1}^*$ and $-3.530i_{t-1}$. These elements of equation C1 had early peaks and troughs in most of the turning-point zones covered. Neither FS^*, which moved late, nor K^* which had almost no turns, could have contributed to the relative accuracy of timing of these estimates.[27]

Importantly, then, these findings indicate that the pervasive leads of new investment commitments in business cycles have been closely associated with the fluctuations in profits, and, to a somewhat narrower

[27] Graphs analogous to those in Chart 10-3 were prepared for estimates from equation C12, which includes, in addition to the factors used in C1, the change in profits, ΔR_{t-1}^*. The latter tends to have early turns, which makes it a potential contributor to the timing of new investment commitments, but its effectiveness in C12 seems close to nil. The curve of OC_{est}^* from C12 is a virtual replica of the estimated series shown in Chart 10-3, panel A.

extent, with interest rates. These two variables can "explain" a large proportion of the cyclical movements in new orders and contracts, whereas the others are almost entirely ineffective in this respect.

Varying the Assumed Timing Relations

When the lags of OC_t^* relative to the explanatory variables are increased, the fits definitely deteriorate (Table 10-8). The $\bar{R}^2$ coefficients reach into the .75 to .85 range for the one-quarter lags; they are con-

Chart 10-3

Regressions of New Investment Orders and Contracts in Constant Dollars on Final Sales, Capital Stock, Corporate Profits, and Interest Rates, Quarterly, 1949–62

$$\widehat{OC}_t^* = -20.7 + .227FS_{t-1}^* - .484K_{t-1}^* + 1.200R_{t-1}^* - 3.530i_{t-1}$$

A. ACTUAL AND ESTIMATED VALUES OF OC_t^*

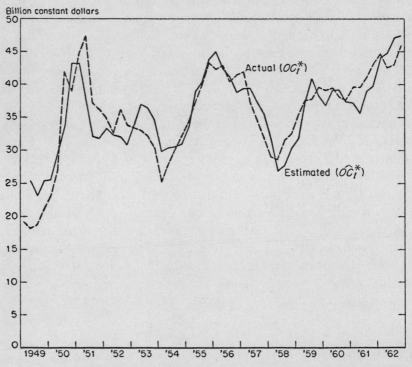

Chart 10-3 (concluded)

B. COMPONENTS OF THE ESTIMATED VALUES AND RESIDUALS

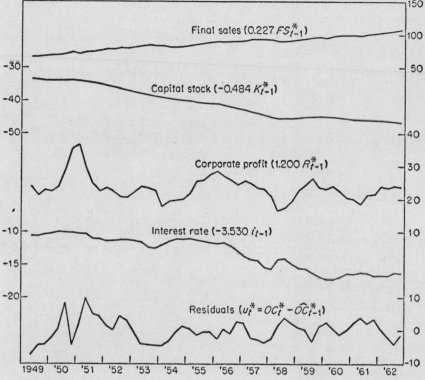

Billion constant dollars

Billion constant dollars

centrated in the .55 to .75 interval for the two-quarter lags, and in the .35 to .55 interval for the three-quarter lags (column 11).[28]

On the whole, the profit variables are rather successful in retaining their significance as the lags are lengthened, whereas the accelerator variables are not (compare the corresponding estimates for the regression sets C, D, and E in columns 2–5 and 6–8 of Tables 10-7 and 10-8). This result suggests that, on the average, the lags of OC^* may be larger

[28] This statement and the following ones are based on more evidence than is presented in Table 10-8. The table omits some regressions, such as E3 and E5 (corresponding to E4 and E6 but without the term OC^*_{t-3}), that add little to the picture provided by our estimates.

Table 10-8
Regressions for Investment Orders and Contracts in Constant Dollars, Two- and Three-Quarter Lags, 1949–62

Regression No.	Constant Term (1)	FS* (2)	K* (3)	CR* (4)	ΔFS* (5)	R* (6)	ΔR* (7)	CF* (8)	i (9)	OC* (10)	Adj. Coeff. of Det. ($\bar{R}^2$) (11)	Stand. Error of Est. (bill. dol.) (12)	Durbin-Watson Statistic [b] (13)
						Regression Coefficients [a]							
				WITH LEADS OF TWO QUARTERS RELATIVE TO OC^*_t								
D1	−19.035 (8.990)	.170 (.048)	−.198[c] (.258)			1.117 (0.203)			−4.054 (2.006)		.589	4.076	0.822
D2	−15.628 (9.026)	.094[c] (.065)	.028[c] (.284)			0.864 (0.246)			−3.384[c] (2.004)	.264 (.152)	.605	3.995	0.820
D3	18.124 (7.762)	.244 (.054)	−.734 (.284)				0.948 (0.326)		−3.652[c] (2.389)		.431	4.793	0.668
D4	8.118[c] (6.323)	.002[c] (.060)	.106[c] (.267)				1.169 (0.258)		−1.267[c] (1.915)	.660 (.116)	.652	3.749	1.278
D5	20.022 (4.559)			.106 (.038)			1.075 (0.360)		3.042[d] (1.061)		.288	5.364	0.613
D6	13.741 (2.970)			−.113[d] (.035)			1.305 (0.229)		−1.255[c] (0.832)	.919 (.105)	.716	3.390	1.720

498

									OC_t^*				
D7	−3.244[c] (5.152)				.121[c] (.133)			1.266 (0.183)	−2.602 (1.134)		.551	4.258	0.830
D8	−0.529 (4.860)				.067[c] (.130)			0.840 (0.220)	−2.202 (1.060)	.351 (.116)	.615	3.947	0.907

WITH LEADS OF THREE QUARTERS RELATIVE TO OC_t^*

									OC_t^*				
E1	−7.605[c] (10.891)	.110 (.061)	.009[c] (.320)			0.770 (0.245)			−3.652[c] (2.432)		.310	4.933	0.540
E2	−6.749[c] (11.304)	.090[c] (.087)	.069[c] (.372)			0.709 (0.309)			−3.482[c] (2.551)	.063[c] (.195)	.297	4.980	0.523
E4	13.541 (7.543)	−.010[c,d] (.077)	.196[c] (.334)				1.300 (0.308)		−1.154[c] (2.294)	.424 (.142)	.433	4.472	0.815
E6	4.862[c] (4.926)			−.202[d] (.041)				1.112 (0.224)	−4.846 (1.195)	.463 (.140)	.566	3.911	0.577
E7	5.915[c] (5.836)				.210[c] (.153)			0.936 (0.204)	−1.609[e] (1.253)		.373	4.702	0.575
E8	6.571[c] (5.988)				.197[c] (.156)			0.839 (0.267)	−1.520[e] (1.272)	.079[e] (.139)	.364	4.735	0.555

[a] See text for explanation of symbols. Standard errors of the coefficients are given underneath in parentheses.
[b] On the meaning and limitations of the Durbin-Watson statistic, see text, above.
[c] Not significant at the 5 per cent level according to the one-sided t test.
[d] Sign is "wrong," i.e., contrary to expectations.

relative to the profit than relative to the accelerator variables.[29] It is not necessarily disturbing for the concept of the longer-term distributed-lag accelerator (although it might seem so at first sight), since that concept is not in any sense adequately tested here; the comparisons concern mainly the applications of different discrete lags.

The coefficients of the interest rate variable (i) appear to be fairly stable in the transition to larger lags: they neither increase nor decrease markedly relative to their standard errors (column 9). Their signs, too, remain in most cases appropriately negative, but their statistical significance is quite low, with few exceptions.

As would be expected, the importance of the autoregressive terms OC_{t-j}^* is reduced substantially as j is increased from one to two quarters and reduced still more for $j = 3$ quarters (Tables 10-7 and 10-8, columns 10). In fact, OC_{t-3}^* is not significant in some cases, e.g., regressions E2 and E8.

Different explanatory variables need not, of course, have the same timing relative to OC_t^*. Another set of equations (group F) was therefore estimated, using for each variable the lead that maximizes its simple correlation with OC_t^*. But there was no improvement over the results reported in Table 10-7. The scope for improvement was limited in the first place, since the correlation-maximizing leads turned out in general to be one-quarter leads.[30]

Additional calculations were made to examine the possibility that second-order lag models are applicable to the determination of new investment commitments. Their verdict was negative: when OC_{t-2}^* was added to the regressions, its coefficients consistently turned out to have very little or no statistical significance.

The Implicit Lag Structure

One can think of two reasons why investment commitments should follow the determinants of investment decisions with gradual distributed lags rather than with short discrete lags. First, the recognition of

[29] Using very different data—annual cross sections and time series for 1935–55—Edwin Kuh reports that "the strongest influence on investment [expenditures] came from lagged (or the average of lag and present) profit and not from current profit, while the influence of capacity pressure appears strongest in the current rather than in the preceding year." This result, then, is qualitatively similar to ours. See Kuh, *Capital Stock Growth: A Micro-Econometric Approach*, Amsterdam, 1963, Chap. 8 and p. 333.

[30] For K^* and ΔR^* simple correlations suggested four-quarter leads, but in the multiple regressions one-quarter leads often proved to be appropriate for these variables, too.

the need for additional productive facilities and the decision to acquire them may be based on a string of past values, rather than on a single value, of certain indicators. Second, even if the decision to invest relates to a whole project, the placement of orders for the project may be spaced over time. The first reason is plausible in that the recognition of the gap between the desired and the actual capital stock probably does require more than a single determinant value, but it is not at all clear that the decision to invest must depend on a *long* sequence of indications. The second reason is independent of the first inasmuch as it suggests some form of a distributed lag even if the need for the investment was recognized with little delay; but the lags involved here could very well be relatively short and clustered. Once the shortage of the available capital stock is perceived, ordering may be expected to follow promptly to implement the investment decision with least delay.

It seems implausible in light of these considerations that the determination of investment commitments should be a process of such slow lagged adjustments as are implied by several regressions in Table 10-6, Group B. These are the equations that show very high coefficients of the lagged dependent variable (OC_{t-1}), e.g., B6, which is a very rudimentary version of a distributed-lag accelerator, where the average lag would be about seven quarters; or B7, which is an analogous model with profits, where the reaction is still more protracted. In such cases, the implied lag pattern indicates little more than the apparent inadequacy of the specifications used.

In contrast, B3 yields the highest correlation in this set, suggesting a much more concentrated lag pattern, with half of the effect on OC_t of a maintained change in the causal factors (as of the time t) requiring no more than 1.4 quarters to work itself out. Two other regressions in this group, B2 and B4, imply similar lagged distributions averaging 1.7 and 1.9 quarters.

It is clear that the estimates of the structure of the lag differ drastically depending on which variables are assumed to have influenced the placing of investment orders through time. They are highly sensitive to b, the value of the coefficient of OC_{t-1}. When relevant causal variables are omitted, or when the included causal variables are weak or irrelevant, that coefficient is very high, giving rise to estimates of apparently unduly long lags.

It is likely that some factors influence investment decisions more gradually and others relatively promptly. In principle, if such influences occur jointly, the net contribution of each ought to be evaluated simultaneously, but in practice it is very difficult to estimate the partial distributed-lag effects of each of the different codeterminants even if there are only a few. The reason is high multicollinearity, as noted in Chapter 7.

The constant-dollar equations in Table 10-7 produce a much narrower range of lags whose duration is relatively short. Regressions C2, C6, and C8 give the best fits with few variables and reasonable estimates for their coefficients. The average lags computed according to the formula $b/(1 - b)$ are here 1.1, 2.4, and 1.6 quarters, respectively, but since the independent variables are for $t - 1$, 1.0 must be added to each of these three figures. With this adjustment, the equations imply that for $q = 0.5$ (that is, to account for 50 per cent of the total long-run reaction involved), the necessary lags n vary from 2.1 to 3.0 quarters; for $q = 0.7$, the range of n is from 2.9 to 4.5 quarters; and for $q = 0.9$, it is from 4.6 to 7.7 quarters.[31] The gist of this analysis is that the lags on balance are probably not very large. Half or more of the value of new investment orders and contracts are placed in the first six or nine months following a hypothetical maintained change in the factors combining to influence the investment decision. Most of the new commitments that remain are made in the next couple of quarters.

Comparisons with Other Lag Estimates

While studies of the determinants of investment expenditures abound, there are very few such studies for investment commitments. Kareken and Solow[32] describe a series of experiments with quarterly regressions in which fixed-investment demand is represented by the deflated series of nonelectrical machinery orders, N_t. They settle on equations relating N_t positively to industrial production and corporate profits and negatively to industrial bond yields. These equations are said to suggest, as a "rough statement," that "of the full long-run effect of the determining variables on new orders, about 45 per cent takes place in

[31] For the formulas linking n and q, see the discussion following equation (Z) near the end of Chapter 9.

[32] John Kareken and Robert M. Solow, "Lags in Fiscal and Monetary Policy," in Commission on Money and Credit, *Stabilization Policies,* Research Study One, Part I, Englewood Cliffs, N.J., 1963, pp. 31–38.

the first quarter in which a change occurs, another 25 per cent in the following quarter, 14 per cent in the next quarter, 8 per cent in the next quarter, and 4 per cent in the quarter after. Thus about 90 per cent of the long-run effect would run its course in a year." [33]

The coefficients of N_{t-1} in the Kareken-Solow estimates, approximately 0.55 or 0.58, are quite close to the coefficients of OC^*_{t-1} in our equations C2 and C8, which are 0.52 and 0.61; consequently, the lag structures computed from these statistics are similar.[34] However, the causal variables in the C regressions have subscripts $t - 1$, while those in the Kareken-Solow regressions have subscripts t. Also, other related equations (notably C6 in Table 10-7, which deserves consideration) show higher coefficients of OC^*_{t-1}. On the whole, therefore, my estimates imply slower lagged reactions than those reported by Kareken and Solow. Whereas they suggest that slightly more than 90 per cent of the hypothetical "total response" of investment commitments would be completed within one year, my results indicate that this proportion is perhaps nearer three quarters (the best estimates, in my view, run from 64 to 86 per cent).

This relatively modest discrepancy has no simple explanation, since the estimates differ in more than one respect. However, one probable reason for it is that N includes only nonelectrical machinery orders, whereas my regressions refer to plant contracts as well as equipment orders, both of these categories being represented in OC^*. Some new industrial equipment is bought in conjunction with the construction of new plants or plant additions, but some is bought for installation in al-

---

[33] *Ibid.,* p. 38. Kareken and Solow first included an industrial capacity variable along with the FRB production index (Z), but that variable lost its statistical significance with the inclusion of net corporate profits (R), and was dropped. Among others, the following estimates were obtained (with $Z = $ FRB index $\times$ 10 and $i = $ bond yield $\times$ 100):

$$N_t = -2513.2 + 1.857Z_t + 1.225R_t - 4.131i_t; R^2 = .778$$
$$\qquad\qquad (0.339) \quad (0.228) \quad (2.543)$$

$$N_t = -1391.1 + .929Z_t + .660R_t - 2.662i_t + .547N_{t-1}; R^2 = .881$$
$$\qquad\qquad (.294) \quad (.193) \quad (1.902) \quad (.090)$$

[34] To show this similarity, let us tabulate for C2 the increments $\Delta q \times 100$ (per cent) as a function of n (quarters), which is the form used in the Kareken-Solow statement.

n	1	2	3	4	5
$\Delta q \times 100$	47.7	25.0	13.0	6.8	3.6

It should be noted that these equations are broadly comparable as far as their independent variables are concerned. The roles of FS^* in our regression and of Z in theirs are probably rather similar. Both equations include profits and interest rate variables. C2 also includes the capital stock (K), which however lacks significance.

ready existing structures. For such independent equipment purchases, the lags involved in placing (as well as in executing) new orders may well be considerably shorter than the lags that relate to industrial plant contracts and to the associated equipment orders. According to one study, only about two months elapse on the average between the realization of the need for a piece of equipment and the date of the purchase order.[35]

In recent work by Hart,[36] deflated capital appropriations by large manufacturing corporations (quarterly NICB data) are related to an index of the ratio of new orders to productive capacity for all manufacturing (called $ORCA$) interpreted as an expectational variable corresponding to the accelerator hypothesis. When App_t is thus regressed on three terms $(ORCA)_{t-i}$, $i = 0, 1, 2$ quarters, an $\bar{R}^2$ of .847 results, indicating a better fit than that obtained from an autoregressive equation linking App_t to App_{t-1} and App_{t-2} (where $\bar{R}^2 = .747$). Starting from a regression of App_t on the three $ORCA$ terms and the lagged interest rate, Hart then adds the autoregressive factors App_{t-1} and App_{t-2} and finds that their contribution is trifling. Indeed, the estimate of the average of the implied lag distribution would seem unacceptable to one who believed that App systematically lags $ORCA$.[37]

There is, however, reason to doubt that such lags should in fact exist. I have suggested elsewhere that the role of $ORCA$ can be explained without reference to the accelerator theory.[38] Changes in that variable reflect mainly the movements in new orders for durable goods which are highly correlated with new investment orders and contracts. Hence,

[35] This result comes from a study, by the National Industrial Advertisers Association, of equipment purchases in manufacturing plants with over 500 employees. It is quoted in Thomas Mayer, "The Inflexibility of Monetary Policy," *Review of Economics and Statistics*, November 1958, p. 364. A similar estimate of the lag by George Terborgh is also cited. Note however that the date of the "realization of the need" appears to be approximated by the date of authorization for the expenditure, and the latter can have a substantial lag behind the timing of changes in the "causal factors" here considered.

[36] Albert G. Hart, "Capital Appropriations and the Accelerator," *Review of Economics and Statistics*, May 1965, pp. 123–36.

[37] The regression coefficients of App_{t-1} and App_{t-2}, with their standard errors in parentheses, are 0.3149 (0.1758) and −0.2314 (0.1310), respectively (*ibid.*, p. 131; I have changed the symbols to correspond to the notation used earlier in this book). Applying the formula $\bar{n} = (b + 2c)/(1 - b - c)$ to these estimates of b and c results in a small *negative* fraction, −0.161. It is true that the applicability of the formula may be questioned because of dimensionality problems. But note also that the regression coefficients of the lagged $ORCA$ terms in Hart's equation are not large relative to their standard errors, whereas the coefficient of the simultaneous term is large and definitely significant.

[38] Victor Zarnowitz, Comment on Reynold Sachs and Albert G. Hart, "Anticipations and Investment Behavior: An Econometric Study of Quarterly Time Series for Large Firms in Durable Goods Manufacturing" in *Determinants of Investment Behavior*, Universities–National Bureau Conference 18, New York, NBER, 1967, pp. 596–99.

ORCA is likely to derive most of its influence from being actually another form of an anticipatory variable, like investment commitments, and similar to as well as, probably, roughly coincident with, capital appropriations.

Integrating the Results on Commitments and Expenditures

Average Lead Times for Business Investment in Plant and Equipment
   Estimates presented in the preceding part of this chapter suggest that new investment orders and contracts lag an average of two to three quarters behind the variables that are presumed to influence investment decisions. Most of the new commitments are probably made within the first year after the motivating change in the investment determinants, although some will no doubt be made later, over a considerable stretch of time. In general, these lags are likely to be quite differentiated and variable, and they seem difficult to define, let alone to evaluate, in any rigorous manner.

   The lags of investment realizations behind new investment commitments can be much better defined and measured. Not surprisingly they tend to be quite substantial. Investment in plant and equipment involves new construction and acquisition of capital goods that must be produced according to the specifications of the investor and prospective user. This process, starting from the new appropriations made or orders placed and ending at the stages of output or expenditures, is ordinarily time-consuming. The lags are gradual, i.e., distributed, but some minimum delay is likely to occur before the new commitment will begin affecting expenditures. The lag distribution may be unimodal, that is, it may incorporate an initial build-up effect of orders. It is probably often skewed as that effect tails off slowly. According to the various estimates reviewed in the last part of Chapter 9, the average lags of business fixed-investment outlays relative to commitments range from three to about five quarters. In the first year after the orders for capital goods had been placed, perhaps only 50 percent of their full long-run effect on spending will have been completed.

   A rough estimate of the time required for plant and equipment expenditures to register major changes in response to factors influencing investment decisions is obtained by adding the two average lags, thus accounting for both the time needed to reach the decision and the time needed to implement it. My estimates for the combined average lag vary approximately between five and eight quarters.

According to the estimates by Kareken and Solow, four to five quarters are required to account for about half of the "full effect" of new orders on production of business equipment. The corresponding "half-life" estimate for the impact of selected determining variables on new orders is one quarter or a little more. These figures add up to an average lag of five to six quarters for the relation between the determining factors and equipment output. This is within the lower part of the range of my estimates.

Frank de Leeuw, in relating plant and equipment expenditures by manufacturers to "capital requirements," internal funds (cash flow), and bond yields, tried Koyck, rectangular, and inverted V (symmetrical triangular) lag distributions.[39] The last approach gave the best result of the three when weights were used which increased for six quarters and declined for another six. Although the lag pattern is in this case quite different, the average lag estimate (about 6.5 quarters) again resembles the others.

In the first of his papers on investment behavior, Jorgenson suggested that "the average lag between change in demand for capital stock and the corresponding net investment is, roughly, 6.5 quarters or about a year and a half."[40] In a related later study, estimated patterns of lagged response based on applications of the general Pascal lag distribution are presented for total manufacturing and several of its major subdivisions.[41] The data are quarterly, for the period 1949–60. The fitted functions imply asymmetrical patterns that typically rise steeply

[39] De Leeuw, "Demand for Capital Goods," pp. 415–19.

[40] Dale Jorgenson, "Capital Theory and Investment Behavior," *American Economic Review,* May 1963, p. 259. In this work, net investment is a distributed-lag function of one or more differences in a computed "desired capital stock" variable and replacement investment is proportional to capital stock. The desired capital stock is estimated from a formula that includes the value of output, price of capital goods, interest, and tax rates on business income. The main aims are to link the investment function to the neoclassical theory of capital, assuming net worth maximization as the objective of the firm, and to generalize the lag structure involved. Possible implications of uncertainty and entrepreneurial preference for internal financing, as well as of short-run fluctuations in the rate of utilization of the capital stock, are disregarded. In practice, the excellent fits obtained by Jorgenson are due in large measure to his use of the OBE-SEC investment anticipations data.

[41] Dale W. Jorgenson and James A. Stephenson, "The Time Structure of Investment Behavior in United States Manufacturing, 1947–1960," *Review of Economics and Statistics,* February 1967, pp. 16–27. Similar estimates for four comprehensive industrial groups are also given.

for three or four of the shortest lags and then tail off gradually in the direction of intermediate and long lags. The average lag for total manufacturing is computed to be 8.5 quarters; the corresponding estimates for the various industries vary from 6 to 11 quarters. These results are for net investment, but those for gross investment are described as quite similar during a long initial phase of about three years following the change in desired capital.

The 1964 study by Meyer and Glauber includes, in addition to an extensive analysis of cross-sectional data, an exploration of investment behavior based on quarterly time series.[42] Their focus is on testing different hypotheses about the determinants of capital outlays of business corporations; while not directly concerned with the estimation of distributed lags in the investment process, their study is instructive in the present context. Meyer and Glauber use different explanatory variables with different timing relative to the dependent variable I_t so as to optimize the over-all fits. Thus the cash flow, capacity utilization, and stock price variables are generally taken with time subscripts $t - 1$, while the interest (industrial bond) rate, which is expected to show a negative coefficient, has the subscript $t - 3$.

The autoregressive factor used most frequently in the Meyer-Glauber study is I_{t-2}. Its coefficients vary greatly depending on the choice of causal variables, a finding that parallels what was observed repeatedly in my own results. For example, the coefficient of I_{t-2} is 0.821 when only cash flow and the capacity factor are used, 0.893 when the interest rate is added, 0.651 when the level of the stock price index is added, and 0.984 when the change in the stock price index replaces the level.[43] Several criteria of accuracy of estimation and forecasting are applied to the different equations but selection of the best one proves difficult, mainly because good structural qualities and superior forecasting performance do not coincide in the same model. The highest-ranking models suggest lag distributions with averages of 5 to 7.5 quarters for the interest rate and 3 to 5.5 quarters for the other variables, allowing for the time subscripts chosen.

[42] Meyer and Glauber, *Investment Decisions*. The data came mainly from Federal Trade Commission–Securities and Exchange Commission sources and cover the period 1949–58 (in forecasting tests, 1949–61). See especially Chapter VII.

[43] *Ibid.*, Table IX-1, p. 215. The authors observe that the last of these estimates comes disturbingly close to one (the "upper limit" for a stable process) and that it "seems unrealistically large" (*ibid.*, p. 216).

At this point it is possible to conclude that the explicit estimates of the average lag of investment in plant and equipment are all substantially the same for the studies based on quarterly postwar data. The Kareken-Solow, de Leeuw, and my own estimates are all concentrated in the range of 5–7 quarters. The results of Meyer and Glauber suggest somewhat shorter mean lags and those of Jorgenson and associates suggest somewhat longer mean lags, varying roughly from 6.5 to 8.5 quarters.[44]

In a sharp contrast to these findings from regressions based on quarterly time series for periods since 1947 are the results of studies of annual data for periods including prewar years. Thus Koyck's estimates of the speed-of-adjustment coefficient λ (see note 23, above) range from 0.7 to more than 0.9 for several industries. This implies that capital stock adjusts very slowly to changes in output: The suggested average lags are often as long as seven years and may exceed ten years. Kuh notes that his time series estimates of the "reaction coefficients" (capital stock slope coefficients) have similar implications, and that a different model by Grunfeld also yields "approximately consistent" results.[45] Long lags of capital expenditures are likewise involved in Eisner's work with company data from the McGraw-Hill annual surveys, where sales changes in each of the six preceding years are used as codeterminants of the current year's outlays.[46]

The lags suggested by the studies of annual data are so long that they are difficult to rationalize. Moreover, independent evidence from surveys of new or expanding manufacturing plants suggests that it takes

[44] Zvi Griliches and Neil Wallace have used Jorgenson's and their own estimates of investment functions to illustrate "the fact that a small difference in the estimated regression coefficients can imply substantial differences in the derived form of the distributed lag" ("The Determinants of Investment Revisited," *International Economic Review*, September 1965, p. 322). Their equation in this comparison yields an implausibly long average lag. However, other estimates presented in the same paper imply lags that are much shorter and closer to the figures quoted in the text above. Thus the average lag of investment expenditures behind the rate of interest and the stock price index is 4.7 quarters, according to "one of the better fitting" equations of Griliches and Wallace (compare Zvi Griliches, "Distributed Lags: A Survey," *Econometrica*, January 1967, p. 30).

[45] Kuh, *Capital Stock Growth*, p. 293. Kuh's reaction coefficients are typically in the neighborhood of 0.08 and do not exceed 0.15 (*ibid.*, Table 9.1, p. 294; on the meaning of such coefficients and their relation to Koyck's coefficients, see notes 19 and 23, above). Grunfeld's estimates are based on annual time series for six large corporations and cover the period 1935–54; they relate gross investment to the capital stock and market value of each firm at the beginning of the year and yield capital stock coefficients ranging from 0.003 to 0.400 (Yehuda Grunfeld, "The Determinants of Corporate Investment," in A. C. Harberger, ed., *The Demand for Durable Goods*, Chicago, 1960, pp. 255–57).

[46] For the most recent reports on this project, see Robert Eisner, "Investment and the Frustrations of Econometricians," *American Economic Review*, May 1969, pp. 50–64; and Eisner, "A Permanent Income Theory for Investment: Some Empirical Explorations," *ibid.*, June 1967, pp. 363–90. For references to earlier reports, see the June 1967 article and Chapter 9, note 32, above.

on the average about seven quarters for a decision to build to result in the completion of the project.[47] The lags estimated from regressions of annual data are often five to eight *years* longer, and it is hard to see why this much time should have to elapse on the average between changes in the investment-motivating factors and the decision to invest. On the other hand, the estimates from the quarterly regressions are certainly much closer to, and seem on the whole reasonably consisaent with, the survey results. The latter are summarized by the following mean lead times (averages for all types of plants weighted by the cost of project), which were obtained by Thomas Mayer from questionnaires sent to companies that were reported by the *Engineering News Report* to be building industrial plant during 1954.

From:	*To:*	No. of Months	No. of Cases
Start of consideration	Start of construction	23	64
Start of drawing of plan	Start of construction	7	61
Placing of first significant orders	Start of construction	2	70
Start of construction	Completion of project	15	77

According to these figures, the average lead of first orders relative to the realized investment is seventeen months, just below the midpoint of the range of 5–8 quarters indicated by my regression estimates. The lead is 4–5 months longer when reckoned from the time of "drawing plans" or making the "final decision." The average interval from the "start of consideration" of a new project to the "first significant orders" is a relatively long one of about 7 quarters; it exceeds considerably the average lags suggested by my regression analysis of new investment commitments. However, the initial stage is here but vaguely denoted; e.g., if "consideration" meant just a feeling that expansion of the productive capacity in the next two years would be desirable, it might bear little relation to the timing of changes in the investment determinants. Even so, this information appears to indicate that the decision taking itself is often viewed as a rather time-consuming process in business firms engaged in expanding plant and equipment.

The possible biases in the survey results point in opposite directions,

[47] Thomas Mayer, "Plant and Equipment Lead Times," *Journal of Business of the University of Chicago,* April 1960, pp. 127–32. See also Thomas Mayer, "The Inflexibility of Monetary Policy," *Review of Economics and Statistics,* November 1958, pp. 362–64.

and their probable net impact is viewed as relatively small.[48] However, it is important to recognize that purchases of industrial equipment include not only items to be installed in new plants or plant additions but also those to be put in old buildings. The lags in decision taking are probably rather short for the latter type of equipment buying, perhaps about two months on the average.[49] To this a delivery lag, which is variable but not longer than several months, would be added, judging from our order-shipment timing comparisons and the average ratios of unfilled machinery orders to monthly sales.

To summarize the evidence, distributed lags of substantial duration prevail in the relations between investment determinants, commitments, and realizations; but the lags are better measured in quarters than in years, and they are believed to have been greatly overstated in some studies based on annual data. As implied in the discussion of this viewpoint by Jorgenson and Stephenson[50] there are several possible reasons for the discrepancy between the annual and the quarterly results, and a full explanation of the discrepancy is not yet available. The authors argue that one reason lies in the misspecification of the lag structure in studies of annual data that rely mainly on the geometric distribution; but they also believe that the discrepancy is too large to be explained only by this source of bias and that "the possibility of other errors of specification in the annual results should be explored."[51]

Investment Functions with Estimated Commitments

The procedural question from the beginning of this chapter may be reconsidered in a more concrete form. Can estimates of investment commitments derived only from previous values of causal variables provide a sufficient basis for the successful projection of investment

---

[48] See *ibid.*, p. 127, note 5, and p. 130; also, William W. White, "The Flexibility of Anticyclical Monetary Policy," *Review of Economics and Statistics,* May 1961, pp. 142–47; and Thomas Mayer, "Dr. White on the Inflexibility of Monetary Policy," *Review of Economics and Statistics,* May 1963, pp. 209–11.

[49] See note 35, above.

[50] "Investment Behavior," p. 26.

[51] In a recent paper, Hall and Jorgenson derive separate estimates of investment functions for equipment and for structures, using annual data for 1931–41 and 1950–63 and distributed-lag estimation methods analogous to those introduced in the earlier Jorgenson studies of investment behavior. The average lags between changes in desired capital and investment expenditures are estimated as approximately 2 years for equipment in manufacturing and 1.3 years for nonmanufacturing equipment, which agrees with the quarterly results for total business fixed investment as reported before. The corresponding averages for structures, however, are much larger: 3.8 years in manufacturing and 7.5 years in nonmanufacturing. See Robert E. Hall and Dale W. Jorgenson, "Tax Policy and Investment Behavior," *American Economic Review,* June 1967, pp. 391–414.

expenditures? An affirmative answer, if true and not due to some fortuitously favorable evidence, would suggest that: (1) the commitments data work well as a representation of the flow over time of aggregated investment decisions; (2) the determinants of the decisions can be specified in a sufficiently correct way; and (3) investment realizations, to which the expenditures are tied up, can be predicted with reasonable accuracy as some lagged function of the decisions to order capital goods. By the same token, the answer could be negative because either (1) or (2) or (3) does not hold. However, these propositions were purposely expressed in broad and cautious terms, and indeed each of them can at best be only partially valid, even if the tests come out favorably. As already noted, the available commitments data undoubtedly have serious shortcomings, and our knowledge of both the determinants of investment decisions and any possible additional factors influencing the rates and timing of expenditures is certainly quite deficient.

In the tests to follow, I shall use the estimates of new investment orders and contracts computed from regression C1 in Table 10-7. The equation is reproduced below:

$$OC_t^* = -20.704 + .227FS_{t-1}^* - .484K_{t-1}^* + 1.200R_{t-1}^* - 3.530i_{t-1}.$$

$$(\text{C1})$$

In Table 10-9, plant and equipment outlays I^* are related to the estimate of OC^* based on (C1). Geometric and second-order lag distributions are applied. The coefficients of $\hat{OC}_{t-1}^*$ are about four times as large as their standard errors in equations with I_{t-1}^* only, but just 1.3–1.5 as large as their standard errors in equations that also include I_{t-2}^* (column 2). In either set, it is redundant to include additional values of lagged commitments: the measured effects of $\hat{OC}_{t-2}^*$, where the circumflex denotes estimates derived from (C1), are negative but apparently not significant (column 3). The coefficients of I_{t-1}^* equal 0.86 and 0.88 in the geometric-lag models and rise to nearly 1.4 in the second-order lag functions, where I_{t-2}^* enters with negative coefficients, −0.48 and −0.46 (columns 4 and 5).[52]

---

[52] These results are at least broadly similar to those obtained in the current-dollar regressions of I_t on actual commitments OC_{t-i} and on I_{t-i} and I_{t-2} (Table 9-3). However, in Table 10-9 commitments have much lower, and lagged expenditures have higher, coefficients. This must be largely due to the change from actual to estimated commitments, but the change from current-dollar to deflated series probably also works in the same direction.

Table 10-9

Regressions for Plant and Equipment Expenditures (I)
in Constant Dollars for Distributed-Lag Functions
with Estimated Commitments, 1949–62

Regression No.	Constant Term (1)	Regression Coefficients [a]				$\bar{R}^2$ (6)	SE (7)	Durbin-Watson Statistic [b] (8)
		$\widehat{OC}^*_{t-1}$ (2)	$\widehat{OC}^*_{t-2}$ (3)	I^*_{t-1} (4)	I^*_{t-2} (5)			
4a	−.462	.140 (.033)		0.861 (0.034)		.9640	1.016	1.168
4b	−.255	.189 (.049)	−.074[c] (.054)	0.883 (0.037)		.9646	1.008	1.324
5a	.942	.052 (.040)		1.396 (0.159)	−.483 (.141)	.9704	0.921	1.663
5b	.992	.084 (.055)	−.043[c] (.051)	1.383 (0.160)	−.460 (.144)	.9702	0.924	1.730

[a] $\widehat{OC}^*$ is the estimate of new investment orders and contracts calculated from equation C1 (see the first line in Table 10-7 and text). Standard errors are given underneath in parentheses.

[b] On the meaning and limitations of the Durbin-Watson statistic, see Table 10-3, note c, and text above.

[c] Positive rather than negative sign would be expected, but the statistical significance of these estimates is very low anyway.

Chart 10-4 shows the estimates of I^*_t computed from equations (4a) and (5a) in Table 10-9. These estimates lie very close to the actual values I^*_t, but they tend to lag behind the latter at turning points by one-quarter intervals. Such lags, of course, are typically associated with regressions that include lagged values of the dependent variable. The estimates from the two equations are closely similar, but (5a) has a marginal advantage, which is also reflected in the summary measures of Table 10-9, columns 6–8. While the (4a) estimates show one-quarter lags at all eight recorded turns in I^*, the (5a) estimates show such lags at six and coincident timing at two of the turns (the troughs of 1958 and 1961).

Clearly, one must expect I^*_t to be less closely associated with the estimates of OC^*_{t-i} than with the actual values. My calculations suggest that the differentials in these effects are substantial. Moreover, in the equations with observed values, OC^* performed well when entered

Chart 10-4

Regressions for Business Fixed-Investment Outlays in Constant Dollars, Based on Distributed Lags with Estimated Commitments, Quarterly, 1949–62

(a) $\hat{I}_t^* = -.462 + .140O\hat{C}_{t-1}^* + .861I_{t-1}^*$

(b) $\hat{I}_t^* = .942 + .052O\hat{C}_{t-1}^* + 1.396I_{t-1}^* - .483I_{t-2}^*$

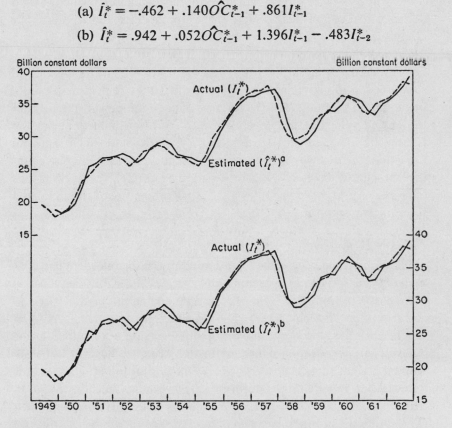

with the subscripts $t - 2$ or even $t - 3$, as shown in Table 10-3, while here $O\hat{C}^*$ must be used with the subscript $t - 1$.[53]

To replace actual commitments by the estimates means in effect to replace new investment orders and contracts by a linear combination

[53] It will be recalled that several causal variables taken with subscripts $t - 1$ make significant contributions in regressions for I^* when included along with OC_{t-2}^* or OC_{t-3}^* (Table 10-3). Now $O\hat{C}_{t-1}^*$ might reflect to some extent these influences, while $O\hat{C}_{t-2}^*$ would not. When $O\hat{C}_{t-1}^*$ is excluded from the equations of Table 10-9, the re-estimated coefficients of $O\hat{C}_{t-2}$ are positive but barely significant. That $O\hat{C}^*$ must be taken with a shorter lead relative to I^* than was applicable to OC^* offsets the potential gain of a longer predictive span that would result from the substitution of estimated for the actual commitments.

of selected "causal" variables or a sum of their estimated influences. The present results and related earlier findings suggest that the anticipatory data definitely contain more information about subsequent investment expenditures than do the causal factors. Perhaps further efforts will produce substantially better specifications which would permit a revision of this verdict, but the prospect seems to me rather doubtful.

With all the necessary qualifications, a modest success can probably be claimed on behalf of the estimated values of OC^*. There is indeed some reason to appreciate the very fact that they remain measurably influential in equations for I^* that also include the powerful effects of the lagged values of the dependent variable. Not only that, but the average lags implied by the estimates of Table 10-9 are consistent with the evidence reviewed in the preceding sections. Taking into account the one-quarter leads of the causal variables in (C1), the average lags of I^* relative to these variables are 7.2 according to equation (4a) and 5.9 quarters according to (5a).

Concluding Remarks

The rather crude aggregate intended to approximate orders and contracts for capital goods is demonstrably associated with several series that can be taken to represent factors influencing private decisions to invest in plant and equipment. The associations are of the type consistent with familiar hypotheses of investment determination. These hypotheses are general, and their formal structure has not yet been worked out adequately. In particular, we know far too little about how the relevant expectations are formed. Investment decisions relate to the expected time-paths of such variables as sales, profits, and interest rates rather than to their past levels or changes; yet it is the past values which alone are known and must serve as proxies for the expectations that are not observable. However, some of the proposed explanatory variables may be more "proxy" than others, in the sense that their theoretical meaning is less clear and that they are likely to prove of little (if any) importance once the other factors are more properly accounted for. Especially, attempts have been made in some recent studies to reduce profits to the role of a proxy variable for the pressure of demand on capacity.[54] The literature makes it only too clear that these

[54] The main proponent of this view is Robert Eisner (see references in note 46, above). However, the evidence on this point is quite mixed. To quote Eisner: "While coefficients of the profit variables

problems are very difficult to handle with the available data and techniques; fortunately, it is not improper to place them outside the scope of this inquiry.

Indeed, in asking whether the constructed order-contracts series fits into the framework of suppositions adopted to explain investment, one is "testing" the data perhaps as much as the hypotheses. An exploratory and experimental approach seems appropriate at this point, despite its lack of rigor. The analysis bears on important issues and should at least give useful hints for further research. Thus it is suggestive that the variables associated with the flexible-accelerator hypothesis work rather better when applied to investment orders than when applied to investment expenditures; that the profit variables are nevertheless still significant (the capacity and profit "principles" need not be mutually exclusive); and that the influence of interest rates conforms to expectations.

As shown in Chart 10-1 and documented later (Chapter 12), new investment orders and contracts turn down well ahead of peaks and turn up before the troughs in general economic activity. In fact, this variable (OC) is an important "leader" that precedes many other economic aggregates and follows few. Most of the series suggested as possible "explanatory" variables for the investment commitments function lag behind rather than lead OC at turning points; it does not seem likely that they could represent the critical factors in the determination of the early timing of OC. However, the changes in profits and sales and the interest rates (inverted) do often turn ahead of new investment commitments as do sometimes also corporate profits proper. The latter appears to be more closely associated with new investment orders and contracts than any other variable examined, as far as the cyclical behavior of the commitments series is concerned.

Some variables that have recently been treated as potentially important determinants of investment were not included in my analysis. Grunfeld (see note 45) has argued that the "market value of the firm" provides a preferable indicator of the expectations governing in-

are uniformly low in cross sections, they are relatively high in most of the time series. Firms apparently tend to make capital expenditures in the period immediately following higher profits, but firms earning higher profits do not make markedly greater capital expenditures than firms earning lower profits. This evidence is consistent with the hypothesis that past profits play some significant role in the timing of capital expenditure but do not affect its long-run average." ("A Permanent Income Theory," p. 386). Since the principal interest of the present study is in the short-term behavior of investment on aggregative levels, my direct concern here is with the time series aspects of the relations involved.

vestment decisions, which suggests that a stock market variable ought to be included in the analysis of orders for plant and equipment. Recent tests indicate that the stock price index makes a significant but not major contribution to the explanation of fixed-investment expenditures.[55] It seems unlikely that this factor will prove much more forceful as an early determinant of investment orders and contracts; moreover the chain of influence in the opposite direction—from orders to stock prices—may also be important, and could disturb this relation.[56] But these matters have yet to be investigated.

Recent studies by Jorgenson and associates provide support for a "neoclassical" model of investment behavior, in which a complex synthetic variable is employed to represent the price (or user cost) of capital services. These contributions, to which references were made before, appeared too late for tests based on Jorgenson's model to be included in this study.

According to a monetary view of business cycles, variations in the rate of growth of the money stock are a major source of changes in spending on current and future output (including consumption as well as investment expenditures).[57] If the rate of change of the money stock is treated as conforming positively to business cycles, its turning points are found to lead at peaks and troughs by long, though variable, intervals. The transmission mechanism involves adjustments in the demands

[55] Griliches and Wallace, "Determinants of Investment Revisited," p. 326, use the Standard and Poor's index of industrial stock prices as of the end of quarter ($t - 2$) and find that past output and interest rates had stronger effects on gross investment in plant and equipment. Meyer and Glauber, *Investment Decisions*, Chap. VII, conclude that the S&P index changes do reflect "an expectational influence at work in business investment decisions," but note that introduction of this variable greatly aggravates the collinearity problem, which is generally serious and difficult in time series regressions for investment; that it is not clear at all how to deflate the stock price index; and that the latter's positive contribution to the explanation of investment occurs chiefly during periods of expansion when the internal funds variable is ineffective (*ibid.*, pp. 152–53 and 172). Christ, *Econometric Models and Methods*, also finds the stock price variable to have a significant positive effect on investment expenditures. D. W. Jorgenson and C. D. Siebert ("Theories of Corporate Investment Behavior," *American Economic Review*, September 1968, pp. 681–712) rank the factor of firm value ("expected profits") as stronger than the accelerator and liquidity factors but weaker than the value of output deflated by the price of capital services (the "neoclassical" variable). For some theoretical objections to the use of market value (as well as profits) as an indicator of desired capital stock, see John P. Gould, "Market Value and the Theory of Investment of the Firm," *American Economic Review*, September 1967, pp. 910–13.

[56] For example, "declines in the level or rate of growth of profits or in factors portending such declines— . . . profit margins . . . or new orders . . . —during the latter stages of business cycle expansions may alter appraisals of common stock values and hence produce a decline in stock prices before the downturn in business" (Geoffrey H. Moore, ed., *Business Cycle Indicators*, Princeton for NBER, 1961, Vol. I, p. 68).

[57] For a summary of this position, see Milton Friedman and Anna J. Schwartz, "Money and Business Cycles," *Review of Economics and Statistics*, Supplement, February 1963.

for, and prices of, various assets, although the early impact is mainly on financial assets. This view implies a causal connection between money and investment and suggests the inclusion of monetary variables in the regression analysis of orders and contracts for capital goods. But the suggested transmission process includes complex intermediate links and lags that may be long and are probably quite variable; the whole subject is as yet little explored and little understood. It is doubtful that the present analysis would gain much if it simply included a measure of monetary changes, but a systematic investigation of the relations involved lies beyond its scope. Of course, monetary changes strongly influence several of the causal variables used in this study, notably the interest rates and the cash flows or internal funds available for investment.

Orders and contracts provide an important link in the analysis of business investment in plant and equipment. It is important to recognize that the latter is a time-consuming process and to utilize this insight in research and prediction. There is need for better data on the early investment stages. Thus a "cleaner" series on new orders for capital goods should contribute substantially to the improvement of analysis and forecasting in this area. That much can be said with considerable assurance, and it is worth emphasizing.

Summary

Business expenditures on plant and equipment (I), taken with appropriate lags, are closely associated with new capital appropriations (App), new investment orders and contracts (OC), and "first anticipations" (A_1). The correlations of I with any of these anticipatory or symptomatic variables tend to be considerably higher than the correlations of I with any of the several "causal" variables that are suggested by various hypotheses about investment determination. In multiple regressions that include both the symptomatic and the causal variables, the former contribute in general more to the statistical explanation of I than do the latter. The causal variables include some that are associated with the flexible-accelerator hypothesis, some that provide proxies for expectational elements and measures of financial factors, and some that stand for the opportunity costs involved. The hypotheses considered are not mutually exclusive and none are decisively refuted by this regression analysis.

If the causal variables in the equations for I_t represent factors that influence investment *decisions,* then they should, when taken with earlier timing, contribute significantly to a statistical explanation of OC_t. In general, they do this, but in different degrees and with important qualifications. It is not difficult to obtain rather good fits for OC, but the best fits result from using simultaneous relationships or short leads of the explanatory variables. The regressions for I_t yield higher $\bar{R}^2$ coefficients with longer predictive leads. As would be expected, OC with its early timing pattern is a good predictor of expenditures but is itself much more difficult to predict.

Final sales, capital stock, profits, and the long-term interest rate together account for 78 per cent of the variance of new investment commitments, when deflated series and one-quarter leads of the independent variables are used. The coefficients of capital stock and of the interest rate are negative; the others are positive. The early cyclical timing of OC is captured rather well in these estimates, owing to the contributions of the profit and interest variables. Of the lagged values of the dependent variable, only OC_{t-1} improves the results significantly. When the explanatory factors are taken with longer leads relative to OC_t, the goodness-of-fit statistics become much less favorable.

The distributed-lag regressions suggest that half or more of the total volume of new investment commitments are incurred in the first six or nine months following a shift in the factors that influence investments decisions. The lags in reaching the decision to go ahead with an investment project are not very long, according to these estimates. This result is believed to be plausible and consistent with other acceptable evidence.

To calculate the average time that outlays on plant and equipment require to register major changes in response to changes in the determinants of investment decisions, one must combine the lag of OC behind the latter factor and the lag of I behind OC. According to my estimates in this and the preceding chapter, the combined average lag varies between approximately five and eight quarters.

Other quarterly regression studies yield for the most part about the same range for the estimates of the average lag between the change in the demand for capital stock and fixed-investment expenditures. This similarity is limited to the averages, as the studies use different forms of lag distribution. In contrast, regression studies based on annual data suggest average lags that are exceedingly long (up to 7–10 years). The estimates of such protracted lags are contradicted by independent evidence from surveys of new investment projects, and it is difficult to justify or accept them.

Calculated series of new investment commitments, $\hat{OC}$, perform fairly well in selected distributed-lag equations for I, but they are much less effective in this role than the corresponding series of *actual* commitments, OC. This confirms that the data on new orders and contracts for plant and equipment, despite their undoubtedly considerable weaknesses, contain definitely more information about subsequent capital expenditures than do several presumably important causal variables linearly combined.

PART IV

ORDERS AND RELATED PROCESSES
DURING BUSINESS CYCLES

11

CYCLICAL CONFORMITY
AND TIMING

Introduction: Why Orders Are Expected to Lead

Earlier findings and general considerations suggest that new or-ders received by manufacturers usually lead at business cycle turns. The strong tendency of manufacturers' orders to lead industrial output and shipments is clearly evident (Chapters 4 and 5). It is also well known that manufacturing activity, as measured by comprehensive series on factory employment and production, has a historical record of a roughly coincident timing at cyclical revivals and recessions.[1] The implication is clear: If the turns of aggregate industrial output are typically synchronous with peaks and troughs of the business cycle, then the like turns in the corresponding total of new orders must typically lead these peaks and troughs. This should hold not only when new orders and production are measured in real terms (quantity index points or constant dollars) but also for current-dollar aggregates, since price movements do not, on the whole, strongly affect the timing characteristics referred to here.

These, however, are merely broad presumptions from which the facts may well deviate. Thus manufacturing, while important, is by no means necessarily predominant in the U.S. economy, and its weight has of late been decreasing. It is possible for movements in this sector to be offset by movements in other parts of the system. Clearly, one can no longer take for granted that fluctuations in manufacturing activity

---

[1] On the timing of factory and nonagricultural employment and of industrial production, see "Lead-ing and Confirming Indicators of General Business Changes" and "Statistical Indicators of Cyclical Revivals and Recessions," in Geoffrey H. Moore, ed., *Business Cycle Indicators*, Princeton for NBER, 1961, Vol. I, pp. 56–57 and 244–45, respectively.

will always conform perfectly to business cycles at large, and it was never true that they must have synchronous timing at each revival and recession. Nevertheless, it still seems reasonable to expect roughly coincident timing for aggregate manufacturing production, as an average tendency over the succession of business fluctuations. This assumption pertains to a weighted average of outputs of all the component industries, not to each of the components. Historically, many manufacturing series show high over-all conformity; that is, the specific-cycle turns in large groups of series on industrial output or shipments tend to cluster about the peaks and troughs of the business cycle. This implies that the turns in the corresponding series on new orders tend to cluster about some earlier dates.

In the production process to which they give rise, new orders for industrial output stimulate ordering of other goods needed by the manufacturer. A firm that expects an increase in customers' orders may try to prepare for the event by stepping up its own buying of materials. If the rise in demand was not expected or if the materials requirements are specialized and difficult to predict, the firm will probably increase its purchases after its order receipts have begun expanding. The impact of the increases in new orders will be reinforced when they are accompanied by increases in the backlog of unfilled orders. When they are sufficiently sustained and associated with prospective capital shortages, the increases in orders received will also stimulate increases in outlays on capital equipment and plant.

The onset of a cyclical rise (decline) in manufacturers' orders indicates, therefore, that an upturn (downturn) of industrial output and employment is soon to follow. It also marks the beginning of a cumulative process whereby the increases (decreases) in orders spread throughout the economy. Thus new orders can be said to lead the business cycle because they lead the output of products to which they give rise and stimulate ordering of other goods needed for that production.

This is a comprehensive yet simple statement which certainly has merit as far as it goes; but saying that new orders lead the business cycle because they lead production is in a sense formal and limited to the surface of the matter. Clearly, the timing of new orders can never be *explained* by reference to the timing of production by the order-receiving industries: The causal connection runs from commitments or sales to output, not the other way around. The second part of the statement, which says that manufacturers' new orders lead aggregate economic activity because they induce further buying, goes deeper. Investment in purchased-materials stocks, which leads at business cycle turns, is doubtless influenced in an important way by changes in manufacturers' unfilled orders. Although the latter depend strongly on changes in the rate at which new orders are received, they also depend on the speed with which orders are executed. That speed, in turn, depends on the conditions of supply as well as the urgency of demand. The cumulation of orders is suggested in various ways by the evidence already reviewed.[2]

If new orders can be expected to lead at business cycle peaks and troughs, how large and regular have these leads been in the past and how dependable do they appear as guides to the future? This is an empirical question, since the general argument above cannot go beyond a qualitative indication of the expected timing sequence.

New Orders for Major Industries and Sectors

The Record of Comprehensive Series

The lack of long comprehensive and consistent series on manufacturers' new and unfilled orders is a serious gap in the stock of the available statistical data. The OBE Industry Survey data include broad aggregates for all durable goods industries and the group of nondurable goods industries reporting order backlogs, which begin in 1939. (See Chapter 3 on the revised series that start in 1947 and are now published by the Census Bureau.) For earlier years, there are the monthly indexes of the value of new and unfilled orders, 1935-39 = 100, computed by the National Industrial Conference Board. They begin in 1929 for new orders and in 1935 for unfilled orders, and extend

---

[2] New investment orders and contracts show strong autoregressive properties: OC_{t-1} retains a major influence on OC_t in any combination with presumptive causal factors (Chapter 10). Where production involves relatively short delivery periods and in industries working largely to stock, new orders are apt to be still more autocorrelated; for example, they tend to be smoother for nondurables than for durables (shipments and production, of course, are generally smoother than new orders; see Chapter 3). Increases in the quantities of advance orders received and on hand anticipate rising production and are therefore likely to be associated with increased purchases of materials (Chapter 8). Finally, large and sustained rises in orders would tend to stimulate capital expenditure projects (as shown below, Charts 12-12 and 12-13 and text).

through mid-1944. They cover ten durable and six nondurable goods industries.[3]

For a still earlier period, 1920–33, indexes of the physical volume of new and unfilled orders (1923–25 = 100) were compiled by the Department of Commerce. Their components fall into six groups: iron and steel; transportation equipment; lumber; stone, clay, and glass; textiles; and paper.[4] The names of these groups might suggest broad industrial coverage, but in fact the basis of these indexes is narrow. However, other, more comprehensive indexes are not available for the period before 1929.[5]

Chart 11-1 presents the three most comprehensive new-order series. These cover both durables and nondurables, but not industries in which new orders are practically identical with shipments, or are assumed to be. Thus, of the major nondurable goods industries, only the four reporting order backlogs are included in the 1939–62 series of the Commerce Department (Office of Business Economics). Again, in the NICB series (1929–44) nondurables are represented only by textiles, clothing, leather, shoes, paper, and chemicals and drugs. Hence the weight of durable goods in these data is heavy.[6]

[3] The components of the new orders index since 1936 are the same as those of the unfilled orders index (see Chapter 6, note 6, for the list of industries covered). The indexes for total manufacturing comprise seventeen series, including a "miscellaneous" category not covered in either the durable or nondurable goods indexes. The weight for each industry was based on the total value of its product as reported in the Census of Manufactures of 1937. The seasonal adjustment of the chain indexes computed for each industry group was made by the NICB. For a more detailed description of the new-order index, see the *Supplement to the Conference Board Economic Record,* Vol. II, December 26, 1940.

[4] In unfilled orders, iron and steel accounts for nearly one-half of the weight total and lumber products for about 20 per cent; in new orders, these weights are approximately reversed. For the composition of the unfilled orders index and the source reference, see Chapter 6, note 4. A description of the new-order index is given in *Survey of Current Business,* September 1928, pp. 19–20. The commodities included and their percentage weights are as follows: Textiles (cotton finishing, hosiery, knit underwear), 15; iron and steel (steel sheets, malleable castings, steel castings, fabricated structural steel, fabricated steel plate, sanitary enamelware), 22; transportation equipment (locomotives, railroad cars), 7; lumber (furniture, lumber, flooring), 50; paper and printing (boxboard, labels, book paper), 5; clay and glass products (terra cotta, illuminating glassware), 2.

[5] On a state basis, a composite index of new orders has been compiled since 1924 by the Associated Industries of Massachusetts. This index (1926 = 100) is based on reports from a sample of 160–260 concerns classified as textile, leather and shoe, metal trade, paper, and "all other" (mostly consumer goods). It has a good record of cyclical conformity, with leads at six of the seven reference turns during 1924–38 and coincident timing at the June 1929 peak. Its average lead, about three months at business peaks as well as troughs, is much shorter than the average lead of the Commerce and NICB series in the same period (approximately six months; see Table 11-1, below).

[6] Most of the time, the course of the corresponding series on new orders for durables only was closely parallel to the course of the series plotted on Chart 11-1, but some differences will be noted later in the timing at individual business revivals and recessions.

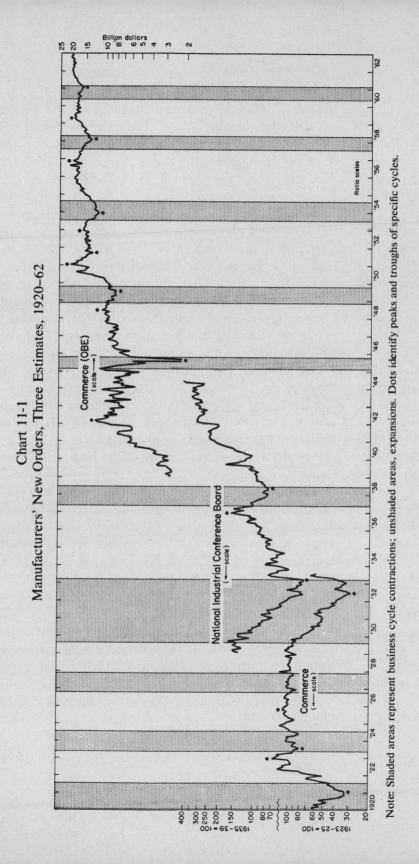

Chart 11-1

Manufacturers' New Orders, Three Estimates, 1920–62

Note: Shaded areas represent business cycle contractions; unshaded areas, expansions. Dots identify peaks and troughs of specific cycles.

The series in Chart 11-1 show leads at virtually all recessions and revivals covered. The first Commerce index had an almost horizontal or just slightly downward trend during 1926–38, with no specific-cycle turns that could clearly be matched with the 1927 trough and the 1929 peak in the business cycle; but the beginning of the rapid decline in this series definitely preceded the general downturn in 1929. The timing of the NICB index at the 1929 peak seems about coincident but is uncertain because this series only began a few months earlier. The OBE series reached an early wartime peak in 1942 and had an "extra" decline in 1951, during the Korean War. These few particular episodes do not detract much from the excellent over-all record of conformity and early timing displayed by these series, especially in the more recent period for which more adequate and comprehensive data are available.[7]

Table 11-1 shows the timing of the series plotted on Chart 11-1 and of the corresponding indexes or aggregates for the durable goods industries at each business cycle turn from 1921–61. It suggests that the conformity to business cycles is high for durable goods orders and perhaps a little lower for nondurable goods orders. The timing of total advance orders, however, is in most instances identical or closely similar to the timing of new orders placed with manufacturers of durables. The leads at peaks are on the average considerably longer than the leads at troughs of the business cycle.

The recessions in 1957 and 1960 were preceded by periods of relative weakness and of labor unrest in manufacturing. Industrial production ceased rising earlier than the outputs of other sectors and of aggregate economic activity. Downturns in new orders gave advance signals of the retrenchment, thus anticipating the business cycle peaks by as much as 19 and 13 months.

During the long expansion of the 1960's, manufacturers' new orders, followed by shipments, declined twice for more than one or two months: in 1962 (very mildly) and in 1966–67 (somewhat more steeply). On both occasions, declines also occurred in other sensitive indicators, but the economy at large experienced only retardations of growth, not general business recessions. However, in the last four months of 1969, new orders in most durable goods industries reached peaks which, along with downturns in other leading indicators, point

---

[7] For more detail, see Victor Zarnowitz, "The Timing of Manufacturers' Orders During Business Cycles," in Moore, ed., *Business Cycle Indicators*, Vol. I, pp. 441–43.

Table 11-1
Timing of Comprehensive Series on New Orders
at Each Business Cycle Turn, 1921–61

		Lead (−) or Lag (+) at Ref. Peaks (months)			Lead (−) or Lag (+) at Ref. Troughs (months)	
	Date of Reference Peak	Durable Goods (1)	Durable and Non-durable Goods (2)	Date of Reference Trough	Durable Goods (3)	Durable and Non-durable Goods (4)
1				July 1921	−6	−6
2	May 1923	−4	−5	July 1924	−12	−12
3	Oct. 1926	−12	−12	Nov. 1927	−4	
4	June 1929	−3		Mar. 1933	−4	−9
5				Mar. 1933	0 [a]	0 [a]
6	May 1937	−5	−5	June 1938	−2	−1
7	Feb. 1945	[b]	[b]	Oct. 1945	−2	−2
8	Nov. 1948	−3	−5	Oct. 1949	−4	−6
9	July 1953	−6	−6	Aug. 1954	−11	−5
10	July 1957	−19	−19	Apr. 1958	−3	−2
11	May 1960	−13	−13	Feb. 1961	−1	−1
12	Av. timing	−8.1	−9.3		−4.9	−4.9
13	Av. dev.	4.9	4.6		2.9	3.0

Source: Measures in lines 1–4 are based on indexes compiled by the Department of Commerce from various individual new-order series (see text and note 3). The indexes were seasonally adjusted for the National Bureau by the Census electronic computer method. Measures in lines 5 and 6 are based on the National Industrial Conference Board indexes (see text and note 2). Measures in lines 7–11 are based on the OBE-Census estimates of the dollar values of manufacturers' new orders (see text). The series used in lines 7–11, columns 2 and 4, was computed by adding the seasonally adjusted figures for new orders of all durable goods industries plus the four major nondurable goods industries reporting unfilled orders: textiles, leather, paper, and printing and publishing.

[a] Excluded from the average.

[b] Not matched. The specific-cycle peak of March 1942 preceded the February 1945 business cycle peak by thirty-five months.

to another and more serious economic slowdown, if not the fifth postwar recession. In this case, the leads seem to be short, perhaps not exceeding two or three months; but this is probably due to inflation as reflected in a strong upward movement in the price components of these series. Real new orders would have shown earlier peaks and longer leads.[8]

Major-Industry Series: Timing at Successive Business Cycle Turns

Table 11-2 shows that each business recession in the post-World War II period was anticipated by downturns in the major-industry series for new orders and that each business revival was anticipated by upturns in these series. Lapses from this pattern were extremely rare. But the leads, while dominating throughout, varied greatly from turn to turn. They were relatively short at the recessions of 1948 and 1953, long at those of 1957 and 1960. New orders also turned upward early in the 1953–54 contraction for most industries, but their leads at other revivals were generally much shorter. The particularly sluggish timing of orders in 1958 deserves special mention as part of the remarkable "V pattern" of this recovery in which so many activities turned sharply upward within an unusually short span of time.

These cycle-by-cycle differences can be seen best in the observations for total durable goods industries. The timing of this aggregate and of total manufacturing as well (first two lines), represents in a sense weighted averages of the leads for the component industries. Simple averages of the leads of the components are similar, but usually somewhat shorter.

It must be emphasized that these comparisons are affected by errors in the reference dates but that direct comparisons between cyclical turning points in two or more specific series are not affected. (The assumption is that the specific turns are identified independently of the reference cycle chronology—otherwise the statement would be invalid. Working rules intended to justify this assumption are generally adopted in the NBER specific-cycle analysis.) The margin of error in the reference dates is unfortunately not something that can be precisely established, although it presumably can be reduced by a systematic review of the evidence including new and revised data. The important point is that the probability of error varies considerably with the type or "profile" of the cyclical reversal. Recessions or recoveries that are widely diffused produce gently rounded turns in the aggregates and are

---

[8] As these observations are added (June 1970), the peak in total advance orders (and in total durables orders) in current dollars can be placed in September 1969. This would be only one month ahead of shipments and two months after the July 1969 peak in the industrial production index. The tentative date for the business cycle peak is November 1969.

Table 11-2

Timing of Value of Manufacturers' New Orders at Each Business Cycle Turn, by Major Industries, 1948–61

Industry	Lead (−) or Lag (+), in Months, of New Orders at Business Cycle Turns							
	Peak Nov. 1948 (1)	Trough Oct. 1949 (2)	Peak July 1953 (3)	Trough Aug. 1954 (4)	Peak July 1957 (5)	Trough Apr. 1958 (6)	Peak May 1960 (7)	Trough Feb. 1961 (8)
All manufacturing	−3	−4	−6	−8	−7	−3	−13	−1
Durable goods industries, total	−3	−4	−6	−11	−19	−3	−13	−1
Primary metals	0	−3	−1	−11	−20	−2	−15	−10
Blast furnaces and steel mills	n.a.	n.a.	0	−11	−27	−2	−15	−11
Fabricated metal products	a	−5	−6	−10	−5	−5	−15	0
Elect. machinery b	−4	−6	−3	−5	−8	−4	−11	+1
Machinery, exc. elect. b	−5	+1	−6	−3	−8	−2	−12	−6
Transport. equip.	c	c	−7	−11	−7	−2	−13	−1
Other durable goods d	−7	−3	−6	−9	−18	−1	−13	−1
Nondurable goods industries, total	−2	+2	−9 e	−8	−7	−4	−12 e	−1
Reporting unfilled orders f	−11	−8	−7	−8	−3	−2	−5	−1
Not reporting unfilled orders g	−3	+3	−9 e	−8	−5	−4	n.t.	n.t.

n.a. = not available.

n.t. = no turn in new orders.

Note: The new Census data (1963 revision) are used for all manufacturing, total durables, and total nondurables for the entire period, November 1948–February 1961, and also for all measures for August 1954–February 1961 for the individual industry groups.

a Timing uncertain. The high in 1948 for this series is April; taking that date as a tentative peak would yield a lead of 7 months.

b Based in part on unpublished data received from the Department of Commerce, Office of Business Economics.

c This series shows a retardation in 1948–49, which began a few months before the 1948 reference peak and ended before the 1949 reference trough, but the precise timing of this episode is not identified.

d Includes professional and scientific instruments; lumber; furniture; stone, clay, and glass; and miscellaneous industries.

e These measures may be questioned because they refer to retardations or very mild and gradual declines whose beginning dates are particularly difficult to identify.

f Includes textiles, leather, paper, and printing and publishing.

g Includes the industries of food, beverages, tobacco, apparel, petroleum, chemicals, and rubber, for which the values of new orders and shipments are assumed to be equal.

particularly difficult to date, whereas the "angular" variety of relatively concentrated turning-point zones is fairly easy to deal with and much less likely to be seriously misdated. Imperfections of data and erratic events affect the former much more than the latter.[9]

The 1954 trough is clearly the "flat bottom" type and its selection was one of the most difficult on record. In choosing August as the reference date, the National Bureau picked a late low month, which had the advantage of pointing to a definite upturn; the uncertainty attaching to an earlier date would have been considerably greater. Recent data revisions, however, suggest that a shift of this reference trough to an earlier month may be advisable. April or May might be a more appropriate selection; if so, the leads in Table 11-2, column 4, would be biased; specifically, they would have overestimated the "true" leads by three or four months.

This is not the place to try to decide what should be the proper date of this or any other reference turn; it is merely suggested that an error in chronology is a possibility. Moreover, since the dates of specific turns are unaffected by errors in the dating of reference cycles, the important fact remains: Troughs in new orders came very early in this turning zone for most of the industries, but the recovery was quite sluggish and shipments did not turn up until much later (Table 4-6, column 6). If the reference trough were shifted to the earlier date, this would mean that orders preceded it by shorter intervals and outputs and shipments lagged it considerably.

It has also been suggested that the reference trough has been placed too late in 1949. The major steel strike that occurred when the contraction had nearly run its course complicates the issue, but so far sufficient evidence has not been offered for shifting this trough to an earlier date.[10] Such a shift would reduce the already short leads of orders (Table 11-2, column 2). The other reference dates in the postwar period are not in serious doubt.

Differences Among the Major Industries

The average leads of new orders at the business cycle turns during 1948–61 varied within the narrow range from 6.6 to 7.8 months for in-

[9] On this point and other problems in determining the reference turns, see Victor Zarnowitz, "On the Dating of Business Cycles," *Journal of Business,* April 1963, pp. 179–99.

[10] See George W. Cloos, "How Good Are the National Bureau's Reference Dates?" *Journal of Business,* January 1963, p. 28; and Zarnowitz, "On the Dating of Business Cycles," pp. 187–88.

dustries as diverse as primary and fabricated metals, transportation equipment, and the group of other durable goods (Table 11-3, column 10).[11] For each of the two machinery industries, the mean lead was about 5 months. The average for the durable goods sector as a whole, estimated as 7.5 months, lies near the top of the observed range.

Of nondurable goods industries, those reporting unfilled orders show more regular and on the average longer leads than do the others, but the difference is not very pronounced. The mean leads for these two groups and the total nondurable goods sector vary approximately between 4 and 6 months.

The over-all timing averages for these series, however, are rather unrepresentative. Separate summaries for peaks and troughs are indicated, since the differences between the two groups of observations are apparently systematic. For each industry, the average lead of new orders turns out to be longer at peaks than at troughs of business cycles, and the differences are substantial (Table 11-3, column 9). For the durable goods industries, the mean leads are about twice as long at peaks than at troughs, judging either from the record of the aggregate series or from averages of the comparisons for the component industries.

Even the separate peak and trough timing averages conceal a great deal of variation. For example, new orders of the primary metals industries were among the first to change direction at the recessions of 1957 and 1960, whereas their leads at the 1948 and 1953 peaks were the shortest on record (Table 11-2). No significant regularities appear in the observed sequences of peaks in the major-industry series for new orders, that is, none of these industries qualifies as a consistently early or a consistently late leader. Table 11-2 suggests that an analogous statement also applies to the timing sequences at revivals. All this, however, is based on very limited evidence for a small number of broadly defined industries. More formal tests applied to a larger number of industry series gave some indication of correlated sequences at troughs, but not at peaks.[12]

[11] The averages for the period since 1953 are larger, reflecting the prevalence of long leads at the cyclical reversals in 1954, 1957, and 1960. Thus the blast furnaces component of primary metals, a series that begins in 1953, shows a mean lead of 11 months.

[12] The leads of new orders for eleven major manufacturing industries were ranked at each of the eight business cycle turns of the 1948–61 period. Coefficients of concordance, W (see Chapter 6), computed for the rankings at peaks and at troughs, were found to equal 0.212 and 0.729, respectively. (This analysis was performed on the OBE series that predate the 1963 revision.)

Table 11-3

Summary Measures of Timing of Value of Manufacturers' New Orders at Business Cycle Peaks and Troughs, by Major Industries, 1948–65

Period Covered [a] (1)	No. of Timing Observations [b] (2)	Bus. Cycle Turns Skipped [c] (3)	Extra Turns in New Orders [d] (4)	No. of Timing Observations at Peaks or Troughs [e] That Are				Av. Lead (−) or Lag (+) (months)		Av. Dev. from Av. Lead or Lag (months)	
				Leads (5)	Exact Coincidences (6)	Lags (7)	Rough Coincidences [f] (8)	Peaks or Troughs [e] (9)	All Turns (10)	Peaks or Troughs [e] (11)	All Turns (12)
ALL MANUFACTURING INDUSTRIES											
1948–65	8	0	4(2)	4			1	−7.2	−5.6	2.9	2.9
				4			2	−4.0		2.0	
DURABLE GOODS INDUSTRIES, TOTAL											
1948–65	8	0	4(2)	4			1	−10.2	−7.5	5.8	5.1
				4			2	−4.8		3.1	
PRIMARY METALS											
1948–65	8	0	8(6)	3	1		2	−9.0	−7.8	8.5	6.2
				4			2	−6.5		4.0	
BLAST FURNACES AND STEEL MILLS [g]											
1953–65	6	0	6(4)	2	1		1	−14.0	−11.0	9.3	6.7
				3			1	−8.0		4.0	
FABRICATED METAL PRODUCTS [h]											
1949–65	7	0	4	3	1			−8.7	−6.6	4.2	3.4
				3			1	−5.0		2.5	
ELECTRICAL MACHINERY [i]											
1948–65	8(1)	0	6(2)	4			1	−6.5	−5.0	3.0	2.5
				3		1	1	−3.5		2.2	
MACHINERY EXCEPT ELECTRICAL											
1948–65	8	0	4(2)	4				−7.8	−5.1	2.2	2.9
				3		1	3	−2.5		2.0	

TRANSPORTATION EQUIPMENT[j]								
1951–65	6	0	6	3		–9.0	–6.8	2.7	3.6
			3	2	–4.7		4.2	
OTHER DURABLE GOODS[k]								
1948–65	8	0	2	4		–11.0	–7.2	4.5	4.6
			4	3	–3.5		2.8	
NONDURABLE GOODS INDUSTRIES, TOTAL[l]								
1948–65	8(4)	0	2	4	1	1	–7.5	–5.1	3.0	3.9
			3		2	–2.8		3.2	
NONDURABLES INDUSTRIES REPORTING UNFILLED ORDERS[m]								
1948–65	8	0	4(2)	4	1	–6.5	–5.6	2.5	2.9
			4	2	–4.8		3.2	
NONDURABLES INDUSTRIES NOT REPORTING UNFILLED ORDERS[n]								
1948–65	6(2)	2	0	3	1	–5.7	–4.3	2.2	3.0
			2	1	–3.0		4.0	

[a] The first date identifies the year of the first reference turn at which the timing of the series could be determined. The last reference turn covered is in each case the 1961 trough, but the count of the "extra" turns in new orders (column 4) is extended through 1965.

[b] The number of reference turns matched by like turns in new orders. The figures in parentheses give the number of minor turns in new orders included in these observations.

[c] The number of reference turns not matched during the periods identified in column 1.

[d] The number of turns in new orders that do not correspond to reference turns. The figures in parentheses refer to minor turns that are included in these observations.

[e] For each item, entry on first line is for comparisons at peaks; entry on second line, for comparisons at troughs.

[f] Includes exact coincidences and leads or lags of one, two, or three months.

[g] Data begin in 1953.

[h] Data begin in 1948 but timing at the 1948 recovery is uncertain; to determine it earlier figures would be necessary.

[j] The pre-1953 measures are based on unpublished data.
Series underwent a retardation in 1948–49, but its timing at the reference dates of the period cannot be adequately determined.

[k] Includes professional and scientific instruments; lumber; furniture; stone, clay, and glass; and miscellaneous industries.

[l] Columns 9, 10, 11, and 12 include two observations relating to retardations that are difficult to date (see Table 11-2, note e). When these are omitted, the average leads are –4.5 for peaks and –3.3 for all turns. The corresponding average deviations are 2.5 and 3.0.

[m] Includes textiles; leather; paper; and printing and publishing.

[n] Includes nondurable goods industries other than those listed in note m, for which the values of new orders and shipments are assumed to be equal. Columns 9, 10, 11, and 12 include one observation relating to a retardation that is difficult to date. When this is omitted, the average leads are –4.0 for peaks and –3.4 for all turns. The corresponding average deviations are 1.0 and 2.7.

The findings for the major-industry series included in Tables 11-2 and 11-3 receive broad support from measures based on the rather detailed industry breakdown available for the pre-1963 OBE data (see Appendix E, part II). The conclusion stands that on some occasions the demand for durable goods, as measured by new orders, has turned well ahead of the rest of the economy, while on other occasions its lead time was short. Different summaries of the data (averages of timing measures at each turn) show considerable agreement on the identity and ranking of these episodes. At the same time, however, the positions of the individual industries in the sequences of the leads shift a great deal between the different episodes, in what may simply be a random fashion.

Confirming evidence on the strong tendency of manufacturers' new orders to lead at business recoveries and (generally, by longer intervals) at recessions also comes from the Standard and Poor's indexes for ten major durable goods industries and four nondurable goods industries (Appendix B, part II).

Conformity to Business Cycles

If matching the business cycle turns is the criterion, the conformity record of the new-order series in Table 11-3 is nearly perfect. None of the series for the eleven industries or groups of industries that report advance orders ($N \neq S$) missed any of the cyclical reversals covered, although in 5 of the 83 opportunities to do so minor turns rather than specific-cycle turns in new orders were involved. Only in the series for nondurable goods manufacturers with no reported backlogs, which represents orders shipped, are some business cycle turns skipped (columns 2 and 3).

However, on the complementary criterion of "extra" turns that do not correspond to business revivals or recessions, the record of these series is not so good. All in all, there are 50 such turns listed (column 4). It is true that this count includes as many as 20 minor turns (figures in parentheses), but these are often difficult to distinguish from specific-cycle turns, except with the full benefit of hindsight. The extra turns must generally be regarded as lapses from conforming behavior. Most of them would probably also represent potentially misleading signals to a forecaster of cyclical reversals.

Had Table 11-3 been limited to the period 1948–61, as defined by the first and last of the reference turns covered, each of the series included would have shown just two extra turning points, since new orders generally declined in 1951 from their early Korean War peaks to resume a more moderate rise in the following year. However, most of these series also show substantial extra declines in 1962 and 1966–67, periods in which there were marked though short-lived retardations in business activity.

The proportion of new-order turns matched varies from 50 to 80 per cent for the different series, with 66.7 per cent being the most frequent figure. These results, which incorporate minor as well as specific-cycle turns, would disqualify most of these series under the conformity test devised by Geoffrey Moore, in which the probability of 0.188 is the maximum acceptance level.[13] If the minor turns were excluded, however, most series would pass the test.

There are only four short lags and three "exact" coincidences among the 89 timing observations included in Table 11-3. Most of the leads are intermediate or long; only 24 (or about 29 per cent) are short, that is, three months or less. Altogether, a little more than one-third of the measures consist of "rough" coincidences or leads and lags not exceeding three months (columns 5–8).

The leads are about equally divided between peaks and troughs (the respective frequencies are 42 and 40). All four lags and 22 of the 31 rough coincidences, however, are at troughs.

Disaggregation has relatively little effect on the over-all conformity and timing record for manufacturers' new orders. This can be seen by comparing the summary statistics in Table 11-3 with their counterparts in Table E-3, which relate to the more detailed industrial breakdown of the orders data (Appendix E, part II).

Differences Among Market Categories

Table 11-4 records the timing of new orders for nine market categories at the five business cycle turns of 1954–61. These measures are

[13] "Statistical Indicators of Cyclical Revivals and Recessions," in Moore, ed., *Business Cycle Indicators,* Vol. I, pp. 206–07. The assumptions underlying Moore's measures are that the probability that a series will rise in correspondence to a given business expansion is one-half and that the results in successive cycles are independent. Both assumptions can be questioned, but Moore found the method workable for rating and screening series to select business cycle indicators. Under these premises, the probability that no failures will occur on five occasions is $(1/2)^5$; that one failure will occur, $5(1/2)^5$; two failures, $10(1/2)^5$; and so on, as given by the binomial expansion. Cumulation gives the probability 0.1875 for as good a result as one lapse, the probability 0.5 for as good a result as two lapses (i.e., two, one, or zero lapses), etc. In Moore's work with conformity indexes based on the reference cycle patterns, series with probabilities of more than 0.188 (or the nearest approximation to that level possible in the given case) were rejected. The probabilities were computed separately for expansions and contractions and combined by multiplication.

Table 11-4

Timing of Value of New Orders at Each Business Cycle Turn,
Nine Market Categories,[a] 1954–61

Lead (−) or Lag (+), in Months, of New Orders at Business Cycle Turns					Av. Lead or Lag (months)			Av. Dev. from Av. Lead or Lag, All Turns (months)
Trough Aug. 1954 (1)	Peak July 1957 (2)	Trough April 1958 (3)	Peak May 1960 (4)	Trough Feb. 1961 (5)	Peaks (6)	Troughs (7)	All Turns (8)	(9)
HOME GOODS AND APPAREL								
−9	−7	−1	−12 [b]	−1 [b]	−9.5	−3.7	−6.0	4.0
NONAUTOMOTIVE EQUIPMENT AND DEFENSE								
−5	−8	−3	+1	−4	−3.5	−4.0	−3.8	2.2
DEFENSE PRODUCTS								
−11	−11	−6	c	c	d	−8.5	−9.3	2.2
OTHER								
e	−8	−1	−5	−5	−6.5	−3.0	−4.8	1.9
AUTOMOTIVE EQUIPMENT								
−8	+2	−1	−3	−1	−0.5	−3.3	−2.2	2.6
MACHINERY AND EQUIPMENT INDUSTRIES								
−5	−8	−2	−8	−3	−8.0	−3.3	−5.2	2.2
MATERIALS, SUPPLIES, AND INTERMEDIATE PRODUCTS								
−10	−8	−3	−15	−1	−11.5	−4.7	−7.4	4.3
CONSTRUCTION MATERIALS, ETC.								
−10	−5	−1	−13	0	−9.0	−3.7	−5.8	4.6
OTHER MATERIALS, ETC.								
−11	−11	−3	−15	−1	−13.0	−5.0	−8.2	5.0

[a] For composition of these categories, see Chapter 3.

[b] The series declined between May and November of 1959; this movement, which ended six months before the onset of the 1960 business recession, was followed by a retardation that lasted through 1960 (Chart 3-3). The above observations are based on the May 1959 high and the January 1961 date terminating the retardation. If these marginal observations are excluded, the average lead for 1954–58 is −5.7 months with an average deviation of 3.1.

[c] Not matched.

[d] Only one observation is available.

[e] Timing uncertain, but the lead appears to be at least 7 months. Including this observation would yield averages of −4.3 for troughs and −5.2 (with an average deviation of 1.8) for all turns.

based on the current Census series (1963 revision) that were introduced and compared with the corresponding shipments data in Chapters 3 and 4 (see, in particular, Chart 3-3). The timing of these series at the 1953 recession is uncertain and not identified in the table, but minimum leads of six months can be established for several categories.[14]

Only one group of consumer goods is included in the table, consisting of nonautomotive household equipment and apparel (first line). New orders for this category led at the turning points of 1953–54 and 1957–58, but showed only a general weakness in 1959–60 that started well before, and continued through, the business contraction of 1960–61. The series for consumer staples has shown no cyclical declines at all in the years covered, but it did undergo retardations in 1953–54 and again briefly in 1957.[15] The totals for consumer durable goods, a series that begins in 1960, declined mildly during the business recession of 1960–61. In short, the behavior of new orders for consumer goods in this period can be described as trend dominated and relatively stable, with low scores on cyclical conformity going to the nondurable, primarily staple products (for which new orders and shipments generally coincide). The few timing comparisons that are available for these series, however, are mostly leads. The latter reflect almost entirely certain early turns in the production of consumer goods, since the observed delivery periods (lags of shipments relative to new orders, in monthly terms) are here usually very short or zero.

In contrast, new orders for machinery and nonautomotive equipment show large fluctuations in conformity to the business cycle movements of 1953–61. Their leads at the two recessions and the three revivals of that period averaged six to eight and three months, respectively (Table 11-4). Since early 1961 these series followed strong upward trends, interrupted by brief and shallow declines in 1962 and more pronounced contractions during the business slowdowns of 1966 and 1969–70.

New orders for defense products are the most erratic. The series

---

[14] The series that begin in 1953 and decline from the outset would presumably have leads of at least months (January–July 1957). This applies to home goods and apparel; equipment and defense products, except automotive; machinery and equipment industries; and the three materials series. The 1953 local high for defense products occurred in February.

[15] The first of these retardations began at least four to six months before the July 1953 peak; it ended October 1964, two months after the reference trough. The second retardation started in February, five months before the business cycle peak, and ended in October 1957, six months before the reference trough.

shows a very large random component in its short up-and-down move-ments superimposed upon a rising trend (Chart 3-3). One would not expect it to respond positively in a regular fashion to business cycles, and it does not, judging from the short record of the recent years. How-ever, large fluctuations in defense purchases could well be a major destabilizing factor in the economy at the high levels that such spend-ing has presently attained. In particular, large declines in defense orders may contribute significantly to a developing weakness. Actually, new orders for defense products did decline substantially *before* the business downturns of both 1953 and 1957, causing subsequent cut-backs in defense output and shipments during and after each of the two business contractions of the 1950's. The orders increased *during* each of these contractions, but very irregularly and apparently too weakly to result in any significant increases of shipments in either of the downswing-and-recovery phases, 1954–55 and 1958–59. In the 1960–61 recession these orders declined a little. Defense expenditures de-clined along with shipments in 1953–55, remained stable in 1957–58, and rose somewhat in 1960.[16]

New orders for automotive equipment moved close to shipments and turned close to business cycle peaks and troughs in the period after 1955 (see Chart 3-3 and Table 11-4). The only long lead was at the 1954 revival. The timing of automotive orders and production, then, was in recent years nearly synchronous with the business cycle turns.[17] Extra movements, however, result in a low conformity of these series. There were definitely two specific cycles between the troughs of 1954 and 1958, with peaks in 1955, troughs in 1956, and lower peaks in 1957. Substantial declines also occurred during the business slowdown of 1966–67. Furthermore, rates of orders and ship-ments of motor vehicles were sharply reduced in the second half of 1959 because of the protracted steel strike and in the latter part of 1964 because of strikes in the automobile industry itself. On the other hand, it is notable that the widespread slowdown of economic activity in 1962 had very little restraining effect on new orders and shipments of automotive equipment.

[16] See the section on "Defense Products" in Chapter 4, with Chart 4-2, for further discussion of military orders, obligations, and expenditures, including a brief account of later developments during the 1960's, which came to be dominated by the Vietnam War and inflation.

[17] The latest contractions in these series started in July 1969 (for production) and in September 1969 (for new orders in current dollars). These downturns might come to be recognized as involving relatively short leads of perhaps four and two months.

New orders for materials, supplies, and intermediate products conformed well to the recent cyclical movements of the economy, as did the corresponding shipments series. Both new orders and shipments turned down before each of the three recessions of the period (1953, 1957, and 1960). The downturns in 1959 preceded the steel strike and led the business peak by long intervals. As elsewhere, early though slow recoveries of orders occurred in the 1953–54 contraction, but the upturns in 1958 and 1961 were nearly coincident with business troughs (Chart 3-3 and Table 11-4). Mild declines in these series mark the business retardation phases in 1962 and 1966–67.

Construction accounts for about one-fourth of total materials, supplies, and intermediate products, and for this part new orders and shipments move closely together. The other, larger part comprises many made-to-order products of the metalworking industries; it shows somewhat greater cyclical sensitivity than do the construction series, and appreciably longer leads of new orders. On the whole, however, the behavior of the two components of total materials has been rather similar (including the most recent episode in which both series on new orders turned down in September 1969, one month ahead of shipments).

Close inspection of the data gives no indication that the categories tend to turn up or down in any particular sequence at business troughs or peaks.

New Orders for Individual Industries or Products

The measures presented in this part relate to thirty series on new orders for a variety of manufactured goods. Six of these are in current dollars, and the rest are in physical units. The data give better representation to the largely made-to-order producer goods than to the largely made-to-stock consumer goods. Most of the former are durables; only four of the series refer to nondurable goods.

Averages, Distribution, and Probabilities of Leads and Lags

The full record of performance at business cycle turns of these series is summarized in Table 11-5. The table leaves no doubt about the strong tendency of new orders for various products to turn down

Table 11-5

Summary Measures of Timing of New Orders[a] at Business Cycle Peaks and Troughs, Thirty Individual Industries or Products, Various Periods, 1873–1957

Period Covered[b] (1)	No. of Timing Observations[c] (2)	Bus. Cycle Turns Skipped[d] (3)	Extra Turns[e] in New Orders (4)	No. of Timing Observations at Peaks or Troughs That Are:				Av. Lead (−) or Lag (+) (mos.)		Av. Dev. from Av. Lead or Lag (mos.)	
				Leads (5)	Exact Coincidences (6)	Lags (7)	Rough Coincidences[f] (8)	Peaks or Troughs (9)	All Turns (10)	Peaks or Troughs (11)	All Turns (12)
WATER-TUBE BOILERS[g]											
1. 1927–57	5	1	2	4	0	1	1	−15.8	−9.2	11.8	10.2
2.	5	1	2	3	0	2	3	−2.6[h]		4.3	
SOUTHERN PINE LUMBER											
3. 1918–54	7	2	4	7	0	0	0	−11.3	−9.1	5.5	4.0
4.	9	0	3	9	0	0	2	−7.3		3.2	
OAK FLOORING											
5. 1913–54	9	1	5	9	0	0	0	−9.2	−8.2	3.6	3.2
6.	9	1	4	9	0	0	2	−7.2		2.9	
CLAY AND GLASS PRODUCTS (2)											
7. 1921–33	3	0	0	3	0	0	1	−8.0	−7.4	3.3	3.1
8.	4	0	0	4	0	0	1	−7.0		3.0	
RAILS											
9. 1873–1949	16	3	9	12	0	4	3	−8.4	−6.9	8.2	6.6
10.	13	6	11	11	1	1	7	−5.0		4.6	
BATH TUBS											
11. 1918–29	3	2	0	3	0	0	2	−5.7[h]	−6.7	4.9	4.0
12.	3	1	0	3	0	0	0	−7.7		2.9	

STEEL SHEETS

13. 1919–33	4	0	0	4	0	0	0	-7.2	-6.2	1.9	2.5
14.	5	0	0	5	0	0	2	-5.4		3.5	

IRON AND STEEL PRODUCTS (6)

15. 1921–33	3	0	0	3	0	0	2	-6.0	-6.1	4.0	3.6
16.	4	0	0	4	0	0	1	-6.2		3.2	

RAILROAD LOCOMOTIVES

17. 1873–1954	18	2	5	17	0	1	5	-7.3	-5.8	5.9	5.4
18.	20	0	3	16	1	3	6	-4.6		5.2	

PAPERBOARD

19. 1924-54	5	1	5	5	0	0	2	-4.4	-5.7	2.5	2.7
20.	5	2	4	5	0	0	1	-7.0		2.4	

PAPER AND PRINTING (3)

21. 1923–33	3	0	0	3	0	0	0	-7.3	-5.7	2.4	4.0
22.	3	0	0	2	1	0	2	-4.0		4.7	

RAILROAD FREIGHT CARS

23. 1873–1954	18	2	6	14	1	3	6	-6.2	-5.6	5.8	4.8
24.	18	2	6	16	0	2	7	-5.0		4.0	

FABRICATED STRUCTURAL STEEL

25. 1910–54	10	1	6	9	0	1	8	-3.4	-5.4	2.6	4.3
26.	10	1	6	10	0	0	3	-7.4		5.1	

LUMBER (3)

27. 1921–33	2	1	0	2	0	0	0	-7.0^{h}	-5.4	3.0	3.3
28.	3	1	0	3	0	0	2	-4.3		3.1	

PAPER, EXCLUDING BUILDING PAPER, NEWSPRINT, AND PAPERBOARD

29. 1937–54	3	1	3	2	1	0	1	-3.7^{h}	-4.7	2.6	2.1
30.	3	1	3	3	0	0	1	-5.7		1.8	

ARCHITECTURAL TERRA COTTA

31. 1919–38	5	0	1	4	0	1	2	-6.4	-4.7	8.9	6.2
32.	6	0	0	4	0	2	2	-3.3		4.3	

(continued)

543

Table 11-5 (concluded)

Period Covered[b] (1)	No. of Timing Observations[c] (2)	Bus. Cycle Turns Skipped[d] (3)	Extra Turns[e] in New Orders (4)	No. of Timing Observations at Peaks or Troughs That Are: Leads (5)	Exact Coincidences (6)	Lags (7)	Rough Coincidences[f] (8)	Av. Lead (−) or Lag (+) (mos.) Peaks or Troughs (9)	All Turns (10)	Av. Dev. from Av. Lead or Lag (mos.) Peaks or Troughs (11)	All Turns (12)
RAILROAD PASSENGER CARS											
33. 1873–1954	20	0	7	12	0	8	6	−3.4	−3.9	8.3	6.8
34.	18	2	8	15	0	3	5	−4.5		5.1	
FURNITURE											
35. 1924–45	4	0	1	3	1	0	2	−4.5	−3.8	4.0	2.8
36.	4	1	1	3	1	0	2	−3.0		1.5	
WOODWORKING MACHINERY											
37. 1923–38	4	0	1	4	0	0	1	−5.8	−3.5	3.1	2.9
38.	4	0	1	3	1	0	4	−1.2		0.9	
TEXTILE PRODUCTS (3)											
39. 1921–33	2	1	3	2	0	0	1	−3.5[b]	−3.5	1.5	4.2
40.	4	0	2	3	0	1	1	−3.5		5.5	
MILL AND INDUSTRIAL SUPPLIES[l]											
41. 1949–54	1	0	1	1	0	0	1	−3.0	−3.0	0.0	0.0
42.	2	0	1	2	0	0	2	−3.0		0.0	
MERCHANT PIG IRON											
43. 1919–26	2	1	0	1	1	0	2	−1.0[b]	−2.8	1.0	1.8
44.	3	0	0	3	0	0	2	−4.0		2.0	

	(1)	(2)	(3)	(4)	(5)	(6)	(7)	(8)	(9)	(10)	(11)
FOUNDRY EQUIPMENT											
45. 1921–54	5	3	3	3	0	2	2	−3.6[h]	−2.6	3.7	2.7
46.	7	0	2	5	2	0	6	−1.9		1.6	
MACHINE TOOLS											
47. 1919–54	7	1	1	6	1	0	5	−3.3	−2.1	2.7	1.8
48.	7	2	2	5	1	1	7	−0.9		1.1	
LAVATORIES											
49. 1918–29	4	1	0	3	0	1	2	−3.5[h]	−2.1	4.0	4.4
50.	4	0	0	3	0	1	1	−0.8		5.4	
KITCHEN SINKS											
51. 1918–29	4	1	0	3	0	1	2	−3.2[h]	−2.0	3.8	4.2
52.	4	0	0	3	0	1	1	−0.8		4.9	
ELECTRIC OVERHEAD CRANES											
53. 1926–45	3	1	1	2	0	1	0	−3.7[h]	−1.7[h]	5.1	4.3
54.	3	1	1	1	0	2	3	+0.3[h]		2.2	
FABRICATED STEEL PLATE											
55. 1924–38	3	0	0	2	0	1	2	−1.7[h]	−1.6	1.8	2.5
56.	4	0	0	2	1	1	2	−1.5[h]		3.0	
OIL BURNERS											
57. 1933–49	1	2	3	1	0	0	1	−2.0[h]	−1.0[h]		1.3
58.	3	2	3	1	0	1	2	−0.5[h]		1.5	
MISCELLANEOUS ENAMELED SANITARY WARE											
59. 1918–29	2	3	0	1	0	1	1	+4.0[h]	−0.8[h]	5.0	4.9
60.	2	2	0	2	0	0	0	−5.5[h]		1.5	
Totals											
61. Peaks	176	31	67	145	5	26	61				
62. Troughs	188	26	63	158	9	21	80				
63. All turns	364	57	130	303	14	47	141				

Notes to Table 11-5

Note: In columns 2–9 and column 11, entries on the first line for each series are for comparisons at peaks; entries on the second line, for troughs. Entries in columns 10 and 12 pertain to all turns (peaks and troughs).

ᵃ The series are ranked by the length of the average lead for all turns (column 10), from longest to shortest. Figures in parentheses indicate the number of items included in the component series of the Department of Commerce index of new orders in physical terms, 1920–33, as follows: Line 7 — terra cotta, illuminating glassware; line 15 — steel sheets, malleable castings, steel castings, fabricated structural steel, fabricated steel plate, enameled sanitary ware; line 21 — boxboard, labels, book paper; line 27 — furniture, lumber (5 kinds), flooring (2 kinds); line 39 — cotton finishing, hosiery, knit underwear.

ᵇ Identifies the complete business cycle phases covered by the given series.

ᶜ Number of recorded timing comparisons (leads, lags, and coincidences) at business cycle peaks or troughs.

ᵈ Number of business cycle peaks or troughs that are not matched by cyclical turns in the given series. Corresponding entries in columns 2 and 3 add up to the total number of business cycle turns (peaks or troughs) covered.

ᵉ Number of specific-cycle peaks or troughs in the given series that do not match business cycle turns. Corresponding entries in columns 2 and 4 add up to numbers of new-order turns (peaks or troughs) covered.

ᶠ Includes exact coincidences and leads and lags of one, two and three months.

ᵍ Index of new orders for stationary water-tube boilers received by a company accounting for a large proportion of the boiler industry.

ʰ Given the numbers of turns covered and the distribution of the timing comparisons by type, the probability of obtaining this result exceeds 0.223 (or the nearest approximation to that level possible). See the accompanying text.

ⁱ Index of new orders received by a cross section of members of the American Supply and Machinery Manufacturers' Association (producers of a variety of supplies such as abrasives, beltings, hoists, saws, tools, etc.).

before the peaks and to turn up before the troughs in aggregate economic activity. For each item, new orders show an average lead at business cycle turns (column 10). These mean leads differ greatly in length, descending from nine months at the top of the table to slightly less than one month at the bottom, but they exceed three months for two-thirds of the list.

Separate averages of the timing observations at peaks and at troughs (column 9) indicate that leads prevail heavily at either type of turn. Of the sixty averages only two are lags, both in very short series (lines 54 and 59). The mean leads are longer at peaks than at troughs for nineteen of the thirty series, and shorter for only nine. The mean leads at peaks range approximately from 16 months to 2, those at troughs from 8 months to less than 1 month.

Timing varies considerably in the successive revivals and recessions, as seen by the average deviations in columns 11 and 12. But leads account for the great bulk (83 per cent) of all comparisons, and short leads of less than 3 months are less frequent than the intermediate and long leads for most of the industries or groups of products included. For all series, if the observations at peaks and troughs are combined, 13 per cent are lags, 14 per cent are exact coincidences, and 39 per cent are rough coincidences.

In Moore's screening procedure for business cycle indicators, the significance of a given record of timing is judged by computing the probability that, for a certain number of reference peaks (or troughs), a specified number of timing comparisons of a given type will be equaled or exceeded by chance.[18] As with conformity, the assumptions are ones on which the binomial distribution can be applied. The maximum acceptance level adopted in this case corresponds as nearly as possible to the probability (0.223) that four or more timing comparisons will appear in a given group (leads, lags, or rough coincidences) when the series covers six reference turns. The longer the series (the more turns it covers), the lower the probability for any given proportion of successes (say, leads for a leading indicator). Thus, the maximum acceptable proportion of failures is directly related to the length of the series.[19]

Separate probabilities were computed for peaks, troughs, and all turns from the distributions of timing observations shown in Table 11-5, columns 5-8. Note h in that table denotes the cases in which these probabilities are sufficiently high to admit, under the assumptions just stated, the null hypothesis that the observed timing distribution may represent merely the working of chance. The underlying probabilities are based on the number of leads at reference turns in the period covered; in another set that was also computed, the probabilities were based on the number of leads at new-order turns covered. The

---

[18] This approach parallels that adopted to evaluate the conformity measures, as summarized in note 13 above. For details, see Moore, ed., *Business Cycle Indicators*, Vol. I, p. 209.

[19] For the timing probability criterion, an exact coincidence was counted as a half-lead and a half-lag. Thus, for leads the "successes" are represented by leads and half the number of exact coincidences and the "failures" by lags and half the number of exact coincidences; while for lags the reverse applies. Of course, a series cannot be both a "significant" leader and a "significant" lagger according to these tests. The test for the significance of rough coincidences treats all leads and lags that are longer than three months as failures. Success in this last test does not preclude a series from also passing the test as a leader (if short leads prevail strongly in its record) or as a lagger (if short lags prevail).

latter probabilities are higher than the former ones for several items, reflecting the fact that extra turns are more frequent than skipped ones. It should be noted that many of the high probabilities relate to short series, that is, items for which the evidence is skimpy.

The probability approach discloses no significant lagging tendency in any of the series but does indicate the significance of rough coincidences (short leads and lags within the range of −3 to +3 months centered on the reference turn) in a few cases. These relate to six items: fabricated structural steel, woodworking machinery, merchant pig iron, foundry equipment, machine tools, and electric overhead cranes. However, the probabilities for leads are also below the acceptable maximum levels in all these cases except one (electric overhead cranes at troughs), and indeed are in most instances lower than or equal to the rough-coincidence probabilities. The evidence of the timing probabilities is summarized in the tabulations below.

Number (and Percentage) of Series for Which

Probabilities Based on	*Leads Are Significant at*			*Rough Coincidences Are Significant at*		
	Peaks	*Troughs*	*All Turns*	*Peaks*	*Troughs*	*All Turns*
Business cycle turns	18(60)	25(83)	27(90)	2(7)	4(13)	3(10)
New-order turns	18(60)	21(70)	20(67)	2(7)	4(13)	2(7)

Conforming Behavior: The Turning Points

Timing regularities should be appraised against the background of conformity measures. A consistent leader is a series that leads at a large proportion of the reference turns *covered*. A series would not deserve a high consistency rating even if it led at each turn *matched*, if it matched only a few of the revivals and recessions through which it passed. However, columns 2 and 3 of Table 11-5 indicate that new orders turn in sympathy with the large majority of peaks and troughs in the business cycles they cover.

Skipped turns are one type of nonconforming behavior. There is no turn in the series that can be matched to a particular business cycle turn. The occurrence in the series of an extra turn which cannot be matched with a peak or trough of the business cycle is another type.

The percentage of matched business cycle turns measures (inversely) the frequency of skipped turns. To allow for the frequency of extra turns, we compare the number of "matchings" with the number of specific-cycle turns in a given series. To take account of both the skipped and the extra turns, we simply average the percentage of business cycle turns matched and the percentage of specific turns matched. Given a sufficient number of observations, the percentages matched can provide meaningful measures of conformity and can be computed separately for peaks and troughs as well as for all turns combined.

Table 11-6 presents the distributions of the conformity measures of the thirty series on new orders for individual industries or products. The average percentages (column 7) are heavily concentrated in the upper end of the scale; two-thirds of them are in the 80–100 range and all but four exceed 70. Typically, the extra turns outnumber the skipped ones in the series examined, and so the percentages of business cycle turns matched tend to be larger than the percentages of new-order turns matched, and the associated probabilities tend to be lower for the former than for the latter measures (compare columns 1 and 4, 2 and 5, and 3 and 6).

The figures in the next to last line of Table 11-6 give a count of the cases in which the number of failures to match a business cycle turn exceeds the acceptable maximum, that is, as good a result as one lapse in five occasions (any instance of an unmatched turn is treated as a lapse in conformity). Specifically, these are the instances where, given the assumptions of the method (see note 13, above), the probability of obtaining the observed result by chance exceeds 0.188 or the nearest approximation to that figure. For peaks, such cases represent 30 per cent of the series covered; for troughs, 20–27 per cent; and for all turns, where more observations are available, 10–17 per cent.[20]

Most of the large probabilities refer to series that are short, covering six or fewer turns. This applies principally to the percentages of business cycle turns matched, where only one of the nine series, with an

---

[20] It should be noted that in these probabilities for all turns no distinction is made between peaks and troughs; the timing measures are treated as being part of a single universe. In a more stringent test, assuming two separate universes, "product probabilities" would be computed by multiplication of the peak and trough probabilities. The product probabilities would be lower than the independently computed probabilities for all turns, and would require a lower maximum acceptance level, say, 0.035. The criterion thus defined would not be passed by any of the series that failed the criterion applied in Table 11-6 (columns 3 and 5, $P > 0.188$ line).

Table 11-6

Thirty New-Order Series for Individual Industries or Products, Distribution by Percentage of Cyclical Turns Matching Business Recessions and Revivals, 1919–38, 1948–57

	Frequency Distributions Based on the Percentages of						
	Business Cycle Turns Matched			New-Order Turns Matched			Bus. Cycle and New-Order Turns Matched,
Percentage of Turns Matched [a]	Peaks (1)	Troughs (2)	All Turns (3)	Peaks (4)	Troughs (5)	All Turns (6)	Av., All Turns (7)
	NUMBER OF SERIES						
100.0	10	15	8	11	12	11	5
90.0–99.9	4	4	5	0	0	1	5
80.0–89.9	6	2	9	4	3	4	8
70.0–79.9	3	6	5	5	6	5	8
60.0–69.9	5	1	1	5	5	4	3
50.0–59.9	0	2	0	3	3	4	0
Less than 50	2	0	2	2	1	1	1
Total	30	30	30	30	30	30	30
$P = .188$ [b]	9	6	3	9	8	5	n.a.
	PER CENT						
Av. % of turns matched [c]	85.0	87.8	86.5	72.4	74.9	73.7	80.1

[a] For columns 1–3: Ratio of the number of business cycle turns matched to the number of business cycle turns covered by the given series, multiplied by 100.

For columns 4–6: Ratio of the number of business cycle turns matched to the number of new-order turns covered, multiplied by 100.

For column 7: Average of the percentages used for the distributions in columns 3 and 6.

[b] Given the numbers of turns covered and matched, the probability of obtaining this result by chance exceeds 0.188 (or the nearest approximation to that level possible). On the assumptions underlying the probability measures, see text.

[c] Average, for all thirty series, of the percentage-matched figures on which the distribution in lines 1–9 is based.

indifferent performance at peaks, is relatively long (Table 11-5, line 23). However, for percentages of new-order turns matched, half of the ten series with high probabilities for at least one type of turn are long series with 10 to 29 observations each.

To sum up, few business cycle turns are skipped by the series on new orders: The proportion is less than 1 in 8. Extra turns in new orders are more frequent, but the fact remains that as many as three-quarters of the recorded specific peaks and troughs in these series can be matched to the peaks and troughs of business at large (Table 11-6).

A Summary of Cycle-by-Cycle Performance

Most of the timing observations for the individual series refer to the business cycle turns of the interwar years, 1919–38; the period after World War II is less well represented. Table 11-7 shows the distribution of the leads and lags of new orders at each of the eight revivals and seven recessions during 1919–38 and 1948–54 (most of the series included failed to match the short business contraction in 1945). Upturns in newly received business are seen to precede each of the troughs in aggregate economic activity by average intervals of about three to six months. Downturns led the business peaks by more variable intervals—by long leads, averaging seven to eleven months, in 1926, 1948, and 1953, and by short leads and rough coincidences, averaging less than one month, in 1920. At the other peaks—1923, 1929, and 1937—the leads averaged three to five months.

Closer inspection of the distributions indicates that a prior turn in most categories of new orders is a highly regular characteristic of a business revival or recession. Leads outnumber lags and coincidences combined at each of the business cycle turns covered, and they outnumber rough coincidences on each occasion except one. Since revivals and recessions are matched by all but a very few of the series, and since the bulk of the matchings are leads, a timing record of substantial consistency results. At ten of the reference turns, leads account for 74–100 per cent of all *possible* comparisons; at the other five, for 53–65 per cent.

Relating the Timing Patterns for New Orders and Shipments

Comparisons by Type of Manufacture

Table 11-8 presents a summary of the timing at business peaks and troughs of two groups of new-order series representing production to

Table

Distribution of Timing of New Orders of Individual Industries or

	Trough April 1919	Peak Jan. 1920	Trough July 1921	Peak May 1923	Trough July 1924	Peak Oct. 1926
				NUMBER OF TIMING		
Lead (−) or lag (+), mos.						
−13 to −24				1	2	5
−7 to −12		2	12	4	3	12
−4 to −6	6	1	3	8	1	4
−1 to −3	8	5	1	6	10	
0		2			1	
+1 to +3		2	4		1	1
+4 to +6	1	2				
+7 to +12		1		2		
				MONTHS		
Av. lead (−) or lag (+)	−2.6	−0.4	−5.2	−4.1	−4.2	−10.4
Av. dev.	1.5	3.3	3.1	3.4	4.1	3.2
				SUMMARY: NUMBER		
Leading	14	8	16	19	16	21
Coincident		2			1	
Lagging	1	5	4	2	1	1
Roughly coincident [a]	8	9	5	6	12	5
Matching the turn, total	15	15	20	21	18	22
Included, total	15	15	20	22	25	26

Note: The table includes observations for the thirty series identified in Table 11-5. Only the measures relating to the periods 1919–38, 1948–54 are included.

order and production to stock. The timing of new orders in either category is shown to be on the average somewhat earlier at peaks than at troughs. The measures offer no evidence of a systematic difference in cyclical timing between the two groups of series. This contrasts with the finding that leads of new orders *relative to shipments* are (as would be expected) longer for made-to-order products than for products made to stock (Chapter 4). According to the averages in column 6, series representing manufacture to stock turned, if anything, somewhat *earlier* than the other series at business revivals and recessions. Hence the measures imply that some industries that customarily fill

11-7

Products at Each Business Cycle Turn, 1919–38, 1948–57

Trough Nov. 1927	Peak June 1929	Trough Mar. 1933	Peak May 1937	Trough June 1938	Peak Nov. 1948	Trough Oct. 1949	Peak July 1953	Trough Aug. 1954
COMPARISONS								
1	2	1			3		1	1
6	6	5		6	4	3	3	4
3	5	4	8	4	2			2
5	4	7	8	3	1	8	3	5
2		3	1	1			1	
1	5	1		3		1	1	
1	1	1	1					
3		1						
−2.8	−4.5	−3.2	−3.1	−3.5	−10.7	−3.7	−7.3	−5.7
6.2	4.5	3.8	1.9	3.2	5.4	1.5	7.1	3.2
OF SERIES								
15	17	17	16	13	10	11	7	12
2		3	1	1			1	
5	6	3	1	3		1	1	
8	9	11	9	7	1	9	5	5
22	23	23	18	17	10	12	9	12
26	26	23	18	17	11	12	12	12

[a] Includes exact coincidences and leads and lags of one, two, or three months.

their orders on receipt or on short notice experience cyclical turns in their activity relatively far ahead of peaks and troughs in general business; their new orders *and their shipments* are early leaders.

Direct evidence on this is given in Table 11-9, part I, which shows the average cyclical timing of new orders and shipments for those industries in our sample for which corresponding series on the two variables are available. The list includes seven items representing manufacture to stock. In this group, turns in new orders preceded business peaks and troughs by greatly varying but predominantly long intervals, as indicated by the measures in columns 4, 7, and 10. Since these goods

Table 11-8
Timing of Thirty Series on New Orders at Business Cycle Turns,
Distribution of Leads and Lags by Type of Turn and Type of
Manufacture, 1873–1957

Line		Leads (1)	Exact Coincidences (2)	Lags (3)	Rough Coincidences[a] (4)	Total (5)	Av. Lead (−) or Lag (+)[b] (months) (6)
			AT REFERENCE PEAKS				
1	Manufacture to order[c]	107	5	22	49	134	−5.7
2	Manufacture to stock[d]	38	0	4	12	42	−6.6
3	Total (30 series)	145	5	26	61	176	−5.9
			AT REFERENCE TROUGHS				
4	Manufacture to order[c]	114	9	15	66	138	−4.2
5	Manufacture to stock[d]	44	0	6	14	50	−4.9
6	Total (30 series)	158	9	21	80	188	−4.4
			AT ALL REFERENCE TURNS				
7	Manufacture to order[c]	221	14	37	115	272	−4.9
8	Manufacture to stock[d]	82	0	10	26	92	−5.7
9	Total (30 series)	303	14	47	141	364	−5.1

[a] Includes exact coincidences and leads or lags of one, two, or three months.

[b] Weighted by the number of observations for each component item.

[c] This group includes all nineteen series in Table 11-5 other than those listed below in note d.

[d] This group includes the following eleven series (see Table 11-5): southern pine lumber, oak flooring, clay and glass products, bath tubs, lumber, architectural terra cotta, textile products, lavatories, kitchen sinks, oil burners, miscellaneous enameled sanitary ware.

have short order periods (columns 2, 5, and 8), their shipments, too, turned substantially ahead of business revivals and recessions (columns 3, 6, and 9).

The made-to-order capital goods in Table 11-9 present a different picture. On the average, turns in new orders for these products anticipated the reversals in aggregate economic activity by from two to six months (the leads tend to be longer at peaks than at troughs). The delivery periods were apparently longer than these leads, so that for most items in this group, and on the average, shipments lagged. The lags are more pronounced at troughs than at peaks. Where shipments of these goods led rather than lagged business reversals, the leads were typically short.

Rank correlations between the columns of Table 11-9 indicate that the average leads of new orders relative to shipments are not significantly associated with the average leads of new orders at business cycle turns. The latter do show positive correlations with the average leads (or lags) of shipments at business turns. (The lags are treated as negative leads.) Also, negative rank correlations exist between the order-shipment leads and the leads and lags of shipments at business revivals and recessions. The correlations vary between ±.5 and ±.8. While these results help to summarize the evidence presented in Table 11-9, one must be cautious in generalizing from them because the samples used are small and perhaps not sufficiently representative.

In Table 11-9, part II, matched data on new orders and production for six individual industries provide some additional evidence. With one exception, the products covered here are also included in part I, and their outputs and shipments are on the whole closely associated. Hence, the net informational gain from these measurements is small.

Whether for items produced to order or to stock, new orders lead output by short intervals averaging about two months (manufacture to order is in these measures represented only by some industrial materials). Output of made-to-stock items, like shipments, shows substantial leads at business cycle turns.

Obviously, at least as far as comparatively small segments of total manufacturing are concerned, long leads of new orders relative to production or shipments in a given industry need not necessarily be associated with long leads of new orders at business cycle turns. The cyclical timing patterns of orders, output, and shipments, which are of course interrelated, are very diverse.

The Dispersion of Turning Points in Paired Series

For any item, the timing of shipments is determined by the timing of new orders and the delivery lag. Suppose the length of the latter is four months, and new orders lead at a given business turn by six months; then the lead of shipments is, of course, two months. This simple relationship between the three timing variables implies that their dispersions are interdependent according to the general formula

Table 11-9

Average Timing of New Orders (N), Shipments (S), and Production (Z) at Business Cycle Turns, Twenty Individual Industries or Products Classified by Type of Manufacture, Various Periods, 1919–54

		At Peaks[c]			At Troughs[c]			At All Turns[c]		
					Average Lead (−) or Lag (+), in Months					
Line	Industry or Product[a] and Period[b] (1)	N vs. S or Z (2)	S or Z vs. Bus. Cycles (3)	N vs. Bus. Cycles[d] (4)	N vs. S or Z (5)	S or Z vs. Bus. Cycles (6)	N vs. Bus. Cycles[d] (7)	N vs. S or Z (8)	S or Z vs. Bus. Cycles (9)	N vs. Bus. Cycles[d] (10)
	I. NEW ORDERS AND SHIPMENTS									
	RAILROAD PASSENGER CARS (OR)									
1	1919–54 (17)	−9.5	−3.8	−6.0	−8.7	+7.2	−1.6	−9.1	+5.6	−3.9
	FABRICATED STRUCTURAL STEEL (OR)									
2	1926–54 (12)	−6.4	+2.2	−4.2	−8.8	+1.2	−7.6	−7.6	+1.7	−5.9
	RAILROAD LOCOMOTIVES (OR)									
3	1919–38 (11)	−5.4	+1.4	−4.0	−9.2	+10.0	−1.3	−7.3	+6.1	−2.5
	RAILROAD FREIGHT CARS (OR)									
4	1919–54 (17)	−6.2	−0.7	−6.8	−5.1	+2.6	−2.3	−6.0	+1.1	−4.4
	ELECTRIC OVERHEAD CRANES (OR)									
5	1926–45 (8)	−6.6	+3.0	−3.7	−4.0	+4.3	+0.3	−5.3	+3.7	−1.7
	MERCHANT PIG IRON (OR)									
6	1919–24 (5)	−4.0	+3.0	−1.0	−4.0	0.0	−4.0	−4.0	+1.2	−2.8
	STEEL SHEETS (OR)									
7	1919–33 (9)	−5.8	−1.5	−7.2	−2.4	−3.0	−5.4	−3.9	−2.3	−6.2
	MACHINE TOOLS (OR)									
8	1927–54 (11)	−4.0	−1.0	−2.3	−2.8	+1.4	−1.4	−3.1	+0.5	−1.8

	I	II	III	IV	V	VI	VII	VIII	IX
9 WOODWORKING MACHINERY (OR) 1923–38 (8)	−3.2	−2.5	−5.8	−1.0	−0.2	−1.2	−2.2	−1.4	−3.5
10 OAK FLOORING (ST) 1913–54 (20)	−3.0	−7.0	−9.2	−0.9	−5.5	−7.2	−1.9	−6.2	−8.2
11 FURNITURE (OR) 1926–45 (8)	−1.0	−1.3	−4.5	−2.5	−0.5	−3.0	−1.9	−0.9	−3.8
12 SOUTHERN PINE LUMBER (ST) 1918–54 (18)	−2.7	−8.6	−11.3	−0.8	−6.6	−7.3	−1.6	−7.4	−9.1
13 PAPER, EXCLUDING BUILDING PAPER, NEWSPRINT, AND PAPERBOARD (OR) 1937–49 (6)	−3.0	−2.5	−5.5	+0.5	−5.5	−5.0	−1.2	−4.0	−5.2
14 KITCHEN SINKS (ST) 1919–26 (6)	−3.0	−2.0	−5.0	+0.7	−4.7	−4.0	−1.2	−3.3	−4.5
15 BATH TUBS (ST) 1919–26 (6)	−0.5	−6.5	−7.0	−0.5	−5.0	−5.5	−0.5	−5.8	−6.2
16 LAVATORIES (ST) 1919–26 (6)	−0.3	−5.0	−5.3	0.0	−4.3	−4.3	−0.2	−4.7	−4.8
17 OIL BURNERS (ST) 1933–49 (7)	0.0	−2.0	−2.0	0.0	−0.5	−0.5	0.0	−1.0	−1.0
18 FOUNDRY EQUIPMENT[e] 1926–38 (6)	+1.7	−6.7	−5.0	−0.3	−2.7	−3.0	+0.7	−4.7	−4.0
19 MISCELLANEOUS ENAMELED SANITARY WARE (ST) 1919–23 (4)	+2.0	+2.0	+4.0	+3.5	−9.0	−5.5	+2.8	−3.5	−0.8
20 Group averages[f] 11 OR items	−5.6	+0.4	−5.0	−4.9	+2.2	−2.8	−5.2	+1.4	−3.9
	(41)	(43)	(46)	(50)	(52)	(51)	(91)	(95)	(97)
21 7 ST items	−1.9	−5.6	−7.4	−0.2	−5.5	−6.0	−1.0	−5.6	−6.7
	(25)	(25)	(27)	(29)	(29)	(30)	(54)	(54)	(57)
22 All 19 items	−3.9	−2.0	−5.9	−3.1	−0.6	−4.0	−3.5	−1.2	−4.9
	(69)	(71)	(76)	(82)	(84)	(84)	(151)	(155)	(160)

(continued)

Table 11-9 (concluded)

| | | Average Lead (−) or Lag (+), in Months | | | | | | | | |
| | | At Peaks^c | | | At Troughs^c | | | At All Turns^c | | |
Line	Industry or Product^a and Period^b (1)	N vs. S or Z (2)	S or Z vs. Bus. Cycles (3)	N vs. Bus. Cycles^d (4)	N vs. S or Z (5)	S or Z vs. Bus. Cycles (6)	N vs. Bus. Cycles^d (7)	N vs. S or Z (8)	S or Z vs. Bus. Cycles (9)	N vs. Bus. Cycles^d (10)
	II. NEW ORDERS AND PRODUCTION									
	MERCHANT PIG IRON (OR)									
23	1919–24 (5)	−5.5	+4.5	−1.0	−5.3	+1.3	−4.0	−5.4	+2.6	−2.8
	STEEL SHEETS (OR)									
24	1919–33 (9)	−3.5	−3.8	−7.2	−2.0	−3.4	−5.4	−2.7	−3.6	−6.2
	OAK FLOORING (ST)									
25	1918–54 (18)	−3.3	−7.2	−9.5	−1.9	−3.7	−6.6	−2.5	−5.3	−8.1
	PAPER EXCLUDING BUILDING PAPER, NEWSPRINT, AND PAPERBOARD (OR)									
26	1937–49 (6)	−4.0	−1.5	−5.5	+0.5	−5.5	−5.0	−1.8	−3.5	−5.2
	SOUTHERN PINE LUMBER (ST)									
27	1919–54 (17)	−0.3	−12.2	−11.3	−2.6	−4.0	−7.3	−1.6	−7.5	−9.1
	PAPERBOARD (OR)									
28	1926–54 (12)	−1.8	−2.6	−4.4	−0.4	−6.6	−7.0	−1.1	−4.6	−5.7
	Group averages^f									
29	4 OR items	−3.2 (13)	−1.7 (13)	−4.9 (13)	−1.8 (15)	−3.8 (15)	−5.6 (15)	−2.5 (28)	−2.8 (28)	−5.3 (28)
30	2 ST items	−1.8 (12)	−9.7 (12)	−10.3 (15)	−2.3 (15)	−3.9 (15)	−7.0 (17)	−2.1 (27)	−6.4 (27)	−8.6 (32)
31	All 6 items	−2.6 (25)	−5.5 (25)	−7.8 (28)	−2.0 (30)	−3.8 (30)	−6.3 (32)	−2.3 (55)	−4.6 (55)	−7.0 (60)

Notes to Table 11-9

ᵃ (ST) signifies goods made primarily to stock; (OR), goods made primarily to order. This classification is identical with the division made in Chapter 4 (Tables 4-1 and 4-2) between the group of eleven items representing manufacture to order and the group of seven items representing manufacture to stock.

The list in part I of the table includes those items in Table 11-5 for which corresponding series on new orders and shipments are available; the list in part II includes those of the items for which corresponding series on new orders and production are available. The items in lines 1–19 are ranked by the length of the average lead of new orders relative to shipments, and the items in lines 23–28 relative to production, beginning in both cases with the longest lead (column 8).

ᵇ The years identify the first and last reference turns matched by both the new-order and the shipment (production) series. Figures in parentheses identify the number of reference turns in the periods thus defined. The periods differ in some cases from those given for the corresponding items in Table 11-5, column 1, because shipments (production) are not always available for the entire interval covered by the new-order series.

ᶜ The averages for new orders versus shipments (production) do not include comparisons at "extra" turns, but only those between specific turns related to the same reference dates. They are therefore not necessarily identical with the corresponding figures in Tables 4-1 and 4-2, columns 9 and 10. The averages for the timing comparisons at business cycle turns include all observations at the reference turns covered by periods identified in column 1 (see note b).

ᵈ These measures are identical with the entries for the corresponding items in Table 11-5, columns 9 and 10, except when the periods covered are different. In general, column 4 ≃ column 2 + column 3; (7) ≃ (5) + (6); and (10) ≃ (8) + (9). More specifically, they are equal to these sums, except in those cases in which any of the reference turns during the period covered were matched by new orders but not by shipments (production), or vice versa.

ᵉ Available information does not permit classification of this item as either (OR) or (ST) (cf. note 4 in Chapter 4). It is excluded from the averages in lines 20–21, but included in the over-all averages in line 22.

ᶠ Weighted by the number of observations for each component item. Number of observations covered is given in parentheses.

for variances of sums or differences. Denote the standard deviation of the timing of new orders and shipments at a business cycle turn as σ_n and σ_s, respectively, and the standard deviation of the timing of new orders relative to shipments (of the "delivery lags") as σ_d. Then, for matched observations relating to a given set of industries or products,

$$\sigma_s^2 = \sigma_n^2 + \sigma_d^2 - 2r_{nd}\sigma_n\sigma_d, \tag{1}$$

where r_{nd} is the coefficient of correlation between the leads (or lags) of new orders at the particular recession or recovery and the corresponding delivery lags.

It is clear that the diversity of supply conditions and business operating policies and practices, as expressed in the variance of the delivery periods (σ_d^2), makes a gross contribution to the dispersion of turns in shipments (σ_s^2); this contribution is in addition to that due to the dispersion of turns in new orders (σ_n^2). This would be the whole story if the delivery lags were independent of the cyclical leads of new orders. The dispersion of shipments would then always be greater than the dispersion of new orders, since, with $r_{nd} = 0$, $\sigma_s^2 = \sigma_n^2 + \sigma_d^2$. If the correlation were negative ($r_{nd} < 0$), this conclusion would be reinforced. In fact, σ_s^2 would then exceed not just σ_n^2 but the sum of both variances ($\sigma_n^2 + \sigma_d^2$). For $\sigma_s^2 < \sigma_n^2$, r_{nd} would have to be positive and larger than $\sigma_d/2\sigma_n$ (i.e., large enough to make $|2r\sigma_n\sigma_d| > \sigma_d^2$).

Economic considerations join the statistical analysis in suggesting the likelihood that $\sigma_s^2 > \sigma_n^2$. Cyclical forces operate primarily on the demand side, giving rise to interdependent and, in a substantial measure, convergent processes. On this premise, one would expect that the cyclical timing of many new-order series would be alike. But, since delivery periods vary among different industries and products, the timing of production and shipments would vary even for items for which the effective demand, as measured by new orders, fluctuated in unison.

On the other hand, anticipations of buyers of materials and investors in equipment could be such as to make for more dispersion in orders placed and less in outputs and shipments. Expectations of, say, a downturn in business may cause purchasers of items with long delivery periods to curtail their orders early and purchasers of items with short delivery periods to do so later. In the extreme case of correct anticipations of this sort, peaks and troughs in outputs and shipments would cluster closely about the dates of business recessions and revivals, and the leads of new orders at these dates would reflect the delivery periods for the products concerned.

Actually, neither of the extreme situations is very realistic, since *close* clusters of turns in either group of series are likely to be the exception rather than the rule. But the weight of our argument favors the presumption that new orders would typically show less dispersion than shipments, and the evidence to be presented is not inconsistent with this hypothesis.

Table 11-10 shows that the dispersion of leads and lags was greater for shipments than for new orders at nine of the eleven business

Table 11-10
Average Timing and Dispersion for Paired Series on New Orders and Shipments at Each Business Cycle Turn, 1919–38
(timing and deviation in months)

Reference Turn	No. of Indust. or Prod. Covered [a] (1)	Timing of New Orders at Business Cycle Turns		Timing of Shipments at Business Cycle Turns		Timing of New Orders at Shipments Turns		Corr. Bet. Avg. Leads in Cols. 2 and 6
		Av. Lead (−) or Lag (+) (2)	Stand. Dev. (3)	Av. Lead (−) or Lag (+) (4)	Stand. Dev. (5)	Av. Lead (−) or Lag (+) [b] (6)	Stand. Dev. (7)	(8)
Trough Apr. 1919	11	−2.6	2.5	0.0	5.0	−2.6	3.7	−.29
Peak Jan. 1920	11	−1.4	4.1	+1.7	7.2	−3.1	6.7	.19
Trough July 1921	11	−5.5	3.0	−5.7	7.9	+0.2	5.9	−.51
Peak May 1923	12 [c]	−4.0 [d]	5.6 [d]	+3.0	4.4	−7.0	5.7	.65
Trough July 1924	11 [e]	−4.1	4.3	+1.0 [f]	7.5 [f]	−5.1	7.2	.23
Peak Oct. 1926	14	−11.5	4.0	−10.1	5.0	−1.4	5.5	.49
Trough Nov. 1927	12	−3.8	6.7	+1.2	6.6	−5.0	4.7	.37
Peak June 1929	12	−5.0	5.0	−1.0	6.8	−4.0	4.9	.07
Trough Mar. 1933	13	−2.3	4.9	+0.8	6.6	−3.1	6.6	.37
Peak May 1937	13	−2.9	2.8	+0.3	3.8	−3.2	3.5	.29
Trough June 1938	13	−4.2	3.0	−0.4	4.2	−3.8	4.4	.39

Note: The observations summarized in this table relate to series identified in Table 11-9.

[a] Equals the number of observations included in each of the averages on the given line, columns 2 to 7, except as noted below.

[b] Taken with opposite sign, these are the inferred average "delivery periods." They equal the algebraic differences of the corresponding entries in columns 2 and 4.

[c] The entries in this line are based on nine observations. Three series of shipments skip this turn.

[d] Two series of new orders skip this turn. If all ten observations are used (instead of the nine that correspond to the shipments turns), an average lead of −4.8 is obtained, with a standard deviation of 5.8.

[e] The entries in this line are based on seven observations. Four series of new orders skip this turn.

[f] Three series of shipments skip this turn. If all eight observations are used (instead of the seven that correspond to the new-order turns), an average lead of +0.4 is obtained, with a standard deviation of 7.2.

cycle turns of the interwar period (cf. columns 3 and 5).[21] Only at the 1923 recession was σ_s considerably smaller than σ_n; at the 1927 recovery the two were approximately equal. In other instances, σ_s/σ_n falls within the range 1.3–2.6.

The standard deviations of the leads of new orders at turns in shipments, i.e., of the delivery periods (σ_d), are also usually smaller than σ_s, but larger than σ_n. (A comparison of corresponding entries in columns 3, 5, and 7 of the table will show two exceptions from either part of this statement.)

The cyclical leads of new orders and the delivery periods are positively correlated in all but two of the eleven episodes covered (column 8). But the correlations are typically not high enough to vitiate the hypothesis that $\sigma_s > \sigma_n$.

Thus, data for individual industries (covering mainly the interwar period) suggest that the cyclical turns of shipments tend to be more widely dispersed than the cyclical turns of new orders: a tentative finding in favor of the hypothesis.[22] The same type of dispersion analysis was applied to the paired aggregative series for 1948–61, first to the pre-1963 OBE data and then to the current Census series when these became available. Table 11-11 presents the results, beginning with those based primarily on the current data.

The first section of the table refers to six major durable goods industries and the group of nondurable goods industries reporting unfilled orders. Standard deviations are larger for shipments than for new orders on four occasions.[23] In the other four episodes the opposite ob-

---

[21] These measures are based on a subsample of observations for paired order and shipments series drawn from the sample of Table 11-9. The number of series included at the successive turns varies, since the series differ in length and timing. Here and elsewhere in the tests discussed in this section only the matching new-order and shipments turns are included, but adding the few unmatched turns would not alter the results in any significant way.

Corresponding measures were also compiled for 1948–54, but only five to seven items are covered. The results tend to confirm the hypothesis. At the peaks of 1948 and 1953, σ_s equals 5.8 and 8.9; σ_n equals 5.8 and 3.9. At the troughs of 1949 and 1954, σ_s equals 5.4 and 5.3; σ_n equals 2.5 and 2.4.

[22] The leads and lags of two series at a common set of reference dates would be influenced in a parallel fashion by any errors in these dates, which may introduce a bias toward positive correlation between such timing observations. However, this should not have any systematic effect on the measures of timing dispersion. A shift in a reference date has the effect of adding a constant algebraically to each of the leads and lags measured from that date; it has no effect at all on the deviations of the leads and lags from their own mean, since these depend only on the dates of the specific turns involved, which are given.

[23] Compare the second and fourth lines of Table 11-11. Because of the disturbing influence of the 1956 steel strike, entries in column 5 exclude primary metals. Inclusion of the observations for this industry would result in a value of σ_n slightly higher than σ_s (the figures are 6.0 and 5.7, respectively).

tains, that is, $\sigma_s < \sigma_n$, but in two of these cases the observed differences are small and probably insignificant. However, σ_n definitely exceeds σ_s at the 1953 recession and the 1961 recovery.

The new data for market categories permit comparisons at the five business cycle turns of the period 1954–61. On two of these occasions, the differences between the standard deviations are very small or negligible, and on two others σ_s is much greater than σ_n. The remaining episode, in which σ_n is clearly larger than σ_s, is for the 1956–57 period, when there was a major steel strike with particularly strong effects on the relative timing of new orders and shipments.

The third section of Table 11-11 is based on the pre-1963 OBE series for seven major durable goods industries and four major nondurable goods industries. These data provide greater diversity of industrial coverage, which is a favorable factor in the present context. Broad coverage seems required by the hypothesis tested inasmuch as it produces that diversity of supply conditions which is expected to make the scatter of turning points on the production side wider than the corresponding scatter on the demand (i.e., new-order) side. The results for this set of eleven industries are again mixed, but the dispersion of turning points is somewhat greater for shipments than for new orders. In four instances, the differences between σ_n and σ_s are negligible (and, incidentially, evenly divided as to their signs). In three others, $\sigma_s > \sigma_n$. Only at the 1961 recovery did σ_n definitely exceed σ_s according to these data.

Finally, for the set of twenty-seven components of the durable goods sector, $\sigma_s \simeq \sigma_n$ at two of the seven business cycle turns covered; $\sigma_s > \sigma_n$, at three of them; and $\sigma_s < \sigma_n$ at two.

To sum up, the measures assembled in Table 11-11 are on the whole consistent with the hypothesis that new orders show more agreement in their timing at business recoveries and recessions than do shipments. However, an appreciable part of the assembled evidence is neutral or unfavorable to the hypothesis. Averages of the standard deviations weighted by the numbers of observations at each turn are larger for shipments than for new orders in all cases, but the margins of difference are small. This is shown in the first two lines of the tabulation on page 566, which are computed from the four sets of measures given in Table 11-11.

Table 11-11

Average Timing and Dispersion for Paired Series of New Orders and Shipments at Each Business Cycle Turn, Major Manufacturing Industries and Divisions and Market Categories, 1948–61

| | Peak Nov. 1948 (1) | Trough Oct. 1949 (2) | Peak July 1953 (3) | Lead (−) or Lag (+), in Months, at Business Cycle Turns | | | | |
				Trough Aug. 1954 (4)	Peak July 1957 (5)	Trough April 1958 (6)	Peak May 1960 (7)	Trough Feb. 1961 (8)
SEVEN MAJOR INDUSTRIES [a]								
New Orders								
Av. lead (−) or lag (+)	−5.4	−4.0	−5.1	−8.1	−8.2	−2.6	−12.0	−2.6
Standard deviation	3.6	2.8	2.1	2.9	4.7	1.3	3.2	3.7
Shipments								
Av. lead (−) or lag (+)	−2.6	−0.8	−1.1	−0.7	−6.7	+1.1	−5.4	−0.1
Standard deviation	4.5	2.3	1.1	2.8	6.2	6.0	5.0	1.0
SIX MARKET CATEGORIES [b]								
New Orders								
Av. lead (−) or lag (+)				−8.0	−6.2	−1.8	−8.3	−1.7
Standard deviation				2.3	4.1	0.9	5.7	1.4
Shipments								
Av. lead (−) or lag (+)				−3.7	−3.8	+0.7	−8.2	−0.3
Standard deviation				3.9	2.9	1.6	5.6	1.1

	ELEVEN MAJOR INDUSTRIES [c]							
New Orders								
Av. lead (−) or lag (+)	−6.6	−3.8	−5.8	−7.5	−8.0	−1.4	−7.3	−2.9
Standard deviation	3.8	2.5	3.4	2.3	3.8	2.7	5.6	2.2
Shipments								
Av. lead (−) or lag (+)	−3.6	−0.8	−1.8	−1.1	−4.6	+0.1	−5.0	−1.6
Standard deviation	4.7	2.3	3.2	4.4	4.9	2.8	5.7	1.2
TWENTY-SEVEN DURABLE GOODS SUBDIVISIONS [d]								
New Orders								
Av. lead (−) or lag (+)		−4.2	−6.8	−6.3	−12.0	−1.7	−8.1	−2.4
Standard deviation		3.0	6.4	2.7	6.2	2.6	5.7	3.0
Shipments								
Av. lead (−) or lag (+)		+0.2	−2.6	−0.3	−7.0	+1.0	−6.1	−0.9
Standard deviation		4.0	5.2	4.4	7.6	2.5	4.2	3.0

[a] Based on new Census data since 1953 and on the older OBE data for the earlier years. The seven industries are primary metals, fabricated metal products, electrical machinery, machinery except electrical, transportation equipment, other durable goods, and nondurable goods industries reporting unfilled orders. All observations for these industries that are listed in Table 11-2 are included, except primary metals at the 1957 peak. The observations for shipments match those for new orders. The numbers of leads or lags included in each of the entries for these seven industries are: column 1, five; columns 2 and 5, six; other columns, seven.

[b] Based on new Census data beginning in 1953. The six market categories are home goods and apparel; nonautomotive equipment and defense; automotive equipment; machinery and equipment industries; construction materials, supplies, and intermediate products; and other materials, supplies, and intermediate products. All observations for these categories that are listed in Table 11-4 are included. The observations for shipments match those for new orders. Each of the entries covers six leads or lags.

[c] Based on OBE data of pre-1963 vintage. The eleven industries are primary metals, fabricated metal products, electrical machinery, machinery except electrical, motor vehicles and parts, other transportation equipment, other durable goods, textile-mill products, leather and leather products, paper and allied products, and printing and publishing. Matching observations only are used for new orders and shipments. The numbers of leads or lags included in each of the entries for these eleven industries are: column 1, seven; columns 2 and 8, eight; columns 3 and 4, ten; columns 5 and 7, nine; and column 6, eleven.

[d] Based on OBE data of pre-1963 vintage. See Table E-1, lines 1–27, for the industries covered and the observations for new orders included in the entries here. The relatively few and uncertain timing measures for the 1948 peak are excluded. Matching observations only are used for new orders and shipments. The numbers of leads or lags included in each of the entries for this group are: columns 2 and 7, twenty-one; columns 3 and 8, twenty; column 4, twenty-two; columns 5 and 6, twenty-five.

Weighted Average Standard Deviation

	Seven Major Industries	*Six Market Categories*	*Eleven Industries*	*Twenty-seven Subdivisions*
$\bar{\sigma}_n$	3.33	2.88	3.27	4.22
$\bar{\sigma}_s$	3.55	3.02	3.65	4.45
$\bar{\sigma}_d$	2.97	2.78	3.29	4.28

The last line of the table lists the corresponding averages of standard deviations for the leads of new orders at turns in shipments. It shows that the dispersion of these delivery lags is either somewhat smaller or about as large as the dispersion of the leads of new orders at business cycle turns.

The leads of new orders at business cycle turns and the leads of new orders at turns in shipments are as a rule positively, but not closely, correlated. The higher these correlations and the lower the relative dispersion of the delivery lags, the greater is the chance that the hypothesis will be contradicted by the data.[24]

Theories of business cycles that stress factors which are supposed to produce comovements of demand across industries would be supported by the finding that new orders and contracts for various types of products tend to reach peaks and troughs at about the same time. Other hypotheses may involve systematic sequential developments on the demand side, rather than more concentrated and randomly ordered turning points, and they may imply different results. Some monetary theories of the cycle might belong to the former category, some investment theories to the latter. Such considerations suggest that an extended and improved analysis along the above lines should be of substantial interest. However, the information on hand is too limited for this task, and more comprehensive data for longer historical periods are not available.

---

[24] Recall that

$$\sigma_s^2 = \sigma_n^2 + \sigma_d^2 - 2r_{nd}\sigma_n\sigma_d$$

[see equation (1), above]. If $0 < r_{nd} > (\sigma_d/2\sigma_n)$ then $\sigma_s < \sigma_n$. In the case of $\sigma_d = \sigma_n$, for exampl , this result would require that r_{nd} exceed $+0.5$; assuming that $\sigma_d = 0.8\sigma_n$, it would require only that r_{nd} exceed $+0.4$.

Unfilled Orders: Aggregate and Individual Series

Measures of cyclical timing and conformity for the series on unfilled orders are presented in several tables. It will be seen that they
parallel to a large extent the measures developed in Chapter 6 for the
relations between unfilled orders and shipments (used as an indicator
of industrial activity). References to these similarities help to shorten
the exposition below.

Durable and Nondurable Manufactures

Table 11-12 lists the timing of the most comprehensive series of
order backlogs at each recession and recovery since 1920. It shows the
same type of differences between peaks and troughs and between
strong and weak backlog expansions as were observed before in Chapter 6 (where the series are plotted in Charts 6-2, 6-3, and 6-4).

Unfilled orders appear to have been relatively small and declining
during most of the 1920's, and their timing then was irregular but on
the average roughly coincident, judging from the rather narrowly
based Commerce index (Table 11-12). They were, of course, very
small in the depression of the next decade, and their broad movements
were then closely synchronous with the course of manufacturing and
general economic activity. But when the backlogs grew very large
relative to production, in the 1940's, their leads at business cycle
peaks as well as at the downturns in manufacturing output and shipments became very long. The tendency of unfilled orders to coincide at
business troughs (Table 11-12, columns 4–6) also recalls the results
obtained from the relative timing analysis of the manufacturing series,
as does the reduction in the leads of durables backlogs at the more recent recessions as compared with the early postwar ones.

The evidence suggests that backlog contractions are often much
slower and longer when they start from very high levels than when
they start at relatively low peaks. Of course, this is not inevitably so.
The reverse could happen if the average rate of *net* backlog liquidation
were sufficiently higher in the cycle with the larger accumulation of unfilled orders. But this is apparently not a very likely situation, for
reasons that are not difficult to perceive. It is in the advanced stages
of vigorous business expansions that unfilled orders become exceed-

Table 11-12
Timing of Comprehensive Series on Unfilled Orders at Each Business Cycle Turn, 1920–61

Date of Reference Peak	Lead (−) or Lag (+), in Months			Date of Reference Trough	Lead (−) or Lag (+), in Months		
	Durable and Non-durable Goods (1)	Durable Goods (2)	Non-durable Goods (3)		Durable and Non-durable Goods (4)	Durable Goods (5)	Non-durable Goods (6)
1 Jan. 1920	+4			July 1921	+6		
2 May 1923	−2			July 1924	−1		
3 Oct. 1926	−10			Nov. 1927	0		
4 Aug. 1929	−4			Mar. 1933	−2		
5 May 1937	−1	−1	−1	June 1938	−1	0	−5
6 Feb. 1945	−26ᵃ	−26ᵃ	−21ᵃ				
7 Feb. 1945	−27	−27	−18	Oct. 1945	0	0	0
8 Nov. 1948	−22	−25	−18	Oct. 1949	−2	−1	−4
9 July 1953	−10	−10	ᵇ	Aug. 1954	0	0	−8
10 July 1957	−7	−5	−20	Apr. 1958	+5	+5	−1
11 May 1960	−6	−7	−4	Feb. 1961	+1	+1	−1
Av. lead (−) or lag (+)				Av. lead (−) or lag (+)			
1920–60	−8.5			1921–61	+0.6		
1937–60	−12.2	−12.5	−12.2	1938–61	+0.5	+0.8	−3.2
Av. dev. 1937–60	8.2	9.0	7.8	Av. dev. 1938–61	1.7	1.4	2.5

Source: Measures on lines 1–4 are based on indexes compiled by the Department of Commerce from individual unfilled orders series (see text and note 2). Measures on lines 5 and 6 are based on the National Industrial Conference Board indexes (see text note 2); and those on lines 7–11, on the OBE-Census estimates of the dollar value of manufacturers' unfilled orders (see text above).

ᵃ Excluded from the average.
ᵇ Not matched. The specific-cycle peak of March 1951 is regarded as an "extra" turn associated with Korean War developments (see Chart 6-4).

ingly high. Buyers then still attempt to place large amounts of new orders. If the net rates of backlog decumulation are to be increased, producers must limit acceptance of new commitments and/or speed up deliveries. Drastic measures of either kind may be necessary to obtain the desired effect, and many manufacturers will probably be partly unwilling and partly unable to take them. Order limitation is known to be practiced in some industries, but it is difficult to detect its effects in the aggregate data. Certain relevant factors are essentially beyond the manufacturers' control, at least in the short run: the capacity limits on the firms' current operations and the rates at which customers try to place new orders, as well as the urgency of their efforts to buy. When all this is considered, it is not surprising that the net outcome should be *gradual* reductions of backlogs from their top levels. But as long as unfilled orders while slowly receding are still voluminous, current manufacturing operations have a firm basis—indeed, here is a factor that can (and at times demonstrably does) contribute substantially toward the maintenance and prolongation of industrial prosperity. Hence, we see the long backlog leads at the peaks of those business cycles to which the large backlog cycles correspond.

Major-Industry Series

The comprehensive series on manufacturers' unfilled orders turned down late in 1946 or early in 1947 and declined gently for a long time before falling off more sharply during the 1948–49 recession (Chart 6-4). Their major downturns thus preceded the 1948 business peak by as much as seven quarters or two years (Table 11-13, column 1). At the next recession, in 1953, the lead of aggregate backlogs was ten months —again quite substantial but less than half as long as at the first postwar expansion. Smaller and less pervasive reductions in this lead can be observed at the 1957 and 1960 recessions, when unfilled orders for all manufacturers and the durable goods sector turned down five to seven months before the reference dates (cf. Table 11-13, columns 3, 5, and 7).

As was shown in Chapter 6, the timing of aggregate backlogs at successive peaks in shipments shifted even more drastically: from very long leads in the late forties and the early downturns in 1952 to short leads and, even, frequent lags during 1957–62. On the hypothesis that this trend is associated with the decrease in the relative size and pro-

Table 11-13

Timing of Value of Manufacturers' Unfilled Orders at Each Business Cycle Turn,
by Major Industries, 1948–61

Industry	Lead (−) or Lag (+), in Months, of Unfilled Orders at Business Cycle Turns							
	Peak Nov. 1948 (1)	Trough Oct. 1949 (2)	Peak July 1953 (3)	Trough Aug. 1954 (4)	Peak July 1957 (5)	Trough Apr. 1958 (6)	Peak May 1960 (7)	Trough Feb. 1961 (8)
All manufacturing	−22[a]	−2	−10	0	−7	+5	−6	+1
Durable goods, total	−25[a]	−1	−10	0	−5	+5	−7	+1
Primary metals	+1	−1	−11	0	−11	+2	−6	+1
Blast furnaces and steel mills	n.a.	n.a.	n.a.	0	−11	+2	−6	0
Fabricated metal products	−3	+2	−10	+2	−15	+1	−5	0
Electrical machinery[b]	−22	−5	−6[c]	+5	−5	−3	−7	+4
Machinery exc. electrical[b]	−21	+2	−17	+3	−7	+3	−5	+3
Transport. equipment	−12	−2	−5[d]	−3	−10	n.t.	n.t.	n.t.
Other durable goods[e]	−7	−2	−4	0	−14	0	−10	0
Nondurable goods industries[f]	−18[a]	−4	[g]	−8	−20	−1	−4	−1

Notes to Table 11-13

n.a. = not available.

n.t. = no turn in unfilled orders.

Note: All measures in columns 4-8 and some in columns 1-3 are based on the new Census data (1963 revision) which begin in 1947 for the over-all aggregates and in 1953 for the component industries. Most of the measures in columns 1-3 are based on the older OBE data.

[a] See Charts 6-3 and 6-4 for the underlying series on backlogs of durable and non-durable goods. For total manufacturing and all durables, both the old data (Chart 6-3) and the new (Chart 6-4) show downward trends through 1947-48 and most of the 1949 recession. For nondurables, Chart 6-3 shows a peak in December 1947. Chart 6-4 shows one in May 1947, which is used here.

[b] The pre-1953 measures are based in part on unpublished data received from the Department of Commerce, Office of Business Economics.

[c] Minimum lead based on the Census series, which declines from its beginning in January 1953. Earlier OBE data show a mild increase between March and July 1953 and hence would indicate a different (coincident) timing of these backlogs.

[d] Timing difficult to establish as unfilled orders were slightly higher in June than in February of 1953, according to the new Census data; February is viewed as the peak date on the basis of the evidence of moving averages. Earlier OBE data point unequivocally to February.

[e] Includes professional and scientific instruments; lumber; furniture; stone, clay, and glass; and miscellaneous industries.

[f] Includes textiles, leather, paper, and printing and publishing.

[g] Not matched. Unfilled orders declined steeply after the March 1951 peak associated with Korean War developments, except for a small increase in November 1952–May 1953 (Chart 6-4).

duction-sustaining capacity of unfilled orders, one would expect it to show up directly in the comparisons involving the specific output or shipments series; its manifestations in the comparisons at turning points in general business activity are of the derived type and may therefore be weaker. Actually, the results of the two sets of measures for the 1948 and 1953 turning-point zones are about the same. However, those for the 1957 and 1960 zones show significant differences. Backlogs led at these recessions, even though they nearly coincided with, or even lagged behind, shipments. As noted before, downturns in manufacturing activity came early on these occasions, which accounts for these observations.

The tendency for the leads of backlogs to become shorter shows up strongly in the measures for the machinery industries as well (Table 11-13). No such indications, however, are obtained for the other major components of the durable goods sector and the nondurable goods industries.

In contrast to the long or intermediate leads at peaks, the timing of unfilled orders at the postwar troughs in economic activity was on the average coincident. Short leads were more frequent at the revivals of 1949 and 1954, intermediate or short lags at those of 1958 and 1961. The timing of order backlogs relative to the corresponding turns in shipments was on the whole very similar (cf. Tables 11-13 and 6-1, columns 2, 4, 6, and 8).

In sum, there were 35 leads and only 1 lag at business cycle downturns. The leads generally exceeded three months; the count includes only 2 rough coincidences. On the other hand, at business cycle upturns there were 12 leads, 9 exact coincidences, and 16 lags. Only seven of these observations were leads and lags exceeding three months and as many as 30 were rough coincidences.

For each of the industries, the average of the timing measures at peaks was a lead. These averaged from -6.8 months for primary metals to -14.0 months for the nondurables group; the figure for all durables is -11.8 months. Of the averages at troughs, seven were short lags and three were short leads; the former varied from $+0.5$ to $+2.8$, the latter from -0.5 to -3.5 months. The recession-revival contrast here is so systematic that no good purpose would be served in discussing the all-turns averages.[25]

The aggregative backlog series covered in Table 11-13 missed business cycle turns in as few as 4 instances out of the 77 opportunities to do so in the years 1948-61. They also had very few extra turns in this period so that their cyclical conformity, allowing for timing differences, was very good. Furthermore, the general smoothness of these series enhances the reliability of this record. However, short but sharp declines in unfilled orders of several industries occurred in 1962, and again in 1966-67, years that witnessed slowdowns in economic activity. Scattered countercyclical movements occurred at other times, notably in primary metals during the 1963-65 period, but these fluctuations have generally been shorter than the movements recognized as specific cycles in the National Bureau studies. The most recent high point in manufacturers' unfilled orders occurred in May 1969, about

[25] The long leads at the early postwar peaks result in large average deviations of the corresponding timing measures. The peak-trough differences could be exaggerated by a few extreme observations with opposite signs. However, this actually does not happen. Medians, which are not affected by extreme items, show much the same type of timing relations as the means, which are so affected.

six months before what now seems a likely date of another business cycle peak.

Again, the patterns observed for the comprehensive series in the current Census compilation are confirmed by the record of the pre-1963 OBE data for the more narrowly defined industrial subdivisions. This supporting evidence is presented in Appendix E, part III.

Market Categories

Table 11-14 shows the timing of unfilled orders for six market categories at each successive business cycle turn during 1954-61.[26] These series begin in 1953 and their timing at the mid-year downturn in business activity is uncertain. Typically, these series were at their highest levels near the beginning of the year. They then declined through the 1953-54 recession, indicating leads of at least five to six months. Information suggests that some of these leads were probably a good deal longer.[27]

Unfilled orders for all categories of nonmilitary items show basically conforming behavior in that their peaks and troughs can be matched with business recessions and revivals, respectively. Extra declines in these series occurred in 1962, but they were relatively mild, except for the backlogs of consumer goods orders. The latter category (home goods, apparel, and consumer staples) also shows a small and hesitant but rather long decline in 1964 and the first half of 1965.

Unfilled orders for defense products, on the other hand, show a rather different time path, with fewer and weaker links to the cyclical movements of the economy. Their highest level in 1953 was reached in June, one month before the reference peak; and their subsequent decline was not reversed until mid-1955. There followed a rise to a high plateau in the fall and winter of 1956-57, then a protracted, gradual decline through 1962, and afterward another upward movement which intensified beginning early in 1965.

All observations at the 1957 and 1960 recessions are leads of backlogs. These vary from three to eleven months, but most fall in the intermediate range of five to eight months (Table 11-14, columns 2 and

---

[26] The data are from the current Census compilation, first published in 1963. They are described in Chapter 6 and shown in Chart 6-6.

[27] Note (Table 11-13, column 3) the ten-month leads of the first two comprehensive backlog series at the July 1953 peak.

Table 11-14

Timing of Value of Unfilled Orders at Each Business Cycle Turn, Six Market Categories, 1954–61

Market Category[a]	Lead (−) or Lag (+), in Months, of Unfilled Orders at Business Cycle Turns					Av. Lead (−) or Lag (+), in Months	
	Trough Aug. 1954 (1)	Peak July 1957 (2)	Trough April 1958 (3)	Peak May 1960 (4)	Trough Feb. 1961 (5)	Peaks (6)	Troughs (7)
Home goods, apparel, and consumer staples	0	−7[b]	−1	−5	+1	−6.0	0
Equipment and defense products, incl. automotive	+4	−5	+4	−11[c]	n.m.	−8.0	+4.0[d]
Defense products	+10	−10	n.m.	n.m.	n.m.	[d]	[d]
Machinery and equipment industries	+4	−5	+4	−5	−3	−5.0	+1.7
Construction materials, supplies, and intermediate products	+1	−5[e]	+1	−3	0	−4.0	+0.7
Other materials, supplies, and intermediate products	0	−8	+2	−6	+1	−7.0	+1.0

n.m. = not matched.

[a] For composition of these categories, see Chapter 3.

[b] Based on the secondary peak of unfilled orders in December 1956. The series reached a primary peak in October 1955, after which it slightly declined in the first and rose in the second half of 1956.

[c] Based on the peak in June 1959, which terminated a distinct but small rise that began in August 1958.

[d] Only one observation is available.

[e] Based on the peak in February 1957. The isolated high values of this series in April–May 1956 are disregarded.

4). Among the timing measures at the 1954, 1958, and 1961 revivals, short lags of one to four months prevail over short leads and coincidences (columns 1, 3, and 5). About all that can be inferred from this limited information is that these patterns are consistent with those observed generally in the industry series.

Individual Industries or Products

Table 11-15 summarizes the record of cyclical performance for sixteen series on unfilled orders. When no allowance is made for differences between the periods they cover, these series are found to vary greatly in their timing. The averages at peaks range from long leads (eighteen months for machine tools) to intermediate lags (five months for foundry equipment). At troughs the variation is less, most series being on the average roughly coincident; the range of the means is here from a lead of four to a lag of seven months. Moreover, the timing of the series often varies considerably from one recession or revival to another.

Another way of describing the situation is to note that as many as 47 observations at peaks, or 72 per cent, are leads, while the lags number 15, or 23 per cent. At troughs, there are almost as many lags as leads, and most of the recorded timing intervals are short, i.e., "rough coincidences" (see the distributions of leads and lags in columns 4–7, particularly the summary in the last three lines).

These over-all measures, however, include the interwar period, when unfilled orders were on the whole small and roughly coincident with production, as well as the recent war and postwar years, when unfilled orders were large and led production at peaks by long intervals. When the pre-1945 observations used in Table 11-15 are separated from the post-1945 ones, a marked contrast is found between the results of the two sets, and it is in the expected direction. For the eleven pre-World War II series,[28] the timing average was −2.1 at recessions and (nearly) coincident at revivals. For all sixteen series covered in Table 11-15, the corresponding averages were −2.2 and +0.2 months in the period before 1945, and −15.8 and −2.5 months in the period after 1945. These figures again demonstrate the prevalence of very long leads of unfilled orders at the postwar recessions compared to

[28] See Table 11-15 for their identification and timing records. The five postwar series are machine tools, paperboard, oil burners, railroad freight cars, and oak flooring.

Table 11-15

Summary Measures of Timing of Unfilled Orders at Business Cycle Peaks and Troughs, Sixteen Industries or Products,[a] Various Periods, 1904–61

Period Covered[b] (1)	No. of Observations[c] (2)	Bus. Cycle Turns Skipped[d] (3)	Extra Spec. Cycle Turns[e] (4)	No. of Timing Observations at Peaks or Troughs That Are				Av. Lead (−) or Lag (+) (months)	
				Leads (5)	Exact Coincidences (6)	Lags (7)	Rough Coincidences[f] (8)	Peaks or Troughs (9)	All Turns (10)
MACHINE TOOLS[g]									
1948–61	4	0	1	4	0	0	0	−18.0	−9.5
	4	0	1	2	0	2	3	−1.0	
PAPERBOARD[b]									
1926–57	6	1	3	6	0	0	2	−13.2	−9.0
	5	1	3	4	0	1	2	−4.0	
OIL BURNERS[i]									
1933–49	2	1	4	2	0	0	0	−12.5	−7.0
	3	1	4	2	1	0	2	−3.3	
TEXTILES[j]									
1923–33	3	0	1	3	0	0	0	−9.0	−4.8
	3	0	1	1	0	2	1	−0.7	
FURNITURE AND FLOORING[j]									
1921–33	3	0	0	3	0	0	1	−5.3	−4.4
	4	0	0	3	0	1	2	−3.8	
UNITED STATES STEEL CORPORATION[h]									
1904–33	8	0	0	6	1	1	4	−3.9	−2.7
	9	0	0	4	2	3	4	−1.7	
RAILROAD FREIGHT CARS[i]									
1927–57	5	1	2	4	0	1	1	−8.6	−2.1
	5	1	2	1	0	4	3	+4.4	

OAK FLOORING[k] 1920–57	9	0	2	6	0	3	4	−4.0	−2.1
	8	0	2	5	0	3	2	0.0	
BRICK AND GLASS[j] 1920–33	2	2	0	1	0	1	2	−0.5	−2.0
	2	2	0	2	0	0	1	−3.5	
WOODWORKING MACHINERY[g] 1921–38	4	0	1	4	0	0	3	−4.0	−1.6
	5	0	1	4	0	1	4	+0.4	
IRON AND STEEL[j] 1920–33	4	0	0	3	0	1	2	−2.8	−1.1
	4	0	0	1	2	1	2	+0.5	
FURNITURE[j] 1924–38	3	0	1	2	1	0	2	−2.7	−0.4
	4	0	1	2	0	2	3	+1.2	
STEEL SHEETS[h] 1919–33	4	0	0	2	1	1	3	+0.2	+0.4
	5	0	0	2	2	1	4	+0.6	
FOUNDRY EQUIPMENT[g] 1926–38	3	0	0	0	0	3	1	+4.7	+3.2
	3	0	0	1	0	2	2	+1.7	
ELECTRIC OVERHEAD CRANES[g] 1927–38	2	0	1	0	0	2	0	+4.5	+3.8
	3	0	1	0	0	3	2	+3.3	
TRANSPORTATION EQUIPMENT[j] 1920–33	3	1	0	1	0	2	1	+2.0	+4.5
	3	1	0	0	0	3	1	+7.0	
Total									
Peaks	65	6	16	47	3	15	26		
Troughs	70	6	16	34	7	29	38		
All turns	135	12	32	81	10	44	64		

Notes to Table 11-15

Note: For each series, the entries on the first line in columns 2–9 are for peaks; the entries on the second line, for troughs.

ᵃ Ranked by the length of the average lead, all turns (column 10), from longest to shortest.

ᵇ Identifies the first and last reference turn that could be matched by the given series.

ᶜ Number of recorded timing comparisons (leads, lags, and coincidences) at business cycle peaks and troughs.

ᵈ Number of business cycle peaks and troughs that are not matched by cyclical turns in the given series. Corresponding entries in columns 2 and 3 add up to the number of business cycle peaks or troughs covered.

ᵉ Number of specific-cycle peaks or troughs in the given series that do not match business cycle peaks or troughs. Corresponding entries in columns 2 and 4 add up to the number of new-order peaks or troughs covered.

ᶠ Includes exact coincidences and leads and lags of one, two, and three months.

ᵍ In current dollars.

ʰ In tons.

ⁱ Number.

ʲ Components of an index, 1923–25 = 100, based on data in physical units.

ᵏ In board feet.

ˡ Number of production days; based on data in value terms.

short leads at the interwar recessions. At revivals, short leads dominate in the postwar period and short lags or coincidences in the interwar period.

All but five of the sixteen series had a downturn (upturn) at each business cycle peak (trough) covered. It appears that unfilled orders for a variety of products rarely fail to participate in a general recession or revival. Some of the series show relatively frequent "extra" turns that imply additional movements shorter than the phases of the business cycle and in opposite direction. These episodes are concentrated in periods of widespread acceleration and retardation of economic activities, during which many different series had extra movements.[29] The average percentage of business cycle turns matched is 92; that of the specific-cycle turns matched is 81. According to these measures, no significant differences seem to exist between peaks and troughs; all but three of the series can be said to have had a good conformity record at either turn.

[29] Extra peaks occurred mainly in 1933–34, 1941–42, and 1950–51; extra troughs, in 1934–35, 1942–44, and 1951. These periods include the "double-bottom" configuration of the early thirties, some particular developments during World War II, and the mild "Korean cycle."

First-Difference Series

While the monthly series of order backlogs for various manufacturing industries are on the whole remarkably smooth, differencing transforms them into series of monthly changes that are typically very erratic. However, longer movements of the specific-cycle type are also definitely recognizable in several of these backlog-change series, even though they are overlaid and somewhat obscured by the short, irregular oscillations (which probably reflect mainly errors of measurement that are brought into sharp focus through the differencing procedure). The largest movements occurred during World War II and the Korean War, with sharp peaks in 1942 and 1951 (Chart 11-2). Smaller cycles appear in the series for all manufacturing and all durable goods industries in 1945–47, 1947–49, 1953–58, 1958–60, and 1960–67. Allowing for the pronounced tendency of the series to lead, all business cycle peaks and troughs in this period are matched by the like turns in these fluctuations. In addition, there are "extra" specific-cycle movements and turns in these series, associated with the business retardations of 1947 and 1966–67. Only in the early sixties did the changes in order backlogs show a prolonged hesitancy, in the form of very slow drifts from small negative to small positive values.

The first-difference series for the major component industries of the durable goods sector disclose similar cyclical patterns in the first decade covered (beginning in 1948). Negative values of ΔU prevail in each of the recessions, 1948–49, 1953–54, and 1957–58. Sharp peaks on the positive side show up during the Korean War period in 1950–51 and are followed by steep declines interrupted by small secondary rises in the first half of 1952. Generally lower positive values are observed at the height of the next expansion, in 1955–56, reflecting the prevalence of downward trends in backlogs during the 1950's. In particular, fabricated metal products and the group of other durables show only small and sporadic positive values of ΔU during the 1955–56 boom. The short and rather weak rise of business activity in 1958–60 leaves less of an imprint on these series, except for sharp fluctuations in primary metals due to the anticipations and effects of the 1959 steel strike. Several of the ΔU series in the early sixties look just like predominantly random short oscillations about the zero level with varying amplitudes. The declines in 1966 and again in 1969–70 (which

Chart 11-2

Month-to-month Change in Manufacturers' Unfilled Orders, Durable Goods Industries, 1939–67

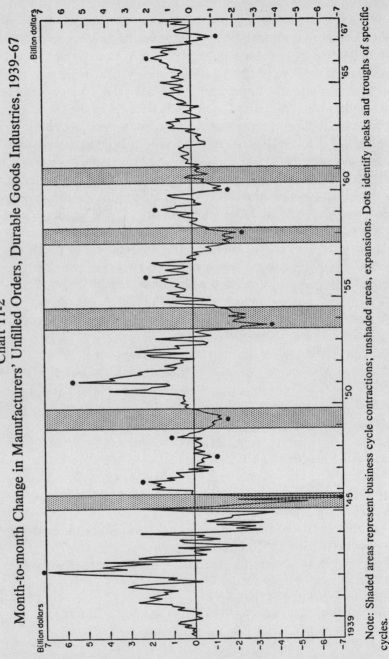

Note: Shaded areas represent business cycle contractions; unshaded areas, expansions. Dots identify peaks and troughs of specific cycles.

began in the last quarter of 1968) are definitely cyclical in most of these series.

It appears that systematic elements are apparently most difficult to discern in the ΔU of those industries which produce mostly to stock and have, therefore, relatively small backlogs. These include the lumber products and the stone, clay, and glass products industries in the "other durables" group and also the nondurable goods industries reporting unfilled orders (textiles, leather, paper, and printing and publishing).

As long as new orders rise more rapidly than shipments, the rate of change in the backlog of unfilled orders (ΔU) will be increasing. But before turning down, new orders are likely to show an increase slower than that of shipments (whose expansion is not as yet so advanced). When this happens, ΔU will be at its peak. This suggests a lead of ΔU relative to N, and therefore often a long lead of ΔU at business cycle peaks. Moreover, another influential factor that can work in the same direction is the size of the total backlog. If unfilled orders have accumulated to large volumes in the expansion, they can sustain a rise in production even after a downturn in currently received orders. Hence, their lead relative to output and shipments is likely to be long. In such cases, then, the lead of ΔU will be long a fortiori.

Confirming evidence is provided below by the timing measures for the change in backlogs of durable goods orders (OBE-Census). These

Reference Peak	Lead (−) of ΔU (mos.)	Reference Trough	Lead (−) of ΔU (mos.)
Feb. 1945	−35	Oct. 1945	−2
Nov. 1948	−5	Oct. 1949	−6
July 1953	−30	Aug. 1954	−11
July 1957	−19	Apr. 1958	−3
May 1960	−15	Feb. 1961	−13
Av.	−20.8	Av.	−7.0
Av. dev.	9.4	Av. dev.	4.0

leads are much longer than those of new orders.[30] There is some indication that the peak leads have, here too, undergone some reduction in

---

[30] The corresponding averages for peaks (1948–60) are −10.2 for N and −17.2 for U. The averages for N and U at troughs (1949–61) are −4.8 and −8.2.

the recent years.[31] The results for total manufacturing are similar. Further documentation, consistent with the same general conclusions, is given in Table 11-16, which shows estimates of the timing of ΔU based on the current Census data for major durable goods industries. Finally, considerable support for our expectations concerning the cyclical timing of ΔU comes from the historical data on order backlogs of the U.S. Steel Corporation (first introduced in Chapter 6). Chart 11-3 presents quarterly first differences in this series (the data were reported quarterly during 1902–10 and monthly during 1911–33). As would be expected, the series (particularly in monthly terms) has a large irregular component, yet it has clearly undergone several longer cyclical movements. Measured trough to trough, six of these major fluctuations stand out. The last of these waves can be divided into two parts (1923–27 and 1927–33), though with some uncertainty since these movements are shallow and obscured by the short, small oscillations around the zero level that dominate this segment of the series.[32]

There is no doubt about the tendency of ΔU for steel products to lead at both the peaks and the troughs of business cycles. The leads are on the average long, even at troughs.[33] They vary greatly, from some in the range of rough coincidences to several exceeding a year or even two. The longest ones, of 27 and 33 months, are associated with the downturns of 1907 and 1918, which terminated the two longest business expansions in the period here covered. On both occasions, large backlog accumulations accompanied major upswings in the economy. In 1917–18 high wartime demand for steel had apparently caused an early downturn and a substantial depletion of the backlogs despite persistently high levels of steel output (Chart 6-1).

[31] The short lead at the November 1948 peak may appear surprising, but it is based on a secondary downturn in ΔU, terminating a mild rise in this series between mid-1947 and mid-1948; the basic trend in ΔU has been downward since 1946. The major peak in 1946 preceded the 1948 recession by 30 months.

The long lead at the July 1953 peak, on the other hand, can be questioned because it covers the entire decline in ΔU after the huge backlog accumulation during the first three quarters of the Korean War. This decline was interrupted by secondary gains in ΔU during the first half of 1952. Using the high value of ΔU in June 1952 to match the 1953 reference date would result in a lead of 13 months (see Chart 11-2).

[32] The series of backlog *levels* (Chart 6-1) has unmistakably passed through two specific cycles in the same years, but these movements were relatively small (except for the decline in 1930–31). It should be recalled that unfilled orders declined substantially and were generally rather small relative to production in the middle and late twenties.

[33] The mean of the leads of ΔU at the eight recessions of 1907–29 is −12.5 months. Omitting the last two observations, which are relatively uncertain, leaves the average unchanged. The mean of the leads at the nine revivals of 1904–33 is −10.3; excluding the last two observations again makes little difference (it reduces the average slightly, to −9.7).

Table 11-16

Timing of Changes in Unfilled Orders at Each Business Cycle Turn,
Seven Major Durable Goods Industries, 1954–61

| Industry | Lead (−) or Lag (+), in Months, of Backlog Change at Business Cycle Turn | | | | | Av. Lead (−) or Lag (+), in Months | |
	Trough Aug. 1954	Peak July 1957	Trough Apr. 1958	Peak May 1960	Trough Feb. 1961	Peaks	Troughs
Primary metals	−10	−28 [a]	−3	−7	−11	−17.5	−8.0
Blast furnaces, steel mills	−10	−28 [a]	−4	−7	−11	−17.5	−8.3
Fabricated metal products	−14	−21 [a]	−5	−6 [b]	−8 [b]	−13.5	−9.0
Electrical machinery	−5	−28	−8	−11 [b]	−13 [b]	−19.5	−8.7
Machinery except electrical	−6	−20	−4	−14	−7	−17.0	−5.7
Transportation equipment	−11	−19 [a]	−6	n.t.	n.t.	[c]	−8.5
Other durable goods	−9	−23	−3	−16 [b]	−10 [b]	−19.5	−7.3

n.t. = no turn.

[a] Based on specific-cycle peaks in 1955. Sharp but isolated peaks in mid-1956, due to large orders for defense products, are disregarded.

[b] Timing particularly uncertain and difficult to establish.

[c] Only one observation is available.

Chart 11-3

Quarter-to-quarter Change in Unfilled Orders of U.S. Steel Corporation, 1902–33

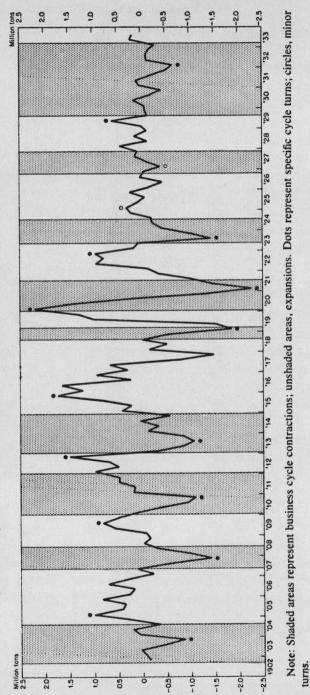

Note: Shaded areas represent business cycle contractions; unshaded areas, expansions. Dots represent specific cycle turns; circles, minor turns.

In other business expansions that also rank high in relative magnitude, 1908–10 and 1921–23,[34] unfilled orders for steel products show smaller rises and the leads of ΔU at peaks are not very long. Steel production increased at particularly high rates in each of these periods, which probably provides a part of the explanation. These were short but vigorous upswings that followed upon fairly severe contractions during which backlogs fell to low levels. It may be helpful to recall that the amplitudes of business expansions are positively correlated with the amplitudes of the preceding (but not of the following) contractions.[35]

Summary

Comprehensive series show that new orders received by durable goods manufacturers led at each business cycle turn of the period 1921–70. Total advance orders (excluding those industries for which order backlogs are not reported) behaved similarly. The leads were, on the average, shorter at the troughs than at the peaks of the cycle—about five and eight months, respectively.

The tendency to anticipate business cycle turns with substantial regularity is shown by the less aggregative series on new orders of the component manufacturing industries. However, the leads of these series varied substantially from turn to turn. They were generally rather long at the recessions of 1957 and 1960 and at the revival of 1954, but tended to be short at the other revivals and at the recessions of 1948 and 1953 (according to preliminary results, probably also at the tentatively dated peak of 1970). For each major industry and for a large majority of the subdivisions, the average lead of new orders was longer at business cycle peaks than at troughs in the postwar periods for which such records can be established.

The new data for market categories confirm the leads of new orders, but they also reveal some rather marked differences in cyclical con-

---

[34] For a ranking of business expansions and contractions according to relative magnitude, based on the average rise and fall in three indexes of business activity, see "Leading and Confirming Indicators of General Business Changes," in Moore, ed., *Business Cycle Indicators*, Vol. I, pp. 91 and 104.

[35] See *ibid.*, pp. 86–93. Another episode that obviously illustrates the same correlation is the sequence of a mild contraction and moderate recovery in 1926–29. Both output and unfilled orders for steel had weak declines followed by weak rises in this period.

formities. The series for machinery and equipment and for materials, supplies, and intermediate products score high on conformity. Very low scores go to nondurable consumer goods, primarily staples made to stock. Automotive orders (differing little from shipments) show turning points that correspond to business cycle peaks and troughs but also marked extra movements. Defense orders are the most erratic, with large autonomous fluctuations.

The early cyclical movements of new orders are still more widely diffused than these series for major industries and their main components would suggest. Leads prevail over lags and coincidences for each item in a fairly large and varied collection of series for individual industries and products. These series cover different periods between 1937 and 1957 but give the best representation to the interwar years. Most of the average leads of new orders fall in the range of three to nine months, according to these data. The leads are in most cases longer at business peaks than at troughs. Their frequencies are generally too high to be attributable to change. Leads at business cycle turns are characteristic of both new orders and shipments (N and S) in some industries that customarily fill their orders on receipt or on short notice.

For these individual series of new orders, too, the over-all degree of conformity to business cycles is high. The series have rarely "skipped" business cycle turns by failing to reverse their own movement in correspondence with a general revival or recession. More frequently they (like the more aggregative series) show "extra" turns, which mark sizable movements that do not match business expansions or contractions. But again, the frequencies of conforming movements are, with few exceptions, too high to be attributable to chance.

For any period, the cyclical timing of S is determined by the cyclical timing of N and the delivery lag (of S behind N). Cyclical fluctuations in aggregate demand may impart considerable similarity to the timing of major turns in many new-order series. The dispersion of cyclical turning points could well be greater for the corresponding series on production and shipments because of the variation in delivery periods among different industries and products. However, convergent and approximately correct anticipations of buyers would work in the opposite direction; e.g., expectations of a recession may cause purchasers of items with long (short) delivery periods to curtail their orders early (late).

Timing dispersion was measured at each of the recessions and revivals covered, for all available sets of paired series on N and S. The evidence for the more aggregative data (several industry and market-group classifications) does not refute the hypothesis that the turning points in new orders are usually more concentrated in time than those of shipments. However, the results here are fairly weak, mainly because the corresponding dispersion figures are often large and not significantly different for N and S. The evidence for the individual series, on the other hand, supports the hypothesis rather strongly, since the dispersion of leads and lags for these was greater for S than for N at nine of the eleven business cycle turns of the interwar period.

Unfilled orders were generally small and their cyclical timing was roughly coincident during the interwar period, judging from a sample of series for individual industries. Subsequently, as shown both by these data and the major-industry aggregates, manufacturers' backlogs of orders grew large and led by long intervals at business cycle peaks, while continuing to be approximately coincident at troughs. The leads were exceedingly long at the recessions of the forties, but were much shorter at the more recent business downturns, from 1953 or 1957 on. These results recall the timing comparisons of unfilled orders with shipments and can be similarly interpreted.

Series on the change in backlogs anticipate both peaks and troughs of the cycle. These leads are often very long, particularly in the late stages of major business expansions, when they signal slowdowns in the rise of new orders that occur well in advance of any slowdowns in the rise of production.

12

PATTERNS AND DIFFUSION
OF CYCLICAL MOVEMENTS

IN THIS CHAPTER, the analysis of the behavior of manufacturers' orders during business cycles is completed and is related to cyclical changes in several variables representing production, the successive stages of business investment, and financing. The measures presented refer to stages of general economic fluctuations. They are designed to distill the major features of those changes in the processes described that occur during expansions, downturns, contractions, and upturns of the economy at large. The focus is on typical patterns, but in some cases the deviations from them in individual historical episodes are also examined. Attention is given particularly to certain factors that are presumed to contribute to the early downturns and upturns in orders and contracts for plant and equipment and in purchases of materials and supplies.

In addition, in this chapter the diffusion of new orders is considered, that is, how the movements in them spread among the different industries during business expansions and contractions. This analysis shows systematic early changes in the scope of the demand for industrial products and how these changes are related to those in the diffusion of production and some other activities.

Manufacturers' Orders and Production
During Business Cycles

Reference Cycle Patterns for Durable Goods Aggregates
Reference cycle patterns provide an instructive device for describing the movements of a series during business cycles. They are similar

to the specific-cycle patterns presented in Chapter 3, but are computed for periods defined by major fluctuations in aggregate economic activity rather than in the particular processes represented by the given series.[1]

Chart 12-1 presents the patterns for new orders received by durable goods manufacturers. It is based on the three compilations of order data described in the preceding chapter (see Chart 11-1 and the text) and covers each of the nine business cycles of the four decades 1921–61. As noted before, the data for the earlier years have a rather narrow coverage, and this limits the comparability of interwar and postwar patterns. A joint evaluation of these measures is thereby impaired but not entirely invalidated.[2]

The huge movements of the thirties stand out conspicuously in two of the patterns: The 1927–33 cycle is dominated by a long and steep decline; and the 1933–38 cycle, by the protracted rise from the nadir of the depression. The pattern for the war cycle, 1938–45, shows another fluctuation of extraordinarily large amplitude. Although the expansion part of this cycle lasted eighty months and the contraction only eight months, the rapid fall of orders in the latter phase matched the amplitude of their rise in the former phase. Relative to their average levels in each episode, new orders for durable goods fluctuated much less during the other business cycles covered. However, their rises during the early expansion stages in the cycle of 1921–24 and again in the two cycles of 1945–54 were vigorous enough; it was the ensuing declines that were brief and shallow. Very mild fluctuations, with shorter rises and longer declines, characterized the behavior of durables orders in the 1924–27 cycle and the two recent cycles of 1954–61.

[1] The series is divided into segments, each of which covers one business ("reference") cycle usually dated from the initial to the final trough. A pattern is computed for each of these successive reference segments. It consists of nine figures, one for each of the consecutive stages of the reference cycle. Stages I, V, and IX are three-month periods centered on the initial, middle, and terminal turns of a business cycle, respectively. Stages II, III, and IV cover successive thirds of the expansion, and stages VI, VII, and VIII cover similar portions of the contraction. All measures are in "reference cycle relatives"—percentages of the average standing of the data during the given business cycle. Thus the construction of a reference cycle pattern is fully analogous to the construction of a specific-cycle pattern (cf. Chapter 3, note 34). For full discussion of the method, see A. F. Burns and W. C. Mitchell, *Measuring Business Cycles,* New York, NBER, 1946, pp. 160–70.

[2] The Commerce-NBER index, mainly reflecting new orders for steel, lumber, and textile products, covers the three cycles of 1921–33. Its behavior in 1929–33 resembled rather well the concurrent behavior of the broader NICB index (Chart 11-1). The NICB index is used in the pattern for the 1933–38 cycle, and the aggregative OBE-Census series cover the five cycles of 1938–61. (The NICB index for 1929–38 was linked to the OBE data, which go back to 1939, by converting the former to a series in millions of current dollars through multiplication by a level-adjustment factor of 18.303.) Considerable similarity is also observed in the movements of the NICB index and the OBE series through most of their overlap period, that is, 1939–41.

Chart 12-1 also confirms the familiar tendency of new orders for durable goods to turn ahead of business cycle peaks and troughs, although some of the leads observed in the monthly data are too short to register as cycle stages. Leads of one to three stages account for six of the nine comparisons at peaks, and leads of one to two stages account for seven of the nine comparisons at troughs.[3]

The nine-point pattern computed by averaging the individual reference cycle patterns of a series stage by stage is designed to bring out the typical features in the behavior of the activity concerned during the business cycle. The assumption of the procedure is that cyclical behavior does have such persistent traits and that they are important; the more valid this assumption is, the more useful the method.

Averages of the single-cycle patterns of new orders (N) of durable goods manufacturers for three selected subperiods and for the total period covered are shown in Chart 12-2, together with the corresponding average patterns for production (Z). The typical expansion interval for new orders covers stages VIII–IV in each case, which involves one-stage leads at both peaks and troughs.[4] The typical expansion interval in production is I–V throughout, which means average simultaneous-stage timing in each subperiod. The correspondence of the patterns for N and Z is impressively close.

Since the specific-cycle amplitudes are typically larger for new orders than for production, one may expect an analogous relationship between the amplitudes of the average reference cycle patterns; but this need not be so, because of timing differences. The average pattern for the postwar cycles in new orders does have a larger rise-and-fall amplitude than its counterpart for production (the figures in reference cycle relatives are 57 and 47, respectively). In some of the earlier cycles this does not hold, but this could be because the series do not strictly correspond.

Comprehensive coverage of manufacturers' unfilled orders is avail-

---

[3] It should be clear that the reference cycle patterns can provide only a general picture of how the major fluctuations in a given series are timed relative to the business cycles, and a rather imprecise and difficult-to-interpret picture at that. This is because the reference cycle stages are often too long for a sensitive timing analysis and, particularly, because they differ in duration as do the individual business cycles. Measures in fixed calendar-time units are therefore definitely preferable for timing studies, and my use of reference cycle patterns for this purpose is strictly peripheral.

[4] When the 1945–49 cycle, which includes the early postwar reconversion period, is excluded, a two-stage lead at the peak is obtained in the average pattern for 1949–61 (i.e., the typical expansion interval for the most recent cycles is VIII–III).

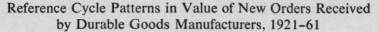

Chart 12-1
Reference Cycle Patterns in Value of New Orders Received
by Durable Goods Manufacturers, 1921–61

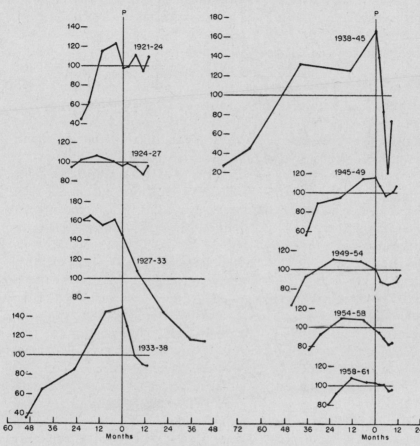

able only for the post-World War II period. Chart 12-3 shows the be-havior of total backlogs of durable goods orders in the four reference cycles of the period 1945–61. The patterns characteristically increase in stages I–IV (but the expansion phase includes only stages I–III in the 1945–49 cycle and only stages II–IV in the 1958–61 cycle). As a corollary, declines in the patterns typically extend at least through the interval between stages IV and IX.

The facts implied by these diagrams have already been encountered earlier in this study, although they were brought out by different

Chart 12-2
Average Reference Cycle Patterns in New Orders and
Production of Durable Goods Manufacturers,
1921–38 and 1945–61

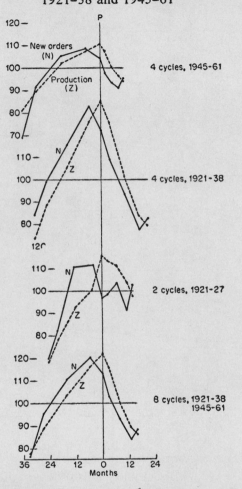

methods and in different forms. Clearly, backlogs of durables orders turned down early at the recent business recessions. Here it is shown that their leads amounted to one or two long expansion stages. At troughs, the timing of the backlogs was in these terms coincident. The patterns retain the intracycle trends, which were downward in the first and last of these episodes. Their amplitudes are large, except for the 1958–61 cycle.

Chart 12-3
Reference Cycle Patterns in Manufacturers' Unfilled Orders, Durable Goods Industries, 1945–61

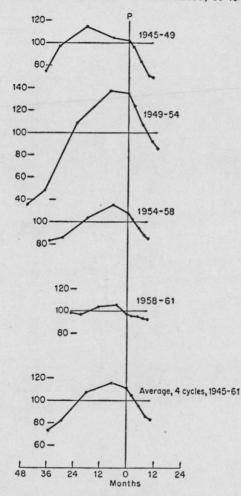

Summary Measures for Selected Products

Chart 12-4 presents average reference patterns for twenty-six series on new orders, production, and shipments, divided into eleven groups for as many commodities. Comparability is assured in that the graphs for the same product cover the same business cycles. The data are for 1919–38. The horizontal scales are drawn up uniformly, ignoring the differences in duration between the cycles covered by the averages.

Chart 12-4
Average Reference Cycle Patterns in New Orders, Production, and Shipments, Eleven Commodities, 1919–38

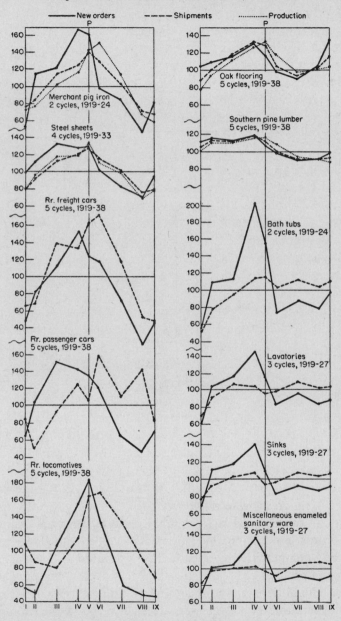

A close look at the chart reveals that in most cases new orders exceed shipments and production in the average amplitude of their movements during business cycles (all patterns are drawn to the same vertical scale). In some instances the differences are very pronounced, in others small (e.g., compare the patterns for locomotives with those for steel sheets). The patterns on the left-hand side of the chart have larger amplitudes on the whole than those on the right. The left-hand patterns represent in part goods made largely to the specifications of industrial buyers and in part heavy equipment produced only upon advance orders. Those on the right represent staples made for sale to builders.

Numerical measures supporting the visual impressions conveyed by Chart 12-4 are presented in Table 12-1. The average reference cycle amplitude (column 3) is computed from the standings of the series in its typical trough and peak stages, as identified in column 2.[5] This figure is in each case smaller than the corresponding measure of the average specific-cycle amplitude (cf. columns 3 and 4). The ratios of the two measures (column 5) roughly indicate the closeness of the relation in time between the specific cycles of a series and the cycles in general business.

Fluctuations in new orders exceed those in shipments and production not only in specific-cycle but also in reference cycle measurements (columns 6 and 7). The three exceptions to this rule (lines 10, 14, and 15) can be traced to loose relationships between the business cycles and specific cycles of the series involved.

Comparisons of the typical expansion intervals in column 2 indicate that new orders for railroad equipment and metal products, which are made to order, led production and shipments by one or two (in one case by three) reference stages. On the other hand, the timing of new orders for the staples used in construction (lines 13–24) was in terms of reference cycle stages coincident with the timing of output and deliveries.[6]

---

[5] Each entry in column 3 is the sum of two average amplitude measures, one for the phase matched with expansions and the other for the phase matched with contractions, with signs disregarded. Cf. Wesley C. Mitchell, *What Happens During Business Cycles: A Progress Report,* New York, NBER, 1951, pp. 51–52 and 100–102.

[6] According to Table 12-1, column 2, eight types of division of reference cycles into "expansion" and "contraction" are found for the series included (the total number of possible divisions in 24; of the schemes that are not represented, all but four indicate typical *lags* at business revivals and/or recessions). It is clear from these calculations that all new-order series lead at both peaks and troughs, while for the series on shipments and production as a group, only half of the measures indicate leads.

Table 12-1

Typical Expansion Intervals and Average Cyclical Amplitudes of New Orders, Shipments, and Production, Ten Commodities, 1919–38

Commodity, Reference Cycle Period, and Series [a]	Specific-Cycle Period [b] (1)	Expansion Interval [c] (2)	Average Amplitude, rise + fall (reference cycle relatives)		Ratios of Average Amplitudes (per cent)			
			Reference Cycles [d] (3)	Specific Cycles [e] (4)	Ref. Cycles to Specific Cycles [f] (5)	Shipments or Prod. to New Orders		
						Ref. Cycles [g] (6)	Spec. Cycles [b] (7)	
MERCHANT PIG IRON, 1919–24 (2)								
1. New orders	1919–24 (2)	VIII–IV	262.0	373.8	70.1			
2. Shipments	1919–24 (2)	I–V	135.1	162.6	83.1	51.6	43.5	
3. Production	1919–24 (2)	I–V	149.7	200.4	74.7	57.1	53.6	
STEEL SHEETS, 1919–33 (4)								
4. New orders	1919–32 (4)	VIII–III	120.7	187.9	64.2			
5. Shipments	1919–32 (4)	I–V	100.3	130.4	76.9	83.1	69.4	
6. Production	1919–33 (4)	VIII–V	115.9	154.8	74.9	96.0	82.4	
FREIGHT CARS, 1919–38 (5)								
7. New orders	1919–38 (7)	VIII–IV	249.4	571.4	43.6			
8. Shipments	1919–38 (6)	I–V	209.9	540.6	38.8	84.2	94.6	

RAILROAD PASSENGER CARS, 1919–38 (5)

9. New orders	1919–37 (7)	VIII–IV	196.0	498.0	39.4		
10. Shipments	1919–39 (6)	I–V	39.2	557.3	7.0	20.0	111.9
RAILROAD LOCOMOTIVES, 1919–38 (5)							
11. New orders	1919–37 (7)	VIII–IV	214.4	537.6	39.9		
12. Shipments	1920–38 (6)	III–VI	152.1	328.2	46.3	70.9	61.0
OAK FLOORING, 1919–38 (5)							
13. New orders	1920–37 (5)	VII–III	64.3	194.9	33.0		
14. Shipments	1920–37 (5)	VII–IV	88.7	145.3	61.0	137.9	74.6
15. Production	1921–38 (4)	VII–IV	77.6	148.7	63.8	120.7	76.3
SOUTHERN PINE LUMBER, 1919–38 (5)							
16. New orders	1920–37 (5)	VII–IV	50.7	106.7	47.5		
17. Shipments	1919–38 (6)	VII–IV	41.6	83.0	50.1	82.0	77.8
18. Production	1918–38 (5)	I–IV	44.1	84.0	52.5	87.0	78.7
BATH TUBS, 1919–24 (2)							
19. New orders	1918–23 (2)	VIII–IV	295.6	381.1	77.6		
20. Shipments	1918–24 (2)	VIII–IV	86.1	156.4	55.0	29.1	41.0
LAVATORIES, 1919–27 (3)							
21. New orders	1918–28 (3)	VIII–IV	156.6	226.7	69.1		
22. Shipments	1919–24 (2)	VIII–IV	44.0	160.4	27.4	28.1	70.8
SINKS, 1919–27 (3)							
23. New orders	1918–28 (3)	VIII–IV	135.2	209.0	64.7		
24. Shipments	1919–24 (2)	VIII–IV	40.6	148.2	27.4	30.0	70.9

597

Notes to Table 12-1

ᵃ The same series are included as in Chart 12-3, except for new orders and shipments of miscellaneous enameled sanitary ware (each of these series covers one complete specific cycle only). The longest reference cycle period covered by each of the series (new orders, shipments and, wherever available, production) relating to the same commodity is the one shown. The number of cycles covered is shown in parentheses.

ᵇ The specific-cycle periods listed are those that best match the reference cycle period for the given commodity. The number of cycles covered is shown in parentheses.

ᶜ Each expansion interval is based on the patterns for *all* reference cycles covered by the given series (as of the time the series was analyzed in the business cycle unit of the National Bureau). The intervals for the following series are based on longer reference-cycle periods than those listed in the table.

New orders: Railroad freight cars, 1879–1938, 16 reference cycles (the expansion interval for the six reference cycles, 1914–38, is also VIII–IV, however); railroad passenger cars, 1870–1938, 17 reference cycles; railroad locomotives, 1879–1938, 16 reference cycles; oak flooring, 1914–38, 6 reference cycles.

Shipments: Oak flooring, 1914–38, 6 reference cycles.

Production: Oak flooring, 1919–49, 7 reference cycles.

ᵈ Based on the reference-cycle periods listed in the table beside the commodity name.

ᵉ Based on the specific-cycle periods listed in column 1.

ᶠ Percentage ratio of the corresponding entries in columns 3 and 4. [= (average reference cycle amplitude ÷ average specific-cycle amplitude) × 100].

ᵍ Average reference cycle amplitude of shipments or production as percentage of average reference cycle amplitude of new orders. Based on corresponding entries in column 3.

ʰ Average specific-cycle amplitude of shipments or production as percentage of average specific-cycle amplitude of new orders. Based on corresponding entries in column 4.

For additional historical perspective, Chart 12-5 shows the reference cycle patterns for unfilled orders of the U.S. Steel Corporation and for steel ingot production, 1904–33. These patterns indicate that new orders for steel must have been increasing in each expansion and decreasing in each contraction at rates substantially exceeding those of output and shipments. The change in backlogs of steel orders was typically positive in expansions and negative in contractions, and these cyclical movements were usually large. This confirms the familiar thesis that the effective demand for steel has long been very sensitive to fluctuations in aggregate economic activity.

The steel industry produces thousands of products, most of which are made according to buyers' specifications regarding shape, dimension, and chemical composition. To the diversity of these made-to-order items corresponds a diversity of their prices and other sales

Chart 12-5
Reference Cycle Patterns in Unfilled Orders of U.S. Steel Corporation and in Steel Ingot Production, 1904–33

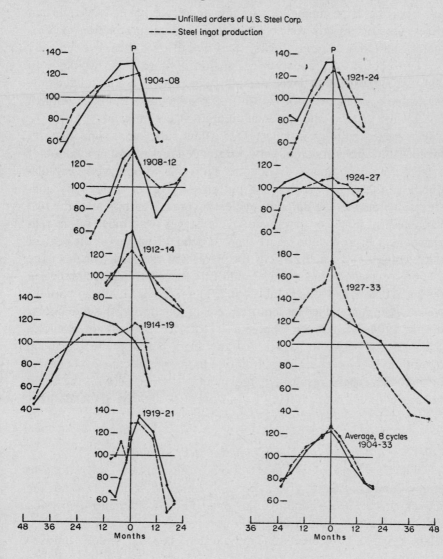

terms including delivery periods. The movements of quantities demanded and produced are no doubt far from simultaneous for these different products; yet their confluence is apparently pronounced, judging from the large amplitudes of the aggregate patterns. At certain times, steel users buy well beyond their current production requirements and build up large stocks; steel output rises then, but typically not fast enough to prevent an expansion in steel order backlogs. In contrast to these boom developments, users' stocks are liquidated during a slump, and current orders shrink; production is cut back, though not as much, eating into the accumulated orders on hand.

The paired patterns in Chart 12-5 show substantial similarity, reflecting the high correlation between unfilled orders and production of steel during each successive cycle. This can be observed very distinctly in the chart, because the patterns for either series vary considerably between the different cycles covered. The timing of the two variables in terms of reference cycle stages was most often synchronous, but production clearly lagged behind backlogs at the peak of the 1914–19 cycle and at both the peak and terminal trough of the 1924–27 cycle. The lag at the height of the large backlog accumulation during World War I was notably long. The reference cycle amplitudes were larger for unfilled orders than for production in the five cycles during 1904–21, but the opposite is true for the last three cycles covered (1921–33). In particular, steel ingot output fluctuated much more than U.S. Steel backlogs (relative to their respective cycle bases) in 1927–33. These results are presumably connected with the trend toward hand-to-mouth buying in the twenties and the associated decrease in the size and role of the backlogs.

Diffusion of Changes in New Orders and Production

Timing analysis reveals that various series on new orders tend to expand and contract at about the same time and in conformity to the movements of the economy at large. Yet considerable dispersion among the corresponding turning points in these series is also evident. Thus cyclical movements in new orders become widely diffused throughout the manufacturing sector of the economy, but it takes time for them to spread from one commodity, firm, industry, or region to another.

How they spread can be summarized by means of diffusion indexes, which can be constructed in various ways. A simple measure of diffusion records only the direction, and not the magnitude, of changes in the component series. It shows in percentage form how many of these series expand at a given time. Two methods of determining when a series is expanding are in use: (1) Historically, specific-cycle expansions and contractions in the series can be dated and used; or, (2) on a more current basis, rises in moving averages of the series can be defined as expansions; and falls, as contractions. Each method presents its own problems and has its own limitations.[7]

Diffusion indexes based on series that reach their peaks and troughs in the vicinity of downturns and upturns in aggregate economic activity (and not much later) persistently lead at these business revivals and recessions, although by variable intervals.[8] Clearly, a diffusion index built from series which lead the reference dates (e.g., new orders) should itself show longer leads than an index representing tardier activities (e.g., production or shipments).

Many diffusion indexes based on short-period moving averages are very choppy. This occurs clearly in indexes computed from data with large, short fluctuations, such as the individual new-order series. Cumulation provides an effective way of suppressing the smaller irregular movements and bringing out the larger cyclical movements in these diffusion indexes. To be sure, the method also reduces substan-

[7] In an historical index (1), a positively conforming series is said to expand in each month that falls between a specific trough and a specific peak in the data; it is said to contract in each month situated between a peak and a trough. This is a simple principle designed radically to smooth out all movements shorter than cyclical, but dating the specific cycles often involves considerable uncertainty. The alternative (2) is to smooth the seasonally adjusted component series by means of moving averages, so as to reduce their irregular, and bring out their cyclical, components. Month-to-month increases or decreases in the smoothed series would then be taken to indicate cyclical expansion and contraction.

For further explanation of these and other measures of diffusion, and applications to new orders and related data, see Victor Zarnowitz, "The Timing of Manufacturers' Orders During Business Cycles." in Geoffrey H. Moore. ed.. Business Cycle Indicators. Princeton for NBER. 1961. Vol. I, pp. 459–73.

[8] Some time prior to the culmination of business expansion the percentage of series reaching peaks begins to exceed the percentage of series reaching troughs, and when this develops the proportion of series expanding starts declining. It does not turn up again until the percentage reaching troughs exceeds that reaching peaks, which happens some time before the central month of the business contraction. This explains the diffusion lead in general terms. Depending on the duration of the "zones" of peaks and troughs and the graduation of the transitions between them, indexes of diffusion will show more or less continuous cyclical fluctuations. See Arthur F. Burns, "New Facts on Business Cycles," in Moore, ed., Business Cycle Indicators, Vol. I, pp. 13–44.

tially the leads of the indexes at business cycle turns.[9] Nevertheless, the diffusion indexes of new orders retain a comfortable lead even after cumulation, as illustrated in Chart 12-6.

The first curve in this chart represents an index based on Commerce series on new orders for twenty-three manufacturing industries. The second shows the diffusion of changes in twenty-four components of the Federal Reserve Board index of industrial production.[10] The strong difference in trends between the two curves is due to technical factors and is of no real interest.[11] The indicated one-to-one correspondence between the diffusion cycles in new orders and production, however, is confirmed by other measures, and I am prepared to accept it as a "real" and significant phenomenon. The movements of new orders preceded those of output at peaks, with leads ranging from two to six months and averaging four. At troughs, the timing of the two indexes was nearly synchronous. It is possible that these comparisons somewhat understate the diffusion index lead of new orders relative to production.[12]

The third and fourth curves in Chart 12-6 record the results of the monthly business survey of the National Association of Purchasing Agents (NAPA) on new orders and production. These indexes are based on 200–225 member reports that reflect in general the conditions in the firms with which the respondents are associated; they are presumably directly comparable, being compiled from materials with a

[9] The cumulated figures are derived by taking the deviations of percentage expanding from 50, or the deviations of the average duration of run from 0, and adding each month's deviation to the sum of the deviations for all preceding months. Hence the peaks in the cumulated figures occur when the deviations shift from positive to negative, and the troughs when they shift from negative to positive.

[10] The production series cover ten durable goods and ten nondurable goods industries as well as four minerals; consequently, the combined weight of the durables is much less here than in the new-order index, which includes the series for the nondurable goods aggregates with and without unfilled orders but mainly reflects the behavior of durables. Month-to-month changes in seasonally adjusted production series (1957–59 = 100) are used, whereas three-month moving averages are applied to the more volatile new-order series.

[11] In the early fifties, new orders contracted while production experienced only a temporary retardation in several industries. Thus the percentage expanding of the new-order series declined below 50 more often in 1951 than did the corresponding measure for the output series, and then, in 1952–53, exceeded that level by smaller margins. This accounts for the stronger upward trend in the output index compared to the new-order index.

[12] The figures for new orders involve considerable smoothing, while those for production do not. One effect of smoothing is to shift the turning points to later dates, thereby reducing the length of the measured leads compared to the true leads. In earlier work, I used somewhat differently constructed indexes of cumulated percentage expanding, which yielded short leads of new orders vis-à-vis output at troughs as well as peaks (see Moore, ed., *Business Cycle Indicators*, Vol. I, pp. 470–73, with Chart 14.9 and Table 14.11).

Chart 12-6

Cumulated Percentage Expanding and Aggregative Series, New Orders and Production, All Manufacturing Industries, 1948–62

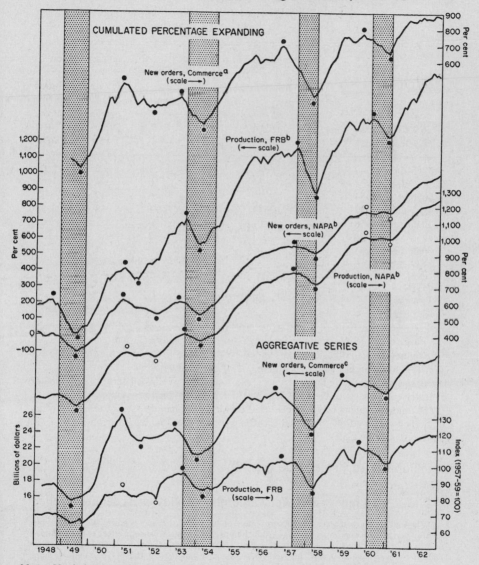

Note: Shaded areas represent business cycle contractions; unshaded areas, expansions. Dots identify peaks and troughs of specific cycles; circles, minor turns or retardations.

a Based on three-month moving averages.

b Based on month-to-month change.

c Six-month moving average centered.

Table 12-2

Timing of Cumulated Diffusion Indexes and
Aggregates of New Orders and Production,
All Manufacturing Industries, 1949–61
[lead (−) or lag (+), in months]

| Date of Business Cycle Turn | Cumulated Diffusion Index | | | | Aggregate Series | |
| | New Orders | | Production | | Value of New Orders[d] (5) | Index of Mfg. Prod. (FRB) (6) |
	Commerce[a] (1)	NAPA[b] (2)	FRB[c] (3)	NAPA[b] (4)		
Trough Oct. 1949	−3	−4	−3	−3	−5	0
Peak July 1953	−3	−3	0	0	−4	0
Trough Aug. 1954	−6	−7	−7	−6	−7	−4
Peak July 1957	−6	−1	0	−1	−8	−5
Trough Apr. 1958	−2	0	0	0	−1	0
Peak May 1960	−4	−2	+1	−2	−12	−4
Trough Feb. 1961	−1	0	−1	0	−1	−1
Average timing						
Peaks	−4.3	−2.0	+0.3	−1.0	−8.0	−3.0
Troughs	−3.0	−2.8	−2.8	−2.2	−3.5	−1.2
All turns	−3.6	−2.4	−1.4	−1.7	−5.4	−2.0

[a] Based on three-month moving averages of 23 seasonally adjusted series.

[b] Computed from diffusion data yielded by the Monthly Business Survey of the National Association of Purchasing Agents, after seasonal adjustment.

[c] Based on month-to-month changes in 24 seasonally adjusted series for the major-industry components of the FRB index of industrial production.

[d] Six-month moving averages centered on the fourth month. The average lead of unsmoothed data for 1949–61 for all turns is a little longer (6.0 months as compared with 5.4 months in the table).

common source, in the same ways (unsmoothed) and for the same time spans (monthly).[13]

The NAPA indexes are very smooth and show well-defined cyclical

[13] The indexes show the cumulated percentage of survey participants reporting an increase plus half the percentage reporting no change from the previous month. The main effect of this treatment here is to raise the level of the figures being cumulated without appreciably altering their cyclical pattern, because the "no change" answers, while often very numerous, constitute a relatively stable series. Two other features of these data may be noted. First, the findings of the NAPA survey are available very early, even before the end of the report month. Second, the seasonal components are very weak in these data, although the survey replies are not explicitly adjusted for seasonal variation. (The series in Chart 12-6 are adjusted; see *ibid.*, p. 471, Chart 14.9, for graphs of unadjusted indexes, 1948–58.)

movements in general conformity to the chronology of the concurrent business fluctuations. However, they closely resemble each other in a way that is difficult to explain or accept as plausible, especially since durable goods manufacturers are well represented in the NAPA surveys. The turning points in the two indexes have been simultaneous since 1954, and the timing of new orders was occasionally sluggish.

Chart 12-6 also demonstrates the close parallelism between cumulated diffusion indexes for new orders and production and the corresponding aggregates. The comparisons, whether for new orders or production, confirm other evidence of high correlations between the scope and the over-all magnitude of cyclical movements in economic aggregates.[14]

Table 12-2 shows the timing of each of the six series included in Chart 12-6 at each successive business turn. According to the Commerce data, both the cumulated percentage expanding and the aggregate of new orders led on each occasion (columns 1 and 5). The FRB data for production, on the other hand, show coincidences or shorter leads at most turns, again both for the cumulated diffusion index and the aggregate (columns 3 and 6). Short leads and coincidences also dominate the timing of the NAPA indexes, where the differences between new orders and production are few and small (columns 2 and 4).

Cyclical Behavior of Investment Commitments and Realizations

New Orders, Construction, and Expenditures for Plant and Equipment

The series on new investment orders and contracts discussed in Chapters 9 and 10 make it possible to construct reference cycle patterns of business commitments on capital account for three complete cycles, 1949–61. Chart 12-7 compares the behavior of the two components of these commitments. It shows that new orders for producer durable equipment and the contracts for industrial and commercial plant construction had rather different patterns of change during the

[14] The burden of proof here is on the Commerce and FRB data, since surveys concerned only with directions of change (such as those of the NAPA) provide no basis for any meaningful aggregation. See *ibid.*, pp. 465–66, with Chart 14.7, for a comparison of interwar data in the same form.

Chart 12-7
Reference Cycle Patterns in Value of New Orders for
Producers' Durable Equipment and of Commercial
and Industrial Building Contracts, 1949–61

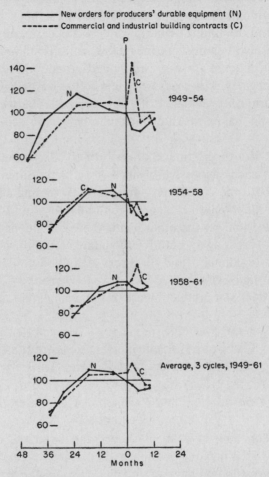

recent business cycles. Contracts ran high early in the contractions of
the 1949–54 and 1958–61 cycles. Equipment orders increased faster
than plant contracts in the early recovery stages of these cycles, and
declined earlier to reach trough levels in mid-contraction—just when
contracts were very high. In the 1954–58 cycle, however, the behavior of orders and contracts was rather similar. In the average pat-

terns for 1949–61, the expansion periods were stages I–VI for plant contracts and VII–III for equipment orders.

Monthly figures on construction contracts are highly erratic (see Chart 9-1, above), and even averages based on them are occasionally strongly affected by chance concentrations of large contracts. The averages based on a few monthly values would presumably be especially prone to such random influences, and the contraction stages are typically short in mild or moderate cycles such as those examined here. There may be little more than this to the peculiar peaks in the patterns for the value of contracts in the contractions of 1953–54 and 1960–61. Since 1919, both commercial and industrial building contracts have led business cycle peaks by 5–6 months and troughs by 1–2 months, on the average. The combined value aggregate had mean leads of 4 months at peaks and 2.8 months at troughs.[15]

Contracts for factory, business office, or store construction are, of course, influenced by financial market conditions and other cost elements as well as by demand factors, though they appear to be less sensitive to the former and more to the latter than are the contracts for residential construction. Historically, long-term interest rates have lagged, as have building costs. Hence, late expansion and the beginning of contraction are unfavorable cycle stages for construction starts, and late contraction and the beginning of expansion are favorable. These are presumably important reasons for the tendency of contracts to lead. Indeed, residential construction contracts or starts have led by such long intervals at some recent business peaks that much of the time they followed a countercyclical course. This behavior has been attributed in the literature to the high sensitivity of the housing market to the supply of mortgage credit. But the leads in industrial and commercial building contracts were much shorter and traces of inverted behavior much weaker than in the residential sector. The big companies that account for the major share of industrial building generate large cash flows of their own and are particularly valuable customers of financial institutions, with high credit ratings and ample

[15] The monthly figures are somewhat less erratic for floor space than for the value estimates of the contracts, and it is the former series that is included in the National Bureau list of "leading indicators." For the timing record of commercial and industrial contracts (floor space) in the period 1919–59, see *ibid.*, App. B. A comprehensive compilation of the principal time series on construction, including the contracts data, is provided in Robert E. Lipsey and Doris Preston, *Source Book of Statistics Relating to Construction*, New York, NBER, 1966.

access to loanable funds most of the time. They are likely to be less deterred by high and rising costs of building and financing than the smaller decision-making units that are active in the residential construction field, and may have stronger motivations against retrenchment.[16]

Chart 12-8 compares new orders for producer durable equipment with the corresponding aggregate for shipments. While equipment orders had their highest standing in stage III or IV, shipments had theirs in stage V. Usually, the lowest values for orders fell in stages VII and VIII; the lowest values for shipments, in stages VIII and IX. In the average patterns, the expansion period for orders is VII–III (indicating two-stage leads at peaks and troughs), while the expansion period for shipments is I–V (coincident timing).

When contracts for industrial and commercial plant (including privately owned utilities) are added to equipment orders, the patterns for the resulting estimates of aggregate fixed-investment commitments (OC) differ but slightly from those computed for only the equipment component (N), as shown by the corresponding patterns in the first two columns of diagrams in Chart 12-8. This similarity reflects the heavy weight of equipment in OC and is somewhat reduced when the reweighted aggregate OC_r is used instead. Even then, however, a considerable family resemblance between these diagrams remains, which presumably testifies to the genuinely large importance of the equipment component within the aggregate of fixed-investment commitments of business.

The value-of-output counterpart to the combined orders-contracts series for plant and equipment is compiled by adding to shipments of equipment-producing manufacturers the value of industrial, commercial, and privately owned utilities construction put in place. Here again the inclusion of the construction estimates apparently has remarkably weak effects, since the S and OC patterns in the first and second

---

[16] In an early (about 1936) unpublished manuscript on building construction, Arthur F. Burns suggested the following reasons for the observed difference in timing: (1) Costs of building and financing usually form a smaller part of total costs for an industrial firm than in residential construction. (2) The incentive to expand plant capacity is greater than the incentive to expand housing capacity, because commodity prices tend to rise faster than rents during a cyclical expansion. (3) The capacity of an industrial plant can typically be modified by changes in the intensity of utilization, whereas the capacity of a house is relatively well defined and less adjustable. Other, more speculative reasons were also mentioned, namely, (4) potential long-run losses of customers' business due to inadequate plant are of greater concern to an industrial company than to an apartment house owner; and (5) big firms, which account for a relatively large proportion of industrial building, often move more sluggishly than do smaller decision-making units.

Chart 12-8

Reference Cycle Patterns in New Investment Orders and Contracts, Value of Capital Goods Shipments and Business Construction Put in Place, and Business Expenditures on Plant and Equipment, 1949–61

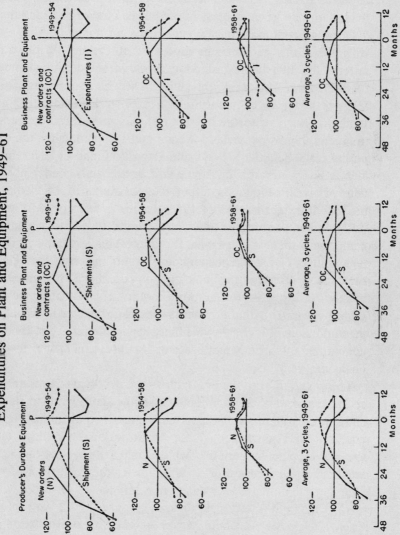

columns of Chart 12-8 are very similar. Yet there must be much less of an undercoverage bias on the construction side in this aggregate of investment realization than in the commitments series, since figures for the value of construction put in place give better representation to the plant component than do the building contracts data.[17]

The diagrams on the right-hand side of Chart 12-8 reproduce the patterns for investment orders and contracts and compare them with the patterns for business expenditures on plant and equipment. The behavior of the latter in each of the three cycles since 1949 has been remarkably similar to the behavior of the value-of-investment series, i.e., the combined aggregate of equipment shipments and construction put in place (cf. the second and third columns of diagrams in the chart). There are several slight lags of expenditures relative to the value of investment goods output, each of one short stage adjoining the business turn (at the peak of 1953 and the troughs of 1954, 1958, and 1961). Some lags of this sort would be expected. The average patterns of the two series, however, hardly differ. This appears sensible, since expenditures on plant and equipment should be closely correlated with the value of output of the capital goods covered. However, there is no reason for the overrepresentation of equipment relative to plant outlays (or vice versa) in the expenditure series. The value-of-output estimates presumably do have this bias, but the similarity of their cyclical behavior to that of expenditures seems to suggest that in this case the bias is not very disturbing.

According to the average patterns (lower-right diagram in Chart 12-8), new orders and contracts for plant and equipment led at both peaks and troughs of the business cycle by two stages (expansion period VII–III), while business fixed-investment outlays tended to coincide (expansion period I–V). Actually, the typical timing of plant and equipment expenditures differs from that of investment orders even more than this measurement in reference cycle stages would suggest. Turns in quarterly data for expenditures tend to *lag* behind business cycle peaks and troughs by short intervals (Chart 9-2).

Both new orders for equipment and business construction contracts usually decline well below their average cyclical levels during contractions in aggregate economic activity (i.e., they fall below the base line

---

[17] Although it should be noted, too, that the use of shipments instead of orders data does nothing to correct any overstatement bias on the equipment side.

of 100 in our diagrams). In contrast, the value of plant and equipment produced and of expenditures on plant and equipment held up well in the mild postwar recessions. The rise-and-fall amplitude in the patterns is considerably larger for new orders and contracts than for the corresponding expenditures or shipments. For example, the averages in reference cycle relatives for 1949–61 are 56 for capital orders and 43 for expenditures.

The Evidence of Historical Series

For the years before World War II, quarterly estimates of plant and equipment expenditures by manufacturers are available, but there is no series on aggregate investment orders. Therefore, the patterns for Chawner's expenditure series [18] are compared with those for the early Commerce-NBER index of orders for durables, 1921–33, and the NICB index of new orders for durable goods, 1933–38 (Chart 12-9). In the two weak cycles of 1921–27 manufacturers' capital outlays for productive facilities typically expanded in stages I–V, showing the same type of average coincident timing as the postwar capital outlays of private nonagricultural business enterprises. In the mild contractions of 1923–24 and 1926–27 and in the sharp but short contraction of 1937–38, manufacturers' expenditures for plant and equipment dipped only slightly below the base line in the immediate vicinity of the terminal trough. This feature, too, broadly recalls the behavior of business capital outlays during the postwar recessions, although investment generally displayed more strength on the later occasions.

The one-stage leads of durables orders are already familiar. The average amplitude of rise and fall was less in these orders than in manufacturers' plant and equipment expenditures. This is probably due to the heavy weight in the orders figures of nonequipment items with smaller cyclical amplitudes, as well as to the use of physical rather than current-value series in the earlier orders index. These estimates of new orders for durable goods are after all far from perfect as a proxy for producer equipment orders.

Chart 12-9 also includes the patterns for the value of commercial

[18] U.S. Department of Commerce, Bureau of Foreign and Domestic Commerce. See Lowell J. Chawner, "Capital Expenditures for Manufacturing Plant and Equipment—1915 to 1940," *Survey of Current Business,* March 1941, pp. 9–15, and further descriptions in *ibid.,* December 1961 and May 1962.

Chart 12-9
Average Reference Cycle Patterns in New Orders for Durable Goods, Value of Commercial and Industrial Building Contracts, and Expenditures on Plant and Equipment, 1921–27 and 1927–38

——————— Plants and equipment expenditures, manufacturing, Chawner (I)

– – – – – Index of new orders, durable manufactures, Commerce–NBER (N)

·········· Value of commercial and industrial building contracts, Dodge (C)

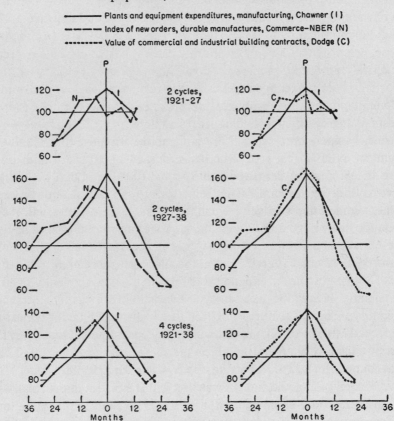

and industrial building contracts for the same groupings of interwar business cycles. Here the typical trough-peak-trough stages are I-V-IX, the same coincident timing as that of expenditures. More sensitive comparisons in monthly terms would be necessary to reveal a tendency for the contracts to lead by short intervals.

It is possible that new investment orders placed with manufacturers had shorter and less regular leads at business cycle turns in the interwar period than after World War II. This is suggested, particularly for the peaks and omitting the two cycles in 1921–27, by comparisons of the patterns for the durable goods orders in Chart 12-1, and also, as a broad approximation, by Charts 12-8 and 12-9. Further evidence comes from new orders for machine tools, for which a relatively long and continuous series is available, which enjoyed early recognition as one of the timeliest indicators of the demand for capital goods.

As shown in Chart 12-10, the demand for machine tools (which, of course, are produced largely to specific orders) has a very high degree of cyclical conformity and sensitivity. The patterns bring out well the contrast between investment behavior in mild cycles (such as 1921–24, 1924–27, and 1958–61) and in other cycles including the most severe ones in 1919–21 and the 1930's.

When the five interwar patterns are combined into one by averaging, an almost symmetrical inverted V pattern is obtained, but this is because the large rises in some of these cycles are nearly balanced by large declines in others. A coincident timing of machine-tool orders at peaks and troughs in general economic activity is suggested. Actually, the analysis of monthly data reveals a slight prevalence of leads over coincidences, but the leads are mostly too short (1–2 months) to show up in longer units such as the reference stages (see Table 11-5, lines 47–48).

The patterns for the postwar cycles have a considerably different appearance. The first one (1945–49) is dominated by a downward trend because of the discontinuation of high wartime demand, but it already shows a distinct lead of orders at the terminal trough. The 1949–54 and the 1954–58 patterns both have sharp peaks in stage III —two stages before the business downturn—and both show retardations before the troughs. The pattern for the 1958–61 cycle is flatter and less regular, but it suggests a similar lead at the peak. Short leads at the troughs of 1954 and 1961 are also visible in these schematized pictures. According to the average pattern for the four postwar cycles, 1945–61, the typical expansion interval for machine-tool orders in this period consisted of stages VIII–III.

If the leads at business cycle peaks of new orders placed with manufacturers increased since World War II compared with the interwar period, two factors may be responsible: (1) Production and shipments of the goods ordered may have acquired leads or longer leads at the recent recessions. The importance of manufacturing has declined;

Chart 12-10
Reference Cycle Patterns for New Orders of Machine Tools,
1919–38 and 1945–61

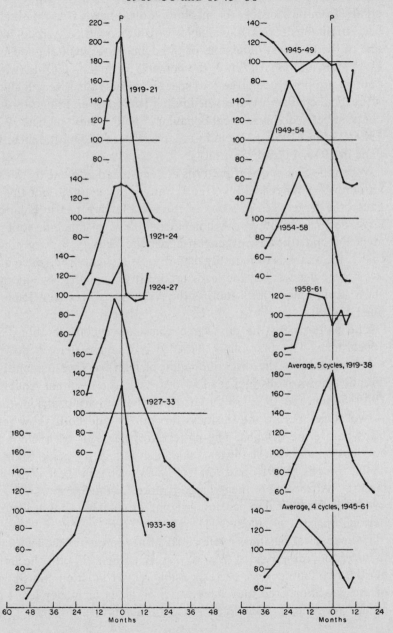

therefore, a downturn in the output of this sector no longer has the prompt and strongly depressing effect upon the economy it used to have. (2) The lags of output and deliveries behind new orders may have lengthened because of greater backlog accumulations in the postwar expansions. The first effect is a structural and presumably long-lasting one. The cyclical role of investment is affected to the extent that capital goods are supplied by the manufacturing sector. The second effect is cyclical, depending on the intensity of demand during the preceding expansion. It is particularly important for investment, since capital goods are produced largely to order, with substantial but variable delivery periods. In the 1940's and 1950's both factors became effective, but there is of course no necessary link between them.

The long leads of machine-tool orders at the postwar recessions can be traced mainly to extensions of the delivery periods, as revealed by the increase in the lags of shipments behind new orders. The timing of machine-tool shipments tends to be roughly coincident, with some tendency toward short leads at business recessions and short lags at revivals.[19]

Fluctuations in Orders, Profits, and Investment

Purchases of Durable Goods and Corporate Profits

One of the factors that may account for the early decline in aggregate new orders during business expansions is the deterioration, from the viewpoint of those who place the orders, of the cost-price relations.[20] Changes in corporate profits after taxes reflect the net over-all effect of changes in cost-price differentials but depend also on changes in the volume of transactions.

According to quarterly estimates by Harold Barger,[21] net corporate profits coincided at two peaks and led at two peaks in the period 1923–37, yielding an average lead of two months. New orders for durable goods (NBER-Commerce and NICB) had leads at all four

[19] For summary measures in monthly terms, see Table 11-9, line 8. At the first three postwar recessions, shipments also reached their top levels at least several months ahead of the measures of aggregate economic activity. However, this factor appears definitely less important in accounting for the long leads of new orders than does the factor of extended delivery periods.

[20] Cf. Geoffrey H. Moore, "Leading and Confirming Indicators of General Business Changes," in Moore, ed., Business Cycle Indicators, p. 65.

[21] Outlay and Income in the United States, 1921–38, New York, NBER, 1942, pp. 297–99.

peaks, which averaged six months. However, in the postwar period, for which more comprehensive and reliable data are available from the Commerce Department, the lead of orders at turns in profits implied in the earlier comparisons disappears and may even be slightly reversed. Both series led at each of the four recessions of 1948–60, and profits showed longer leads on three of these occasions; but the differences between these measures were mostly small and the mean leads closely similar (8 months for profits and 7.5 months for orders).

Profits, like new orders, also led at business recoveries. In the interwar period, the mean leads at troughs differed very little from those at peaks for both variables; again, orders turned earlier in most cases. At the four postwar recoveries, 1949–61, profits led three times and coincided once. New orders led four times, twice by slightly shorter intervals than profits. The mean leads in this period were 4 months for profits and 3.5 months for orders.[22]

Chart 12-11 indicates that a close positive association exists between purchases of durables—mainly materials inputs and producer equipment—and total net profits of what is no doubt the major group of purchasers, namely, U.S. corporations. Certainly the similarity of reference cycle patterns in new orders for durable goods and in corporate profits for the two most recent cycles (1954–61) is striking. In the two earlier cycles (1945–54), there are larger divergences between these patterns, but the correspondence is still very marked. It is, in fact, more pronounced than would appear from cycle-stage averages, because in the early fifties both orders and profits had a double-peak pattern, which in Chart 12-11 is visible only in profits. According to the diagrams, profits led orders at the 1948 peak and the early downturns in the Korean period, and lagged slightly at the revival of 1961 (all these are one-stage timing differences). At the other revivals covered, in 1949, 1954, and 1958, as well as the recessions of 1957 and 1960, the two series turned in the same business cycle stage.[23]

Of course, even a very high correlation does not necessarily denote a meaningful direct association. Thus, new orders and profits could both be jointly determined by some third factor, e.g., sales of the ordering firms. Furthermore, should the association be in fact a direct

---

[22] For a detailed record of leads and lags of these series through 1948, see Moore, ed., *Business Cycle Indicators*, Vol. I, App. B.

[23] For a graph of corporate profits after taxes, seasonally adjusted, 1948–61, see Chart 10-4.

Chart 12-11
Reference Cycle Patterns in New Orders for Durable
Goods and Corporate Profits After Taxes, 1945–61

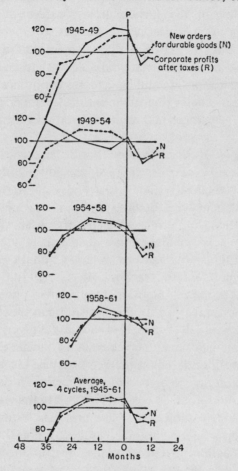

one, the familiar problem of the direction of causation must be faced. Rising profits may stimulate orders; but rising orders, too, may have strong stimulating effects and lead to higher levels of activity and higher profits.

Mutual interaction in partnership with other important factors is no doubt the broadest and, hence, the most accommodating concept for this relation (as for so many others), but to acknowledge this does not deny that proximate cause-and-effect connections may be involved.

What is suggested, rather, is that a search for such connections here is likely to be difficult. Cyclical developments are cumulative, and factors involved in them may alternate in the roles of "cause" and "effect," depending on the span of time considered or the stage of the process. If this is the case, timing comparisons, which sometimes provide helpful clues to the direction of causation, are apt to give mixed results of limited informational value. At least, however, it is clear that the cyclical movements in orders and profits are closely correlated; the relationship is important and it deserves further exploration, especially in the context of the determination of investment (Chapter 10).

Profit Variables and Investment Commitments

The chain of influence running from profits to orders is widely believed to be particularly important for investment goods. The decision to invest depends on the profits expected from the contemplated investment—this much is neither questioned nor as such is an operational statement. The expected profits depend on the demand for the products concerned, on the technologically determined capital requirements (production function), and the relative prices of factors of production—all as perceived by the decision maker who must try to predict these elements over a span of the future, given limited knowledge even of the past and the necessity of facing risk and uncertainty.[24] This list does not include current and past profits, but then the determinants that it does include are not directly observable (which is usually the case for variables required by purely theoretical analysis). In any empirical application, proxy variables must be used, and profits are frequently cast in this role. It has been argued that this lacks theoretical justification, at least "at the level of the individual firm with free access to capital markets," but with the qualification that "it is possible that the supply of money capital may itself be a function of current profits. . . . For lack of better information, investors of funds may be guided considerably by current and past profits in their estimates of the return and risk on contemplated investment. One might

---

[24] See Robert Eisner and Robert H. Strotz, "Determinants of Business Investment," in Commission on Money and Credit, *Impacts of Monetary Policy*, Englewood Cliffs, N.J., 1963, Chaps. I and II; and Robert Eisner, "The Aggregate Investment Function," *International Encyclopedia of the Social Sciences*, 1968, Vol. 8, pp. 185–94.

expect that in the case of large firms, however, it would pay the market to sustain the cost of securing better information."[25]

As a practical proposition, in a world of imperfect and costly information, the guiding role of past and present profit experience in the formation of profit expectations could well be considerable. But this, in any event, is a hypothesis about empirical regularities, and its validity can only be tested against the data; it cannot be determined on a priori grounds. It is true that the past may offer no relevant information for the basic decision on whether or not a new investment project is worth undertaking, and that such judgments should probably seldom be strongly affected by the record on profits. However, in addition to this basic decision there are subsidiary decisions, including a major one that concerns the choice of the proper *time* for the implementation of an investment project that has already been approved. This timing decision is likely to depend more on profits. This is so inasmuch as the net impact of changes in sales and in cost-price relations registers in the financial record which the firm uses to appraise its current and near prospects.

Lags may be expected to occur in this process, if only because it takes time for the firm to evaluate changes in its income and expenditure flows, but such lags need not be long and may be quite variable, even if the influence of profits were strong. Thus it is conceivable that some firms treat their current profits, which were realized on past investments, as unbiased estimates of profits expected from planned investments. Then, for them, current profits alone would be decisive, the variability of the underlying conditions being such that historical experience is considered no longer relevant.[26] In other cases, however, past experience may, on the contrary, carry considerable weight in the implementation of investment decisions. Implementation may be delayed until past changes add up to trends on which expectations can more safely be based. This would be so where short-term changes are viewed as too volatile to be relied upon, but longer changes are not. Limited information and discounting for risk and uncertainty would work in this direction.

There are no good reasons for expecting much uniformity in these

[25] Eisner and Strotz, "Determinants," pp. 124–25.
[26] Compare the "implicit expectations" analysis in Edwin S. Mills, *Price, Output, and Inventory Policy,* New York, 1962, Chap. 3.

relations across different industries, types of investment projects, business conditions, etc. However, firms may often view the movements in industry- and economywide aggregates as more "permanent" than deviating movements in their own microdata for the same variables (e.g., sales).[27] If this is so in the present context, then the influence on business investment of *aggregate* profits may well be considerably stronger than the presumably varying relationships among the corresponding microvariables would seem to imply.

A different reason for viewing profits as a determinant of investment lies in any preferences for internal financing that may exist. If imperfections are present in the capital market, such preferences acquire an objective basis. This argument may appear unconvincing, particularly for the large corporations which usually have easy access to sources of money capital. It also implicitly gives more weight to cash flow, a more comprehensive factor than (net) profits.[28]

Data on profit margins (profits before taxes per dollar of sales, R/S) will now be used, to de-emphasize the financial aspect of profits and to focus instead on the role of profits as an indicator of price-cost relations and of prospects for investment projects. This also serves to make some allowance for the role of sales. Chart 12-12 compares the reference cycle patterns for R/S with those for new investment orders and contracts, OC. The R/S series refers to all corporations and is compiled by the Federal Trade Commission–Securities and Exchange Commission; the OC series is familiar from Chapters 9 and 10.

Given moderately rising marginal cost curves and fairly rigid short-run price behavior in the manufacturing sector, profits would tend to be a positive function of sales, since fluctuations in sales are paralleled by changes in the degree of capacity utilization. However valid this common explanation, positive correlations between profits and sales are often observed and accepted as a feature of short-term business developments. But R is definitely much more variable than S; therefore, the R/S ratios reflect much more the changes in R than in S. Indeed, the cyclical patterns for R/S in Chart 12-12 strongly resemble

[27] This hypothesis was found by Eisner to be consistent with his regression estimates of investment functions based on firm and industry data from the McGraw-Hill capital expenditure surveys. See references in note 24 above and in Chapter 10, note 46.

[28] The two variables are as a rule highly correlated in the short run. There is, however, some evidence that profits are more effective than cash flow in influencing investment commitments (Chapter 10).

Chart 12-12
Reference Cycle Patterns in New Capital Appropriations,
New Investment Orders and Contracts, and Profits per
Dollar of Sales, 1949–61 and 1954–61

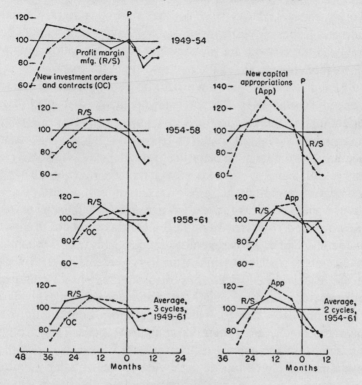

the corresponding patterns for total after-tax profits in Chart 12-11. They show that forces causing deterioration (from the producer's point of view) of cost-price relations can become effective enough in the mid-stages of a business expansion to result in an early downturn in profit margins. The peaks in the patterns for R/S fall in stage III (except in the 1949–54 cycle when the series had two peaks, the first in stage II, which was early in the Korean War period, and the second, much lower one in stage V). Thus R/S led by two long cycle-stages relative to the recent peaks in aggregate economic activity and by one or two stages relative to the peaks in new investment orders and contracts, OC.

The tendency of R/S to lead at troughs is barely evident in the patterns, nor does R/S turn up ahead of OC; at the 1961 recovery the opposite was, in fact, the case.

New capital appropriations by manufacturers (App) had larger amplitudes of rise and fall than OC in the two business cycles covered by these data (1954–61). They also led OC at peaks by one cycle-stage, as can be seen by comparing the corresponding patterns in the two columns of Chart 12-12. At peaks in R/S, capital appropriations had either roughly coincident or lagging timing, but they definitely led at the 1961 trough.[29]

Profits and profit margins, then, have patterns of cyclical behavior that are substantially similar to the patterns of durable goods orders and investment commitments. The timing of these series is either approximately simultaneous or, at least at peaks, it is the profit variables that lead On the aggregate level, considering the chain of influence that is running in the opposite direction, i.e., from orders to profits, it would seem that the time dimension of this feedback effect is likely to be quite different. Sustained increases in new orders will be translated into higher gross revenues and probably also into higher net revenues, while sustained decreases will have the contrary effects. Since the realization and recording of profits takes time, the process can be expected to involve significant lags.[30] This is particularly true of investment orders–contracts, which often require considerable time to be taken into production, executed, and paid for—facts suggesting that these commitments can generate profits only with distributed and frequently long lags. Since our data provide no evidence of such lags of profits, a tentative inference from them is that in the short run the effect of profits on orders and contracts is stronger than the feedback

[29] See Thomas M. Stanback, Jr., and Howard Sherman, "Cyclical Behavior of Profits, Appropriations and Expenditures: Some Aspects of the Investment Process," *Proceedings of the Business and Economic Statistics Section,* American Statistical Association annual meeting, September 1962, pp. 274–86. Using quarterly data for 1953–61 (NICB series on appropriations and FTC-SEC series on profits), Stanback and Sherman concluded (p. 284) that "there appears to be a significant similarity in the patterns of cyclical movements in profits and appropriations for the aggregate and most of the industry series. Among the industry series conformity is highest with appropriations lagged one quarter in over half of the cases, with coincident timing in most of the remainder. . . . There is some evidence . . . that the relationship between the two variables is more consistent at downturns than at upturns. The relationship also improves when rises or declines in profits are widespread among the various manufacturing industries."

[30] Note that this refers directly to the firms that receive orders, whereas the earlier argument about the likelihood of relatively short lags in the chain of influence running from realized profits to investment commitments referred to the behavior of the firms that place orders. For the aggregate of all firms, of course, orders received equal orders placed; hence, no operational distinction can be made along these lines.

effect running in the opposite direction. However, profits and investment commitments may well be subject to common influences and they
doubtless interact; hence, one must beware of any simple assertions
of unidirectional causal relations among these variables.

New Orders Received and Capital Appropriations and Outlays

A sustained rise in demand will tend to increase profits and stimulate expectations and investment, but the process, as suggested above,
is probably often a protracted one. Thus the curves in Chart 12-13 suggest that cyclical fluctuations in industry expenditures on plant and
equipment (I) follow with long lags the fluctuations in new orders for
products of the given industry (N).[31] A positive association between N
and I seems to exist in each of the several major manufacturing industries covered, but at times the lags are so long that the series appear to
be related in an almost inverted fashion (see the graphs for primary
metals in 1958–61 or for electrical machinery in 1953–55). At times,
too, new orders experienced short cyclical movements which could not
be matched with similar lagged movements in the corresponding investment outlay series (e.g., the 1952–53 rise in primary metals orders).

Clearly, investment in plant and equipment depends on various
other factors in addition to the course of demand for the investor's output. Hence, one would not expect it to be closely related to new orders, and in fact the relations are not close. Nevertheless, the cyclical
fluctuations in the paired series show a high degree of conformity, as
indicated by a comparison of the numbers of turns covered and
matched. The matched peaks and troughs represent 88 per cent of all
turning points covered in the expenditure series and 80 per cent of
those covered in the new-order series. All but three of the forty-six
timing comparisons made, or 93 per cent, were leads of orders. By
industries, the mean leads vary from two to three quarters, except for
one lead of 11 months in primary metals. On the average for eleven
industries, new orders led expenditures by 8 months, with a mean deviation of 4 months. The series on investment expenditures show a
preponderance of lags at business cycle troughs, but at peaks the
series are for the most part roughly coincident and not very regular,
with leads nearly as frequent as lags.

[31] This analysis is based on the major-industry data published prior to the 1963 revision of the
Industry Survey series for new orders, etc.

Chart 12-13
New Orders Received and Expenditures on Plant and
Equipment, Seven Major Manufacturing Industries,
1948–61

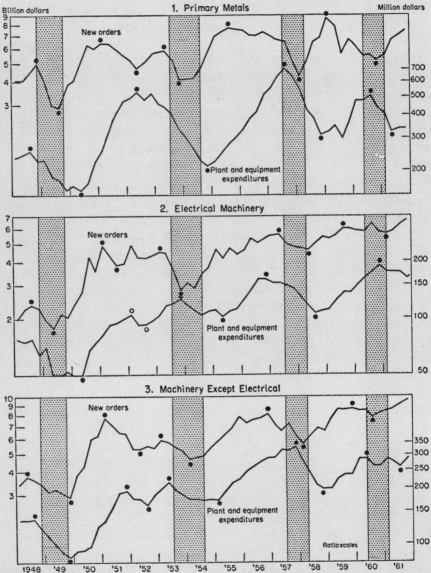

Chart 12-13 (continued)

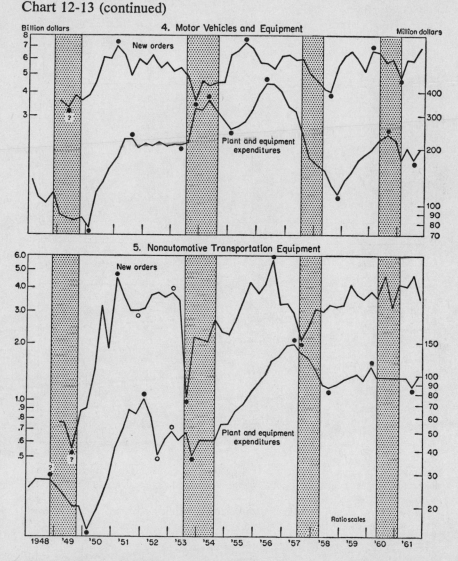

4. Motor Vehicles and Equipment

5. Nonautomotive Transportation Equipment

New orders received by such industries as nonelectrical machinery and nonautomotive transportation equipment reflect decisions to acquire capital goods by private domestic producers. Outlays on such goods are a major component of equipment expenditures. It is of interest to note that the relations between new orders and fixed-investment outlays are closer for these industries (especially nonelectrical

Chart 12-13 (concluded)

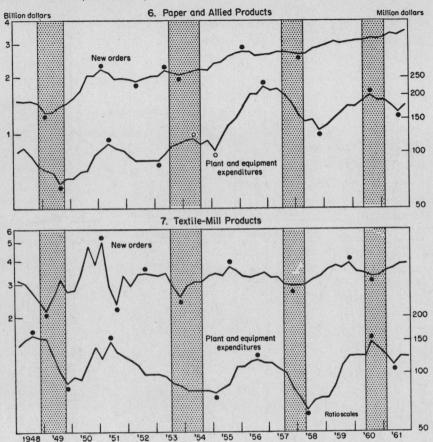

Note: Shaded areas represent business cycle contractions; unshaded areas, expansions. Dots identify peaks and troughs of specific cycles; circles identify minor turns or retardations.

Source: Securities and Exchange Commission and U.S. Department of Commerce, Office of Business Economics.

machinery) than for the others. The weakest association is found for motor vehicles in the period approximately through 1954.[32]

[32] In these years, mainly under the impact of heavy defense spending, new orders and shipments for the motor vehicles industry followed considerably different time-paths (see Chart 4-3; for civilian motor vehicles these N and S series are nearly alike). Plant and equipment outlays of motor vehicle manufacturers were then much better correlated with S than with N. Since 1955, N and S for this group moved rather closely together, and both series show a definite association with fixed-investment expenditures.

The finding that cyclical movements in incoming business typically begin and end several months ahead of the corresponding movements in plant and equipment expenditures becomes more significant when these leads are either as long or longer than the intervals between investment decisions and expenditures. The evidence appears in comparisons of the OBE series on new orders with data from NICB new capital appropriations, and with the OBE-SEC figures on capital outlays. Chart 12-14 presents the sequences of related turning points in these series. It suggests a tendency for appropriations (App) to lag behind orders received by the same industry (N), though the timing relations between these variables are rather irregular. In 1953–61, App lagged behind N in fourteen instances, but there were as many as nine coincidences. Although there were only four leads of App over N, they were long enough to offset the lags in two industries and to outweigh them in one. Capital outlays (I) lagged behind N and App in each industry by similar intervals. As shown by the accompanying figures, these intervals averaged six to ten months for most industries.

Timing Comparisons: Average Lead (−) or Lag (+),
in Months, 1953–61

	Prim. Met.	Elec. Mach.	Mach. exc. Elec.	Motor Veh. and Equip.	Other Transport. Equip.	Paper and Allied Prod.	Textile-Mill Prod.
N and App	−4.2	−0.8	0.0	+2.0	−5.2	0.0	−2.4
App and I	−9.6	−6.8	−10.2	−6.6	−4.0	−10.0	−7.8
N and I	−13.8	−7.8	−9.0	−6.0	−8.0	−9.0	−10.2

Limitations of materials and technique prohibit any firm inferences from these figures. But they seem at least consistent with the notion that sufficiently pronounced and prolonged expansions in new orders for manufacturers' output stimulate, and contractions discourage, the approval and implementation of capital expenditure projects of the companies concerned. This result is, of course, anything but surprising. It would be expected on any version of the flexible-accelerator hypothesis but also on the hypothesis that investment responds positively to rising and negatively to falling profits. If manufacturers'

Chart 12-14

Timing of Cycles in New Orders Compared with Cycles in New Capital Appropriations and in Plant and Equipment Expenditures, Seven Major Manufacturing Industries, 1953–61

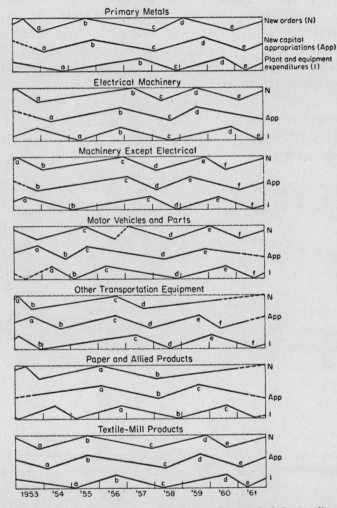

Note: Identical letters denote cycle turns that can be matched. Broken lines between points indicate retardations; broken lines at the beginning or end of the period covered indicate uncertainty regarding the direction of cyclical movement.

Source: U.S. Department of Commerce, Office of Business Economics; Securities and Exchange Commission; and National Industrial Conference Board.

profits tend to move with output and sales, the short-term expectations of profits should be much influenced by changes in new orders, which anticipate the movements of production. The business climate in the period covered by these comparisons was probably not conducive to the development of any sharp differences between the short-run and the longer-term business outlook. It was a period in which business conditions were mostly favorable and capacity utilization rates mostly high; the external disturbances impinging upon the economy were relatively short and not very strong, except during the Korean War. Hence, there are good reasons why the trends in new orders, through their effects upon actual and anticipated profits, should have had a major influence on the industrial producers' decisions regarding investment in plant and equipment.

Diffusion Indexes for Orders, Profits, and Investment

Chart 12-15 assembles some diffusion indexes based on series for the variables now under discussion: new capital appropriations (App), new orders for durable goods (N), corporate profits (R), and business expenditures on plant and equipment (I). These indexes show the percentages of series in the given group that undergo expansion; they are based on moving averages, like the indexes in Chart 12-6, but unlike the latter are not cumulated.

The monthly index for N includes 36 series for durable goods industries and is presented in the form of percentages of series expanding over nine-month spans.[33] There is a very definite correspondence of cyclical movements in this index and in the diffusion index of new capital appropriations (compare the first two curves in Chart 12-15). The index for appropriations, being quarterly, is of course considerably smoother than the monthly index for orders, but the two show similar broad fluctuations of approximately coincident timing.[34]

Also included in Chart 12-15 is a diffusion index of profits based on the quarterly financial reports of large numbers of manufacturing cor-

[33] The index is plotted in the sixth month of the span. Its component series are not separately published, but the index itself is released regularly and charted in the monthly *Business Conditions Digest* (Bureau of the Census). The other index series shown in Chart 12-15 are published in the same source. All series are seasonally adjusted. I am indebted to the Bureau of the Census for the historical data for the series.

[34] The appropriations index is based on three-quarter changes and plotted in the third month of the second quarter. The two indexes thus have spans of equal length (nine months) and are similarly centered.

Chart 12-15
Diffusion Indexes of Capital Appropriations, New Orders for Durable Goods, Corporate Profits, and Industrial Production, 1948–67

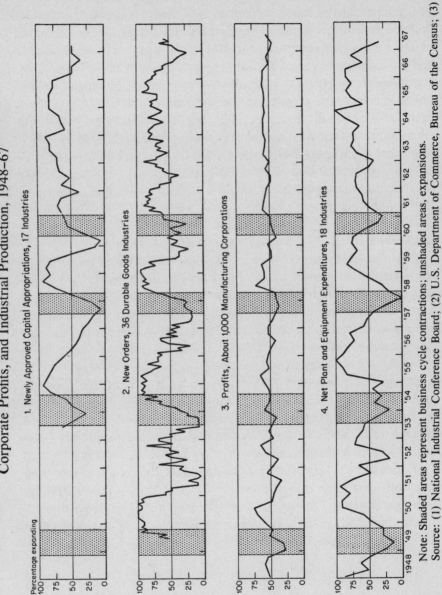

Note: Shaded areas represent business cycle contractions; unshaded areas, expansions.

Source: (1) National Industrial Conference Board; (2) U.S. Department of Commerce, Bureau of the Census; (3) First National City Bank of New York; (4) U.S. Department of Commerce, Office of Business Economics, and the Securities and Exchange Commission. Series 1, 2, and 3 are currently published in Bureau of the Census, *Business*

porations (approximately 600 in the fifties, presently about 1,000). This index refers to one-quarter spans and thus involves no smoothing (it is plotted in the first month of the second quarter). It fluctuates within a relatively narrow range, most of the time between 35 and 65 per cent and never beyond the 25–75 per cent band, which primarily reflects the large size of the samples covered.[35] Nevertheless, these percentages, too, show clusters of locally high values in the expansion years (1950, 1955, 1958–59, and 1961) and of locally low values in the recession or retardation periods (1949, 1951, 1953, 1957–58, 1960, 1962, and 1967). And the timing of these maxima and minima tends to be roughly synchronous with the timing of the corresponding values in the indexes for new orders and capital appropriations.

The index shown on the last line of Chart 12-15 is based on the quarterly surveys of business expenditures on new plant and equipment conducted by the Department of Commerce–Securities and Exchange Commission (OBE-SEC). It has one-quarter spans and is plotted in the first month of the second quarter. Since it is not smoothed and is calculated from a limited number of industry series, it shows relatively frequent, large, and irregular oscillations, but its longer, cyclical movements are for the most part clearly recognizable. These movements are much earlier than those in the corresponding aggregate of business fixed-capital outlays. The latter shows roughly coincident timing at business cycle peaks and short lags at troughs, while the diffusion index leads at peaks by long, and at troughs by intermediate or short, intervals.[36] However, the diffusion indexes for new investment commitments are even earlier leaders than those for expenditures, reflecting the timing sequence of the corresponding aggregates. The cyclical reversals in the percentage-expanding series for business capital outlays lag systematically behind the reversals in the indexes for new capital appropriations and new orders for durable goods (curves 1, 2, and 4 in Chart 12-15). The lags relative to the appropriations index average 8.5 months at peaks and 6 months at troughs in the period

[35] For a given type of economic process, unit of analysis, etc., it is clearly far more likely that 10 component series would all expand or contract simultaneously than that 500 would do so. But here there are other sources of difference as well, since the indexes refer to different variables and units (industries, firms).

[36] The leads of the index at peaks ranged from 13 to 27 months and averaged about 20 months; the leads at troughs ranged from 1 to 7 months and averaged about 4 months.

1954–61; the lags relative to the new-order index average 6 months at peaks and nearly 5 months at troughs in the period 1950–61.[37]

Materials Purchases, Inventory Changes, and Credit Conditions

Moore has suggested that "tight credit conditions and piling up of inventories" contribute to the early declines in orders during business expansions, along with "unfavorable cost-price relations."[38] The last factor was considered in the previous sections; the first two factors will be given some attention now.

New orders for materials increase sharply in the initial stage of a business expansion. Total stocks of purchased materials usually continue to decline in this stage, but the rate of disinvestment begins decreasing late in the contraction. At that time, new orders turn up for many products of the firms holding the inventories, giving rise to or reinforcing expectations of an upswing in demand. Then, an increasing number of firms, facing the upswing, hasten to end further disinvestment and to build up their working inventories. Shipments of materials rise too, but at a lower rate than new orders, so that producers' order books lengthen, i.e., commitments to supply materials increase. Purchasers, however, not only add to their outstanding orders but presently succeed in increasing their stocks on hand. In fact, the largest increases in these stocks take place early in expansion, in stage-to-stage intervals I–II and II–III.

All this is indicated by the patterns in the first two columns of Chart 12-16, which are based in part on grouped pre-1963 OBE data on new orders and shipments. The patterns for the purchased materials inventories (M) refer to the Commerce series in book values.[39] Studies of the cyclical behavior of inventories support this analysis.[40]

In the late stages of expansion, the pace of increases in demand typically slackens. Though it is by no means demonstrated, it is plausible that the very increases in inventories which occurred during the

---

[37] All in all, these comparisons yield twelve lags of the investment expenditures index and one case of coincidence. But the lags, while persistent, varied considerably in length (from 1 to 13 months). It should be noted that some of the dates involved in these observations represent marginal and inevitably uncertain selections.

[38] "Leading and Confirming Indicators," p. 65. He adds that "opposite conditions are associated with the early upturns in new orders during contractions."

[39] The stage-to-stage changes in inventories (ΔM) are plotted at points in time separating the stages (the values of the reference cycle patterns in M are centered on the stage intervals).

[40] See Chapter 8 for references to the work by Abramovitz, Stanback, and others, and for an account of other aspects of inventory behavior at each stage of fabrication.

Chart 12-16

Reference Cycle Patterns in New Orders and Shipments of Manufacturers of Materials, Inventories of Purchased Materials, Bank Loans, and Bank Interest Rates, 1949–61

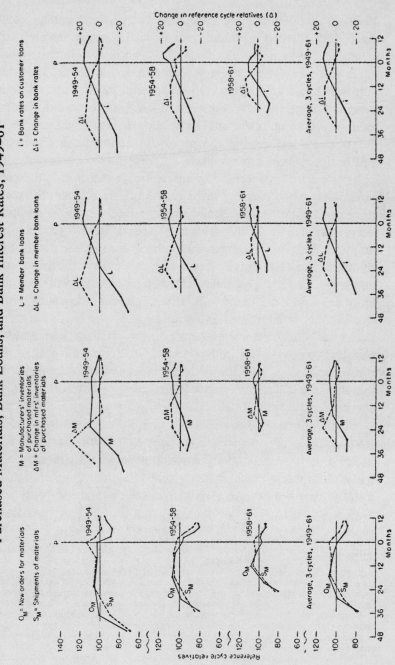

recovery on an impressive scale now act as a deterrent against further massive stockpiling. Certainly pronounced retardations are evident in inventory fluctuations. The stage-to-stage changes in materials inventories form an almost inverted pattern relative to that of inventories proper in Chart 12-16. Thus, in the second half of expansion new orders for materials begin to decline, while output and deliveries of materials flatten out. Inventories continue to rise throughout the expansion but at a declining rate; inventory investment turns down early.

Inventory purchases and financing are a major source of the demand for business loans, which brings up a point about the influence of credit conditions. From stage to stage of the business cycle, the pattern of movement in commercial bank loans (L) has a very similar appearance to the course followed by purchased-material inventories (compare the diagrams for totals and changes in the two middle columns of Chart 12-16).[41] The similarity extends to the patterns of stage-to-stage changes (L and M). The differences between the patterns are in part of technical origin and not essential as far as the cyclical aspect of this relation is concerned.[42]

The patterns in bank interest rates on short-term business loans, i (a quarterly series of the Federal Reserve Board), also bear a strong family resemblance to the patterns in L and M. (Compare the corresponding diagrams in the last three columns of Chart 12-16.) These high positive correlations in each successive cycle among inventories, loans, and interest rates indicate strong influences arising from shifts of demand. To finance the net additions to inventories (and for other business purposes), increasing amounts of loans are sought, which drives up interest rates. Banks strive to satisfy the loan demands of regular customers as far as possible, even when funds are scarce.[43]

[41] The patterns for commercial bank loans are based on the monthly FRB series for *total* loans of reporting member banks. Inventory borrowing is known to represent a large part of total business borrowing and a major use of *short-term* bank credit. Close associations between manufacturers' inventories and short-term bank loans have been shown and analyzed in Doris M. Eisemann, "Manufacturers' Inventory Cycles and Monetary Policy," *Journal of the American Statistical Association,* September 1958, pp. 680–88.

[42] The most significant difference observable is that loans often start rising earlier than inventories and start declining later. The average expansion period in the chart is VII–VI for loans (L) and II–V for inventories (M). This seems largely due to trend differences, which are only partially eliminated by the adopted technique since the patterns abstract from the intercycle but retain the intracycle trend components. The timing discrepancies are decreased when first differences in the patterns are calculated to obtain the diagrams for ΔL and ΔM, a step that further reduces the effect of trends.

[43] They do so by reducing excess reserves, selling securities, and borrowing. (See Phillip Cagan, "Interest Rates and Bank Reserves—A Reinterpretation of the Statistical Association," Jack M.

But one can also see in these patterns some elements of a simple negative relation between price and quantity demanded. The largest decreases in the interest rates $(-\Delta i)$ occur in mid- or late contraction, and the lowest levels of the rates are observed at the end of the downswing and early in the recovery. The credit ease may contribute to the fact that new orders for materials firm up shortly before the business trough and show the highest rate of rise between the first two stages of expansion (I–II), while ΔL and ΔM both reach their peaks in the interval II–III. Again, the largest increases in the bank interest rates $(+\Delta i)$ occur in mid-expansion, in the stage intervals II–III and III–IV, a timing which agrees with that of the early weaknesses or declines in new orders and with slowdowns in the rate of borrowing and inventory investment.

Forward Buying and Supply Conditions

The early spurts of new orders in postwar business recoveries, visible in the patterns for durable goods and the market category of materials (Charts 12-1 and 12-16), have been accompanied by definite shifts toward slower deliveries by the "vendors." The graphs of cyclical movements in the vendor performance index [44] show in most cases an increase between stages VII and II (Chart 12-17). Thus, according to a sample of purchasing agents, suppliers have increasingly quoted longer times to delivery even before the general business upturn. The post-Korean patterns show the largest values of this index in the expansion stages II and III and relatively low values around the business peaks and in contractions.

The increase in the quoted lead times to delivery induces, with short lags, a protective reaction on the part of the industrial purchasers. Thus, in the initial stages of business expansions more companies report ordering at least sixty days in advance of anticipated needs than at other times, according to survey data of the National

Guttentag and Phillip Cagan, eds., *Essays on Interest Rates,* New York, NBER, 1969, Vol. I, pp. 223–71.) Elsewhere Cagan has shown that interest rates on bank loans, along with other rates, have a generally lagged timing at business cycle turns, but that the lags have become shorter and less differentiated over the years, indicating increasing sensitivity of the financial markets to cyclical business developments; see his "Changes in the Cyclical Behavior of Interest Rates," *Review of Economics and Statistics,* August 1966, reprinted as Occasional Paper 100, New York, NBER, 1966.

[44] This index, based on the monthly survey of members of the Purchasing Agents Association of Chicago, was introduced in Chapter 8 (see Chart 8-2 and text).

Chart 12-17
Reference Cycle Patterns in Indexes of Vendor Performance and Buying Policy and Changes in Unfilled Orders, 1949–61

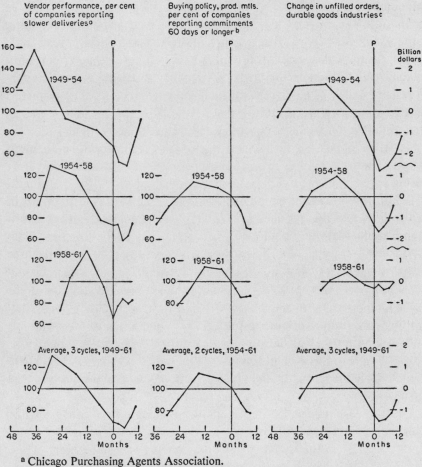

ᵃ Chicago Purchasing Agents Association.
ᵇ National Association of Purchasing Agents.
ᶜ OBE-Census. Deviations from cycle base.

Association of Purchasing Agents (Chart 12-17). The patterns for this buying policy index rise fairly sharply to their highest relative standings in stages III and IV, then decline similarly to level off before the end of contraction.[45]

[45] For a discussion of a related purchasing policy index of the PAA of Chicago, see Chart 8-2 and text in Chapter 8.

Delivery slowdowns and increases in backlogs of unfilled sales orders are symptoms of rising demand pressures as seen from the suppliers' side; increases in the average time covered and total amounts of outstanding purchase orders are the corresponding symptoms as seen from the buyers' side. Changes in unfilled orders (outstanding orders) for durable goods are shown in the patterns of deviations from the cycle base (last column of Chart 12-17). These patterns certainly resemble the others in the chart, particularly those of the vendor performance index. The largest cyclical increases in backlogs occurred at mid-expansion or earlier, in stages II and III; the largest decreases, shortly after the peak of business activity, in stages VI and VII.

It is an important fact that these indicators of relative demand pressure start declining so early during a business expansion and start rising so early during a contraction or recovery. Well before the general downturn, the rate and scope of the rise in demand (new orders) begin to decline, and this reduces first the growth and then the level of uncompleted orders and contracts. The decline in unfilled orders is accompanied by speedier deliveries, which causes firms to reduce forward buying of materials and parts. The first signs of weakness may be connected with residential construction or new investment commitments of the business sector, but suppliers of consumer goods may be involved as well.[46] Stronger efforts are then made to adjust inventories downward, and investment in inventories begins declining (although total stocks on hand still increase). *Mutatis mutandis,* analogous (but not symmetrical) developments tend to accompany the process of recovery.

Summary

Most reference cycle patterns for new orders for durable goods register leads that vary from one to three cycle-stages. Contrasts between business contractions of different severity, and between business expansions of different vigor, are strongly reflected in the amplitudes of these patterns. Reference cycle patterns for production show smaller amplitudes than the corresponding constructs for new orders, and a

---

[46] See Arthur F. Burns, "Business Cycles," in *International Encyclopedia of the Social Sciences,* 1968, Vol. 2, pp. 238–39, for an account of these components of the "gathering forces of recession."

more nearly coincident timing. The patterns for unfilled orders demonstrate that in business cycles with vigorous expansions the typical sequence is first a rapid rise in the backlog and then an early and slow decline continuing through the contraction stages. By contrast, in "weak" cycles that fail to include a full-grown boom, the backlog rise is smaller and slower, often reaching its highest point in the peak stage.

New orders and contracts for plant and equipment attained their highest cyclical standing at or after the midpoint of recent business expansions, in stage III or IV; but shipments and installations, as well as the corresponding capital outlays, continued to rise until the peak or the early-recession stage (V or VI). While new investment commitments had their lowest cyclical standing either in mid-contraction or in the next stage (VII or VIII), investment realizations, whether measured by the value of output or expenditures, had theirs in the trough stage. The amplitudes of rise and fall over the business cycle, as shown by the typical patterns, are considerably larger in fixed-investment commitments than in realizations.

The evidence for the period between the two world wars, which is rather fragmentary, suggests that the timing of new orders was then less often leading and more often coincident than in the post-World War II cycles; this is so according to the patterns for durable goods and, particularly, for such capital goods as machine tools. To the extent that this represents a systematic change, it can be related to (1) the lead of manufacturing output at peaks in recent business cycles (in the past, when manufacturing had greater weight in the economy, declines in this sector had stronger and prompter effects and therefore more nearly coincident timing); (2) the long lags of production behind new orders at the recessions of the 1940's and 1950's because of very large accumulations of unfilled order backlogs in the preceding expansions.

The reference cycle patterns in new orders of durable goods manufacturers and in corporate profits after taxes show marked similarities, and so do the patterns in corporate profit margins and in new investment commitments (orders and contracts and capital appropriations). In the postwar cycles for which these measures are available, profit margins turned down earlier than investment commitments.

The influence of profits may be due to their acting as proxies for changes in internal funds, cost-price relationships, and business expectations, so that the role of this variable, even though apparently strong, is ambiguous. However, the use of profit margins presumably helps to reduce the financial aspect and to bring out more strongly the other aspects of the profit-investment relationship.

Orders and profits may well be jointly determined by other factors, and they certainly interact. Sustained increases (decreases) in new orders received are apt to be translated, via output and sales, into higher (lower) profits. However, this process is likely to involve relatively long lags of profits behind orders received, whereas the causal chain that "starts" with profits suggests that profits should lead or coincide with orders placed. For the aggregate of all firms the distinction between orders received and placed is immaterial. The fact that aggregate profits seldom lag but frequently lead or coincide with orders suggests that the influence of profits on orders is the stronger one.

The cyclical fluctuations in industry expenditures on plant and equipment tend to follow with long lags the more pronounced and prolonged expansions and contractions in new orders received by the given industry. New capital appropriations tend to coincide approximately with, or lag shortly behind, these orders, for most of the major industries covered. These results are consistent with both the flexible accelerator and the profits hypotheses about investment determination.

New orders for materials usually turn up ahead of the business cycle trough, then increase sharply in the initial stage of expansion, while stocks still decline but at considerably lower rates. Although shipments of materials rise more slowly than orders, purchasers soon succeed in adding not only to their stocks on order but also to stocks on hand. In the later stages of business expansion, there is typically a retardation in purchasing, which may partly represent reactions to the earlier massive stockpiling. Both the levels and stage-to-stage changes in the cyclical patterns for commercial bank loans and bank interest rates on short-term business loans resemble quite well the patterns for purchased-material stocks. These relations reflect the shifts in demand for bank credit by business and the effects of such shifts on interest rates. But there is also evidence that the largest increases (decreases) in bank interest rates occur in mid-expansion (mid-contraction), and this may contribute to the similar timing of the first declines (rises) in purchases of materials and parts. Still another reason for such early declines in new orders during business expansions lies in the concurrent reductions of delivery lags and of forward buying.

Diffusion indexes show that the percentage of industries with rising new orders typically turns up early in a business contraction and turns down early in an expansion. The *scope* of cyclical movements in the demand for industrial outputs evidently undergoes large fluctuations of its own that lead the fluctuations in aggregate demand by long intervals. The percentage-expanding indexes for new orders received by durable goods industries show roughly coincident timing with the indexes for new investment commitments and profits. Such diffusion series based on leading indicators can be particularly helpful in revealing and locating the strengths and weaknesses that often develop early in business contractions and expansions. The percentage-expanding indexes for production and business capital outlays lag behind those for new orders and capital appropriations and profits (although they, too, have considerably earlier timing than the corresponding aggregates of output and investment expenditures).

13

MAIN RESULTS AND
CONCLUSIONS

IN THE PRECEDING CHAPTERS of this book, there was presented, first, an exploration of the changes during business cycles in the effective demand for industrial products, as reflected in the fluctuations of orders placed with manufacturers. The second subject studied was the response of industry to these changes: the adjustments of output and shipments, the implications of changes in unfilled orders, and the problem of determinants of inventory investment. The third subject was business investment in plant and equipment, included because new orders received by industries that produce machinery and equipment represent an early stage of the process, along with the contracts for industrial and commercial construction. Here the principal topics included the cyclical behavior of investment orders and contracts, their main determinants, and their relation to such measures of investment commitments and realizations as capital appropriations and outlays.

It is difficult to synthesize briefly the results of such a study, but it is desirable to try. This necessitates concentration on selected points of importance. The more detailed findings are given in the summaries that conclude the substantive chapters of this book, and they need not be repeated here.

Typical Developments and Relationships

Let us reconstruct what appears to be the typical sequence of events in the response of producers to fluctuations in demand. One of the earliest signs of a business revival, at a time when general economic activity is still depressed, is an upturn in the proportion of industries (and companies) that experience increases in new orders. This is followed by an upturn in the proportion of industries (and companies) that start increasing their output rates. Later, as the expansion of demand widens, aggregate new orders turn up, preceding the revival in aggregate industrial production. At business recessions, there is characteristically an analogous sequence of downturns in these diffusion indexes and aggregates.

As a rule, the expansion in demand soon carries new orders above the levels of production and shipments. Hence, unfilled orders accumulate. They increase faster than shipments, and average delivery periods lengthen. When at a later date new orders start declining, current production will continue to rise to fill the volume of order backlogs. The latter continue increasing, too, although at a slower pace; they turn down only when new orders fall below the level of shipments.[1] Even then, output may still move up for some time, but its curtailment will inevitably follow. The ensuing contraction in the industry's activity is, however, slower than the contraction in new orders, because production and deliveries tend to exceed the concurrent inflow of new business, as manufacturers work off the backlogs of their past commitments. Unfilled orders begin to decrease faster than shipments, and average delivery periods shorten. When current demand (new orders) turns up again, its level is likely to be initially lower than that of output—too low in the view of most firms to justify an immediate reversal of their contractive production policies. The direct effects of the increase in new orders will then be limited to a slowdown in backlog decumulation and, perhaps, in the rate at which output declines. But as soon as the recovery of new orders carries them above the levels of current production, the latter will most likely turn up. Backlogs by then will be increasing, too, which brings us back to the beginning of the cycle.

As this account implies, new orders generally tend to lead production. For goods made to order, they do so by longer intervals and more

---

[1] If the contraction in new orders is so weak or short as to expire before descending to the concurrent levels of production, it may not bring about any decline in activity at all, but merely reduce the rates of increase in backlogs and output. A new expansion in demand will then put an end to these retardations and induce an accelerated increase in output and deliveries. Most of the "extra" turns in new orders are associated with those expansions or contractions in these series that fail to reach up or down to the levels of current industrial operations.

regularly than for goods sold from stock, and they also lead shipments. The leads are on the average longer for durable than for nondurable manufactures. The largest delivery lags are for heavy made-to-order equipment and defense products, the smallest for items that are relatively standardized. Many consumer goods and some materials are shipped promptly upon receipt of order, from stock. Among the goods made to order, those serving investment in producers' durable equipment and plant are particularly important. New orders and construction contracts for such capital goods are similar to new capital appropriations in their early cyclical timing, and they anticipate investment activity, whether the latter is measured by output or expenditure. The relations are distinctly of the distributed-lag type, and the average lags of business expenditures on plant and equipment behind the new investment commitments tend to be substantial; it may take three to four quarters after commitment for about half of the capital outlays to be made. These lags appear to be positively associated with the height of the backlog-shipments ratio, and thus probably with the degree of capacity utilization, in the capital-goods-producing industries. Similarly, turning-point comparisons show that new orders usually precede deliveries by longer intervals at peaks than at troughs, presumably because the capacity position of many of the supplying firms is strained at the top levels of production.

The relative amplitudes of cyclical, irregular, and seasonal fluctuations are systematically larger for new orders than for the corresponding series on production and shipments. This is so partly because output is limited by capacity, while demand (new orders) is not. Another reason lies in manufacturers' efforts to stabilize production. Firms seek to make their output variability as small as possible; and they are probably more strongly motivated and apparently more successful in this endeavor in those industries that face greater instability of demand (i.e., greater variability of cyclical and irregular movements in incoming business) than in industries where demand is more stable. In production to order, scheduling of operations on advance orders and adjustments in delivery periods are the instruments whereby the course of output and shipments can be made considerably smoother and subject to smaller cyclical fluctuations than the course of new orders. The variability of production relative to demand is thereby reduced, particularly in the machinery and equipment industries.

Total business expenditures on plant and equipment, like the corresponding value-of-output series, also show considerably smaller percentage changes than the aggregate of new investment orders and contracts.

Industries that produce largely to order hold a small proportion of their inventories in finished form. These are mainly stocks of output already sold and in transit to the buyers, and their short-term changes are largely random. Firms whose unfilled orders expand are likely to increase their buying of materials, inasmuch as such orders represent goods that are presold but yet to be produced. Materials and goods in process (which depend positively on the rate of output) account for the bulk of the inventories in production to order. In contrast, inventories in industries that produce mainly to stock include a large component of finished goods, subject to unintended changes reflecting errors in sales forecasts. These inventories can act as "buffers" or output stabilizers and at times they do so because they lag behind other activities (e.g., production may still expand after sales have turned down). However, comparisons of average amplitudes of real new orders, shipments, and output suggest that such effects of finished stocks are on the whole weak in comparison to the stabilizing role of changes in order backlogs. Finished inventories and unfilled orders show quite different patterns of movement, which reflect their very different sources and composition. The treatment of order backlogs as "negative inventory" may therefore be very misleading. Both analytical considerations and empirical results indicate that one should expect inventory behavior to differ systematically between industries producing mainly to stock and industries producing mainly to order, as well as between stages of fabrication.

The tendency of new orders to turn before both the revivals and the recessions in aggregate economic activity is general and pronounced, as is their characteristic of leading production in the industry receiving the orders. The average leads at business cycle peaks were longer than those at troughs for a large majority of the series, but the leads varied considerably from turn to turn, as well as among the different industries. New orders for durable goods other than defense products show particularly high cyclical conformity and consistent leading records. The series for nondurable goods industries also led at most of the postwar recessions and recoveries, but they scored low on conformity for the industries that do not report backlogs of unfilled orders (mainly producers of staple consumer goods). The main categories with early cyclical timing were new orders for machinery and equipment and for construction and other materials that are likewise associated with investment.

· The leads of aggregate advance orders averaged about five months at troughs and eight months at peaks of the business cycles in the period since 1921, but they appear to have been much shorter in the decade before World War II and much longer at most peaks of the postwar period. These differences are related to those observed for unfilled orders, which had generally small volumes and roughly coincident timing before and during the depression of the thirties but grew very large in the period covering World War II and the Korean War and led by long intervals at the peaks of the latter period. When backlogs are large at the height of the cycle, they can sustain production for some time, even when the currently received orders are declining. This tends to prolong the expansion and to extend the leads of orders at the peaks. A counteracting factor is the growth of manufacturing capacity, which was reflected in lower backlog-shipments ratios (shorter average delivery periods) at the successive peaks preceding the three post-Korean recessions of 1953–60.

Another reason for the longer leads of new orders at some of the recent business cycle turns is that these intervals include appreciable leads of manufacturers' outputs. This probably reflects the reduced relative importance of manufacturing in the economy: reversals in the activity of this sector now have weaker and slower effects on the other sectors, which may mean either longer leads or "extra" movements (as in 1967 when the declines in new orders and industrial production failed to cause a general downturn).

Other Findings

Over short spans of time, advance orders provide the best available predictor of output and shipments in those sectors where production to order is generally important. On the other hand, such orders themselves are particularly difficult to forecast with operationally acceptable errors, which in fact helps explain why the goods concerned are being manufactured to order. However, the problem of how the aggregates for the major categories of new orders are determined should be analyzed. What is particularly needed is a tested and validated explanation of the early timing of new investment commitments. Only modest progress has been made in this area, partly because the available data are inadequate. The evidence is consistent with the hypothesis that changing relations among costs, prices, and sales, as summed up in the profit variables (the levels, changes, margins, and diffusion of profits), account in a substantial degree for the cyclical behavior, and especially the tendency to lead, of new investment commitments (orders and contracts and capital appropriations). However, profits may also act in some measure as proxies for expectational and financial factors. The reverse chain of influence, from investment commitments to profits, also has a logical claim to existence, but it seems less important in the short run, according to the observed characteristics of the relationships involving these variables.

The accelerator hypothesis, in its current flexible or distributed-lag form, is likewise not inconsistent with the evidence presented. However, it appears less suited as an explanation of short-term movements and turning points in new orders and contracts for plant and equipment, although it may well be more successful as an explanation of longer trends in this variable. There are indications that interest rates have been moderately influential in the determination of fixed-investment commitments, including their cyclical leads, in the postwar period. In real terms, about four-fifths of the variance of new investment orders and contracts in the next quarter can be "explained" by final sales, capital stock, profits, and the long-term interest rate. While this result is significantly improved by the use of a distributed lag with geometrically declining weights, the estimates suggest that reaching the decision to go ahead with an investment project does not involve very long lags.[2]

The usefulness of orders data can also be demonstrated in the analysis of investment in stocks of materials and supplies. Purchases of materials vary positively with new and unfilled orders for products

[2] This finding appears reasonable and is consonant with some persuasive independent evidence. Of course, there are many important open questions in this field that remain unexamined, notably the role of changes in the money supply and other general monetary and financial factors (except insofar as it is reflected in the effects of the interest rate and some other variables).

of the purchasing firms, as well as with expectations of higher prices and longer delivery periods (increases in the backlogs on the suppliers' books are likely to stimulate such expectations). The adjustments to changes in demand are rather prompt for the outstanding orders that represent "stocks on order" for materials; they are slower and smaller for stocks on hand. Information of this sort travels faster than goods. Ordering is a cumulative process, and cyclical rises (or declines) of orders spread vertically as well as horizontally through large areas of the economy.

Finally, there are various additional factors that modify the processes and intervene in the relationships analyzed in this book, and a few may be mentioned. The accumulation of advance orders and extensions of terms to delivery tend to benefit the suppliers in times of generally high and rising demand, but as long as some firms have sufficient reserve capacities they will fill orders more quickly than others, thereby attracting a greater share of the incoming business. Thus, retardation in filling orders is promoted by the diffusion as well as the intensity of increases in demand, but it is counteracted by competition. Price increases may serve to ration demand and check the growth of order backlogs, but in times of generalized demand pressures both the selling prices of an industry and its unfilled sales orders tend to rise. Over time, changes in unfilled orders reflect the varying degree of excess demand and are positively correlated with price changes.

Data Required for Further Research

There is a definite need for statistics on flows of new orders placed and stocks of orders outstanding.[3] These should be monthly or at least quarterly time series classified by industries in which the orders originated and by broad categories of product. To have such data for producer durable equipment would be of great benefit in studies of the determinants and behavior of fixed investment. For this purpose, these series would complement the similarly classified data on new construction contracts and would be related to data on profits, output, capacity utilization rates, new and unfilled sales orders, etc., for the industries

[3] It will be recalled that the bulk of the available information on orders comes from companies that receive, not from those that place, the order.

concerned. Likewise, information on purchase orders placed and outstanding for materials would be highly useful in studies of inventory fluctuations. It is true that the new Census series for market categories provide some substitute information in lieu of the unavailable data of the type just described (I have used those series for just this purpose in parts II and III of this book), but this information is limited to comprehensive aggregates that are rather crude for the intended use. Collection of the data from companies that place the orders would permit the compilation of much "cleaner" series as well as the needed disaggregation by industry.

PART V

APPENDIXES

APPENDIX A

TIME SERIES ON ORDERS, SHIPMENTS, PRODUCTION, AND INVENTORIES

Coverage in Table A-1

This appendix covers most of the statistical materials employed in this book. In addition to the series catalogued in Table A-1, data on price changes, construction contracts, investment expenditures, and other selected variables have been used.

The distribution of the time series included in Table A-1 by economic variable is as follows:

New orders (N)	108 series
Shipments (S)	95 series
Production (Z)	22 series
Unfilled orders (U)	88 series
Canceled orders (C)	3 series
Inventories (H)	20 series
Total	336 series

The series in constant dollars for N, S, and U are not listed separately. Such deflated series have been constructed for several major-industry groups in the Monthly Industry Survey of the Office of Business Economics (OBE) of the U.S. Department of Commerce for those categories in part I of the table for which the Federal Reserve Board (FRB) production indexes (Z) are also included.[1] Another

---

[1] See column 3 of Table A-1 for the listing of the principal variables for each group, industry, or product category.

Table A-1
Basic Characteristics and Sources of Data for New and Unfilled Orders, Shipments, Production, and Inventories

Line	Industry, Market Grouping, or Product Category	Comparable SIC Industries[a] (1)	Market Grouping[b] (2)	Comparable Series Used[c] (3)	Period Covered[d] (4)
	I. MONTHLY INDUSTRY SURVEY, OBE-CENSUS, AND INDUSTRIAL PRODUCTION INDEXES, FRB[e]				
1	All manufacturing industries	19–39	All	N,S,Z,U,H	1939–66
2	Durable goods	19;24;25; 32–39	All exc. CS	N,S,Z,U,H	1939–66
3	Primary metals	33	OM	N,S,Z,U,H	1948–66
4	Blast furnaces, steel mills	331	OM	N,S,U	1953–66
5	Iron and steel foundries	332	OM	N,S,U	1948–62
6	Nonferrous metals	333–6[f]	OM	N,S,U	1948–62
7	Other primary metals	339	OM	N,S,U	1948–62
8	Fabricated metal products	34	HG,CM,OM	N,S,Z,U,H	1948–66
9	Heating and plumbing	343	CM	N,S,U	1955–62
10	Structural metal work	344	CM	N,S,U	1955–62
11	Tin cans and other	341,2,5,6,7,9	HG,OM	N,S,U	1955–62
12	Electrical machinery	36	ND,OM,HG	N,S,Z,U,H	1948–66
13	Electrical generator apparatus	361,2	OM	N,S,U	1948–62
14	Radio, TV, and communication equip.	365,6	HG,ND	N,S,U	1948–62
15	Other electrical equip.	363,4,7,9	OM	N,S,U	1948–62
16	Machinery exc. electrical	35	ND,OM	N,S,Z,U,H	1948–66
17	Metalworking machinery	354	ND	N,S,U	1948–62
18	General industrial machinery	3561,4,7,9	ND	N,S,U	1948–62
19	Special-industry machinery	355	ND	N,S,U	1948–62
20	Engines and turbines	351	ND,OM	N,S,U	1948–62
21	Construction, mining, and material-handling machinery	353	ND	N,S,U	1948–62
22	Office and store machines	357	ND	N,S,U	1948–62
23	Agricultural implements	352	ND	N,S,U	1948–62
24	Household and service appliances	358	ND	N,S,U	1948–62
25	Other machinery and parts	3544,5;3599; 3562,5,6	OM	N,S,U	1948–62
26	Transport. equip.	37	AE,ND,OM	N,S,H	1948–66
27	Motor vehicles and parts	371,5,9	AE	N,S,Z	1948–66
28	Motor vehicles	3711	AE	N,S,U	1949–62
29	Parts and accessories	3714	AE	N,S,U	1948–62
30	Nonautomotive transport. equip.	372,3,4	ND,OM	N,S,Z,U	1948–66
31	Aircraft	372	ND,OM	N,S,U	1949–62
32	Other nonautomotive transport. equip.	373,4	ND	N,S,U	1949–62

(continued)

Table A-1 (continued)

Line	Industry, Market Grouping, or Product Category	Comparable SIC Industries [a] (1)	Market Grouping [b] (2)	Comparable Series Used [c] (3)	Period Covered [d] (4)
33	Other durable goods industries	24;25;32;38; 39;19	HG,ND,CM, OM	N,S,Z,U 661	1948–66
34	Lumber and wood products	24	CM,OM	N,S,U	1953–62 [g]
35	Furniture	25	HG,ND	N,S,U	1953–62 [g]
36	Stone, clay, and glass products	32	CM,OM,HG	N,S,U	1948–62
37	Prof. and scientific instruments	38	ND,OM,HG	N,S,U	1953–62 [g]
38	Miscellaneous incl. ordnance	39;19	HG,OM,ND	N,S,U	1953–62 [g]
39	Nondurable goods industries, total	20–23,26–31	All exc. ND	N,S,Z,H	1939–66
40	Reporting unfilled orders	22,26,27,31	HG,CS,CM, OM	N,S,Z,U	1939–66
41	Textile-mill products	22	OM,HG	N,S,Z,U	1948–62
42	Leather and leather products	31	OM,HG	N,S,Z,U	1948–62
43	Paper and allied products	26	OM,CM,CS	N,S,Z,U,H	1948–62
44	Printing and publishing	27	CS,OM	N,S,Z,U	1948–62
45	Not reporting unfilled orders	20,21,23,28, 29,30	All exc. ND	$S(=N),Z$	1939–66

MARKET CATEGORIES [h]

Line	Industry, Market Grouping, or Product Category	Comparable SIC Industries [a] (1)	Market Grouping [b] (2)	Comparable Series Used [c] (3)	Period Covered [d] (4)
46	Consumer staples	20(excl. 209); 21;2645,6; 271,2,3; 283,4	CS	N,S,U	1953–66
47	Home goods and apparel	]	HG	N,S,U	1953–66
48	Consumer durables (other than automobiles)	251;326; 3421,3,5; 363,5;385, 7;391	CD	N,S,U	1960–66
49	Automotive equip.	3011;371,3, 5,9	AE	N,S,U	1953–66
50	Nonautomotive equip. and defense	]	ND	N,S,U	1953–66
51	Defense products	366;3721;19	DP	N,S,U	1953–66
52	Other	]	OE	N,S,U	1953–66
53	Machinery and equip. industries	35(excl. 352, 9);36(excl. 363,5,6); 3731;374	ME	N,S,U	1953–66
54	Materials, supplies, and intermediate products	[k]	MS	N,S,U	1953–66
55	Construction materials, etc.	[k]	CM	N,S,U	1953–66
56	Other materials, etc.	[k]	OM	N,S,U	1953–66

(continued)

Table A-1 (continued)

Line	Industry, Market Grouping, or Product Category	Comparable SIC Industries [a] (1)	Market Grouping [b] (2)	Comparable Series Used [c] (3)	Period Covered [d] (4)
	II. MONTHLY INDEXES (1949 = 100), STANDARD AND POOR'S [1]				
57	Composite index	m	m	N,S,U	1949–58
58	Steel	33;34	OM,CM	N,S,U	1949–58
59	Metal fabricating (nonferrous)	33;34	OM,CM	N,S,U	1949–58
60	Machinery, industrial	35	ND	N,S,U	1949–58
61	Machine tools	354	ND	N,S,U	1949–58
62	Electrical equipment	36	ND,OM	N,S,U	1949–58
63	Aircraft	372	ND,OM	N,S,U	1949–58
64	Auto parts	371	AE	N,S,U	1949–58
65	Lumber	24	CM,OM	N,S,U	1949–58
66	Building materials	24;32	CM	N,S,U	1949–58
67	Cement	324	CM	N,S,U	1949–58
68	Textiles	22	OM,HG	N,S,U	1949–58
69	Floor coverings	227	HG	N,S,U	1949–58
70	Shoes	314	HG	N,S,U	1949–58
71	Paper	26	OM,CM	N,S,U	1949–58
	III. COMPOSITE INDEXES				
	NATIONAL INDUSTRIAL CONFERENCE BOARD				
72	All manufacturing	n	All(probably)	N,S,U	1929–44 for N and S; 1935–44 for U
73	Durable goods industries	n	All exc. CS	S,U	
74	Nondurable goods industries	n	All exc. ND	S,U	
	DEPARTMENT OF COMMERCE				
75	Total (composite) index	o	HG,ND,CM, OM	N,U	1920–33
76	Iron and steel	331,2;343,4; misc.	CM,OM	N,U	1920–33
77	Transportation equipment	3731;3741,2	ND	N,U	1920–33
78	Lumber products	241,2;25	HG,ND,CM	N,U	1920–33
79	Stone, clay, and glass products	3229;3251,9	CM	N,U	1920–33
80	Textile products	2251,4;2261; 2295	HG,OM	N,U	1920–33
81	Paper and printing	2621;2631; 2641;2751	OM	N,U	1921–33 for N; 1923–33 for U
	MC GRAW-HILL				
82	Nonelectrical machinery, total	351,3,4,5,6, 7 [p]	ND	N	1949–66
83	Nonelectrical machinery, export	p	ND	N	1957–66

(continued)

Table A-1 (concluded)

Line	Industry, Market Grouping, or Product Category	Comparable SIC Industries [a] (1)	Market Grouping [b] (2)	Comparable Series Used [c] (3)	Period Covered [d] (4)
	ASSOCIATED INDUSTRIES OF MASSACHUSETTS				
84	Composite index for Massachusetts [q]	[q]		N	1924–41
	UNITED STATES STEEL CORPORATION				
85	Steel, unfilled orders [r]	33	OM	U	1902–33
	IV. SERIES FOR INDIVIDUAL INDUSTRIES OR PRODUCTS [s]				
86	Merchant pig iron [t]	3312	OM	N,S,Z,H	1919–26
87	Steel sheets [t]	3312	OM	N,S,Z,U,H	1919–36
88	Rails [t]	3312	OM	N	1870–1950
89	Fabricated steel plate [t]	3312	OM	N	1923–40
90	Fabricated structural steel [t]	3441	CM	N,S	1909–56
91	Water-tube boilers [t]	3443	CM	N	1927–58
92	Oil burners [t]	3433	CM	N,S,U,H	1929–53
93	Bath tubs [t]	3431	CM	N,S,H	1917–31
94	Lavatories [t]	3431	CM	N,S,H	1917–31
95	Kitchen sinks [t]	3431	CM	N,S,H	1917–31
96	Miscellaneous enameled sanitary ware [t]	3431	CM	N,S,H	1917–31
97	Machine tools	3541,2	ND	N,S,U,C	1919–63
98	Machine tools, export orders	3541,2	ND	N,S	1946–63
99	Foundry equipment	3559	ND	N,S,U	1921–56
100	Electric overhead cranes	3536	ND	N,S,U	1925–46
101	Woodworking machinery	3553	ND	N,S,U,C	1921–40
102	Mill and industrial supplies	3291;353,4,5 a.o. [u]	ND,CM,OM	N	1948–58
103	Aircraft and parts	3721,2,3,9	ND,OM	N,S	1948–63
104	Railroad freight cars [t]	3742	ND	N,S,U	1870–1956
105	Railroad passenger cars [t]	3742	ND	N,S	1870–1956
106	Railroad locomotives [t]	3741	ND	N,S	1870–1955
107	Architectural terra cotta [t]	3259	CM	N	1919–40
108	Southern pine lumber [t]	2421	CM	N,S,Z,H	1916–56
109	Oak flooring [t]	2426	CM	N,S,Z,U,H	1912–56
110	Furniture	2511,2;2521 [v]	HG,ND	N,S,U,C	1923–46
111	Boxboard and paperboard [t]	2631	OM	N,Z,U,H	1923–56
112	Paper, excl. building paper, newsprint, and paperboard [t]	2621	OM	N,S,Z,H	1934–55

Notes to Table A-1

ᵃ In terms of 1957 Standard Industrial Classification (SIC) system. For more detail and descriptions of the industries, see Bureau of the Census, *Manufacturers' Shipments, Inventories, and Orders: 1947–1963 (Revised)*, Washington, D.C., 1963, App. B, pp. 122–25.

ᵇ According to the source cited in note a. For an explanation of the symbols and industrial content of each grouping, see lines 46–56.

ᶜ N = new orders; S = shipments; Z = production; U = unfilled orders; C = canceled orders; H = inventories (= inventories of purchased materials plus goods in process plus finished goods). The inventory series have been used in various contexts (in particular, for the stock-backlog ratios), but only a few are presented and analyzed at greater length. The inventory series for individual product categories in part IV of the table are labeled H for uniformity, but they represent finished-goods stocks.

ᵈ Where new orders (N) are included, the periods are those covered by the analysis of N. The comparisons with shipments generally cover the same periods for the series in parts I–III, but some of them cover shorter periods in part IV. The comparisons with production often cover shorter periods (in part I, mostly 1948–58).

ᵉ Current values of N, S, and U are reported by the Department of Commerce, Office of Business Economics (OBE) and the Census Bureau in millions of dollars. For the major industries, these series have also been adjusted for price variation; the deflated (constant-dollar) series were used in comparisons with the Federal Reserve Board production indexes (Z). The series on new orders (N) are net of cancellations.

ᶠ In a sequence of this type, single figures modify the last digit in the number of a group or industry that is listed first. Thus, in the present case, the reference is to the groups 333, 334, 335, and 336; the sequence 3421,3,5 in line 48 stands for industries 3421, 3423, 3425; and analogously elsewhere in this column and in some footnotes below.

ᵍ For the combined "lumber and furniture" industry group, and for the combined "instruments and miscellaneous including ordnance" industry group, there also exist data for 1948–52.

ʰ Census series (1963 revision) beginning in 1953. Earlier estimates from industry data used in Chapter 4 for comparisons with production indexes are not listed.

ⁱ Includes SIC industries 225,7; 23; 314,5,6,7,9; also, the industries listed on line 48.

ʲ The ND group includes industries listed on line 51 and those in the "other" group (line 52), namely, 252,3,4,9; 3511; 3522; 353; 3541,2,8; 355,6,7,8; 361; 3731; 3741,2; 381,2,3,4.

ᵏ The MS category (line 54) consists of groups CM and OM (lines 55 and 56, respectively). CM includes SIC industries 241,2,3,9; 2661; 2816; 285; 295; 32 (excluding 3221); 3429; 343,4,8. OM includes SIC industries 2211; 2221; 2231; 224,6,8,9; 244; 261,2,3,5; 2641,2,3,4,9; 274,5,6,7,8,9; 2812,3,4,5,8,9; 282,6,7,9; 2911; 2992,9; 302,3,6,7; 311,2,3; 3221; 33; 3411; 3491; 345,6,7,9; 3519; 3544,5; 356,9; 362,4,7,9; 3722,3,9; 3681; 3872; 395,8,9.

ˡ Indexes of current-dollar value of manufacturers' orders and shipments (1949 = 100) reported monthly in Standard and Poor's *Industry Surveys*. New orders are gross of cancellations. Only an approximate classification of the series on a two- or three-digit basis and in terms of the market groupings is possible. For more information on these data, see Appendix C.

ᵐ Includes SIC industries 22; 24; 26; 314; 32–36; and 371–2, as listed before in this column, lines 58–71. Also includes some companies in other industries where the coverage is considered too narrow to warrant publication of separate industry indexes. The market groupings included, as listed in column 2, lines 58–71, are HG, AE, ND, CM, and OM. The consumer staples group, CS, is probably represented weakly or not at all.

[n] Monthly indexes of current-dollar value (1935–39 average = 100) computed by the chain-index method and seasonally adjusted by the NICB. Chain indexes were derived for each industrial group and combined with weights based on each industry's value of product according to the 1937 Census of Manufactures. The coverage of the composite indexes is as follows. Durable goods: Automobile equipment (for *N*, since January 1935), building equipment, electrical equipment, metal products, iron and steel, machinery, nonferrous metals, office equipment (for *N*, since January 1935), railroad equipment (for *S*, since June 1930), house furnishings (for *N*, since January 1934; for *S* since January 1935), cement (for *S* only), and glass (for *S* only). Nondurable goods: Boots and shoes (for *N*, since January 1934), chemicals and drugs, clothing (for *N*, since January 1935; for *S*, since January 1933), leather (for *N*, since January 1935), paper manufactures, textiles, and rubber goods (for *S* only). Also miscellaneous industries (n.e.c.; for *N*, since January 1935). New orders are gross of cancellations.

[o] Based on the monthly indexes of physical volume of new and unfilled orders (1923–25 average = 100), as listed below on lines 76–81. The commodities included are as follows. For *N* – Iron and steel: steel sheets, malleable castings, steel castings, fabricated structural steel, fabricated steel plate, enameled sanitary ware; Transportation equipment: locomotives, railroad cars; Lumber products: furniture (factories in the Grand Rapids district), lumber (pine, fir, redwood, and walnut), flooring (oak, maple, etc.); Stone, clay, glass: terra cotta, illuminating glassware; Textiles: cotton finishings, hosiery, knit underwear; Paper and printing: boxboard, labels, book paper. For *U* – Iron and steel: pig iron, enameled sanitary ware, orders of the U.S. Steel Corporation and of the Independent sheet-steel manufacturers (as compiled by the National Association of Sheet and Tin Plate Manufacturers); Transportation equipment: ships, freight cars, locomotives; Lumber: oak and maple flooring, Grand Rapids district furniture orders; Stone, clay, glass: common brick, face brick, paving brick, illuminating glassware; Textiles: as for *N*, plus pyroxylin-coated textiles; Paper: boxboard.

[p] Indexes of gross current value of new orders; begin in 1949 for total new orders (1950 = 100) and in 1957 for export orders (1957 = 100). Since March 1963, calculated on the base 1957–59 average = 100. Component-industry indexes are available for pumps and compressors, engines and turbines, construction machinery, mining machinery, metalworking machinery, office equipment, other industrial machinery (with one subcomponent, chemical process equipment). Seasonal adjustments are made by McGraw-Hill for total nonelectrical machinery orders and total export orders. The data for the component industries are unadjusted.

[q] Index of gross current value of new orders (1926 = 100). Based on reports from 160–260 concerns in these classifications: textiles, leather and shoes, metal trades, paper, and "all other" industries (mostly consumer goods such as optical, confectionery, jewelry, rubber, plastics, and some electrical appliances). The sample, then, consists mainly of firms in the industry groups 22, 26, 31, 34, 36, and 39 and market groupings HG, CM, and OM.

[r] Total; end of quarter prior to June 1910; thereafter end of month; in thousands of long tons.

Notes to Table A-1 (concluded)

ˢ Mostly trade association data. Sources, by line number: 86—American Pig Iron Association; 87—National Association of Flat Rolled Steel Manufacturers; 88, 104–106—Partington (Brookings Institution), Iron Trade Review (*Steel*), *Railway Age,* American Railway Car Institute; 89, 92, 107—Bureau of the Census; 90—Bureau of the Census and American Institute of Steel Construction; 91—Large boiler-producing companies; 93–96—Bureau of the Census and the Enameled Sanitary Ware Manufacturers' Association; 97, 98—National Machine Tool Builders' Association; 99—Foundry Equipment Manufacturers' Association; 100—Electric Overhead Crane Institute; 101—Association of Manufacturers of Woodworking Machinery; 102—American Supply and Machinery Association; 103—Bureau of the Census and Civil Aeronautics Administration; 108—Southern Pine Association; 109—National Oak Flooring Manufacturers' Association; 110—Seidman & Seidman (factories in Grand Rapids, Michigan, district); 111—National Paperboard Association and Bureau of the Census; 112—American Paper and Pulp Association.

The series on orders for rails and aircraft and parts (lines 88 and 103), and those for railroad freight cars before 1913, for railroad passenger cars before 1934, and for railroad locomotives before 1941 (lines 104–106) are quarterly. All the other series are monthly.

New-order series on lines 89, 90, and 92 are reported net of cancellations; those on lines 97, 98, 99, 101, and 110, gross and net; and all others, gross only.

ᵗ Series in physical units, as follows (by line number): 86, 88—thousands of long tons; 87, 89, 90, 107, 111, 112—thousands of short tons; 91—heating surface and steam capacity indexes, 1947–49 = 100; 92–96—thousands of pieces; 104–106—number; 108, 109—millions of board feet.

The other series in part IV are in current-value units, as follows: 97, 98—average monthly shipments 1926 = 100, 1945–47 = 100 (for 1919–58, gross); thousands of dollars, millions of dollars (1921–40, 1945–66, gross and net); 99—monthly average shipments, 1922–24 = 100, 1937–39 = 100, 1947–49 = 100 (1921–40, gross; 1940–56, net); 100, 101—thousands of dollars; 102—July 1948 = 100; 103—millions of dollars; 110—number of days' production (value).

ᵘ Index of new orders received by a cross section of members of the American Supply and Machinery Manufacturers' Association, producers of a variety of supplies such as abrasives, beltings, hoists, saws, tools, etc.

ᵛ Wooden furniture, Grand Rapids district.

source of undercount is in the labeling of the inventory series as H, even where more than one such series has been used. For the comprehensive aggregates and several industry groups in the OBE-Census compilation, the analysis involved total inventories and finished-goods inventories, and in some cases purchased materials and goods in process as well. However, these distinctions by stage of fabrication were not considered sufficiently important for the present classification to be shown in the (already rather elaborate) table.

The OBE-Census Series

The main data on manufacturers' orders, shipments, and inventories come from two agencies of the U.S. Department of Commerce. The Office of Business Economics (Monthly Industry Survey, 1939–63) and the Bureau of the Census, which began processing the OBE surveys in the spring of 1957, released revised series (M3-1) in 1963, and has published the data regularly since then. The Commerce series, insofar as they were available to me for use in this book, are listed in Table A-1, lines 1–56, along with some corresponding components of the industrial production index of the Board of Governors of the Federal Reserve System.

The new Census data were used for the most comprehensive aggregates — all manufacturing, durable goods, and nondurable goods industries — in the period since 1947, and for the broad industry groups and market categories in the period since 1953. In the earlier years, only the older OBE series are available for the two-digit industries and their combinations.

Unpublished monthly series covering the period 1948–62 have been received through the courtesy of the OBE and were used to analyze the cyclical timing and some other aspects of new and unfilled orders and shipments of twenty-eight three- or four-digit industries in the durable goods sector. These are pre-1963 revision data, as are also the series for four industry groups in the nondurable goods sector which report unfilled orders. The new Census series produced in the 1963 revision are not published in comparable industrial detail, except as charts.[2] It was therefore not possible to use the revised data for the period since 1953 to replicate the full analysis of the older OBE data for industrial subdivisions. However, limited use could be made of the new series for the three- or four-digit industries through inspection of the charts and presentation of some published descriptive statistics based on these data.[3]

---

[2] See Bureau of the Census, *Chart Book—Manufacturers' Shipments, Inventories, and Orders: 1953–1963 (Revised)*, Series M3-1 Supplement, Washington, D.C., 1964.

[3] See Table 3-5 and the accompanying text. The statistics on the average percentage changes and related measures are given in Bureau of the Census, *Manufacturers' Shipments, Inventories, and Orders: 1947–1963 (Revised)*, Washington, D.C., 1963, App. F.

Classification by Industries and Market Groupings

Most of the series included in Table A-1 are broadly identified in terms of the products covered. The series in column 1 are classified by the industries into which the products apparently belong. The industry assignment was determined by comparing, in as much detail as possible, the description of the series with the description of the industry as given in the 1957 Standard Industrial Classification (SIC) manual. Some of the assignments, however, are merely approximate or tentative, as information was lacking to make a better determination.

The pre-1963 OBE series were derived from Internal Revenue Service (IRS) classifications, which in turn were based on the 1945 SIC. The new Census series are classified according to the 1957 SIC. In Table A-1, the 1957 SIC is applied throughout for uniformity of treatment.[4]

The new Census series include a classification by market groupings similar to that used in the FRB index of production. These are categories that distinguish between final products and semifabricated goods and materials, and between consumer goods (home goods and apparel and staples) and producer goods (nonautomotive equipment, construction materials, and other materials). There is a separate automotive equipment grouping and a defense products subgroup (which, however, must be combined with nonautomotive equipment as far as the feasible classification of our series is concerned). In short, there are six market categories: home goods and apparel (MG); consumer staples (CS); automotive equipment (AE); nonautomotive equipment and defense (ND); construction materials, supplies, and intermediate products (CM); and other materials, supplies, etc. (OM). In column 2, the series are classified according to these categories, by means of those generalizations and approximations as were considered best for the purpose. The series for these groupings and some additional ones (consumer durables other than automobiles, defense products, other nonautomotive equipment, machinery and equipment industries, and

---

[4] A detailed table, "Composition of Monthly Industry Survey Categories in Terms of 1957 Standard Industrial Classification System," is given in the 1953 Census Bureau source cited in note 2; see App. B, pp. 122–25. For another helpful table, "Conversion of 1945 Standard Industrial Classification System to Obtain Comparable Monthly Industry Survey Benchmark Levels," see *ibid.*, App. C, pp. 126–30.

total materials, supplies, and intermediate products) are described in
Table A-1, lines 46–56.[5]

Composite Indexes and Series for Individual Industries or Products

Part II of the table includes monthly indexes of new and unfilled
orders and shipments compiled for fourteen manufacturing industries
by Standard & Poor's. These series, as well as a composite index from
the same source, refer to current dollar values of N, U, and S and
have been used for 1949–58. Some further detail on them is provided
in Appendix C.

Part III is a catalogue of additional monthly indexes and aggregative series for N, S, and U. All but two of the series cover years before
or during World War II. The indexes compiled by the National Industrial Conference Board are for 1929–44 and 1935–44 and distinguish
between the durable goods sector and the nondurable goods sector of
manufacturing. They are based on series in current-dollar values (lines
72–74). The indexes compiled by the Department of Commerce for
1920–33 are based mainly on trade association series for individual-
product categories in physical units and are of rather limited coverage.
The indexes of new orders and of unfilled orders are not strictly comparable but are similar (lines 75–81). There is also one state index of
new orders, for 1924–41, by the Associated Industries of Massachusetts (line 84) and one company series of unfilled orders in physical
units, for 1902–33, by the U.S. Steel Corporation (line 85). The postwar indexes in this section of the table are the McGraw-Hill series
showing the relative changes in the value of new orders for nonelectrical machinery, total, and for export (lines 82 and 83).

Part IV is a listing of series of narrower coverage, for individual industries or types of product, which can generally be assigned to four-
digit industries. Of the 26 different industries or product categories
included, 11 represent the metalworking industries; 5, primarily nonelectrical machinery; 4, nonautomotive transportation equipment; and
the rest are for paper, furniture, lumber, and clay products. The market

---

[5] A classification of the Monthly Industry Survey categories in terms of the market groupings is
given in Appendix B of Census, *Manufacturers' Shipments* (1963), pp. 122–25.

groupings to which these products belong are essentially industrial equipment and construction and other materials and supplies, i.e., *ND*, *CM*, and *OM*. The series for 19 of the items are in physical units; the others are in current-dollar values. Except for a few quarterly series, the data are monthly as are all the series in the other parts of the table. Most of the series are gross of cancellations but for several items data on canceled and/or net orders are available. Trade associations provide the main source for these series, but some are collected by the Bureau of the Census (see Table A-1, note s).

Some Further Notes on the Composition of the Catalogued Data

The titles of the series included in Table A-1 already indicate that the data give a considerably better representation to durables than to nondurables and to goods used primarily by producers than to goods used primarily by consumers. The classifications in columns 1 and 2 clearly support the inference that our collection of series is heavily weighted with items serving investment in producers' durable equipment and new construction.

To be sure, the distinctions concerned are of necessity to some extent arbitrary and questionable. Producer goods have been defined to include finished goods used by business and all goods that require further fabrication whether destined ultimately for producers or consumers.[6] Because it comprises all commodities that are to undergo further processing, the producer goods category thus defined is certainly much larger than the consumer goods category, which consists only of finished goods of types used primarily by consumers. However, such considerations do not impair the usefulness of the more detailed classifications adopted in Table A-1 or the validity of the derived finding that data relating to manufacturers' orders represent predominantly goods which, in their present form, are demanded mainly by producers (business firms) rather than consumers (households). But it is also necessary to note the importance, among these goods, of materials that may be worked into either consumer goods or finished producer or capital goods. Moreover, government purchases

[6] Cf. Moses Abramovitz, *Inventories and Business Cycles*, New York, NBER, 1950, p. 359, n. 4.

surely account for a substantial proportion of manufacturers' orders, as indicated by the series for the "defense products" (government orders for other goods are not identified). Finally, export orders (i.e., new business received by domestic concerns from foreign buyers) also represent a significant, if smaller, component of the universe of orders held at any time by the U.S. industry.

The industrial composition of data on new orders and, particularly, of data on unfilled orders is associated with differences in the significance of orders for companies in different segments of manufacturing. In some industries new orders are customarily filled from stock. They are therefore practically identical with shipments. Here backlogs of unfilled orders are zero or insignificant, except perhaps at peak levels of demand when firms operate close to capacity, are unable to fill on receipt all new orders they can get, and are willing to accept some new business for future delivery. On the other hand, where production is to specification only, orders cannot be filled immediately and are therefore all of the "advance orders" variety. Today, however, many large manufacturing corporations produce highly diversified outputs that consist partly of goods made to stock and partly of goods made to order.

Accurate knowledge of the relative volume of the two modes of production within companies is not available. Consequently, it is impossible to differentiate systematically and with some acceptable degree of precision between advance orders and orders for items shipped directly from stock. Compilers of aggregate orders series note as one source of their difficulties that many companies do not maintain records on new orders for shelf goods (goods in stock).[7] In the OBE-Census data, there are figures on new orders, as well as on shipments, for all manufacturing industries, but for a large group of nondurable goods industries unfilled orders are not reported and there shipments and new orders are assumed to be equal. However, it is admitted that "a number of nondurable goods industries which are presently not considered as 'production to order' industries do operate on a backlog basis."[8] On

[7] See Walter W. Jacobs and Genevieve B. Wimsatt, "An Approach to Orders Analysis," *Survey of Current Business*, December 1949, p. 24 (Technical Appendix). Also, "Inventories, Shipments, Orders, 1929–1940," *Supplement to the Conference Board Economic Report*, Vol. II, National Industrial Conference Board, December 26, 1940, p. 8. However, orders supplied directly from stocks of finished goods on hand would then probably be recorded in some other form such as sales in the manufacturers' in-stock departments.

[8] Census, *Manufacturers' Shipments* (1963), p. 12.

the other hand, also according to the Census source, "there are a number of industries in the durable goods area which characteristically produce only for stock."[9] A comprehensive study of industry practices and structure as they relate to production to stock and to order was reported to be under active consideration in 1963 by the Bureau of the Census.[10]

As shown in Chapter 2, a criterion exists for judging approximately the relative importance of production to order in a given industry or for a given type of product. The method requires corresponding data on finished-goods inventories (Q) and unfilled orders (U) and consists in comparisons of the average levels of these variables. Prevalence of manufacture to stock is indicated if typically $Q > U$; prevalence of manufacture to order, if typically $Q < U$. The application of this criterion yields results that are more difficult to interpret for value aggregates that cover heterogeneous industry groups than for series relating to more narrowly defined industries or product categories, particularly those in physical units. But despite some ambiguities, due mainly to aggregation, the classifications based on the average ratios $\bar{Q}/\bar{U}$ are on the whole quite reasonable. This judgment is supported by the consistency of the results obtained not only with general information about the industries involved but also with specific and apparently systematic differences in relative amplitudes and timing between series relating to goods made largely to order and series relating to goods made largely to stock (Chapters 3 and 4).

The evidence of the $\bar{Q}/\bar{U}$ ratios assembled in Table 2-1 suggests that production to order, as defined by this criterion, carries a heavy weight within the aggregate of durable goods industries, and particularly in the metalworking, machinery, and nonautomotive transportation equipment industries. On the other hand, production to stock appears to dominate in the automotive assembly operations, the heterogeneous "other durables" group, and the aggregate of nondurable goods industries. Within the latter, only textiles, leather, paper, and printing and publishing are shown as reporting unfilled orders in the OBE-Census data. Among the individual-industry or product series for which the ratios were examined, there are about as many staples made

9 *Loc. cit.*
10 *Ibid.*, p. 20.

ordinarily to stock as items subject to various specifications and made largely to order. However, among the individual series that were subjected to the full analysis of relative amplitudes, timing, etc., the industries or product categories representing production to order exceed those representing production to stock by 11 to 7. Statistics on new orders as distinguished from shipments are simply more likely to be collected and are therefore more readily available in industries where advance orders are of greater relative importance.

While the differences in the relative importance of production to order are important enough in the present context to warrant these references,[11] an attempt to apply the dichotomous classification by type of manufacture to all items in Table A-1 was abandoned after preliminary work revealed the extent of difficulty and potential pitfalls that would inevitably beset such an undertaking. However, the Census-OBE work on the 1963 revision of the shipments and orders series produced some pertinent new information, a summary of which is presented in Table A-2.

This table contains, first, the over-all response rates of companies in the sample reporting shipments and covers forty-eight selected industry groups (column 1). It also provides some information about the sample design for the new series (note a).[12] The coverage was about 70 per cent for both the durable goods and the nondurable goods aggregates, but it was much less, between 40 and 50 per cent, for some industries consisting mainly of small firms, for example, lumber, furniture, and textiles. Against this background, Table A-2 lists, for each of forty-nine industry groups, the percentage of shipments accounted for by the companies that also report unfilled orders (column 2). The over-all figure for the durable goods sector was 65 per cent in August 1962, while that for the nondurable goods sector was only 38 per cent. Aircraft and electrical communication equipment show the highest coverage of unfilled orders, with figures of 96 and 91 per cent, and several industries in machinery, metalworking, and transportation equipment have entries in the 65–89 per cent range. On the other hand,

[11] In addition to Table 2-1 and its accompanying text, relevant information is given in Table 2-4; Chapter 3, passim (particularly in the discussion of Table 3-8); Chapter 4, passim (Tables 4-1, 4-2, 4-4, and their discussion); and Chapter 11 (Table 11-5).

[12] For a more detailed account, see Census, *Manufacturers' Shipments* (1963), Chap. IV and Table D, pp. 9–12.

Table A-2
Response Rate in Reporting Shipments and Percentage of Reported Shipments (S) Accounted for by Companies Also Reporting Unfilled Orders, August and October 1962

Line	Industry Group	Response Rate[a] in Reporting S (1)	Share of S Accounted for by Cos. Reporting Unfilled Orders[b] (2)
1	All manufacturing industries	70%	n.a.
2	Durable goods industries	72	65%
3	Primary metals	87	68
4	Blast furnaces and steel mills	97	74
5	Iron and steel foundries	74	82
6	Nonferrous metals	71	52
7	Other primary metals	80	76
8	Fabricated metal products	57	54
9	Metal cans, barrels, and drums	95	2
10	Hardware and structural steel	56	72
11	Other fabricated metal products	52	58
12	Machinery except electrical	67	69
13	Engines and turbines	94	86
14	Farm machinery	83	22
15	Construction, mining, and materials handling	72	59
16	Metalworking machinery	67	89
17	Miscellaneous equipment	49	70
18	Special-industry machinery	51	72
19	General industrial machinery	69	73
20	Office and store machines	84	88
21	Service industry machinery	56	86
22	Electrical machinery	78	73
23	Transmission and distribution equipment	81	82
24	Electric industrial equipment apparatus	79	80
25	Household appliances, including radio and TV	78	51
26	Communication equipment	91	91
27	Electronic components	66	66
28	Other electrical machinery	67	64
29	Transportation equipment	86	74
30	Motor vehicles, trucks, and bodies	91	54
31	Aircraft and parts	87	96
32	Other transportation equipment	78	78
33	Lumber products	43	30

(continued)

Table A-2 (concluded)

Line	Industry Group	Response Rate[a] in Reporting S (1)	Share of S Accounted for by Cos. Reporting Unfilled Orders[b] (2)
34	Furniture	48%	72%
35	Stone, clay, and glass products	65	28
36	Scientific and other instruments	76	47
37	Other durable goods	66	65
38	Nondurable goods industries	69	38
39	Textile mill products	50	45
40	Leather and leather products	62	38
41	Industrial products and cut stock	57	16
42	Other leather products	63	43
43	Paper and allied products	74	42
44	Pulp and paper	87	57
45	Paperboard containers	66	26
46	Printing and publishing	49	28
47	Newspaper, books, and periodicals	57	9
48	Other publishing and printing	40	48
49	Industries with unfilled orders, total[c]	n.a.	60
50	Nondurable goods industries with unfilled orders[d]	n.a.	38

n.a. = not available.

Source: Bureau of the Census, *Manufacturers' Shipments, Inventories, and Orders: 1947–1963 (Revised)*, Washington, D.C., 1963, Table D (for column 1) and Table E (for column 2), pp. 10–11.

[a] As of October 1962. Based on the sample for the new Census series, a probability sample selected as a subsample of the 1959 Annual Survey of Manufacturers. All companies with 1,000 or more manufacturing employees were included with certainty (with a sampling weight of 1.00). Smaller companies were sampled with probabilities proportional to their employment size within each industry category stratum. Approximately 7,500 companies were thus drawn for the panel, according to the Census source (p. 9). The over-all response rates, from which a selection is given below in this table, are in *ibid.*, Table D, together with response rates for the "certainty class" and three other sample weight ranges.

[b] As of August 1962. Measures the percentage of total shipments of each industry group that is accounted for by those companies in the group that also report unfilled orders.

[c] Includes all durable goods industries, textiles, paper, printing and publishing, and leather, except for the following: wooden containers; glass containers; metal cans, barrels, and drums; building paper; and automotive assembly operations.

[d] Includes textiles, paper (excluding building paper), printing and publishing, and leather.

even in these areas, the coverage of unfilled orders is much lower in some industries, although not below 50 per cent, except in two cases.[13] Elsewhere among the durables, it is weak (about 28–47 per cent) for lumber, stone, clay, and glass products, and instruments. Among the nondurable goods industries, the highest coverage is 57 per cent (pulp and paper); the lowest is 9 per cent (newspapers, books, and periodicals).

This evidence is, of course, not conclusive, because a company that does not report unfilled orders may nevertheless hold such orders. However, it is certainly suggestive and it is, on the whole, consistent with some other information I was able to assemble. It is to be hoped that more documentation on the importance of new advance orders and unfilled orders will be provided in the future work by the Bureau of the Census.[14]

[13] The two are farm machinery and equipment (22 per cent) and metal cans, barrels, and drums (2 per cent). The latter industry has been excluded from the group of industries with unfilled orders in the new Census data (see Table A-2, note c). (However, for "heavy type" steel barrels and drums alone, the $\bar{Q}/\bar{U}$ ratios in Table 2-1 indicate relatively very large backlogs in the period 1933–54.)

[14] This is particularly needed, since the proper benchmark levels for the order series are not known. The initial level of unfilled orders was established by applying the ratio of December 1947 unfilled orders to 1948 sales (shipments) for the reporting companies to the total 1948 sales estimates. Figures for earlier and subsequent months were computed from that point. New levels were established similarly by using the August 1962 U/S ratios. See Jacobs and Wimsatt, "Approach to Orders Analysis," p. 24; and Census, *Manufacturers' Shipments* (1963), p. 12.

APPENDIX B

SUPPLEMENTARY MEASURES OF TIMING: STANDARD AND POOR'S DATA

I. Relative Timing of New Orders and Shipments

Standard and Poor's Corporation (S&P) has compiled estimates of relative changes in the value of manufacturers' shipments, new and unfilled orders, and inventories. These monthly indexes begin in 1949, and their analysis in this book extends through 1958. For this period, they were published in relatives, 1949 = 100, unadjusted for seasonal variation; the seasonal corrections, where needed, have been made by the National Bureau.[1]

The S&P sample reporting the sales (value of shipments), orders, and inventory figures comprises several hundred companies, including the largest ones in each of the major industries covered.[2] The companies are grouped into industries, so there is no overlap in coverage between the industry indexes. Some industries such as auto parts and chemicals were said to be quite well represented; others, such as textiles, considerably worse. In general, the coverage in these indexes is substantially narrower than that in the Commerce (OBE) data for the same period.

[1] The data for 1949–56 appear in Standard & Poor's, *Industry Surveys, Trends and Projections*, Section 6, November 15, 1956, under the heading "Progress Report of Industry." Later issues of this release continued the series in the same basic form. The December 15, 1960, issue of S&P *Trends and Projections* (section 5) presents revised "Progress Report of Industry" data in relatives, 1957 sales = 100, for the period January 1949 through October 1960. The December 6, 1962, issue carries the data forward through October 1962.

[2] The orders are reported on an "as received" basis, like the Commerce data; the inventories include stocks in all stages of fabrication. New and unfilled orders and shipments are reported independently. This information, and that in the text concerning the coverage, comes from conversations with S&P personnel engaged in the preparation of the data. Published information about these S&P indexes is very limited.

Being shorter than the Commerce series, the S&P indexes offer fewer timing observations per industry and, being based on smaller samples, they are also more erratic. Considerable uncertainty attaches therefore to some of the dates of their specific-cycle turns. However, in the few cases where the S&P and the OBE data can be roughly matched in terms of industrial coverage, there is a good deal of correspondence between their relative movements, probably because the indexes are based on reports from most of the largest firms in the industries covered. Several of these industries are sufficiently concentrated that the series may be fairly representative, despite the relatively small number of companies participating in the S&P surveys. The evidence for the most comprehensive series that can be compared is presented in Chart 2-1 and the related text; there, one substantial difference in the broad movements of these series was found and explained by the behavior of cancellations. The following timing comparisons provide additional documentation of the good correspondence between the results of the two independent compilations. The tendency for the matched turning points to coincide is certainly pronounced.[3]

*Lead (−) or Lag (+) in Months of Standard and Poor's
Indexes at Turns in OBE Series*

	At 1949 Troughs	At 1951 "Korean" Peaks	At 1954 Troughs	At 1956 Peaks	At 1958 Troughs
New Orders	0	0	+2	−6	+1
Shipments	0	0	0	0	−1

Chart B-1 presents the paired S&P indexes of new orders and shipments for all but a few of the component industries and for all companies included.[4] The series are of unequal quality, since the value of such small-sample estimates is lower, the smaller the average size and the more widely varying the experience of the firms in the given in-

---

[3] The only example of a larger deviation from synchronous timing seems to be at the 1956 peaks in new orders, but even this is not a real exception. The 1956 turning dates for new orders are based on marginal considerations, and comparing them may be misleading. A glance at Chart 2-1 shows that the first decline in the two series started at the same time, at the beginning of 1956.

[4] The latter series, labeled the "composite" indexes, are weighted averages of the component-industry indexes, but they also include a few companies in industries for which no separate indexes are published because of insufficient coverage.

Chart B-1
Standard and Poor's Indexes of Value of Manufacturers' New Orders and Shipments, Thirteen Major Industries, 1949–58

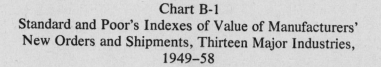

——— New orders
------ Sales

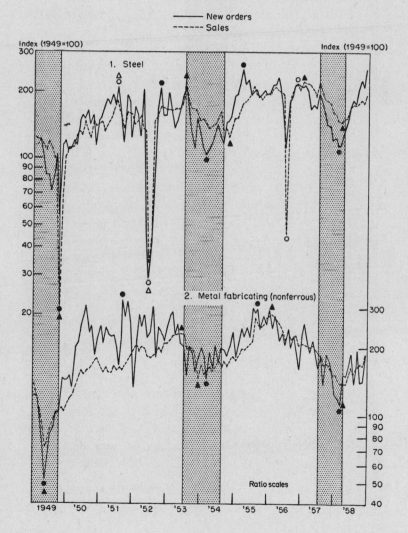

Chart B-1 (continued)

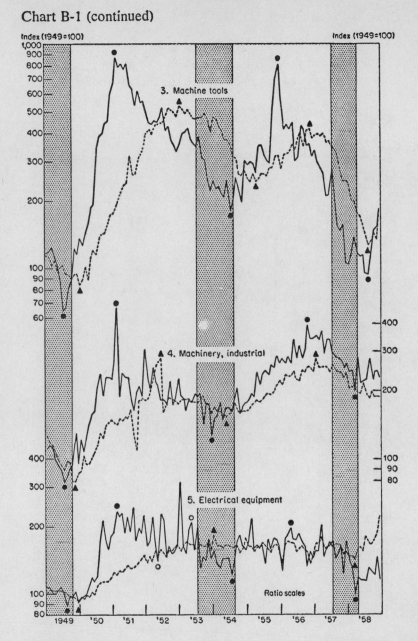

Chart B-1 (continued)

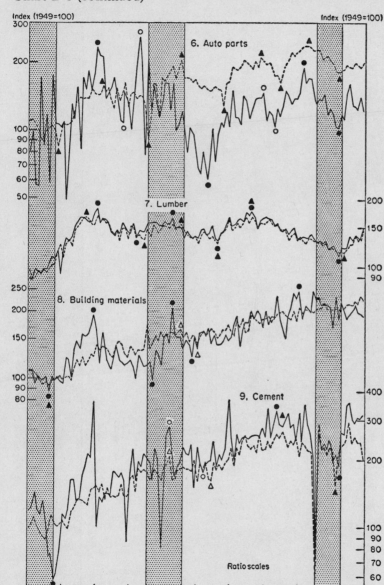

Index (1949=100)

Index (1949=100)

6. Auto parts

7. Lumber

8. Building materials

9. Cement

Ratio scales

1949   '50   '51   '52   '53   '54   '55   '56   '57   '58

Chart B-1 (continued)

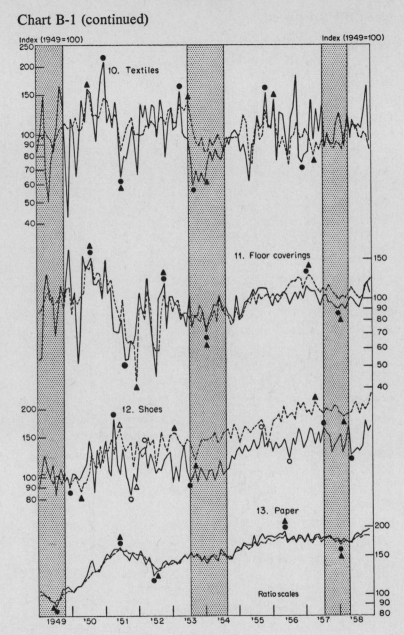

Index (1949=100)　　　　　　　　　　　　　　　Index (1949=100)

10. Textiles

11. Floor coverings

12. Shoes

13. Paper

Ratio scales

1949　'50　'51　'52　'53　'54　'55　'56　'57　'58

Chart B-1 (concluded)

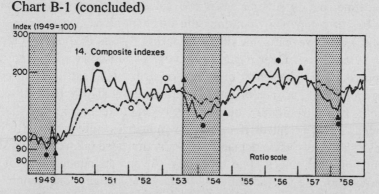

Note: Shaded areas represent business cycle contractions; unshaded areas, expansions. Dots identify peaks and troughs of specific cycles in new orders; black triangles, sales (value of shipments). Circles and white triangles identify short cycles or retardations in new orders and sales, respectively.

Source: Standard and Poor's Corporation. Seasonal adjustments by the National Bureau of Economic Research.

dustry. Thus industries such as textiles or shoes must have a considerably weaker representation in a survey of this sort than, say, steel or industrial machinery. But we are not concerned here with "universe" estimates for either new orders or shipments of any industry. Our interest is solely in the relations among the different activities covered, and in this respect the S&P indexes deserve some attention. Hence, we examine all the available evidence. However, to avoid a virtual duplication of the graphs, Chart B-1 does exclude the indexes for the paper industry, which resemble closely the corresponding OBE series in Chart 4-3. Also excluded from the graphical presentation are the indexes for the aircraft industry, which offer few advantages over the comprehensive Census estimates of new orders and shipments of aircraft manufacturers. The latter series, which are quarterly, were presented in Chart 4-4. The cyclical course of the corresponding S&P indexes is similar but obscured by exceedingly large and erratic month-to-month oscillations for new orders.

There is one disturbing factor as far as our comparisons are concerned, however, and while its influence cannot be evaluated with the information available it is potentially serious. Some of the companies reporting shipments (sales) in the S&P sample do not report new orders. In each industry the coverage for either activity is consistent over time, but in several cases the sales series represents a larger number of companies than does the corresponding new-order series.

Our graphs reveal some of the apparent results of these discrepancies in coverage. Over a period of years, total new orders and total shipments of a given firm or group of firms will tend to have equal average values: sooner or later, whether immediately from stock or months hence from future output, any orders (except for a few that are canceled) will be filled. If in certain industries new orders rise high above shipments when demand expands, they also fall well below shipments in slack times. The tendency toward an equalization of the averages for the two activities is largely a cyclical phenomenon. But Chart B-1 shows considerable departures from this pattern for some of the industries in the S&P sample. In particular, new orders remained below shipments throughout 1953–58 for auto parts and shoes (graphs 6 and 12). These instances of incongruent behavior cannot be ascribed to the form in which these series are presented.[5] They occur in industries in which the companies reporting new orders are substantially fewer than those reporting shipments, and are presumably due to these discrepancies in coverage between the two variables.[6]

Table B-1 lists the timing comparisons that can be made between the specific turns in new orders and shipments for fourteen pairs of Standard and Poor's series. The observations refer to a short period marked by three revivals and two recessions, all of them mild, and by the Korean War, which was accompanied by buying waves of many products. The peaks and troughs in the S&P indexes, like those in the Commerce series, are concentrated in zones that are apparently associated with these business reversals or transitions. But the indexes, somewhat more often than the Commerce series, failed to turn

[5] The Standard and Poor's series are published as indexes based on the average monthly values of new orders and sales in 1949. Because of the recession, the average levels of new orders in 1949 were lower than those of sales for several industries. We were able to make some rough allowances for this fact by expressing both the new orders (N) and the sales (S) of an industry as percentages of its average monthly *sales* in 1949. (This arrangement makes the relative position of the paired index series similar to what would be obtained by plotting to a common scale the corresponding value aggregates, as was done in the charts for the OBE series presented earlier in this volume.) After the adjustments, the series still show some persistent deviations from the expected tendency for the across-the-cycle averages of N and S to be approximately equal.

[6] The discrepancy in coverage would have no significant effect on the relation concerned if no significant difference existed in the behavior of new orders between those companies in the sales sample that do and those that do not report new orders. Indeed, the building materials industry conforms well to the expected pattern, even though the coverage discrepancy is here particularly large, with the average value of new orders in 1949 being somewhat less than half the average value of sales.

in one or other of these zones, in particular during the Korean period (see the note to Table B-1 and the text above on the differential behavior of gross and net new orders in that period).

Table B-1 shows that at the shipments troughs connected with the 1954 revival new orders led in most industries by substantial intervals, whereas their leads in the 1949 upturn zone were fewer and on the whole shorter. At the 1958 recovery, the timing of orders and shipments was roughly coincident. This is similar to what was found for the OBE series in Table 4-5. For the corresponding columns of peak observations, broad comparisons of the same type reveal more differences.

The accompanying tabulation shows the breakdown of the timing comparisons based on the Standard and Poor's and the OBE data for 1949–58. The similarity of the two distributions is considerable.

	Standard and Poor's, Thirteen Industries		Office of Business Economics, Eleven Industries	
	No.	Per Cent	No.	Per Cent
Long leads (over 3 months)	18	36.7	18	39.1
Short leads (1 to 3 months)	16	32.7	15	32.6
Exact coincidences	11	22.4	8	17.4
Short lags (1 to 3 months)	4	8.2	4	8.7
Long lags (over 3 months)	0	–	1	2.2
Total	49	100.0	46	100.0

II. Timing of Orders at Business Revivals and Recessions

Table B-2 presents the record of cyclical timing of the S&P indexes of new orders. Some broad similarities exist between this record and that shown in Table 11-2 for the OBE-Census series on new orders for the major manufacturing industries. The average leads for seven component series in that table at the revivals of 1949, 1954, and 1958 are −4.0, −8.1, and −2.6 months, and at the recessions of 1953 and 1957, −5.1 and 9.9 months, respectively.[7] According to these data, therefore,

[7] The industry groups included are primary metals, fabricated metal products, electrical machinery, nonelectrical machinery, transportation equipment, other durable goods, and nondurable goods industries reporting unfilled orders.

Table B-1
Timing of Standard and Poor's Indexes of Value of Manufacturers' New Orders at Turns in Corresponding Indexes of Shipments, 1949–58

	Lead (−) or Lag (+) in Months of New Orders at Turns in Shipments in Turning Zone Associated with				
Industry	1949 Revival: Trough (1)	1953 Recession: Peak (2)	1954 Revival: Trough (3)	1957 Recession: Peak (4)	1958 Revival: Trough (5)
Durable goods industries					
Steel	0	−9	−8	−2 [a]	−1
Metal fabricating (nonferrous)	0	−3 [a]	−3	−5	−1
Machine tools	−6	−23	−9	−11	0
Machinery, industrial	−4	−6 [a]	−5	−3	n.i.
Electrical equipment	−4	−8 [a]	n.s.	n.s.	0
Auto parts	n.i.	−15	−6	−2	0
Lumber	n.i.	−3	0	0	−2
Building materials	0	−3 [b]	−2 [b]	n.s.	n.s.
Cement	n.s.	0	−3	−2	+1
Nondurable goods industries					
Textiles	n.i.	−3	−5	−3	−4
Floor coverings	n.i.	0	0	−1	−1
Shoes	−4	−11	−2	+3	+3 [a]
Paper	+1	n.t.	n.t.	0	0
Composite index [c]	−3	−6	−8	−8	0
Component industries, average	−2.1	−7.0	−3.9	−2.4	−0.5
(No. of observations)	(8)	(12)	(11)	(11)	(11)

n.i. = not identified (timing of new orders and/or sales uncertain).

n.s. = no turn in sales at this recession or revival.

n.t. = no specific-cycle turn in either new orders or sales.

Note: A few of the Standard and Poor's series show additional cyclical movements during the Korean period, 1950–52, and some of the turning points in these movements can be matched. Note, however, that the trough dates for steel fall in June 1952, a month of widespread work stoppages in the industry (like the previous troughs of October 1949; see Chart B-1), but they seem to approximate well the turning dates between falls and rises in new orders and sales. The resulting observations, excluded from the table because of the marginal nature of some of the movements and the uncertain dating of some of the turns involved, are listed below with the proper reservations (notes a and b are the same as for the table proper).

	Peaks (1950–51)	Troughs (1951–52)		Peaks (1950–51)	Troughs (1951–52)
Steel	0	0	Floor coverings	0	−4
Auto parts	−2	−9 [a]	Shoes	−2 [b]	−1 [a,b]
Lumber	+4	−3	Paper	0	−1
Textiles	+6	0			

Notes to Table B-1 (concluded)

^a The turning point of new orders used in this comparison is a minor or "subcycle" turn rather than a specific-cycle turn (see Chart B-1).

^b The turning point of shipments used in this comparison is a minor or "subcycle" turn rather than a specific-cycle turn (see Chart B-1).

^c Includes companies in industries other than those shown above. For some industries, no separate indexes are presented in the Standard and Poor's *Industry Surveys* because the coverage, or the number of firms reporting, is considered too small. For one industry — aircraft — indexes of both new orders and shipments are available, but timing of the highly erratic new-order series could not be satisfactorily ascertained (see text).

the shortest leads occurred at the 1958 revival and the longest at the 1957 recession, while the 1949, 1953, and 1954 episodes have intermediate ranks in the succession from shorter to longer leads. The component-industries averages listed in Table B-2 yield the same ranking of the five business cycle turns. Moreover, the average leads of new orders computed from Table E-2 for fourteen selected industrial subdivisions also give the same ranks to the five turning-point zones of the 1949–58 period.[8] This type of agreement between different sets of data seems encouraging; it is probably significant. There is, of course, no reason to expect that such data would reveal close similarities of detail. (As noted elsewhere, individual timing observations can be very sensitive even to small discrepancies between series at the critical turning points.)

There is one conspicuous difference between the timing records here compared, namely, that most of the Commerce series show cyclical downturns in 1952 and 1953 which anticipate the business peak of July 1953, while most of the S&P indexes do not (see Table B-2, column 2, and Tables 11-2 and E-2, columns 3). What this means is that in the Commerce series those contractions that followed the Korean buying surge are clearly separated from the contractions associated with the 1953 business recession by upward movements which, though mostly mild, are long and distinct enough to be recognized as specific expansions. In several S&P indexes, on the other hand, the corresponding movements are weaker or shorter or both, and are best viewed as merely retardations superimposed upon the contrac-

[8] These industries are iron and steel; primary nonferrous metals; electrical generator apparatus; other electrical equipment; metalworking machinery; general industrial machinery; special-industry machinery; aircraft; motor vehicle parts and accessories; lumber; stone, clay, and glass products; textiles; leather; and paper. The average leads of new orders according to these data are, in months: in 1949, −3.9; in 1953, −4.3; in 1954, −7.2; in 1957, −10.6; and in 1958, −2.1.

Appendix B

Table B-2
Timing of Standard and Poor's Indexes of Value of Manufacturers' New Orders at Each Business Cycle Turn, 1949–58

Industry	Lead (−) or Lag (+) in Months of New Orders at Business Cycle Turns				
	Trough Oct. 1949 (1)	Peak July 1953 (2)	Trough Aug. 1954 (3)	Peak July 1957 (4)	Trough April 1958 (5)
Durable goods industries					
Steel	0	−9	−6	−28 [a]	−2
Metal fabricating (nonferrous)	−5	n.m. [b]	−5	−22	−1
Machine tools	−3	n.m.	−1	−19	+4
Machinery, industrial	−3	n.m.	−8	−9	−1
Electrical equipment	−2	n.m. [c]	−1	−15	−1
Aircraft	−3 [d]	n.m.	−11	−11	−6
Auto parts	n.i.	n.m. [e]	−4	−5	−1
Lumber	n.i.	−3	0	−23	−1
Building materials	−2	−3	−9	−6	−3
Cement	0	n.m. [f]	n.m. [f]	−14	−1
Nondurable goods industries					
Textiles	n.i.	−3	−11	n.m.	n.m.
Floor coverings	n.i.	−9	−7	−6	−4
Shoes	+2 [d]	n.m.	−13	0	+1
Paper	−3	n.m.	n.m.	−14	−3
Composite index [g]	−3	n.m. [h]	−6	−14	−1
Component industries, average	−1.9	−5.4	−6.3	−13.2	−1.5
(No. of observations)	(10)	(5)	(12)	(13)	(13)

n.i. = not identified (timing uncertain).

n.m. = not matched.

[a] A secondary peak led the July 1957 business downturn by 8 months.

[b] A minor peak, leading the July 1953 business downturn by 4 months, can be distinguished.

[c] A minor peak, leading the July 1953 business downturn by 2 months, can be distinguished.

[d] Based on a tentative trough date.

[e] A minor peak, leading the July 1953 business downturn by 15 months, can be distinguished.

[f] A minor contraction in this series began 4 months, and ended 5 months, earlier than the business contraction of July 1953–August 1954.

[g] S&P total index of the value of manufacturers' new orders. Covers companies classified into the fourteen industries listed on the lines above plus a few companies in industries for which no separate indexes were published because of inadequate coverage.

[h] A minor peak, leading the July 1953 business downturn by 6 months, can be distinguished.

Table B-3
Timing of Standard and Poor's Indexes of Value of Manufacturers' Unfilled Orders at Each Business Cycle Turn, 1949–58

Industry	Lead (−) or Lag (+), in Months, of Unfilled Orders at Business Cycle Turns				
	Trough Oct. 1949 (1)	Peak July 1953 (2)	Trough Aug. 1954 (3)	Peak July 1957 (4)	Trough April 1958 (5)
Durable goods industries					
Steel [a]	−1	−18	0	−9	+2
Metal fabricating (nonferrous)	0	−19	−1	−5	+7
Machine tools	0	−19	+4	−15	+8
Machinery, industrial	0	−15	+5	−4	+8
Electrical equipment	+8	−6	+11	0	−3
Aircraft	n.i.[b]	+3	+1	−6	−5
Auto parts [a]	+9	−12	−1	−2	+1
Lumber [a]	−4	−8[c]	−7	−22	−1
Building materials	+1	−3[c]	+3	−1	+1
Cement [a]	n.i.[d]	n.m.[e]	−4	0	+1
Nondurable goods industries					
Textiles [a]	−5	−3[c]	−5	0	−4
Shoes [a]	+6	−7[c]	−4	n.t.	n.t.
Paper	−4	+2[c]	−3	−15	+1
Composite index [f]	−2	−12	+2	−4	0
Component industries, average	+0.9	−8.8	−0.1	−6.6	+1.3
(No. of observations)	(11)	(12)	(13)	(12)	(12)

n.i. = not identified (timing uncertain).

n.m. = not matched.

n.t. = no turn.

[a] Seasonally adjusted for NBER by Census Method II. The seasonal variations were found to be large in one of these series (shoes) and mild or moderate in the other five. The remaining series required no seasonal adjustments.

[b] This series rose steeply in 1949 and through the rest of the 1948–53 expansion. Its lowest values in 1949 were in January and February.

[c] Timing is measured from the second of the two peaks that each of these series reached during the period 1950–53. (The series peaked first during the early phase of the Korean War in 1950–51, then contracted, and expanded again in 1951–53. Each of the remaining series in this table shows only one major peak during the same period.)

[d] This series rose steeply through 1949 and 1950, except for a short decline (not a cyclical contraction) in August–October 1949.

[e] This series reached a high peak in January 1951, then declined through April 1954. No major countermovement interrupted that contraction, and the series shows no cyclical downturn that can be matched with the 1953 business peak.

[f] S&P total index of the value of manufacturers' unfilled orders. Covers companies classified into the industries listed on the lines above plus a few companies in industries for which no separate indexes were published because of inadequate coverage.

tions that began early in 1951, not as cyclical expansions. This point
has already been documented, in Chapter 2, for the estimates of total
advance orders. As suggested there, it is probably a consequence of
the temporary increase in cancellations, especially of military orders.

Table B-3 shows the timing of S&P indexes of unfilled orders at the
five business cycle turns of 1949–58. This record, too, is in a broad
agreement with that of the OBE-Census series as presented in Table
11-13. According to both tables, the longest leads of the backlogs (of
about 9–12 months in the over-all aggregates and on the average) occurred at the business peak of 1953. The leads at the 1957 peak tended
to be shorter (4–7 months when judged by the corresponding summary
measures). Short leads or coincidences prevailed at the 1949 trough,
short lags or coincidences again at the troughs of 1954 and 1958.

APPENDIX C

PRICE DEFLATORS FOR SELECTED MANUFACTURING INDUSTRIES

THE OBE SERIES of new orders and shipments of the major manufacturing industries, in current-dollar values, were adjusted for changes in prices by means of indexes based mainly on selected components of the monthly Wholesale Price Index of the U.S. Department of Labor, Bureau of Labor Statistics (BLS). These deflators are price indexes on the base 1947–49 average = 100.[1] They were applied to the monthly series in the OBE compilation for 1948–58.[2]

To deflate the series for motor vehicles and parts, the WPI component for motor vehicles (code 11-8) was used directly. Similarly, the price index for pulp, paper, and allied products (code 09) was judged to be applicable as reported to the series for paper and allied products. For the other major industries in the OBE compilation, however, price deflators had to be calculated from selected components of the WPI and, in a few cases, from some other price or cost (in particular, average hourly earnings) indexes. Table C-1 identifies these component indexes and the weights used to combine them into the deflators for the major industries or industry groups.

Comprehensive series of deflated values were constructed by adding up the appropriate industry series in constant dollars. These include the aggregates for (1) all durable goods industries (combining seven industries, namely, primary metals, fabricated metal products, electrical machinery, other machinery, motor vehicles, other transportation equipment, and other durable goods); (2) nondurable goods industries reporting unfilled orders (combining four industries, namely, textiles, leather, paper, and printing and publishing); (3) all nondurable goods industries (the preceding aggregate plus that for nondurable goods industries not reporting unfilled orders; see Table D-1, line 60); and (4) all manufacturing industries – the sum of the aggregates for all durables and all nondurables, that is, the series included in (1) and (3) above.

[1] That base replaced the 1926 = 100 base in the extensive revision of the WPI in 1952. The revision doubled the number of commodities and quotations covered. The revised index has been published in complete detail for the period back to January 1947. (More recently, since January 1962, the WPI has been computed on the base 1957–59 = 100.) The index is a chain of relatives each calculated by the Laspeyres formula. For further details on the construction of the index, see references in Table C-1, notes a and b.

[2] See the section, Series in Constant Prices, in Chapter 3.

Table C-1
Component Indexes and Weights Used
in Calculating the Price Deflators

Line	Component-Index Series [a]	BLS Code Number (1)	Value of Trans- actions (millions of dollars) [b] (2)	Relative Importance Within Industry (per cent) [c] (3)
PRIMARY METALS				
1	Iron and steel	10-1	10,420.0	68.1
2	Nonferrous metals	10-2	4,882.7	31.9
3	Total		15,302.7	100.0
FABRICATED METAL PRODUCTS [d]				
4	Metal containers	10-3	819.2	9.2
5	Hardware	10-4	1,001.3	11.2
6	Plumbing equipment	10-5	366.6	4.1
7	Heating equipment	10-6	1,029.0	11.5
8	Fabricated structural metal products	10-7	2,123.7	23.8
9	Fabricated nonstructural metal products	10-8	3,171.9	35.6
10	Cutlery	12-6-7	144.5	1.6
11	Metal household containers	12-6-8	253.3	2.8
12	Total		8,909.5	100.0
ELECTRICAL MACHINERY				
13	Electrical machinery and equipment	11-7	2,585.7	45.6
14	Household appliances	12-4	2,194.2	38.7
15	Radio, television, and phonographs	12-5	895.7	15.8
16	Total		5,675.6	100.0
MACHINERY EXCEPT ELECTRICAL				
17	Machinery and motive products	11	28,687.3	146.6
18	*minus* Electrical machinery and equipment	11-7	2,585.7	13.2
19	*minus* Motor vehicles	11-8	6,535.0	33.4
20	Total		19,566.6	100.0
NONAUTOMOTIVE TRANSPORTATION EQUIPMENT [e]				
21	Railroad equipment index [f]	n.a.	n.a.	65.7
22	Av. hourly earnings index, shipbuilding [g]	n.a.	n.a.	9.8
23	Av. hourly earnings index, aircraft [g]	n.a.	n.a.	7.6
24	Floating equipment, ICC cost index [h]	n.a.	n.a.	6.1
25	Foundry and forge shop products	10-1-5	n.a.	1.5
26	Machinery and equipment, special-purpose index	11 exc. 11-8	n.a.	2.2

(continued)

Table C-1 (concluded)

Line	Component-Index Series[a]	BLS Code Number (1)	Value of Transactions (millions of dollars)[b] (2)	Relative Importance Within Industry (per cent)[c] (3)
27	Nonferrous metal mill shapes	10-2-5	n.a.	1.1
28	Finished steel	10-1-4	n.a.	3.6
29	Fabricated structural metal products	10-7	n.a.	2.4
30	Total			100.0
	OTHER DURABLE GOODS INDUSTRIES			
31	Lumber and wood products	08	5,363.3	35.4
32	Household furniture	12-1	1,865.6	12.3
33	Commercial furniture	12-2	594.1	3.9
34	Other household durable goods	12-6	1,596.8	10.5
35	Nonmetallic minerals—structural	13	2,789.8	18.4
36	Miscellaneous	15	6,095.6	40.2
37	minus Manufactured animal feeds	15-2	3,152.4	20.8
38	Total		14,683.8	100.0
	TEXTILE-MILL PRODUCTS			
39	Textiles and apparel	03	19,770.7	175.2
40	minus Apparel	03-5	9,198.6	81.5
41	Floor covering	12-3	715.6	6.2
42	Total		11,287.7	100.0
	LEATHER AND LEATHER PRODUCTS			
43	Leather	04-2	967.0	27.2
44	Footwear	04-3	1,868.7	52.5
45	Other leather products	04-4	721.4	20.3
46	Total		3,557.1	100.0
	PRINTING AND PUBLISHING			
47	Av. hourly earnings index[g]	n.a.	n.a.	50.0
48	Newsprint	9-32	454.8	24.7[i]
49	Printing paper	9-31-11	95.7	5.2[i]
50	Book paper	9-31-21	371.8	20.1[i]
51	Total		922.3	100.0
	NONDURABLE GOODS INDUSTRIES NOT REPORTING UNFILLED ORDERS			
52	Processed foods	02	31,807.3	46.0
53	Apparel	03-5	9,198.6	13.3
54	Chemicals and allied products	06	10,754.2	15.6
55	Rubber and rubber products	07	2,051.8	3.0
56	Tobacco mfrs. and beverages	14	4,776.6	6.9
57	Manufactured animal feeds	15-2	3,152.4	4.6
58	Petroleum and products	05-5	8,926.8	12.9
59	minus Crude petroleum	05-5-6	1,590.8	2.3
60	Total		69,076.9	100.0

Notes to Table C-1

n.a. = not applicable.

[a] All series except those identified on lines 21–24 are indexes for groups or subgroups in the BLS Wholesale Price Index, 1947–49 = 100. The BLS code numbers for these indexes are listed in column 1. The price data used in constructing the WPI are those which apply at primary market levels, that is, the first important commercial transaction for each commodity. Most of the quotations are the selling prices of representative manufacturers or producers, or prices quoted on organized exchanges or markets. For a description of the WPI, see U.S. Department of Labor, *Techniques of Preparing Major BLS Statistical Series,* BLS Bulletin 1168, Washington, D.C., 1954, Chap. 10.

[b] Transactions are reported in the Census of Manufactures for 1947 and used as basic weights in the 1952 revision of the WPI. Interplant transfers were excluded insofar as available data permitted. Data for agricultural and extractive industry products were obtained from the *Agriculture* and *Minerals Yearbooks* for 1947; import data cover the year 1947, as reported by the U.S. Department of Commerce.

[c] Refers to each of the ten major industries or group of industries in the OBE *Industry Survey.* These industries are identified below in the body of the table.

[d] Instead of computing the weighted averages of the eight component indexes listed below (lines 4–11), a simpler method of calculation was used. The primary metals index (combining 10-1 and 10-2; see lines 1–3, above) were multiplied by 179.8, and the result was subtracted from the metal and metal products index (code 10) multiplied by 279.8. The weights 179.8 and 279.8 correspond to the 1947 transaction values of $15,302.7 million and $23,814.4 million, respectively. This method is equivalent to computing the weighted averages of the six component indexes listed on lines 4–9 (i.e., omitting cutlery and metal household containers, which have very small weights; see lines 10 and 11).

[e] The weights are based, approximately, on the 1947 values of private purchases of aircraft, ships and boats, and railroad equipment. The criterion assigns much greater weight to the railroad component of nonautomotive transportation equipment than later developments would justify, and much smaller weight to the aircraft component (the former is nearly two-thirds, the latter about one-seventh).

[f] U.S. Department of Commerce price deflator for railroad equipment, with linear extrapolation.

[g] Index numbers, 1947–49 average = 100, based on the monthly BLS series on gross average hourly earnings per worker in the corresponding industries (in dollars). The series used are estimates first published in June 1953.

[h] Interstate Commerce Commission cost index for floating equipment, account 56, with linear extrapolation.

[i] Based on the corresponding values of transactions in column 2, for which the sum ($922.3 million) is treated as representing 50 per cent of the within-industry weights.

APPENDIX D

AVERAGE MONTHLY PERCENTAGE AMPLITUDES AND RELATED MEASURES FOR NEW ORDERS, PRODUCTION, AND SHIPMENTS: ADDITIONAL EVIDENCE

MONTHLY PERCENTAGE CHANGES in the seasonal, trend-cycle, and irregular components, as well as some related measures, have been computed for many time series on new orders (N), shipments (S), and production (Z) in the process of adjusting these data for seasonal variation. Such statistics were presented and discussed in Chapter 3 for groups of series matched by industry and period. In Table D-1, estimates of the same type are shown for selected industries and products, including several cases where data on N and S or Z correspond only approximately, having overlapping rather than coextensive periods of coverage.[1]

The comparisons in Table D-1 indicate again, with strong regularity, that the mean amplitudes of the seasonally adjusted series and of their cyclical and irregular components are greater for new orders than for shipments, often by large differentials. The same is generally true for the original (unadjusted) series and the seasonal components. Furthermore, the average amplitudes for production also are systematically smaller than the corresponding measures for new orders. In fact, they

[1] The items in this category are machine tools, lumber, oak flooring, printing and publishing, and leather and leather products. In one case, there is also an analogous divergence in product coverage (for the iron and steel and metal products series in lines 1–3). Measures based on exactly matched series are available for the remaining items: electric overhead cranes; railroad freight cars; southern pine lumber; furniture; paper, excluding building paper, newsprint, and paperboard; boxboard and paperboard; printing and publishing; leather and leather products. See Table D-1, column 1.

Table D-1
Average Monthly Percentage Amplitudes and Related Measures of the Irregular and Cyclical Components of New Orders, Shipments, and Production, Selected Industries, 1919–58

Line	Variable and Period Covered[a] (1)	Average Monthly Amplitude[b] of					Ratio, $\bar{I}/\overline{Cy}$ (MCD[b] in brackets) (7)	ADR[b] (8)
		$\overline{Or}$ (2)	$\overline{Se}$ (3)	$\overline{Cyl}$ (4)	$\bar{I}$ (5)	$\overline{Cy}$ (6)		
IRON AND STEEL — METALS[c]								
1	N, 1920–33	12.3	8.1	9.1	7.7	4.4	1.8[3]	2.01
2	Z, 1919–39	8.7	3.9	7.5	5.6	5.5	1.0[2]	3.59
3	Z, 1924–39	13.2	3.0	6.1	4.0	4.0	1.0[2]	3.47
MACHINE TOOLS[d]								
4	N, 1940–56	19.4	7.7	16.2	14.8	6.4	2.3[3]	1.80
5	S, 1945–56	10.9	7.8	6.4	5.4	2.8	1.9[2]	2.03
ELECTRIC OVERHEAD CRANES								
6	N, 1925–46	50.1	19.6	43.1	40.5	8.6	4.7[5]	1.63
7	S, 1925–46	28.3	10.3	24.7	23.9	6.7	3.6[4]	1.58
RAILROAD FREIGHT CARS								
8	N, 1941–56	154.2	98.0	143.7	157.6	21.8	7.2[n.a.]	n.a.
9	S, 1941–56	17.4	8.5	14.0	11.2	7.0	1.6[4]	2.21
LUMBER INDEX[e]								
10	N, 1920–33	13.8	9.5	9.4	8.2	3.5	2.3[3]	2.12
11	Z, 1919–39	n.a.	n.a.	4.0	3.0	2.0	1.5[2]	2.56
12	N, 1953–62	9.1	5.4	6.2	6.0	1.6	3.7[3]	1.44
13	Z, 1947–56	n.a.	n.a.	3.5	3.3	1.0	3.4[5]	1.84
OAK FLOORING								
14	N, 1936–56	17.1	8.9	13.2	11.9	3.9	3.1[4]	2.02
15	S, 1941–55	n.a.	n.a.	n.a.	6.2	2.6	2.3[n.a.]	1.98
SOUTHERN PINE LUMBER								
16	N, 1929–56	10.8	7.6	7.7	7.2	2.6	2.7[4]	1.73
17	S, 1929–56	n.a.	7.0	n.a.	4.9	2.2	2.3[n.a.]	1.93
18	Z, 1929–56	n.a.	4.7	n.a.	4.2	2.1	2.0[n.a.]	1.82
FURNITURE[f]								
19	N, 1923–46	36.8	26.4	18.1	17.5	4.8	3.7[4]	1.87
20	S, 1923–46	13.1	10.3	8.0	7.2	2.7	2.7[3]	2.17

(continued)

Table D-1 (concluded)

Line	Variable and Period Covered[a] (1)	Average Monthly Amplitude[b] of					Ratio, $\bar{I}/\overline{Cy}$ (MCD[b] in brackets) (7)	ADR[b] (8)
		$\overline{Or}$ (2)	$\overline{Se}$ (3)	$\overline{Cyl}$ (4)	$\bar{I}$ (5)	$\overline{Cy}$ (6)		
PAPER, EXCLUDING BUILDING PAPER, NEWSPRINT, AND PAPERBOARD								
21	N, 1934–55	7.2	5.7	4.3	3.7	1.7	2.2[3]	1.96
22	S, 1934–55	6.5	5.7	3.0	2.6	1.3	2.0[n.a.]	1.70
23	Z, 1934–55	n.a.	n.a.	2.3	1.8	1.2	1.5[n.a.]	2.05
BOXBOARD AND PAPERBOARD[g]								
24	N, 1923–32	9.3	7.3	5.1	4.9	1.0	4.8[6]	1.59
25	Z, 1923–32	8.2	6.6	4.8	4.6	1.1	4.1[5]	1.64
26	N, 1933–42	10.4	7.3	6.4	5.2	2.9	1.8[3]	2.35
27	Z, 1933–42	7.9	6.6	4.4	3.3	2.4	1.4[2]	2.53
28	N, 1938–56	8.4	6.0	5.5	4.9	1.6	3.1[3]	1.72
29	Z, 1938–56	7.4	6.9	3.4	3.0	1.4	2.2[3]	1.62
PRINTING AND PUBLISHING[h]								
30	N, 1949–58	11.8	8.2	7.6	7.5	1.0	7.2[6]	1.43
31	S, 1939–58	8.1	7.1	3.5	3.2	1.1	3.0[3]	1.76
LEATHER AND LEATHER PRODUCTS[h]								
32	N, 1949–58	19.2	14.3	11.6	11.4	1.7	6.6[6]	1.61
33	S, 1939–58	11.4	9.5	5.7	5.2	1.5	3.5[4]	1.81

n.a. = not available.

Source: In addition to notes c to h for this table, see Appendix A.

[a] N denotes new orders; S, shipments; and Z, production. Dates indicated are the earliest and latest years covered.

[b] For description of these measures, see Chapter 3, pp. 110 ff. Following the notation in that chapter, $\overline{Or}$ denotes the original series; $\overline{Se}$, the seasonal component; $\bar{I}$, the irregular component; $\overline{Cy}$, the cyclical component; and $\overline{Cyl}$, the seasonally adjusted series.

[c] Line 1: iron and steel, index of new orders in physical terms, 1923–25 average = 100, Department of Commerce; line 2: pig iron production, monthly, daily averages in long tons, F. R. Macaulay (for NBER), Iron Age; line 3: metal products index, NBER.

[d] National Machine Tool Builders' Association. Value in current dollars. New orders are net of cancellations. The figures for the corresponding series of gross new orders, 1940–56, show generally smaller amplitudes, as follows: 14.4, 7.1, 11.7, 10.4, 5.3, 2.0[3], 1.88 (compare with the entries in line 4, columns 1–8, respectively).

[e] Line 10: index of new orders in physical terms, 1923–25 average = 100, Department of Commerce; lines 11 and 13: indexes of physical volume of production, 1947–

Notes to Table D-1 (concluded)

49 average = 100, Federal Reserve Board; line 12: Department of Commerce (OBE), value in current dollars.

  ᶠ Seidman & Seidman. In numbers of days' production. Series refer to the manufacturers in the Grand Rapids district.

  ᵍ Lines 24–25: boxboard; lines 26–29: paperboard. National Paperboard Association and Bureau of the Census. In thousands of short tons.

  ʰ Department of Commerce (OBE). Value in current dollars.

are even smaller than the figures for shipments in the two cases where series on all three variables are matched, which suggests that some stabilization here is attributable to stock adjustments.[2]

Rank correlations based on these and other (Standard and Poor's) data show that the cyclical amplitudes tend to be positively associated with the irregular amplitudes, less so with the seasonal ones (see tabulation below). Rankings according to the corresponding component amplitudes in N and S show particularly high correlations.[3]

New Orders		*Shipments*		*New Orders and Shipments*	
Variables (ranks)	r_s	*Variables (ranks)*	r_s	*Variables (ranks)*	r_s
$\overline{Cy}$ vs. $\bar{I}$	.85	$\overline{Cy}$ vs. $\bar{I}$	.85	$\overline{Cy}_n$ vs. $\overline{Cy}_s$	1.00
$\overline{Cy}$ vs. $\overline{Se}$	.65	$\overline{Cy}$ vs. $\overline{Se}$	.57	$\overline{Se}_n$ vs. $\overline{Se}_s$	0.81
$\overline{Se}$ vs. $\bar{I}$	.86	$\overline{Se}$ vs. $\bar{I}$	.80	$\bar{I}_n$ vs. $\bar{I}_s$	0.95

The new orders-to-shipments amplitude ratios computed from the data in Table D-1 are positively associated with the variability

  [2] Compare the estimates for southern pine lumber, lines 14–16, and for paper excluding building paper, etc., lines 19–21. The ratios of average monthly amplitudes of shipments to those of new orders and production are as follows:

	Cyclical		Irregular		Seasonal	
	$\overline{Cy}_s/\overline{Cy}_n$	$\overline{Cy}_z/\overline{Cy}_s$	$\bar{I}_s/\bar{I}_n$	$\bar{I}_z/\bar{I}_s$	$\overline{Se}_s/\overline{Se}_n$	$\overline{Se}_z/\overline{Se}_s$
Southern pine lumber	.83	.95	.69	.86	0.99	.67
Paper, excl. bldg. paper, newsprint, and paperboard	.78	.94	.69	.72	1.00	n.a.

  [3] The correlations for new orders are based on twenty-eight series, including some that have not been matched with shipments. Those for shipments are based on twenty-one series, including some that have not been matched with new orders. The correlations involving both N and S are based on matched series for nine items (eight in the case of the seasonal amplitudes).

measures for new orders. (The same also applies to statistics based on Standard and Poor's data.) The rank correlations, approximately significant at the 3 to 8 per cent levels, are as follows: $\overline{CyI}_n$ versus $\overline{CyI}_n/\overline{CyI}_s$, .57; versus $\bar{I}_n/\bar{I}_s$, .59; versus $\overline{Cy}_n/\overline{Cy}_s$, .65; versus $\overline{Se}_n/\overline{Se}_s$, .71.

In addition to the average amplitudes, Table D-1 includes indexes of the number of months required for cyclical dominance (MCD) and of the average duration of run (ADR). As the $\bar{I}/\overline{Cy}$ ratios are systematically larger for new orders than for shipments and outputs, the related MCD figures tend to be so, too. (However, note that the MCD are

Table D-2
Average Monthly Percentage Amplitudes and Related Measures of the Irregular and Cyclical Components of New Orders, Shipments, and Production, Summary by Groups of Series, 1919–58

Line	Variable and Number of Series Covered [a] (1)	Average Monthly Amplitude [b] of $\overline{Or}$ (2)	$\overline{Se}$ (3)	$\overline{CyI}$ (4)	$\bar{I}$ (5)	$\overline{Cy}$ (6)	Ratio, $\bar{I}/\overline{Cy}$ (MCD [b] in brackets) (7)	ADR [b] (8)
NEW ORDERS AND SHIPMENTS [c]								
1	N(23)	30.2	16.6	23.2	22.2	4.6	4.4[4.8]	1.69
2	S(23)	13.0	8.6	8.2	7.3	2.6	3.1[3.9]	1.88
NEW ORDERS AND PRODUCTION [d]								
3	N(8)	10.1	7.3	7.4	6.6	2.8	2.6[3.5]	1.91
4	Z(8)	8.0	5.7	4.6	3.7	2.5	1.8[2.7]	2.41
NEW ORDERS AND SHIPMENTS AND PRODUCTION [e]								
5	N(31)	27.0	14.9	19.6	18.2	4.1	3.9[4.5]	1.75
6	S and Z(31)	12.2	8.1	7.3	6.4	2.5	2.7[3.6]	2.02

[a] N denotes new orders; S, shipments; Z, production. Numbers of series used to compute the $\bar{I}$, $\overline{Cy}$, $\bar{I}/\overline{Cy}$, and ADR figures in columns 5–8 are given in parentheses. The other entries (in columns 2–4 and the MCD figures in column 7) are based on smaller numbers of observations because the required measures have not been computed for all series. The number of series omitted from these averages varies from one to four for lines 1–4 and from one to six for lines 5 and 6.

[b] See Table D-1, note b.

[c] Includes Standard and Poor's indexes for fourteen industries and series on N and S for nine items covered in Table D-1.

[d] Includes series on N and Z covered in Table D-1.

[e] Includes the N series from lines 1 and 3, the S series from line 2, and the Z series from line 4.

equal for N and Z in lines 26–27, column 7; as noted before, these measures are considerably less sensitive than the $\bar{I}/\overline{Cy}$ ratios.) Again, the ADR values tend to be larger for S and Z than for N, as would be expected, although there are a few exceptions (column 8).

Table D-2 contains a summary in the form of averages for broad groups of items, suppressing the industry detail. The contents covers both the Standard & Poor's indexes and the series that are included in Table D-1. These group averages demonstrate the strength and persistence of the rule that new orders are subject to larger and more frequent fluctuations of all sorts than are either production or shipments. Invariably, whether in the years before or after World War II,[4] the average cyclical, seasonal, and irregular amplitudes were larger for N than for S or Z. New orders also had systematically larger irregular-cyclical amplitude ratios, and larger numbers of months required for cyclical dominance, i.e., for the $\bar{I}/\overline{Cy}$ ratios to fall below 1. Finally, they show shorter average durations of run, that is, of a unidirectional movement. These characteristic differences still persist among averages that cover larger numbers of series for which the decomposition measures were computed, including noncorresponding series on N, S, and Z.[5]

[4] The comparisons with production in Table D-2, lines 3 and 4, include five pairs of series for the interwar period. The comparisons with shipments on lines 1 and 2 include fourteen pairs of series (the S&P indexes) for the post-World War II period. The tabulation below sums up the evidence for these two groups of series.

	$\overline{Or}$	$\overline{Se}$	$\overline{Cyl}$	$\bar{I}$	$\overline{Cy}$	$\bar{I}/\overline{Cy}$	ADR	MCD
INTERWAR PERIOD								
N	10.7	7.6	8.4	7.4	3.2	2.6	1.97	3.6
Z	8.3	5.7	5.4	4.1	3.0	1.8	2.76	2.6
POST-WW II PERIOD								
N	23.9	12.7	18.0	17.1	3.7	4.4	1.64	4.7
S	12.6	8.8	7.6	7.0	2.2	3.4	1.86	4.1

[5] This is shown by the following summary for forty-one series on new orders and forty-five series on shipments and production.

	$\overline{Or}$	$\overline{Se}$	$\overline{Cyl}$	$\bar{I}$	$\overline{Cy}$	$\bar{I}/\overline{Cy}$	ADR	MCD
N	28.7	16.1	22.5	21.8	4.6	4.1	1.72	4.4
S	12.8	8.3	7.7	7.0	2.6	2.8	1.96	3.6

APPENDIX E

NEW ORDERS AND SHIPMENTS FOR INDUSTRIAL SUBDIVISIONS, 1948–62

I. Measures of Relative Timing

Table E-1 presents measures based on the most detailed industry breakdown available for the OBE data of the pre-1963 vintage. This analysis had been completed before the revision that produced the current Census series going back to 1953. The older series begin for the most part in 1948 and end early in 1962. They suffer from the smallness of some of the samples and the difficulty of assigning to relatively narrow industry categories the dollar figures reported by multiproduct companies. Figures on this level of disaggregation are not published, and only restricted use could be made of them, in compliance with the wishes of the compiling agency.[1] But the comparability of the paired series is not in question, and, with proper caution, they are believed to deserve attention for the limited purpose of this analysis.

Primary Metals

Table E-1 groups the industrial subdivisions of the detailed OBE set by the major durable goods industries as listed in Tables 4-5 and 4-6, thereby facilitating comparisons between these tables; but in making such comparisons the very unequal weights of these subdivisions must be taken into account. Thus within the primary metals group, iron and steel, being about twice as large, in terms of the average levels of orders or sales, as the other two component industries taken together,

---

[1] In particular, I am not at liberty to reproduce the charts on which the following analysis is based, although references to them must be made to describe the behavior of the series. In footnotes attached to Table 4-6 I point out the significant difficulties that have been encountered in dating the turning points in the series; the charts are available to support the decisions made.

Table E-1

Timing of Value of New Orders at Turns in Shipments, by Business Cycle Turning Zones, Thirty-one Industrial Subdivisions of Manufacturing, 1948–61

	Lead (−) or Lag (+) in Months of New Orders at Turns in Shipments in Turning Zone Associated with										Av. Lead (−) or Lag (+) in Months		
	1948 Recession:	1949 Revival:	Korean War[a]		1953 Recession:	1954 Revival:	1957 Recession:	1958 Revival:	1960 Recession:	1961 Revival:			All
			1950–51:	1951–52:									
Industry	Peak	Trough	Peak	Trough	Peak	Trough	Peak	Trough	Peak	Trough	Peaks	Troughs	Turns
	(1)	(2)	(3)	(4)	(5)	(6)	(7)	(8)	(9)	(10)	(11)	(12)	(13)
PRIMARY METALS													
1. Iron and steel	−1	−1	−4	0	0	−11	−2	−1	−4	−9	−2.2	−4.4	−3.3
2. Primary nonferrous metals	0	+1	−4	0	−1	0	+1	0	−2	−3	−1.2	+0.8	−0.2
3. Other primary metals	−6	−4	−7[b]	0[b]	0	−7	−1	−3	−3	−3	−3.4	−3.4	−3.4
FABRICATED METAL PRODUCTS													
4. Heating and plumbing[c]							+2	−4	−1	−8	+0.5	−6.0	−2.8
5. Structural metal work[c]	n.i.	−7[d]	−1[d]	−4[d]	−6[d]	−12[d]	+3	−6	−7	−4	−2.0	−5.0	−3.5
6. Tin cans and other[c]							−3	−2	−2	−1	−2.5	−1.5	−2.0
ELECTRICAL MACHINERY													
7. Electrical generator apparatus	−4	−2	n.s.	n.s.	−2	−7	0	−1	+5	+7	−0.2	−0.8	−0.5
8. Radio, TV, and equip.	+4	−6	0	+3	0	−2	−1[b]	−2[b]	n.i.	n.i.	+0.8	−1.8	−0.5
9. Other electrical equip.	n.i.	−11	n.s.	n.s.	−4	−7	0	0	0	−8	−1.2[e]	−6.5[e]	−4.3[e]
MACHINERY EXCEPT ELECTRICAL													
10. Metalworking mach.	n.i.	−6	−15	n.t.	n.t.	−17	−13	−1	n.s.	n.s.	−14.0	−8.0	−10.4
11. General mach.	−3	−4	−7[b]	−2[b]	−5	−7	−8	−6	+3	−4	−4.0	−4.6	−4.3

				REPORTING	UNFILLED ORDERS[m]								
12. Special mach.	n.i.	-7	-6	0	n.i.	n.i.	-5	-9	n.s.	n.s.	-5.5	-5.3	-5.4
13. Engines and turbines	n.i.	-2	n.s.	n.s.	-23	-1	-20	-8	-6	-3	-16.3	-3.5	-9.0
14. Construction mach.	n.i.	-7	-8	-1[b]	0[b]	-6	-10	0	-8	0	-6.5	-2.8	-4.4
15. Office and store machines	n.i.	-7	-4[f]	0[f]	-4	+1	n.s.	n.s.	-2[b]	+3[b]	-3.3[g]	-0.8[g]	-1.9[g]
16. Agricultural implements	-1	0	-3	+1	n.t.	-3	-1	0	-2	n.i.	-1.0	-1.3	-1.1
17. Household and service appliances	n.i.	n.i.	[h]	+1	+1	-11	-4	0	-5	-2	-2.7	-3.5	-3.1
18. Other mach. and parts	n.i.	-6	n.s.	0	0	-5	-9	-5	-5	-2	-4.7	-4.5	-4.6
TRANSPORTATION EQUIPMENT													
19. Motor vehicles	n.a.	n.i.	+5	-5[b]	-13[b]	-10	-3[b]	0	-1	0	-3.0[l]	-3.8[l]	-3.4[l]
20. Motor vehicle parts and accessories	-1	-6	-6[b]	0[b]	-3	+9	-9[b]	-1	-4	+1	-4.6[l]	-3.0[l]	-3.8[l]
21. Aircraft	n.a.	n.s.	n.s.	n.s.	-10	n.m.	-14	-11	n.o.	n.o.	-12.0	-11.0	-11.7
22. Other nonautomotive transportation equip.	n.a.	-12	n.s.	n.s.	-5[b]	-12	-8[b]	-3	n.i.	n.i.	-6.5	-9.0	-8.0
OTHER DURABLE GOODS INDUSTRIES													
23. Lumber[j]	-2[k]	-5	0	-3	-1	-1	-4	0	0	-1	-2.0	-0.7	-1.2
24. Furniture[j]	-2[k]	0[k]	-3[k]	0[k]	-2[k]	-1	-2	0	0	0	-1.0	-0.3	-0.6
25. Stone, clay, and glass prod.	+2	-2	-6	-6	0	0	-6	0	0	0	-1.2	-0.4	-0.8
26. Professional and scientific instruments[j]		+4	-2	0	-7	-7	-8	-5	-6	-11	-7.0	-7.7	-7.4
27. Miscellaneous incl. ordnance[j]	n.i.	-5[l]	-2[l]	+2[l]	-11[l]	-3	-2	+1	+2	+1	0	-0.3	-0.2
NONDURABLE GOODS INDUSTRIES													
28. Textile-mill prod.	-2[b]	-5	-4	-7	-1	-1	-6	-2	-5	-6	-3.6	-4.2	-3.9
29. Leather and leather prod.	-2	-5	0	-3	-3	-3	+1	-5	-2	n.i.	-0.6	-4.0	-2.1
30. Paper and allied prod.	-7	0	-4	-3	-3[b]	+1	0	+4	n.t.	n.t.	-3.5	+0.5	-1.5
31. Printing and publishing	n.t.	n.t.	n.t.	n.t.	n.t.	+1	+1	+1	-1	0	0	+0.5	+0.2

Notes to Table E-1

n.a. = data for new orders not available.

n.i. = not identified (timing of new orders and/or sales uncertain).

n.m. = not matched.

n.o. = no turn in new orders at this recession or revival.

n.s. = no turn in sales at this recession or revival.

n.t. = no turning points at this recession or revival.

ᵃ These pairs of peaks or troughs represent "extra" turns, not related to a cyclical recession or revival recognized in the National Bureau chronology.

ᵇ Based on minor but well-established turns in new orders and/or shipments. Included in the averages.

ᶜ The series for these components of the fabricated metals industry have been seasonally adjusted for the NBER by the Census electronic-computer method.

ᵈ Timing measures for total fabricated metal products. Not included in the component-industry averages of lines 4–6, columns 11–13.

ᵉ Two timing comparisons can be made for this industry in addition to those listed in the table, since the series declined between February-March 1955 and March 1956. If these comparisons (+1 for peaks, 0 for troughs) were included, the averages would read −0.8, −5.2, and −3.2 for peaks, troughs, and all turns, respectively.

ᶠ The turns in shipments mark a retardation here rather than a contraction, but the observations are sufficiently firm to be included in the averages. (The series show pronounced upward trends.)

ᵍ Two timing comparisons can be made for this industry in addition to those listed in the table, since the series declined briefly in the second half of 1955. If these comparisons (−2, −2) were included, the averages would read −3.0, −1.0, and −1.9 for peaks, troughs, and all turns, respectively.

ʰ Both series declined in the second half of 1950 and the first half of 1951, but their relative timing is uncertain because of double-turn configurations. However, roughly coincident patterns or short lags of new orders are suggested. Taking them into account would lead to somewhat smaller average leads than those shown in the table.

ⁱ Two timing comparisons can be made for this industry in addition to those listed in the table, since the 1955–58 declines in new orders and sales were interrupted by short but marked increases in the second half or last three quarters of 1956. These additional comparisons and the averages which would include them are:

	Lead (−) or Lag (+) at		Av. Lead (−) or Lag (+) Incl. Additional Comparisons		
	Troughs 1956	Peaks 1956–57	Peaks	Troughs	All Turns
Motor vehicles	−2	0	−2.8	−3.0	−2.9
Motor vehicle parts and accessories	−3	−2	−4.3	−2.8	−3.6

ʲ The series on new orders for these industries begin in 1953 and their timing at peaks corresponding to the 1953 recession cannot be determined. For the earlier years data are available on lumber and furniture (combined) and on professional instruments and miscellaneous including ordnance (combined). The series for new orders have been seasonally adjusted for the NBER by the Census electronic-computer method.

ᵏ Timing measures for lumber and furniture. Not included in the component-industry averages of lines 23 and 24, columns 11–13. Included in the turning-zone averages of line 28, columns 1–5.

ˡ Timing measures for professional and scientific instruments and miscellaneous including ordnance. Not included in the component-industry averages of lines 26 and 27, columns 11–13. Included in the turning-zone averages of line 28, columns 2–5.

ᵐ The series for new orders in this group, and the series for leather shipments, have been received from the Department of Commerce in seasonally unadjusted form only. They have been seasonally adjusted for the NBER by the Census electronic-computer method.

influences the over-all results most strongly. In primary nonferrous metals, shipments follow new orders closely with short lags, while in the other two industries N and S show larger amplitude and timing differences.

The dates of the major steel strikes are marked by precipitously low levels of shipments for the iron and steel industry: October 1949, June–July 1952, July 1956, and August–October 1959. New orders also show declines in these months but much smaller ones. In 1949 and 1952 the strike months were surrounded by sufficiently low and broad valleys in these series to qualify as specific-cycle troughs. In 1956 and 1959, however, this was not the case, despite the particular gravity of the 1959 strike. In 1952, 1956, and especially in 1959, new orders reached very high levels in some of the months preceding the strike, indicating intensified protective purchasing in anticipation of the work stoppage. However, in 1949 there is little evidence of such precautionary buying. The 1959 strike was followed by a strong but very brief recovery in new orders for iron and steel products. Apparently the users soon found that, given the signs of weak demand ahead, their steel inventories, greatly expanded due to the prestrike buying hike, were still ample. This gave rise to much concern about the "steel cycle." Similar but much weaker developments took place in connection with the two earlier strikes, particularly that of 1952.

The steel strikes left relatively weak impressions on the other components of the primary and fabricated metals industries, according to our orders and sales data.

Fabricated Metal Products

Of the three components of the fabricated metal products group, heating and plumbing is the smallest, structural metal work the intermediate, and tin cans and other the largest. The latter shows the smallest divergences between N and S and the shortest order leads of the three. The heating and plumbing subdivision includes construction materials and equipment, items which are produced largely to stock (such as sanitary ware and oil burners; see Table 4-2). Structural metal work, on the other hand, includes some important products made mainly to order and with much longer delivery periods (such as fabricated structural steel; see Table 4-1), although it contains a variety of standardized metal items for buildings as well. The records for the components of the fabricated metals group are still too aggregative and too short (they begin in 1955) to bring out these distinctions well.

Electrical Machinery

Radio, television, and communications equipment constitute the largest component of the electrical machinery group. New orders and shipments for this industry show strong upward trends, substantial declines in 1951 and 1953–54, and very mild cyclical fluctuations in 1956–62. There is much jagged month-to-month movement in new orders around the fairly smooth shipments series but larger and more systematic divergences seem to have occurred only in the early Korean period and in 1953–54. The timing of the two series is, by and large, approximately coincident, as might have been expected. The rest of the electrical machinery group consists in large part of products used by industry rather than households; electrical generating and transmission equipment, the second largest component of the group, is, of course, entirely of this nature. Here a few longer order leads are encountered, but coincidences and short leads are more common (and there are also a couple of disturbing lags). Most of the average measures are rough coincidences. The charts indicate that new orders and shipments became generally much more similar in the second half of the period than they were in the first, and this behavior is reflected in the greater frequency of the coincidences.

Machinery Except Electrical

The N-S relationships in the subdivisions of the nonelectrical machinery group vary a great deal. The differences apparently mainly reflect the contrast between heavy made-to-order industrial machinery and standardized types of equipment and appliances.

Metalworking machinery, the largest of the components, in which sales grew rapidly in the early 1950's and again after 1958, shows very long leads on three out of five occasions (two at peaks). This industry produces mainly machine tools, for which we have long separate records confirming the tendency of new orders to turn down well ahead of the peaks in shipments (Table 4-1). However, metalworking machinery orders and shipments moved quite closely together after mid-1958, incidentally skipping the 1960 contraction. No similar development can be observed in engines and turbines, the only other machinery industry with very long order leads. In this, the smallest of our components of the nonelectrical machinery group, new orders show very large irregular month-to-month movements but also large cyclical fluctuations around the contrastingly smooth sales.

General and special industrial machinery, two components of intermediate and similar size, have average leads of new orders exceeding four and five months. These summary figures may understate somewhat the typical leads here, especially for special industrial machinery (judging from the frequency of longer leads). A similar statement can be made for construction machinery and other machinery, where the means are also somewhat larger than four months.[2]

In household appliances and service-industry machinery, the leads of new orders appear to be relatively short, particularly toward the end of the period covered; the average lead here is about three months. Finally, at the other end of the scale from metalworking and engines and turbines are office and store machines and agricultural implements, in which new orders lead shipments by mean intervals of only 1 to 2 months. The former is an industry with a rapid growth in sales interrupted only by mild fluctuations. Except in 1948–49 and the early Korean period (1950–51), the divergences between N and S are small. They are much larger, both cyclically and month-to-month, in agricultural implements, where the series show less growth and more fluctuations, but the leads of orders are consistently short.

---

[2] Other machinery, a sizable category, comprises valves and fittings, fabricated pipe, ball and roller bearings, and machine shops (jobbing and repair). It is industry group 359 in the 1945 Standard Industrial Classification (the OBE series here used are derived from Internal Revenue Service classifications, which are based on the 1945 SIC). Ranked by the average monthly value of new orders in 1961, this industry is the third largest in the nonelectrical machinery group, following metalworking and agricultural machinery. Special and general industrial machinery rank fourth and fifth, office machines and household appliances sixth and seventh, construction and mining machinery eighth, and engines and turbines ninth.

Transportation Equipment

In the transportation equipment group, motor vehicle orders are particularly difficult to interpret, as noted in Chapter 4. Also, their relation to shipments in the earlier part of the period is blurred. Separating manufacturers of complete motor vehicles from those who turn out only parts and accessories shows that these irregularities relate to the former, not the latter. After 1955, the two series for motor vehicles followed a closely similar course. In parts and accessories, the relation has been more consistent throughout, with new orders fluctuating more and moving ahead of shipments. Here too, however, some tendency toward shorter leads and smaller differences in amplitude is visible in the second half of the period.

In aircraft, there is a striking contrast between the huge cyclical and month-to-month fluctuations of new orders and the smoothness of the value of shipments. When converted to quarterly values, the OBE series resemble closely the Census–Civil Aeronautics Commission series shown in Chart 4-1. The data confirm that aircraft account for the bulk of total nonautomotive transportation equipment and are mainly responsible for the behavior of new orders and shipments in that division as a whole (see Chart 3-4). The leads in the monthly series can be established only crudely because of the large erratic component in orders, but there is no doubt that they are long. The remainder of nonautomotive transportation equipment shows little growth compared to aircraft, less erratic movements in new orders, and shipments that follow orders more faithfully. Although some of the comparisons at peaks are obscured by short extra movements in orders, the evidence suggests that the leads in this category are often long, too. One would expect this, since the series include railroad equipment and shipbuilding, but it must be noted that they also cover a variety of smaller standardized items such as boats, motorcycles, and bicycles.

Other Durable Goods Industries

The measures for "other durables" confirm earlier results by showing short leads or coincidences for lumber and for stone, clay, and glass products, where production to stock prevails, and for furniture, where orders can be promptly handled in batches. The timing of new orders and shipments is rather irregular but on the average synchronous for the combination of miscellaneous manufacturing industries that includes ordnance and accessories. These measures are of little use, since they refer to a highly heterogeneous residual category that, regrettably, cannot be subdivided.[3] That the defense products as a whole had mostly long lags of shipments, is shown in Chapter 4. On the other, hand, it is of interest, although perhaps a little surprising, that the order leads are as long as seven months on the average for professional and scientific instruments.[4]

II. Timing of New Orders at Business Cycle Turns

Table E-2 shows the timing of the subdivision series for new orders at each of the recessions and revivals of the period 1948–61. Once more, leads of new orders can be seen as predominant at every major reversal in aggregate economic activity, but also as varying greatly from turn to turn. The ranking of the episodes by the averages for the twenty-seven subdivisions of the durable goods sector is almost the same as the ranking by length of lead of aggregate new orders for the sector (see Table E-2, line 32, and Table 11-2, line 2). Starting with the longest leads, one finds that the 1957 peak ranks first, followed by the peaks of 1960, 1953, and 1948. Among the leads at troughs, which are generally shorter, those at the 1954 revival rank first, followed in descending order by 1949, 1961, and 1958.[5]

The over-all cyclical conformity of the series here examined is high. The proportions of business cycle turns and new-order turns matched are 92.8 and 78.0 per cent, respectively, for the twenty-seven subdivisions of the durable goods sector, according to Table E-3, columns 2–4. The corresponding percentages for the six major durable goods industries (based on observations for 1948–61 only) are 100.0 and 88.2.

[3] This combination consists of SIC major groups 19 and 39 (classification of 1945). Group 19, ordnance, includes artillery, small arms, ammunition, tanks, etc. The other, miscellaneous, includes jewelry; musical instruments; toys; sporting goods; pens, pencils, and other office and artists' materials; costume novelties, fabricated plastics products; brooms, matches, candles, and other miscellaneous manufacturing industries.

[4] This is the 1945 SIC major group 38, covering laboratory, scientific, engineering, medical, and mechanical measuring instruments; photographic and optical goods; and watches and clocks. Four of the observations for this industry are based on well-identified turning-point dates. The last one is more doubtful, perhaps overstating the lead.

[5] The last two have reversed positions in the ranking for total durables but the same positions in the ranking according to the averages for the six major durable goods industries. The leads at both the 1958 and the 1961 troughs were short in most cases, and the differences between them are small.

Table E-2
Timing of Value of New Orders at Each Business Cycle Turn, Thirty-one Industrial Subdivisions of Manufacturing, 1948–61

Industry	Lead (−) or Lag (+) in months of New Orders at Business Cycle Turns							
	Peak Nov. 1948 (1)	Trough Oct. 1949 (2)	Peak July 1953 (3)	Trough Aug. 1954 (4)	Peak July 1957 (5)	Trough April 1958 (6)	Peak May 1960 (7)	Trough Feb. 1961 (8)
PRIMARY METALS								
1. Iron and steel	0	−1	0	−11	−8	−2	−15	−11
2. Primary nonferrous metals	+1	−4	−1	−6	−18	−1	−13	−1
3. Other primary metals	−5	−4	0 [a]	−5	−20	−2	−13	−2
FABRICATED METAL PRODUCTS [b]								
4. Heating and plumbing [b]					−15	−1	−6	−1
5. Structural metal work [b]					−2	−5	−10	−2
6. Tin cans and other [b]					−6	−2	−5	−2
Total products	n.i.	−5 [c]	−6 [c]	−10 [c]				
ELECTRICAL MACHINERY								
7. Electrical generator apparatus	−4	−6	0	−5	−12	−4	+4	+4
8. Radio, TV, and equipment	0	−9	−3	−2	−1 [a]	−3 [a]	n.a.	n.i.
9. Other electrical equipment	+1	−5	−6 [d]	−5	−5	+1	−8	−7
MACHINERY EXCEPT ELECTRICAL								
10. Metalworking machinery	n.i.	−3	n.m.	−9	−19	+1	−5 [b]	−7 [b]
11. General machinery	−2	−2	0	−7	−5	−2	0	−2
12. Special machinery	n.i.	−3	n.t.	n.t.	−7	−4	−1	−1
13. Engines and turbines	−4	+2	−23	−7	+14	−2	−16	−3
14. Agricultural implements	0	+1	−20	0	n.m.	n.m.	−12	n.i.
15. Construction machinery	n.i.	−6	n.i	n.i	−9	+1	−11	−4

AVERAGE LEAD (−) OR LAG (+), IN MONTHS

Industry	1	2	3	4	5	6	7	8
16. Office and store machines	n.i.	−10	−4	−6	−2[a]	−5[a]	−5[a]	−5[a]
17. Household and service appliances	−4	−9	−6	−7	−14	−4	−11	−2
18. Other machinery and parts	n.i.	−2	−4	−3	−20	−1	−8	−6
TRANSPORTATION EQUIPMENT								
19. Motor vehicles	n.a.	n.i.	−13[a]	−8	−8[a]	+5	+4	−1
20. Motor vehicle parts and accessories	−1	−5	−10	−8	−7[a]	−1	−14	0
21. Aircraft	n.a.	−3	−7	−11	−11	−9	n.t.	n.t.
22. Other nonautomotive transportation equipment	n.a.	−6	−12	−7	−7[a]	−2	n.i.	n.i.
OTHER DURABLE GOODS INDUSTRIES								
23. Lumber[e]				−3	−16	−1	−10	−2
24. Furniture[e]				−9	−20	+2	−10	0
Series 23 and 24 combined	−5[f]	−5[f]	−5[f]					
25. Stone, clay, and glass products	+1	−3	−4	−7	−23	−1	−10	−1
26. Professional and scientific instruments				−4	−15	−4	n.m.	n.m.
27. Miscellaneous incl. ordnance[e]				−9	−18	−1	−1	0
Series 26 and 27 combined	n.i.	−3[g]	−13[g]					
NONDURABLE GOODS INDUSTRIES REPORTING UNFILLED ORDERS[b]								
28. Textile-mill products	−8[a]	−8	−9	−9	−9[a]	−5	−5	−7
29. Leather and leather products	−13	−3	−7	−6	−6	−1	+3	n.i.
30. Paper and allied products	−9	−3	−3[a]	−7[a]	−3[f]	0	n.t.	n.t.
31. Printing and publishing	n.t.	n.t.	n.t.	n.t.	−11	+2	+1	0
32. 27 industrial subdivisions of durable manufactures	−1.7	−4.1	−6.8	−6.5	−11.6	−1.8	−7.7	−2.5
(No. of observations)	(13)	(22)	(20)	(23)	(26)	(26)	(23)	(22)

Notes to Table E-2

n.a. = not available.

n.i. = not identified (timing uncertain).

n.m. = not matched.

n.t. = no turn in new orders.

ᵃ Based on a minor but well-established turn in new orders. Included in the averages.

ᵇ The series on new orders for these components of the fabricated metals industry begin in 1955. They have been seasonally adjusted for the NBER by the Census electronic-computer method.

ᶜ Timing measures for total fabricated metal products. Included in the turning-zone averages of line 32, columns 2–4.

ᵈ The series underwent a major contraction between February 1951 and March 1954, which was interrupted by a retardation in the second half of 1951 and 1952. This comparison is based on the secondary peak of new orders in January 1953, which ended that retardation.

ᵉ The series on new orders for these industries begin in 1953 and their timing at peaks corresponding to the 1953 recession cannot be determined. For the earlier years data are available on lumber and furniture (combined) and on professional instruments and miscellaneous including ordnance (combined). The series have been seasonally adjusted for the NBER by the Census electronic-computer method.

ᶠ Timing measures for lumber and furniture. Included in the turning-zone averages of line 32, columns 1–3.

ᵍ Timing measures for professional and scientific instruments and miscellaneous including ordnance. Included in the turning-zone averages of line 32, columns 2–3.

ʰ These series were received from the Department of Commerce in seasonally unadjusted form. They have been seasonally adjusted for NBER by the Census electronic-computer method.

ⁱ Based on a secondary peak of new orders. The first peak occurred in May 1956, i.e., fourteen months before the reference date.

The relative frequency of leads at business cycle peaks also is just a little lower for the less aggregative series (83.3 per cent as compared with 95.5 per cent for the six major industries), while the proportions of leads at troughs are virtually identical (86.5 and 87.0 per cent). One difference that may be significant, however, is that short leads at peaks are more frequent among the observations for the industrial subdivisions. Rough coincidences account for 25.6 per cent of the measures in this set, while the corresponding figure for the six major industries is 13.6 per cent.[6]

---

[6] The proportions of rough coincidences among the timing observations at business cycle troughs are much higher and very similar in the two sets: 51.7 and 52.2 per cent for the twenty-seven subdivisions and the six major industries, respectively. The tabulation below gives the distribution

The four nondurable goods industries that report unfilled orders have, as a group, relatively low proportions of turns matched (61.3 per cent, whether based on business cycle turns or on new-order turns), but this is due mainly to the poor conformity record of one series, printing and publishing. Here too, leads of new orders prevail decidedly, accounting for 84.4 per cent of the observations at peaks and 75.0 per cent of those at troughs.

Clearly, a two-digit industry can contain subdivisions with quite different timing patterns. Nonelectrical machinery, for which a relatively fine breakdown is available in these data, offers the best example of this in the contrast between the short leads of general machinery and the long leads of engines and turbines (see Table E-3, lines 11 and 13).

Again, there is a strong tendency for the leads to be longer on the average at peaks than at troughs; there are only four exceptions to this rule among the thirty-one series covered. The peak-trough differences are often large and probably significant. Convincing formal tests of this are hard to get because of the small numbers of observations available per series, but the high degree of consensus among the series in showing these differences strongly suggests that there is a real dichotomy here, at least for the postwar cycles.

Long leads of new orders dominate the averages at business cycle peaks for most of the component industries, according to Table E-3, column 5. Their prevalence is indicated particularly among the series for nonelectrical machinery, nonautomotive transportation equipment, and other durable goods industries.[7] Eighteen of these mean leads range from 8 to 15 months and seven are about 5 or 6 months each. In

of the leads and lags for the subdivision data, which is based on Table E-2, lines 1–27, and underlies some of the statements just made.

Number of Timing Observations

	Total	Leads	Exact Coin- cidences	Lags	Rough Coin- cidences
At peaks	78	65	8	5	20
At troughs	89	77	4	8	46

[7] The leads at peaks for electrical machinery components average appreciably less than the corresponding measures for this industry as a whole, as given in Tables 11-2 and 11-3. Elsewhere, too, there are differences between the two sets of measures, but they are on the whole not large, and a rough reconciliation is possible when account is also taken of the discrepancies between data of different vintages.

Table E-3
Summary Measures of Timing of Value of New Orders at Business Cycle Turns, Thirty-one Industrial Subdivisions of Manufacturing, 1948–61

Industry	Period Covered[a] (1)	No. of Observations[b] (2)	Business Cycle Turns Skipped[c] (3)	Extra Turns in New Orders[d] (4)	Av. Lead (−) or Lag (+) (months)			Av. Dev. from Av. Lead or Lag (months)		
					Peaks (5)	Troughs (6)	All Turns (7)	Peaks (8)	Troughs (9)	All Turns (10)
PRIMARY METALS										
1. Iron and steel	1948–61	8	0	2	−5.8	−6.2	−6.0	5.8	4.8	5.2
2. Primary nonferrous metals	1948–61	8	0	2	−7.8	−3.0	−5.4	7.8	2.0	4.9
3. Other primary metals	1948–61	8	0	2	−9.5	−3.2	−6.4	7.0	1.2	4.1
FABRICATED METAL PRODUCTS										
4. Heating and plumbing[e]	1957–61	4	0	0	−10.5	−1.0	−5.8	4.5	0.0	4.8
5. Structural metal work[e]	1957–61	4	0	2	−6.0	−3.5	−4.8	4.0	1.5	2.8
6. Tin cans and other[e]	1957–61	4	0	0	−5.5	−2.0	−3.8	0.5	0.0	1.8
ELECTRICAL MACHINERY										
7. Electrical generator apparatus	1948–61	8	0	2	−3.0	−2.8	−2.9	5.0	3.4	4.2
8. Radio, TV, and equip.	1948–61	6	2	4	−1.3	−4.8	−3.0	1.1	2.9	2.0
9. Other electrical equip.	1948–61	8	0	2	−4.5	−4.0	−4.2	2.8	2.5	2.6
MACHINERY EXCEPT ELECTRICAL										
10. Metalworking machinery	1949–61	6	1	1	−12.0	−4.5	−7.0	7.0	3.5	4.7
11. General machinery	1948–61	8	0	2	−1.8	−3.2	−2.5	1.8	1.9	1.8

706

12. Special machinery	1949–61	5	2	2	−4.0	−2.7	−3.2	3.0	1.8	1.8
13. Engines and turbines	1948–61	8	0	0	−14.2	−2.5	−8.4	5.2	2.5	7.0
14. Agricultural implements	1948–60	5	2	2	−10.7	+0.5	−6.2	7.1	0.5	7.8
15. Construction machinery	1949–61	5	2	2	−10.0	−3.0	−5.8	1.0	2.7	3.4
16. Office and store machines	1949–61	7	0	2	−3.7	−6.5	−5.3	1.1	1.8	1.5
17. Household and service appliances	1948–61	8	0	2	−8.8	−5.5	−7.1	3.8	2.5	3.1
18. Other machinery and parts	1949–61	7	0	2	−10.7	−3.0	−6.3	6.2	1.5	4.4
TRANSPORTATION EQUIPMENT										
19. Motor vehicles	1953–61	6	0	4	−5.7	−1.3	−3.5	6.4	4.4	6.2
20. Parts and accessories	1948–61	8	0	4	−8.0	−3.5	−5.8	4.0	3.0	3.5
21. Aircraft	1949–61	5	2	2	−9.0	−7.7	−8.2	2.0	3.1	2.7
22. Other nonautomotive transportation equip.	1949–61	5	2	2	−9.5	−5.0	−6.8	2.5	2.0	2.2
OTHER DURABLE GOODS INDUSTRIES										
23. Lumber[f]	1954–61	5	0	0	−13.0	−2.0	−6.4	3.0	0.7	5.3
24. Furniture[f]	1954–61	5	0	0	−15.0	−2.3	−7.4	5.0	4.4	6.7
25. Stone, clay, and glass products	1948–61	8	0	2	−9.0	−3.0	−6.0	7.5	2.0	5.5
26. Professional and scientific ins.[f]	1954–61	3	2	2	−15.0	−4.0	−7.7	[g]	0.0	4.9
27. Miscellaneous incl. ordnance[f]	1954–61	5	0	0	−9.5	−3.3	−5.8	8.5	3.8	6.2
NONDURABLE GOODS INDUSTRIES REPORTING UNFILLED ORDERS										
28. Textile-mill products	1948–61	8	0	2	−7.8	−7.2	−7.5	1.4	1.2	1.4
29. Leather and leather products	1948–61	7	0	2	−5.8	−3.3	−4.7	4.4	1.8	3.8
30. Paper and allied products	1948–61	6	2	2	−5.0	−3.3	−4.2	2.7	2.4	2.6
31. Printing and publishing	1948–61	4	4	0	−5.0	+1.0	−4.0	6.0	1.0	4.5
32. 27 industrial subdivisions of durable manufactures[h]		167	13	47	−7.8	−3.6	−5.6	5.5	2.7	4.3

Notes to Table E-3

ᵃ The dates identify the years of the first and the last reference turn at which the timing of the series can be determined. For some industries, the series begin in 1949. Even where the 1948 data are available, it is in some cases impossible to determine the timing of the series at the 1948 recovery without still earlier figures. In one case (line 14) the timing of the series at the 1961 recovery is similarly uncertain.

ᵇ The number of reference turns in periods identified in column 1 that are matched by like turns in new orders.

ᶜ The number of reference turns not matched during the periods identified in column 1. The sum of the corresponding entries in columns 2 and 3 gives the maximum number of timing observations possible for these periods.

ᵈ Refer to periods identified in column 1. In all but a few cases, these turns relate to the extra movements during the Korean period 1950–52. Some of these turns are minor rather than major or specific-cycle, but all are clearly identifiable.

ᵉ Series begins in 1955.

ᶠ Series begins in 1953; timing at the 1953 recession uncertain.

ᵍ Only one observation is available.

ʰ Summary of the timing measures for the industries listed in lines 1–27. Entries in columns 2–12 are totals. Entries in columns 13–18 are averages weighted by the number of observations for each item.

contrast, none of the averages for troughs exceeds 8 months and only four exceed 6 months. Seventeen fall in the range of 3 to 6 months and ten are shorter still (column 6). The dispersion of timing is as a rule less for the trough than for the peak observations (columns 8 and 9).

III. Timing of Unfilled Orders at Business Cycle Turns

The full record for the series on order backlogs of industrial subdivisions mainly confirms the patterns observed for the more comprehensive series in the current Census compilation. A summary presentation of the results will therefore be sufficient. Table E-4 strongly demonstrates three points. First, unfilled orders for durable goods show high cyclical conformity in the period covered, in the sense of having matching business cycle turns, with very few exceptions, and very few extra movements and turns (columns 2–4).[8] Second, the peaks in these

---

[8] Among the few series for which these measures indicate low cyclical conformity are those for electrical generators, radio and television, and office and store machines. In unfilled orders for these industries, upward trends tend to overwhelm the cyclical fluctuations.

series tend to precede the end of business expansions, frequently by long intervals (column 5). Third, the upturns in backlogs occur more often after than before the end of business contractions, tending to lag the revivals by short average intervals (column 6).

The lapses from one-to-one correspondence between business cycle reversals and backlog turns amounted to about 6 per cent of the relevant "opportunities to match." For the subdivisions of durable manufactures (Table E-4, lines 1–26, columns 2–4), the totals are as follows: number of observations, 163; business cycle turns skipped, 10; extra turns, 11. For the nondurable goods industries, the proportions of unmatched turns, particularly of extra turns in the backlog series, are considerably larger (see lines 27–30, columns 2–4).

Virtually all of the series have average leads at business recessions.[9] These vary from four months for household appliances to seventeen months for leather products (column 5). The nondurable goods industries show some of the earliest downturns, but the leads are on the average large—from seven to twelve months—for each of the industry groups covered, except electrical machinery. This is broadly consistent with the corresponding measures for the comprehensive series, which also fall in the same range of long leads (see Table 11-13). The averages are not swayed by a few very long leads, and in general the effect on them of extreme observations is moderate.[10]

Two-thirds of the timing averages at troughs are rough coincidences, but lags outnumber leads for an equally large proportion of the industries. There are very few long leads of unfilled orders at the recent business revivals, but long lags do appear in some averages.

To sum up, leads of intermediate or long duration appear to be characteristic of the timing of unfilled orders at business recessions, at least in the recent decades. On the other hand, rough coincidences with some tendency to lag prevail at business revivals. These features are clearly demonstrated by the data for both the major industries

---

[9] The two exceptions are again the industries with strong upward trends in backlogs (radio and television, and office and store machines).

[10] Thus, the use of medians instead of means would not alter the results in any essential way. The mean-median differences are as often negative as positive. Also, they are on the whole not large relative to the averages involved. Where the median leads are smaller than the mean leads, the average discrepancy is 2.5 months, and in the opposite case it is 1.6 months.

Table E-4

Summary Measures of Timing of Unfilled Orders at Business Cycle Turns, Thirty Industrial Subdivisions of Manufacturing, 1948–61

Industry	Period Covered [a] (1)	No. of Observations [b] (2)	No. of Business Cycle Turns Skipped [c] (3)	No. of Extra Turns [d] (4)	Av. Lead (−) or Lag (+) (months)		Standard Deviation	
					Peaks (5)	Troughs (6)	Peaks (7)	Troughs (8)
PRIMARY METALS								
1. Iron and steel	1948–61	8	0	0	−7.0	−0.5	3.4	1.8
2. Primary nonferrous metals	1948–61	8	0	0	−6.8	−0.5	5.4	0.5
3. Other primary metals	1948–61	8	0	0	−12.2	+1.0	8.2	1.2
FABRICATED METAL PRODUCTS								
4. Heating and plumbing [e]	1957–61	4	0	0	−5.0	+5.0	1.0	3.0
5. Structural metal work [e]	1957–61	4	0	0	−6.0	+4.0	1.0	2.0
6. Tin cans and other [e]	1957–61	4	0	0	−11.5	0	1.5	0
ELECTRICAL MACHINERY								
7. Electrical generator apparatus	1949–61	5	2	1	−4.5	+8.7	2.5	4.8
8. Radio, TV, and equipment	1949–61	5	2	2	+0.5	+0.3	2.5	4.5
9. Other electrical equipment	1949–61	7	0	0	−5.3	+3.5	2.5	3.3
MACHINERY EXCEPT ELECTRICAL								
10. Metalworking machinery	1949–61	5	2	0	−14.5	+5.0	4.5	2.4
11. General machinery	1949–61	7	0	0	−7.3	+3.5	4.0	4.2
12. Special machinery	1949–61	7	0	0	−10.7	−0.8	9.1	3.6
13. Engines and turbines	1949–61	7	0	0	−10.7	+2.5	4.8	4.4

710

	[a] 1	[b] 2	[c] 3				
14. Agricultural implements	1948–60	7	0	0	−8.5	+6.3	2.6	1.7
15. Construction machinery	1949–61	7	0	0	−11.7	+1.5	5.4	3.4
16. Office and store machines	1949–61	5	2	4	+2.0	+1.7	2.0	3.4
17. Household and service appliances	1949–60	6	0	2	−4.3	+0.3	2.5	6.8
18. Other machinery	1949–61	7	0	0	−10.3	+2.8	6.2	0.4
TRANSPORTATION EQUIPMENT								
19. Motor vehicles	1949–61	7	0	0	−5.7	+4.0	1.9	5.7
20. Motor vehicle parts and accessories	1948–61	8	0	0	−11.5	+0.8	5.0	1.3
21. Aircraft	1949–60	4	2	0	−5.5	+5.0	4.5	7.0
22. Other nonautomotive	1949–61	7	0	0	−9.0	+2.0	2.9	1.9
OTHER DURABLE GOODS INDUSTRIES								
23. Lumber[f]	1953–61	6	0	2	−6.3	−2.0	2.6	0.8
24. Furniture[f]	1953–61	6	0	0	−9.7	−1.3	7.3	1.9
25. Stone, clay, and glass	1948–61	8	0	0	−12.8	+0.2	9.9	3.0
26. Professional and scientific instruments[f]	1953–61	6	0	0	−9.0	+1.0	4.2	7.8
NONDURABLE GOODS INDUSTRIES								
27. Textile-mill products	1948–61	7	1	3	−10.0	−3.8	5.9	2.7
28. Leather and leather products	1948–61	8	0	2	−17.0	−1.8	2.5	1.9
29. Paper and allied products	1948–61	6	2	2	−16.3	−2.3	4.0	2.5
30. Printing and publishing	1948–61	7	1	2	−6.5	−0.7	7.1	4.5

[a] The dates identify the years of the first and last reference turn at which the timing of the series can be determined.

[b] The number of reference turns matched by like turns in unfilled orders.

[c] The number of reference turns not matched. The sum of the corresponding entries in columns 2 and 3 gives the maximum number of observations possible for the period identified in column 1.

[d] Turns that mark extra movements in unfilled orders not corresponding to business cycle expansions or contractions.

[e] Series begins in 1955.

[f] Series begins in 1953.

711

(Table 11-13) and their subdivisions (Table E-4). The accompanying tabulation shows the distribution of leads and lags for the twenty-six components of durable goods manufactures.[11]

	Number of Timing Observations				
	Total	*Leads*	*Exact Coin-cidences*	*Lags*	*Rough Coin-cidences*
At peaks	76	72	1	3	13
At troughs	87	22	14	51	57

[11] This count covers the series listed in Table E-4, lines 1–26. It is also of interest to compare this distribution with its counterpart for new orders (see note 6, above).

APPENDIX F

EXPORT ORDERS AND SHIPMENTS

INFORMATION ON EXPORT ORDERS can be helpful for an analysis of foreign trade problems and outlook. Also, separation of home orders from foreign orders is desirable, since the former should be more valuable as tools and guides for the appraisal of domestic economic developments than are the aggregates that include both categories.

Although this study is not concerned with foreign trade problems as such, it is of interest here to examine the relation between foreign orders and shipments and to compare it with the relation between domestic series for these variables. Data available for such comparisons, however, are limited to certain types of capital equipment and to the recent postwar years.[1]

Since 1957, the economics department of the McGraw-Hill Publishing Company has compiled monthly indexes of export orders for nonelectrical machinery. The goods covered by this series comprise about 15 per cent of the value of U.S. exports (about $3 billion out of a total of some $20 billion in 1961). The sample of reporting firms is said to be small, but the index behaves sensibly in the light of the evidence on actual exports of nonelectrical machinery as reported by the Commerce Department. The curves in Chart F-1 for export orders and exports suggest a relationship similar to that observed for the longer and more comprehensive series on capital goods orders and deliveries. It indicates that both the longer swings and the short irregular movements tend to be much larger in orders than in exports. Indeed, some distinct but short movements, such as those in the second half of 1957 and of 1961, are entirely "smoothed out" in the export series.

[1] The relation between export orders and exports is discussed in Hal B. Lary, "The United States in a Changing World Economy," *Forty-second Annual Report of the NBER*, June 1962, pp. 96–99. The analysis that follows is based in part on Lary's study.

Chart F-1
Export Orders and Exports, Nonelectrical Machinery, 1956–62

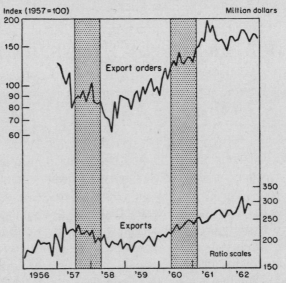

Note: Shaded areas represent business cycle contractions in the United States; unshaded areas, business expansions. Series are seasonally adjusted.

Source: Export orders: McGraw-Hill Publishing Company. Exports: U.S. Department of Commerce (derived from the foreign trade statistics by selection of items represented in the export series).

The movement of the curves also suggests that exports of the machines lag behind new orders by substantial intervals.[2]

Monthly data on export orders for machine tools are prepared by the National Machine Tool Builders' Association. They go back to 1946 for the metal-cutting type and to 1956 for the metal-forming type. This compilation relates to a small subgroup of the products covered in the McGraw-Hill sample (exports of machine tools, mostly metal-cutting, amounted to little more than $200 million in 1961), but it offers series extending over a longer period, and not only for gross orders, but also for shipments and cancellations. The NMTBA export orders and shipments data are highly erratic but are also subject to

[2] The series are too short to offer conclusive evidence. Nevertheless, it is clear that orders led exports at the 1957 peak, since they were falling at the beginning of the year and exports did not start declining steadily until August (after having reached an isolated peak in March). Orders also show a sharp trough in August 1958, exports a shallow trough in March 1959 (Chart F-1).

pronounced longer fluctuations. Chart F-2 shows them in the form of four-month moving averages of the seasonally adjusted figures.[3]

An outstanding feature of recent developments in machine tool export orders was their sharp increase in 1950 and an equally sharp decrease in 1951 — a movement due mainly to large orders placed here by the United Kingdom for rearmament purposes after the start of the Korean War. The corresponding movements in shipments followed with long lags of 18 to 24 months (the latter figure measures approximately the distance between the peaks). It is clear that the flow of orders underwent much dampening in the production-scheduling process.

Before and after the disturbing impact of the Korean crisis, the lag of export shipments behind new orders was quite regular: about six to nine months in the smoothed or eight to ten months in the unsmoothed data. Even smaller movements such as the double-turn patterns at the peaks of 1956–57 and 1960–61 and at the troughs of 1958–59 were transmitted from new orders to shipments with stable lags, suggesting fairly uniform average delivery periods in the export business of this rather closely defined industry.

Except in the Korean period, fluctuations of export orders do not seem to be very much larger than those of export shipments for the machine tools. It should be noted, however, that the unsmoothed series show larger amplitude differences between orders and shipments than do the moving averages plotted in the chart.[4]

Changes in export orders and in home orders for machine tools show considerable similarity on several occasions. Both series rose to sharp wartime peaks in February 1951 (compare Charts F-2 and 2-3). The declines that followed ended in 1954 — in July for gross domestic orders and in September for gross export orders. The two series reached their next peaks again two months apart in the same sequence (domestic

[3] The MCD (months required for cyclical dominance) index is four months for these series. See Chapter 3 for an explanation of this measure.

[4] Smoothing reduces the amplitudes more for export orders than for export shipments because the short-period variability is greater in orders than in shipments. Although the MCD's are the same for orders and shipments, the more sensitive amplitude measures show the differences in variability to be considerable. The summary figures are as follows (using symbols explained in Chapter 3):

	$\overline{Cyl}$	$\overline{I}$	$\overline{Cy}$	$\overline{I}/\overline{Cy}$	ADR	MCD
Gross orders	20.4	19.0	5.4	3.5	1.78	4
Net orders	23.5	21.7	5.8	3.7	1.78	4
Shipments	13.4	12.4	3.9	3.2	1.77	4

Chart F-2

Gross and Net Export Orders and Export Shipments, Metal-cutting Machine Tools, 1946–63

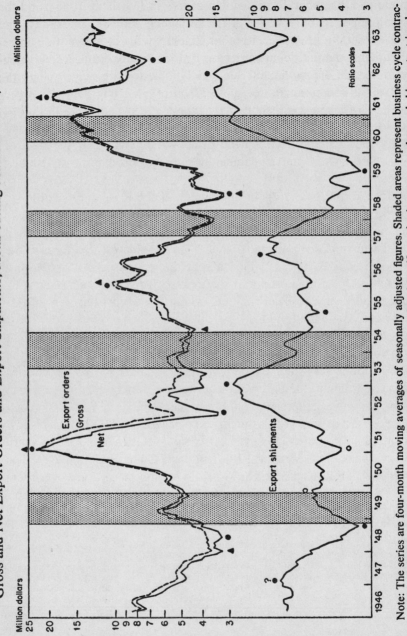

Note: The series are four-month moving averages of seasonally adjusted figures. Shaded areas represent business cycle contractions; unshaded areas, expansions. Dots identify peaks and troughs of specific cycles in net new orders and shipments; triangles, gross new orders. Circles identify minor turns in shipments.

Source: National Machine Tool Builders' Association.

orders in December 1955, foreign orders in February 1956), and the same happened once more at the following troughs (in August and October 1958). However, at other times, divergent rather than correlated demand conditions at home and abroad are indicated. In particular, domestic orders declined in 1959–60, matching, with a lead, the 1960–61 business recession in the United States, while foreign orders reached high levels during that recession. On the other hand, foreign orders contracted in 1961–62, while domestic orders expanded.

APPENDIX G

REGRESSIONS OF SHIPMENTS ON NEW ORDERS: FIRST RESULTS BASED ON DATA FOR 1948–58

THESE REGRESSIONS use the OBE series compiled before the 1963 revision. The results are inferior to those of the more advanced and complete analysis based on the revised Census data and discussed in Chapter 5. They must be treated with caution but are nevertheless of interest as supplementary evidence.

Relations with Variable Discrete Lags and with Several Lagged Terms

Table G-1 draws on Hyman Steinberg's calculations for the National Industrial Conference Board, which cover the period from 1952 to mid-1957.[1] Columns 1–7 in the first part show the simple correlations between new orders and shipments when the former series are assumed to lead the latter by intervals varying from 0 to 6 months. The highest coefficients, and the leads that yield them, are identified. These coefficients vary from .769 for primary metals to .834 for machinery. In terms of the proportion of the variance of shipments accounted for by new orders (r^2), the corresponding range is .591 to .696 (columns 8–9). As leads longer or shorter than the "optimal" are taken, the correlations decline, but slowly. The declines are continuous, with few exceptions. In contrast to these relatively high correlations, the single

[1] Hyman Steinberg, "Influence of New Orders on Sales," "More on Relating Durables Orders to Sales," and "Relationship Between Ordering and Sales, Part III—Transportation Equipment Industry," *Conference Board Business Record,* September 1957, October 1957, and January 1958, respectively.

r coefficient reported for transportation equipment is as low as .49.[2] This is disturbing even for this highly heterogeneous industry, where particularly large aggregation errors may mar estimates of the relationship between total S and N.[3]

Apart from transportation equipment, the maximum-correlation lags of S in Table G-1 agree fairly well with their counterparts in Table 5-1. According to both tables, two-month lags yield the best results for the total durable goods sector, and zero or one-month lags for the metalworking industries. Three-month lags work best for nonelectrical machinery in Table 5-1 and for total machinery in Table G-1.

When new orders of several past months are used jointly as independent variables (Table G-1, lower panel), the highest partial regression coefficients turn out to be associated with the same lags of shipments as those that yielded the highest simple correlations.[4] This might suggest the existence of certain well-behaved linear relationships between S and N, involving unimodal lag distributions.[5] However, the information provided at this point is certainly insufficient to support such inferences, and perhaps all that can be said here is that the intercorrelations among the independent variables (i.e., the autocorrelations of new orders) are apparently not such as to disturb the correspondence between the correlation and regression coefficients observed for these samples.

The equations in Table G-1 include from two to four N_{t-i} terms

[2] The five-month lag of S behind N is said to maximize simple correlation, and Steinberg does not show the corresponding r coefficients for other lags (*Conference Board Business Record,* January 1958, pp. 23–24). However, working with earlier data, Steinberg obtained the highest r (.42) for a two-month lead of N and observed generally higher correlations for the short leads (of 0 to 3 months) than for the longer leads (of 4 to 6 months), as shown by a graph in the September 1957 issue of the *Business Record* (p. 426). Furthermore, in this book, the highest r for transportation equipment in 1953–65 was obtained for simultaneous timing of N and S; the lowest, for the six-month lead of N (Table 5-1). These coefficients show a relatively wide range, from .772 to .865, but they are all much higher than Steinberg's coefficient for 1952–57.

[3] It will be recalled that in the automotive and nonautomotive parts of this industry the relative importance of production to order is sharply different (see Chart 3-4 and text, Chapter 4, "Timing Differences Among the Major Industries"). The distribution of lags in shipments for total transportation equipment could therefore be bimodal, with short lags prevailing for automotive and long lags for nonautomotive orders. If so, the over-all lag may be quite unrepresentative and unstable. It would strongly depend upon changes in the product mix of the industry group as a whole, and these may at times be large, particularly due to shifts in the weight of the important defense-goods component of transportation equipment output.

[4] See the items on lines 1–5 of Table G-1 that are included in notes b and c and the items on lines 6–10 that are included in note e.

[5] See Chapter 5, "Regression Estimates and Turning-Point Estimates," text and note 40, for a statement of conditions under which the maximum-correlation timing would correspond to the mode of the lag distribution.

Table G-1
Correlations Between New Orders (N) and Shipments (S), Assuming Various Lags, Durable Goods Industries, 1952–mid-1957

A. SIMPLE CORRELATIONS

Line	Industry[a]	Simple Correlation Coefficients (r) for Assumed Lead in Months of New Orders Over Shipments							Timing That Maximizes Simple Correlation	
		0 (1)	1 (2)	2 (3)	3 (4)	4 (5)	5 (6)	6 (7)	Lead of New Orders (mos.) (8)	(r^2) (9)
1	Durable goods, total	.763	.792	.819[b]	.812	.798	.778	.741	−2	.671
2	Primary metals	.769[b]	.754	.693	.709	.696	.587	.583	0	.591
3	Fabricated metal products	.805	.814[b]	.784	.760	.747	.735	.750	−1	.663
4	Machinery, total	.778	.806	.830	.834[b]	.831	.823	.804	−3	.696
5	Transportation equipment, total						.49[e]		−5[e]	.24

B. MULTIPLE REGRESSIONS OF S_t ON SELECTED VALUES OF N_{t-i} ($0 \leq i \leq 5$)

Line	Industry[a]	Constant Term (1)	Regression Coefficients of							
			N_t (2)	N_{t-1} (3)	N_{t-2} (4)	N_{t-3} (5)	N_{t-4} (6)	N_{t-5} (7)	R (8)	R^2 (9)
6	Durable goods, total[d]	6,103	−.0435	.0117	.3019[e]	.2700			.929	.863
7	Primary metals	614	.4282[e]	.2759	.2133				.813	.661
8	Fabricated metal products	467	.2116	.2341[e]	.0905				.856	.733
9	Machinery, total	1,450				.2062[e]	.1407	.1678	.886	.785
10	Transportation equipment, total	1,675				.1183	.1318	.1743[e]	.61	.37

Notes to Table G-1

Source: *Conference Board Business Record,* October 1957 and January 1958 (articles by Hyman Steinberg).

[a] The estimates for total durable goods are based on data for January 1953–July 1957 (see note d). The estimates for the other industries are based on data for January 1952–June or July 1957. Monthly seasonally adjusted series have been used in all these calculations.

[b] Figures denote the highest correlation coefficients and thus also the leads that maximize the simple correlations between S_t and N_{t-i} ($i = 0, 1, \ldots , 6$ months). These leads are listed in column 8, and the squares of the highest correlation coefficients are listed in column 9, lines 1–5.

[c] The results for other leads are not available, but they are said to be worse in terms of correlation between S and N. See note 2 in the text.

[d] This regression equation is based on data for January 1953–July 1957.

[e] The highest regression coefficient in each of the fitted equations.

with selected lags i. These are presumably significant, but the reliability of the regression coefficients cannot be appraised in the absence of calculated standard error statistics. The proportion of the variance of S_t that is statistically explained does increase substantially when two or more N_{t-i} terms are used instead of one (compare the r^2 and the R^2 coefficients in column 9). However, for transportation equipment R^2 is still only .37. And the sums of the regression coefficients vary from 0.424 to 0.704 for the five equations in Table G-1, lines 6–10, thus falling short of unity by large margins.[6]

Applications of a Modified Koyck Model of Lag Distribution

My own first attempts to analyze the distributed-lag relationships between new orders and shipments centered on regression equations of the form

$$S_t = k + aN_{t-j} + bS_{t-1} + u_t. \tag{G-1}$$

This is analogous to the well-known model by Koyck (see equations 2–4 and their explanation in Chapter 5), except that N_{t-j} is used instead of N_t, and a constant term k is admitted. The lead j is

[6] Adding up the entries in columns 2–7 in each of the lines 6–10 of Table G-1 gives the following figures: durable goods, 0.5401; primary metals, 0.7041; fabricated metal products, 0.6590; machinery, 0.6052; and transportation equipment, 0.4244.

an estimate of the timing that maximizes the simple correlation between S and N. The (G-1) model would be a logical one in pure production to order, with j representing the minimum period needed for production and delivery and also the "normal" or most frequent delivery
lag.[7]

Ideally, if these hypothetical conditions were fully satisfied and the
S-N relations were linear and stable on the aggregation levels used, the
sum $(a + b)$ and the intercept k would equal, or at least closely approximate, the values 1 and zero, respectively. Actually, Table G-2 shows
positive and in some cases large values of k and sums $\Sigma = a/(1 - b)$
that are considerably smaller than 1, except for the paper industry
(columns 3 and 7). In principle, $\Sigma (= a + ab + ab^2 + \cdot \cdot \cdot)$ should show
the complete cumulative response of S to a unit change in N maintained
"forever." Given that N represents net new orders and that both N
and S are expressed in the same units (millions of dollars), this "total
effect" should equal unity.[8] In fact, the estimates of Σ in Table G-2
vary from 0.373 to 0.982; three exceed 0.8, six exceed 0.6, and two are
less than 0.5.

It is clear that these results leave a great deal to be desired. In particular, they are definitely inferior to estimates from Koyck distributed-
lag regressions that have the same form as equation (G-1) except
that j is taken to equal zero. Thus most of the Σ estimates in Table 5-5
exceed 0.9, and several are not significantly different from 1.0. Also,
the constant terms in these regressions are small, in most cases probably not different from zero (see also text in the sections on geometric-
lag models in Chapter 5). It seems unlikely that this contrast between
the estimates in this appendix and those in Chapter 5 is due to the differences in vintage and coverage between the data used in the two
analyses. Rather, the principal reason for the inferiority of the results
shown in Table G-2 lies probably in the difference between the
models, that is, in the omission of the terms N_{t-i}, where $0 \leqslant i \leqslant j$,
from equation (G-1).

Errors from this source should be particularly large where j is unduly
high. The eleven-month lag of shipments of nonautomotive transportation equipment presents a drastic case, although such long delivery

---

[7] See Chapter 5, note 19 and accompanying text. Equation (G-1) is the estimated form of the
equation shown in the note.
[8] See "Estimates of Geometric Lag Distributions" in Chapter 5.

periods are undoubtedly quite prevalent in this industry. The four-month lag for primary metals raises doubt in view of the different results obtained elsewhere.[9]

The new-order variables with zero or short leads, N_{t-i}, which are not included in the (G-1) model, may well be correlated with S_{t-1}. Such correlations would cause the estimated coefficients of S_{t-1} in Table G-2, column 5, to be overstated. Indeed, these b coefficients are generally higher than the b' coefficients of S_{t-1} in Table 5-5, column 3. Furthermore, the a estimates of the coefficients of N_{t-j} in Table G-2, column 4, are generally lower than the a' estimates of the coefficients of N_t in Table 5-5, column 2. This presumably reflects the importance of production to stock and for relatively short delivery periods, which is allowed much greater and more direct expression in Table 5-5 than in Table G-2.

A larger value of b indicates that more time is required to account for any given proportion q of the total effect Σ, according to the formula $q = 1 - b^n$, where n is the time interval required. Columns 8–10 of Table G-2 list the values of $n = \log (1 - q)/\log b$, for $q = 0.5$, 0.7, and 0.9. These lags are on the whole much larger than their counterparts in columns 6–8 of Table 5-5. The latter are underestimates, according to our "best" average-lag measures for the corresponding industries, which include the results of second-order distributed-lag functions and the instrumental-variables approach (Table 5-8, column 4). Still, there can be little doubt that the figures in Table G-2 definitely overstate the lags of shipments for the same reason that they overstate the b coefficients. Moreover, according to the lag structure assumed in Table G-2, the count of the n intervals starts from the month $t - j$, the time index of the new-order variable in these regressions. If this were allowed for, the bias of overestimation of the lags would appear still larger.

Despite these deficiencies, some aspects of the results reported in

[9] According to Table G-1, line 2, $j = 0$ for the corresponding series in 1952–57. According to Table 5-1, $j = 1$ for the new Census data on primary metals orders and shipments in 1953–63. These figures do not necessarily imply either inconsistency or calculating errors, but they do indicate that the correlations between S_t and N_{t-i} can deviate little for different lags i in any given period and that the maximum-correlation lags j may depend sensitively on the choice of the period covered. For example, the second highest r coefficient for primary metals in 1948–58 equals .794 for $i = 3$, as compared with $r = .798$ as shown in Table G-2. The maximum-correlation lags in 1953–65 could well be shorter than their counterparts in the earlier postwar years. This would be consistent with some evidence of the turning-point comparisons in Chapter 4 (Table 4-6 and text) and of the U/S ratios in Chapter 6 (Charts 6-4 and 6-5).

Table G-2

Distributed-Lag Regressions of Shipments on New Orders,
Eight Major Manufacturing Industries, 1948–58

| Line | Industry | Simple Correlations[a] for Selected Lags | | Distributed-Lag Equations[b] | | | | | | Lags[d] Necessary to Account for | | |
| | | Lag j (mos.) (1) | r (2) | Constant Term k (3) | Regression Coefficients[c] a (4) | b (5) | R^2 (6) | Sum of Implicit Coef.[d] (7) | 50 (8) | 70 (9) | 90 (10) |
									Per Cent of Col. 7		
1	Primary metals	4	.798	213.30	.2202 (.0681)	.6705 (.0767)	.789	.668	1.7	3.0	5.8
2	Fabricated metal products	2	.853	33.06	.0895 (.0172)	.8887 (.0200)	.952	.801	5.9	10.2	19.5
3	Machinery exc. electrical	4	.854	35.51	.0419 (.0099)	.9438 (.0118)	.983	.745	12.0	20.8	39.8
4	Electrical machinery	2	.815	17.37	.0608 (.0122)	.9298 (.0137)	.976	.866	9.5	16.5	31.6
5	Nonautomotive transport. equipment	11	.572	37.48	.0327 (.0137)	.9323 (.0210)	.952	.484	9.9	17.2	32.9
6	Other durable goods[e]	1	.942	65.55	.0735 (.0147)	.9018 (.0156)	.968	.749	6.7	11.7	22.3
7	Textile-mill products	3	.640	111.82	.0609 (.0204)	.8367 (.0368)	.829	.373	3.9	6.8	12.9
8	Paper and allied products	2	.982	8.41	.3069 (.0128)	.6876 (.0128)	.979	.982	1.9	3.2	6.1

Notes to Table G-2

Note: The data come from the OBE Industry Survey and are monthly and seasonally adjusted; the unit is $1 million for both new orders (N) and shipments (S). They cover the period 1948–58 for all industries, except nonautomotive transportation equipment, where the period covered is 1949–58. The numbers of correlated observations per industry vary from 108 to 131. Adjustments for numbers of observations and constants lower the R^2 coefficients in column 6 only slightly, to figures ranging from .777 to .967.

[a] For zero-order correlation between S_t and N_{t-j}.

[b] Measures in columns 3–10 are based on least-square regressions of S_t on N_{t-j} and S_{t-1}: $S_t = k + aN_{t-j} + bS_{t-1} + u_b$.

[c] Figures in parentheses are calculated standard errors.

[d] In column 7, the sum equals $a/(1 - b)$. For explanation of the measures in columns 7–10, see text. The lags are in months.

[e] Includes professional and scientific instruments; lumber; furniture; stone, clay, and glass; and miscellaneous industries.

Table G-2 are acceptable and instructive. First, new orders taken with leads j retain substantial effects upon current shipments S_t in face of the strong autoregressive terms S_{t-1}. The coefficients a, while small in comparison to the b's, are all significant according to conventional statistical criteria.[10]

Second, the table displays pronounced interindustry differences that are consistent with other evidence. At one extreme, there is nonautomotive transportation equipment (line 5), an industry in which production is predominantly to order, delivery periods are typically long, and highly irregular inflows of orders are translated into relatively smooth outflows of shipments. The correlations between S_t and N_{t-j}, while moderate, are much better for long lags (j of 9 to 11 months) than for shorter lags. Also, the transition from simple to distributed lags improves the association greatly in this case (where $r^2 = .327$, $R^2 = .952$). At the other extreme, the correlations between S_t and N_{t-j} for the paper industry (line 8) already are very high when discrete lags of one or two months are assumed. They are not much increased by the addition of the S_{t-1} term (from $r^2 = .966$ to $R^2 = .979$). The regression coefficients and related lag-distribution measures indicate that the delivery periods for paper products are typically short.

[10] The ratios of these estimates to their standard errors exceed 4 for five industries and 2.38 for all (Table G-2, column 4). By the one-tailed t test, this means that all these coefficients (expected to be positive) differ significantly from zero, at least at the 1 per cent level. However, no conclusive tests can be offered here, because the appropriateness of both the model and its estimation by simple least squares can be questioned (see also the section on "Estimates of Geometric Lag Distributions" in Chapter 5).

Timing comparisons at turning points and ratios of unfilled orders to shipments lead to the same general conclusions about these industries.[11]

Nonelectrical machinery has the second longest delivery periods according to the estimates in Table G-2. Electrical machinery and the metalworking industries have generally shorter lags. For the group of "other durable goods," as for paper, the correlations yielded by simple lags are very high and the gain from using the distributed-lag formula is small. This, it will be recalled, is a group of industries working predominantly to stock. The textile industry shows the second lowest correlation coefficients (both simple and multiple) in the set, but the improvement due to the application of the distributed lag is here large. This is consistent with our earlier inference regarding the highly heterogeneous product mix of this industry, but it also suggests that a substantial proportion of textile output is produced to order with varied but generally not very long delivery periods.

Using the OBE series for 1948–58, the eight industries included in this analysis were ranked according to the average lead of new orders at cyclical turns in shipments. These ranks show a positive correlation with the ranks based on lags j in Table G-2, column 1. (The Spearman coefficient, adjusted for tied ranks, is .720.) They also show a correlation of .762 with ranks assigned according to the sums of j and the corresponding entries in column 8 of the table.[12] The correlation of the latter ranks with ranks based on the U/S ratios for the corresponding industries (see "Backlog-Shipment Ratios" in Chapter 6) is as high as .905. According to all of these various measures, paper, textiles, the other durables group, and primary metals have relatively short delivery lags and low U/S ratios, while fabricated metal products, the two machinery industries, and nonautomotive transportation equipment show increasingly long delivery periods and high U/S ratios.

[11] On the relative timing of cyclical turns in these and other OBE series for N and S, see "Major Industry Aggregates and Their Components" in Chapter 4, with Tables 4-6–4-8. The backlog-shipments ratios are discussed in Chapter 6 with the aid of Tables 6-5 and 6-6. On the particular characteristics of the paper industry, see also Chapter 2, note 15, and the accompanying text.

[12] It may be noted that this result does not depend on the (arbitrary) choice of column 8 ($q = 0.5$): one might just as well have used the figures from column 9 or 10, for example. While the lags n increase with q, the industry ranks according to n are the same for any q.

APPENDIX H

NOTES ON SOME THEORETICAL ASPECTS OF VARIABLE DELIVERY PERIODS

Joint Optimization of Delivery Period and Price

Consider a firm that sets the delivery period (k) as well as the price (p) in its offer to customers, aiming for an optimal (profit-maximizing) combination of p and k. Other things being equal, let prompter delivery indicate improved quality of the product, i.e., let it increase demand (the quantity of product ordered per unit of time, q^d) but also costs (the average production costs, c, of the quantity supplied per unit of time, q^s).[1] This gives the following demand (D) and cost (C) functions, which are of the simple static type and assumed to be continuous and differentiable:

$$q^d = D(p, k), \qquad \text{(H-1)}$$

where $D_p = \dfrac{\partial D}{\partial p} < 0$ and $D_k = \dfrac{\partial D}{\partial k} < 0$;

$$c = C(q^s, k), \qquad \text{(H-2)}$$

where $C_k = \dfrac{\partial C}{\partial k} < 0$.

Suppose p and k are changed by small amounts and in such a way as to have equal and opposite effects upon the rate of ordering and sales.

---

[1] This view of k as an aspect of product quality permits application in the present context of a simple and effective technique used in Robert Dorfman and Peter O. Steiner, "Optimal Advertising and Optimal Quality," *American Economic Review*, December 1954, pp. 826–36.

If the rates of quantities ordered and supplied are thus kept constant,[2] we get

$$\frac{dp}{dk} = -\frac{D_k}{D_p} \qquad\qquad \text{(H-3)}$$

and

$$dc = C_k dk. \qquad\qquad \text{(H-4)}$$

The economic meaning of equation (H-3) is the marginal rate of substitution of price for delivery period, given a certain quantity ordered, $q^d = $ constant. A system of downward sloping indifference curves is thus conceived,[3] each of which is a locus of all combinations of p and k that are associated with a given value of q^d.

The net effect on profit of small changes in price and delivery period, which leave unchanged the quantity the firm sells ($q = q^d = q^s$), is the difference between the effect on the gross revenue of the change in price ($= qdp$) and the effect on total costs of the change in the delivery period ($= qdc$). By substitution from equations (H-3) and (H-4), this net effect on profit equals

$$qdp - qdc = -q\left(\frac{D_k}{D_p} - C_k\right) dk. \qquad\qquad \text{(H-5)}$$

The condition for the "joint optimum" (profit-maximizing combination) of p and k is that this whole expression be equal to zero. This will be so necessarily if, and only if, the parenthetical expression in equation (H-5) equals zero. Otherwise, one could always choose dk (with the compensating dp) such that $dp > dc$, i.e., profit could still be increased. Hence it is required that [4]

$$C_k = -\frac{D_k}{D_p}. \qquad\qquad \text{(H-6)}$$

In Figure H-1 this condition is satisfied, for example, at $k = OA$, $p = OB$, and $c = OC$. The "indifference curve" MM represents all the combinations of values of p and k at which the quantity ordered

---

[2] Equation (H-3) is obtained by differentiating (H-1) totally to get $dq^d = D_p dp + D_k dk$ and setting $dq^d = 0$. Equation (H-4) is the form to which the differential of (H-2) reduces when $dq^s = 0$.

[3] Since $D_p < 0$ and $D_k < 0$, dp/dk must, according to (H-3), be negative.

[4] This is the necessary condition for a maximum profit (if π is net revenue or profit taken as a function of p and k, then $d\pi = 0$, that is, $\partial\pi/\partial p = \partial\pi/\partial k = 0$). To this the sufficient condition should be added, that is, the second-order partial derivatives of the profit function must be assumed to be negative at the point where $\partial\pi = 0$.

Figure H-1

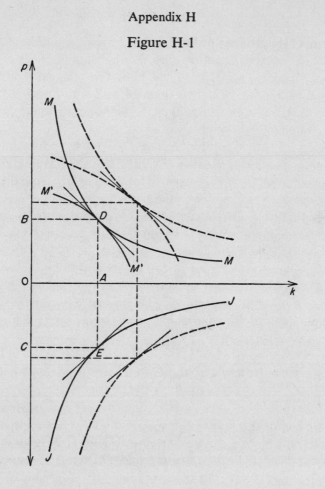

equals a given amount, say, q_1. The curve JJ shows the costs per unit (c) of supplying this same quantity at various delivery periods (k). The slope of MM at point D equals the slope of JJ at point E (note that p and c are measured vertically from the origin O). Hence $dp/dk = dc/dk$, as required by equation (H-6).

Both MM and JJ are assumed to be convex relative to the origin. However, this need not necessarily be so. The convexity of the MM curve means that buyers are ready to pay increasing price premiums for each additional unit reduction in k. Their own production (input) requirements may indeed be such as to make this advisable. But it is also possible that the buyers' willingness to pay for the additional unit decreases in k would gradually decline; the initial speed-up may be needed and valued most, the further ones less and less. The locus of the equivalent $p - k$ combinations (given q_1) would then be a concave curve such as, e.g., $M'M'$ in Figure H-1. The convexity of JJ means that equal additional reductions in k are associated with rising increments in costs. This should be typical, although it is quite possible to conceive situations in which it would not be.[5]

Equation (H-6) can be rewritten as $-D_p = D_k/C_k$, a form convenient to interpret verbally. If the rate of increase in sales attributable to the incremental outlay for delivery-period reduction (D_k/C_k) exceeded the rate of decrease in sales due to the higher price charged to cover the cost increase ($-D_p$), then it would still pay the producer to spend more for a further delivery speed-up. In the opposite case, c should be somewhat decreased, thereby allowing k to lengthen.

Formally, the above argument can be applied to *any* level of orders received and filled, so that its generality is not unduly restricted by the assumption of a constant q. The broken curves in Figure H-1 suggest an application to a level of orders that is higher than q_1.

Reactions of Price and Delivery Period to Demand Fluctuations

An expansion of demand will in all likelihood be accompanied by increases in both p and k, as illustrated in Figure H-2. Each of the convex curves in this diagram has the same meaning as curve MM in Figure H-1 and corresponds to a given quantity ordered, q_i. The higher and further to the right the curve, the larger the amount of orders per period to which it refers, i.e., $q_2 > q_1$, etc. To simplify presentation, the J-type curves, such as JJ in Figure H-1, are here omitted. Short heavy lines tangential to the M curves are drawn through those points at which the slopes of the paired M and J curves are assumed to be equal. These points are connected by the lines AA, BB, CC, and DD, each of which thus represents one of the many different sequences of

---

[5] The applicability of the preceding analysis—equations (H-1)–(H-6)—is not affected by whether the curves are convex or concave. For example, in Figure H-1, $M'M'$ is drawn with the same slope as MM. Each of these curves, together with JJ, satisfies equation (H-6). It would also seem sensible to impose certain limits upon the range of variation of p and k, but this again does not prejudge the form of the MM curve. The convex curve, e.g., may have at its ends two segments parallel to the p and k axes, respectively. The concave curve would not reach to either axis.

Figure H-2

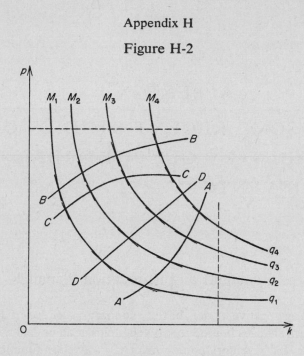

the combinations of p and k that may result from an increase of demand from q_1 through q_4. Figure H-2 merely illustrates these various possibilities; it provides no tool for discrimination among them. In one example p increases relatively fast and k relatively slowly (AA). In another, the reverse applies (BB). Each path corresponds to a different combination of the M and J "maps" and depends on the varying slopes and positions of the curves of either set.[6]

It is clear that the diagram simply gives graphical representation to developments that differ essentially with respect to the relative importance of price and backlog adjustments. The broken lines perpendicular to the axes depict the extreme alternatives in which either p or k alone would bear the brunt of the adjustment. For these extremes to be realized, either MM or JJ would have to be nearly horizontal in one case, nearly vertical in the other. That is, there would be no significant substitutability of p and k.

[6] Figure H-2 employs the arbitrary short-cut device of keeping the M map constant, implicitly varying the J map, but one could just as well reverse this procedure. The curves in either set may run parallel or deviate in one direction or the other (as M_3 or M_4). Conceivably, the maps could even show a negative slope for a part of the $p - k$ curve (e.g., CC).

APPENDIX I

ON SOME RECENT STUDIES OF INDUSTRY OUTPUT-ORDER-INVENTORY RELATIONS

Cost Functions and Production Planning

The current aggregative models of the economy either do not deal with the short-term changes in production schedules at all or deal with them indirectly via the inventory equations. The production functions they include are of the conventional type, relating output to inputs of labor and capital and to trends in technology; they are much more likely to reflect long-term tendencies than short-term adjustments. Such models are not focused on how previous commitments, expectations, and cost considerations influence the short-term production decisions. They are not constructed to handle the relationships in question, which require considerable disaggregation, such as the distinction between production to stock and to order. Yet a complete model which employs reasonably short unit periods such as quarters and includes equations for components of effective demand, output, and inventories must have some implications about the over-all mechanism underlying short-term production decisions.

These decisions, having the objective of minimizing cost over a time horizon, must involve the parameters of the relevant cost functions. This theme is developed in recent studies of production planning, which are largely microeconomic and normative.[1] This work applies

[1] C. C. Holt, F. Modigliani, J. F. Muth, and H. A. Simon, *Planning Production, Inventories, and Work Force*, Englewood Cliffs, N.J., 1960. Also see C. C. Holt and F. Modigliani, "Firm Cost Structures and the Dynamic Responses of Inventories, Production, Work Force, and Orders to Sales Fluctuations" in *Inventory Fluctuations and Economic Stabilization, Part II*, Joint Economic Committee, Washington, D.C., 1961.

mainly to firms that produce to stock according to sales expectations derived in some assumed manner. Unfilled orders are treated as if they were equivalent to negative inventories. This approach may be appropriate in some individual cases, but it is not generally applicable and it is surely incorrect where aggregates, e.g., industry data, are concerned. As was shown in Chapter 2, some products are typically produced to stock, others to order. The aggregates of inventories and of unfilled orders refer in large measure to different products. Hence the concept of "net inventory," taken to mean the value of product inventory minus the value of order backlogs, may be meaningless even for a single firm. For an industry, which usually means a group of multi-product firms, the aggregates of stocks of goods and backlogs of orders are likely to be still more heterogeneous, since their composition would differ not only in terms of the "product mix" but also in terms of the "company mix."

The production studies work with quadratic functions for several cost categories: (a) costs of hiring and layoffs, overtime, machine setups, etc., which are incurred when the production rates are changed to absorb the fluctuations in sales; (b) costs of holding inventory and of unmet orders (stock-outs), which are incurred when the fluctuations in sales are absorbed by variations in inventories and in unfilled orders. Given the parameters of the cost functions, a linear "decision rule" is derived which links the scheduled production rate to forecasts of orders or sales, to the actual rate of output or labor input in the preceding period, and to the inventory situation at the time. Forecasts of sales in several future periods may be averaged, with the largest weight being given to the nearest and the smallest weight to the distant future. This would have the effect of smoothing output relative to the *expected* demand in production to stock (though smoothing relative to actual sales need not be assured because of possible errors of forecasts). The scheduled output rate is positively associated with the initial rate of production and size of the employed work force, since cutbacks in operations, either through layoffs or through underutilization of labor, are costly. Finally, the larger the product inventory on hand, the smaller is the rate of output needed to meet the given sales expectations (and the greater the need to lower the inventory for cost reasons). Hence the association between scheduled output and finished unsold inventory is, ceteris paribus, a negative one.

In production to order, the situation is in large part different. Other things being equal, output is positively related to the backlog of unfilled orders, just as it is negatively related to finished inventory in production to stock. It is also plausible that the costs of holding unfilled orders are quadratic. When the backlog becomes small, costly production cutbacks may have to be made and when the backlog becomes large, sales may be discouraged by the lengthening of the delivery periods. But one must not expect the effect of unfilled orders on production to be a stable function of some cost parameters. This effect reflects in a summary fashion the relationship between orders received in the past and current output resulting from the processing of some of these orders; and, as suggested by earlier analysis, this relation involves distributed and probably variable lags. Also, where output depends in a large measure on prior orders, it is correspondingly less closely guided by sales forecasts or expectations.

Short-Run Behavior of Production

If only because of grave aggregation problems, it is difficult to apply the lessons from the literature on quadratic cost functions and the associated linear decision rules—essentially a normative micro-analysis—to comprehensive industry data. Moreover, unfilled orders and finished-goods inventories are in large measure determined by the demand forces and are only in part controllable "decision variables." Nevertheless, a few ambitious efforts were made recently to apply models similar to those proposed by Holt et al. in *Planning Production* to the current Census data for the major manufacturing industries. The study by David A. Belsley[2] makes a clear distinction between production to stock and production to order. Belsley's results consist of a large number of direct and indirect estimates derived from several sets of regressions. Here it will only be possible to consider the primary direct estimates from his basic regression output.[3]

Belsley derived series for gross value of production (call it Z'_t) from

[2] *Industry Production Behavior: The Order-Stock Distinction*, Amsterdam, 1969.

[3] Belsley attempted in ingenious ways to develop separate estimates of reaction coefficients for the production-to-stock and production-to-order components of each of the major durable goods industries that report unfilled orders. But this can only be done indirectly, through transformations based on a number of particular assumptions of varying degrees of plausibility. The resulting estimates of the "structural" model, which contains unobserved variables, are difficult to evaluate. In any event their consideration seems logically posterior to the task of interpreting the underlying regressions whose coefficients furnished the inputs for the transformations.

the monthly Census data on shipments and finished inventory change (S_t and ΔQ_t) according to the identity $Z'_t \equiv S_t + \Delta Q_t$. He then computed regressions of Z'_t on Q_{t-1}, ΔQ_{t-1}, U_{t-1}, N_t, and Z'_{t-1}, using the monthly, seasonally adjusted Census series on finished inventories and unfilled and new orders for the period from January 1953 to November 1964. In two other sets of estimates, S_t and ΔQ_t were cast in the role of the dependent variable, while the above five series were used in each case as the explanatory variables. Finally, all these computations were performed again on series deflated by wholesale price indexes, 1957 = 1.00. Data for twelve industries reporting unfilled orders were thus processed.

As would be expected, the correlations obtained for the equations with either Z'_t or S_t as the dependent variable are generally very high (the $\bar{R}^2$ coefficients exceed .9 in all but a few cases and often exceed .95), while the correlations for the ΔQ equations are very low and frequently insignificant. It is disturbing that some of the equations contain many identity elements.[4] Of more interest are the regression estimates. For example, the undeflated value-of-output equations for three large durable goods industries are as follows:

Primary metals

$$Z'_t = -56.10 + .268Q_{t-1} + 1.706\Delta Q_{t-1}$$
$$\;\;\;\;\;\;\;(101.04)\;(.072)\;\;\;\;\;\;\;(0.458)$$

$$+ .051U_{t-1} + .302N_t + .476Z'_{t-1};\; \bar{R}^2 = .880$$
$$\;\;\;(.012)\;\;\;\;\;\;\;\;(.031)\;\;\;\;\;\;(.050)$$

Machinery except electrical

$$Z'_t = 6.03 + .119Q_{t-1} - .315\Delta Q_{t-1}$$
$$\;\;\;\;(23.62)\;(.039)\;\;\;\;\;\;(.205)$$

$$+ .011U_{t-1} + .218N_t + .651Z'_{t-1};\; \bar{R}^2 = .991$$
$$\;\;\;(.004)\;\;\;\;\;\;\;\;(.024)\;\;\;\;\;\;(.052)$$

Transportation equipment

$$Z'_t = 319.27 + .384Q_{t-1} + 3.688\Delta Q_{t-1}$$
$$\;\;\;\;\;(111.48)\;(.169)\;\;\;\;\;\;\;(0.980)$$

$$+ .0002U_{t-1} + .135N_t + .717Z'_{t-1};\; \bar{R}^2 = .957$$
$$\;\;\;(.004)\;\;\;\;\;\;\;\;(.030)\;\;\;\;\;\;(.051)$$

[4] Thus Z'_t is related to Z'_{t-1}, Q_{t-1}, and N_t for industries without unfilled orders, where $N_t \equiv S_t$; yet here $Z'_t \equiv N_t + Q_t - Q_{t-1}$. More generally, consider also that $Z'_t \equiv N_t + \Delta Q_t - \Delta U_t$ and that the series on the value of output, shipments, inventories, and unfilled orders typically show high serial correlations.

Since many orders require little time for production and many are sold and shipped from stock, N_t should have a substantial effect on Z_t' and does. But in the above industries, manufacture to order with longer production and delivery periods is important, and hence earlier orders also influence current output. These distributed-lag relations presumably account in large part for the autoregressive properties of the output series as reflected in the major importance of the term Z_{t-1}'.[5] Simple aggregates of unfilled orders would not be expected to influence output as effectively as do the recent values of new orders taken with regression-determined weights (as in the equations of Chapter 5, for example). In any event, the combination of N_t and Z_{t-1}' works to suppress the effect of the backlog factor, U_{t-1}. Indeed, the observed residual effects of U_{t-1} are generally small and in some instances not significantly different from zero.

It is possible to interpret these relations differently, stressing that N_t stands for sales expectations and that the coefficient of Z_{t-1}' reflects the costs of changing the rates of production. These conceptions, which correspond approximately to some of the ideas underlying Belsley's analysis, are probably partly valid, but on the basis of the available evidence, I believe them to be secondary to the aspects noted in the preceding paragraph.

Given the sales expectations that govern production to stock, the possession of large quantities of unsold finished inventory would tend to inhibit a company in its production of those goods that are made in anticipation of market sales. Hence, as already noted, a negative influence on output of finished stocks on hand is expected. But anticipations of high sales may stimulate output sufficiently to result also in additions to inventory. However, adjustments of inventory by means of output changes are not necessarily timely or efficient. They are subject to forecast errors and may be impeded by lack of flexibility on the

---

[5] The ratios of regression coefficients to their standard errors tend to be very large (exceeding 7.0) for both N_t and Z_{t-1}'; the corresponding t ratios for the other variables are generally much smaller (in the 1 to 5 range). For industries in which production to order is particularly important, such as those making machinery, equipment, and instruments, the t values for Z_{t-1}' exceed 10.0 and are much larger than the corresponding statistics for N_t. In contrast, the t ratios are typically greater for N_t than for Z_{t-1}' in the equations for industries in which production to stock and short delivery periods are characteristic, e.g., stone, clay, and glass; furniture; paper; and printing. These results are all consistent with our explanations. They are reported in Belsley, *Industry Production Behavior*, App. D ("The Basic Regression Output"). (We are referring to the regressions based on monthly, seasonally adjusted data. The use of seasonally unadjusted data naturally results in giving relatively more importance to N_t and less to Z_{t-1}'.)

input side due to fixed commitments, etc. Also some inventories result from production to order and consist of sold stocks in transit. These factors can produce elements of a positive association between output and finished inventory, which complicates the situation. In Belsley's equations, the coefficients of Q_{t-1} (call them λ_1) are typically positive but those of $\Delta Q_{t-1}(\lambda_2)$ are negative and considerably larger. Such a combination implies a negative net effect of Q_{t-1} (equal to $\lambda_1 - \lambda_2$) and a larger positive effect of Q_{t-2} (equal to $-\lambda_2$).[6]

Define the average production period for the made-to-order (oth) part of an industry's output as $x = \bar{U}/\bar{Z}^o$ and the average inventory-sales ratio for the made-to-stock (sth) part as $y = \bar{Q}/\bar{S}^s$. Then the relative importance of production to stock versus production to order can be expressed as:

$$\frac{\bar{Z}^s}{\bar{Z}^o} = \frac{\bar{Q}/y}{\bar{U}/x} = \frac{\bar{Q}x}{\bar{U}y},$$

on the assumptions that in these steady-state values Q appears solely in production to stock and U in production to order and that $\bar{S}^s = \bar{Z}^s$. In Chapter 2 of this book, the $\bar{Q}/\bar{U}$ ratios were used to rank the industries and products according to the relative importance of production to stock versus production to order. But, if the above formulation is correct, $\bar{Q}/\bar{U}$ may not be an appropriate means of such ranking. Conceivably, the x/y ratios could so vary among the industries as to make the ranking of the latter by $\bar{Z}^s/\bar{Z}^o$ differ significantly from the ranking by $\bar{Q}/\bar{U}$. Actually, however, this argument, made by Belsley,[7] is unconvincing for several reasons. It depends itself on the implicit premise that Q is to be assigned to production to stock only and U to production to order only, as already noted and also, basically, on the stability of the x and y values and on the not necessarily plausible assumption that $\bar{S}^s = \bar{Z}^s$. Moreover, as shown by John A. Carlson,[8] the U/S ratio used in this book and elsewhere as an indicator of an industry's average delivery period, is in a sense independent of the relative importance of production to order. If $r = S^o/S$ is the proportion of total shipments

---

[6] Note that $\lambda_1 Q_{t-1} - \lambda_2(Q_{t-1} - Q_{t-2}) = (\lambda_1 - \lambda_2)Q_{t-1} + \lambda_2 Q_{t-2}$. For primary metals and transportation equipment, λ_2 is positive and very large, but for each of the other industries, λ_2 is negative. These exceptions are difficult to understand, but they refer to particularly recalcitrant cases. The relations for primary metals are disturbed by the effects of the major steel strikes, and transportation equipment is an exceedingly heterogeneous industry.

[7] *Industry Production Behavior*, pp. 149–51.

[8] "The Production Lag," preliminary draft, July 1970.

that goes to fill backlog orders, then U/rS would be the average delivery period for items produced to order. The average delivery period on the rest of shipments is approximately zero, neglecting the short response time in filling orders from stock. Combining U/rS and zero with weights of r and $(1 - r)$, respectively, gives U/S as the average delivery period for all shipments. Finally and most importantly, the evidence of the $\bar{Q}/\bar{U}$ ratios is generally sensible and consistent with other information, as demonstrated in this study. No contrary evidence is presented by Belsley, who reports a "frustrated attempt to rank industries" without trying to implement the proposed $\bar{Q}x/\bar{U}y$ measures (which, of course, are not directly observable).

Another interesting study of manufacturers' short-term production decisions [9] focuses on how they vary between cyclical expansions and contractions and employs the stock-adjustment model of inventory investment. Recognizing that this model applies to production to stock and accepting the evidence of the $\bar{Q}/\bar{U}$ ratios for determining the prevalence of that type of manufacture versus production to order, Moriguchi limits his statistical work to a few products made primarily to stock in the cement, paper, and lumber industries. Monthly data, 1949–60, for current production are regressed on current sales (shipments), alternative variants of sales anticipations, and lagged finished stock. Dummy variables are used to study separately the seasonal influences, the role of changes in capacity utilization, and the other effects of the distinction between business cycle prosperity and recession. Moriguchi's results suggest, among others, that the speed with which inventories are adjusted to the desired levels is reduced in recession because of manufacturers' skepticism about anticipated sales, even though lower capacity utilization in the same phase would counsel the opposite reaction, i.e., faster adjustments of the rate of production for stock.

Unfilled Orders and Finished Stocks

A study by Gerald Childs [10] contains estimates of manufacturers' unfilled orders and finished-goods inventories based on monthly regres-

[9] Chikashi Moriguchi, *Business Cycles and Manufacturers' Short-Term Production Decisions,* Amsterdam, 1967.
[10] *Unfilled Orders and Inventories: A Structural Analysis,* Amsterdam, 1967. (This monograph, as well as those by Belsley and Moriguchi, is published in the North-Holland Publishing Company series, "Contributions to Economic Analysis.")

sions for 1953–64, each of which includes as the independent variables Z'_{t-1}, Q_{t-1}, and U_{t-1} as well as certain lagged or future values of new orders. The latter are used to represent forecasts of demand (new orders), which are either assumed perfect (with N_{t+i}, $i = 0, 1, 2$, included in the equations) or alternatively are taken to be autoregressive (N_{t-i}, $i = 1, 2, 3$). The desired level of inventories is assumed to depend linearly on the current value of either new orders or shipments only, although no rationale is provided for these seemingly arbitrary and quite restrictive specifications. Combinations of these alternatives define several variants of the model.[11]

Two of the variants use the lagged "net inventory," $Q_{t-1} - U_{t-1}$, as one of the determinants. As argued before, this is not likely to be a meaningful concept. The coefficients of this stock-backlog difference factor seem to reflect mainly the high positive autocorrelations that are characteristic of both U and Q.[12] By the same token, in the other two variants, where lagged backlogs and finished stock are included as separate independent variables, U_{t-1} dominates the equations for U_t, and Q_{t-1} dominates the equations for Q_t.

The previous value of output, Z'_{t-1}, appears in all estimated relationships, predominantly with a negative net effect on U_t and a positive one on Q_t. The explanation given is that production fills some of the backlog orders and that some of the output is being added to the finished-goods stock.

The coefficients of Q_{t-1} in the equations for unfilled orders are negative and at least twice as large as their standard errors, while the coefficients of U_{t-1} in the equations for finished-goods inventories are positive and appear for the most part to be reasonably significant. But in production to order, finished-goods inventories would not be expected to depend systematically on unfilled orders except perhaps indirectly or as a reflection of common growth trends of the industry.[13] Similarly, for items sold from stock, there is no relation to be expected between the finished-goods inventories and the unfilled order backlogs,

[11] There are four variants applied to U_t and then again to Q_t, thus making a set of eight regressions for each of the seven industries covered, including all manufacturing, total durables and four major components, and total nondurables.

[12] These coefficients are therefore always negative in the equations for U_t and positive in the equations for Q_t. On these and other results discussed below in this section, see Childs, *Unfilled Orders*, Tables 5-1 through 5-16, pp. 68–83.

[13] The behavior of finished inventories that are already sold and held only transitorily before delivery to the buyer is largely random (see Chapter 10). However, the greater the order backlog, the higher the rates of production are likely to be, for they may be associated with shipping delays and hence with larger stocks of finished goods in transit.

since there is no tendency for backlogs to accumulate in the first place. Logic and evidence indicate, as shown earlier, that U and Q typically refer to different goods. And the backlogs of goods made to order are likely to be essentially independent of the inventories of goods made to stock, unless the two categories of product are complementary or unless further expansion of production for one of them imposes a limitation on the other because of an effective capacity constraint.[14] Childs notes that the signs of the cross-effects of Q_{t-1} and U_{t-1} are those that would be expected if the items produced to stock were used as inputs in production to order. It is not known to what extent such input-output relations actually exist within the industries concerned. The suggested explanation provides one interesting possibility but does not preclude others.[15]

The impact on unfilled orders of past and current new orders (N_{t-i}, $i = 0, 1, 2, 3$) is positive and on the whole highly significant, as would be expected. It is also not surprising that future new orders, N_{t+1} and N_{t+2}, have virtually no effect upon current backlogs, U_t. This merely shows that outputs manufactured to order are *not* typically based on *forecasts* of demand, an aspect that is largely ignored in Childs's specifications.

In contrast to their strong positive effects on U_t, the new-order variables are, with few exceptions, very weakly, if at all, related to the finished-goods inventories. However, the coefficients of N_{t-1} in several regressions for Q_t are significantly negative. Some of these new orders are no doubt filled from stock, which should be a partial reason for this relation. A capacity constraint could also contribute to this result, since an increase in the demand for goods produced to order would then be associated with a reduction in the output of goods produced to stock.

[14] The assumption of independence in the absence of either or both of these two conditions (complementarity and capacity constraint can, of course, coexist) is made by Childs, *Unfilled Orders*, p. 42.

[15] Under the input hypothesis, a rise in Q_{t-1} enables production to order to be increased in period t, thereby reducing the end-of-period backlog, U_t. Also, a rise in U_{t-1} makes it advisable to increase Q_t so that back orders can be more efficiently filled in the near future (see *ibid.*, p. 84). An alternative pair of hypotheses is: (a) that a rise (fall) in backlogs on the order-oriented side of the industry leads to the expectation of higher (lower) sales on the stock-oriented side; (b) that a rise of demand is met first by reductions in unsold stocks of some products and next by backlogging of orders for others (and analogously for a fall of demand).

Index

Abramovitz, Moses, 44n, 50n, 355n, 384, 384n, 403, 632n, 662n

Accelerator theory of investment, 353, 468, 492, 493, 646

Advance orders, 2; for durable and nondurable goods compared, 32; and irregular movements, 103–105; microforecasts of, 61–62; as predictors of output and shipments, 645–46; and unfilled orders related to production, 250

Aggregation problem, 11–12, 12n, 52, 53, 56

Aircraft. *See* Transportation equipment, nonautomotive

Alchian, Armen, 303n

Almon, Shirley, 460

Alt, Franz L., 196n

American Face Brick Association, 19

American Furniture Mart, 41n

American Paper and Pulp Association, 21n

American Supply and Machinery Manufacturers' Association, 546

Amplitude of fluctuations: average, of component movements, 110–20; average, of specific cycles, 121–27; of business cycles, *see* Business cycles, Contractions, Expansions; in investment in plant and equipment, 412ff; in new orders, production, and shipments, 641–42; of new orders vs. shipments, 2–3, 22, 70ff, 78–83, 90–94, 689–92; of output in deflated series, 105–10

Ando, Albert, 457n

Anticipations surveys: of capital expenditures, 427, 433–42, 462, 465–75, 515–16, 618ff; of sales, 62–68, 69, 560

Apparel industry. *See* Home goods and apparel

Architectural terra cotta, 122–23, 543, 655

Arrow, Kenneth J., 304n

Associated Industries of Massachusetts, 655

Autocorrelated disturbances in shipments regressions, 234–40

Automotive equipment and parts. *See* Transportation equipment, motor vehicles and parts

Autoregressive components, 159, 159n, 205; in investment in plant and equipment estimates, 492ff, 507

Average duration of run, 111ff, 120

Average hourly earnings, 334, 684

Backlog-shipment ratios, 261–62, 289–93; and competition, 299–300; and delivery-period lags, 279, 281–83, 306; for durable goods industries, 259–60; factors affecting, 270; industry averages for, lags and, 283–88; and inventory investment, 354–58, 375, 375n; and investment in plant and equipment, 483; for nondurable goods industries, 258; peak and trough values for, 278–81; and price adjustments, 296, 329; in steel industry, 246–49; and timing measures in major-industry series, 267–70; and unfilled orders, 264–65; and variable lag hypothesis, 226–27

Backlogs. *See* Unfilled orders

Ball, R. J., 282, 282n

Bank interest rates. *See* Interest rates

Bank loans, 632–35

Barger, Harold, 615

Belsley, David A., 734, 734n, 736n, 737, 738n

Bennett, W. A., 22n

Blast furnaces and steel mills: amplitude of new orders vs. shipments, 75, 79, 80, 82, 179, 181, 186, 189, 193, 194, 201, 202, 206, 209, 210, 213n, 216, 217, 227, 229, 231, 232; backlog-shipment ratios, 259, 280, 284; timing of new orders at business cycle turns, 531, 534; timing of unfilled orders at business cycle turns, 570, 583; unfilled orders vs. shipments, 268